Timor-Leste

Challenges for Justice and Human Rights in the Shadow of the Past

Timor-Leste

Challenges for Justice and Human Rights in the Shadow of the Past

Edited by
William Binchy

CLARUS
PRESS

Trinity College Dublin
Asian Law and Human Rights Series

Published by
Clarus Press Ltd,
Griffith Campus,
South Circular Road,
Dublin 8.

Typeset by
Compuscript Ltd,
Bay 11a, Shannon Industrial Estate
Shannon, Co Clare.

Printed by
MPG Books Ltd
Victoria Square, Bodmin, Cornwall.

ISBN
978-1-905536-21-4

Preface

Timor-Leste has had a troubled history and faces an uncertain future. Having experienced colonisation for centuries followed by the Indonesian occupation, with all its abuses of human rights, Timor-Leste emerged as an independent state, based on the rule of law and on respect for human rights. The last few years have shown that no society is simple and that the complex influences of the past continue to shape political, social and cultural realities.

This book seeks to examine contemporary challenges for justice and human rights in the shadow of the past. It approaches the task from a broad, interdisciplinary perspective, conscious of the need to integrate insights not only of scholars immersed in human rights, international criminal justice and customary law, but of others whose backgrounds are in international relations, history, anthropology, demography, sociology, geography and ecology. We were fortunate in assembling a strong international team of contributors, all presenting careful objective analysis but equally committed to the future wellbeing of this fragile state.

Dr. Aoife Nolan, of Queen's University Belfast, played a crucial role in the editing process and ought rightly to be recorded as co-editor though she generously disclaims that title. Her work is very much appreciated. Sincere thanks are due to David McCartney, Managing Director of Clarus Press, for his huge industry and enthusiasm in bringing the project to fruition. Dr. Hilary Delany, Head of the Law School of Trinity College Dublin, has been a constant source of encouragement and support.

We are most grateful to the Irish Department of Justice and Irish Aid for their financial support for this project. Ireland, a small country that has also emerged from a history of colonisation, finds it easy to empathise with Timor-Leste, its complex history and its challenges in building up democratic structures that are sensitive to human rights.

The book is the first in Trinity College Dublin's Series on Asian law and Human Rights.

William Binchy
5 January 2009

Contents

Contributors

Dr. Gernot Biehler is Lecturer in Law at Trinity College Dublin. He has published extensively in German, English and Russian in the fields of administrative, public and international law. His books include *Procedures in International Law* (2008), *International Law in Practice: an Irish Perspective* (2005) and *Auswärtige Gewalt, Auswirkungen auswärtiger Interessen im innerstaatlichen Recht* (2005).

William Binchy is Regius Professor of Laws at Trinity College Dublin and a Commissioner of the Irish Human Rights Commission . He established, and lectures on, a course on the Legal System of Timor-Leste in the Master of Laws degree programme at Trinity and has acted as a consultant to Irish Aid in relation to the justice system of Timor-Leste.

Guy Cumes is Lecturer in Law at Charles Sturt University. His publications include "Murder as a Crime against Humanity in International Law: Choice of Law and Prosecution of Murder in East Timor", 11 European Journal of Crime, Criminal Law and Criminal Justice 40 (2003).

Dr. Fernand de Varennes is Associate Professor at the School of Law at Murdoch University at Perth. A former Director of the Asia-Pacific Centre for Human Rights and the Prevention of Ethnic Conflict and the founding Editor-in-Chief of the Asia-Pacific Journal on Human Rights and the Law, his publications include *Language, Minorities and Human Rights* (1996) and *A Guide to the Rights of Minorities and Language* (2001). He has worked with the United Nations' Working Group on the Rights of Minorities, UNESCO and the OSCE's High Commissioner on National Minorities.

Dr. Clinton Fernandes is Senior Lecturer in Strategic Studies at University College, the University of New South Wales. He specialises in international relations and strategy. He is the author of *Reluctant Saviour: Australia, Indonesia and the independence of East Timor* (2004) and *Reluctant Indonesians: Australia, Indonesia and the future of West Papua* (2006).

Carolyn Graydon worked with East Timor asylum seekers in Australia between 1994 and 1998. From 2001 to 2003 she worked as a Human Rights Officer under UN missions based in the Oecussi Enclave, Ermera and Dili districts. Since 2003 she has regularly undertaken human rights work in Timor-Leste, including participating as an investigator in the secretariat of the

UN Independent Special Commission of Inquiry to investigate responsibility for key incidents in the 2006 crisis.

Laura Grenfell lectures in human rights law, constitutional law and comparative constitutional law at the University of Adelaide. She has published widely in the areas of feminist theory and transitional justice. Her article, "Legal Pluralism and the Rule of Law in Timor Leste", was published in the Leiden Journal of International Law in 2006.

Dr. Susan Harris Rimmer is Research Officer at the Centre for International Governance and Justice and is President of Australian Lawyers for Human Rights. She is the author of *Transitional Justice and the Women of East Timor*. Her article, "'Orphans' or Veterans? Justice for Children of War in East Timor", published in the Texas International Law Journal (2007), won the 2006 Audre Rapoport Prize for Scholars on the Human Rights of Women.

Dr. Jeff Kingston is Professor of History and Director of Asian Studies at Temple University, Japan. He has published widely on East Timor and has produced two books examining social change in contemporary Japan.

Dr. Jackson Nyamuya Maogoto is Senior Lecturer in Law at the University of Manchester. He has authored and co-authored four books, including *Battling Terrorism: Legal Perspectives on the Use of Force and the War on Terror*, (Ashgate, 2005) and *Legal Control of the Private Military Corporation*. (Palgrave Macmillan, 2008).

Dr. Joseph Nevins is Associate Professor of Geography at Vassar College. His publications include *A Not-so-distant Horror: Mass Violence in East Timor* (2005). He is a founding member of the East Timor Action Network and a founder and board member of La'o Hamutuk.

Rod Nixon completed a doctorate on *Integrating Indigenous Approaches into a 'New Subsistence State': The Case of Justice and Conflict Resolution in East Timor* at Charles Darwin University. He has considerable work experience in East Timor and was senior researcher with the ARD/USAID East Timor land programme (2003-2005). He has published widely on East Timor, including a chapter in Dennis Shoesmith ed., *The Crisis in Timor-Leste: Understanding the Past, Imagining the Future* (2007) and (with Tanja Hohe) *Reconciling Justice: "Traditional" Law and State Judiciary in East Timor (2003).*

Dr. Simon Philpott is Senior Lecturer in International Politics at Newcastle University. He served as a UN accredited observer of the independence referendum in East Timor of 1999. He is at present researching Western media representations of Asian cultures, countries and peoples, funded by a British Academy Larger Grant.

Sarah Staveteig is completing her doctorate on Genocide and Fertility: How Mass Violence Shaped Women's Reproductive Trajectories in Bosnia-Herzegovina and Rwanda, at the University of California, Berkeley. She was awarded the UC Institute on Global Conflict and Cooperation Dissertation Fellowship in 2007. She has published widely on themes relating to demography and sociology.

Dr. Clive R. Symmons is Research Associate in Law at Trinity College Dublin and Adjunct Professor at NUI Galway Maritime and Ocean Policy Centre. He has written extensively on international law; his book, *Historic Waters in the Law of the Sea: A Modern Re-appraisal*, was published by Brill in 2007.

James T. Thomson is Senior Associate at Associates in Rural Development (ARD), Inc., an international development consulting firm in Burlington, Vermont. He has participated in ARD's work for the USAID Timor Leste Land Law Program and in similar work relating to Mali, Botswana, Namibia and Malawi.

Dr. Dominik Zaum is Lecturer in International Relations at the University of Reading. He is the author of *The Sovereignty Paradox: The Norms and Politics of International Statebuilding* (OUP, 2007) and is co-editor of *The United Nations Security Council and War* (OUP, 2008).

Dr. Spencer Zifcak is Professor and Director of the Institute of Legal Studies at Australian Catholic University. He has held appointments as Visiting Fellow at Wolfson College, Oxford and New York University and was an Australian Vice-President of the International Commission of Jurists for ten years.

PART I

Justice Systems in Historical and Cultural Perspective

Non-State Actors as Agents of Order: *Suco* Justice and Dispute Resolution Systems in East Timor

Rod Nixon[1]

SUMMARY

Although Portuguese colonial influence over the eastern half of the island of Timor dates back half a millennium, the authority of the *liurais* (kings) who ruled the Timorese micro-kingdoms remained largely intact until the early 20th century. After the suppression of the 'Great Rebellion' that broke out in Manufahi in 1911, the Portuguese consolidated their rule over the province by incorporating the *suco*s (integrated clusters of hamlets)[2] of the territory into sixty administrative *posto*s which became the new interface between the colonial administration and the largely intact administrative systems of the *suco*s. This development sealed the end of the feudal punishment regimes of the various kingdoms, yet also preserved the legitimacy of the administrative and conflict resolution systems that prevailed within the *suco*s until the end of the Portuguese period. These mechanisms maintained their currency throughout the 1975–99 occupation, as a preferred alternative to the Indonesian courts. The legitimacy of *suco* justice and conflict resolution mechanisms continued to prevail in the wake of the Indonesian withdrawal, throughout the passage of the transitional administration, and into the new era of East Timorese statehood. East Timor's robust mediation and conflict resolution mechanisms continue to provide a workable means of resolving a

[1] I thank Kevin Sherlock for providing me with access to rare materials, for providing translations from Portuguese of a number of items (including a part of das Dores' 1903 work) and for providing comments on a draft of this paper. I also thank all those with whom I worked – especially Tanja Hohe and Edwin Urresta – over the period during which the field data presented in these pages was collected, and those from USIP, USAID, ARD Inc. and the various Government of East Timor institutions who provided support and assistance to the research process. I am grateful to James T. Thomson and William Binchy for suggesting that I prepare this paper and to Dennis Shoesmith from Charles Darwin University for his feedback and encouragement.

[2] The term 'village' is sometimes used in the Timorese context to refer to the integrated clusters of hamlets comprising the *suco*. In deference to the argument of Capell (1944:198) that the nature of Timorese settlement is too dispersed to conform to the concept of the village, the term is avoided where possible in the present work.

wide range of disputes, not least in relation to the high proportion of disputes pertaining to land and property. The durability and utility of *suco* conflict resolution mechanisms in East Timor demonstrates the positive influence which non-state actors can play in promoting order in emerging states with low levels of formal governance capacity.

Introduction

Since the commencement of the War against Terror, increased attention has been focussed on the problem of weak states and the need to prevent these from degenerating further to the realm of the failed and collapsed.[3] These latter, dire levels of state capacity and reach have been associated with the increased involvement of non-state actors, sometimes portrayed in a sinister light in the weak state literature. As described by Rotberg (2002a; 2002b; 2003), non-state elements typically include terrorists and warlords who invade the state mandate as the state itself (usually rotting internally from maladministration and corruption) retreats to the capital, its regional influence extending only to milk available sources of mineral wealth. As the states' rapacious and decadent leaders reap the rewards of political office, the terrorists and warlords expand their grip over abandoned tracts of state land, posing a threat not only to the local population, but also to the stability of the region and the world. Such a portrayal, however, fails to do justice to those non-state actors who have local legitimacy and whose existence and influence supports order and stability, including in contexts where state actors are failing to produce similar outcomes.

The fact that political and social modernisation is a gradual process is reflected in the retention, by more than a third of the world's most developed nations, of unelected monarchs as heads of state.[4] Yet international state-building efforts in emerging nations can place such strong emphasis on democratic rights and legal processes that the transitional role of locally legitimate actors becomes at risk of being ignored, potentially with serious consequences. In this regard, McGeough (2004) argues that in Iraq, the US-led coalition reduced

---

[3] See, for example, Australian Foreign Minister Alexander Downer's statement concerning (2004) the need to address the 'risks posed by state and institutional weakness in the Pacific.' For Australia, one manifestation of this commitment has been the Regional Assistance Mission to the Solomon Islands (RAMSI).

[4] Taking member-states of the Organisation for Economic Cooperation and Development (OECD) as an example, the following twelve (out of a total of thirty) have monarchs as heads of state: Australia, Belgium, Canada, Denmark, Japan, Luxemburg, Netherlands, New Zealand, Norway, Spain, Sweden, and the United Kingdom. Note that this is an observation rather than an argument in favour of monarchs as heads of state in developed societies.

their chances of producing stability at an early stage, by sidelining the same Iraqi tribal leaders who assisted them prepare for the actual invasion.[5]

The discipline of the social sciences recognises that different historical circumstances have produced different kinds of human societies, with different capacities for such undertakings as surplus generation and public administration. As demonstrated by the new states of the South Pacific, countries composed predominantly of subsistence farming communities with no autochthonous experience of state development, typically struggle when faced with the challenge of operating in accordance with the modern state model. In such countries (referred to by the writer elsewhere as New Subsistence States),[6] the state will commonly (a) lack the capacity for surplus generation and administration crucial for effective state administration activities, and (b) have citizenry who, in the terms articulated by Weber (1978:227), are more inclined towards the observance of 'traditional authority' than state authority with its rationality-based democratic and legal institutions. In such contexts, the state may hold no monopoly over political legitimacy and may be incapable of delivering even modest benefits. Meanwhile, where the legitimacy and service-delivery capacity of non-state actors has never been extinguished in the course of an organic process of modernisation, they may retain the ability to contribute to order.[7] In a weak state that *never was a state*, non-state actors perceived as legitimate by the population might not just be considered threats to state development or symptoms of state failure; they can also be seen as important elements for the construction of a stable future.

The objective of this chapter is to explore the concept of legitimate non-state actors as agents of order in relation to the case study of East Timor. The exploration focuses on *suco* justice and dispute resolution processes, with

---

[5] This ill-fated oversight has been explored at length by McGeough (2004) in a critique titled *Mission Impossible: The Sheikhs, the US and the Future of Iraq*. In his study, McGeough refers to the role played by tribal leaders in planning the overthrow of the regime of President Saddam Hussein, together with US intelligence agents. However, after the invasion had commenced and just as the Sheikhs were preparing to play their own hand in removing Saddam Hussein from office, the US made the decision to ignore a pact they had made with tribal leaders, and enter Baghdad independently. Shamed deeply by such disrespect for the role of the tribes in determining the future of Iraq, the sheikhs became alienated from the US-led intervention, and McGeough (2004:26–30) profiles the case of one sheikh who initially worked with the US to plan the ousting of Saddam Hussein, yet who ended up supporting the resistance against the US-led invasion.

[6] See Nixon (2006). For broad discussion concerning the difficulties associated with introducing the modern state model in all social contexts, see Migdal (1988) and Latouche (1996[1989]).

[7] See Dinnen (2003) for a discussion on the benefits of restorative justice (facilitated by non-state actors) in the Pacific islands.

particular focus on the mediation of land disputes. The term '*suco*' (sometimes referred to as 'princedom' in English) is used in reference to these systems because the *suco* is the largest indigenous unit of Timorese political organisation to remain in existence following the elimination of the kingdoms, or *reinos*, in the early 20th century. Although the *suco* may not have been a universal element of socio-political organisation throughout Timor, it appears to have been sufficiently common to merit use in this context.[8] The chapter draws on historical sources and recent scholarship, supplemented by both qualitative and quantitative data accumulated by the writer in association with several research projects.[9] The chapter commences with an overview of historical developments of the early colonial period, and descriptions of indigenous systems of justice dating from that time. This is followed by a discussion of developments that occurred during the late Portuguese and Indonesian periods, and how these contributed to the ongoing strength of *suco* administration and justice practices. A further section describes the contemporary nature of these justice and dispute resolution systems and a final section reviews attempts and proposals in the post-Indonesian period for their integration into the state framework. This latter discussion pertains both to the period of UN transitional administration, and the period since the inauguration of the *República Democrática de Timor-Leste* (RDTL).

A Geographic Overview

Lying approximately seven hundred kms to the northwest of Darwin, Timor is an island of about 30,000 square kms[10] located in the 'non-volcanic Outer Arc' (Metzner 1977:21; Glover 1986:8) on the south-east perimeter of the Indonesian archipelago. The island is roughly between fifty and one hundred kms wide and close to five hundred kms long, with a range of mountains running from end to end. The highest point, at 2,960 metres,[11] is Mount Ramelau in the eastern part of the island. As described by the geographer

---

[8] See Hicks (1976:4–8). See also Davidson (1996:109-12), who discusses variations to the *suco* model of socio-political organisation.

[9] These include a 2002 United States Institute of Peace (USIP) investigation of the interface between formal and traditional justice systems during the period of United Nations (UN) transitional administration, and a study of land dispute mediation systems completed in 2003 as part of the ARD East Timor Land Law Program (LLP) that was supported by the United States Agency for International Development (USAID).

[10] According to a GIS database based on data orthophoto data collected by the Australian Defence Forces in August 2001 (accessed through the East Timor National Directorate of Land and Property), the area of East Timor is just under 15,000 square kms. Farram (2004:31) notes that estimates of the land mass of the whole island vary from 26,000 to over 33,000 square kms.

[11] According to the government website (*Turismo Timor-Leste* 2005).

Joachim Metzner (1977:22), the topography of the island is the product of 'a turbulent geological past...broadly characterized by a core of rugged hill and mountain land consisting of a confused mass of knife-edged, highly dissected ridges trending in various directions and craggy upland blocks....'

Unlike the many volcanic islands of the region,[12] the geology of Timor is characterised by marine sediments and clays (Metzner 1977:21; Fox 1988:261). An implication of this is that the island's soils are considered more 'fragile' than those of the volcanic islands. The cultivation potential of the island is further limited by the steep slopes that cover close to half the surface area, making the thin layer of soil vulnerable to erosion from the severe monsoonal rains that lash the landscape seasonally. North of the mountain range, these rains come between November and April, and are followed by an extensive dry season that results in widespread water shortages, imposing a further limitation on agricultural potential. Areas to the south and east of the range experience a later wet season and a less arduous dry season (MAFF[13] 2004:1).[14] The unpredictability of the yearly rainfall is yet another factor that impacts upon agricultural production capacity, and droughts are likely to result in severe food shortages or famine (Ormeling 1957:21,239-240).[15] According to Fox (1988:262), the capricious nature of the natural aquifer system, in which water is 'trapped in limestone deposits by irregular sheets of clay,' complicates the matter of water supply even further, since earth tremors may interrupt the flow of spring water emanating from these aquifers, making new springs appear elsewhere. Fox explains that the hydrological features of Timor have implications on human settlement possibilities, necessitating 'a scattered form of settlement and cultivation.' As discussed below, the geographical

---

[12] From his extensive travels in the area, Wallace (1962[1869]:4–5) commented on the great degree to which the 'Malay Archipelago' was the product of, and was subject to, volcanic activity. Wallace observed (1962:5) that 'Timor itself consists of ancient stratified rocks, but is said to have one volcano near its centre.' Glover (1986:8) notes that 'Timor is the largest island in the non-volcanic Outer Banda Arc, which also includes the islands of Buton, Baru, Savu, Semau, Roti, Leti, Tanimbar, Kai and Seram.' A 'volcanic Inner Arc' includes the islands of Alor, Bali, Ceram, Flores, Java, Lombok, Sumatra, Sumbawa and Wetar (Metzner1977:21).

[13] (East Timor) Ministry of Agriculture, Forestry and Fisheries.

[14] See also Ormeling (1957:11–29), Metzner (1977:61–84), Glover (1986:8-11), Fox (1996:1–2).

[15] All in the context of increasing population pressure and the use of shifting cultivation practices unsupported by sufficient anti-erosion controls. Writing in the mid-1950s primarily in relation to West Timor, Ormeling noted (1957:240) that '[a]lready conditions are constantly changing for the worse. Migrations among the growing mountain population bring only temporary relief. In the new settlement areas more land is cleared for cultivation, burning takes place more frequently, fallow periods are shortened and, since anti-erosion measures are almost lacking, erosion is speeded up. Concentrations of growing cattle herds in lantana-free districts lead to the same results. Thus, the anthropogenic destruction spiral causes general deterioration of both man and his environment.'

constraints of Timor have influenced the nature of the political systems that have developed on the island.

Human Societies and Political Systems

According to Glover (1986:212), who undertook detailed archaeological work in eastern Timor in 1966–67, the evidence 'suggests that Timor was occupied before 13,500 years ago by groups, probably few in number...dependent on naturally-occurring food sources.' Agricultural production practices, supported by animals (pigs) and technologies (pottery) providing modest surplus storage capacity, appear to have commenced on Timor around five millennium ago. In the words of Glover (1986:12), '[a]bout 4500 years ago substantial changes occurred in the pattern of this archaic Timorese culture, for pigs and pottery then appeared in the archaeological record.'[16] Glover speculates (1986:204) that the introduction of these important new economic features may indicate 'an immigration of agricultural peoples into Timor some 5000 years ago,' considering 'the well documented reluctance of hunter-gatherers to take up agriculture except under considerable pressure and continuous example.'

The rich diversity of ethnic groups to have migrated to Timor, as reflected in a range of 'physical types' and fourteen or more languages, has drawn considerable comment from observers.[17] From his own review of the literature, Ormeling (1957:67) concluded that 'the Timor archipelago is a transition area, where an Indonesian-Malay and a Melanesian population component meet and influence each other.' With respect to linguistic diversity, Fox (1996:2–4) refers to the prevalence in Timor both of Austronesian languages related to those spoken on Flores, the Maluku islands and Solor; and of Trans-New Guinea languages related to those spoken on the nearby islands of Alor, Kisar and Pantar, as well as the *Vogalkop* region of Irian Jaya. In Ormeling's (1957:236) assessment, despite their differences,[18] 'the various ethnic groups have developed a striking similarity in their material culture – shifting cultivation being the base of economy for all groups.'

---

[16] According to Glover (1986:202–203), the 'butchering marks' found on pig bones aged between 2,000 and 1,500 years (approximately), 'lend a certain amount of support for the introduction of metal into Timor well before the arrival of the Portuguese.'

[17] See, for example Forbes (1989[1885]:424–25,464–67), Moura (1937:475–76), Gonçalves (1937:444–47), Capell (1944:194–96), Ormeling (1957:66–67), Hicks (1972:97), Glover (1986:12), Fox (1996:2–4), Gunn (1999:32) and Hull (2000:1).

[18] According to Ormeling (1957:74), the 'Indo-Malay affected part of the population' (including the Belunese and Rotinese of West Timor) are more enterprising than the Melanesian population, utilizing 'the natural resources more fully' and engaging 'in a greater variety of economic activities.' Fox (1988:259-60,269), however, rejects these assertions, arguing for example that the Rotinese were slower to adapt to the introduction of maize than the (Melanesian) Atoni Pah Meto (People of Dry Land).

Whereas elsewhere in the archipelago fertile soils and high rainfall characteristics supported the development of technically and administratively complex societies with broad-spanning interdependencies and surplus-generation capacities,[19] the geographic constraints of Timor were unconducive to such a development trajectory.[20] In contrast to the irrigation-based states of Java with their webs of inter-reliant communities and bureaucratic service delivery, the political structures that developed in Timor prior to the colonial consolidation of the late 19th and early 20th centuries, were characterised by unstable head-hunting micro-kingdoms constantly warring over entitlement to draw tithes from the narrow margin of surplus produced by subsistence farmers, supplemented by benefits derived from trading in such items as beeswax and sandalwood (*Santalum album*).[21] The latter commodity was

[19] Commenting on state development on parts of Java, Legge (1964:5) remarks that '[w]here intensive agriculture prevailed, it was not possible for each village to be a completely closed and selfsufficient [*sic*] unit. Such agriculture required cooperation for the maintenance of the irrigation system on which a series of villages depended. It thus called for some sort of unit to overarch the individual communities. Hence the growth of principalities, supported by agricultural tribute and supplying in return a necessary bureaucratic service.'

[20] As archaeologists (Denham *et al.*, 2003:192–93) point out in relation to abandoned irrigation systems in Kuk Swamp (Papua New Guinea) dating to several thousand years prior to the development of irrigated agriculture in Mesopotamia, the necessary geographic conditions for state development are insufficient cause for it to occur in the absence of human motivation. It would also appear clear, however, that without the necessary geographic conditions, state development has little or no chance of occurring as an autochthonous process. The writer has discussed this subject elsewhere (Nixon 2006).

[21] In an analysis focussing on the warring kingdoms of southwest Timor in the 19th century, McWilliam (1996:128-29), describes how the Nabuasa progress from being a 'warrior clan' on the periphery of one 'ruling center' or micro-kingdom, to a ruling centre in their own right, with their own peripheral and deferential warrior clans. This account demonstrates why traditional Timorese states were inherently unstable in terms of their core-periphery dynamic, since the peripheral warrior clans of any one state, charged with responsibility for waging headhunting expeditions into outlying areas to facilitate a flow of wealth and authority to the centre, could be tempted to rebel against the principal central clan and establish themselves as centres in their own right, with satellites of their own.

Documentation from the Portuguese colonial administration confirms that the Timorese political organisation in the east of the island were similarly characterised by unstable and opportunistic alliance patterns and core-periphery dynamics into the late 19th century, at least in relation to their interaction with the Portuguese colonial administration. In 1870, following a term of Governor of Portuguese Timor, Antonio Joaquim Garcia reported to his superiors in Macau (Garcia [1870] in Sherlock 1986a:62) that 'one cannot have nor should have real confidence in the *regulos* [*liurai*s] even in those said to be vassals, for all of them are linked, some by barlaques (marriage) and other by blood oaths, and when they give 200 men to help the Government they give an equal or larger number to the enemy, and it is believed, Your Excellency, that this is without fail; there is one difference to be noted – that all the *regulos* inclined towards the Government give to it their best people, and, in time of combat, if realising that we have the advantage, those who are fighting on behalf of the enemy join with ours, and the action is soon decided; however, if they realise that we are at a disadvantage in position or strength, they are the first to betray us.'

already renowned for its quality in pre-colonial times, and Boxer (1960:350) remarks that '[l]ong before Vasco da Gama rounded the Cape of Good Hope, Timor was known to the Chinese as their best source for the supply of sandalwood.'

Notwithstanding the subsistence basis of Timorese society and the ongoing warfare, the political structures that characterised the Kingdoms of Timor were highly ritually complex. Wehali, the ancient centre of ritual Timorese power situated towards the south coast of the island to the west of the present border, is perhaps the most recognised example of Timorese ritual complexity. Once headed by a powerful but 'passive' Tetum ruler known as the 'Great Lord' or '*Maromak Oan*' (Child of God), Wehali was closely connected to the vast realm of Sonba'i to the west of Wehali inhabited by the *Dawan* speaking Atoni, and possessed ritual power that spread widely throughout the island. Fox (1982:23–25) describes how the power of Wehali was not based primarily on military might but derived from the nature of its matrilineal descent practices in a land dominated by patrilineal descent systems, and because of the 'female principle of authority' which featured so strongly in Wehali society. As a centre of ritual power that traditionally dispersed its men in marriage to outside areas, Wehali is believed to have gained wide influence as a source of *liurai*s (kings) to other princedoms throughout the island, placing it in a key position in relation to the island's trade in sandalwood and beeswax.[22] Although Wehali retains an historic profile in Timorese culture for the influence it once held,[23] it was physically destroyed in 1642 as an outcome of the development of geopolitical tensions involving new players, themselves attracted to Timor by the abundant supplies of sandalwood (Boxer 1960:350; Schulte Nordholt 1971:163–65: Hicks 1976:4).

In the course of the ensuing colonial consolidation of Timor (discussed below in relation to East Timor), most *liurai*s would ultimately be disempowered

---

[22] Fox (1982:23–25) remarks that '[t]o appreciate the importance of Wehale, it is essential to realize that its significance had nothing to do with military strength or prowess, but rather with an ideology of spiritual authority – a kind of receptive powerlessness that left it open to protection and vulnerable to intrusion. This is because, in the idiom of the Timorese, Wehale epitomized the female principle of authority.' See also Fox (1996:10-14) for a summary of analysis concerning the nature of power in Wehali and surrounding areas, under the subheading 'Timorese Ideas of Political Authority.' See also Francillon (1980:251–53,259-61), Schulte Nordholt (1971:232–39) and Farram (2004:36–37).

[23] In 2002, in the context of a discussion about the *Negara Timor Raya* (Nation of the Land of Timor) movement, a *katuas* (elder) from near Suai (now living in Australia) asserted to the writer that 'Kupang was never given to Indonesia. Timor is *still* one country. The story of Timor has nothing to do with the story of Indonesia…[and]…Wehali is Timorese, not Indonesian.'

and the *suco*s from which their kingdoms were composed, integrated into colonial administrative units. Yet the demise of the formal authority of the *liurai*s would by no means precipitate the destruction of the ritual and administrative authority that prevailed within the *suco*s, which became integrated into the Portuguese system of colonial administration. Indeed, the continuing strength and viability of the *suco* administrations after their integration into the Portuguese colonial administration supports the assertion of one commentator (Davidson 1996:11) that even prior to the subjugation of the *liurai*s in the early 20th century, it had long been the *chefe de suco* (chief of *suco*) whose 'primary authority' was most respected by the Timorese.[24] As Berlie (2000:139-40) later noted, at a point when East Timor was emerging from almost a quarter century of Indonesian occupation and preparing for transition to national independence, the hereditary authority of *chefe*s *de suco* remained a fundamental feature of life throughout this territory, the economy of which remained overwhelmingly characterised by subsistence agriculture.

At the comparative level, even if traditional Timorese social structures lack the administrative and organisational capacities which developed on Java, commentators (Glover 1986:12; Capell 1944:196) have remarked that the Timorese social institutions are highly structured in comparison to the Melanesian 'big-man' systems to the east, notwithstanding the mixed ethnic origins of the population that includes a Melanesian component. In this respect, Glover (1986:12) asserts that 'Timor is basically Indonesian in culture and not Melanesian,' and that:

> Timorese culture can be distinguished from that of Melanesia by a number of traits such as a developed class system with hereditary chiefs, cattle-keeping, the predominance of cereals including wet rice over root crops,

[24] An account related to the writer by a *Naizuf Mnasi* (senior ritual leader) from *Nuno Heno* (meaning 'many languages' in the local *Bikeno*) in Oecusse (interviewed in March 2003), begins with reference to a time when the island of Timor was already populated, yet had no *raja*s. Then eventually, four brothers with advanced ritual powers arrived in different parts of the island, each becoming a *liurai*. It was the brother Benu Sila who settled in Oecusse, and so advanced was his ability to promote fertility and bring rain, that people of many languages joined together to follow him, a development now reflected in the name of the settlement. Such origin myths are common in Timor (see Schulte Nordholt 1971:159-63,232–38) and raise the question (Davidson 1994:112) of whether there was a separate class of *liurai*s in Timor, and if so, 'where did they come from?' The possibility that in most cases, the *suco* was an early form of social organisation pre-dating the arrival of the *liurai*s provides a possible explanation for the ease with which *suco* administration systems were integrated into the colonial administration following the elimination of the kingdoms.

metal working (iron for swords, and gold and silver for ornaments), weaving of cotton, and a partial market economy with the production of goods for sale and export.

The Long Process of Colonial Consolidation

As documented by historians,[25] the Portuguese first reached Timor in the early 16th century following the 1511 conquest of the key trading port of Malacca. No substantial settlement was constructed in the region, however, until 1566, at which time Portuguese Dominican priests built a fort on Solor Island, to the north of Timor and the east of Flores. From this settlement originated a Portuguese-native *mestiço* population who came to be known as the *Topasses*, and who followed the Portuguese settlers to Larantuka on eastern Flores after the Dutch conquered the Solor fort in 1613. As the Dutch and the Portuguese settled into a regional conflict that would last almost half a century, the Dominican priests and their *Topasse* allies expanded their alliances over the island of Timor, with the *Topasses* establishing a trading base at Lifau, in what is now the East Timorese enclave district of Oecusse in 1641.[26] Nominally identifying themselves as Portuguese and cooperating with the Portuguese colonial authorities on an opportunistic basis, the *Topasses* developed as an independent force in their own right, cultivating strong local connections on the island of Timor and proceeding to dominate the sandalwood trade.[27] By the early 1660s when the Portuguese and Dutch finally resolved to end their

---

[25] See, for example, Boxer (1960:350-54), Vaz (1964), Fox (1996:5–7), Gunn (1999:51–67), Schulte Nordholt (1971:159-81), Farram (2004:37–41).

[26] According to Fox (1996:7), this occurred after the native ruler of Oecusse was converted to Catholicism by a Dominican priest.

[27] Soon after the establishment of the *Topasse* presence at Lifau, the *Topasse* officer Captain Major Francisco Fernandes led the expedition that razed Wehali in 1642. This expedition, which also subdued (although without destruction) the allied realm of Sonba'i, served as retaliation against an emerging relationship between the realm of Wehali and the Dutch, and also advanced *Topasse* control of sandalwood trading, (Fox 1996:5–7; Schulte Nordholt 1971:163–165; Farram 2004:37–41). Note also that it was not only the *Topasses* who were equivocal about cooperating with the Portuguese authorities. Although Church officials would enjoy good relations with the *Topasses* (Fox 1996:6), relations between the Church and the Portuguese state weakened enduringly in 1622 when the Vatican introduced a new policy of controlling Catholic missions directly instead of through the Portuguese royalty. There are indications that the few Church officials stationed in Timor were preoccupied more with trade and other matters than with proselytising, much to the irritation of the Portuguese administration (Crowe 1996:27, 34–36). In this respect, despite numerous Timorese leaders apparently declaring themselves Christian following the demonstration of 'Christian' power that resulted in the destruction of Wehali in 1642 (Schulte Nordholt 1971:165), Wallace would observe over 200 years later (1962[1869]:151) based on his travels in Timor in 1861, that '[e]xcept a few half-breeds in the town, there are no native Christians in the island of Timor. The people retain their independence in a great measure, and both dislike and despise their would-be rulers, whether Portuguese or Dutch.'

regional conflict, *Topasse* powerbrokers were endeavouring to influence developments over the entire island (Boxer 1960:352).

After almost two hundred years of engagement with Timor, the Portuguese finally established a permanent settlement at Lifau on Timor in 1702. It was at this point the Portuguese first bestowed military ranks upon Timorese leaders for the purpose of integrating them into the framework of an incipient Portuguese colonial administration.[28] At Lifau the Portuguese faced constant insurgencies until being forced by the *Topasse*s to relocate to Dili in 1769. During the first half of the 18th century, the *Topasse*s also tried repeatedly[29] but ultimately without success, to dislodge the Dutch from their base in Kupang. The scale of the *Topasse* defeat on their final attempt in 1749 was such that the Dutch were subsequently able to gradually expand their influence over much of the western half of the island, which at this time and for long after was regarded as being composed (see Figure 1)[30] of the two native kingdoms of Bello (comprising up to fifty smaller kingdoms) in the east, and Servião (comprising around 16 smaller kingdoms) in the west (Boxer 1960:352–54; Fox 1996:8). If the *Topasse* defeat and the subsequent expansion of Dutch influence in the west was the beginning of the eventual colonial division of Timor, then this process was extremely drawn out. Farram (2004:41) points out that following the *Topasse* defeat of 1749 the island became 'divided into three spheres of influence,' with the Portuguese in the east, the *Topasse*s in the centre and the Dutch in the west. Whereas all three of the powers endeavoured to expand their control during the second half of the 18th century, the Dutch and the Portuguese had very little authority outside their respective settlements of Kupang and Dili during this time.

---

[28] According to Boxer (1960:353), Timorese leaders were 'inordinately proud of their honorific military ranks,' which included the rank of colonel for 'tribal heads' and lower ranks for other local system officials. The ranks changed over time, and by the late Portuguese period (Barata 1963:25–26) the rank system entitled a *liurai* or *régulo* (head of kingdom) to the rank of major; a *chefe de suco* (chief of *suco*) to the rank of *capitão* (captain); a *chefe de suco dependente* (deputy *suco* head) to the rank of *tenente* (lieutenant), and; a *chefe de povoações* (hamlet chief) to the rank of *sargento-ajudante* (assistant sergeant). See also Gonçalves (1937:457), Saldanha (1994:46) and Berlie (2000:145), who refers to the strong links between the first governor (Antonio Coelho Guerreiro) and 'local *adat* [customary laws, values and belief systems].'

[29] *Topasse* assaults on Kupang were made in 1735, 1745, and 1749 (Fox 1996:8).

[30] Note that in view of the shifting alliances characteristic of the Timorese kingdoms of the period, the border between the kingdoms of Servião and Bello indicated on Affonso de Castro's map of 1867 (see Figure 1 below) may not reflect the situation in the mid-18th century.

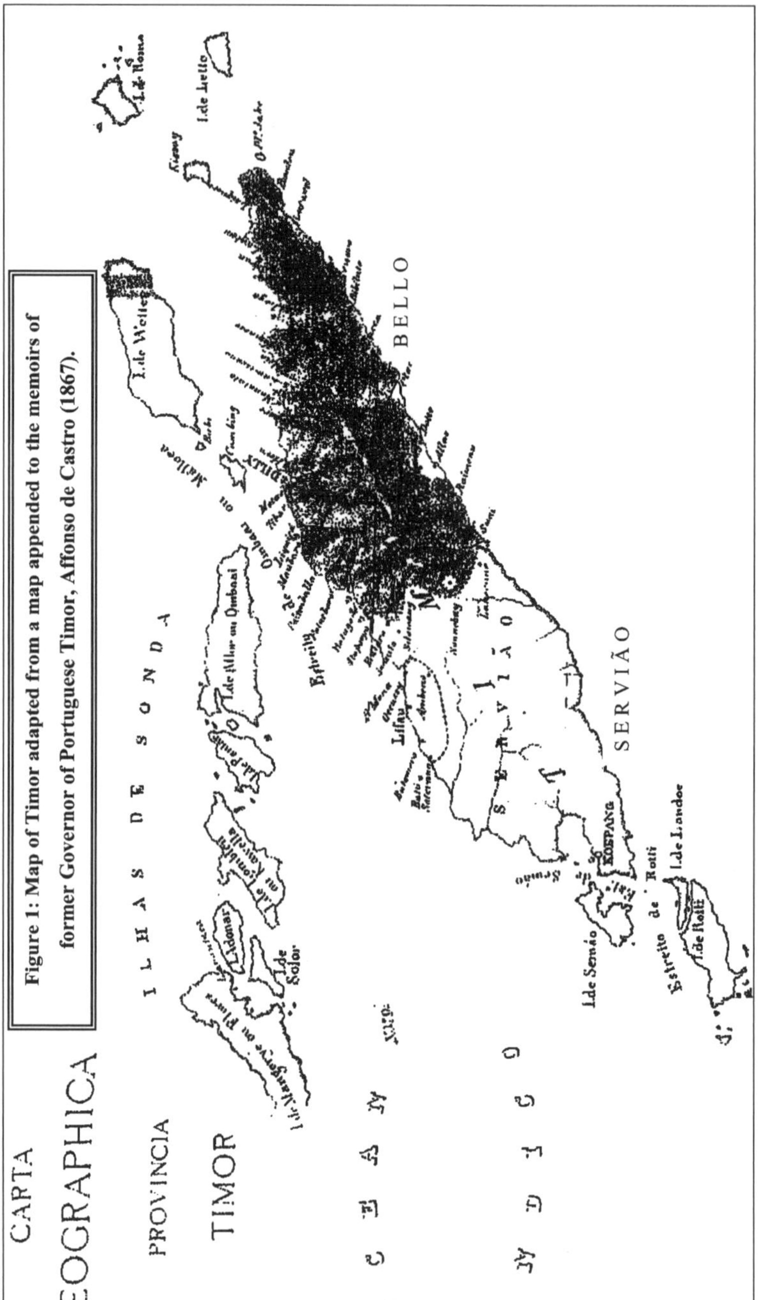

Figure 1: Map of Timor adapted from a map appended to the memoirs of former Governor of Portuguese Timor, Affonso de Castro (1867).

As historians of Portuguese Timor have highlighted,[31] the Portuguese made few advances towards consolidating control of the eastern half of the island until the late 19th or early 20th century. By the 1850s, sandalwood stocks had become severely depleted, influencing Portuguese authorities in Macau to cut shipping services to Timor for almost four decades.[32] The territory experienced economic malaise while warfare between Timorese kingdoms and insurgencies against the Portuguese administration remained common features. The comments of British visitors to Portuguese Timor during this period were commonly scathing,[33] yet no less so were the comments of some Portuguese observers, whose accounts similarly portray the colonial administration of Portuguese Timor as under-resourced and lethargic with minimal reach into the interior. A Portuguese officer, believed to have been *Segundo Tenente* (Second Lieutenant) João Monteiro Pinto da Fonseca Vaz ([1870] in Sherlock 1986a:73),[34] published the following account of his 1869 visit to the Portuguese fort at Batugadé:

> It is notable that the Portuguese, having been in Timor for centuries, have paid no attention to taking advantage of some strategic points which nature would seem to be indicating. The result of this is that, with insufficient forces and stationed in completely dominated places, we are everywhere at the mercy of the good or ill will of the indigenes…[who]…if they should

---

[31] See, for example, Boxer (1960:335) and (Fox 1996:8).

[32] For an historical overview of the financial crisis faced by Portuguese Timor during this period, see Davidson (1994:83–87).

[33] Based on his visit to Dili in 1861, Wallace (1962[1869]:144–51) referred to a 'most miserable' Portuguese government, incompetent military officers, officials who robbed the natives and an administrative centre with the aesthetic attributes of a 'poor native town.' He also noted that exquisitely dressed administrative officials and military officers proliferated 'in a degree quite disproportionate to the size or appearance of the place.' Henry Forbes (1989[1885]:415–17), who visited Portuguese Timor in the early 1880s with his wife Anna, observed that '[t]he lack of money to carry out efficiently the necessary municipal arrangements was painfully evident.' Forbes quickly determined the need to reside at elevated altitude when in the vicinity of Dili, in order to avoid the 'pestilence that nightly rises from the marshes surrounding the town,' although even this precaution did not prevent Anna Forbes catching fever, which she describes in detail in her own account (Forbes 1987[1887]:287–300). References to the hazardous nature of the Dili environs during this period were frequent, such that in the words of Gunn (1999:130), Portuguese Timor became '[n]otorious as a graveyard for residents and travellers alike.'

[34] Based on a detailed search of the Macau archives, Kevin Sherlock has compiled collections of articles (see Sherlock 1986a; Sherlock 1986b) on 'Timor in the Portuguese Periodical Press of the Far East' published during this period. A series of articles appear under the (often truncated) title 'Voyage of the Corvette *Sá da Bandeira* to Timor and Operations against the Ruler of Cová.' Although these articles are signed only with the initials 'F.V.,' it is the view of Sherlock (based on a review of the manifest of the *Sá da Bandeira*) that the initials are likely to be those of Joáo Monteiro Pinto da Fonseca Vaz.

have had some energy they would already have long ago put an end to that same shadow of dominion which they still today treat with contempt.

The stockade of Batugadé is also of loose stone...The few cannon with which it is fortified, respectable for their antiquity, are always pointing obstinately towards the same side; and there is no way of moving them...since the two wooden trestles on which each is mounted resist it. If necessity obliges the firing of a shot, the piece with which it is one is immediately castigated for its act...bringing the trestles crashing down.

Notoriously short of funds,[35] the Portuguese administration in the 19th century depended on Timorese *liurai*s (as well as locally recruited and more highly regarded *moradore*[36] forces) for the security of the territory. However, as indicated in the following account of Antonio Joaquim Garcia ([1870] in Sherlock 1986a:62),[37] who had recently completed a term as interim governor; mobilising local support to help wage war against rebel kingdoms could take considerable patience:

...not having the military strength ...to promptly subdue any attempt at rebellion against the legally constituted authorities, is subject to the will of different *regulos* [*liurai*s] who make up their minds to support the Government with amazing slowness, and, even then, only after having carried out some tests at what they call an *estillo*,[38] which turns out to be the bringing together of the so-called men of war, which may take many days or even months; then they are tested for strength, many being rejected as a result of this trial. After that they go on to behead dogs, cocks, sheep, pigs and buffaloes in order to observe the way in which they fall, the

[35] In relation to his recently completed term of governorship of the Portuguese Timor, Antonio Joaquim Garcia ([1870] in Sherlock 1986a:62) referred to the severe financial conditions in the colony that necessitated the prioritisation of expenditure. Garcia remarked that 'I always had a lack of means to pay the public employees, whom I left with eight months in arrears, not failing however to have had the regular soldiers' wages paid up-to-date.'

[36] According to Garcia ([1870] in Sherlock 1986a:67) the most reliable local troops at this time were the *Moradores de Dilly*, who could be even sent if necessary to arrest *liurai*s and other native officials, thereby saving 'a good sum of florins' on the cost of regular Portuguese soldiers. In later periods as the various kingdoms were integrated into Portuguese rule, the term was applied more broadly to locally recruited troops (for example, see Barata 1963:25). Literally meaning 'citizen,' in Portuguese, the Timorese came to understand the term to mean 'warrior' as a result of the common Portuguese practice of drafting citizen (*moradore*) forces for security purposes. One of the results of this practice, as the writer found in the course of fieldwork in 2002, is that in the present day, *suco* security officers in some parts of Timor are referred to as *moradore*s.

[37] See also Forbes (1989[1885]:444–46) for a further description of the warrior selection process.

[38] Literally meaning 'style' in Portuguese, but comparable in the Timorese context to the Malay/Indonesian term *adat*.

> direction in which the head is turned, and if the intestines are perfect; if the heads fallen at random are turned towards the side of the enemy, they become discouraged, some retiring to their houses, and the *regulos* do not then have the power to bring them together again; the rest march on, but always with the idea and fear of being defeated by the enemy. There is nobody who can make them deviate from these heathen manners and customs. It is worthy of note that this is the case only when it is to assist the Government, because when they are attacked they defend themselves courageously without resorting to the so-called *estillo*.

Although patterns of power would change after the elimination of the kingdoms, the dependence on elements of Timorese social organisation for the security and administration of the territory would remain a feature of colonial administration in Timor until the end of the Portuguese period. This feature of colonial rule would have bearing on the nature of justice and conflict resolution processes practiced throughout the 20th century, as well as on ongoing tensions between some ethic groups.[39]

Despite and because of the prevailing economic stagnation,[40] the period between 1851 and 1916 is significant, firstly because it was during this period that the colonial powers in Timor sought to reach agreement about the location of their respective domains in the Timor region and assert control over their colonial subjects, and secondly because of associated social and political changes that occurred. In his account of 'The Partitioning of Timor by the Portuguese and the Dutch,' Farram (1999:42–48)[41] outlines how a series of disputes between the Dutch and the Portuguese over their various claims in the Timor region during the first half of the 19th century led to these powers meeting in Dili on 1st August 1851 for the purpose of commencing negotiations concerning their respective territories. Whereas a treaty was finally concluded in 1859 (Farram 1999:44), this by no means finalised

[39] Characteristic of warfare between Timorese kingdoms, wrote one Portuguese observer (das Dores 1903:29), was the 'inveterate practice among the natives to burn the settlements of the defeated who had fled, a practice always adopted by the Portuguese authorities who at times had seemed more savage than them.' The destruction of rebel villages, and the exploitation of antipathies between ethnic groups to facilitate the suppression of rebellions appears to have persisted into the late Portuguese period, as seen in relation to the involvement of native auxiliaries and Makassae villagers in the destruction and looting of Naueti settlements following the 1959 rebellion in the Uatolari sub-district of Viqueque (Chamberlain 2005:16–18; Gunn 2006:4). It appears likely that the events of this period exacerbated tensions that persist in the area to the present day, particularly in relation to competing land ownership claims.

[40] As discussed in the main text, many of the measures introduced by the Portuguese were designed (often without success) to raise revenue for the colonial administration.

[41] See also Saldanha (1994:38-39).

negotiations because no specific borders had yet been determined and neither the Dutch nor the Portuguese had asserted control over their territories by this time. By 1916, however, both the Dutch and the Portuguese had finally consolidated control over their respective colonies after hundreds of years of presence in the region, and a final border settlement was able to be reached.[42]

Gunn (1999:160-61) describes how in the years following the 1859 treaty between the Portuguese and Dutch (the 'Lisbon Treaty'), the Portuguese created 'the embryo of the modern politico-administrative system on Timor,' by establishing district military commands in Alas, Batugadé, Buursuco,[43] Cailaco, Dili, Lautem, Manatuto, Maubara, Oecusse,[44] Vermasse[45] and Viqueque. It was through these commands that the colonial administration sought to rule Timor indirectly through the agency of the leaders of the Timorese *reino*s, or kingdoms. As clear from the accounts of colonial officials cited earlier, however, maintaining the allegiance of the *régulo*s or *liurai*s during this period remained an ongoing challenge, and one not helped by the Portuguese administration's new resolve to use the *finta* (customary tribute) system as a means for raising revenue for the colonial administration.

With sandalwood stocks exhausted since the early decades of the 19th century, the new revenue raising effort centred on coffee,[46] and historians (Gunn 1999:160-63; Davidson 1994:90-95; Clarence-Smith 1992:4–6) have outlined in detail the difficulties faced by a succession of Portuguese governors in the second half of the 19th century as they sought to make coffee production a viable industry from which the colonial administration could benefit. The original initiative launched by Governor Affonso de Castro in the early 1860s required that every family plant 600 coffee trees and that a proportion of the harvest be collected via the *finta* system in each *reino* and forwarded to the colonial administration, minus a proportion to be kept by each *liurai* for facilitating the process. Yet despite the increase in coffee production that ensued as a result of the distribution of coffee

---

[42] In fact the determination of the borders has been a gradual process, and negotiations and disputes continue in some areas. The process of border demarcation continues, for example, in the enclave district of Oecusse, and has led to a number of misunderstandings and incidents. In a recent press statement released by United Nations Office in Timor-Leste (UNOTIL), reference (UNOTIL 2005) is made to these.

[43] Elsewhere (Sherlock 1983:49), the spelling 'Bobucusso' is used. Forbes (1989[1885]:473) uses 'Bibiçuçu'

[44] According to Gunn (1999:160), the Oecusse command was not established until 1863, whereas the other commands were established earlier.

[45] More usually spelt 'Vemasse.'

[46] According to Gunn (1999:160), '[t]hose kingdoms not cultivating coffee were obliged to offer up one-tenth of their rice-harvest.'

seedlings, no proportionate increase in government earnings followed. This eventually led to a series of more resolute attempts at colonial domination, ultimately resulting in the introduction of the *capitação* (head tax) in 1908.[47] There is broad agreement among commentators[48] that the intensification of colonial control, and in particular the introduction of taxes, increased dissatisfaction with the Portuguese colonial administration and contributed to the factors that led to the 'Great Rebellion' of 1911. The rebellion itself, which began in Manufahi under the leadership of Dom Boaventura and spread to other parts of Portuguese Timor including Dili, was only suppressed after a bloody campaign involving over 12,000 troops (many brought in from other colonies) and the use of the *Pátria*, a Portuguese gunboat, for shelling rebel positions.[49]

The suppression of the Manufahi rebellion can be seen as a turning point in the administration of the colony. In terms of practical effects on the Timorese socio-political structure, the suppression of the 'Great Rebellion' resulted in a dramatic change in the power held by the colonial administration vis-à-vis the power held by the *liurai*s. Although a number of *liurai* families would continue to access privileges and hold authority in different forms into and beyond the 20th century,[50] at the level of day-to-day administration, the office

---

[47] According to Davidson (1994:104), the *capitação* (paid in Mexican *pataca*) initially applied only to adult males. The next year, however, all males of sixteen years or over were required to pay the tax. The preferred method of payment of the *capitação* was cash.

[48] See Clarence-Smith (1992:5), Davidson (1994:100-104), Jolliffe (1978:35) and Gunn (1999:169).

[49] It is of historical note that the last major rebellion of the Portuguese period occurred in 1959. For a brief overview of rebellions in Portuguese Timor, see Saldanha (1994:43), according to whom '[a]pproximately 550 large and small scale rebellions are recorded to have been staged by the people of East Timor against the power of the oppressor.' Also see Gunn (1999:160), who engages with earlier commentators to issue a reminder that not all of the rebellions were 'necessarily anti-colonial,' since many were primarily motivated by friction *between* kingdoms.

[50] Despite the dramatic intensification of Portuguese power following the suppression of the Manufahi rebellion, it appears clear that some elements of *reino* organisation persisted for some time. It is likely, for example, that ongoing hostilities from the *reino*-period formed the basis of the 'local jealousies and rivalries' referred to by Callinan (1984[1953]:155) which contributed to incidents of 'slaughter' between native groups from different regions during WWII. According to the detailed evaluation of Timorese authority structures in the mid-20th century produced by Kevin Sherlock (1983:15), reference to *liurai*s (as distinct from *chefes de suco*) and *reinos* (kingdoms) continued to appear in official records into the second half of the 20th century. Implying a gradual reduction in the profile of the *reinos*, however, Sherlock also notes that '[i]t would appear that the *suco*...or princedom, a grouping of *povoações* or settlements, was the largest indigenous political unit still in widespread and effective operation in East Timor in the 1945–1975 period.' Concerning the *liurais* themselves, post-war observers (Landman and Plant 1948 Part 1:229) noted that '[t]he few remaining kings are recognised by the Government and are granted many privileges: their homes are provided by the Administration and they are free of the burden of head tax. The do not appear to have any very clearly defined legal powers, but apparently handle matters concerning native custom...' For a discussion on the authority wielded by *liurai*s in more recent times in militias, resistance movements and politics, see Farram (2006).

of *suco* head (*dato*,[51] or *chefe de suco*) became the highest level of traditional authority across most of Portuguese Timor. Capell (1944:198) refers to this development as follows:

> At the present time the *dato*, as I gathered from conversation in a refugee camp, is rather an exalted personage with whom the average commoner has little to do. This is obviously the result of the political eclipse of the *leo-rai*, and to this a great revolt against the Portuguese in 1911–12 largely contributed. After putting down that revolt, the Portuguese abolished for the most part these petty kings and divided their authority among the *dato* ruling different *suku*. Where the *leo-rai* is still found, he almost always represents a broken succession, the present ruler being elected from leaders of groups who were faithful to Portugal during the revolt, and not necessarily related in any way to the old rulers.[52]

When British representative C.H. Archer (1941:7) visited Portuguese Timor in 1941, therefore, he observed the following system of colonial administration in the districts:

> The circumscription [district, from *circunscrição*] is divided into a number of smaller administrative posts under officials known as "chefes de posto." It is the duty of these officials to collect the head taxes, supervise the work of the natives in their area, and attend to all the minor details of administration. They are assisted by native chiefs as unpaid functionaries and by bands of volunteers, known as "Moradoors" [*sic*], who are also unpaid, and form the greatest value to the government.

[51] Note that the term '*dato*,' although often used in reference to the *suco* head, is also used (Saldanha 1994:45) as a term of address for other leaders of royal descent, including *liurais*.

[52] It is understood that the refugee camp referred to by Capell was at Bob's Farm near Armidale, Australia. See also Hicks (1976:7–8), concerning the disempowerment of the *liurai* in relation to his Tetum case-study. According to Hicks, 'the term *liurai* came to be applied to the chiefs, whose office was another innovation' of the colonial administration. As Hicks describes in relation to his case-study, the indigenous political structure at this level is somewhat more complex (see also Figure 2 in this chapter for an indication of this complexity in relation to the Atoni *suco* structure). Generally, however, an appreciation of the extent of the new socio-political reality in Portuguese Timor post-1912 is facilitated by reference to Forbes' profile of Timor in the 1880s. As described by Forbes (1989[1885]:425), '[t]he whole of East Timor is apportioned out under certain chiefs called *Leoreis* [*sic*], each of whom is independent and absolute in his own kingdom. At present there are forty-seven of these; but many of them possess far greater influence than, and exercise a sort of vassalage over, the others. Each *Reno* [*sic*], or kingdom, is divided into districts each of which is called a *Suku* [*sic*], ruled over by a *Dato*, who receives his orders from the Leorei by a special officer appointed for that purpose. The Dato has under him two other officials, a *Cabo* and a *Tenente* [both terms adapted from the Portuguese, Forbes suggests] who assist him in the regulation of the Suku.'

It is also of note that at least by the early post-war period, the boundaries of the old kingdoms had ceased to play any role in the administration of the colony, and that by this time, '[t]he divisions between the Postos cut across the ancient kingdom boundaries' (Landman and Plant 1948 Part 1:229).[53] As indicated in Archer's account (above), it was at the level of the *posto* that the colonial administration interfaced with the traditional administrative system that continued to operate within the *suco*s. Whereas the realm of *posto* administration and beyond was the preserve of European or European*ised* [54] officials, the realm within the *posto* continued to be administered in accordance with the principles of 'traditional authority' under a system of indirect rule.[55] With the exception of the war years (1942–45), this administrative approach continued until the end of the Portuguese period in the mid-1970s, and was reflected, for example, in post-war regulations concerning the taxation of native subjects. The native head-tax regulations distinguished clearly between native subjects, and the *assimilado*s (assimilated natives) who were eligible for exemption from native head-tax on the basis of '[h]aving abandoned entirely the uses of intimate customs of the socially aggregated natives,' developed competence in the spoken and written Portuguese language, adopted monogamy[56] and achieved 'a professional art or office compatible with the European civilisation.'[57] As specified in the regulations, *assimilado*s shared their eligibility for exemption from the native head-tax with traditional leaders 'who have a minimum of 50 natives who pay their taxes.' In such a way was the indigenous elite separated into those whose status was based upon the

[53] Note that numerous changes to the administrative boundaries of Portuguese Timor were made during the 20th century. For details of these changes see Vaz (1964:55–87).

[54] In reference to *assimilados*, who receive further attention in the main text.

[55] Saldanha (1994:52) remarks that this administrative model was eminently suited to the under-resourced nature of the Portuguese colonial administration, and that it also supported the functioning of the most fundamental units of social organisation (*sucos* and *povoações*) in accordance with local expectations. As distinct from the administration of the overall colony, asserts Saldanha, '[t]he East Timor people hold the leadership of their *suco* in high esteem. Therefore, the replacement of a *liurai* [*chefe de suco*] is of great importance. It surpasses the importance of the replacement of an *administrador de posto* or *concelho*, as well as the replacement of a governor because the formal officials were elected by the colonial government. The *chefe de suco, however*, was elected by the people based on inherited power. They respected this institution of power transfer.'

[56] As documented by observers (Moura 1937:487; Gonçalves 1937:451–54), polygamy and concubinage was common throughout Timor, although largely restricted to *liurai*s and *chefe*s (Forbes 1989[1885]:458). Polygamy, at least, continues to be practiced, despite the influence of the Catholic Church.

[57] Drawn from complete English translation of post-war head-tax regulations titled 'Regulation of Census and Collection of Native Head-Tax,' appended to a despatch sent to the Australian Department of External Affairs by the Australian Consul to Portuguese Timor, Charles Eaton, on 26th February 1947 (Eaton 1947 Despatch No.2:7–9).

abandonment of native practices, and those whose status was based upon the perpetuation of native practices within the *sucos*.[58] Of course, the great majority of Timorese remained for the most part insulated from the world beyond their own *posto*,[59] and lived in a universe governed by the expectations and traditions of their ancestors, at least so far as these were interpreted by successive generations of traditional leaders.[60] Through this system of colonial administration were key elements of *suco* justice and dispute mediation preserved in Portuguese Timor until the end of the Portuguese period.

TIMORESE PRINCIPLES OF JUSTICE AND CONFLICT RESOLUTION: ACCOUNTS FROM THE COLONIAL PERIOD

Early Observations

The accounts of observers and officials from colonial times provide a sketch of Timorese justice and conflict resolution practices in the period prior to colonial consolidation. These accounts demonstrate not only the severity of the justice regimes that prevailed prior to the disempowerment of the *liurai*s, but also that in terms of key *principles* of Timorese justice, there are great consistencies between the pre-pacification period and the present day. An historic overview outlining the consistency of some of these principles contributes balance to the legitimate emphasis placed (Mearns 2002:26,30-32) on 'so-called "traditional"' justice as comprising a diversity of systems experiencing a constant process of change.

By the time Scottish naturalist Henry Forbes travelled in the interior of Timor in the early 1880s, European law had already begun to encroach. Complete

---

[58] The social reality, of course, is likely to have been less clear-cut, and chiefdom even appears to have been a means in itself by which the descendents of traditional leaders, through access to education, could transcend native society. In this respect, Hicks (1983:30) found in his research that the sons of traditional leaders would often consider themselves too educated to accept leadership positions in the *suco*. As explained by Hicks, 'Education had raised him above his father's level, and he often refused to accept a post which involved a diminution of his prestige.'

[59] Hicks (1983:24) notes that the requirement for a '*giu de transito*,' or 'transit pass' for travel outside of the *posto*, was maintained until the end of the Portuguese period, thereby limiting the extent to which Timorese villagers were able to visit other *postos* and interact with their inhabitants. Later, the Indonesian administration imposed similarly tight controls over movements within East Timor, requiring that travel passes (now known as '*surat jalan*') be carried specifying the details of each journey. Officially, at least, these controls were withdrawn in the late 1980s in association with the new 'openness' policy (Saldanha 1994:172–73; Budiardjo and Liong 1984:216–27).

[60] Note that administratively, according to a detailed review of records and published accounts concerning both indigenous and colonial administrative units (Sherlock 1983:76), Portuguese Timor by 1950 was comprised of fifty-four *postos* comprising 411 *sucos*. By 1968, this had increased to fifty-six *postos* comprising 415 *sucos*.

colonial consolidation, however, still remained several decades away. In his travels in Timor, Forbes (1989[1885]:431,472,477) noted the presence of *keros*; structures on which the imitation or real bodies or severed heads of thieves were impaled, sometimes in the company of the severed heads of livestock they had stolen.[61] Forbes (1989[1885]:432) remarked that it was clear he was 'travelling in a lawless land,' as 'it was the most inaccessible peaks and isolated crags that were crowned by dwellings.'[62]

From early accounts, it is clear that prior to pacification, *liurai*s and other *reino* officials held great power within their kingdoms. As lords of the land, *liurai*s had ultimate authority on justice matters, and the repertoire of measures available to them was by no means confined to routines for the negotiation of compensation and the promotion of reconciliation between affected parties.[63] Forbes' detailed commentary (1989[1885]:473) highlights the power of the *liurai* at this time when the *suco*s of Timor remained integrated into the networks of kingdoms. It is also apparent in his account that beneath the ultimate authority of the *liurai*, many justice matters were resolved, one way or another, between the families of the individuals involved, and that retribution in some form was a key principle:

> The *Leorei* is judge as well as king, but acts only, however, on the rare occasions when a case is brought before him on complaint, his judgement being for the litigants always a costly boon. Every man or his family exacts justice by his own individual arm on the person or his family by whom he has been wronged. If the wrong-doer has goods or chattels on which a fine may be levied, the wronged as a rule exacts a fine in expiation. Homicide is revenged by death, but this penalty can be averted by the payment of the equivalent in money or goods demanded by the relatives, and the substitution of some one of the offender's family to take the place of the slain. A robber taken in the act used to be executed on the spot – and is even now when the avenger is likely to escape punishment by the European

[61] Forbes (1989[1885]:477) observed the impaled skull of a horse thief, attached by the horse's halter to the impaled (and 'grinning') skull of a horse, and noted that '[a] horse once stolen is gone for good, it would seem.' The rationale of killing the stolen (and recovered) horse is not fully explained, but it may have been perceived as a means of balancing the death of the thief. In the present day (as outlined later in this chapter), the family of a livestock thief would be expected to return stolen stock, and also provide a further animal to be consumed at a reconciliation ceremony.

[62] As noted by Metzner (1977:16–17) pacification in the early 20th century precipitated new settlement patterns and associated demographic changes, since the population was able to settle more fertile areas once freed from the risk of attack by head-hunters from rival groups.

[63] As discussed later in this chapter, compensation and reconciliation procedures are fundamental elements of contemporary conflict resolution approaches throughout East Timor.

> authorities, who have rightly interfered with the old savage administration of justice in the rajahships – and if the theft consisted of a living animal the head of the animal was struck off and affixed near that of the robber on a stake.

Forbes goes on to explain that potentially all crimes 'could be avenged by death,' but that payment of an appropriate penalty could avert the need for this outcome *except* in cases of adultery with a member of the *liurai*s' family, and in cases involving witchcraft. For both of these offences, writes Forbes, the offender would be punished with 'impalement with all his family, and confiscation of their goods for the benefit of the accuser and of the lord of the soil.' Indeed, there are indications that such dire punishments may have been widespread throughout the kingdoms of Timor. Farram (2004:90-91) refers to *Raja* or *Kaizer* Bil Nope of Amanuban in West Timor, who ruled until 1910 and was recognised by Dutch authorities as a *raja* 'of the old stamp.' A main factor contributing to *Kaizer* Bil's reputation was his use of severe and pitiless punishments, which included turning offenders into 'human *sate*s' then hanging them in trees as a deterrent to other potential miscreants. Whereas the power to impose such punishments was taken from the *liurai*s after pacification, it is reported (Landman and Plant 1948 Part 1:229) that *liurai*s retained the power to 'have their subjects beaten' until WWII.

As well as highlighting the potential severity of justice measures under *liurai* authority, the passage by Forbes cited above includes reference to a range of features which continues to have bearing on Timorese justice and conflict resolution practice in the present day. Notable aspects include the importance of compensation in settling disputes (including disputes related to cases of homicide) and the role of the family in seeking justice on behalf of members. Forbes also noted the emphasis in Timorese society on the importance and effectiveness of reconciliation between conflicting groups, a matter discussed below under a separate sub-heading. By the late colonial era most of the excessive and inhumane pre-pacification dispute resolution and 'justice' practices had been eliminated following the disempowerment of the *liurai*s. Some practices, however, have yet to be successfully controlled; including the problem of retributive killings in response to perceived acts of sorcery (see below). For greater clarity, various aspects related to Timorese conceptions of justice which received commentary during the colonial period, are outlined thematically as follows:

Barlaque

A characteristic of eastern Indonesia and Timor which has drawn anthropologists to the region is the prevalence of cross-cousin marriage patterns involving complex systems of obligations between wife-givers and wife-takers.[64] Like other observers, Forbes (1989[1885]:457–59) recorded details concerning marriage exchange, *barlaque* (bride-wealth) payments, residence protocols and rights concerning offspring and property.[65] His account (with special emphasis on elite unions) provides particular details of practices in the south-central region of Portuguese Timor, indicating a diversity of marriage practices within this region with respect to protocols requiring (or not requiring) the payment of bride-price and the apparent existence of both patrilineal and matrilineal systems. Notwithstanding the diversity of marriage practices in eastern Timor, bride-wealth payments remain commonplace. Although the practice might be seen from an anthropological perspective as an *exchange* process, *barlaque* can also be conceptualised as a form of compensation.[66] In accordance with *suco* principles of justice, for example, payments to compensate for some sexual crimes approximate the level of the bride-price. The economic principle also becomes clear in the event a couple marry, but the family of the husband is unable to pay the bride-wealth. In this instance, notes Moura (1937:479), the husband must go to serve the family of the bride.

Justice and Conflict Resolution in a Cultural Context

There are indications that during the late 19th century and the first decades of the 20th century attempts were initiated to systematically document the *usos e costumes* (practices and customs) of the various parts of Portuguese Timor.[67] Although the end result of these particular initiatives is unclear, the customs and social systems of East Timor (including justice aspects) appear to have been given increased attention from the 1930s onwards, at least in a general sense. As well as contributing information on Timorese approaches to justice and conflict resolution matters, these profiles highlight the extent to which concepts of justice are grounded in the societies of which they are a part. In their studies of *adat*[68] rights and common law among the indigenes of Portuguese Timor, Gonçalves (1937) and Moura (1937) emphasise the role of ancestors and *lulik* (sacred) objects, rituals and values in Timorese social organisation.[69] Broadly, this is

[64] See Fox (1980:329-30), who also clarifies that in fact a 'large number – possibly a majority - of the societies of eastern Indonesia do not structure their alliances on the basis of exclusive cross-cousin marriage.'

[65] Moura (1937:479,487) and Gonçalves (1937:451–54) also give attention to these areas, including divorce arrangements. See also Berlie (2000:142).

[66] Although practices will vary, Capell (1944:201) draws on Martinho to outline a scenario whereby '[t]he girl's parents receive buffaloes, horses, jewels and money and give back clothing and pigs to the value of a third of what was received by them. The difference represents the actual value of the bride.' As described, such a routine provides for both ritual exchange and economic compensation.

[67] For further details, see the *Boletim Oficial do Governo de Timor* (1932:1–4) and Corrêa (1934/35:351).

[68] Malay/Indonesian term used in reference to customary laws, values and rituals. *Lisan* is a corresponding term used widely throughout Timor.

[69] See also Berlie (2000) for commentary on these papers.

illustrated in reference to such diverse aspects as the historical role of oracles for determining, by such means as the augur of a decapitated dog's kidneys, the wisdom of waging war against another kingdom (Moura 1937:485); shamanic 'healing' conducted by *matadocs* (Moura 1937:477–78);[70] and an existential realm featuring a range of mystical objects and spirit-creatures, including some (such as the *buan*) of malevolent nature (Gonçalves 1937:448–49).[71] These references indicate the extent to which the spirit world was (as it largely remains in Timor)[72] a constant presence in everyday life. As described by Capell (1944:208), the reality of the spirit world is such that denied suitable honours at burial, one's own ancestors might turn evil in spite, and seek 'opportunities to wreak vengeance in sickness or other punishments.' In this regard, the Timorese *uma lulik* (sacred house) serves as a physical site dedicated to the honouring of ancestors and the storage of objects that belonged to them, alongside other objects of historical significance.

Role of Ancestors in Justice

As discussed later in this chapter, the desire to avoid dishonouring one's ancestors remains strong in Timor to the present day, since giving one's family a bad name could invoke the wrath of the ancestors, potentially leading to sickness or death. In this motivation can be seen the link between existential beliefs and the promotion of order and (culturally specific) concepts of justice; since blemishing the family name through committing social transgressions, or failing to atone for such actions, is a sure means of offending the ancestors. In the accounts of Moura and Gonçalves, this link is illustrated in relation to the formalisation of contracts, as well as in relation to the determination of a suspect's guilt and other aspects of criminal law. In relation to the former, both Gonçalves (1937:456) and Moura (1937:482) note the importance of oaths in the pre-literate culture of Timor, including the practice of swearing oaths with the hand on a *lulik* object (which Gonçalves speculates is derived from Christian practice). *Lulik* phenomena used and referred to in oaths would include God (or *Maromak*), the (Portuguese) flag and the sacred crocodile.[73]

---

[70] Note that Capell (1944:205–06) uses the term *matan do:k*; Hicks (1976:112) the term *matan do'ok*.

[71] For detailed descriptions of the nature of the witch-like *Buan* in Tetum society, and the shamanic practices used to counter its 'influence,' see Hicks (1976:110-13). See also Capell (1944:205–07).

[72] This assertion is substantiated with examples and other evidence in later sections of this chapter.

[73] Origin myths in Timor commonly involve crocodiles, and there are said to be people who can communicate with crocodiles using a special (sung) language. Historical writings (Capell 1944:211–212; Schulte Nordholt 1971:322–23) indicate that in Kupang in West Timor in earlier times, young girls would be periodically 'married' (sacrificed) to crocodiles as part of succession celebrations. As Forbes (1989[1885]:405) illustrates in reference to his visit to the island of Buru in the Moluccas, the crocodile is also considered sacred in other parts of the region. See Forbes (1989[1885]:442–46) for a broader description of *lulik* objects and practices in Timor.

Meanwhile, *adat* practices employed in the determination of guilt and innocence would include shamanic rituals through which the identity of perpetrators would be determined through communion with the spirit world (Moura 1937:483; Capell 1944:205-6). Clearly lacking robustness by modern justice standards, such practices (conducted by a *matadoc*) may serve as a general deterrent against criminal activity. Potentially, the possibility of shamanic 'investigations' may also influence offenders to own up to their misdeeds in the physical world in preference to having matters addressed by the enraged spirits of ancestors with their fearsome powers, thereby accelerating processes of reparation and reconciliation within the community. In an equatorial region such as Timor with a subsistence economy and an abundance of tropical diseases, there is every chance that one who has incurred the wrath of the ancestors will experience ill-fortune sooner or later. The existence of the ancestors and the powers they hold exerts a powerful influence over social conduct, and if the Timorese remain unusually eager to admit to crimes, then the vigilance of the ancestors may be a reason why.[74]

The Compensation Principle

The Portuguese, outlined Forbes (1989[1885]:474), were strongly opposed to the 'taking of life,' and the [gradual] expansion of their authority was influencing an effect whereby 'causes before the Rajah are becoming more frequent in order to obtain the fines which the wronged claims from the wrong-doer for his offence, which in former times, if not paid, would have been atoned for by his head.' In reference to the question of the extent to which traditional justice is in fact traditional, Forbes' account provides an example of how traditions can change while remaining based on similar principles or values. Throughout the region, procedures already prevailed for determining the reparation payable to compensate for a death, in the event the death is not

---

[74] This tendency was indicated to the writer in the course of interviews with CivPol officers (UN civilian police) in Timor in October 2002. The tendency was such that on some occasions numerous individuals would confess to having committed the same crime. Note that *lulik* rituals continue to be practised in various forms. In late 2002, a sum of money was stolen from *malai* (foreign) friends of the writer outside a government office in Dili. After conventional attempts to recover the money failed, a *lulik* ritual (with a number of components) intended to curse the perpetrator was prescribed by concerned locals. A central element of the procedure required a return to the scene of the crime every day for a week, at the time of day the crime occurred. A ring of white candles had then to be placed around the site of the theft with a red candle (the last to be lit) in the centre. In this case the money was never returned and the fate of the perpetrator remains unknown. However, the very public and prolonged nature of the ritual would have ensured that its conduct was widely communicated by word of mouth. The perpetrator, had his belief in *adat* not been compromised by 'rationalization' and 'disenchantment' (Weber 1976[1919]:155]), clearly major threats to the viability of *suco* justice, may well have had cause for alarm.

revenged with a payback killing. Based on his research, Forbes (1989[1885]:404,450) outlines protocols from Timor and Buru in the Moluccas, each based on the particular value of each part of a person's body. An example of a similar payment protocol recently documented in Timor by the writer is provided later in this chapter, indicating that the validity of this compensation principle has not yet been extinguished.

Based on a case-study of Liquiça to the west of Dili, Moura (1937:483) presents an outline of *direito penal* (criminal law) which indicates how broadly the compensation principle characterised approaches to justice and conflict resolution in that region in the early 1930s. The resolution of such diverse crimes as murder, sexual crimes, theft, defamation and corporal crimes would require payments to the victim. In the case of crimes such as murder and theft, compensation was an alternative to the penalty of death which, especially in earlier times, might have been imposed on the perpetrator as a vendetta.[75] In the case of murder, Moura indicates that in Liquiça the family of a murdered individual would be due a gong, a traditional necklace, ten liras, one hundred florins and a buffalo. Non-payment of the required amount would place the perpetrator at risk of being killed by a member of the victim's family.[76] For the Liquiça region, Moura reports that adultery could be compensated with the payment of twenty florins to enable the husband of the woman to 'wash the face,' although, were the woman the wife of a senior traditional leader, both she and her collaborator would risk death.[77] Meanwhile, the resolution of cases of rape and defloration would also require payments. Capell (1944:205) remarks generally that payment to compensate for defloration would 'correspond to that of the marriage price,' which would vary between regions. As discussed in the later sections, there are broad similarities between the protocols documented in the first half of the 20th century and those which prevail in the present day.

Collective Responsibility

The extent to which crimes manifest themselves as disputes between all members of families or other groups is emphasised by both Forbes (1989[1885]:473) and Moura (1937:483), with the result that all members of the family or clan of a perpetrator become responsible for contributing to the

---

[75] Without knowing for sure, Forbes (1989[1885]:464) was 'strongly of impression…that the *vendetta* exists among' the Timorese. See also Berlie (2000:143).

[76] In a variation of this protocol, Forbes (1989[1885]:473) reports that in Bibiçuçu, the payment of compensation to atone for murder would be complimented by 'some one of the offender's family to take the place of the slain.'

[77] See also Moura (1937:480), Capell (1944:205) and Berlie (2000:142) for further commentary on this matter. Note that in the event a husband is not satisfied with compensation to 'wash the face' and divorce results, the return of the bride-price would be expected.

compensation due to the family of the victim. As discussed later in this chapter, this practice of collective responsibility continues and, alongside the vigilance of the ancestors and their capacity to implement punishments, acts as a further disincentive against committing crimes and repeat offences; the latter especially likely to test the goodwill and patience of a community through the ongoing compensation obligations imposed.

Reconciliation

The importance of reconciliation ceremonies between conflicting groups was noted by colonial observers, including at the level of kingdoms. Forbes (1989[1885]:449–51) refers to a chance meeting between his Timorese servant, and a warrior who had beheaded the servant's father during an earlier war between kingdoms. Inquiring if his servant held any bitterness towards the warrior, the servant replied that he did not, as the kingdoms now had peaceful relations between them and all heads had now been returned. For as the taking of heads was a great part of warfare between kingdoms in Timor,[78] so the return of the carefully preserved heads to the families of the victims was integral to the procedure for restoring peaceful relations between the warring kingdoms. Forbes (1989[1885]:451–52) refers to large assemblies attended by member of both kingdoms, where heads would be returned by each side accompanied by small gifts to signify friendship. The restoration of good relations would be sealed by 'a boisterous feast, concluded by heavy drinking, and...wild dancing,' and by ritual affirmations of blood-brotherhood. The latter ritual, observed Forbes, 'is the same in substance whether between two individuals or large companies.' This ritual involved the swearing of an oath of friendship, accompanied by the consumption of local liquor mixed with the blood of the respective parties and the planting of a tree as witness to the bond. Forbes was advised that this ritual of conciliation was 'almost never...violated at least between individuals.' Head-hunting is now only a part of Timor's past history; however reconciliation ceremonies remain an important component of justice and dispute resolution processes to the present day.[79]

---

[78] Capell (1944:217–18), with his linguistic interest, noted that special words existed for such things as headless corpses and the 'head sword' used for separating the head from the body. He also asserted that '[c]utting off an enemy's head was the custom that remained longest alive in the mind of the native out of all his old customs.' According to Forbes (1989[1885]:451), the desire to avoid decapitation was such that the warriors of the south coast kingdom of Kabalaki would go to war 'with their legs tied under their horses' bellies, so that, in case of their being wounded or killed, they may be carried back to their own village with their heads on their shoulders.' For details of ritualistic aspects of headhunting based on research in West Timor, see Middelkoop (1963), Schulte Nordholt (1971) and McWilliam (1996).

[79] Realistically, there is reason to believe the emergence of new periods of conflict or instability can threaten the permanence of acts of reconciliation, and create the space for acts of revenge. This matter receives attention later in this chapter in respect to the violence that occurred in rural areas in the course of the 1975 civil war in East Timor.

Sorcery

The Timorese, wrote Forbes (1989[1885]:438) could not understand 'why any one should ever die unless he be killed,' and were inclined to attribute deaths to sorcery. Until (and unless) the practice was prohibited by colonial authorities, therefore, the sorcerer believed responsible for a death was liable to be executed. Although it is difficult to identify any mitigating aspects stemming from the persecution of alleged sorcerers, it is likely that in the conservative social context of subsistence societies, fear of being identified as a sorcerer encourages a certain community mindedness whereby individuals become highly motivated to fit in with the group.[80] From Capell's description (1944:206) of the shamanic process for determining the identity of the sorcerer, it would appear likely that any errant individual would live in fear of the *matadoc*, lest the *matadoc* use the occasion of a shamanic investigation into a death to 'take vengeance without fear of retribution' on any member of the group with a history of showing disrespect towards the conventions and leaders of the *suco*.

Of course, subsistence societies are notoriously predisposed towards superstitious beliefs and the persecution of alleged sorcerers, a reality highlighted by the Knauft (1987) study of 'violence in simple human societies.' In his detailed study of homicide rates among the Gebusi of lowland New Guinea, Knauft reports (1987:459) that, although relatively 'non-competitive and politically decentralised' and normally exhibiting 'self-effacing, nonhierarchical [*sic*], and mutually deferential' conduct towards one another, Gebusi society is characterised by a very high rate of homicide. Based on a genealogical survey of a band of Gebusi covering the period 1940–1982, and subsequent investigation concerning the cause of each of the three hundred and ninety-four deaths that occurred during this time, Knauft (1987:462–66) found that almost one third of deaths among the Gebusi were due to homicide.[81] Furthermore, and of particular interest in relation to the present theme, Knauft (1987:460-64) found that the

---

[80] To give an example from elsewhere in the region, Knauft (1987:464–65) found in his study of sorcery-related homicide among the Gebusi of the New Guinea lowlands that the determination of the identity of a sorcerer might be based simply on an individual's reputation as 'a bad person' or other intangible reasons. As in Timor, however, the formal process for determining the identity of the sorcerer would be a highly ceremonial 'spiritual inquest' involving a séance through to daylight. It would appear clear that in a subsistence social context, the danger of being identified as a sorcerer would encourage conformist behaviour. As Knauft (1987:466) remarks in relation to the Gebusi, '[m]en and women who are by temperament more aggressive, outspoken, or assertive appear from my observations to be more much more likely targets for sorcery accusations, particularly as they get older. Conversely, persons who are good-humoured and accommodating tend to be immune to such accusations.'

[81] Correlated to this dire statistic, Knauft (1987:466) calculates that by middle-age, approximately sixty-five percent of Gebusi men have committed homicide.

main reason for this high frequency of homicide among an otherwise peaceful society was retaliation for acts of 'sorcery.'[82] Overall, and reflecting the kinds of conclusions arrived at by Forbes in Timor, Knauft (1987:466) found that among the Gebusi, over one quarter of all deaths from sickness 'precipitated the murder of another person for allegedly practicing sorcery.'

From the information available, it is difficult to estimate the frequency of retributive killings for perceived acts of sorcery during colonial and pre-colonial times in Timor. It is clear that the Portuguese regarded the practice of killing alleged sorcerers as a matter of the utmost seriousness, although it is likely that many 'sorcerers' were killed without the knowledge of the administration. An early instance of the Portuguese administration intervening to prevent a series of planned sorcerer executions is described in a document written by José de Mello Gouveia, Minister and Secretary of State for Marine and Overseas Affairs, dated 31st August 1871 (in Sherlock 1986b:49). Gouveia's account suggests that although the matter was regarded as of great importance, actual interventions were probably not routine events:

> Having been presented to His Majesty the King the official letter of 21st of June last, no.142, in which the Governor of the Province of Macau and Timor communicates that the *regulo* of Vemasse, in Timor, having ordered to be put to death, on the pretext of the crime of witchcraft, two families of his territory, and the commander of that *concelho*, Lieutenant José dos Santos Vaquinhas, learning of this order, succeeded in preventing the execution, and placed under arrest the officers to whom the *regulo* had entrusted it, who were going to be detained in the capital for some time; and that the Governor of the District had placed a fine on the same *regulo* of four hundred rupias and 50 men for public works during the summer; the families happily saved from death being kept safe in the capital as residents: the same August Lord orders, through the State Secretariat for Marine and Overseas Affairs, to be communicated to the aforesaid Governor of Macau and Timor that the news was very pleasing to him of the act performed by the said Lieutenant which is very worthy of praise, as well as the mentioned measures meriting his royal approval; and, in the same way, are worthy of praise the efforts employed by the Governor of the District to put an end beneficially to the

[82] Note that Knauft (1987:462–63) found homicide rates to have fallen in the latter period covered by the study, leading to the conclusion that homicide rates were higher prior to the advance of western administration from colonial engagement onwards. Note also that Knauft (1987:462–65) remarks that retaliation for sorcery-related killings among the Gebusi is uncommon, and that there is more commonly 'a general feeling in the community that a lethal sickness sender in the group has been expunged.'

> questions between the *regulos*, using in this commission several officers, and among them the Lieutenant-at-orders João Alves da Costa, whose good service is taken into just consideration.

Despite such a celebrated victory, continued references to sorcery retribution in Timor in the twentieth and twenty-first centuries indicate that the Portuguese administration was unable to eliminate the practice. Writing in the early 1940s, Capell (1944:210) refers to folklore tales from central Timor concerning *suanjis*,[83] a term used in the eastern archipelago in reference to individuals with the ability to transform themselves into animals. Capell describes how the 'soul-stuff' of a malignant *suanji* may exit its own body for the purpose of undertaking werewolf-like activities aimed at 'seizing the soul-substance of sleepers,' potentially leading to sickness and death. This malignant 'soul-stuff' might be fleetingly seen in the form of a rodent, as it returns via the anus to the body of its temporarily vacated (hence sleeping) owner.[84] Of a number of witchcraft-related cases brought to the attention of UN civilian police (CivPol) during the period of UN transitional administration that followed the Indonesian withdrawal in late 1999, one involved the burning of four houses belonging to the same family in the enclave district of Oecusse. Upon investigation it was discovered that the houses had been destroyed by a group of youths on the instructions of the *chefe de suco*, in retaliation for the alleged practice of sorcery. Whatever the real reason for this act of retribution, the burnings were said to have been ordered after 'witnesses' claimed to have observed rats exiting the anuses of women living in the houses, a sure sign of sorcery (as discussed above).[85] As with other *suco* justice and conflict resolution principles, the consistency of key aspects associated with sorcery retribution between colonial times and the present, highlight the extent to which subsistence belief patterns have been preserved in East Timor throughout the various historical periods; each of which has failed to generate substantial development.

* * *

The lack of modernisation to have occurred in Portuguese Timor by the late 1960s and early 1970s was reflected in the number of anthropologists attracted to the territory wishing to research traditional societies. Fieldwork undertaken during

---

83 The Tetum term is '*buan*' (Hicks 1976:110; Hull 2000:65).

84 According to the information provided by Capell (1944:210) the chances of seeing the 'soul-stuff' as it returns to the sleeping body of its owner, may be improved by turning the body of the suspected *suanji* around; confusing and hence delaying the returning fiend. See also Hicks (1976:110-11) for a description of beliefs relating to the possession of individuals by malignant spirits, based upon fieldwork undertaken among the Tetum in the 1960s.

85 Interview (Dili, November 2002) with the former Commander and Deputy Commander of Oecusse CivPol during 2000 and 2001.

this time led to works by Hicks (1976) on the Tetum, Traube (1986) on the Mambai, Forman (1980) on the Makassae, Friedberg (1980) on the Bunaq and Clamagirand (1980) on the Kemak. The resulting, albeit incomplete, mosaic of ethnographic data demonstrates the extent to which social order within the *sucos* of Portuguese Timor continued, until the close of the colonial era, to resemble the model of 'traditional authority' described by Weber.[86] And whereas the anthropologists attracted to Portuguese Timor during this time were commonly motivated (Hicks 1976:11; Traube 1986:xi,xii) to seek out the most remote, traditional and pagan communities in order to study the most pristine pre-literate traditions before they were 'overtaken by Westernization' (Hicks 1976:2–3), the kinds of beliefs they succeeded in documenting are almost certain to have been widely shared, at the general level, even in those places already exposed to Christian thought and other corrupting influences. As is addressed later in this paper, belief in witchcraft and magic remains widespread even among those with tertiary education, and the ritual sacrifice of animals is a routine occurrence in a range of public administration contexts. It is clear, therefore, that the process of Westernisation has taken longer to overtake East Timor than some might have expected, an outcome with real implications on public expectations concerning justice and conflict resolution, especially in rural areas.

The flourish of social research of the 1960s and early 1970s was brought to an end in Portuguese Timor by a series of developments that followed the 25th April 1974 revolt of the Armed Forces Movement in Portugal in which the regime of Marcello Caetano, successor to the veteran dictator António de Oliveira Salazar, was overthrown.[87] Amid the new environment of political freedom in Portuguese Timor a brace of political organisations emerged. The most notable of these included the UDT *(União Democrática Timorense*, or Timorese Democratic Union); the ASDT (*Associação Social Democrata Timorense* or Timorese Social Democratic Association) and its radically fashioned successor party FRETILIN (*Frente Revolucionária de Timor-Leste Independente* or Revolutionary Front for an Independent East Timor); and, the pro-Indonesian APODETI (*Associação Popular Democrática Timorense* or Timorese Popular Democratic Association). Less than one and a half years after the overthrow of the Caetano regime in Lisbon amid an increasingly complex and difficult decolonisation scenario, the backward tranquillity of the territory was rocked by a coup that unfolded in Dili on 10th August 1975,

[86] See in particular Hicks (1976:4–7), who describes the interface between the *suco* administration and the Portuguese colonial system at the time of fieldwork in the 1960s.

[87] Salazar, due to poor health, left office in 1968 and was succeeded by Professor Marcello Caetano. See Hill (2002:28-34) for a discussion of the evolution of aspects of the Portuguese corporatist system under Caetano, and resulting developments in Timor.

and then a bloody counter-coup that commenced less than two weeks later on 19th August. Amid a brief but bloody civil war, the Portuguese administration abandoned Dili for the nearby island of Atauro on 27th August, leaving the victorious political organisation, FRETILIN, to run an *ad hoc* administration in the territory for a period that barely exceeded three months. Over the course of this period, the FRETILIN administration was forced to respond to a series of border incursions launched by Indonesian forces. These incursions were followed, on 7th December 1975, by a full Indonesian invasion.[88]

Party politics and the prospect of decolonisation emerged in East Timor at a time when cold war considerations influenced strategic developments both globally and regionally, and there is no doubt that this factor contributed to Timor's slide into chaos. However, there is equally no doubt that local rivalries and weaknesses (including political inexperience) contributed to the disaster that unfolded in the territory, as East Timor's youthful new political elites responded to the environment of competitive politics by entering into patterns of exaggerated posturing[89] and bickering over unsubstantial political differences.[90] Colonel Mario Lemos Pires, the final Portuguese governor of

---

[88] For accounts and commentary pertaining to this period, see Nicol (1978), Jolliffe (1978), Hill (2002), Dunn (1996), Taylor (1991), Gunn (1999), ACFOA (1975), CAVR (2004; 2005) and Ramos-Horta (1987).

[89] FRETILIN's claim (in Nicol 1978:79) to be 'the only legitimate representative of the people of East Timor' made on 12th September 1974, only months after the formation of the organisation, appears frivolous and provocative in the absence of an election. Similarly, elements of the FRETILIN program (in Hill 2002:85) declaring that 'cooperatives will be the base of economic and social life of East Timor,' and that 'all large farms will be expropriated and returned to the people and...used within the cooperative system' were unnecessarily sensational. As Nicol (1978:83) notes, the FRETILIN agricultural agenda 'sounded more radical and dramatic than it really was,' since large farms were few in number and most land was already accessible to the population. Nicol's assessment is supported by the results of a national survey of non-customary primary industry land recently conducted by the writer (Nixon 2005:8), in which it was found that only 47,000 hectares of agricultural land in East Timor (equivalent to three per cent of land area) has been alienated from customary tenure in the history of the territory. Notwithstanding the small amount of land involved, FRETILIN's 'revolutionary front' approach would have done little to appease their main political rivals in the UDT party, a number of which had links with the small plantation agriculture sector.

[90] Dunn (1996:53) has remarked that when political organisations first formed in East Timor following the events in Lisbon of April 1974, there was broad common ground concerning the policies of the two major parties, UDT and ASDT/FRETILIN. The ideal time-frame within which independence from Portugal would be realised, emerged as one area of difference between the two organisations, even though each of the parties proposed different time-frames themselves at various times. The early time-frame proposed by ASDT/FRETILIN leader Francisco Xavier do Amaral was ten years, with lesser periods suggested thereafter. UDT proposals, meanwhile, ranged between twenty years and three years (Nicol 1978:69,77–78,80). Although relations between UDT and ASDT/FRETILIN remained amicable for some time, they are said to have deteriorated in the second half of 1974 with the return from Lisbon of a group of left-wing student radicals affiliated with FRETILIN. Nicol (1978:107) makes particular reference to Roque Rodrigues (later appointed defence minister of the RDTL after independence on 20th May 2002), for whom 'anyone in any way opposed to the [expeditious] independence of East Timor was an enemy of the state, a traitor.'

East Timor who arrived in Dili on 18th November 1974 (Nicol 1978:84) to oversee decolonisation, observed (in CAVR 2004) during the 2004 CAVR proceedings that East Timorese society was unprepared for engagement with party politics. Despite the antipathy that developed between the UDT and ASDT/FRETILIN, Pires asserts that ideology had little to do with party support, and that 'most people were in one party or another mostly due to their friendship or because they were contacted at an early stage.' This conclusion is supported by Xanana Gusmão, former FRETILIN member and resistance leader who eventually became president of the RDTL on 20th May 2002 following the completion of the period of UN transitional administration. As Gusmão (2000:19) explains in relation to the period of political liberalisation in Portuguese Timor, there was substantial pressure, at least among the community of civil servants in Dili, to identify with either UDT or FRETILIN:[91]

> People were incited to violence and I began to understand the mobilisation to action. I struggled between getting involved and keeping to the sidelines. It was not that I did not want to join in, but I could see that the situation could easily get completely out of hand...Friends avoided me until I identified myself politically, in writing, and once again I was greeted and could greet others with closed fist, the Fretilin salute! At first, friends and colleagues in the UDT continued to raise their hands and greet me. Then came indifference, until finally it became obvious that we were avoiding each other. This really was not what I had wanted. UDT parents, Apodeti uncles, Fretilin children. What shit this freedom was!

The increasing antipathy between the major parties, their willingness to use martial means to realise political objectives, and the tendency of sections of the state security forces to align themselves politically, ultimately proved explosive.[92] In the ensuing chaos, recent political alliances and doctrines

---

[91] With APODETI receiving support only from (Gusmão 2000:19) '[a] few frustrated racist [anti-Portuguese] individuals.'

[92] Perhaps drawing on the martial heritage that characterised the Timorese micro-kingdoms of former days, each of the major political parties was to develop or engage an armed wing of some kind. In recent testimony, Tomas Gonçalves (in CAVR 2004), the son of APODETI co-founder Guilherme Gonçalves, has indicated that APODETI sought assistance from the Indonesian military for the formation of an armed wing in August 1974, within three months of APODETI's establishment. Similarly, Nicol (1978:101,164–65,194–95) makes numerous references to the FRETILIN 'army' or People's Security Organisation (PSO) that was in existence by the time of his visit in early 1975, and which was directly responsible to FRETILIN Vice-President Nicolau Lobato. Although FRETILIN forces staged a mini-coup in Oecusse in mid-June 1975 (Jolliffe 1978:273), it was UDT that launched the attempted coup in Dili that commenced on the evening of 10th August 1975 (Jolliffe 1978:120-43;

sometimes blurred, as ancient rivalries emerged and opportunities for retributive killings were created.[93] Whereas the political history of East Timor is a separate study in itself, the events of 1974 and 1975 already indicated that the development of a functional state in this subsistence territory would be a challenging affair, even without the additional complexities posed by the presence and geopolitical aspirations of Indonesia. As will be addressed later in this chapter, this reality has bearing on the utility of non-state actors as agents of order in the post-independence period.

The Indonesia Period: Developments and 'Development'

As briefly discussed earlier, both the Portuguese and the Indonesian chapters of East Timor's history are remarkable for the limited modernisation of economy and society that unfolded during these respective periods. In the case of the Indonesian occupation of East Timor, this outcome was *despite* the vast Indonesian central government spending that was channelled into East Timor between the 1970s and the 1990s, partly reflecting the general difficulty of promoting development in a territory under foreign occupation.[94]

Dunn 1996:150-58; CAVR 2005 Part 3:40-45; Taylor 1991:50-65; Nicol 1978:302), with the support of police commander Lieutenant Colonel Rui Maggiolo Gouveia and the police force. According to the Australian *Transportes Aéreos de Timor* (Timor Air Transport ,or TAT) pilot Roger Rudduck (interviewed by telephone 6th February 2006), who assisted with the coup and later bombed FRETILIN positions (with grenades designed for rifle-launch taped into beer glasses) using a TAT commercial aircraft, the reason why UDT launched the coup at this time was because they were convinced that FRETILIN was planning to launch their own coup on the following day, upon the return of the senior FRETILIN member José Ramos-Horta from Darwin. Ultimately, links between FRETILIN and the military ensured that FRETILIN was able to eclipse UDT in terms of trained personnel and access to weapons, after FRETILIN launched a counter-coup on the night of 19th August 1975. Accordingly, after two weeks of civil war that commenced following the FRETILIN counter-coup, FRETILIN forces were in the ascendancy and UDT forces were fleeing to the west towards the border with West Timor (Jolliffe 1978:122,129-33; Taylor 1991:51; CAVR 2005 Part 3:42).

93 The investigation of the Commission for Reception, Truth and Reconciliation in East Timor (CAVR) found (CAVR Part 3:42) that the highest death rate during the civil war period was 'in the rural areas, where tensions based on long-standing clan feuds and personal grudges, intensified by more recent militant party ideological divisions, exploded into violence.' See also Hicks (1983:22), who reflects in relation to this period that 'Western notions of right wing and left wing, capitalist and communist, were meaningless to the vast majority of the Timorese population' and suggests that 'old rivalries and loyalties' dating back to the 19th century or longer may have played a role in fuelling the 1975 conflict.

94 As characterised by Beazley (1999:12–13), Indonesia's strategy for the integration of East Timor was 'based on a combination of tight internal security and efforts to promote economic and social development.' Yet as she observes, with up to fourteen battalions stationed in East Timor, with intelligence activities operating throughout the communities, and with Indonesian security activities frequently resulting in acts of terror and intimidation, the internal security agenda acted to suppress the social and economic development component of the equation. Writing for the Australian Agency for International Development in early 1999, Beazley remarks that whereas Indonesian security forces are 'said not to be severely threatened by guerrilla resistance or civilian unrest, the intensity of their approach has ensured that any progress made through development spending in order to placate the people has been neutralised.'

Commentators (Saldanha 1994:180-82; da Costa and Soesastro 2002:2–3) have remarked that the initial upheaval of the invasion years was followed by a period of high economic growth rates (up to ten percent) from 1983 until the onset of the Asian economic crisis in 1996.[95] Yet this high growth rate was fuelled not by local productivity increases derived from structural changes to the economy but by a steady flow of Indonesian government capital directed at infrastructural development and administration activities, estimated to have approximated US$100 million annually in the 1980s (da Costa and Soesastro 2002:2–3) and referred to by Soesastro (1989:207) as 'by far the largest central government financial allocations (on a per capita basis) of any region in Indonesia.'[96] According to Saldanha (1994:168–69) the province remained almost fully dependent on support from Jakarta, with 'authentic income of East Timor' averaging less than five percent of 'total regional income.' The contribution of private sector capital to the overall economic growth rate was minimal since East Timor attracted almost no private investment throughout the entire Indonesian period.[97] The development process itself has been characterised by Saldanha (1994:131–178) as centrally controlled (from Jakarta) and of a 'high technology' nature (focussed largely on construction)[98] such that it could only be undertaken with imported labour from elsewhere in Indonesia. As a process often remote from the skill bases, needs and participation of local communities, the Indonesian development program caused resentment through the involvement of large numbers of outsiders, and focussed on the development of physical infrastructure at such a rate that it was 'difficult for the other sectors to

[95] The effects of the Indonesian *crismon* (monetary crisis) resulted in growth rates slowing to four percent in 1997 and then minus two percent in 1998 (da Costa and Soesastro 2002:2).

[96] Assessments (Soesastro 1989:220; Saldanha 1994:142–43) suggest that the amount of public investment during the 1980s had the potential to be even higher than this, had budget execution rates not been so low. In this regard Soesastro points to the 'low absorptive capacity' as a factor, while Saldanha refers to an inefficient government 'apparatus.' Even so, Soesastro (1989:214) has calculated that economic growth in the province between 1983 and 1986 was approximately fifty percent above the growth rate nationally. Notwithstanding the substantial nature of the Indonesian resources directed at East Timor, it should also be noted that a significant proportion of the funds were for payment of military salaries, much of which is reported to have been repatriated to other parts of Indonesia (Soesastro 1989:214).

[97] The lack of private sector investment has been attributed to limited investment incentives combined with a prominent range of investor disincentives, including the security situation, land access delays, corruption and transport challenges and infrastructure deficiencies (Saldanha 1994:151–52,176–78; da Costa and Soesastro 2002:2–3; Soesastro 1989:216–17). Indicating the severity of the situation, Soesastro (1989:216–17) reports that manufacturing comprised less than one per cent of GDP in 1986 and showed no signs of improvement.

[98] See Saldanha (1994:145). Perhaps the construction-centred nature of the development program is best illustrated by the roadwork program. According to official figures (BAPPEDA 1997:325 Table 8.1.2), East Timor had 6,363 kms of roads by 1996, of which 3,513 were sealed. Vehicle testing figures (BAPPEDA 1997:332 Table 8.2.5) indicate that the roads catered for a fleet of registered vehicles that had expanded from 118 in 1978 to 4,969 in 1996.

catch up' (Saldanha 1994:146). The integrity of this non-participatory and overly rapid development agenda suffered further compromise because of the tendency for 'extravagance and corruption' within the civil service.[99]

The disparity between investment and development outcomes appears clear in the case of the healthcare system. Official *Badan Perencanaan Pembangunan Daerah* (Indonesian Regional Development Planning Board, or BAPPEDA) figures (BAPPEDA 1997:105-07, Tables 4.2.1, 4.2.2, 4.2.3) indicate substantial expansion of public health facilities and staffing levels over the period of Indonesian control. Between the mid-1980s and 1996, hospitals increased from five to ten, public health centres increased from one hundred and seventeen to two hundred and eighty-seven, and pharmacies increased from three to seventeen. Staffing levels also increased dramatically and national figures prepared by the Ministry of Health Republic Indonesia (MHRI) indicate (MHRI 2000:33–52) that by 1997, the health personnel to population ratio in East Timor compared favourably to other parts of Indonesia. In 1997, East Timor had the third highest ratio of total health personnel to population, and the third highest ratio of nurses to population in the country. Whereas the military presence in East Timor may have been a contributing factor to this relatively high staffing ratio, the figures suggest relatively high staffing ratios even in unrelated technical areas. Of the twenty-seven provinces in Indonesia in 1997, for example, East Timor had the ninth highest ratio of midwives to population. Yet despite the investments in public health infrastructure and personnel, East Timor compared poorly with the rest of Indonesia over a range of crucial health outcomes, with Indonesian Ministry of Health and World Health Organisation (WHO) data indicating that the infant mortality rate in East Timor in 1997 was over seventy per thousand, the highest of any province and close to twice the national average (MHRI 2000:129 Figure V.B.1; WHO 2006:13). Furthermore, life expectancy rates were reported to be significantly lower than the national average, at 55.3 for men and 58.6 for women, compared with a national average of 61.5.[100]

---

99 See Saldanha (1994:143). It seems likely that the 'extravagance and corruption' may have been promoted partly by the unrelenting flow of central government development funds. Saldanha (1994:145) notes in this respect that unlike other regions, East Timor 'does not have to consider whether development funds are available or not because it is already a commitment of the central government to accelerate the development of the area.' In an indictment of the business skill of local contractors, Saldanha (1999:165) refers to a tendency among contractors to spend advance payments for contracts on personal electrical goods instead of the supplies and equipment necessary to complete the contracts, with the result that the money is wasted and the contracts not completed.

100 See UN (2000:52–54,119), which source refers to WHO warnings about the accuracy of health data from the Indonesian period. In reality, the health status of the population of East Timor during the Indonesian period may have been significantly worse than indicated by the figures referred to in this section. Life expectancy may have been as low as fifty (UN 2000:52).

Numerous factors appear to have contributed to the poor health outcomes achieved by the Indonesian health service in East Timor, including the underlying fact that the territory was experiencing political conflict, and was under occupation. In this respect, according to a news report written by journalist Karen Polglaze in early 1999 (Polglaze 1999), villagers at this time were often afraid to go to the health clinics, while (the mostly Indonesian) public health staff had similar concerns about visiting the villages. Other reasons that have been suggested (Beazley 1999:33–35) for East Timor's poor health statistics include cross-cultural and communication difficulties, avoidance of health services by young women concerned about being coerced into 'over zealous' birth control programs, the Indonesian practice of attracting inexperienced medical staff to hardship posts like East Timor,[101] and shortages of medical supplies.[102]

Similarly, although the primary and secondary education sectors expanded dramatically during the Indonesian period, official data from the Indonesian Statistics Centre (*Biro Pusat Statistik* or BPS) indicates that overall education outcomes in the territory were extremely poor in comparison with all other Indonesian provinces.[103] Commentators (Beazley 1999:48–51; Jones 2000:46–53) have suggested a range of factors contributing to the poor educational outcomes achieved during the Indonesian period, including; the legacy of the Portuguese neglect of the education sector; communication difficulties between the often newly graduated Indonesian teachers (usually from Java or elsewhere in Indonesia) and their Timorese students; nutritional and health deficiencies among students preventing concentration and educational performance;[104] lack of attendance for different reasons, including the fears of

[101] According to Beazley (1999:35), medical doctors are unable to graduate in Indonesia until they have accrued five years 'easy' experience or three years experience in a 'difficult' post. In East Timor, the doctors would reportedly be given responsibilities beyond their experience and competence, contributing to poor health outcomes.
[102] See also UN (2000:53–54).
[103] Assimilated BAPPEDA data (Jones 2000:45–47, Tables 1–2; BAPPEDA 1997: 77–78, 87–92, Tables 4.1.3, 4.1.3a, 4.1.9, 4.1.10) indicates that over the period of Indonesian control, the entire education system underwent massive expansion, with the primary school sector alone expanding from forty-seven schools with 13,500 students in 1976/77 to seven hundred and thirty-six schools with 143,958 students in 1996/97. However, statistical data from the (pan-Indonesian) 1995 Intercensal Population Survey (BPS 1996:129, Table 10.9) indicates that by the mid-1990s, 69.9 per cent of East Timorese (the highest rate in Indonesia) had either never attended or not yet completed primary school. Correspondingly, at 13.4 per cent, East Timor had by far the lowest rate of primary school completion of all Indonesian provinces.
[104] The Indonesian invasion impacted dramatically on agricultural cycles and stock numbers at least into the 1980s, with consequences on the nutritional status of the population. For commentary related to this area see Saldanha (1994:339), Aditjondro (1994:12–13,35), CAVR (2005 Part 3:84–85).

parents that their daughters would fall prey to state birth control programs; and irregular and corrupt classroom practices that served to compromise the learning environment. An outcome of this combination of factors included high drop-out rates and the highest repeat rate in Indonesia (Beazley 1999:50). High drop-out rates are also believed (Anderson 1993:25) to have plagued the thousands of East Timorese students who went to Indonesian universities to study, while the quality of tertiary education available within the province during the Indonesian period is reported to have rivalled the school system in terms of poor learning outcomes.[105] As a related point, it might be noted that despite the doubtful standards and low graduation rates, the education programs of the Indonesian years did succeed in awakening a broad cross-section of the East Timorese youth to the possibilities of life outside the confines of subsistence agriculture. As commentators (Soesastro 1989:219; Saldanha 1994:167; Jones 2000:54) have noted, the scale of this awakening appears to have been matched only by the magnitude of the job shortage faced by East Timorese youth once out of the school system (as discussed below), with the resulting gulf between aspirations and opportunities adding to resentment against the Indonesian administration.[106]

Despite the tripling in size of the public administration during Indonesian times from 11,299 in 1985 to 33,078 in 1996 (BAPPEDA 1997:61, Table 3.2.8), the opportunities for local staff to accrue meaningful experience in government service remained limited in a provincial administration that was both dominated at senior level by appointees from elsewhere in Indonesia, and heavily controlled by the central government in Jakarta.[107] Furthermore,

[105] The main university established in East Timor during the Indonesian period was the *Universitas Timor Timur* (East Timor University or UNTIM). Funded by the provincial government it was established on the initiative of Governor Mario Carrascalão (1982–1992) and opened in 1992 (Saldanha 1994:124; Beazley 1999:52; Jones 2000:50). According to Beazley (1999:52), UNTIM suffered from a lack of learning materials, a high student to lecturer ratio, 'lack of a stimulating academic environment,' and insulation from outside knowledge and participation. The result of this combination of factors was said to be that 'few, if any graduates' were able to find work, with many complaining about educational standards. In the post-independence period, UNTIM has transformed into the *Universidade Nacional Timor Lorosa'e* (East Timor National University, or UNTL). Much teaching remains based on the original curriculum, and the institution continues to attract criticism. In a radio interview in April 2006, José Ramos-Horta (in *Saturday Extra* 2006), speaking as Senior Minister of Foreign Affairs and Cooperation, despairs that many of UNTL's 8,000 students are enrolled 'in a particular degree that was invented by the Indonesian side, and is almost useless, and they call it Social Politics…In my own ministry I have already said, no-one with that degree will be allowed into the Foreign Ministry.'

[106] As Jones (2000:54–55) noted as the dust began to settle after Indonesia's withdrawal, future governments would also come under pressure to meet the aspirations of the country's youth.

[107] See Saldanha (1994:139), Soesastro (1989:221), Beazley (1999:24–27), Taylor (1991:132–33).

the influx of up to several hundred thousand migrants from other parts of Indonesia who arrived during the Indonesian occupation presented stiff competition for any Timorese trying to participate in other sectors of the formal (as opposed to the subsistence) economy.[108] Altogether, the limited opportunities for the Timorese to participate meaningfully and in significant numbers in the administration of the territory or in other areas of the post-subsistence economy, served to minimise the extent to which the Indonesian drive to develop the territory resulted in any kind of broad social and economic modernisation.

In the area of agricultural policy, the Indonesian administration emphasised agricultural self-sufficiency (including in rice production), but it has been asserted (Soesastro 1989:222–28) that the promotion of areas of comparative advantage (including estate crops and livestock) would have been a better approach. In fact, recent survey work indicates that the plantation forestry sector was expanded under Indonesian administration, and that of the 14,213 hectares of state plantation identified in East Timor in 2005, about 13,616 hectares (about ninety-six per cent) dates from the Indonesian period.[109] Still, despite the growth of the sector under Indonesian administration, the total area of government plantation forestry in east Timor at the conclusion of the Indonesian era appears to have amounted to only 14,188 hectares, just under one percent of the land area of the territory.[110]

---

[108] Beazley (1999:15) estimates that by the late 1990s, between 150,000 and 200,000 Indonesian immigrants were residing in East Timor, where their presence presented formidable challenges to any Timorese seeking to engage in commerce. Perhaps because of the subsistence history of the territory, the Timorese are not known for their strong entrepreneurial skills. This weakness has received comment from a number of writers (Soesastro 1989:212; Saldanha 1994:193; Beazley 1999:22,28) and is sometimes the subject of jokes and comments among the Timorese. Soesastro (1989:212–15) has remarked that East Timor was not the only province where the entrepreneurial ability of outsiders (which included the Bugis and the Makassarese) eclipsed those of the local population and Beazley refers to the resentment caused by the common sight of immigrant workers and entrepreneurs throughout the markets and along the roads, driving taxis and tending stalls and shops.

[109] Based on field work coordinated by the writer in 2005 (see Nixon 2005). It is of interest that whereas six of the twenty-eight forestry sites (over one fifth) established during the Portuguese period are now under claim by members of the community, only one of the twenty forestry sites established during the Indonesian era are under claim. Given the far greater land area covered by the Indonesian period plantations, this would appear to indicate that the Indonesian forestry service put considerable effort into negotiating appropriate arrangements with land owners during the site selection phase, whatever the failings of the Indonesian administration in other areas.

[110] The eventual delivery to the East Timorese of long-term benefits associated with timber industry (had the territory remained integrated with Indonesia) would have also depended on the establishment of local value-adding activities in which the East Timorese had the opportunity to participate. However, given prevailing employment and migration patterns as well as skill levels among the East Timorese, it is unclear that this would have happened.

Coffee, East Timor's main estate crop and a sector that could have benefited from modernisation, appears to have either stagnated or gone backwards during the Indonesian period. During this time it was controlled by the military monopoly PT Salazar/PT Batara, a concern which purchased coffee from farmers at one quarter of the market value.[111] According to Soesastro (1989:225) coffee production became even more smallholder dominated in the Indonesian period than it was during the Portuguese period, with smallholder operations increasing from sixty per cent (of a total of 48,000 hectares of coffee producing land)[112] during Portuguese times to eighty per cent during Indonesian times.[113] Because of the poor understanding of coffee crop management among smallholders, East Timor passed through this period of its history with no modernisation of its most important cash crop, a development which has contributed to the uncertain future facing the coffee industry in the present day.[114] An insight into the limited extent to which modern approaches influence the management of coffee crops in the present day in East Timor, might be gauged from the reported opposition of coffee smallholders to the practice of pruning, which despite its proven benefits in terms of improved crop productivity is opposed on the grounds that it can harm the spirits living within the coffee trees.[115]

[111] According to Soesastro (1989:225) the fixing of coffee purchase prices at a low rate was justified by the military 'on the grounds that coffee producers have tended to use their increased earnings for festivities.'

[112] Note that this amounts to around three per cent of the land area of East Timor.

[113] Primary industry survey work coordinated by the writer in 2005 confirms this conclusion. The survey data (see Nixon 2005:19-23) indicates at least twelve instances where plantations were abandoned by Portuguese-era planters following the events of 1975, and subsequently harvested by smallholder groups. Note also that Soesastro (1989:225) refers to a coffee replanting program aimed at quadrupling coffee production that was planned by Indonesian authorities for implementation in the late 1980s, yet there is no record of this program having been commenced. No quadrupling of coffee production appears to have occurred, and the documented increase in annual exports (FAO 2005) between the early 1990s and the years 2001–2003 (from 8,000 tons annually to 14,000 tons annually) is able to be explained by other developments. According to coffee specialist David Boyce (email correspondence dated 10th August 2006), who has worked with the United States supported National Cooperative Business Association (NCBA) since it broke the military monopoly on coffee purchasing in East Timor in 1994, the increase is more likely to have resulted from NCBA's policy of offering farmers four times the price for coffee cherries that was previously offered by the military monopoly, thereby leading to the export of coffee that would otherwise have been consumed by households or sold at local markets. Boyce knows of no new areas of coffee plantation dating to the late 1980s.

[114] For an overview of the East Timor coffee sector, see Deutsch, who refers (2004:3–11) to a range of issues facing the industry including ageing and neglected coffee plants of low productivity, ageing and diseased shade trees, and an absence (within this smallholder dominated industry) of routine pruning and replanting programs.

[115] Based on email correspondence (dated 11th June 2006) from David Boyce.

Justice in the Indonesian period

New justice experiences in East Timor that unfolded during the Indonesian period included exposure to the Indonesian justice system, and the systems of revolutionary justice practiced in resistance-held areas (FRETILIN *zonas libertadas* or 'liberated zones') during the second half of the 1970s. Political objectives influenced the implementation of both systems, and for this and other reasons it is clear that neither served to convince the East Timorese of the superiority of post-subsistence forms of justice and conflict resolution. One outcome of this was that *suco* justice principles continued to be reaffirmed and drawn on throughout the period of Indonesian occupation.

Although East Timor was officially declared an Indonesian province on 17th July 1976 (Republic of Indonesia 1977:96–97 Annex XIII), it was some years before Indonesian security forces were able to assert control over the majority of the countryside. Up until the late 1970s the FRETILIN-led resistance held considerable territory, being forced to give up the last of its *zonas libertadas* only following a massive Indonesian onslaught that commenced in September 1978.[116] The first years following the Indonesian invasion coincided with the rise within FRETILIN of a key group of radicals[117] and the official adoption by the FRETILIN party of a Marxist ideological orientation. This officially occurred in May 1977 at a meeting from which the incumbent FRETILIN president, the moderate Francisco Xavier do Amaral, was absent, and was accompanied by the formalisation of a hardline position against negotiation with the Indonesians (Gusmão 2000:47–49; CAVR Part 5:32).[118] These developments bode ill for President Francisco Xavier do Amaral and his followers. In September 1977, do Amaral was arrested after FRETILIN Vice-President Nicolau Lobato signed an order accusing him of charges that included treason and defeatism, following do Amaral's support for the policy

---

116 After first launching intensive campaigns in the west and central regions of the territory, Indonesian forces then forced FRETILIN's armed wing, the *Forças Armadas de Libertação Nacional de Timor-Leste* (Armed Forces for the National Liberation of East Timor, or FALINTIL), accompanied by tens of thousands of civilians, to retreat to the sanctuary of Mount Matebian in the east. Following a subsequent Indonesian 'encirclement and annihilation' campaign that targeted this region, Indonesian forces succeeded in destroying the last FRETILIN-administered area in the east of the territory in November 1978. The fall of Matebian was accompanied by great loss of life and weapons, and was a great blow to the resistance. FALINTIL units were reduced to isolated bands and the East Timorese population was forced to live in Indonesian-controlled areas (Budiardjo and Liong 1984:66–67; CAVR 2005 Part 5:26).

117 Notably including António Duarte Carvarino (Mau Lear) and Vicente dos Reis (Vicente Sa'he), both of whom had been studying in Lisbon at the time of the Armed Forces Movement revolt (Taylor 1991:48; Hill 2002:66–67; Nicol 1978:102–7).

118 Referred to in CAVR (2005 Part 5:32) as the 'principle of "Negotiation – No and Never."'

that the civilian population sheltering in the 'liberated zones' should surrender and move to Indonesian-controlled areas to reduce hardship. Following his arrest, supporters of do Amaral were publicly executed or otherwise mistreated. Do Amaral himself was beaten and kept in a hole,[119] before eventually escaping during an attack by Indonesian forces.[120]

The purges carried out against supporters of Xavier do Amaral were not the first to take place, and the identification of 'reactionaries' and 'traitors' had already occurred in the *zonas libertadas* prior to the targeting of the FRETILIN President.[121] More generally, according to the CAVR inquiry (2005 Part 5:12–14), FRETILIN detention, interrogation and justice dispensation practices were frequently *ad hoc* and unsystematic and too often resulted in brutal outcomes.

No less harrowing was the experience of justice under the Indonesian state. As the findings of the CAVR inquiry make clear, trauma from activities perpetrated by state institutions was a common part of life for the East Timorese under Indonesian occupation.[122] Anyone associated with pro-

---

[119] A common form of incarceration used in FRETILIN-controlled areas (CAVR 2005 Part 5:12).

[120] In the wake of the purge, Vice-President Nicolau Lobato ascended to the Presidency on 16th October 1977 (CAVR 2005 Part 3:77–78; Cristalis 2002:113–24, Gusmão 2000:49; Niner, in Gusmão 2000:49). The increase in influence of prominent left-wing cadres was reflected in their appointment to senior positions. António Duarte Carvarino replaced Nicolau Lobato as vice-president (CAVR 2005 Part 5:26; Niner, in Gusmão 2000:63). Vicente dos Reis is also known to have been appointed to the post of FRETILIN Prime Minister by the time of his death in February 1979 (Taylor 1991:97). Although the date on which he was appointed to the position of Prime Minister is unclear, in May 1976 dos Reis occupied the more junior position of Minister of Labour and Welfare (CAVR 2005 Part 5:5). Note that in the months following the major Indonesian assault on FRETILIN-controlled territory that commenced in September 1978, all three leaders were killed. In the void that remained, Xanana Gusmão emerged as a promising new leader (Gusmão 2000:65–68; Budiardjo and Liong 1984:69-70; CAVR 2005 Part 5:26; Shoesmith 2003:240). At a meeting of the FRETILIN central committee in April 1984, both the Marxist orientation and the anti-negotiation position were dropped (CAVR 2005 Part 5:32). The FRETILIN purges of the 1970s continue to generate ill-will, and in a recent speech, RDTL President Xanana Gusmão (2006) criticised FRETILIN for having failed to apologise and reconcile with families of those killed by FRETILIN in the 1970s because of their rejection of Marxist-Leninism. President Gusmão referred to requests he had made of FRETILIN in 2000, including that the party review Xavier do Amaral's case, as 'he was not a traitor of our country…[but]…simply did not accept the ideology issued by the Central Committee of Fretilin in May 1977.'

[121] See CAVR (2005 Part 5:19-20)

[122] A concise summary of the crimes committed by the Indonesian state between 1975 and 1999 is outlined in CAVR (2005 Part 8:6–7). Indicating the systematic nature of state violence during this period, the commission found that the 'highest levels of the security apparatus and the civil administration' were complicit in the perpetration of war crimes and crimes against humanity, whereby 'Indonesian security forces implemented a programme of widespread and systematic arbitrary detention, which routinely involved the torture of thousands of East Timorese non-combatants.'

independence activities was particularly at risk, not only from extra-judicial acts of brutality from the security forces, but also from the corrupt use of the judicial system itself. In the course of their investigation, CAVR (2005 Part 8:7) documented 'several hundred' cases where multiple Indonesian officials (including judges, security officials and even defence counsels) had collaborated to undertake 'sham trials' of independence activists. According to the CAVR, '[t]hese trials involved the systematic use of torture to produce confessions, the fabrication of evidence and the manipulation of judicial proceedings.'[123]

It is clear that the routine perpetration of crimes against humanity by the Indonesian administration failed to engender confidence in state institutions in general and in the state justice system in particular. Accordingly, the validity of *suco* principles of justice and conflict resolution received reinforcement while the state justice system was viewed with suspicion and contempt. As Soares (2001:40-41)[124] remarks:

> During the 24 years of Indonesian administration, although the government recognised the existence of traditional institutions, they were given no role to play as had been the case of the previous colonial governments. Nevertheless, those 24 years were also characterised by the degradation of public credibility on the judicial system. This has prompted people to rely on traditional ways of solving disputes rather than on state groups...

* * *

The range of variables considered in foregoing pages indicates that despite the resources Indonesia channelled into East Timor to promote development, very little meaningful modernisation of economy and society (including preferred forums for justice and dispute resolution) took place, even if *expectations* of a post-subsistence lifestyle among the younger generations were aroused by the expanded basic education program. Clearly there were broad and acute failings in the Indonesian approach, however the challenges of development also faced by a range of other subsistence societies in the region serve to highlight the relevance of Saldanha's observation (1994:131) that 'to date there is no model which can...change a traditional society into a modern one.' Whatever might have been possible under different

[123] See also Beazley (1999:24).

[124] See also Soares (2000:287–88) for further discussion of the 'degradation' of the credibility of the formal justice sector during Indonesian times.

circumstances, East Timor towards the conclusion of the Indonesian period of administration remained, by a clear margin, the least urbanised of all Indonesian provinces (MHRI 1999:11, Figure II.A.3), with only 10.1 per cent of the population urbanised in 1998.[125] Furthermore, with four hundred and fourteen of its four hundred and forty-two villages (around ninety-three per cent) still officially considered 'backward' in 1995 (MHRI 2000:17, Figure II.B.3), East Timor at the conclusion of the Indonesian period remained among the least developed regions in the archipelago.

Old Authorities in a New Era

Although there are some indications that the power of the ancestors may be receding,[126] there is also evidence from recent years that *suco* leaders in East Timor continue to be respected for their ability to communicate with *Maromak* and with the ancestors, and it is likely that such perceived abilities will influence the selection of *chefe*s *de suco* to a greater or lesser extent for some time, regardless of the technical process for determining who fills this post.[127] The ancestors continue to take interest in who is appointed to senior positions in the village hierarchy, and an account recorded in Oecusse in 2002 highlights the dangers of disregarding ancestral will. During 1998, a man without the correct lineage was appointed *chefe* of Bobometo *suco*. In the position for only one year, he was murdered by militia during the violence of 1999. The following year he was replaced by another incumbent, also lacking the correct lineage, who died unexpectedly in November 2002. The people of the *suco* then went to the family of the man they knew should be *chefe*. They said there

---

[125] The next lowest rate of urbanisation was in Lampung (Southern Sumatra) with 16.8 per cent (MHRI 1999:11, Figure II.A.3)

[126] See James T. Thomson's paper in this volume for a discussion on this theme.

[127] In 2004, the RDTL government passed legislation (RDTL 2004) prescribing procedures for the conduct of ballots for the 'secret, free, equal and direct' election of *suco* chiefs and councils (the latter to consist of the *suco* chief, the chief of every *aldeia* in the *suco*, two women, a 'young person' of each gender and a further *suco* elder). The composition of the *suco* councils is based on progressive principles, and as suggested by Grenfell (2006:331), probably influenced by the Community Empowerment Project (CEP) initiated under UNTAET. Although elections were held for the *suco* chiefs and councils in 2005, it remains to be seen if the legal requirement for the representation of young people and women on the councils results in significant changes to *actual* authority relations within the *suco*s. The legislation appears focussed on extending state 'legitimisation' to a level of social organisation which already has popular (and *adat*) legitimacy (as well as facilitating the operation of party-politics at *suco*-level). As noted by electoral observers (Caputo and Jungwirth 2005:1) East Timor's formal governance structure extends down only to sub-district level, so although *suco* councils will be able to make recommendations, they will have 'no powers or resources.' For this reason, *suco* authorities will be regarded in this paper as 'non-state actors,' albeit (at least to the extent that the complexity of *suco* administrations is reflected in the new *suco* council framework) state-recognised non-state actors.

was no one else in the *suco* willing to accept responsibility for the position of *chefe*, and pressured the appropriate individual to accept his inherited obligations.[128]

Accounts of *lulik* practices conducted at another *suco* during the Indonesian occupation and the final rampages of the integrationist militia, serve to illustrate how survival requires excellent relations with the ancestors, and respect for those able to communicate with them. In Oecusse, it is the *naizuf mnasi* (senor ritual leader of the *suco* and ideally, although not necessarily, *chefe de suco* as well) who possesses the ability to communicate with *Maromak* and with people's ancestors, in order to work magic that can make people invisible to their enemies. Although this magic dates back to the days of the head-hunting micro-kingdoms, when it would be used by each warring side to ensure the victory of its *meo*s (warriors), it was also used in 1999, when villages fled to the hills to hide from rampaging militia members.

Other examples of the role of *adat* in public administration encountered by this writer include frequent references to the need for animal sacrifices in connection with *posto* administration and various primary industry activities.[129] A further example from mid-2003 relates to the proposed sacrifice of a black dog at midnight in association with the opening of a USAID-funded project office sited in a rehabilitated building in the campus of the national university in Dili, however this particular proposal was altered to a religious blessing at the request of expatriate project officials.[130]

A National Network of Non-State Actors

Although it would be tempting to consider that East Timor was an administrative *tabula rasa* following the Indonesian withdrawal, this assessment would ignore the range of administrative, justice and reconciliation tasks that were coordinated and performed at *posto* and *suco* level throughout

---

128 See also Ospina and Hohe (2001:63–82) and Mearns (2002:47) for further examples of this feature of the political life of rural East Timor.

129 For example, *posto* administration officials in Aileu in 2002 described their monthly practice of sacrificing a goat in the *posto* administration compound to ensure condition good relations with the ancestors. Also, the writer found while surveying primary industry sites in East Timor in 2005 that *suco* administration officials will often refer to the need for the sacrifice of a buffalo and a pig in relation to the (re)commissioning of such primary industry facilities as fish farms. Although the theoretical objective of animal sacrifices is to appease the ancestors and therefore increase the productivity of the facility being commissioned, the ultimate (human) consumption of the sacrificed animals (paid for out of the public administration budget) may also be a factor contributing to the popularity of the practice.

130 The writer was working for this project at the time.

East Timor in the immediate post-conflict period. In fact, a national network linking elements of the *suco* administrative system had already been a feature of the resistance movement during the occupation, with *nurep*s (from *Núcleos de Resistência Popular*, or nucleus of popular resistance) organised at *suco* level and *celcom*s (from *Célular da Comunidade*, or community cell) at the level of the *povoações* or hamlet. Characteristically, those who participated in this national resistance network at grassroots level across the country also held positions of authority in the (traditional) *suco* administration system.[131] This overlap between *suco* authorities and the national resistance shadow organisation was manifested in the district leadership of the national resistance council in the final form it took in 1998, as the *Concelho Nacional da Resistência Timorense* (CNRT).[132]

In 1999, after the announcement that a referendum would be held on East Timor's future, the CNRT umbrella organisation served as the hub of the pro-independence support network that quickly developed in preparation for the 30th August 1999 ballot.[133] Significantly in relation to the theme of public administration, justice and conflict resolution in the *suco*, the CNRT administration also played a role in the post-conflict administration of the territory following the mayhem and violence associated with the pro-independence vote and the Indonesian withdrawal. The turmoil unleashed in September 1999 is estimated to have resulted in over half the population being forced to leave their homes, of whom a quarter of a million either elected to flee to West Timor, or were intimidated into doing so (CAVR 2005 Part 3:145).[134] Yet the return of displaced persons commenced quickly. By mid-October, more than two thousand refugees had been flown back to East Timor by UNHCR flights from Kupang, and negotiations were underway with

[131] Informed primarily by interviews with former CNRT officials in the districts of Aileu and Oecusse in November 2002. Note that a national shadow administration utilising *suco* structures can be traced back to the FRETILIN resistance administration established in areas outside of Indonesian-held territory following the invasion, as well as the interim administration that FRETILIN developed after crushing the UDT coup attempt in 1975 (CAVR 2005 Part 5:4–6). See also McWilliam (2005:34–38) for an historical and anthropological overview of this area.

[132] The former name of the council was the *Concelho Nacional da Resistência Maubere* (CNRM). The term 'Maubere,' which had associations with the FRETILIN party, was replaced with 'Timorense' to make the name of the council inclusive of all those parties supporting independence. For commentary on the CNRT see Federer (2005:53–55).

[133] For further information on the 1999 referendum on independence and CNRT's role in the campaign, see de Araujo (2000:112–17) and Federer (2005:54). Note that the CNRT was formally dissolved prior to the 30th August 2001 election for a Constitutional Assembly.

[134] An early humanitarian assessment (UNOCHA 1999:13) estimated that over seventy-five per cent of East Timor's population had been displaced and that over seventy per cent of housing, utilities and public buildings had been destroyed.

Indonesian authorities for the return of refugees by road (UNOCHA 1999:1–2). In this territory from which the Indonesian regime had vanished and in which the UN transitional authority took an extended period to become established,[135] an *ad hoc* administration incorporating *suco* authority structures played a prominent role in filling the vacuum of state authority. An important component of the responsibilities performed by the *ad hoc* administration concerned the screening of returnees in order to identify those suspected of participation in militia crimes, and the diversion of these individuals into traditional compensation and reconciliation programs at the *suco* level (as described in the next section). According to a UN official who arrived in late 1999 to serve as District Administrator with the UN Transitional Administration in East Timor (UNTAET),[136] an *ad hoc* administration had already formed consisting of an overlapping network of CNRT and *suco* officials,[137] which by December 1999 was processing the re-integration of several hundred returned refugees and former militia members per day.

Suco Justice and Dispute Resolution in a New State

The conclusion of Indonesian rule created the possibility of new social research concerning *suco* justice and dispute resolution processes in the post-occupation period. Based on the writers' involvement in research activities relating to this area, a range of aspects of *suco* justice and dispute resolution in East Timor are presented in the remainder of this chapter.[138] Although there are concerns about the extent to which legal principles and international human rights standards (particular for women, children and vulnerable persons) are observed in *suco* justice proceedings, there is little doubt that *suco* proceedings have played a major role in the resolution of conflicts between individuals and families (hence contributing to order and stability) in the period during which the East Timorese state has been struggling to develop a credible state justice sector. The difficulty of this latter challenge was highlighted emphatically when it was announced in January 2005 that all twenty-two Timorese judges had failed their evaluations at the conclusion of

[135] UNTAET officials and CivPol officials interviewed by the writer in 2002 commonly referred to the delays associated with the establishment of a UN administrative presence in rural East Timor during the early UNTAET period. See also Smith with Dee (2003:60) and King's College (2003:Para.211).

[136] Interviewed in Dili (November 2002).

[137] As mentioned earlier, traditional leaders featured prominently in the CNRT structure in the districts. In the course of interviews with former CNRT officials in Oecusse and Aileu districts in 2002, for example, the writer was informed that the CNRT district secretary for Aileu was a senior *lia nain* ('keeper of the word'), and that the CNRT spokesperson for Oecusse had been a *meo* (senior warrior). Other former CNRT officials interviewed also had positions in the traditional administration.

[138] See also Mearns (2002).

a probationary period of over four years, reducing the number of qualified judges to four internationals (JSMP 2005; Clausen 2005). Such developments illustrate the difficulty of developing formal state institutions in a New Subsistence State and highlight the value of non-state actors with the capacity to provide justice and conflict resolution services in a weak state environment.

The following profile illustrates approaches to a range of justice and conflict resolution aspects, and indicates that many of the underlying principles of *suco* justice and conflict resolution documented by colonial-era visitors to East Timor appear to have retained their currency to the present day. The initial profile is largely based on qualitative fieldwork undertaken by the writer in association with a 2002 study concerning the interface between traditional justice institutions and the formal justice system under UNTAET.[139] The latter section on land dispute resolution draws on several national surveys undertaken in 2003 and 2004 as part of the East Timor Land Law Program.[140]

Justice and Conflict Resolution

Consistent with the observations of colonial observers referred to earlier, the close social environment which is a corollary of East Timor's subsistence rural economy continues to mean that committing a social transgression is perceived by others less as the crime of an individual than as a community problem affecting many. A crime or dispute is therefore likely to attract the interests of a large number of people anxious to establish what has gone wrong and how to arrive at a resolution. In the *suco* environment, where people live in close proximity to one another and to each other's relatives for their entire lives, the promotion of peaceful relations between individuals and families is of utmost importance. Sometimes such an outcome might not be produced by the courts, since sending an offender to jail could potentially remove a productive worker from a family and possibly also deny the family of a victim from receiving compensation. Some may fail to understand why an offender is sent to jail to be fed and clothed and taught Portuguese or English (thereby having their employment prospects improved), while victims are forced to continue eking out

[139] This research was supported by the United States Institute of Peace (USIP) project on peacekeeping and the administration of justice. For the full report, see Hohe and Nixon (2003). The profile in the main text is based mainly on fieldwork undertaken by the writer in the districts of Oecusse and Aileu in 2002, and also on interviews with elders from elsewhere and with individuals who worked in the areas of justice, policing and peacekeeping during the UNTAET period.
[140] The East Timor Land Law Program was supported by USAID and administered by ARD, Inc. The surveys referred to in this chapter concern land dispute mediation (Urresta and Nixon 2004a) and land rights systems (Urresta and Nixon 2004b).

a living on the land! As articulated by a community leader in Oecusse,[141] 'People in the *suco* live and drink together, and if someone goes to jail, then even after being there for twenty years, the bad feeling will remain...If people can sit together, however, then the problem may be resolved.' In the context of the village, therefore, admittance of guilt or error, followed by *compensation* and *reconciliation*, remain fundamental to notions of justice and conflict resolution:

> With stealing or killing, we must first negotiate and pay compensation. And then drink *tuasabu* [distilled palm wine] to conclude the reconciliation. If the problem happens again, the community will inform the police and the courts. But it is very important to first make a decision in the community.[142]

As discussed earlier, the desire to prevent one's family from acquiring a bad name provides strong motivation to resolve a dispute, especially since, from the Timorese perspective, permitting one's family name to be tarnished could attract the wrath of the ancestors. From a practical perspective, it is often *suco* elders, with their superior ritual power and ability to communicate with and appease the spirit world, who are chosen to preside over the dispute resolution process. This process often involves a degree of 'forum shopping' as the parties (supported by senior family members) find a mediator who the parties agree is fair on all sides. Its also appears clear from the land dispute mediation data, that the use of witnesses is common practice in local justice and dispute resolution proceedings and that the accounts of witnesses are treated with great respect.[143] Figure 2 below indicates the path to resolution which a dispute may follow among the Atoni of Oecusse district, where there is an overlap between ritual and administrative authority in the *suco*.[144]

The conflict resolution process requires that the entire history of the conflict be told, as many conflicts go back years or even generations. After compensation has been negotiated, the way is clear for the parties to reconcile. Although both parties would normally contribute to a conflict resolution process, the party responsible for causing the problem – if this has been determined – would be expected to provide the major share of the provisions for the reconciliation feast (in addition to any compensation payable for the actual offence, as discussed below) such as a head of cattle or a goat. The

---

141 *Meo* (senior warrior/*suco* security officer), Oecusse, November 2002.

142 *Naizuf* (senior ritual leader), Oecusse, November 2002.

143 For further details, refer Urresta and Nixon (2004a:46, Figs. 27 and 28).

144 Elsewhere (including among the Mambai), *suco* leaders refer to distinctions which exist between the ritual and administrative systems of the *suco*. See also Mearns (2002:38-39) for commentary on the course through which a conflict might progress until final resolution.

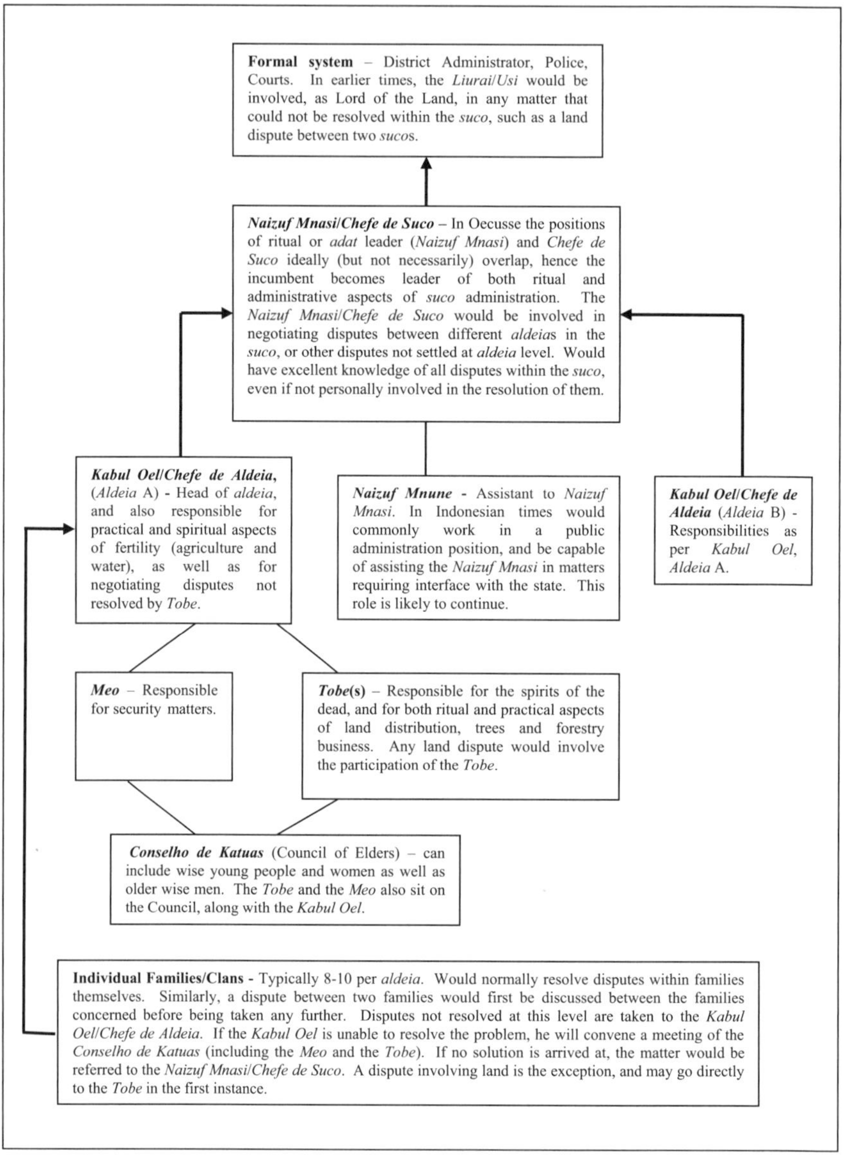

Figure 2: Possible course of dispute resolution/criminal proceedings in Oecusse, where ritual and legal authority commonly overlaps (to be read from bottom to top).[145]

---

[145] Based on a discussion held with a meeting of *naizufs* in Oecusse, November 2002.

other party would contribute such items as drums of distilled palm wine (*tuasabu*) and rice. Senior members of the community, having presided over conflict negotiation proceedings and reconciliation negotiations, may expect modest compensation for their time.

Compensation

Although there is variation, the payment of compensation is generally likely to conform to the 'value' of the crime committed, as outlined in the relation to the following range of offences:

Theft of an Animal

Compensation for the theft of a goat would normally require the return of the goat (or its replacement with another). Depending on circumstances and region, further compensation may also be required.

Compensation for a Killing in Oecusse (the Eight Steps):[146]

Reminiscent of the accounts collected by Forbes in Timor and Buru in the Moluccas, protocols for compensating for a death based on the value of the various parts of the body persist. The following account is from Oecusse:

(i) First you must pay for the head, as a symbol of the whole human being, whose life you took. Cost: approximately US$100
(ii) For the social function of the person, you must pay a *poe aluk* (small bag from which food is given out to others), or maybe US$25
(iii) For the sadness you produced, for destroying peace and love, you must pay nine traditional ('Hollander') coins or about US$45 (depending on personal circumstances, as with all categories).
(iv) For the genitals, about US$50
(v) For the two eyes and the mouth (depending on family name), you must pay $US50, or maybe more.
(vi) For the brain, the thoughts and the rationality, about US$300 (the price for a specific kind of traditional necklace).
(vii) For the teeth and for the tongue, because the dead cannot speak again, you must pay one head-dress worth about US$100.
(viii) For the left body and the right body, 16 traditional coins are payable for each side (about US$80 each).

Sexual Crimes

As in the colonial period, compensation is payable for sexual transgressions. In the case of rape, or if a man makes a woman pregnant but wishes not to

[146] As related by a *meo* and former CNRT official in Oecusse.

marry her, the compensation is likely to be similar to the *barlaque* (or bride price) which itself differs from region to region. In fact with rape, the preferred option is for the parties to marry, and for the union to be legitimised with the exchange of cattle, pigs, *tais* (woven cloth) and other items in accordance with the formal marriage protocol. However, if the parties are unwilling to formalise the union, then the family of the rapist still must pay compensation (thereby also providing for the security of any child conceived). The idea that a woman might be encouraged to marry someone who raped her is a clear example of where *suco* justice conflicts with human rights principles. However, it is also reported that many 'rapes' initially occur as consensual acts, agreed to on the basis that marriage will follow. The claim that an act of rape took place is said to often result in cases where the man subsequently reneges on the promise to marry. Again, compensation is also payable in relation to adultery, as in earlier times, as well as in cases of domestic violence. Although the compensation protocol can make crimes against women appear as property offences, in the context of *suco* life, compensation can also be seen as a means of discouraging rape as well as a means by which pride may be recovered and by which a family may be compensated for the cost of raising a child.[147]

* * *

On the topic of compensation generally, the practice is clearly so well established that it is difficult to conceive of Timorese justice being dispensed without it. As Mearns (2002:55) recommends, the state justice system in East Timor 'should embrace…victim compensation,' along with a range of other established justice principles.

Suco Authorities and Land Dispute Resolution

Two studies undertaken as part of the East Timor Land Law Program (LLP) during 2003 and 2004 provide insight into the prominent role of non-state actors in land administration and the resolution of land disputes throughout East Timor. The first of these studies, of which the key findings are presented in the following pages, concerns land dispute mediation systems.[148] The land dispute mediation study was based on interviews with one hundred and forty-two key persons throughout the country, each of whom was qualified to provide certain information about land dispute resolution practices in their

---

[147] See Mearns (2002:40-42) for further commentary on this area.

[148] For the complete *Report on Research Findings and Policy Recommendations for a Legal Framework for Land Dispute Mediation*, see Urresta and Nixon (2004a). See also Meitzner Yoder (2003) for a discussion of the 'uses and limitations of traditional systems in addressing rural land disputes in East Timor.'

geographic regions. These informants included *chefe*s *de suco*, district administrators, sub-district administrators,[149] land and property officers, court officials, and Non-Government Organisation (NGO) representatives.[150] In order to establish the extent to which the views and perceptions of the 'common citizen' conformed to the views and perceptions of those included in the sample of *suco*, state and NGO officials, interviews were also conducted with members of a randomly selected sample of household heads (totalling sixty-one respondents) from the two sub-districts of Ermera *Kota* and Manatuto *Kota*.[151] Parts of a separate study into land rights systems (from 2004) based on interviews with seven hundred and seventeen randomly selected respondents from across eleven sub-districts in East Timor, are also drawn on in this section.[152]

The Importance of Land Dispute Resolution Capacity

In a subsistence economy such as that of East Timor, where the great majority of the population rely on access to land for their livelihood, it might be expected that land conflicts are a main cause of disputes between individuals and communities. In fact the land dispute mediation survey data indicates that land disputes represent *almost half of all disputes* which authorities (*suco* or state) are called upon to resolve. As part of the survey, eighty-nine district, sub-district and *suco* administrative officials (*not* including land and property

---

[149] Note that many sub-district administration officials also hold senior positions in the traditional authority system.

[150] District-level officials (including district administrators, land and property officer, clergy and NGO personal) were interviewed in all thirteen districts. Also in each district, two sub-districts were randomly selected, and the sub-district administrators interviewed. In each of the selected sub-districts, two *suco*s were randomly selected, and the *chefe*s *de suco* interviewed. This process was used to introduce an element of randomness to the selection of key informants at sub-district and *suco* level.

[151] Ermera *Kota* is a densely populated sub-district in a rich coffee growing area. It is known to land and property officials as a high-conflict sub-district. By comparison, Manatuto *Kota* is a low-density sub-district known to have fewer land disputes. Note that both sub-districts are district-centre sub-districts, and that it is likely that the inhabitants of the more remote sub-districts in each of the respective regions would have had *even greater* respect for traditional social institutions than those surveyed. Note that respondents were chosen on the basis of being the heads of households in closest proximity to sets of navigational coordinates chosen randomly using a Geographic Information System (GIS) program. The coordinate sets were located by field teams using hand-held Global Positioning System (GPS) equipment.

[152] Again, as in relation to the land dispute mediation study, the household random selection component used a GIS approach, with coordinates located using hand-held GPS units. The eleven sub-districts in which fieldwork was undertaken were selected so as to include both rural and urban areas. They were located in the following districts: Bobonaro (Balibo and Maliana), Covalima (Suai Kota and Tilomar), Dili (Dom Aleixo, Metinaro and Nain Feto), Lautem (Lautem and Lospalos) and Oecusse (Oesilo and Pante Macassar). For the complete *Report on Research Findings, Policy Options and Recommendations for a Law on Land Rights and Title Restitution*, see Urresta and Nixon (2004b).

officers)[153] were asked (a) how many disputes had come to their attention over the past year and (b) how many of these concerned land. Collectively, the officials were able to recall a total of one hundred and eighty-nine disputes, of which eighty-seven (forty-six per cent) concerned land. This data indicates the importance of mechanisms supporting the swift resolution of land disputes, in order that losses to economic productivity caused by drawn-out land conflicts are minimised.

It might be speculated that as the population density of East Timor continues to increase, there is a strong likelihood that land disputes will become even more frequent. In this respect, recent information[154] suggests that the 2004 population of 924,642 may double within sixteen years, resulting in the doubling of East Timor's crude population density from around sixty-two people per square kilometre in 2004, to around one hundred and twenty-four people per square kilometre in 2020.[155] Although increased urbanisation may relieve rural areas of the full force of this population increase, acute land administration challenges would still be likely to result. Subsistence agricultural systems may be pressed perilously close to their limits,[156] and a logical result of this would be increased land conflict.

Suco Authorities and Land

Data from both the land rights study and the land dispute mediation study indicates that *suco* authorities retain strong legitimacy in relation to important decisions concerning land. For example, when asked 'who should make a compulsory decision (arbitrate) concerning a land dispute or claim, in the event that such a decision must be made,' a substantial majority of the seven hundred and seventeen respondents interviewed for the land rights study chose senior *katuas* (elders) in preference to any other authority (see Figure 3 below).

---

[153] The eighty-nine respondents consisted of district administrators, sub-district administrators and *chefes de suco*. Data from land and property officers was not included, since one of their main roles is to address land and property disputes.

[154] For an overview of data from the 2004 United Nations Population Fund (UNFPA) East Timor Census, see UNFPA (2005).

[155] Based on a land area of 14,959 square kms calculated using GIS data derived from the August 2001 aerial photo series prepared by the Australian Defence Force.

[156] Fox (1988:274–275) makes a related assessment in regard to West Timor, remarking that '[a]t 30 persons per sq km, it is still possible to rely on a traditional swidden mode of subsistence based primarily on maize; at 140 persons per square km, this is utterly impossible.'

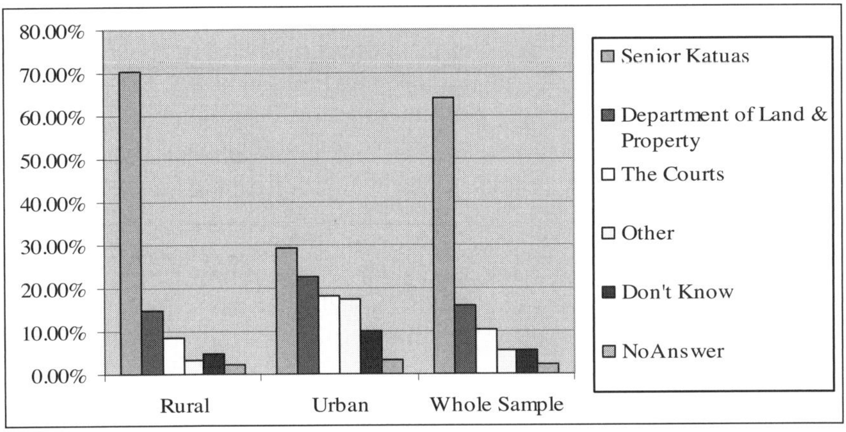

Figure 3: Respondents' views concerning who should make a compulsory decision concerning the resolution of a land dispute or claim, in the event a compulsory decision must be made.[157]

As indicated in Figure 3 above, the proportion of rural respondents who indicated a preference for 'senior *katuas*' to arbitrate land disputes where necessary was over seventy per cent; yet even in urban areas, almost thirty percent of respondents indicated that they would prefer senior *katuas* to make such a compulsory decision in preference to any other authority. Significantly, the category of senior *katuas* was the largest single category, ahead of both the Department of Land and Property and the courts. The popular legitimacy attributed to these non-state actors is a measure of their ability to contribute to social order and warns against dismissing them as feudal artefacts or impostors intruding on the state mandate (particularly given such limited state service delivery capacity as prevails at present). As outlined in Figure 4 below, earlier findings from the 2003 land dispute mediation study (both key persons and random selection components) also support the conclusion that members of the *suco* administration (the *chefe de suco* often in combination with other *katuas* or traditional leaders) are perceived as the most legitimate authorities in relation to decisions concerning land:

[157] Based on interviews with seven hundred and seventeen respondents; six hundred and one from rural sub-districts (including district-centre sub-districts) and one hundred and sixteen from sub-districts in urban Dili.

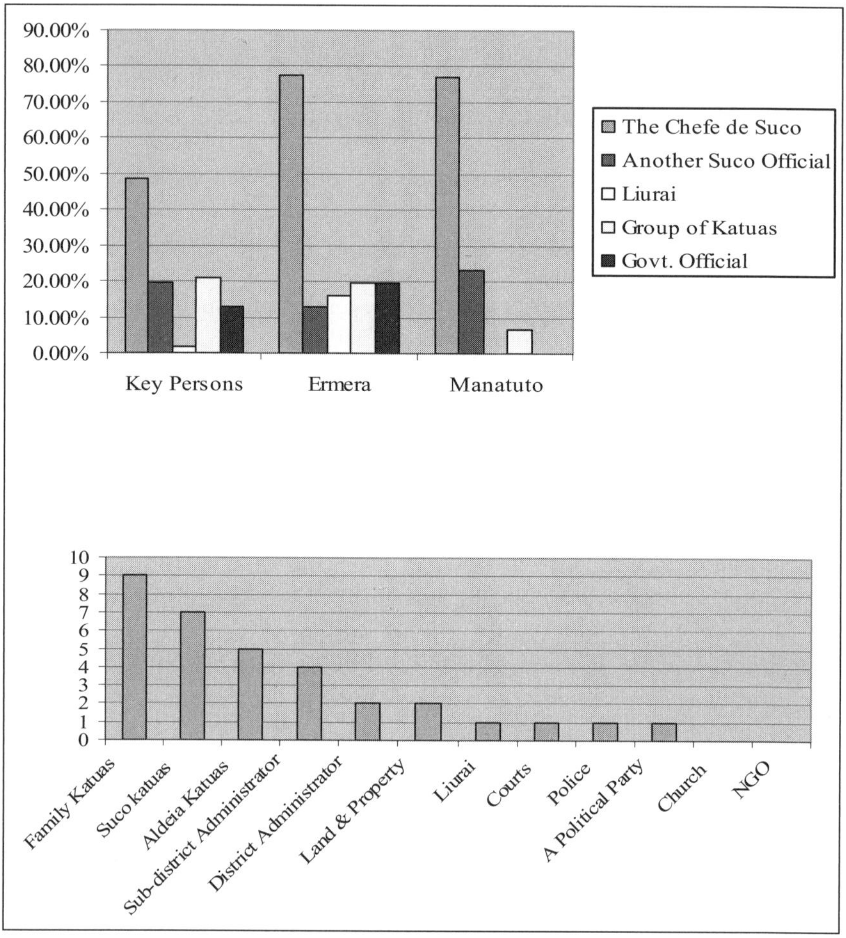

Figure 4: Who has major responsibility for decisions about land in the *suco*?[158]

Land Dispute Mediation Forums

Of the sixty-one randomly selected East Timorese citizens interviewed in Ermera and Manatuto, at least eighteen (around a third) had been involved in one or more land disputes in the past. Collectively, in order to resolve their land disputes, these eighteen parties had participated in a total of thirty-three

[158] Note that multiple responses were provided by informants. The key person sample included one hundred and one respondents. The Ermera and Manatuto samples included thirty-one and thirty respondents respectively.

land dispute resolution forums, at various levels. As indicated in Figure 5 (below), the great majority of these forums (totalling twenty-five) were at the level of the family, *aldeia*, *suco* or sub-district (where officials are commonly also members of the traditional authority system):

The general indication is that individuals prefer to resolve disputes at as local a level as possible (and preferably within or close to the *suco*). As discussed earlier, however (see Figure 2 above), it also appears clear that access to multiple forums is required to enable disputes to proceed from the *aldeia* or *suco* level to the sub-district level or beyond, until such a point where disputants participate in a forum able to facilitate resolution. The need for multiple forums may arise because of the need to find an individual with the necessary personal background to preside over a particular case, or because the dispute is of a nature requiring a higher level authority than that available in the *aldeia* or *suco* (such as a land or boundary dispute between *two sucos*, for example). Informants indicate that the three most important qualities required in a mediator are neutrality, honesty, and good background knowledge of the problem and the community involved.[159] However, in communities with deep and complex alliance networks, the task of finding a mediator whose qualities are respected by all conflicting parties is not always easy, and access to a range of forums is important. With respect to disputes between *sucos*, it is likely

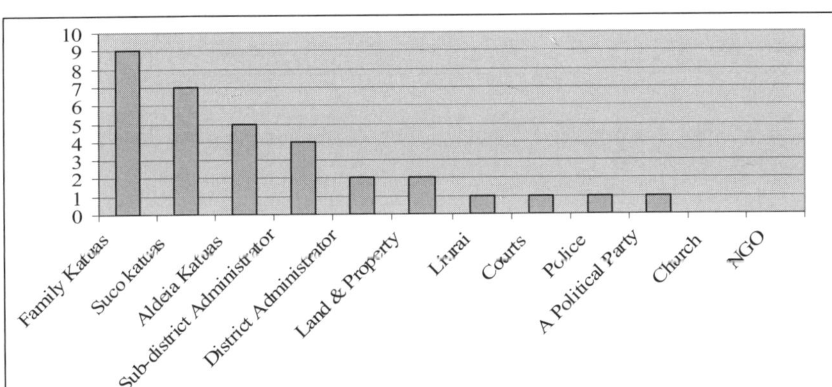

Figure 5: Total land dispute mediation forums used by (18) randomly selected respondents with past involvement in land disputes.

159 For further details, see Urresta and Nixon (2004a:45, Fig. 26).

that in the past, these would often have been resolved by *liurai*s or other members of the *reino* administration. As a result of the colonial history of East Timor, however, and as indicated in the data (see Figures 4 and 5 above) *liurai*s have a reduced role in the present day, and the task of resolving conflicts between *suco*s can fall to any of a number of authorities (traditional *or* state). An outline of a range of land dispute types (intra-*suco* and inter-*suco*) and indications of their relative commonality and ease of resolution is presented in Figure 6 below:

From Key Persons Sample (101 respondents)

Land Dispute Type	Common	Not Common	No Answer	Easy to Resolve	Difficult to Resolve	No Answer
Ownership Dispute	79.2%	18.8%	2.0%	63%	34%	3%
Parcel Boundary Dispute	74.3%	22.8%	3.0%	58%	38%	4%
Inheritance Dispute	73.3%	24.8%	2.0%	67%	29%	4%
***Suco* Boundary Dispute**	53.5%	1.0%	45.5%	29%	66%	5%
Harvest Rights Dispute	34.7%	1.0%	64.4%	67%	29%	4%
Other Dispute (please state)	2.0%	1.0%	97.0%	1%	9%	90%

Figure 6: Which kinds of land disputes are most/least common, and which kinds are easy/difficult to resolve?

As indicated in Figure 6 (above), most respondents consider ownership disputes, parcel boundary disputes, and inheritance disputes to be relatively common. However, the majority of respondents also consider these three kinds of intra-*suco* land disputes to be easy to resolve. Although considered less common, harvest rights disputes are also in the 'easy to resolve' category. Most difficult to resolve of all, are boundary disputes *between suco*s. Although considered less common than other land disputes, sixty-six per cent of respondents consider these disputes to be in the 'difficult to resolve' category.

Overall, the information suggests a high level of capacity *within* the *suco* regarding the resolution of intra-*suco* land disputes, and suggests that (a) *suco* authorities should be encouraged to maintain their dispute resolution activities and that (b) these activities should be legitimised in some way by the state.[160] Meanwhile, the data also identifies *disputes between sucos* as a category of land dispute that could benefit most from the scarce amount of state support available. In this respect, it is of note that even though inter-*suco* boundary disputes are *less* common than other kinds of land disputes in the *suco*, this does not mean that they are rare. In fact, sixty-five per cent of the key persons sample indicated they knew of one or more cases of boundary disputes between *sucos*.[161]

As outlined in Figure 7 (below), the importance of the availability of a range of conflict resolution forums is demonstrated strongly in relation to perceptions concerning the most appropriate authorities for managing the resolution of disputes *between sucos*:

As indicated in Figure 7, respondents collectively suggested numerous authorities who they considered should be involved in the mediation of border disputes between *sucos*, with many indicating the appropriateness of an

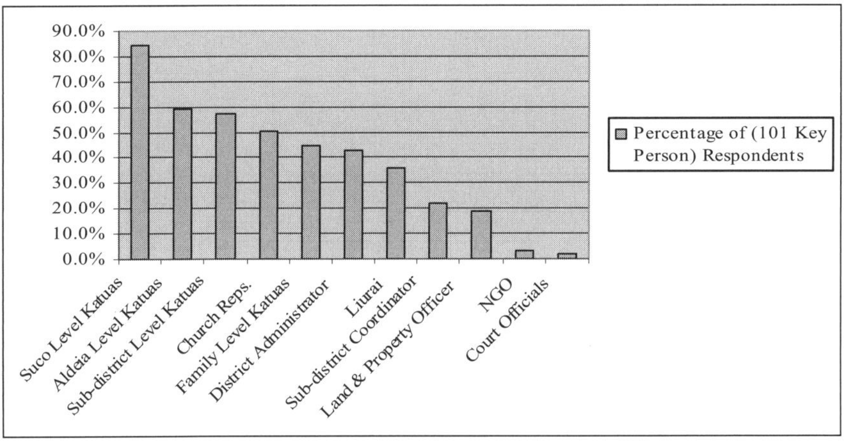

Figure 7: Most appropriate authorities for managing the resolution of inter-*suco* boundary disputes.[162]

---

[160] The matter of promoting more secure land rights for women and other vulnerable groups (a challenge in many societies) receives attention in a later section. The point being argued here is that in a weak state environment, an authority structure *for the delivery of any rights to anyone* is a fundamental requirement for maintaining order.

[161] The total sample included one hundred and one persons (consisting of *chefes de suco*, sub-district administrators, district administrators and land and property officers).

[162] Note that respondents were able to list multiple authorities.

individual from *above* or *beyond* the *suco* level. The resolution of inter-*suco* disputes may never have been easy, but whereas in former times, the *liurai* (as lord of the land) or other members of the *reino* administration may have had the capacity to force a resolution to a boundary dispute between *suco*s by threatening to either seize the land or simply ban the use of it to any party,[163] it appears that in present times, the role of resolving disputes between *suco*s is ascribed to no single authority. In fact this would be difficult in such a social context as that in East Timor, where even district administrators or land and property officers could have family links which could affect their neutrality in relation to particular cases. As seen in Figure 7, therefore, the potential involvement of a range of non-state and/or state actors is considered appropriate for the management of inter-*suco* land conflicts, highlighting again the necessity of access to a range of mediation forums for the resolution of disputes.[164]

As depicted in Figure 8 below, it appears that a distinction between 'traditional' institutions (the *aldeia*, the *liurai*) and 'formal' institutions (district administration and courts) is fairly clearly perceived, at least by the respondents included in the sample of district and sub-district administrators, *chefes de suco* and land and property officers included in the key persons sample:

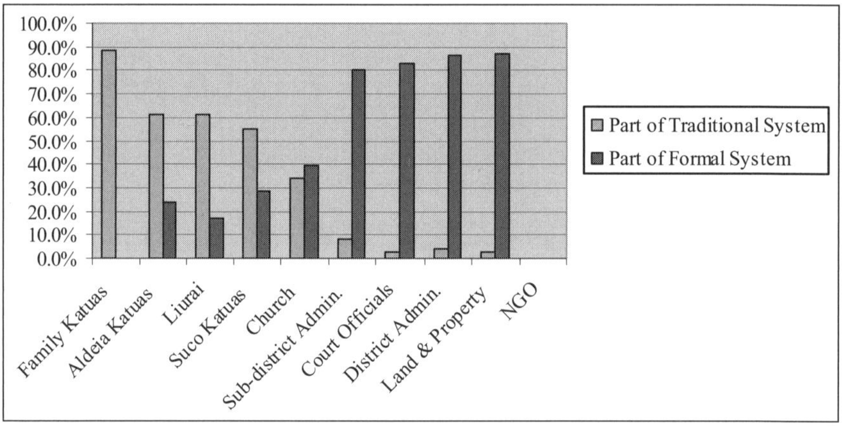

Figure 8: Perceptions of (101) key persons concerning which forums are part of which system (traditional or formal)[165]

[163] For this insight, the writer is indebted to Father Richard Daschbach of Kutete, Oecusse.

[164] See also Meitzner Yoder (2003:12), whose findings suggest the need for a combination of *suco* and state authorities in connection with the resolution of inter-suco land disputes. This consideration would be accommodated by the land dispute mediation model discussed later in this chapter.

[165] Responses indicating 'both systems' were not numerous and are not included. 'No answer' responses not included.

There are, however, other indications that in the area of process, 'formal' procedures often yield to popular expectations based upon *suco* justice practice. Not only did two court officers consulted in relation to the land dispute mediation study indicate that it is 'very important' for *katuas* to attend court proceedings relating to land disputes, but in earlier research, district and sub-district administration officials consulted in relation to broader justice and conflict resolution practices indicated that the processes employed in district and sub-district administration offices were often identical to the processes employed in traditional forums; being based around the negotiation of compensation, followed by reconciliation.[166] There have even been reports of public prosecutors employing this same approach.[167] In one instance, an accomplished mediator interviewed by the writer was both a sub-district administration official and a senior *lia nain* (with some years of tertiary education).[168] If people approached him about a dispute requiring resolution, they could choose to proceed either using the 'formal' system (effected in the sub-district administration compound) or the 'traditional' system (effected in the *suco*). The resolution and negotiation component would be the same in either case, and followed either way by a reconciliation feast in the village! It is likely therefore, that the main components of a 'traditional' agreement apply quite widely in East Timor. According to the sample of key persons, included in the key person sample, the most important elements of a traditional agreement are (1) a traditional reconciliation ceremony or *biti boot* (referred to by fifty-one per cent of the sample), (2) a written agreement or declaration (referred to by twenty-four per cent of the sample), (3) a penalty (referred to by fourteen per cent of the sample) and (4) a ritual oath or (Ind.) *sumpah adat* (referred to by nine per cent of the sample).[169]

Relative Effectiveness of Non-State and State Land Dispute Mediation Mechanisms

From the historical and recent overviews of East Timor *suco* justice already presented, it is clear that these systems have shortcomings, particularly in such areas as women's rights. Yet in a post-conflict society such as that of East Timor, or in any subsistence society endeavouring to conform to the

[166] Based on interviews with two sub-district administration officials in Aileu, and the district administrator of Oecusse (November 2002).

[167] UN human rights official (Dili, November 2002).

[168] This is by no means an unusual overlap of responsibilities in the East Timorese context, and the individual in question had also been a senior member of the CNRT.

[169] The data are based on the top four common responses to an open-ended question directed at members of the key-persons sample. The sample included one hundred and one persons; valid responses numbered ninety-one.

administrative standards of post-industrial societies, the institutions of the state may also face formidable challenges. In order to understand the perceptions of public administration officials concerning the relative strengths (respectively) of traditional justice mechanisms and courts, members of the key person sample were asked to comment on a number of factors, as outlined in Figure 9 below:

The data outlined in Figure 9 above indicate that members of the key person sample (composed of district administrators, sub-district administrators, *chefes de suco* and land and property officials)[170] consider traditional dispute resolution forums superior to the courts over a broad range of areas. In fact, considering that the majority of the sample was drawn from the ranks of East Timorese public servants, the data indicates an extraordinarily strong level of confidence by 'state actors' in the conflict resolution approaches of Timorese 'non-state' institutions. It is such features of New Subsistence States, which complicate black and white distinctions between the (legitimate) state on the one hand, and (insidious) non-state sectors on the other. As indicated in the data (Figure 9 above), the great majority of the sample of administrators perceived that traditional justice forums were cheaper, more accessible, faster, less corrupt, more supportive of reconciliation between parties and easier to understand than the courts. The fact that no such response was indicated in

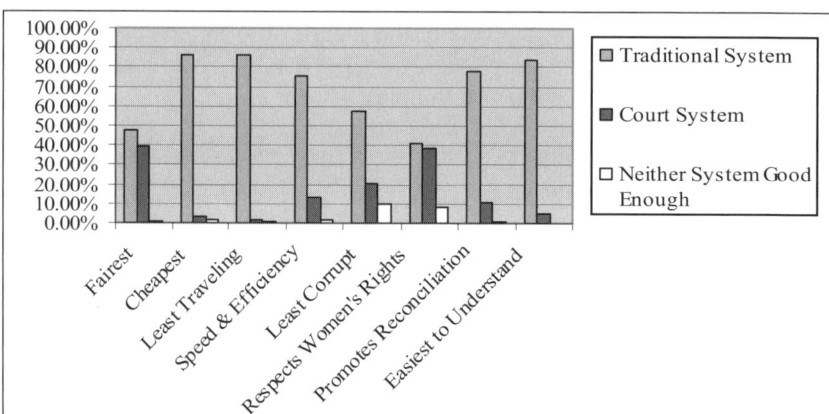

Figure 9: Perceptions of members of key persons sample concerning which system (traditional or courts) is best (total sample 101).

170 The key persons (administrative) sample was overwhelmingly male.

relation to the 'fairness' and 'women's rights' categories might at least indicate a consciousness concerning the need for improvement in these areas.[171]

The views of representatives of women's organisations in East Timor are also insightful in relation to the relative strengths of the two systems (see Figure 10 below):

Although the sample is only small (thirteen) due to the number of women's organisations operating throughout the districts, the data outlined in Figure 10 (above) suggest that representatives of women's organisations (women's reps.) may have similar perceptions to administrators (as presented in Figure 9) across a number of key variables. The most notable exception is in relation to the category of women's rights, where most women's representatives perceive court justice to be superior. However, whether this is an informed perception, or based on an idealised understanding of what *should* happen in a court, is difficult to know, given the possibility (as suggested by the data) that for many women, accessing the courts in relation to a dispute could be too expensive and time consuming an option. Furthermore, the contrast between the perception that traditional justice is 'fairer' and the perception that court justice is more 'respectful of women's rights,' is an intriguing matter worthy of further investigation.

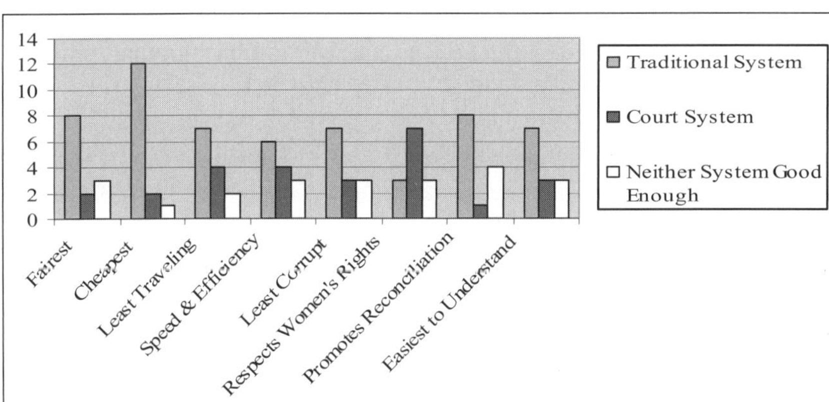

Figure 10: Perceptions of representatives of women's organisations concerning which system (traditional or courts) is best (total sample 13).

[171] For further reading on the area of traditional justice and gender rights in East Timor, see Swaine (2003) and Graydon (2005).

Again, the apparent awareness both among administrators and women's representatives that traditional dispute resolution forums may be deficient in relation to women's rights, might be seen as an encouraging sign, along with other data indicating that at grassroots level, women are beginning to demand more rights concerning land in their communities.[172]

Suco justice and the State

Notwithstanding the reality that *suco* justice principles and processes have in all probability played the dominant role in the resolution of disputes in the post-Indonesian period, little has been done in the way of formally integrating these processes into a state framework. During the UNTAET period, the interface between state or 'formal' law and traditional dispute resolution practices was largely characterised by a policy vacuum, that perhaps stemmed from the inability of UNTAET to either formally condone *suco* justice practices which might conflict with international law, or prohibit practices that in fact contributed to the maintenance of order under the UN mandate.

Although a mixture of Indonesian and UN regulations applied during the UNTAET period, in reality (especially in the more remote areas), CivPol and the courts simply did not have the resources to ensure that all crimes and conflicts were resolved in accordance with formal legal principles. The result was that when cases did come to the attention of UN staffers, these officials applied their own discretion concerning how the cases would be addressed. Typically, outcomes were influenced by the cultural background, policing experience and motivation of individual officers (which varied considerably), resulting in an unsystematic and *ad hoc* approach.[173] As articulated by one CivPol officer,[174] the operational parameters within which UN police could operate were broad:

> CivPol were 'permitted' to do just about anything to resolve matters. The UN's 'expectation' was very grey. My experience is that the UN wouldn't have known or have cared how this was done. In practice, a whole spectrum of resolution methods was utilized from a warning, through to traditional resolution, to arrest and detention for matters that went to a court process.

---

[172] For further details, see Urresta and Nixon (2004a:37, Fig. 16)

[173] Researching this matter in October and November 2002, the writer was told of instances where CivPol from various countries would vigorously debate which approach to take with a case, based on the practice in their respective home countries.

[174] Written correspondence (received in November 2002) from Australian CivPol officer who served in Baucau and Oecusse during the UNTAET period from November 1999 onwards.

Notwithstanding the general scarcity of policy guidelines, several initiatives were attempted under the UN mandate aimed at integrating traditional justice approaches into a formalised structure. The most notable of these was the community reconciliation program of the Commission for Reception, Truth and Reconciliation (CAVR), which was mandated to promote national reconciliation after the period of political conflict and the events of 1999.[175] Under the provisions of UNTAET *Regulation 2001/10* (UNTAET 2001, Sections 22–32), perpetrators of non-serious crimes could apply to participate in a community reconciliation process by submitting a written statement including 'an admission of responsibility' for crimes, a voluntary request to participate in a community reconciliation process, and 'a renunciation of the use of violence to achieve political ends'. Specifically, Schedule 1 of *Regulation 2001/10* limited community reconciliation to offences 'such as theft, minor assault, arson (other than that resulting in death or injury), the killing of livestock or destruction of crops,' and stated that under 'no circumstances, shall a *serious criminal offence* be dealt with in a Community Reconciliation Process.'[176]

Where accepted for community reconciliation, the offender would be brought before a community reconciliation hearing. The panel presiding over this hearing would be chaired by a regional commissioner and also include between two and four community representatives.[177] At this hearing, statements would be invited from the offender, victims of the offender, and other community members with further information. The panel, under Section 27.7 would determine an appropriate 'act of reconciliation', which could involve '(a) community service, (b) reparation; (c) public apology; and/or

---

[175] See also Lundry (2002), who comments on the restorative nature of the program and suggests (2002:2,9-10) that the large number of former militias and the limited capacity of the courts to process them is likely to have been a factor in the decision to authorise an integrated approach in this instance. Note also that even though the first CAVR community reconciliation hearing did not take place until *after* East Timor became independent on 20th May 2002 (and therefore after the conclusion of the UNTAET mandate), the community reconciliation program is discussed at this point in the text because it was established under an UNTAET regulation during the UNTAET period of administration.

[176] As outlined under UNTAET *Regulation No.2000/11 on the Organization of Courts in East Timor* (UNTAET 2000a), and UNTAET *Regulation No.2000/15 on the Establishment of Panels with Exclusive Jurisdiction over Serious Criminal Offences* (UNTAET 2000b) the term 'serious criminal offence' refers to acts of genocide, war crimes, crimes against humanity [including extermination, enslavement, enforced disappearance], murder, sexual offences and torture.

[177] Section 4.3 of UNTAET *Regulation 2001/10* determined that the Commission be composed of between five and seven commissioners and a further twenty-five to thirty-five regional commissioners, whose duties would include facilitating Community Reconciliation Agreements in the districts. The regulations required that a minimum of thirty per cent of the national and regional commissioners should be women. Similarly, the community reconciliation panels were also required to reflect '[a]ppropriate gender representations.'

other act of contrition.' Non-compliance with this 'act of reconciliation' would make the offender liable to a fine of up to US$3000, imprisonment for up to a year, or both.

The community reconciliation process outlined by the CAVR sought to assimilate indigenous practices relating to reparation and reconciliation into a legal, but restorative-based, framework. Modifications to common *suco* practice included the prominence of women on the community reconciliation panels and the restriction on the ability of community reconciliation panels to hear serious crimes (thereby requiring panels to forfeit the right to independently decide which cases should be addressed locally and which should be referred to higher authorities). In these respects the community reconciliation process perhaps differed from what local Timorese authorities might have implemented themselves, and as they appear to have implemented in other cases as the earlier discussion concerning the CNRT *ad hoc* administration suggests. By the completion of the CAVR mandate, more than 1,541 'community reconciliation statements' had been facilitated (CAVR 2005 Part1:36), an accomplishment of no small measure and a demonstration of the potential effectiveness of integrated approaches to justice and conflict resolution in subsistence social environments where indigenous administrative capacity remains robust.

A further integrated justice initiative known as the Oecusse Diversionary Justice Program (ODJP), which was given 'conditional and partial' approval by the Deputy Special Representative of the Secretary General (DSRSG) of the UN for use for a limited period.[178] The ODJP was partly based on a New Zealand 'diversionary justice' model designed to divert proceedings and punishments for minor crimes away from the mainstream criminal justice system. As applied in Oecusse, it incorporated elements of *suco* justice, but modified where 'found inconsistent with human rights norms [especially in relation to women and minority groups], or unreasonable [or] disproportionate in the facts and circumstances of a given case.' The ODJP was approved in Oecusse in relation to theft, minor assaults and attempted assaults, land disputes and 'certain offences committed during the pre and post consultation time...[not including]...murder, rape or serious bodily injury.' The program was subsequently used to process twenty-three land disputes and three criminal cases.

---

[178] Information on the ODJP is based on an extensive written account (received in October 2002) of the program provided by a UN judicial officer who worked in Oecusse during 2000 and 2001 and from an interview (in Dili, November 2002) with the officer who commanded the Oecusse district CivPol at the time the ODJP was used. Note that a similar system was proposed for Covalima district.

Although maintaining many elements of *suco* justice practice, the program favoured restorative labour instead of compensation, and endeavoured (probably optimistically) to exclude the consumption of distilled palm wine from reconciliation ceremonies:

> In [the] customary system apart from compensating the victim [the] accused had to arrange a feast, and share…[*tuasabu*]…with the victim and all persons participating in the process. We considered the…[*tuasabu*]…unhygienic and such approval would encourage alcoholism in the rural areas. We wanted to stop this practice and ultimately succeeded in abolishing [it]. This element of the process was abolished with the active cooperation of the community leaders.

The specific reasons *why* the ODJP was authorised for Oecusse were because of (1) the 'physical isolation of the enclave,' (2) the 'non-existence of judicial infrastructure and human resources,' (3) 'ambiguity as to the applicable law,' and (4) the 'absence of legal culture.'

In fact, with reasonable interpretation, most of the circumstances that supported the authorisation of the ODJP in Oecusse during the UNTAET period could be said to have applied to most of East Timor for much of the post-Indonesian period. While the 'absence of a legal culture' among the rural subsistence population is clear, the process of developing a legal culture in the courts has also proved challenging. For the historical reasons discussed earlier, the absence of skilled individuals has proved a major handicap, and as Australian Federal Court Judge Justice Shane Marshall remarks (2005:8) in relation to his assessment of the East Timorese justice system, the majority of the 'first eight judges and two prosecutors…sworn in on 7th January 2000…had little or no practical experience and certainly none had served as a judge or prosecutor.' The implications of this capacity deficiency quickly became apparent. According to a former UN district legal affairs officer for Liquiça,[179] a request for an arrest warrant to be signed (relating to a rape) by a member of the newly appointed judiciary in Dili resulted in the following outcome:

> The paperwork came back from Dili with six arrest warrants for the witnesses and one summons for the victim.

[179] Interviewed in Dili, February 2005.

As observed earlier, confirmation of the difficulty of developing judicial capacity in East Timor was provided in early 2005 when all twenty-two East Timorese judges failed their evaluations.

In the late UNTAET period, a shift appears to have taken place *against* traditional justice and dispute resolution practices (notwithstanding the weakness of the courts), and a regulation circulated in April 2002 is said to have required that once crimes and disputes enter the 'formal system,' they should remain there.[180] After assuming office at independence on 20th May 2002, the FRETILIN government also demonstrated a modernist, pro-courts position on the matter of justice. This was somewhat at odds with the understanding of *adat* leaders and other members of the community, who often express the view that *adat* justice and state justice should somehow work together.

In the years following independence, several organisations presented dispute resolution models for the consideration of the FRETILIN Government, which incorporated principles derived from *suco* justice practice.[181] The model advanced by LLP (presented to the Government of Timor-Leste in 2004, but not yet passed),[182] was based upon the research findings and conclusions profiled in the previous section of this chapter and proposed a legal framework whereby the state (via the Directorate of Land and Property and its trained mediators) would support the mediation of land disputes in accordance with commonly understood principles. The model can be seen as a mechanism which would legitimise, strengthen and accelerate a conflict resolution approach that is already well understood in the community. The proposed model would support such aspects as the identification of suitable mediators for inclusion on a mediation panel, the buttressing of these mediation panels with trained mediators from the Directorate

[180] This development was reported by a CivPol district commander interviewed in November 2002, but the writer has not personally sighted the document. This reported development could have been a product of the pro-courts emphasis of members of the Constitutional Assembly voted into existence on 30th August 2001, and which assumed full office at independence on 20th May 2002.

[181] The model discussed in the main text pertains to the proposed LLP *Legal Framework for Land Dispute Mediation*, of which full details are available in Urresta and Nixon (2004a). Other projects/organisations have also proposed mediation models, most notably the Peace and Democracy Foundation, which presented a mediation model for consideration in November 2004. See also Mearns (2002:55–56).

[182] By the end of its term of office in mid-2007, the FRETILIN Government had begun to favour mediation as the first level of dispute resolution for *all* civil cases. This is understood to be due to the difficulties experienced in attempting to resolve civil cases in the courts. Accordingly, the FRETILIN Justice Ministry was considering preparation of a General Law on Dispute Mediation. At the time of writing, it is unclear which policy approach the new *Aliança para Maioria Parlamentar* (AMP) Government will take, although the writer understands the new Justice Minister to be supportive, in principle, of mediation.

of Land and Property, and the registration of settlements. Although traditional reconciliation ceremonies would be encouraged, the mandatory presence of trained Land and Property mediators on all mediation panels supported by the Directorate of Land and Property could potentially advance the gradual secularisation of dispute mediation processes, at the same time as promoting the rights of women and members of vulnerable groups. In time, state actors could become as much a part of mediation proceedings as *adat* actors are in the present day, hopefully without weakening the capacity for grassroots resolution of conflicts during times, as in the period following the mid-2006 political crisis, when state capacity becomes critically diminished. Ultimately, a broadened model based on similar principles could provide an alternative to the court system in relation to a range of disputes, similar to or more extensive than those deemed appropriate for the diversionary model trialled in Oecusse under UNTAET.

Conclusion

With varying levels of success, numerous actors operating above the level of the *suco* have endeavoured to influence developments in Timor over the last five centuries. They include the *Liurai*s, the Dutch, the Portuguese, the Catholic Church, the *Topasse*s, the Japanese, the *ad hoc* FRETILIN government of 1975, the Indonesians, the UN and the new RDTL state (with its international support base). Many of these actors have been transient, and no broad and substantial modernisation of society and economy has been produced by any of them, which provides some explanation as to why traditional authority structures have retained legitimacy to the present day. While there were already reports in 2002 that some traditional leaders were becoming unsure of the breadth of their authority amid the new emphasis on 'the rule of law,' it is likely, especially in rural areas, that traditional authority structures will retain their legitimacy into the medium-term future.

The disintegration of state authority and administration capacity that unfolded in mid-2006 highlights the advantages of a conservative position concerning the jettisoning of established systems of dispute resolution, even though these systems might be imperfect. Certainly, *suco* authorities are deficient when it comes to resolving cases of violence against women, and ongoing reports of revenge attacks on alleged 'sorcerers' emphasise the need for strategies to address this particular aspect of the *adat* justice sphere.[183]

[183] The burning of three 'witches' in Liquiça was reported by the Australian Broadcasting Corporation (ABC) in January 2007 (ABC 2007). See also Mearns (2002:45–46). The writer has found that the fear of sorcerers is not confined to uneducated rural dwellers, but that it can also be shared by young tertiary educated adults. Despite this, however, education would appear a major component of the solution for revenge attacks on sorcerers.

However, the many shortcomings of the justice systems of the *suco*s must be balanced against the weak points of the courts *and* the capacity for these existing and functioning *suco* forums of dispute resolution to be improved and supported to accommodate human rights concerns. As in other New Subsistence States in the Pacific and elsewhere, the case supporting *suco* justice and conflict resolution systems in East Timor is that they remain accessible even after state agencies, for any number of reasons (that might include civil war, logistical difficulties of one sort or another or fiscal crisis) have ground to a halt.

References

ABC (Australian Broadcasting Corporation). 2007. 'Three Suspects Arrested for Killing of Timorese "Witches."' ABC news report dated 10th January 2007. Sighted at http://www.abc.net.au/news/newsitems/200701/s1824785.htm, 11th January 2007.

ACFOA (Australian Council for Overseas Aid). 1975. *Report on Visit to East Timor for the ACFOA Timor Task Force*. October 1975. Canberra: ACFOA.

Aditjondro, George J. 1994. *East Timor: An Indonesian Intellectual Speaks Out* (ACFOA Development Dossier No. 33). ACFOA: Canberra.

Anderson, Benedict. 1993. 'Imagining "East Timor,"' *Arena*, No.4, April-May 1993, pp. 23–27.

Araujo, Fernando de. 2000. 'The CNRT Campaign for Independence,' in *Out of the Ashes: Destruction and Reconstruction of East Timor* (edited by James J. Fox and Dionisio Babo Soares), pp. 106–25. Crawford House: Adelaide.

Archer, C.H. 1941. 'Timor (Portuguese) Report.' Australian National Archives Series No. A981, Barcode No. 181029. Sighted at http://naa12.naa.gov.au/scripts/Imagine.asp, 7th June 2006.

BAPPEDA (Indonesian Regional Development Planning Board). 1997. *Timor Timur Dalam Anchor 1996 (East Timor in Figures 1996)*. BAPPEDA (in cooperation with the Statistical Office of East Timor Province): Dili.

Barata, Filipe José Freire Themudo. 1963. 'Timor, esse Desconhecido,' *Estudos Políticos e Sociais*, Vol. 1, No. 3, 1963, pp. 659–84.

Beazley, Harriot. 1999. *East Timor: Background Briefing for Project Identification Mission*. Prepared for AusAID in association with the Australian National University (ANU) Indonesia Project, March 1999. ANU Canberra.

Berlie, Jean A. 2000. 'A Concise Legal History of East Timor,' in *Studies in Languages and Cultures of East Timor*, Vol. 3, pp. 138-57.

Boletim Oficial do Governo da Colonia de Timor (BOGCT). 1932. 'Circular aos Senhores Comandantes Militares e Administradores de Circunscricões

Civis,' BOGCT XXXIII, Supplement to No. 48, pp. 1–4, 28th November 1932.

Boxer, Charles R. 1960. 'Portuguese Timor: A Rough Island Story: 1515-1960,' in *History Today*, Volume X, No. 5, May 1960, pp.349–55.

BPS (*Biro Pusat Statistik*). 1996. *Penduduk Indonesia: Hasil Survei Penduduk Antar Sensus 1995* (Population of Indonesia: Results of the 1995 Intercensal Population Survey). BPS: Jakarta.

Budiardjo, Carmel and Liem Soei Liong. 1984. *The War Against East Timor*. Zed Books: London.

Callinan, Bernard. 1984 [1953]. *Independent Company: The Australian Army in Portuguese Timor 1941–43*. William Heinemann: Richmond.

Capell, A. 1944. 'Peoples and Languages of Timor,' in *Oceania*, Vol. 14, No. 3, March 1944, pp. 191–219 (continued Vol. 14, No. 4, June 1944, pp. 311–37, and Vol. 15, No. 1, September 1944, pp. 19–48).

Caputo, Joe and Gary Jungwirth. 2005. 'Report on a Visit to Observe the Village Chief and other Suco Elections in Aileu District, Timor-Leste: 29 June to 6 July 2005.' Report by Councillors Caputo and Jungwirth (respectively from the Moreland and Hume City Councils, Australia) sighted at http://www.moreland.vic.gov.au/pdfs/aileu%20visit%20to%20observe%20suco%20elections%20report.pdf, 2nd February, 2007.

Castro, Affonso de. 1867. *As Possessões Portuguezas Na Oceania*. Imprensa Nacional: Lisbon.

CAVR (Commission for Reception, Truth and Reconciliation). 2004. 'CAVR Update/Dec 2003 – Jan 2004' (including appendix titled 'Report on Hearing on Internal Political Conflict 1974–1976: CAVR National Public Hearing, 15-18 December 2003), sighted at http://www.easttimor-reconciliation.org/cavrUpdate-Dec03Jan04-en.html, 23rd November 2005.

\- 2005. *Final Report of the Commission for Reception, Truth and Reconciliation in Timor-Leste* (preliminary version). CAVR: Dili.

Chamberlain, Ernest. 2005. *Faltering Steps: Independence Movements in East Timor in the 1950s and 1960s*. E. Chamberlain (self-published monograph): Point Lonsdale, Victoria.

Clamagirand, Brigitte. 1980. 'The Social Organization of the Ema of Timor,' in *The Flow of Life: Essays on Eastern Indonesia* (edited by James J. Fox), pp. 134–51. Harvard University Press: Cambridge, Massachusetts.

Clarence-Smith, W. G., 1992. 'Planters and Small Holders in Portuguese Timor in the Nineteenth and Twentieth Centuries,' sighted at http://www.gov.east-timor.org/MAFF/ta000/TA051.pdf, 4th November 2005 (originally published in *Indonesian Circle*, No. 57, March 1992).

Clausen, Lisa. 2005. 'East Timor Judges Fail Their Test,' in *Time Asia*, 14th February 2005, No. 6.

Corrêa, Armando Pinto. 1934/35.[184] *Gentio de Timôr*. Lucas and Co: Lisbon.

Costa, Helder da and Hadi Soesastro. 2002. *Building East Timor's Economy, Comparing Experiences with State Building in Asia and Europe: The Cases of East Timor, Bosnia and Kosovo*. Council for Asia Europe Co-Operation report sighted at http://www.caec-asiaeurope.org/Conference/Publications/costasoesastro.PDF, 17th July 2006.

Cristalis, Irena. 2002. *Bitter Dawn: East Timor, a People's Story*. Zed Books: London.

Crowe, Louise M. 1996. 'The Impact of the Indonesian Annexation on the Role of the Catholic Church in East Timor.' Unpublished MA thesis, Northern Territory University: Darwin.

Davidson, Katharine G. 1994. 'The Portuguese Colonisation of Timor: The Final Stage, 1850 – 1912.' Unpublished PhD thesis, University of New South Wales: Sydney.

Denham, T.P., S. G. Haberle, C. Lentfer *et al*., 2003. 'Origins of Agriculture at Kuk Swamp in the Highlands of New Guinea,' *Science*, Vol. 301, 11 July 2003, pp.189–93.

Deutsch, Carrie. 2004. *Overview of the Coffee Sector in Timor-Leste*. Oxfam: Dili.

Dinnen, Sinclair. 2003. 'Restorative Justice in the Pacific Islands: An Introduction,' in *A Kind of Meaning: Restorative Justice in the Pacific Islands* (edited by Sinclair Dinnen, with Anita Jowitt and Tess Newton Cain), pp. 1–34. Pandanus Books: Canberra.

Dores, Raphael das. 1903. *Apontamentos para um Diccionario Chorographico de Timor*. Imprensa Nacional: Lisbon.

Downer, Alexander. 2004. International Security – Making Progress in Uncertain Times. Speech by the Australian Minister of Foreign Affairs to the International Institute for Strategic Studies, London, 5th July 2004. Sighted at http://www.foreignminister.gov.au/speeches/2004/040705_int_security.html, 16th November 2006.

Dunn, James. 1996. *Timor: A People Betrayed* (second edition). ABC Books: Sydney.

Eaton, Charles. 1947. 'Despatch No. 2 [1947],' Department of External Affairs Despatch from the Australian Consul to Portuguese Timor, Charles Eaton, dated 26th February, 1947. (Australian) Department of External Affairs File No. P46/67/2.

FAO (Food and Agricultural Organisation). 2005. 'Food and Agricultural Indicators: Timor Leste,' FAO country data sheet (prepared October 2005) sighted at http://www.fao.org/es/ess/compendium_2005/pdf/ESS_TIL.pdf, 10th August 2006.

[184] Front cover: 1935; title page: 1934.

Farram, Steven G. 1999. 'The Two Timors: The Partitioning of Timor by the Portuguese and the Dutch,' in *Studies in Languages and Cultures of East Timor*, Vol. 2, pp. 38-54.

- 2004. 'From "Timor Koepang" to 'Timor NTT': A Political History of West Timor, 1901–1967.' Unpublished PhD thesis, Charles Darwin University: Darwin.

- 2006. 'The Enduring Influence of Timor's Traditional Rulers: Liurais and Rajas in Politics, Resistance Movements and Militias,' in *Crossing Cultures: Art, Politics and Identity* (edited by Sylvia Kleinert), pp. 70-85. CDU Press: Darwin.

Federer, Juan. 2005. *The UN in East Timor: Building Timor-Leste, a Fragile State*. Charles Darwin University Press: Darwin.

Forbes, Anna. 1987 [1887]. *Unbeaten Tracks in Islands of the Far East: Experiences of a Naturalist's Wife in the 1880s*. Oxford University Press: Singapore.

Forbes, Henry O. 1989 [1885]. *A Naturalist's Wanderings in the Eastern Archipelago*. Oxford University Press: Singapore.

Forman, Shepard. 1980. 'Descent, Alliance, and Exchange Ideology among the Makassae of East Timor,' in *The Flow of Life: Essays on Eastern Indonesia* (edited by James J. Fox), pp. 152–77, notes pp. 340-44. Harvard University Press: Cambridge, Massachusetts.

Fox, James J. 1980. 'Models and Metaphors: Comparative Research in Eastern Indonesia,' in *The Flow of Life: Essays on Eastern Indonesia* (edited by James J. Fox), pp. 327–33. Harvard University Press: Cambridge, Massachusetts.

- 1982. 'The Great Lord Rests at the Centre: The Paradox of Powerlessness in European-Timorese Relations, in *Canberra Anthropology*, Vol. 5, No. 2, October 1982, pp. 22–33.

- 1988. 'The Historical Consequences of Changing Patterns of Livelihood on Timor,' in *Contemporary Issues in Development* (edited by Deborah Wade-Marshall and Peter Loveday), pp. 259–79. Australian National University North Australian Research Unit: Casuarina.

- 1996. 'The Paradox of Powerlessness: Timor in Historical Perspective,' paper presented at the Nobel Peace Prize Symposium *Focus on East Timor*, University of Oslo, 9th December 1996.

Francillon, Gerard. 1980. 'Incursions upon Wehali: A Modern History of an Ancient Empire,' in *The Flow of Life: Essays on Eastern Indonesia* (edited by James J. Fox), pp. 248-65, notes pp. 347–49. Harvard University Press: Cambridge, Massachusetts.

Friedberg, Claudine. 1980. 'Boiled Woman and Broiled Man: Myths and Agricultural Rituals of the Bunaq of Central Timor (translated from the French by Elizabeth Traube),' in *The Flow of Life: Essays on Eastern*

Indonesia (edited by James J. Fox), pp. 266–89, notes pp. 349–51. Harvard University Press: Cambridge, Massachusetts.

Glover, Ian C. 1986. *Archaeology in Eastern Timor, 1966–67*. Department of Prehistory, Research School of Pacific Studies, Australian National University: Canberra.

Gonçalves, Luiz da Cunha. 1937. 'Adatrecht van Portugeesch Timor (1933). [Part] I. Direito Consuetudinário dos indigenas de Timôr,' *Adatrechtbundel*, Vol. 39, 1937, pp. 443–58.

Graydon, Carolyn. 2005. 'Local Justice Systems in Timor-Leste: Washed up, or Watch this Space,' *Development Bulletin*, No. 68, 2005, pp. 66–70. Sighted at http://devnet.anu.edu.au/GenderPacific/pdfs/09_gen_legal_graydon.pdf, 19th March 2007.

Grenfell, Laura. 2006. Legal Pluralism and the Rule of Law in Timor-Leste,' *Leiden Journal of International Law*, 19 (2006), pp. 305–37.

Gunn, Geoffrey C. 1999. *Timor Loro Sae: 500 Years*. Livros do Oriente: Macau.

- 2006. 'Revisiting the Viqueque Rebellion of 1959.' Draft paper sighted at http://www.geoffreycgunn.com/material/draft_viquequerebellion.pdf, 19th May 2006.

Gusmão, Xanana. 2000. *To Resist is to Win!: The Autobiography of Xanana Gusmão* (edited by Sarah Niner). Aurora Books: Ringwood.

- 2006. 'President of Republic's Message to Fretilin,' speech by President Xanana Gusmão broadcast on 22nd June 2006 (unofficial English translation distributed by the Asia Pacific Solidarity Coalition). Sighted at http://www.etan.org/et2006/june/30/22xana.htm, 6th February 2007.

Hicks, David. 1972. 'Timor-Roti: Eastern Tetum, Atoni,' in *Ethnic Groups of Insular Southeast Asia, Volume I: Indonesia, Andaman Islands and Madagascar* (edited and compiled by Frank M. Lebar), pp. 97–105. Human Relations Area Files Press: New Haven.

- 1976. *Tetum Ghosts and Kin*. Mayfield: Palo Alto, California.
- 1983. 'Unachieved Syncretism: The Local-Level Political System in Portuguese Timor, 1966–1967,' *Anthropos*, No. 78, 1983, pp.17–40.

Hill, Helen. 2002. *Stirrings of Nationalism in East Timor, FRETILIN 1974–78: The Origins, Ideologies and Strategies of a Nationalist Movement*. Otford [*sic*]: Sydney.

Hohe, Tanja and Rod Nixon. 2003. *Reconciling Justice: 'Traditional' Justice and State Judiciary in East Timor*. Research report produced for the United States Institute of Peace Project on Peacekeeping and the Administration of Justice. January 2003. Available at http://www.ids.ac.uk/ids/law/pdfs/hohendixon.pdf

Hull, Geoffrey. 2000. *Tetum Language Manual for East Timor* (fourth edition). Academy of East Timor Studies, University of Western Sydney: Sydney.

Huntington, Samuel P. 2003 [1993]. 'The Clash of Civilizations,' in *International Politics: Enduring Concepts and Contemporary Issues* (sixth edition, edited by Robert J. Art and Robert Jervis). Longman: New York.

Jolliffe, Jill. 1978. *East Timor: Nationalism and Colonialism*. University of Queensland Press: St. Lucia Qld.

Jones, Gavin. 2000. 'East Timor: Education and Human Resource Development,' in *Out of the Ashes: Destruction and Reconstruction of East Timor* (edited by James J. Fox and Dionisio Babo Soares), pp. 44–56. Crawford House: Adelaide.

JSMP (Judicial System Monitoring Programme). 2005. 'Justice Update' (for the period 24th January – 1st February 2005). Issue No. 3/2005.

King's College. 2003. *A Review of Peace Operations: A Case for Change: East Timor*. Report produced by the Conflict, Security and Development Group, King's College, London, dated 10th March 2003. Sighted at http://www.jsmp.minihub.org/Reports/otherresources/Peace4Timor_10_3_03.pdf, 23rd October 2006.

Knauft, Bruce B. 1987. 'Reconsidering Violence in Simple Human Societies: Homicide among the Gebusi of New Guinea,' *Current Anthropology*, Vol. 28, No. 4, August – October 1987, pp. 457 – 500.

Landman, J. R. and H. T. Plant. 1948. 'Notes on Portuguese Timor -I,' *South Pacific* (journal of the Australian School of Pacific Administration), Vol. 2, No. 11, August 1948, pp. 225–31 (continued [Part 2] in Vol. 3, No. 1, September 1948, pp. 1–8 and [Part 3] in Vol. 3, No. 2, October 1948, pp. 34–39.

Latouche, Serge. 1996 [1989]. *The Westernization of the World* (translated from French by Rosemary Morris). Polity Press: Cambridge.

Legge, J.D. 1964. *Indonesia*. Prentice-Hall: Englewood Cliffs, New Jersey.

Lundry, Chris. 2002. 'Indigenous Justice and the Rule of Law in East Timor: *Lisan*, the United Nations, and the Reintegration of Militia Members.' Paper presented at the conference on East Timor in Transition: Past, Present and Future, Northern Illinois University, 12th – 13th April, 2002.

MAFF (Ministry of Agriculture, Forestry and Fisheries). 2004. *Policy and Strategic Framework*. MAFF, Dili, 15th September 2004.

Marshall, Shane. 2005. 'The East Timorese Judiciary: at the Threshold of Self-Sufficiency?' Address delivered to the Conference of Supreme and Federal Court Judges in Darwin, January 2005. Sighted at http://www.law.ecu.edu.au/news/pdfs/Justice_Marshall_100505.pdf, 31st January 2007.

McGeough, Paul. 2004. *Mission Impossible: The Sheikhs, the US and the Future of Iraq*. Quarterly Essay Issue No. 14, 2004.

McWilliam, Andrew. 1996. 'Severed Heads that Germinate the State: History, Politics and Headhunting in Southwest Timor,' in *Headhunting and the*

Social Imagination in Southeast Asia (edited by Janet Hoskins), pp. 127–66. Stanford University Press: Stanford, California.

- 2005. 'Houses of Resistance in East Timor: Structuring Sociality in the New Nation,' in *Anthropological Forum*, Vol. 15, No. 1, March 2005, pp. 27–44.

Mearns, David. 2002. *Looking Both Ways: Models for Justice in East Timor*. Research report produced for Australian Legal Resources International. November 2002.

Meitzner Yoder, Laura Suzanne (assisted by Calisto Colo, Zacarias F. da Costa and Francisco Soares). 2003. 'Custom and Conflict: The Uses and Limitations of Traditional Systems in Addressing Rural Land Disputes in East Timor.' Unpublished *Deutsche Gesellschaft Für Technische Zusammenarbeit* (German Technical Cooperation, or GTZ) discussion paper prepared in August 2003 for 'Land Policy and Administration for Pro-Poor Rural Growth' workshop held in Dili, December 2003.

Metzner, Joachim K. 1977. *Man and Environment in Eastern Timor: A Geoecological Analysis of the Baucau-Viqueque Area as a Possible Basis for Regional Planning* (Development Studies Centre Monograph No. 8). The Australian National University: Canberra.

MHRI (Ministry of Health Republic Indonesia). 2000. *Indonesia: Health Profile 1999*. MHRI: Jakarta.

Middelkoop, Pieter. 1963. *Head Hunting in Timor and its Historical Implications*. Oceania Linguistic Monograph No. 8 (a). University of Sydney: Sydney.

Migdal, Joel S. 1988. *Strong Societies and Weak States: State-Society Relations and State Capabilities in the Third World*. Princeton University Press: Princeton, New Jersey.

Moura, Jacinto Jose do Nascimento. 1937. 'Adatrecht van Portugeesch Timor (1933). [Part] II. O Direito Consuetudinário em Timôr,' *Adatrechtbundel*, Vol. 39, 1937, pp.475–87.

Nicol, Bill. 1978. *Timor: The Stillborn Nation*. Visa: Melbourne.

Nixon, Rod. 2005. *Non-Customary Primary Industry Land Survey: Landholdings and Management Considerations*. ARD/USAID East Timor Land Law Program report, Dili, August 2005.

- 2006. 'The Crisis of Governance in New Subsistence States,' *Journal of Contemporary Asia*, Vol. 36, No. 1, pp. 75–101.

Ormeling, F. J. 1957. *The Timor Problem: A Geographical Interpretation of an Underdeveloped Island*. J.B. Wolters: Jakarta.

Ospina, Sofi and Tanja Hohe. 2001. *Traditional Power Structures and the Community Empowerment Project: Final Report*. Research report produced for the World Bank. September 2001. Sighted at http://info.worldbank.org/etools/docs/library/139608/finalreport.pdf, 5th September 2006.

Polglaze, Karen. 1999. 'Growing Concern over Health Issues.' Australian Associated Press report dated 7th April 1999, posted on Action in Solidarity with Asia and the Pacific website. Sighted at http://www.asia-pacific-action.org/southeastasia/indonesia/netnews/1999/and14_v3.htm#Growing%20concern%20over%20health%20issues, 21st July 2006.

Ramos-Horta, José. 1987. *Funu: The Unfinished Saga of East Timor*. Red Sea Press: Trenton, New Jersey.

RDTL (*República Democrática Timor-Leste*). 2004. *Law No. 2/2004 on the Election of Suco Chiefs and Suco Councils*. Unofficial translation sighted at http://www.unotil.org/legal/RDTL-Law/index-e.htm, 2nd February 2007.

Republic of Indonesia. 1977. *Decolonization in East Timor*. Republic of Indonesia Department of Information: NP.

Rotberg, Robert I. 2002a. 'The New Nature of Nation-State Failure,' in the *Washington Quarterly*, Vol. 25, No. 3, Summer 2002, pp. 85–96.

- 2002b. 'Failed States in a World of Terror,' *Foreign Affairs*, Vol. 81, No. 4, July - August 2002, pp.127–40.

- 2003. 'Nation-State Failure: A Recurring Phenomenon?' National Intelligence Council Discussion Paper, dated 6th November 2003. Sighted at http://www.dni.gov/nic/PDF_GIF_2020_Support/2003_11_06_papers/panel2_nov6.pdf#search=%22nic%20rotberg%20%22nation-state%20failure%22%22, 9th October 2006.

Saldanha, Joao Mariano de Sousa. 1994. *The Political Economy of East Timor Development*. Pustaka Sinar Harapan: Jakarta.

Saturday Extra. 2006. 'Timor-Leste,' radio documentary produced for the *Saturday Extra* program (presented by Geraldine Doogue), broadcast on ABC Radio National on 15th April 2006. Transcript sighted at http://www.abc.net.au/rn/saturdayextra/stories/2006/1609955.htm#, 12th August 2006.

Schulte Nordholt, H. G. 1971. *The Political System of the Atoni of Timor* (translated from the Dutch by M. J. L. van Yperen). Martinus Nijhoff: The Hague.

Sherlock, Kevin. 1983. 'East Timor: Liurais and Chefes de Suco: Indigenous Authorities in 1952.' Unpublished evaluation of indigenous political units in Portuguese Timor in the mid-20th century. Darwin.

- 1986a. 'Timor in the Portuguese Periodical Press of the Far East, Part Two: 1870.' Unpublished compilation of periodical extracts in Portuguese, accompanied by English translations by Kevin Sherlock. Darwin.

- 1986b. 'Timor in the Portuguese Periodical Press of the Far East, Part Three: 1871.' Unpublished compilation of periodical extracts in Portuguese, accompanied by English translations by Kevin Sherlock. Darwin.

Shoesmith, Dennis. 2003. 'Divided Leadership in a Semi-Presidential System,' in *Asian Survey*, Vol. XLIII, No. 2, March/April 2003, pp. 231–52.

Smith, Michael G. (with Moreen Dee). 2003. *Peacekeeping in East Timor: The Path to Independence*. International Peace Academy Occasional Paper Series. Lynne Rienner Publishers: Boulder (Colorado).

Soares, Dionisio Babo. 2000. 'Challenges for the Future,' in *Out of the Ashes: Destruction and Reconstruction of East Timor* (edited by James J. Fox and Dionisio Babo Soares). pp. 282–97. Crawford House: Adelaide.

- 2001. 'A Brief Overview of the Role of Customary Law in East Timor,' in *Working in East Timor: Culture, Customs and Capacity Building*, pp. 24–43. UNTAET Language and Training Unit: Dili.

Soesastro, M. Hadi. 1989. 'East Timor: Questions of Economic Viability,' in *Unity and Diversity: Regional Economic Development in Indonesia since 1970* (edited by Hal Hill), pp. 207–29. Oxford University Press: Singapore.

Swaine, Aisling. 2003. *Traditional Justice and Gender Based Violence*. International Rescue Committee research report dated August 2003. Sighted at http://www.jsmp.minihub.org/Traditional%20Justice/Reports/Swaine_Gender%20Report/SwaineGenderReport.doc, 19 March 2007.

Taylor, John G. 1991. *Indonesia's Forgotten War: the Hidden History of East Timor*. Pluto Press: Leichhardt.

Traube, Elizabeth G. 1986. *Cosmology and Social Life: Ritual Exchange among the Mambai of East Timor*. The University of Chicago Press: Chicago.

Turismo Timor-Leste. 2005. 'About Timor-Leste: Geography,' sighted at http://www.turismotimorleste.com/en/about/geography/, 9th September 2005.

UN (United Nations). 2000. *Building Blocks for a Nation*. Common Country Assessment produced by the UN country team in East Timor, dated November 2000. UN: Dili.

UNFPA (United Nations Population Fund). 2005. 'Timor-Leste: World Population Day…' (Brochure produced for the World Population Day in Timor-Leste, providing summary of demographic data from the 2004 Timor-Leste UNFPA Census), UNFPA, Dili, 11th July 2005.

UNOCHA (United Nations Office for the Coordination of Humanitarian Affairs). 1999. *United Nations Consolidated Inter-Agency Appeal for East Timor Crisis*. Prepared by the UNOCHA Complex Emergency Response Branch, October 1999.

UNOTIL (United Nations Office in Timor-Leste). 2005. 'Dialogue Agrees on Preventative Actions to Reduce Tensions in Oecusse Border Areas.' Press release dated 15th October 2005. Sighted at http://www.unmiset.org/UNMISETWebSite.nsf/60325cf12626b2a349256f0a003ef7d8/b7e4140edaa5ae164925709b00126399?OpenDocument, 17th March 2006.

UNTAET (United Nations Transitional Administration in East Timor). 2000a. *Regulation No. 2000/11 on the Organization of Courts in East Timor*.

UNTAET regulation dated 6th March 2000. Sighted at http://www.un.org/peace/etimor/untaetR/Reg11.pdf, 21st March 2007.
- 2000b. *Regulation No .2000/15 On the Establishment of Panels with Exclusive Jurisdiction over Serious Criminal Offences*. UNTAET regulation dated 6th June 2000. UNTAET: Dili. Sighted at http://www.un.org/peace/etimor/untaetR/Reg0015E.pdf, 21st March 2007.
- 2001. *Regulation No. 2001/10 on the Establishment of a Commission for Reception, Truth and Reconciliation in East Timor*. UNTAET regulation dated 13th July 2001. Sighted at http://www.un.org/peace/etimor/untaet R/Reg10e.pdf, 20th March 2007.

Urresta, Edwin and Rod Nixon. 2004a. Report *on Research Findings and Policy Recommendations for a Legal Framework for Land Dispute Mediation*. ARD/USAID East Timor Land Law Program, Dili, February 2004. Available at http://www.jsmp.minihub.org/Traditional%20Justice/Reports/LLP_Mediation%20Report/LLPMediationReportEnglish.pdf
- 2004b. *Report on Research Findings and Policy Recommendations for A Law on Land Rights and Title Restitution*. ARD/USAID East Timor Land Law Program, Dili, November 2004.

Vaz, J. Ferraro. 1964. *Moeda de Timor*. Banco Nacional Ultramarino: Lisbon.

Wallace, Alfred Russel. 1962 [1869]. *The Malay Archipelago: The Land of the Orang-Utang and the Bird of Paradise*. Dover: New York.

Weber, Max. 1976 [1919]. 'Science as a Vocation,' in *From Max Weber: Essays in Sociology* (translated, edited and with an introduction by H. H. Gerth and C. Wright Mills). Pp. 129–56. Oxford University Press: New York.
- 1978. *Economy and Society* (edited by Guenther Roth and Claus Wittich), Volume I. University of California Press: Berkeley.

WHO (World Health Organisation). 2006. Country Health Profile: Indonesia. Sighted at http://www.searo.who.int/LinkFiles/Indonesia_indonesia1.pdf, 21st July 2006.

Harnessing Local Law in the Post-Conflict State: The Case of Timor-Leste

Laura Grenfell

1. Introduction

> We need to study the customary law of the people, the property regime, the practices and customs, and to promulgate special laws for them, because it is a grave error to believe that the laws that govern us ... can be applied to ... the Timorese; the social conditions, the property regime, the customs in Timor are quite different ... which is why no one here respects and understands our laws.... [1]

This lament regarding the gulf between the local customary laws of the Timorese and state law could almost be read as emanating from Timor-Leste's last foreign administrator, the United Nations (UN). However, they are the words of a controversial Portuguese Governor who administered Timor-Leste in 1897, more than a century before the September 1999 arrival of UN Transitional Administration for East Timor (UNTAET). Of note is that few studies of local customary laws were conducted in the period between the two administrations and to this day formal state recognition has still not been given to such laws in Timor-Leste.

While the question of local customary law has not commanded much interest internationally, events in Dili in mid 2006 turned the world's attention to the implications of the weak state justice sector in the United Nations' so-called "success story" of Timor-Leste. The world watched as a stand-off between members of the security sector escalated into violence, and as gangs terrorized

[1] Governor Jose Celestino da Silva (1897) Relatorio das Opera~oes de Guerra no Districto Autonomo de Timor no Anno de 1896, Enviado ao Ministro e Secretario D'Estado dos Negocios da Marinha e Ultramar pelo Governador do Mesmv Districto 42-43 translated by Laura Meitzner Yoder, "Custom, Codification, Collaboration: Integrating the Legacies of Land and Forest Authorities in Oecusse Enclave, East Timor" (PhD, Yale University, May 2005) pp.291–292 (on file with author).

ordinary civilians in the capital through arson, looting and assault. To respond to this crisis, an international force of peacekeepers was mobilized and over 300 people were detained.[2]

The UN sought to understand the events through the Report of the United Nations Independent Special Commission of Inquiry for Timor-Leste.[3] This report found that the crisis occurred largely because of the weakness of State institutions and the rule of law.[4] Despite this weakness and the 'minimal functioning' of the judicial system,[5] it recommended that the more serious offences be prosecuted by state courts, where international judges should preside in order to prevent political interference.[6] The report emphasised that, to avoid a culture of impunity, the community's expectations of 'justice' had to be fulfilled through 'formal justice'.[7] But, it is the contention of this paper that, if a culture of impunity is to be avoided, attention must also be turned to the prosecution of those perpetrators arrested for the more minor offences of arson, looting and assault and whether the state courts have the capacity to deal with these cases. It may now be time to heed Governor Da Silva's advice and give serious consideration to the integration of some aspects of local customary law into the state legal system. While the idea of incorporating local customary norms into the state legal system is not a new one, it is one largely neglected in post-conflict literature. On the whole this literature has given little attention to extant informal and indigenous mechanisms and how they can be integrated to serve and strengthen justice in a post-conflict situation.[8]

---

2 The local non-governmental organisation Judicial Systems Monitoring Programme (JSMP) reported in July 2006 that as of 11 July 2006 the international force had detained 278 persons: JSMP, Detention and Trials during the Recent Unrest, Justice Update 7/2006.

3 Report of the UN Independent Special Commission of Inquiry for Timor-Leste, Geneva, 2 October 2006.

4 As above at para 221, "Part VI. Conclusions and Findings".

5 As above at para 176 the report states: "... in reality Timor-Leste has what might be described as a minimally functioning judicial system".

6 As above at para 230; recommendation 6.

7 As above at para 213.

8 According to a literature survey, there is little written on countries in Asia and Africa, (in other words, countries with strong legal pluralism): Alexandra Barahona De Brito *et al.*, (eds), *The Politics of Memory: Transitional Justice in Democratising Societies* (2001), "Bibliographical Survey" pp.315–351. The exception is the gacaca process in Rwanda which has commanded some attention in the literature. See, for example, Timothy Longman, "Justice at the Grassroots? Gacaca trials in Rwanda" in Naomi Roht-Arriaza and Javier Mariezcurrena (eds), *Transitional Justice in the Twenty-First Century: Beyond Truth Versus Justice* (2006) 206. See generally, Jennifer Widner, "Courts and Democracy in Post-Conflict Transitions: A Social Scientist's Perspective on the African Case" (2001) 95 American Journal of International Law 64.

This paper first argues that the state legal system reached a crisis point even before the events in Dili of April–May 2006. It briefly traces the nature of an alternative form of justice, local customary law, and its history of operation in Timor-Leste, arguing that it has been continuous in most regions since prior to the beginning of Portuguese colonization. The paper then examines the status of local customary law since the 1999 ballot, tracing its interaction with the state from the early days of UNTAET's administration to the process of drafting the nation-state's first constitution that was adopted two months before independence on 20 May 2002. This exploration ventures some reasons why local customary law was virtually ignored by those at the top level during these periods, despite its continued use at the bottom level by locals and the repeated calls for its formal recognition and integration. The next part demonstrates that some key actors and mechanisms have taken steps towards the formal recognition of local customary law. It argues that these initiatives provide useful models for the integration of aspects of local customary law into the formal legal system: these models should be given greater attention given the present culture of impunity and the inability of the current state legal system to ease this problem. While local customary law should never be romanticized, as it entails a number of risks that can impact most on the vulnerable members of society, most of these risks may be alleviated through the supervision of the state. A form of 'state law pluralism'[9] may remedy some of problems facing Timor-Leste justice system.

2. Crisis before 'The Crisis'?: The Weaknesses of the State Justice System

There are signs that some improvements are taking place in Timor-Leste's formal justice system. For example, in late 2005 the number of trials being conducted in the Dili District Court increased[10] and in early 2006 the Government enacted the new Penal Code and Criminal Procedure Code, the latter of which aims to simplify criminal procedure, particularly for minor offences. Despite this, in April 2006, shortly before the crisis and at the end of the UN's extended mandate, the future for the state justice sector looked bleak. The UN Secretary-General (SG) observed that the sector "remains one of the most critical areas in need of continuing assistance".[11]

---

[9] This form of pluralism, sometimes dubbed 'weak' or 'juristic', is where the state law incorporates (parts of) other legal systems. It sits in contrast to deep legal pluralism where two or more systems of law exist separately. See generally, Sally Engle Merry, 'Legal Pluralism: Review Essay', (1988) 22 Law and Society Review 869.

[10] JSMP, Recent Developments in the Courts, November 2005.

[11] United Nations Security Council, End of Mandate Report of the Secretary-General on the United Nations Office in Timor-Leste (for the period from January 14 to 12 April 2006), S/2006/251 (2006) para 14.

The SG's report cited problems at a number of levels: the slow process of law-making; the lack of experienced and trained personnel amongst court administrators, the prosecution, defence, and the bench; and poor case-management.[12] While the assistance of a high number of international personnel enabled the completion of 826 cases in the first third of the year, the report noted that "approximately 2500 cases are still pending".[13] From the figures it appears that this constitutes a full year's backlog of cases. The fact that only one court, the Dili District Court,[14] was properly operating in Timor-Leste means that the state justice system was arguably at a crisis point even before the violence erupted.

Months of sporadic violence placed even greater pressure on the state court system. While charges relating to detention were held, trials both in and outside Dili were completely disrupted during the crisis.[15] At the end of June 2006 the UN SG requested his Special Envoy to conduct an assessment mission in Timor-Leste. The Mission observed that the challenges facing the formal legal sector are a combination of a misguided linguistic policy, a lack of capacity and resources, and poor management. It noted that there is "a serious lack of public confidence" in the state legal system and that women and minors in particular experience problems in accessing the system.[16] For example, the most commonly reported crime in Timor-Leste is domestic violence and yet only one in four cases of domestic violence reported to police proceed to the state legal system for prosecution.[17]

None of these findings of the assessment mission is new: they have been repeatedly articulated previously both by indigenous NGOs monitoring the justice system, such as the Judicial Systems Monitoring Programme, as well as the UN in its reports.[18]

---

[12] As above at paras 14–15.

[13] As above at para 15.

[14] The three other courts operate less regularly. The Baucau District Court holds hearings once a week while the Oecusse and Suai District Courts hold hearings on a monthly basis but these hearings are often adjourned because of transport issues or the lack of personnel. See JSMP, Recent Developments in the Courts, Justice Update 22/2005.

[15] JSMP, Detention and Trials During the Recent Unrest, Justice Update 7/2006, p 4ff. Security Council, Report of the Secretary-General on Timor-Leste Pursuant to Security Council Resolution 1690 (2006), S/2006/628 (2006) (8 August 2006), para 85.

[16] Security Council, Report of the Secretary-General on Timor-Leste Pursuant to Security Council Resolution 1690 (2006), S/2006/628 (2006) (8 August 2006), para 85.

[17] As above at para 103. There are some cultural reasons for the few number of prosecutions arising from domestic violence reports: see Laura Grenfell, "Legal Pluralism and the Rule of Law in Timor-Leste" (2006) 19 Leiden Journal of International Law 305 at 312.

[18] See for *e.g.*, JSMP, "Overview of the Justice Sector: March 2005" (March 2005); United Nations Security Council, End of Mandate Report of the Secretary-General on the United Nations Office in Timor-Leste (for the period from January 14 to 12 April 2006), S/2006/251 (2006).

What is new in this report is the mission's conclusion that these challenges are so huge that it is necessary to set up an independent and comprehensive review of the justice system.[19] This review would produce a strategic plan to guide the overall development of the state legal system. Apart from stating that the review should consult all relevant parts of the Government and civil society, the report does not clarify how this review may take place. However, this review may provide a much needed opportunity for Timor-Leste to consider whether its state legal system could be bolstered through the integration of some aspects of local customary law. The SG does not comment specifically on this issue but he does note elsewhere in the report that the process of community reconciliation could be promoted by the use of mechanisms "that have gained meaning in people's lives because of their customary basis and proven effectiveness".[20] Furthermore, the report states that the current capacity deficit could be remedied by harnessing the "unused capacity"of traditional leaders.[21] These may be subtle allusions to the system of local customary law that operates in most regions of Timor-Leste.[22] The following section examines the position of non-state local customary mechanisms of justice as administered by local leaders.

3. History and Nature of Local Customary Law

According to experts, formal legal systems never held great sway in Timor-Leste. The state legal system was weak during the periods of both occupation and colonisation, which has meant that local customary law, sometimes referred to as *adat* or lisan,[23] has continued in operation until today.[24]

During their four centuries of colonial rule beginning in 1556[25] the Portuguese were more interested in tax collection and trade[26] than broader state

[19] Security Council, Report of the Secretary-General on Timor-Leste Pursuant to Security Council Resolution 1690 (2006), S/2006/628 (2006) (8 August 2006) paras 88 and 90.

[20] As above, para 49.

[21] As above, para 33.

[22] Admittedly, as a body composed of state members, it is perhaps not surprising that the UN does not place greater emphasis on the possible use of non-state law.

[23] Adat is the Indonesian word for the sacred laws or beliefs systems on which local law is based. In Tetun the word is lisan.

[24] See Tanja Hohe and Rod Nixon, Reconciling Justice: 'Traditional' Law and State Justice in East Timor- (Final Report) (2003) (report prepared for the United States Institute of Peace), 27 and J. A. Berlie, 'A Concise Legal History of East Timor' in Studies in *Languages and Cultures of East Timor* (2000), Volume 3.

[25] This is the date of the first Portuguese settlement at Lifau (in the present day Oecussi). It was not until the beginning of the eighteenth century that a Portuguese Governor was appointed in East Timor. For a history of East Timor, see J. G. Taylor, *Indonesia's Forgotten War: The Hidden History of East Timor* (1991); J. Dunn, *Timor: A People Betrayed* (1996), Chapter 2.

[26] See Hohe and Nixon, *supra,* note 24, at 27.

administration and hence colonial rule did not have a significant impact on local power structures and systems of law.[27] The Portuguese ruled through a system which bestowed military power onto local chiefs who were expected to provide strong loyalty to Portugal and maintain law and order, a form of indirect rule.[28] Berlie states that up until the twentieth century 'the local native authorities had considerable judicial power' but it is not apparent that a separate system of native courts was recognised by Portugal.[29] In 1910 the Republic of Portugal was founded and rule became more direct.[30] During Portuguese colonial rule, Timor-Leste was divided into nine administrative districts[31] and it is reported that 'four courts of justice existed in Dill, Bacau, Suai and Oecussi'.[32] Contrary to Governor Da Silva's advice, Portugal promulgated few laws specifically for Timor-Leste.[33] However, this minimal outside interference allowed local legal systems to continue operating.[34]

A greater impact was felt by the imposition of the Indonesian legal system during the occupation (1976–1999).[35] Timor-Leste was subject to laws adopted by Indonesia's national legislative council and only civil matters were

---

[27] *ibid.*, More generally, Taylor states 'the salient features of East Timorese society remained in the mid twentieth century much as they had been at the time of the Portuguese arrival': see J. G. Taylor, *Indonesia's Forgotten War: The Hidden History of East Timor* (1991), 15.

[28] See J. A. Berlie, 'A Concise Legal History of East Timor' in *Studies in Languages and Cultures of East Timor* (2000), Volume 3 at 145. Geoffrey Hull states that 'Portuguese rule was accepted because, before the mid-nineteenth century at least, there was minimal interference in indigenous affairs, and this allowed the local kings to maintain the social status quo.' G. Hull, 'East Timor and Indonesia: The Cultural Factors of Incompatibility' in *Studies in Languages and Cultures of East Timor* (2000), Volume 4, at 60. Taylor comments that indirect rule was partly attributable to the fact that the Portuguese were unable to administer successfully the interior: as above at 10.

[29] See Berlie, *supra,* note 24 at 147.

[30] After World War Two, Portugal recognised East Timor as one of its 'overseas provinces', rather than a colony. See Berlie, supra, note 24, at 148 who says that a 'politico-administrative statute for Timor was published in the Organic Law of the Portuguese Overseas (no 2066)' in June 1953. This was during the dictatorship of Antonio de Oliveira Salazar (1932–1968). It is possible that this issue was formalised earlier by the Portuguese Constitution in 1951. However, see J. Dunn, *East Timor: Rough Passage to Independence* (2003), 32 who says that this status was declared in 1963.

[31] The nine districts were Dili, Lautem, Viqueque, Bacau, Manatuto, Suro, Ermera, Bobonaro, and Oecusse.

[32] See Berlie, *supra*, note 24, at 150.

[33] Berlie, *supra*, note 24, at 149.

[34] Hohe and Nixon, *supra*, note 24, at 27. Taylor states that conflict in the region between the Dutch, the Portuguese and the Topasses (a mestizo group from the Portuguese settlement of Palau Solor and Larantuka (Flores)) in the eighteenth century left 'Timorese society relatively free from incursion and disruption': *supra*, note 25, at 5. He comments that East Timorese communities were successful in restricting 'Topasse and European influence and control to the political sphere of princely kinship alliances': at 9.

[35] East Timor became annexed as the 27th province of Indonesia in 1976.

left to the local level to deal with.[36] According to one report, during the occupation, Indonesia passed a law that 'permitted no local traditional institution to exist apart from those adopted by the national legislative body'.[37] Due to widespread perceptions of its corruption, the local population viewed the Indonesian legal system with deep distrust.[38]

This general distrust of the state meant that locals would rarely access the formal legal system, except when it came to report serious cases such as murder.[39] The formal legal system was seen as a last resort. Overall, Berlie sums up that: 'The continual influence of traditional law, shows that colonial and indigenous legal and political systems existed in parallel.[40] Thus the post-colonial legacy was one of two separate legal systems operating in parallel without recognising each other.[41]

Before tracing how local customary law fared in the period after the Indonesian withdrawal following the 1999 independence ballot, it is important to point out three things. First, local customary law is a system of social relationships: it applies to disputes relating to property and land, marriage and other relationships, and crimes.[42] Second, no single local system of customary law stretches in influence across all regions of Timor-Leste; instead there are numerous local systems of law that share some underlying principles. While it is not possible to generalise much about these principles, it is fair to state that local systems of customary law in Timor-Leste are based on very different value systems to Western legal systems. For example, local legal systems use a form of arbitration to deal with disputes, where a local spiritual leader (lia nain) or village chief (chefe) listens to the parties before informing them of the

---

36 See Hohe and Nixon, *supra*, note 24, at 27.

37 S.R. Quast, International Legal Assistance Consortium, Report on East Timor (March 2002), at 22. Dabo Soares explains that this law (UU No 5 Tahun 1974 tentang Pokok Pemerintahan di Daerah), adopted in 1974, "permits no local traditional institution to exist apart from those adopted by the national legislative body": Dionisio da C Babo Soares, "A Brief Overview of the Role of Customary Law in East Timor", paper presented at a symposium on East Timor, Indonesia and the Region organised by the Universidade Nova de Lisboa, July 2000) p 10.

38 See Hohe and Nixon, *supra*, note 24, at 7; see also 26–7.

39 See Hohe and Nixon, *supra*, note 24, at 19, 26.

40 Berlie, *supra*, note 24, at 149. This is confirmed by Taylor who states that the 'two political systems, the colonial and the indigenous co-existed' but in a 'rather uneasy truce': see *supra*, note 25, at 12.

41 While the local system continued informally to serve locals who lived in village structures, particularly in rural areas, the Portuguese legal system predominantly seems to have served the non-East Timorese as well as some urban East Timorese. What is apparent is that local systems of law remained strong and operational, although they could not escape outside influence entirely.

42 See Hohe and Nixon, *supra*, note 24; Tanja Hohe, "Justice without Judiciary in East Timor" (2003) 3/3 Conflict, Security and Development 335.

required means of reconciliation. Third, the continued operation of local customary law since Portuguese colonisation is partly a result of a number of its positive attributes: (i) it is accessible, physically and financially, especially for those people living in remote rural areas because it takes place in the local hamlet or village; (ii) it is sensitive to the social norms lived by the people and thus more likely to be accepted; and (iii) it promotes a social norm centrally important to Timorese life, reconciliation (badame). Reconciliation is considered essential not only between the living but also with one's ancestors.[43]

4. UN Missions in Timor-Leste: State Law and Local Customary Law

Local customary law did not register on UNTAET's radar until it was well into its mission. Established by the UN Security Council in October 1999 the mission had a wide mandate to administer the territory of Timor-Leste until such time as it became officially independent.[44] UNTAET began the process of rebuilding Timor-Leste's formal legal system with its first regulation in late November 1999. This set out that the applicable law was the Indonesian law that operated prior to 25 October 1999.[45]

A few days later UNTAET's third regulation[46] set out the powers of the Transitional Administrator (TA) to appoint judges. In March 2000 the TA issued Regulation 2000/11 for the organisation of courts in Timor-Leste, stating in section 1 that: 'judicial authority in East Timor shall be *exclusively* vested in courts that are established by law and composed of judges who are appointed to these courts in accordance with UNTAET Regulation No

[43] See Hohe and Nixon, *supra*, note 24, p 23.

[44] SC Res 1272 (4057th mtg, 25 October 1999), UN Doc S/RES/1272 (1999).

[45] This was the date of UNTAET's establishment. Indonesian law was to apply in so far as it did not conflict with standards set out in the Universal Declaration on Human Rights and the six core UN human rights treaties: See Sections 2 and 3 of UNTAET Regulation No 1999/1 On the Authority of the Transitional Administration in East Timor, UNTAET/REG/1999/1 (1999). The six core treaties are: the 1966 International Covenant for Civil and Political Rights, 999 UNTS 171 and its Protocols; 1966 International Covenant for Economic, Social and Cultural Rights, 999 UNTS 3; 1965 International Convention for the Elimination of All Forms of Racial Discrimination, 660 UNTS 195; 1979 Convention on the Elimination of Discrimination Against Women, 19 ILM 33 (1980); 1984 Convention Against Torture and Other Cruel, Inhuman or Degrading Treatment, 23 ILM 1027 (1984); 1989 Convention on the Rights of the Child, 28 ILM 1448 (1989). In addition, six Indonesian statutes were declared inapplicable and capital punishment was abolished.

[46] On the Establishment of a Transitional Judicial Service Commission, UNTAET/REG/1999/3 (1999). For analysis of the establishment of East Timor's formal criminal legal system, see S. Linton, "Rising from the Ashes: The Creation of a Viable Criminal Justice System in East Timor" (2001) 25 Melbourne University Law Review 122.

1999/3'.[47] Subsequently UNTAET established four district courts in Dili, Bacau, Suai and Oecussi, an arrangement, which mirrored pre-LJNTAET administration.[48] Together with the Court of Appeal, these courts currently constitute the formal state legal system in Timor-Leste.[49]

Despite the urgency to restore law and order, UNTAET clearly gave some thought to the establishment of Timor-Leste's formal legal system. However, the Administration believed it was building the justice system from scratch. UNTAET's Acting Principal Legal Advisor from this period, Hansjoerg Strohmeyer, writes that the "empty shell" metaphor was often used in UNTAET's early days in Timor-Leste.[50] While there was an awareness that some areas, such as education, only needed "resuscitation", there was the belief that a new legal framework had to be built in order to "avoid a law vacuum".[51] However, there is no evidence of any UNTAET regulation or policy regarding the role of local customary law and how it could assist in maintaining law and order.[52] Possibly this was due to

---

47 (Emphasis added). UNTAET subsequently established District Administrations in the thirteen districts established by Indonesia and created sub district offices numbering sixty, each of which contain about eight villages. In June 2000 the Special Panels for Serious Crimes was established pursuant to section 1 of UNTAET Regulation 2000/15 On the Establishment of Special Panels for Special Crimes, UNTAET/REG/2000/15 (2000), to exercise jurisdiction over the 'serious crimes' of murder and sexual offences committed between 1 January 1999 and 25 October 1999. This limit on temporal jurisdiction does not apply to genocide, war crimes, crims against humanity and torture which are also within the subject matter jurisdiction of the Special Panels.

48 UNTAET/REG/2000/11 (2000) initially stipulated the establishment of eight district courts (Section 7) but this was later amended to four courts by UNTAET/REG/2000/14 (2000) (Section 2).

49 East Timor's highest court is the Supreme Court of Justice but, under s 164 of the 2002 Constitution, the Court of Appeal can exercise its functions until such time as it is established. The JSMP reports that the Court of Appeal did not function from November 2001 to June 2003 due to the lack of judges. This meant that no appeals could be heard during this 18 month period: Judicial Systems Monitoring Programme, Overview of the Justice Sector: March 2005 (March 2005), at 20.

50 Hansjorg Strohmeyer, 'Making Multilateral Interventions Work: The U.N. and the Creation of Transitional Justice Systems in Kosovo and East Timor', (2001) 25 Fletcher Forum of World Affairs 107 at 109. Other reports use similar language that is potentially misleading and could be misread as suggesting a terra nullius doctrine. For example, the description "complete legal vacuum" is used in the report by Kings College, London. However, only a few paragraphs later there is discussion of "the continued widespread reliance on traditional or customary justice mechanisms": King's College London, A Review of Peace Operations: A Case for Change- East Timor (10 March 2003) paras 217, 219.

51 As above at 109, 111. It is more correct to say that a legal vacuum existed in regards to the treatment of serious crimes.

52 Note that there is some evidence that by the end of 2000UNTAET had developed a proposal for using local customary law in resolving land disputes. Daniel Fitzpatrick, who spent three months with UNTAET's Land and Property Unit, states: "In general terms, a three-tier system is proposed: traditional processes, then mediation and, failing that, judicial determination.": (2000) 15 Pacific Economic Bulletin 152 at 158.

UNTAET's limited detailed knowledge of the local justice systems and how they function.[53]

On the ground, the result of this initial UN policy vacuum in regards to the role of local customary law was that a range of approaches was used in relation to local law by various UN staff. For example, some UN CivPol officers used local law, while others refused.[54] This predictably led to 'a certain degree of confusion, particularly amongst the East Timorese'.[55] It was not until September 2001, almost two years into UNTAET's mission, that a workshop was held to discuss the manner in which local customary law could be used to complement the formal justice system.[56] According to Hohe and Nixon, this interest in local law was largely due to pressure relating to land disputes and in the following month LTNTAET prepared a report on establishing a co-ordinated approach to the issue of local customary law.[57] At this time it dawned on UNTAET, as it had on Governor da Silva in 1897, that local processes could be utilised to advantage so as to complement state law in the administration of a weak state.

In fairness, this was one of the first times that the UN was involved in the administration of a whole nation-state and it had little experience in building state legal systems 'from scratch'. The UN's response to this challenge, articulated in the 2000 "Brahimi Report", was to recommend the development of a "common UN justice package" which would allow UN personnel to apply an interim legal code until the rule of law was established locally.[58] If

---

[53] The first detailed report on local law came out in 2001. See D. Mearns, Variations oil a Theme: Coalitions of Authority in East Timor, (2001) (report prepared for Australian Legal Resources International). See also D. Mearns, Looking Both Ways: Models for Justice in East Timor (2002) (report prepared for Australian Legal Resources International); Hohe and Nixon, *supra*, note 24, at 40. Presumably this initial policy vacuum resulted from a combination of a lack of resources and poor communication channels between the local community and the UN administration.

[54] See Hohe and Nixon, *supra*, note 24, at 40. Note that from early 2000 onwards, UNTAET showed interest in traditional mechanisms of conflict resolution in its approach to policing: see Security Council, Report of the Secretary-General on the United Nations Transitional Administration in East Timor (for the period 27 January–26 July 2000), UN Doc S/2000/738, (26 July 2000), at para 46.

[55] As above.

[56] Security Council, Report of the Secretary General on the United Nations Transitional Administration in East Timor (for the period from 25 July to 15 October 2001), S/2001/983 (2001), at para 18.

[57] Hohe and Nixon relate that the report was prepared by the Office of the National Security Advisor: *supra*, note 24, at 41.

[58] Security Council, Comprehensive Review of the Whole Question of Peacekeeping Operations in All Their Aspects, A/55/305-5/2000/809 (21 August 2000) para 81. Acting on these recommendations, the United States Institute for Peace in conjunction with the Irish Centre for Human Rights has developed four model codes. Given the unlikelihood that the UN will administer territory on the same scale as Timor-Leste, these codes are now envisaged as a tool that could assist national personnel in law reform. See Vivienne O'Connor, "Traversing the Rocky Road of Law Reform in Conflict and Post-Conflict States: Model Codes for Postconflict Criminal Justice as a Tool for Assistance" (2005) 16 Criminal Law Forum 231 at 251 and generally.

implemented in a situation such as that of Timor-Leste, this package may have eased the confusion of UN personnel in administering the law in Timor-Leste. However, more critically, it would have created greater confusion for local Timorese to whom the interim laws would have been aimed. Overall, the recommendation is largely misguided in that it fails to consider fully the intended subjects, and the legitimacy, of such imposed laws. In post-conflict situations it is not simply a matter of ensuring that laws comply with human rights standards: the maintenance of law and order requires that laws be predictable and familiar to all levels of society, especially the illiterate and vulnerable, and enjoy a measure of local legitimacy.

The UN Secretary General later revised the UN's position in his 2004 report on "The Rule of Law and Transitional Justice in Conflict and Post-Conflict Societies".[59] The report recognises the danger of a one-size-fits-all formula and it urges that "due regard must be given to indigenous and informal traditions for administering justice," for if these traditions are "ignored or overridden, the result can be the exclusion of large sectors of society from accessible justice".[60] This shows a shift from an international focus to the national and the local as well as a questioning of the assumption that international actors can provide comprehensive cure-all solutions for post-conflict problems.

Another formal opportunity for top-level actors to engage with local customary law arose during Timor-Leste's constitution-making process from late 2000 to March 2002. The following section traces the path by which the Constitution was drafted and it explores the reasons why local customary law was not given clear recognition.

5. Local Customary Law and the Constitution

5.1 The Constitution Making Process

To analyse the Constitution's provisions on local customary law, it is at first necessary to consider briefly the process used to draft the Constitution.

[59] Security Council, Report of the Secretary-General on the Rule of Law and Transitional Justice in Conflict and Post-Conflict Societies, S/2004/616 (2004).
[60] As above at para 12.

In late 2000 the TA, in consultation with a National Council of local leaders,[61] negotiated Timor-Leste's path to independence, setting out a timetable for elections and constitution-making. It was decided that an elected body should draft the Constitution, rather than leaving it to an appointed body of lawyers and experts, and that the process should include a period of consultation. The Constituent Assembly was elected on 30 August 2001, with Fretelin almost winning a majority of two-thirds needed to adopt the constitution.[62] This position of dominance in the Assembly enabled Fretelin to use the draft Constitution it had penned in Australia[63] in 1998 as the basis for the drafting process.[64]

The Assembly was given only a short time-frame in which to consult with the people and to draft a Constitution. Altogether the Assembly had a little less than six months in which to complete this process[65] before it was adopted on 22 March 2002.[66] The Assembly had at its disposal the following forms of assistance to assist it with the drafting process: (i) public hearings; (ii) foreign experts, and; (iii) consultations. The first two were somewhat limited forms of assistance: public hearings were held but they were restricted to invited

---

[61] The "National Consultative Council" was set up by UNTAET Regulation I999/2 (2 December 1999; to bolster the democratic local legitimacy of the TA's mandate to make and execute laws. This body was reformed in mid 2000 so as to make the body more broadly representative. The "National Council" was formed by UNTAET Regulation 2000/24 (14 July 2000). See also UNTAET Regulation 2000/33 (26 October 2000). The body comprised 36 members from sectors of the East Timorese community including 10 politicians and a representative from each of the 13 districts.

[62] The Constituent Assembly comprised 88 members. Women won more than a quarter of the seats. The ASDT gave Fretelin the support it needed for a two-thirds majority.

[63] See Anthony Regan, "Constitution-Making in East Timor: Missed Opportunities" in Babo Soares *et al.*, (eds), *Elections and Constitution-Making in East Timor* (2003) 39; Alipio Baltazar, "An Overview of the Constitution Drafting Process in East Timor" (2004) 9 East Timor Law Journal.

[64] Note that 4 other parties also submitted draft constitutions when the assembly began its process but that Fretelin's draft was chosen as a result of its majority.

[65] Initially UNTAET Regulation 2001/3 gave the Assembly a period of 90 days to draft the constitution once they first sat as a body. This short time frame caused much concern and a few advocates raised suggestions that the Constitution be an interim constitution as in South Africa. This was pushed by the Catholic Church. An articulate plea for an interim constitution was written by Aderito de Jesus Soares who was later elected to the Constituent Assembly: see "For an Interim Constitution" (2001) 2/5 The La'o Hamutuk Bulletin. Eventually the period was extended by a further 90 days. It was adopted with 72 votes in favour, 15 against and 1 absence. The Carter Center, "The East Timor Political and Election Observation Project Final Report" Atlanta: The Carter Center, April 2004 at 41. Brandt notes that despite the short time frame, the Constituent Assembly spent 21 of the initial 90 days in debating the internal rules of procedure: see Michele Brandt, *Constitutional Assistance in Post-Conflict Countries. The UN Experience: Cambodia, East Timor and Afghanistan* (UNDP Report, June 2005) p 16.

[66] It was adopted with 72 votes in favour, 15 against and 1 absence. The Carter Center, "The East Timor Political and Election Observation Project Final Report" Atlanta: The Carter Center, April 2004 at 41.

guests,[67] while foreign experts numbered a little more than a dozen.[68] The consultations deserve some consideration as such mechanisms can be an indicator of local desires.

Two sets of local consultation took place. The first set was organized by the UN: it appointed Constitutional Commissions for each district that conducted month-long civic education programmes in each sub-district in mid 2001.[69] In total, 212 public consultations took place with approximately 38,000 people attending. The Commissions aimed to inform and familiarise the local people with the objectives of the constitutional consultation process and the main constitutional issues facing Timor-Leste.[70] In 2001 the results from these consultations were compiled and presented to members of the Constituent Assembly, as an UNTAET regulation required the Assembly to "give due consideration" to the results.[71]

The second set of formal local consultations took place after the Constituent Assembly had adopted a draft of the Constitution and the draft was then translated into Tetum, English and Indonesian.[72] The Constituent Assembly conducted this week-long consultation process itself in late February 2001; its members held hearings in each sub-district to explain the content of the

[67] According to the UNHCHR report of 1 March 2002, public hearings were "held over a period of only one to three days, at short notice and involved only a small number of invited individuals and groups": UN Doc E/CN.4/2002/39 (1 March 2002 Report), para 46

[68] According to Louis Aucoin, the Asia Foundation provided nine foreign advisors who authored papers on constitutional issues such as customary law, international law, judicial independence, human rights and public participation. In addition, UNTAET established a Secretariat for the CA to coordinate the advice of foreign advisors and local actors. The Secretariat provided 5 foreign advisors (4 Portuguese and 1 Canadian): Louis Aucoin, "The Role of International Experts in Constitution-Making: Myth and Reality" (2004) 5 Georgetown Journal of International Affairs 89 at 94.

[69] UNTAET Directive 2001/2. Each Constitutional Commission comprised 5–7 Commissioners as well as an Advisor and a Rapporteur.

[70] See Constitutional Affairs Branch, Office of Political Affairs, UNTAET, Executive Summary of the Constitutional Commission Public Hearings, Dili, September 2001. This can be found at http://www.un.org/peace/etimor/DB/dbl90901.htm last accessed on 30 June 2006.

[71] Under Regulation 2.4 of UNTAET Regulation 2001/2 it was set out that: "In its deliberations, the Constituent Assembly should give due consideration to the results of the consultations conducted by any duly constituted Constitutional Commission or Commission.". A copy of the Executive Summary of the Constitutional Commission Public Hearings can be found at http://www.un.org/peace/etimor/DB/db190901.htm last accessed on 30 June 2006.

[72] Note that a survey conducted by the Asia Foundation in January 2002 before the formal consultations found that only 22% of voters said a member of the constituent assembly had consulted them on the new constitution. However, 67% of voters said they would like to be consulted about the constitution before its final approval and 87% of voters said they believe that public participation is important. There are no statistics on the outcome of the first set of consultations. See Asia Foundation, Timor Lorosa 'e: National Survey of Citizen Knowledge 2002 p 28.

Constitution and gather suggestions.[73] The suggestions compiled from these hearing were presented to the Assembly in mid March 2002 and some minor amendments were made to the draft constitution.[74]

The following section considers to what degree the issue of local customary law was a concern voiced in the consultations and whether the Assembly translated this concern into the final text of the Constitution. Constitutions are important moments that enable a break from the past and the founding of a new order. Ackerman call this rupture a "constitutional moment",[75] but constitutions are an equally good opportunity for some reflection on the necessity of engagement between the modern state and local traditions. The desire to break with the past does not negate a weak state's need to harness the power of local traditions.

5.2 Constitutional provisions on Local Customary Law

The status of local customary law at the constitutional level generally involves the possibility of three options: recognition, special entrenchment or abolition. The first two options should also draw in debate about local customary law's relationship with constitutional rights. As explained below, this debate was almost non-existent in Timor-Leste's constitution-making process.

Section 2(4) of Timor-Leste's Constitution, which deals with the status of local customary law, provides:

> 4. The State shall recognise and value the norms and customs of East Timor that are not contrary to the Constitution and to any legislation dealing specifically with customary law.[76]

---

[73] Note that the Carter Center report argues that the public hearings were limited to informing the public of the contents and did not involve the solicitation of public input: Carter Center, "The East Timor Political and Election Observation Project Final Report" Atlanta: The Carter Center, April 2004 at 44.

[74] Baltazar writes that eight of these twenty-one amendments were recommended by the people generally while the remainder were the result of recommendations made by civil society: Alipio Baltazar, "An Overview of the Constitution Drafting Process in East Timor" (2004) 9 East Timor Law Journal at 4. According to the Carter Center, "Observers suspected that the Assembly did not intend to make any significant changes to the constitutional draft, and ultimately they did not.": at 45

[75] Bruce Ackerman, *The Future of Liberal Revolution* (Yale University Press, New Haven 1992) p 57.

[76] The influences for this provision cannot be traced to the constitution of one of East Timor's lusophone brothers in Southern Africa, Mozambique, because, as mentioned earlier, Mozambique's Constitution does not include any provision dealing with pre-colonial, customary law. After the revolution in Mozambique in 1975, customary law and local courts were replaced with law created by Popular Assemblies and administered by Popular Tribunals. This unwritten law was based on a concept labelled "Popular Justice" and it sought to ignore customary law that conflicted with the state's new normative standards of human rights and gender equality: see Welsh *et al.*, in Armstrong (ed) *Women and Law in Southern Africa* (1987) 105.

This provision signals the first option, namely that of recognition. But the provision is weak and ambiguous in that it does not specify that courts are to apply them as being part of the body of Timor-Leste's formal law.

It is telling that no provisions for local customary law were included in Fretelin's initial draft of 1998. They were initially added as an afterthought in late 2001.[77] By the final draft, however, the constitutional recognition of custom had moved up in the order of the Constitution to sit uncomfortably with the principle of constitutionalism in section 2. On the advice of an international advisor, the wording was changed from the December 2001 draft so as to envisage the possibility of future legislation to set out specific guidelines regarding local law and custom. A more dramatic change was the scrapping of the constitutional recognition of traditional authority in the final draft, the reasons for which are not entirely clear.[78]

The lack of a provision dealing with local customary law in the initial Fretelin draft perhaps demonstrates the belief held in some quarters that many of the elite members of Fretelin have little interest in local customary law. This disinterest could be a result of a number of factors: First, the party's overwhelming desire to have a "modern" constitution; second, a rejection of a system wherein power is based on ancestry; such a system does not accord with Marxist Leninist principles espoused early on by Fretelin's leaders, and; third, a discontinued connection with traditional structures due to the years in exile spent by most of Fretelin's leaders. However, it is not possible to argue

77 This is apparent from a draft of East Timor's Constitution dated 7 December 2001. This draft notes the addition of a new section, between sections 13 and 14 (dealing with national languages and symbols respectively), entitled "Customary Law and Traditional Authorities". It provides: "(1) The State shall respect the diversity of rules and customs as long as they are not contrary to the Constitution. (2) The State shall recognise and value traditional authorities legitimised by the communities, shall establish how they should operate and their relationship with other institutions and accommodate their participation in the economic, social and cultural life of the country." Like the relevant provisions of the South African Constitution, this section deals with two important elements of traditional life: customary law and traditional authorities. However, the language in this case is very weak and does not speak of 'protection'. In addition, there is no mention of a role for traditional authorities in local or national government. The proposed context of this section leads one to believe that customary law was considered by the drafters to be more of a symbolic matter than a matter pertaining to law and governance.

78 For the section, see above. In an "Options Paper for the Constituent Assembly", Constitutional Advisor Anthony Regan writes that there was no evidence of interest in establishing a formal role of traditional leaders, either at the national level or at the local level as the basis for local government. However, he notes that there may be some interest in such leaders having a role in elected local government or dispute settlement at the local level: document produced for the Asia Foundation, dated 30 November 2001, on file with author.

that Fretelin was disinterested in tradition altogether. To the contrary, Hohe argues that Fretelin played upon tradition in their election campaign leading to the August 2001 election. She claims that it 'manipulated' indigenous values and symbols, as well as the history of the resistance fight to gain election.[79] There is possibly a fourth factor: it could be that Timor-Leste's elected leaders did not want to have their power rivaled and diminished by unelected leaders who derive their authority through ancestry. Fretelin's leaders wanted strong centralised power.

If there is some truth in these four possible factors, how was section 2(4) added to the Constitution? Here it is useful to look at the result of the first set of consultations conducted by the Constitutional Commissions in mid 2001. The Executive Summary of this process sets out sixteen issues that were clearly a concern at the local level. Some of these are more symbolic issues such as the flag, the name of the country and so forth. Others are more substantive such as language, defence and security, the structure and system of government, human rights and, moreover, local customary law and values. The report states:

> There was wide support for the continued use of traditional forms of law making and law-enforcement to complement conventional laws. The role of the "Adat" (unwritten customary law) in relation to the state justice system was a common topic. The people, in general, emphasised that the preservation of "Adat" should be reflected in the future constitution.[80]

Despite the "wide support" for local customary law[81] at the local level recorded in this September 2001 report, it appears that the Constituent Assembly gave the matter little attention. In other transitional countries such as Papua New Guinea and South Africa this matter was considered worthy of some debate and a number of constitutional provisions but in Timor-Leste it was given cursory thought.

The report also states that it was proposed at the local level that traditional authorities be given a "prominent role in solving local disputes and conflicts ... [and that] the future role of the traditional authority ...[should] be proposed

---

[79] See Tanja Hohe, "Totem Polls: Indigenous Concepts and "Free and Fair" Elections in East Timor" (2002) 9 International Peacekeeping 69 at 70.

[80] See Constitutional Affairs Branch, Office of Political Affairs, UNTAET, Executive Summary of the Constitutional Commission Public Hearings, Dili, September 2001. This can be found at http://www.un.org/peace/etimor/DB/dbl90901.htm last accessed on 30 June 2006.

[81] As above.

to be reflected in the constitution."[82] The final text does not reflect this local desire. This could be because the Assembly chose to disregard the consultations conducted by the UN[83] on the ground that the UN had dominated this particular consultation process[84] and that the Commissioners lacked legitimacy because they were unelected.[85] In the end, the Assembly failed to make reference to any of the Commissions' district reports in the drafting debates.[86]

This problem of limited local consultation and the lack of a feeling of local ownership over the process drew the attention of the UN High Commissioner for Human Rights (UNHCHR) on 1 March 2002:

> [I]n emphasising the 'representative democratic' model of government, the work of the Assembly itself seems to minimise the right of individuals in East Timor to participate in political life by contributing to political debate surrounding the Constitution. ... [T]here is a popular perception that, to a larger extent, the drafting process has focused on the prepared drafts of political parties, rather than incorporating comments or suggestions from ongoing consultations or the public hearings. As a result, there appears to be a limited sense of ownership of the process amongst civil society and already a questioning of the responsiveness of the Assembly to its constituents.[87]

It was a result of sustained pressure from civil society and from leaders such as Xanana Gusmao and Bishop Belo that the second set of consultations was conducted.[88] However, this consultation was "time-limited and not

---

[82] As above.

[83] Baltazar comments that the members of the Constitutional Commissions were concerned that the Constituent Assembly would not read their reports and hence requested to participate in the sessions so as to brief the Assembly: Alipio Baltazar, "An Overview of the Constitution Drafting Process in East Timor" (2004) 9 East Timor Law Journal at 5.

[84] Carter Center, "The East Timor Political and Election Observation Project Final Report" Atlanta: The Carter Center, April 2004 at 44.

[85] As above.

[86] Carter Center at 44. See also Jonathan Morrow and Rachel White, "The UN in Transitional East Timor: International Standards and the Reality of Governance" (2002) Australian Yearbook of International Law 1 at 38; Nancy M Lutz, "Constitutionalism as Public Culture in East Timor", paper presented at the Law and Society Association Meetings, Pittsburgh, June 7, 2003 at I.

[87] UN Doc E/CN.4/2002/39 (1 March 2002 Report), para 46. The report continues: "There were serious concerns regarding the extent to which the Assembly members were receptive to the submissions of those outside the political party members."

[88] Michele Brandt, Constitutional Assistance in Post-Conflict Countries. The UN Experience: Cambodia, East Timor and Afghanistan (LTNDP Report, June 2005) p 17. Brandt writes that some members of the Constituent Assembly privately maintained that the consultation process was an exercise in public relations only: as above.

widespread", and the draft constitution was, according to the UNHCHR, made available to civil society "at a very late stage", restricting the ability of groups and individuals to analyse and comment on the draft.[89] The results of the second local consultations were never made available to the public by the Assembly.

There was, however, some pressure in regards to local customary law from within the Constituent Assembly itself. Some of the minor parties involved in the drafting process, such as KOTA, the traditionalist party with two seats, made a suggestion to have an Upper House of traditional leaders (called *liurais*).[90] It is not clear as to the form in which this body was proposed,[91] but it appears to have been dismissed with little, if any, debate. Timor-Leste's traditional leaders were unable to mobilise much pressure to bear on this proposal.[92]

Due to the fact that local customary law is neither formally recognised nor codified in Timor-Leste, it may have been difficult for traditional leaders in Timor-Leste to envisage that the Constitution could affect their traditional decision-making powers. However, women's groups did raise the question of the relationship between state sanctioned equality and local customary law. Through a petition they requested that the constitution regulate the traditional system and its impact on women. Article Eight of *The Women's Charter* presented to the Assembly with 8000 signature,[93] states:

---

[89] UN Doc E/CN.4/2002/39 (1 March 2002 Report), para 47.

[90] Rod Nixon, "Indonesia West Timor: The Political-Economy of Emerging Ethno-Nationalism" (2004) 34 Journal of Contemporary Asia 163 at 177. According to Hohe, "[P]olitical legitimacy in traditional Timorese societies derives from appointment through ritual authorities, the leaders that are connected to the ancestors.": Tanja Hohe, "Totem Polls: Indigenous Concepts and "Free and Fair" Elections in East Timor" (2002) 9 International Peacekeeping 69 at 81.

[91] It is not clear whether the proposed body would function along the lines of the pre-1958 House of Lords in the United Kingdom, or of a more limited nature like a Council of Traditional Leaders in South Africa.

[92] Perhaps the problem was that traditional leaders had no existing institutional standing in East Timor. While many traditional leaders had been conscripted by the Indonesian Government to assist in governing local districts, this had not taken place on the same uniform institutional basis as in South Africa under apartheid. Thus East Timorese traditional leaders did not have the same vested interests to protect in the constitutional dispensation as their South African brothers who had been institutionalised by the apartheid regime. Furthermore, traditional leaders do not appear to have organised themselves into a vocal lobby group. For these reasons, the issue of constitutional recognition of traditional leadership, in some shape or form, seems to have slipped out of the text of the constitution and left traditional leaders without constitutional standing.

[93] The Charter was prepared by the Gender and Constitutional Working Group. It appears in (2001) 2/5 La'O Hamutuk Bulletin 2. Note that versions of some of these Charter rights were incorporated into the Constitution but many have weak enforcement mechanisms.

> The Constitution must guarantee equal rights to inheritance, and regulate the dowry system to prevent violence against women. Women must be guaranteed participation in traditional decision-making processes.[94]

Once again the Assembly chose to ignore the debate. It may have believed that the Constitution was not the right avenue for regulating these specific issues and that local customary law should be left to regulate itself on an informal basis. Alternatively it may have decided that the uncertainty in the area would be clarified by the Constitution's guarantee of equality, section 17, or through future legislation under section 2(4).

The international community perhaps had some sway over the process. In this regard, the influence of Timor-Leste's lusophone brothers, Portugal and Mozambique, needs to be considered. A reading of Mozambique's 1975 Constitution (based on the Portuguese) shows the extensive degree to which it was the model for Timor-Leste's Constitution. Interestingly, Mozambique's 1975 Constitution did not entrench local customary law and indeed it makes no mention of custom whatsoever.

Apart from the lusophone connection, some international influence can be traced to the United Nations[95] but there is contention on the extent to this influence.[96] Core UN documents clearly influenced the drafting, as the *Universal Declaration of Human Rights* (UDHR) was treated as a yardstick throughout the process. Section 23 of the Constitution provides that: "Fundamental rights enshrined in the Constitution ... shall be interpreted in accordance with the *Universal Declaration of Human Rights*" and the Constitution includes an extensive list of rights. According to Babo Soares, provisions dealing with human rights were approved unanimously by all parties in the Assembly "despite fears that traditional groups might refuse to back them, since women and children have a unique place in traditional

---

[94] As above.

[95] Note that in January 2002 some members of US Congress wrote to the Assembly, voicing their concern about the short time frame given to the drafting process and encouraging the Assembly to extend the time so as to "enable more thorough discussions and additional consultation within the Constituent Assembly and throughout East Timor": Letter from eight members of US Congress to the Speaker of the Constituent Assembly dated 10 January 2002.

[96] See Louis Aucoin, "The Role of International Experts in Constitution-Making: Myth and Reality" (2004) 5 Georgetown Journal of International Affairs 89; Jonathan Morrow and Rachel White, "The UN in Transitional East Timor: International Standards and the Reality of Governance" (2002) Australian Yearbook of International Law 1 at 41.

customary law".[97] Despite this tension with local customary law, local support for human rights seemed to be high, with influential local leader Bishop Belo announcing: "It is our dream to build a society founded on the values enshrined in the *UDHR*. These are the values that guided and inspired our struggle for independence."[98]

This sentiment upholding human rights is apparent in the wording of Article 2(4) of the Constitution, which states that local norms and customs must 'not [be] contrary to the Constitution'. This means that they are subject to the extensive bill of rights entrenched in Timor-Leste's Constitution,[99] as well as international conventions, such as core human rights treaties, which are given special status by Article 9 of the Constitution.[100] Thus, local customary law recognised by the state would need to be consistent with all the international human rights conventions to which the state has acceded.

However, there is a provision in the Constitution which points to the possibility of a formal engagement between the state legal system and traditional legal systems, which resolve disputes by various forms of

---

[97] Dionisio da Costa Babo Soares, "The Challenges of Drafting a Constitution" in Babo Soares *et al.*, (eds), *Elections and Constitution-Making in East Timor*" (2003) at 27.

[98] Bishop Carlos Belo, Sydney Morning Herald, "To forge a future, Timor needs justice for the past", 28 August 2001. According to the Executive Summary of the Constitutional Commissions, "it was widely felt that these should be based on the universal principles of the declaration of the United Nations Charter of 1948" (ie the UDHR): Constitutional Affairs Branch, Office of Political Affairs, UNTAET, Executive Summary of the Constitutional Commission Public Hearings, Dili, September 2001 at 8.

[99] East Timor's Constitution has special sections regarding the rights of women, children, youth, the elderly, disabled citizens and the diaspora (Arts. 17–22). It guarantees an extensive list of civil and political rights (Arts. 29–49) and social, economic and cultural rights and duties (Art. 50–61). Note, however, that the enforcement provisions for these rights are not particularly strong. Under Art. 27, the independent office of the Ombudsman only has the power 'to examine and seek to settle citizens' complaints against public bodies, certify the conformity of the acts with the law, prevent and initiate the process to remedy injustices'.

[100] Article 9(3) provides: "All rules that are contrary to the provisions of international conventions, treaties and agreements applied in the internal legal system of East Timor shall be invalid". East Timor has acceded to a number of international conventions. For example, in 2003, one year after independence, it acceded to almost all of the core UN human rights conventions: the International Covenant on Civil and Political Rights (ICCPR), the International Covenant on Economic, Social and Cultural Rights, the Convention on the Elimination of Discrimination against Women, the Convention against Torture, and the Convention on the Rights of the Child (see *supra*, note 45 for publication details). Paragraph 2 of Article 9 provides that the act of accession to an international treaty transforms it into state law: "Rules provided for in international conventions, treaties and agreements shall apply in the internal legal system of East Timor following their approval, ratification or accession by the respective competent organs and after publication in the official gazette."

arbitration. Dealing with the structure of the court system, Article 123 provides:

Article 123 Categories of courts

1. There shall be the following categories of courts in the Democratic Republic of East Timor:

    (a) The Supreme Court of Justice and other courts of law;
    (b) The High Administrative, Tax and Audit Court ...;
    (c) Military Courts. ...

5. The law may institutionalise means and ways for the non-jurisdictional resolution of disputes.[101]

One interpretation of subsection 5 is that it is an opening for legislation to allow a formal engagement with local systems of dispute resolution, which are clearly beyond the present jurisdiction of the formal court system.

To sum up, the final text of the Constitution places the reference to local custom, contained in section 2(4), quite high in the order of the Constitution's "fundamental principles". However, the reference is limited and vague and it does not seem to reflect the strength of local sentiment on this issue.

Ultimately, one of the reasons for this relative dearth of local norms in the Constitution was that one party dominated the drafting process and the leaders of that party were heavily influenced by international norms, mostly of lusophone origin. Fretelin's domination of the Assembly meant it was not forced to make the constitution-making process more inclusive and consultative. The party had a draft before the Assembly met, and according to observers, the final text "did not vary significantly" from this initial draft.[102] The end result is a system of constitutional principles that are mainly foreign and unfamiliar to the local population.

The consequence for the legal system has been confusion: the police and courts are uncertain as to whether and when local customary law is applicable

[101] Emphasis added.

[102] Louis Aueoin, "The Role of International Experts in Constitution-Making: Myth and Reality" (2004) 5 Georgetown Journal of International Affairs 89 at 94. See also Hilary Charlesworth, "The Constitution of East Timor, May 20, 2002" (2003) 1 International Journal of Constitutional Law 325 at 328.

and are therefore making arbitrary decisions on the matter.[103] Furthermore, there is confusion at the village level as to the relationship between local leaders and the government. The Constitution was an opportunity for Timor-Leste to make a symbolic and concrete break with its colonial past by clearly incorporating Timorese values and laws. It is now a question of whether other initiatives can fill this gap.

6. Some Steps Towards Recognition

Since independence, some important steps have been made towards the formal recognition and integration of aspects of local customary law. These steps have been taken directly by some of the country's leaders, mainly non-Fretelin party leaders, in conjunction with civil society, as well as indirectly by transitional justice mechanisms, such as the Commission for Reception, Truth and Reconciliation (known by its Portuguese acronym 'CAVR'). This section briefly discusses the contributions of some of these actors and mechanisms.

6.1. Civil Society and Leaders

In mid 2002 local NGO the Judicial Systems Monitoring Programme (JSMP) organised a workshop on formal and local justice system, thus enabling debate and dialogue to emerge. The workshop's participants came from almost every district of Timor-Leste and included traditional leaders, NGO workers, academics, and employees of the state and the CAVR. Among its recommendations was a request that the state recognise local justice subject to international human rights law guarantees of non-discrimination.[104] This was followed by an international conference hosted by the Asia Foundation in mid 2003.[105] The conference was opened by President Gusmao, a non-Fretelin leader, who recommended that serious reflection was needed on the question of integrating the positive aspects of local law.

Some key NGO initiatives on non-state justice have focused on civil matters, which are currently not prioritised by the over-burdened state court system.

---

[103] For example, the courts have been grappling in an *ad hoc* fashion with the questions of whether local law can be legitimately used as a criminal law defence, as a ground for dismissing a case, to mitigate a sentence, or in sentencing generally. These cases have been reported by the JSMP – see the following reports: *The Role, Practice and Procedure of the Court of Appeal* (28 June 2005), at 15; *Press Release: Judge Applies Customary Law in a Criminal Case* (19 May 2005); *Overview of the Justice Sector: March 2005,* (March 2005), at 14–15; JSMP, *The Interaction of Traditional Dispute Resolution with the Formal Justice Sector in Timor-Leste, Justice Update 23/2005,* Dili November 2005.

[104] JSMP, Findings and Recommendations: Workshop on Formal and Local Justice Systems in East Timor (July 2002) p 15.

[105] The conference was entitled "Traditional Conflict Resolution & Traditional Justice in Timor-Leste".

They propose the use of mediation for these matters. Mediation is seen as a vehicle that focuses on the similarities in Timor-Leste's various *lisan* systems.

One of these civil matters in the spotlight is land law, an area whose importance is underlined by the fact that land disputes have considerable potential to fuel conflict. This problem of land law is exacerbated by the legacy of a complex framework of laws from the country's history of colonisation, occupation and administration.[106]

The majority of land disputes are resolved outside the state legal system using a process of arbitration or mediation. These disputes comprise a significant proportion of all disputes addressed at the local level.[107] US-AID funded Associates in Rural Development (ARD) conducted research into local forms of mediation and alternative dispute resolution in relation to land law and found that local fora were overwhelmingly preferred to formal state courts for settling land tenure disputes because the former are faster, cheaper, easier to access and more sensitive to local norms. The ARD subsequently drafted a number of pieces of legislation for the government, based on the results of its surveys, including a decree law, *Official Mediation Process of Land Conflicts,* which is still being considered by the Council of Ministers. This Bill gives recognition to local mediation by requiring that it be the first option for land dispute resolution, followed by the court system in the case that mediation is unsuccessful or impossible.

Another local initiative has been to establish a mediation model for civil cases generally.[108] The idea is that a mediation model could become the 'one common model to be used in all communities'.[109] The aim of this proposed model, spearheaded by the Peace and Democracy Foundation and sponsored by the then Minister for Foreign Affairs, Jose Ramos Horta (another non-Fretelin leader), is to improve local dispute resolution and 'correct the problems with the customary practice'. The initiative recognises the negative aspects of local customary law and seeks to remedy them while retaining the core of the customary process. Thus the model seeks to implement an alternative mechanism that is 'more transparent' and 'can reduce

---

106 See D. Fitzpatrick, *Land Claims in East Timor* (2002).

107 E. Urresta and R. Nixon, Timor-Leste Land Law Program, Report on Research Findings and Policy Recommendations for a Legal Framework for Land Dispute Mediation (February 2004).

108 Peace and Democracy Foundation, Report about Research on Customary Dispute Resolution and Proposed Mediation Model for the Democratic Republic of Timor-Leste (November 2004) (document on file with author).

109 *ibid.*, at 9.

discrimination suffered by women and young people in the local legal sphere.'[110] The model uses mediation instead of the system of arbitration most commonly used at the local level because it allows the parties to the conflict to find a solution to their problem with the assistance of a mediation team made up of customary leaders, as well as representatives of women, youth and religion. The pilot for this project was completed in December 2005 but an assessment of the project has been held up by the recent events in Dill.

6.2. Timor-Leste's Commission for Reception, Truth and Reconciliation (CAVR)

CAVR is a transitional justice mechanism set up in early 2002 to deal with minor criminal offences that took place in the twenty-five year period between Portugal's Carnation Revolution, which led to its withdrawal in 1974, and the Indonesian withdrawal in 1999.[111] Originally an initiative of the CNRT Congress,[112] the proposal took form through UNTAET's Office for Human Rights and a committee comprised of local NGOs after some consultation in the districts. Clearly there was the understanding at many levels that the state legal system would not have the capacity to deal with all the offences that were perpetrated. CAVR was set up so as to complement the state legal system, which, through the Serious Crimes Unit, would deal with the more serious crimes.

One central aspect of CAVR was its Community Reconciliation Process (CRP), which was a hybrid mechanism that combined practices of local justice, mediation, arbitration and aspects of civil and criminal law.[113] The flexibility of this hybrid mechanism allowed for the inclusion of different elements of local traditional practice *(lisan)* from community to community,[114] which in turn encouraged local ownership over the process. In

---

[110] *ibid.*, at 5.

[111] See UNTAET Regulation No. 2001/10 On the Establishment of a Commission for Reception, Truth and Reconciliation in East Timor UNTAET/REG/2001/10 (2001).

[112] The CNRT, the National Council of Timorese Resistance, was the umbrella group for nationalistic political parties. It formally dissolved in 2001.

[113] The procedure for CRPs was not prescribed by the above regulation but was left to the discretion of the CAVR by section 27(2) of the above regulation. See generally Part IV of the Regulation. For a description of this hybrid procedure, see *Chega!, Report of the Commission for Reception, Truth and Reconciliation*, Part 9.1.1 at para 2.

[114] According to *Chega!*, the basic procedure of the nahe biti boot ritual (where a mat is spread out for the process of dispute resolution) is a cultural constant across Timor-Leste and hence it figured in most hearings: Part 9; para 23. See p 7 of Part 9 for a description of this ritual. Note that participants in nahe biti boot believe that their ancestors are witness to this ritual and validate the outcome. In this sense the ritual provides a means of reconciliation with the dead.

each village, perpetrators of politically-related minor offences such as arson, theft or minor assault, were invited to voluntarily make a full confession of their crime.[115] This confession was initially set out in writing and referred to the Office of the General Prosecutor to check that it dealt only with minor offences.[116] The oral confession then took place in the community's local language in front of the victims and community, as well as a panel comprised of a Regional Commissioner and local community leaders, including spiritual leaders and one or two women.[117] In each case the panel brokered an agreement between the victim and the perpetrator on an act of reconciliation to be carried out by the perpetrator. In line with local customary practices, the perpetrator was required to make an apology or repayment to the victim, or agree to do community service. The agreement was then registered at the district court: this was designed to guarantee that the reconciliation would be carried out, that the form of reconciliation was proportionate to the crime and that human rights were not violated. The perpetrator could then become immune from prosecution in the state legal system.[118] In effect, the formal system of registering agreements strengthened the process by giving it state sanction.

Over a period of four years, CAVR's CRP successfully heard 1371 cases and the body produced a lengthy final report, *Chega!*.[119] Unlike the state legal system, the process was carried out mainly by Timorese nationals, and it required the assistance of only a few international advisors. Out of a population of one million, an estimated 40,000 people (almost 5% of the population) attended and participated in a CRP.[120]

---

115 Note that perpetrators could not be compelled to participate in the process

116 Section 23 of the above regulation provides that before the process could begin the perpetrator was required to submit a written statement to the Commission outlining their crime and their desire to participate in a CRP. Where there was evidence of a serious crime, the matter had to be adjourned and referred to the Office of the General Prosecutor.

117 Section 26.1 stipulates that in establishing the panel the Regional Commissioner should "endeavour to have appropriate gender representation within the Panel". This provision was necessary given that in most districts, political and spiritual leaders are male.

118 Judicial consideration of agreements was stipulated by section 28 of the above regulation. If the court approved and the perpetrator carried out their act of reconciliation, the court could grant the perpetrator immunity from civil and criminal actions: see sections 31-32. However, failure to fulfil the obligations in the agreement could incur imprisonment for up to a year or a fine up to $3000: section 30.

119 Executive Summary, p 23. Note that 1541 depositions were made.

120 *Chega!*, Part 9, para 153.

Burgess speculates that this may be "the only face of justice" that many East Timorese have seen since independence.[121] According to the *Chega!* report, some community leaders believe the process has helped to reinvigorate local customary law.[122] At the same time the process involved the training of approximately 1000 East Timorese locals as panel members in basic skills in mediation and dispute resolution.[123]

The process has been hailed as a success[124] and there are now calls for the process of community-based reconciliation to continue.[125] Part of its success can be attributed to its ability to harness local customary law procedures and the participation of local spiritual leaders. While it was a state mechanism of transitional justice, it was clearly a grass-roots approach to justice.

The relative success of CAVR's CRPs raises the question as to whether the idea of state-sanctioned local fora dealing with minor criminal offences is simply a pipe dream or a concrete proposal that may reduce the burden on Timor-Leste's state court system so that it can deal with serious offences. The CRP has provided a good testing ground for the efficacy of this hybrid model. It has carved out a relatively cheap and fast, state-sanctioned path by which perpetrators can seek reconciliation both with the living and the dead in their communities. Civil society has shown some support for the model's future use as a 'first-option' complement to the state court system.[126]

---

[121] Patrick Burgess, "Justice and Reconciliation in East Timor: The Relationship Between the Commission for Reception, Truth and Reconciliation and the Courts" (2004) 15 Criminal Law Forum 135 at 153, 157. See also *Chega!*, Part 9, para 143.

[122] *Chega!*, Part 9, para 52.

[123] *Chega!*, Part 9, para 153.

[124] According to Patrick Burgess, a mid-programme survey was conducted in 2003. Interviews with CRP participants were positive, with 90% of interviewees saying they were satisfied with the results of the CRP. While every interviewed perpetrator felt the process had helped to repair their relationship with the conununity, a majority of interviewed victims stated that the process had assisted the level of community respect accorded to them and enabled an understanding of the perpetrator's motivations. See Burgess, "Justice and Reconciliation in East Timor: The Relationship Between the Commission for Reception, Truth and Reconciliation and the Courts" (2004) 15 Criminal Law Forum 135 at 151–152. See also JSMP, Unfulfilled Expectations: Community Views on the CAVR's Community Reconciliation Process, Dili, August 2004 and Piers Pigou, *The Community Reconciliation Process of the Commission for Reception, Truth and Reconciliation* (Report for UNDP Timor-Leste) (April 2004).

[125] See *Chega!*, Part 9 at paras 173–174; see also JSMP, Unfulfilled Expectations: Community Views on the CAVR's Communify Reconciliation Process, Dili, August 2004, pp.15, 41–42.

[126] La'o Hamutuk writes that it would support "the creation of a system of alternative dispute resolution for minor crimes and grievances, perhaps similar to the community reconciliation processes used by CAVR": Reviewing the East Timor Commission for Reception, Truth and Reconciliation (CAVR) (2003) 4/5 The Lao Harnutuk Bulletin 1 at 1. See www.laohamutuk.org/Bulletin/2003/Nov/bulletinv4n5.html#cavr<last accessed 21 November 2006.

Now it is incumbent on the Government of Timor-Leste to give some serious consideration to this proposal, as state endorsement is essential.

It is most likely that some modifications may need to be made to the CAVR's CRP model if it is to be used as a first-option for hearing minor criminal offences and perhaps also for civil matters. For example, it may be necessary to make the applicable criminal penalties heavier so as to have a greater deterrent effect.[127] This in turn may require a higher level of investigation, and greater respect for procedural safeguards. The district courts would need to step in and deal with the case if participants refuse this first-level option or want to appeal its decisions.[128] A legal advisor in each district could advise panels and participants as to procedural safeguards and monitor proceedings.[129] Furthermore, more work may need to be done in encouraging the participation of women.[130] Even though female Regional Commissioners set a good example, few women reportedly participated in the CRPs either as victims or as perpetrators.[131] Such modifications should be determined by consultation with all the key actors, governmental and non-governmental, in this field.

---

127 The CAVR did not see its role as one of punishing deponents. Instead, it sought to facilitate reconciliation and for this reason the 'acts of reconciliation' imposed by CRP panels were relatively lenient. They included the reparation of public buildings, the erections of a village flagpole and tree planting: see *Chega!* Part 9, paras 80, 112, 134 and p 22. Unlike the CAVR's CRP, the proposed model would be dealing with ordinary minor offences rather than minor offences that took place on a massive scale during a time of conflict. This different context would require not only an act of reconciliation but also the imposition of heavier penalties because of the higher likelihood of repetition. In this regard, suspended sentences may be appropriate but the punishment of imprisonment may be more appropriate for a District Court to dispense. Corporal punishment is unconstitutional pursuant to sections 30(4) and 25(5) of the Constitution.

128 The difficulty in ensuring that adequate records of matters are kept means that hearings should be held de novo in the District Court in the case of an appeal.

129 This legal advisor would need to be well versed in the relevant constitutional principles that provide safeguards to parties.

130 Some consideration would need to be given to the composition of the panels. The panels could comprise members elected to the suco council, although this may raise separation of powers issues. Note that East Timor's 2004 Law on Election of Suco Chiefs and Suco Councils reserves a minimum of three seats for women on each suco council. Decisions should be made by consensus or by majority vote.

131 See JSMP, *Unfulfilled Expectations: Community Views on the CAVR's Community Reconciliation Process* (August 2004), pp.37–39 and 48, Monika Schlicher, East Timor Faces Up to its Past: The Work of the Commission for Reception, Truth and Reconciliation (Watch Indonesia!, Missio 2005) p 25. Schlicher points out that, while some women were prevented from giving public testimony by their husbands, others simply had to fulfil duties at home or were spoken for by a male 'head of household'. According to *Chega!*, women comprised 21.4% of all deponents: Annex 2, Data and Statistical Methods, para 13. Note that a minimum of thirty per cent of regional commissioners were required to be women: section 11. I of UNTAET Regulation No. 2001/10 On the Establishment of a Commission for Reception, Truth and Reconciliation in East Timor UNTAET/REG/2001/10 (2001).

Overall, Timor-Leste's state leaders need to consider an overhaul of its state justice system so as to integrate forms of local practices to complement the work of state courts.[132] It is apparent that local leaders and civil society have the capacity to, and the interest in, developing some less formal parts of Timor-Leste's justice system as a first-level option for both civil and criminal matters. It is also apparent that the state court system is over-burdened and near crisis point.

It is valuable to note that informal models of justice are gradually taking root in Western legal systems as Western legislators realise the benefits of recognising and incorporating them.[133] In addition, indigenous mechanisms are being incorporated into state legal systems. For example, in Australia, Aboriginal Courts have been established in many regions that enable Aboriginal elders to participate in the sentencing of Aboriginal offenders who have pleaded guilty,[134] through the form of a sentencing circle. Like the CRP, these are hybrid models that link elements of local customary law with state mechanisms.

7. Caution

Before concluding, it is necessary to sound some caution in relation to two main aspects of this proposal. First, as President Gusmao warned in his opening speech at the Asia Foundation conference in 2003, traditional forms of justice can carry dangers that impact most heavily on the most vulnerable sections of society. These dangers arise from the potential for arbitrariness, bias and corruption. However, these dangers are a strong reason favouring state intervention and the extension of its control over local customary law

[132] Such proposals for integrating local practices with the state justice system have been made in regard to other transitional countries, such as Afghanistan, that do not enjoy strong state legal systems. See Ali Wardak, "Building a Post-War Justice System in Afghanistan" (2004) 41 Crime, Law and Social Change 319.

[133] Informal justice mechanism in the criminal context include victim/offender mediation, family group conferencing, victim assistance programmes, victim offender panels, and plea bargaining. See generally Hilary Astor and Christine Chinkin, *Dispute Resolution in Australia* (2002). See also John Braithwaite, *Crime, Shame and Reintegration* (1989); Heather Strang and John Braithwaite (eds), *Restorative Justice: Philosophy to Practice* (2000).

[134] There is much variation between these courts in the regions of Australia. For example, in Victoria these courts are called "Koori courts": see Magistrates' Court (Koori Court) Act 2002 (0ic) and <www.magistratescourt.vic.gov.au> last accessed 22 November 2006. In South Australia some of these courts are called "Nunga courts" but they have no specific legislative basis. In New South Wales these courts are known as "sentencing circles". In Western Australia, Aboriginal courts known as "community courts" are being set up following recommendations of a recent Western Australian Law Reform Commission report into Aboriginal customary law and the justice system. For this report, see <www.lrc.justice.wa.gov.au/> last accessed 22 November 2006.

through research, resources, and legislation.[135] Timor-Leste's history makes it clear that local people would prefer to use local customary practices than court systems based on alien western principles, and they will continue to do so in an unsupervised manner, despite the dangers, unless the state becomes party to the process. The oft-cited risks in integrating indigenous or informal forms of justice are that it may lead to the operation of different standards of justice, or the possibility of forum shopping. But this danger is already present in the current situation where traditional practices operate unsupervised and defendants face the possibility of double jeopardy. These dangers will not disappear if the state simply turns a blind eye. Thus it is best for the state to attempt to reach out to informal justice and regulate it using some of the various safeguards that have been devised in order to protect the most vulnerable sections of society. For example, Article 2(4) of the Constitution states that local norms cannot be contrary to the Constitution (and its bill of rights) or the international (human rights) conventions incorporated into state law by the Constitution. The gradual introduction of constitutional human rights norms into the local sphere through training and education programmes should assist in protecting the most vulnerable sections of society. In addition, state supervision and registration of mediated disputes may lead to better enforcement: the problem of poor enforcement has marked and undermined the force of local customary law, particularly in the area of domestic violence.[136]

A second reason for caution is that the proposal requires the extension of state control.

This may be a tall order for a relatively inexperienced transitional government to deliver. However, the groundwork already performed by the CAVR's process of community reconciliation bodes well on this front and the proposal will take some pressure off the over-burdened state court system. More critically, this extension of state control may put the state into a collision

[135] Note that the CRP's model demonstrates that the codification of local customary law is not necessary and that some flexibility in the incorporation of local customary procedures is essential for the purposes of local participation and acceptance.

[136] Aisling Swaine comments that: 'Local justice has little power to enforce its ruling, whether that is in regard to the compensation payment or the prevention of further violence. Men are not forced to take responsibility for their violent acts...': Swaine, International Rescue Society, Traditional Justice and Gender Based Violence (August 2003). Note that in the area of domestic violence, women should continue to have an option between using the court system at the first level or having the matter resolved locally through mediation. See Laura Grenfell, "Legal Pluralism and the Rule of Law in Timor-Leste" (2006) 19 Leiden Journal of International Law 305 at 333–334 and 327. See also JSMP, *The Law of Gender-Based Violence in Timor-Leste, April–November 2005* (February 2006).

course with strong forces in civil society, parts of which may object to constitutional norms overriding traditional norms. This will require the exercise of much skill and sensitivity on the part of the state: proper consultation with all key players is essential to overcome this challenge.

8. Conclusion

The challenges currently facing the state legal system in Timor-Leste threaten to undermine judicial legitimacy and to encourage people to take law into their own hands. An opportunity was lost in the constitution-making process to avert this possibility through the clear recognition and integration of local customary law into state law. This moment was not fully realised and the consequence is that the Constitution looks prematurely irrelevant as a map of justice. However, recent developments such as the CAVR and civil society projects indicate that the prospects for the integration of local customary law into the formal legal system are strong. The models demonstrate that customary law is not necessarily inimical to human rights principles and that local customary law has something beneficial to offer Timor-Leste's state justice system. While more work needs to be done in order to reconcile local customary norms and human rights norms, a path has already been sketched out.

Justice in East Timor: Super-Naturally-Based Local Enforcement Systems Focusing on Renewable Natural Resources

James T. Thomson

I. Introduction

This paper starts not with the courts, law and legislation, but rather with critical problems in the governance and management of three cornerstone East Timorese Renewable Natural Resources (RNR): forests and arable soils as two linked RNR on the one hand, and fisheries on the other. The paper poses the following problem: what kinds of institutional arrangements might best enable the East Timorese – citizens, resource users, and state officials, including those associated with the justice sector – to control destructive overuse of these valuable RNR that could threaten their sustainability. These resources can properly be considered "cornerstone" in the sense that they provide essential inputs to Timorese human production systems – forestry, agriculture and fishing. Thousands of East Timorese base their livelihoods on these resources and, in uncertain times, will have few resources upon which to fall back if these resources fail.

The threat of overuse has been, since time immemorial, the classic problem in RNR Governance and Management (hereinafter "RGM"). When demand for an RNR exceeds supply, i.e., the flow of "resource or use units"[1] that a

[1] Elinor Ostrom makes a useful distinction between *resource systems* and *resource units*, in the context of the following observation:

> Resource systems are best thought of as stock variables that are capable, under favorable circumstances, of producing a maximum quantity of a flow variable without harming the stock or the resource system itself. Examples of resource systems include fishing grounds, groundwater basins, grazing areas, irrigation canals, bridges, parking garages, mainframe computers, and streams, lakes, oceans and other bodies of water. Resource units are what individuals appropriate or use from resource systems. Resource units are typified by the tons of fish harvested from a fishing ground, the acre feet or cubic meters of water withdrawn from a groundwater basis or an irrigation canal ... the central processing units consumed by

specific RNR can produce in a given place in a given time period, then resource degradation will inexorably follow. Only three ways exist to avoid this negative outcome: (1) institute and enforce a stint that brings demand back into balance with supply; or (2) identify and apply RNR enrichment strategies that increase the supply and so reestablish the balance with demand; or (3) adopt a combination of the two approaches – stint *and* enrichment – to address successfully an overuse problem.

A key assumption of this paper is that both stint and enrichment approaches depend for their ultimate success on *robust, reliable institutional arrangements* that permit communities (a) to establish rules that define clearly approved forms of behavior concerning access to and exploitation of threatened RNR, and to apply those rules both to their own members and, as well, to outsiders who want to use the renewable natural resources in question.

Though easily stated, these are not trivial problems. Solutions can and must be imagined; but the test of a putative "solution" is its *feasibility* in practice, within the constraints set by user group, community and national government capacities (and those of any intermediate governance instances). As will be discussed below, the essential challenge is not "coming up with a set of formal rules," but thinking through ways – reliable ways – in which any possible set of rules – institutional arrangements – can be translated into practice, i.e., converted into *working rules* (Commons: 143–53), that incorporate the monitoring, enforcement, sanctioning, resource mobilization and "fine-tuning" processes and functions essential to convert formal into *working* rules.

In a new country such as East Timor, with comparatively weak and, in the very recent past, unstable representative, technical and judicial institutions at the national level, one can reasonably anticipate that these kinds of non-trivial problems will pose enormous challenges that may well exceed the capacity of national institutions to solve.[2] The question then becomes: are there any alternatives to or supports for national institutions that might render these challenges more manageable?

> those sharing a computer system ... The distinction between the resource as a stock and the harvest of use units as a flow is especially useful in connection with *renewable* resources, where it is possible to define a replenishment rate. As long as the average rate of withdrawal does not exceed the average rate of replenishment, a renewable resource is sustained over time. (Ostrom, 1990: 30)

[2] As of early April 2007, the Government of East Timor was still struggling with the problem of establishing basic governance arrangements (Mydans).

The answer that this essay proposes[3] by way of alternatives to national institutions is *local institutional capital,* i.e., the rules, procedures and processes – institutional arrangements – that indigenous groups – clans, communities, RNR user groups and the like – have established and applied over the centuries. Such arrangements typically evolve over time in response to changing conditions.

While no more perfect than formal institutions, local institutional arrangements typically offer significant advantages in certain situations. They are often well adapted to local circumstances; they are often also thoroughly understood by many stakeholders involved in or affected by their operations in light of long years of interactions that those same stakeholders have conducted within such arrangements.

If one is seeking to promote or consolidate a *rule of law* system, one can posit that there might well be a strategic advantage in beginning with rules that people already understand, in terms of their weak points, the costs and advantages of using them, etc. From the perspective of a potential *rule of law* actor or stakeholder, *knowing what to expect from a system amounts to a risk management device.* A programmatic commitment to replacing local institutional capital with new, state-created sets of institutional arrangements with which few if any local stakeholders have much experience can easily, at least in the initial stages (two decades?) merely *intensify the risks* to which local users might expose themselves by invoking those rules. Telling illustrations of that issue, viewed from the perspective of local rural rule users in East Timor, are documented in Urresta (Nixon *et al.*, 2004) *passim,* especially p. 18, which presents Figure 36, below, illustrates some of the other perceived advantages of such local institutional capital.

Note particularly the last item in Figure 36, "Easiest to Understand," which reveals a decided preference for "Traditional System" over "Court System" (83.2% v. 5%). For a number of highly rational reasons detailed in previous questions in that figure and related not just to familiarity with institutional arrangements but also reflecting litigants' evaluations of a range of transactions costs found in both systems (cheapest, limited travel, quick turn-around, least corrupt, and best at promoting reconciliation, i.e., settling problems through proceedings that offer litigants high assurance that their problem *will stay settled* so that they can get on with their lives rather than expending more resources on bickering with each other) rural residents place high value on those local institutional arrangements for mediation.

[3] This answer is based on applied qualitative research conducted in 2005 in six rural sites scattered across East Timor.

Figure 36: Do local systems or courts offer the highest quality of service in the range of areas presented below? (Q51)

Question 51 Key persons Admin – 101 respondents

Which System is Best

Area of Service	Traditional Total	%	Court System Total	%	Neither Total	%	No Answer Total	%
Fairest System	48	47.5%	40	39.6%	1	1.0%	12	11.9%
Cheapest System	87	86.1%	3	30%	2	2.0%	9	8.9%
Least Amount of	87	86.1%	2	20%	1	1.0%	11	10.9%
Fast and Efficient	76	75.2%	13	12.9%	2	2.0%	10	9.9%
Least Corrupt System	58	57.4%	21	20.8%	10	9.9%	12	11.9%
The Most Respect for	41	40.6%	39	38.6%	8	7.9%	13	12.9%
Promotes Reconciliation between Conflicting	79	78.2%	11	10.9%	1	1.0%	10	9.9%
Easiest System to Understand	84	83.2%	5	5.0%	0	0.0%	12	11.9%

Many such local institutional arrangements, as this essay will argue, are reasonably well designed, efficient and effective. But they do have their weaknesses. It is here where well designed state interventions can make signal contributions by strengthening existing local institutional capital and, in the process, creating opportunities for national governments to "burden shed" or off load responsibilities from their institutions, some of the institutions of which may be stretched close to the breaking point, to more robust local institutions. Such shifts of responsibility, as this paper will argue, may incorporate attractive incentives for local communities and RNR users in the sense that both may find themselves in a position to exercise more effective stewardship over local RNR that they value highly than could the national government working alone.

It is, however, even more likely that local RGM efforts will require occasional support from national government institutions to consecrate the authority of local institutional capital and those who operate such institutions, and to provide them the legitimacy and back-up support that they require to function efficiently. Such opportunities to exploit institutional design opportunities to strengthen overall (hybrid national/local) systems so that they can better serve citizens are more common than is often supposed. Capitalizing on such opportunities is not without special costs, *e.g.*, those who want to engage in effective institutional design must be willing to take the time necessary to understand how such institutions function, their strengths, weaknesses, levels of public support, and ways in which they can be strengthened, rendered more accountable. But the payoffs of those investments can be rewarding, particularly when they enable citizens to play greater roles in self-governance and RNR stewardship.

The paper contains four sections beyond (1) this introduction: (2) an analytic framework that identifies six functions that robust, effective local institutional arrangements must carry out; (3) a description of the context in which forestry/arable soils and fisheries RNR problems occur in contemporary East Timor; (4) an examination of three case studies that shed light on the workings of local institutional arrangements, their strengths and the sources of their weaknesses; (5) conclusions drawn from the case studies and their implications for approaches that the Government of Timor-Leste (GOTL) might adopt to enable RNR users to serve as better, more effective stewards of the RNR upon which they and their families depend for survival.

II. Analytic Framework

At certain risk of belaboring the obvious, let me begin with a commonplace observation: *laws do not apply themselves*[4]. All functional legal systems must therefore solve six generic problems, including (1) establishing a set of rules that can be applied. Once rules are established, if they are to play any role in shaping desired behavior, *e.g.*, promoting RNR stewardship and discouraging undesirable behavior such as RNR overuse, degradation and eventual destruction (2) *somebody* has to monitor the behavior of those meant to comply with the rules and, in instances of identified infractions, (3) somebody must mete out punishments. (4) Somebody must also resolve any disputes arising from enforcement proceedings ("I *didn't* do it!" or "Yes, I'm guilty but the penalty you're imposing is *unjust!*") in a way that the parties find "reasonable" (just, equitable, not so costly as to preclude fair access by the less well off, etc.) and that will elicit their acceptance and support. In addition, (5) results of monitoring and enforcement proceedings must be regularly disseminated so that those willing to comply in good faith with the rules know that in so doing they're not behaving as feckless "suckers," i.e., stinting while others ride free on their sacrifices (Elinor Ostrom, 1995: 97).

[4] There are few exceptions to this assertion. One might cite queuing among West African sahelian pastoralists, several groups of whom not infrequently arrive with their thirsty herds at a well at roughly the same time. Despite the obvious sounds of distress emanating from cattle that have not had water for 48 hours, pastoralists respect the queue without any interventions by the national *gendarmes*. But this example doesn't really invalidate the assertion if one remembers that the pastoralists in question are all armed in one way or another and queue-jumping, under the circumstances, is a fighting offence.

Carrying out those five functions successfully implies that the user group, community, local government, state or other entity that has devised the rules is also (6) capable of mobilizing the resources – manpower, money, materials – required to make rules, monitor compliance with them, sanction identified infractions, resolve disputes and disseminate information in a timely fashion about the results of monitoring and enforcement operations. In a new country like East Timor, with weak national and regional institutions, governmental instability at the national level (Mydans: A3) and, at least initially, limited resources at that level, it's not obvious that the national government can regularly and reliably mobilize the human and material resources necessary to carry out these six indispensable functions. If, as currently seems the case in East Timor, lawyers, judges and trained, reliable police are scarce human resources, it is not clear that upgrades in legal system efficacy, efficiency and "justice" can be achieved with any degree of certainty over the short term through formal, national-level governmental agencies.

This raises, at least by implication, the question of whether, in East Timor, alternatives exist to *national government* rule-making, monitoring, enforcement, dispute resolution, information dissemination and mobilization of the resources required to carry out these six functions. The answer to that question, revealed by qualitative applied research conducted in 2005 under auspices of the USAID-financed Land Law Project on the *governance* and management of common property renewable natural resources in rural areas spread across the country is, quite simply, "yes" (Thomson *et al.*, 2005, *passim*). The renewable natural resources (RNR) in question range from those best described as *fugitive* (*e.g.*, fish) to those clearly more *stable* (forests). The RNR governance and management (RGM)[5] perspective adopted in this paper offers potentially useful insights concerning approaches to sustainable stewardship of RNR and ways in which the national government of Timor Leste might more reliably promote and achieve preferred outcomes in RNR stewardship.

The paper examines particularly the extent to which existing local institutional arrangements might provide reliable frameworks through which

[5] While "NRM" – natural resources management – is a more familiar acronym than "RGM," a consensus growing among those who view themselves as RNR professional managers recognizes that many of the most critical obstacles to better outcomes are "political" and "institutional" in nature – *e.g.*, land and RNR tenure rules; empowerment of resource users to play diverse roles in the *governance* and management of the RNR they exploit; policy issues, such as whether or not to establish enabling frameworks that encourage RNR users to take greater responsibility for stewardship of the renewable resources upon which they depend for survival, etc. [USAID, 2002: Nature, Wealth and Power, *passim*.]

the six RGM functions noted above could be regularly and robustly implemented, and ways in which the central government might support local people's efforts to shoulder responsibility for RGM activities. If innovations in this regard appear feasible, this raises the possibility of *positive sum* "burden shedding." Through this policy process, the central government could divest itself of certain day-to-day functions by devolving to a variety of local communities, local government unit leaders, non-governmental professionals and RNR user groups responsibility for the bulk of RGM activities, while retaining *oversight* and *back-stopping functions* (in particular for enforcement and technical assistance). Oversight, if real and effective, can be helpful in establishing for local RGM officials incentives to conduct themselves as true stewards of the RNR user group's or community's interest in ensuring the sustainability of target renewable resources. The knowledge that authorized outsiders will, from time to time, ask pointed questions about the "health" of the resource in question constitutes an incentive[6] to discourage local RGM officials from ceding to the temptation to enrich themselves at the expense of other members of the group or community through authorizing, *e.g.*, formally illegal harvesting of the target RNR.

III. Forests, Arable Soils and Fisheries: The Contexts of Three RNR with Critical Roles in East Timor's Future

Forests, Arable Soils and Agriculture

The importance of such institutional innovations arises not only from the current weakness of East Timor's central government technical ministries and associated agencies, but from a serious negative dynamic powered by three distinct factors: the country's typology, its dominate agricultural system and a reported increase in the population growth rate following East Timor's second independence in 1999, when the Indonesian occupiers withdrew and thousands of East Timorese guerrilla fighters were able, after a quarter

[6] Note that the existence of such an "incentive" does *not* guarantee that local RGM officials will not from time to time cede to the temptation to profit from illicit exploitation of an RNR, for the stewardship of which they bear prime responsibility. Particularly as such resources – coastal fish, tropical hardwoods and the like – gain in value as demand presses upon supply rational people must anticipate these kinds of incidents. Those who think they can may well bend, or try to bend, RGM rules. Under such circumstances survival, much less sustainability of valued RNR may well become problematic (Klare: 202-08 for examples drawn inter alia from Borneo; Thomson *et al.*, 2004, *passim,* for cases from Indonesia, Democratic Republic of Congo, and ten other Asian and African countries).

century's absence, to return to their loved ones. We examine each of these points in turn.

Typology: East Timor is, to put it mildly, a rugged country. Seventy percent (70%) of the land surface is distributed on slopes of 40% gradient or greater. Annual precipitation ranges between 500 mm on the drier north coast and 2,000 mm in some of the mountains. Even at the lower end of that rainfall range, soil erosion on 40% slopes can threaten sustainability of agricultural production systems, most particularly when vegetative cover has been stripped from the land, as an official publication of the country's Ministry of Agriculture, Forestry and Fisheries notes:

> The topography consists of a narrow plain around the coast and a central mountain range dominating the country. The north coast is the driest area with some 500 mm of rain while the highlands can have over 2000mm.
>
> The steep slopes that dominate most of the country with heavy rainfall translate into heavy erosion once the tree cover is removed. Deforestation (due to sandal wood cutting, fires, land clearing, or goats eating the young plants) initiates a process of land destruction that is very difficult to reverse or even stop. (East Timor: 1)

Dominant Agricultural Systems: Slash and burn hillside agriculture and bottomland irrigated rice production systems both depend heavily on ensuring reforestation of exhausted hill soils rotated out of production and into fallow. Trees, bushes and grasses can all help stabilize soils on steep slopes and encourage percolation of water into hillside soils and thus into the aquifers that channel water productively into the springs, creeks and rivers. These supply, among other services, water to irrigated perimeters. Without woody and vegetative cover on hillsides, heavy rains can transport tons of soil off those slopes through sheet and gully erosion. Soils eroded from such terrain end up in irrigated perimeters, where they often smother the country's most productive agricultural surfaces in sand and gravel.

Swidden Agriculture: the Essentials

The logic of swidden or slash and burn agricultural systems is that trees felled and burned on newly opened fields release nutrients that their extensive root structures allow them to recover from soil depths well below those commonly exploited by crop roots (a.k.a. "nutrient pumping"). Such systems work either well or with acceptable efficacy in producing staple food crops so *long as fallows last the number of years required to allow trees to capture nutrients necessary to fertilize crops,* and if farmers can somehow stabilize exposed soils *in situ*. Agroforestry systems, which combine trees and field crops, often achieve the latter outcome with reasonable efficiency.

The two systemic weak points of swidden systems are those just mentioned: fallows of length insufficient to ensure release of adequate nutrients on farm fields when farmers burn felled trees, and mechanisms inadequate to stabilize surface water flows in ways that both protect soils/encourage production and encourage percolation.

Population Growth: When populations are stable and man/land ratios low, organizing fallows of length sufficient to restore woody vegetation and thus natural nutrients poses few insurmountable problems. But rising population growth rates threaten the equilibria of such arrangements. As populations grow in agricultural economies such as East Timor's, in the absence of alternative (generally urban) employment possibilities or effective agricultural intensification schemes, pressures on the land intensify, crop yields rapidly dwindle, and impoverished farmers shorten fallows as they find themselves compelled to move on to new lands more quickly. Once the lower, gentler slopes have been fully claimed and/or exploited, the search for new fields leads people inexorably into steeper and more fragile environments. Clearing steeper lands in turn poses a new range of virulent threats to system stability.

A Standard Strategy to Counter Negative Land Use Dynamics: These three factors can predictably lead to the negative dynamics mentioned above. One common strategy to break the cycle of negative dynamics associated with overusing steep lands typically involves efforts to change the shape of slopes through terracing. This kind of civil engineering takes a slope and converts it into a "stepped" series of flat surfaces by introducing:

- vegetative bunds (bands of soil constructed on the contour and usually covered with grass [*Vetiver is* a favorite in tropical areas] and/or shrubs and trees),
- agroforestry interventions that combine trees and crops in ways that stabilize soils,
- cultivation on the contour and in-field soil manipulations such as tied ridges, and/or
- other formal soil erosion control works.

This "simple" engineering change of terracing a slope can radically modify not only the dynamics of surface water management and soil erosion, but create opportunities for green (vegetative matter) and brown (livestock waste products) manuring options while simultaneously enhancing the economic feasibility of chemical fertilization. The ideal scenario complements terracing with a range of permanent forage crops (trees and bushes) created on those terraces which provide feed for domestic livestock that could, in turn, generate manure to fertilize fields. Introducing livestock into nutrient recycling processes, while simultaneously creating flat surfaces cultivated along contoured furrows subdivided by tied ridges that the farmer constructs at intervals across each furrow to capture and stabilize surface water flows creates an "engineered" natural system that enables farmers to capitalize their investments in applications of chemical fertilizers (to supply missing nutrients) that complement nutrients already present in locally-produced green and brown manures, rather than watch both natural and chemical fertilizers disappear off steep slopes with eroding top soils.

The weakness in this approach is that it fails to address a standard problem in watershed governance and management: water flows downhill and, as Chairman Mao was reported to have argued in Communist China, based on his observations of the watershed management experiences of the community of Tachai, it makes no sense to install soil and water erosion control infrastructure on lower reaches of a watershed if the upper reaches haven't already been treated so that surface water flows can be controlled and will not wash out terraces, bunds and other erosion control structures lower down.

Fisheries

Fisheries play a not insignificant role in the standard East Timorese diet. Yet inshore fisheries on the country's long coastline are threatened by the depredations of paired trawlers operating huge, weighted seine nets which they drag along the bottom to dislodge and capture all forms of fish life. In so doing they devastate the ocean floor fisheries habitat in which a variety of species grow to maturity. It would appear that the Government of East Timor concluded a verbal agreement in 2006, apparently with either a Thai or a Taiwanese fishing company. The agreement would seem to authorize this form of destructive fishing, which could be expected to occasion two negative consequences for East Timor's population. First, insofar as the projected destruction of coastal fisheries occurs it will materially reduce fishing opportunities available to Timorese artisan fishers whose small boats are probably best suited in any case to fishing coastal waters since they can easily regain land in the event of inclement weather, and may well not be seaworthy in off-shore waters during such conditions. Second and quite apart from the loss of employment, while the government may recover some revenue under this arrangement in the form of licensing fees collected from non-national fishing firms authorized to fish East Timor's coastal waters, there is a serious question whether those revenues outweigh the loss of fish protein in the diets of urban and rural East Timorese, particularly those in the poorer classes. Fish taken by foreign vessels are far more likely marketed in the home countries of those vessels, where citizens' purchasing power is greater, rather than in East Timor.[7]

The same coastal fisheries subject to destructive over fishing by foreign trawlers can likewise be threatened if rivers emptying into the sea from the country's hilly uplands transport so much bedload (soil, sand, gravel, rocks) that they progressively bury fertile habitats – spawning grounds and fingerling nursery sites.

Regulating access to these coastal inshore fisheries and controlling the capture gear used in such areas raises a series of problems beyond the capacity of most coastal fisher communities to tackle.[8] These include legally establishing and patrolling a national coastal domain so that ships using fishing gear of high capture potential (with simultaneously devastating effects on in-shore fisheries) can be legally precluded from fishing in national waters and destroying productive fish habitat, and then putting in place a coast guard force capable of enforcing those regulations.

On the other hand, East Timor does have some coastal lagoons, many of which incorporate mangrove swamps. These lagoon habitats frequently serve as nurseries both for crustaceans like shrimp and anadramous fish species that leave their normal saltwater habitat to breed in fresh or brackish waters. These fisheries, while a specialized subset of the larger-scale coastal fisheries, nevertheless contribute significantly to East Timor's fishery resources.

IV. Three illustrative Case Studies

This section provides brief descriptions of two (and a half) case studies. The first two deal with forestry RGM problems; the last highlights issues in fisheries governance and management. The intent in presenting these case studies is not to suggest that they are in any sense "modal" cases for East Timor. They do, however, illustrate a set of common problems involved in the challenge of ensuring that laws and rules, including those incorporated in

---

[7] Rod Nixon, personal communication. 21 January 2007.

[8] It is worth noting in this regard that efforts to protect coastal fisheries by reestablishing erstwhile systems of local stewardship, often under the control of community elders, have experienced enough success in regenerating fisheries in Palau and other countries in the Pacific's Micronesia Region that a number of Caribbean countries have followed suit, working with local communities to protect individual reefs. But these local systems do require outside back-up for enforcement actions (Pala: 1 ff.)

local level institutional arrangements, function effectively. People *must* meet these challenges if they wish to improve their stewardship of renewable natural resources. It is worth adding, in a law and development context, that solving these inter-linked challenge can create a foundation of stabilized relationships upon which more sophisticated institutional arrangements can be constructed. Among these are various value-adding processes that transform raw renewable resources into inputs for more sophisticated domestic and foreign economies and so establish conditions for job creation in processing industries that, over time, can significantly reduce direct demand for some RNR.

The cases also highlight types of enabling frameworks the East Timorese national government legislators could envisage if they desired to reinforce community and resource user group stewardship of some of the countries critical RNR.

IV.A. First Case Study: Forestry in Suco Leohitu[9]

It is important to begin by noting that because of Suco Leohitu's geographic circumstances the community confronts certain problems that many other East Timorese communities are spared. On the other hand, residents clearly benefit from other elements of the community's geographic setting. Leohitu is situated on East Timor's far western border. This places it within easy reach of East Timorese renegade militiamen who fled the country to take up residence in West Timor, a constituent part of Indonesia, in the aftermath of the United Nations-sponsored vote on independence in 1999. Members of these militia groups threw in their lot with the Indonesian colonizers and participated in the campaign of terror designed to ensure a "no" vote throughout East Timor on the question of "second independence." When the outcome took the form of a resounding affirmation by East Timorese of their desire for independence from Indonesia, militia members concluded their behavior had made them *persona non grata* in their own country and so they fled to West Timor, destroying property (particularly dwellings and domestic livestock) and lives in the border region as they went. Once installed in refugee camps in West Timor they discovered that the Government of Indonesia (GOI) had little intention of rewarding them for their services and apparently expected the

[9] Information presented in this case study is drawn from an appendix of "Initial Assessment, 'When the Ancestors Need Help:' Renewable Natural Resources and Institutional Design in Contemporary East Timor" entitled "TimorLeste Renewable Natural Resources Case Study No. 3: Community Forestry in Suco Leohitu, Balibo Subdistrict, Bobonaro District," pp.1–15. Land Law Project Deputy RNR Research Team Leader Carlos Alves and several Government of East Timor officials conducted the initial investigation of this case.

militiamen to figure out how to sustain themselves without (or with only limited) GOI handouts.

As Leohitu lands contain a large stock of mature tropical hardwoods, the community soon became a target of East Timorese renegade militiamen's armed, cross-border forays to fell and export valuable hardwood logs back into Indonesia (West Timor) where they could easily sell them to raise funds. This scale of problem, village leaders recognized, exceeded their capacities and required interventions by higher governmental levels (which they were actively soliciting at the time of this field work in November 2005).

The geographic circumstance that explained the community's forests was the very rich soils in the area, apparently volcanic in origin but, in any case, sufficiently rich that local fields can be cultivated for long periods without losing their fertility. Since fields do not have to be fallowed frequently, trees in forested areas within Leohitu's jurisdiction grow quite large (and so become very valuable).

Leohitu residents have, by their own account, taken full advantage of this situation, by establishing years ago policies prohibiting unauthorized felling of trees on village lands and requiring that all felled trees be replaced with new saplings. Fleeing East Timorese militiamen torched dwellings of villagers who had fled the conflict; 200 families of the latter returned while international NGOs were active in the area and received assistance in reestablishing themselves, but 600 other families came back after the NGOs had departed. Many of those families needed wood to reconstruct dwellings and farm building.

To deal with this situation village elders (*katuas*) established a rule that anyone wishing to fell a tree had to obtain authorization from the community council, and a council member had to accompany the felling party to guard against over-cutting. Villagers subsequently established a monitoring system staffed by individuals selected by each of the Leohitu lineages. While they were supposed to patrol village lands weekly, it seems likely that actual patrols occurred much more rarely. This seems, however, to have reflected the realities of the post-war situation: community farmers had no reason to clear more land than they had previously, council members closely controlled felling for house construction and, given the overall stability of the village landscape, any illicit felling would in any case be quickly remarked by someone in the population. So the monitoring system seems to have functioned irregularly if at all, but apparently without any ill effects on the community's stewardship of its forests.

During the post-war reconstruction, moreover, World Vision, an international NGO provided materials and training to community members in the propagation and planting out of forest species including mahogany (*Pterocarpus indica*), teak (*Tectona grandis*) and sandalwood. When the first 10,000 seedlings were ready to transplant, villagers sited them above all on field boundaries as a strategy to solidify their land tenure claims. During the site visit team members observed lines of flourishing saplings on field boundaries on community lands. This lends credibility to Leohitu leaders' account of their tradition of forest stewardship.

IV. B. Second Case Study: Forestry in Lore Reserved Forest[10]

This case highlights the powerful threat that market pressures can constitute to renewable natural resources – in this case a large forest – where institutional arrangements are so weak, whether local, national, or a combination of both, that they are incapable of effectively controlling access to and regulating harvesting of a specific renewable resource. When those who constitute potential users of the resource exist in poverty and market demand for the resource is already powerful and intensifying, prospects for long-term sustainability of that resource must be considered dim at best.

> The Lore Reserved Forest Area case study can accurately be characterized as a cautionary tale. It exemplifies in graphic detail the kind of rapid degradation of renewable natural resources that can be unleashed in rural settings in East Timor when a series of perverse incentives combine to overwhelm local interest in sustainable use of an environment (Case Study No. 5, p. 1).

East Timor's war for independence against occupying Indonesian forces gave rise to a cadre of hardened guerrilla fighters; those who survived the 25-year conflict presumably felt entitled to some recognition of their sacrifices to achieve the national public good of independence. The new Alkatiri government (20th May 2002–2006) acceded, however, to the UN forces' insistence that only literates should be accepted as soldiers in the new East Timorese army. Many of the guerrillas had either skipped a number of years

---

[10] Information presented in this case study is drawn from an appendix of "Initial Assessment, 'When the Ancestors Need Help:' Renewable Natural Resources and Institutional Design in Contemporary East Timor" entitled "Lore Reserved Forest, Case Study No. 5: Illegal Logging in Lore Reserved Forest, Designated for National Park Status, Lantern District, East Timor" pp.1–8. Land Law Project Deputy RNR Research Team Leader Carlos Alves and several Government of East Timor conducted field investigations of this case and formulated initial results. Lantern District borders the East Timor Sea in far southeastern East Timor.

of schooling or lost whatever literacy skills they may have had before they joined the clandestine movement. All those individuals were precluded as a matter of government policy from joining the new army.

This decision left most guerrillas, once demobilized, with few useful peacetime skills and precious few prospects of being able to support themselves and whatever families they had. In a remote rural area of far south-eastern East Timor, located in Lautem District near Lore Reserved Forest, demobilized guerrillas opted to return to their home communities where they took advantage of a legal authorization contained in UNTAET Regulation No. 17, of 2000. This rule permitted a family to clear three cubic meters (m^3) of wood annually to open a garden or field in a forest. Retired guerrillas resident in the forest itself or in neighboring areas rapidly cleared lands within Lore Reserved Forest Area, rich in old growth timber and biodiversity and slated to become a national park.

Residents of a community, *Suco Lore 1*, composed of some 90 families living in six different hamlets spread across community lands, are the source of information about this case and were interviewed in November 2005.

Failure of Local Efforts to Curtail Logging in Lore Reserve Forest

To prevent the looming destruction of this forest the six *chefes de aldeia* of *Suco Lore 1* established a *tarabando* (ritual prohibition) on cutting in September 2001. This action can be seen as evidence of community residents' and leaders' awareness of this developing tragedy of a common pool resource, where no one is making effective efforts to control access to the forest or regulate harvesting therein. Neither the community and its leaders nor, as we will shortly see, state officials, have been able to develop and operate meaningful *human* monitoring and enforcement arrangements to control access to Lore Reserved Forest and to regulate harvesting there.

In consequence, as popular belief has eroded in the power of departed ancestors to sanction the living for violating *tarabando* prohibitions,[11]

[11] Rod Nixon, a long-time observer/lapplied researcher concerning events in rural East Timor, expressed in a personal communication (21 January 2007), his sense that popular belief in the capacity of the ancestors to intervene in the affairs of the living was, essentially, "alive and well" in many parts of the country. The *intense* activity deployed by rural residents on All Hallow's Eve (31 October) in cemeteries throughout the country where their ancestors are interred tends to corroborate Nixon's observation. If this is the case, popular beliefs could offer a very useful element that might be utilized to strengthen RNR stewardship in many parts of the country.

temptations to cut wood to earn money for current family expenses (*e.g.*, children's school fees, manufactured goods not available locally) proved irresistible for some.

This paper takes the position that such behavior can only with extreme difficulty be considered "a moral failing." The men who cut, transform and sell timber in Lore Reserved Forest appear to be honoring a very common, strongly-felt human imperative to take care of their families. One can imagine that since the state has provided them with no competitive (and legal) alternative through which they might earn a living, most feel little compunction to desist.

Suco Lore 1 is located, furthermore, far from markets and has limited transportation infrastructure, so moving any locally produced, valuable products to the nearest markets also poses difficulties. When regional entrepreneurs – some allegedly based in Los Palos, capital of Lautem District – who own trucks with the capacity to transport raw logs, locally-fashioned planks and the like offered to pay cash at the stump for felled hardwoods, with payments ranging from $100/m^3$ for the cheapest varieties of timber (*Canarium spp*.) up to $250/m^3$ for redwood (*Pterocarpus indica*), teak (*Tectona grandis*) and even $400/m^3$ for ebony. Faced with these lucrative offers and few if any other economic opportunities, various residents, including the exclandestine fighters, entered into relationships with illicit timber merchants. A lively market, based on felling hardwoods in Lore Reserved Forest, quickly arose. To meet market demand and earn more cash, many residents by their own account and in violation of the LJNTAET rule, cleared more than one field or garden (i.e., more than the authorized 3 m^3/year).

Local loggers justified their actions in light of the usual practices of shifting cultivation (which the UNTAET regulation recognizes). To add fertilizer to the soils of newly cleared gardens and fields, farmers burn felled wood to release valuable minerals into the soil. Even if the trunk and larger branches of mature hardwoods are sold as raw wood or transformed into planks and other marketable commodities, the remaining smaller branches and litter provide more than enough wood to fuel fires in the newly created arable areas. From the perspective of locals wood sales simply provide an additional source of income, in cash rather than in subsistence crops.

In the absence of other economic opportunities, the pressure for residents to engage in such activities mounts. Under the circumstances, those who fail "to get while the getting is good" are in fact playing the role of fools. While heads of other families fell and sell timber to benefit their families, at least in the short run, those who stint expose their families to a future of confirmed poverty. Note that Suco Lore 1 residents estimate that if their behavior continues unmodified, they will have hollowed out Lore Reserve Forest by the end of 2008. They have a clear perception of the danger of abandoning principles of RNR stewardship and over-cutting Lore Forest.

Failure of National Efforts to Curtail Logging in Lore Forest

Up to June 2005 the national forestry department had but a single forester posted to Los Palos, capital of Lautem. During the intervening five months the department hired two additional civil servants and contracted two more private individuals. All five "foresters", however, are posted in Los Palos, lack transportation and communication equipment, and are, additionally, responsible for other large forests scattered across Lautem District, in which formally illegal logging occurs as well. To complicate matters, the Bacau District Court dismissed a case that foresters, the police and the national attorney general brought against an individual accused of transporting illicit logs. The officials' indictment asserted that the accused had violated three separate regulations, two emitted by UNTAET (banning both illegal logging and cutting in reserved areas and as well, Indonesian forestry regulations incorporated at independence into the corpus of East Timor's laws). The court nonetheless found that there was no legal basis for the indictment (perhaps legitimately, *e.g.*, on grounds of inadequate proof; it was not possible to obtain a copy of this decision while the team was in the area) and dismissed the charges. This case, widely discussed both following the initial arrest and after dismissal, has reportedly led many residents of Lautem District to conclude that the Government will not enforce laws against illegal logging and trafficking in illicit timber.

In consequence residents of Suco Lore 1 now take the position that they had better "get while the getting is good", meaning that in the absence of effective government monitoring and enforcement of any rules that might ban illegal logging, it seems pretty clear that there will be no meaningful official attempt to curtail logging in Lore Forest. That being the case, local residents who fell the most hardwoods will likely be most successful in enriching themselves in the short term. Many rural East Timorese anticipated that peace would bring opportunities for enrichment; logging seems, particularly in isolated areas of Lautem District, to offer the greatest prospect of achieving that objective.

Observations and Conclusions: Lore Forest Case

Belief in the supernatural power of the ancestors to punish those who violate the rules of conduct that the ancestors establish (with the ritual assistance of the current set of elders [*katuas*], some of who will likely also be local government officials) has waned in many parts of the country if not everywhere. Thus elders slaughtering animals to establish a ritual prohibition on a defined form of behavior, *e.g*., logging within the boundaries of Lore Reserve Forest, is a procedure that, in and of itself, will contribute little to any effort to establish order in exploitation of resources within the Forest. While official Government rules currently restrict cutting, those rules do not enforce themselves any more than do *tarabando*. The missing link in both cases is supplementary human monitoring, following by enforcement proceedings that local residents consider to be fair and reliable.

The Government of East Timor did establish, on April 14, 2004, Decree-Law No. 5/2004, entitled "On Community Authorities". It authorizes *chefe de suco* to carry out activities focused on "protection of the environment" (Section 2, No. 2, Para. f). This is a significant step in the right direction, insofar as it empowers communities to initiate action to address environmental problems that they identify. Beyond that, however, lie the problems of achieving consensus on *what to do,* then how to do it, including crafting rules for behavior with which community residents are comfortable, determining how to conduct monitoring, enforcement, dispute resolution and how to mobilize the resources necessary to conduct these activities.

Given the current market value in East Timor (and throughout south and southeast Asia) of wood as a commodity, and given the poverty that most residents of Suco Lore 1 experience on a daily basis, efforts by conscientious local leaders committed to ensuring the sustainability of Lore Reserve Forest may not produce positive results, at least from the leaders' perspective. Community leaders (elected officials, elders) would have to organize a human monitoring system to support *tarabando* established to control or ban cutting. If they succeeded, those accused of violating such rules would often reside, and vote, in the wards of elected officials. Accused persons would most likely plead poverty as a justification for their actions in violating a logging ban *tarabando* and with that plea would very likely obtain community empathy, particularly under current circumstances where "everybody is doing it".

This highlights a difficulty in enforcing rules initiated by local bodies: unless community sentiment supports them, the best-designed monitoring systems will very likely fail for lack of co-monitoring by community residents who are often the best informed about activities concerning RNR that they value. Rules imposed from the national level without prior consultation with residents will likely be regarded as opposed to community interests (although community leaders and even many followers might well grasp the long-term value of regulations that establish order and predictability in exploitation of RNR, as measures necessary to ensure renewable resource sustainability). Monitoring and enforcement of national rules might well suffer the same reluctance of community members to engage in co-policing. Unless official governments (national government, national government agencies such as the Forest Department, District and Sub-District administration divisions, elected community governments) can support their own RGM access and use rules with a minimum of reliable monitoring and enforcement, users will rapidly conclude that efforts to support national rules are rather pointless, even if some users might be willing to identify those who violate national rules.

Given the poverty that former guerrillas now resident in communities adjacent to Lore Forest confront, local leaders have petitioned the national government for economic assistance. As these communities are situated quite close to the East Timor Sea, Suco Lore 1 petitioners have specifically requested that local people be provided with fishing gear and training in its use. But this approach would create few if any direct incentives to discourage further unregulated logging within the reserve forest, and it would fail to capitalize on skills that local people already possess.

A more productive approach might involve the Government providing support in the form of subsidized financing for logging and wood processing equipment and careful training in its use. Such an approach would involve undeniable risks, but also create opportunities to change villagers' perceptions of their long-term interest in Lore Forest. If equipment and training were accompanied by information about the value of the processed wood products that they were producing, and assistance in moving those products to market, *e.g.*, through a producers' cooperative of the sort that coffee growers have utilized to their great economic benefit in East Timor, residents of communities adjacent to Lore Forest would have reason to strong economic reason to reassess their interest in and therefore their relationship to the forest. If they came to see it as a vital, potentially perennial source of inputs for local, lucrative wood processing enterprises, they might well conclude that making, monitoring and enforcing access and harvesting rules along lines developed by Leohitu residents, was very much in their self interest, and that uncontrolled logging and "hollowing out" of Lore Forest was simply no longer acceptable. A "cross-visit" that took a half-dozen notables from Suco Lore 1 to Leohitu for discussions with their counterparts there on the feasibility and organization of forest monitoring and enforcement systems might well provide all the "instruction" that Lore people would need.

At that point, it might well be possible to engage some of the ex-guerrillas, who lived and fought in Lore for 25 years, as monitors with a mandate perhaps to regulate access to Lore Forest, but certainly to control logging there.[12] External technical assistance, whether provided by Government foresters or external advisors, could be enlisted to develop a cutting plan for the forest, or sections of the forest that could be mapped using GIS technologies, registered and assigned to the nearest village. Making the permanent assignment of harvesting rights contingent on respect for the harvesting plan, and investment in reconstituting the forest with valuable species, *e.g.*, mahogany, sandalwood, teak and the like, might further clarify the interests of residents in organizing themselves to exert collective stewardship over their section of the forest.

The Government would clearly have to clarify rules concerning illegal logging, and ensure that they were applied in cases of infraction. Otherwise, residents of communities surrounding Lore Forest might well conclude that they had better "get while the getting is good", before others poached the timber for which they would, in any case, be held responsible.

The Government might enact, as well, enabling legislation that would permit communities surrounding the forest (and other groups elsewhere in the country interested in acquiring authority over valuable local RNR) to constitute special districts responsible for governing and managing specified sections of the forest. This legislation could be drafted to empower special districts to establish their own police forces that could work in tandem with policing units of national agencies, *e.g.*, foresters or fishery technicians.

IV.C. Third Case Study: Potential for Off-Loading National Government RGM Functions to Local Users and the Viability of Local Institutional Arrangements

This third case involves one of East Timor's coastal lagoon fisheries, Bemalae, situated 80 km west of the capital, Dili, on the country's north coast. The lagoon sits astride the boundary dividing Attabai and Balibo Subdistricts within Bobonaro District. Its size varies with the season but, during the height of the dry season, it probably measures little more than a hectare in extent.

[12] Rod Nixon notes (personal communication, 21 January 2007) that "Major-General Mike Smith, who helped plan the 1999 intervention and who served as Deputy Force Commander of the PKF contingent ... came up with the idea that ex-FALINTIL (guerrillas) should have been employed as forest guards ..." The logic of this approach obviously appealed to an individual with more experience in East Timor during a critical period than the author has.

Bemalae's productivity as a lagoon fishery derives from features of the natural system that creates it. The annual rainy season begins in this part of East Timor in November, gathers strength through December and January and then tapers off during February and March until the dry season begins in early April. As the rainy season gathers force, several streams pour fresh water into the lagoon until it fills. When fresh water fills Bemalae to the maximum extent it floods a woody "upstream" plain inland from the coast which serves as a fisheries spawning ground and "nursery". Usually in February, the fresh water flood also forces a short passage to the sea through the lowest point in the wide sand bar that seals the lagoon off from the ocean during eight months of the year. While the passage remains open (generally for about two months, into April), Bemalae fingerlings move down it to the sea and mature anadramous fish (principally mullet, mackerel and eel, plus tiger and white shrimp species) run upstream to spawn on the floodplain in their "home waters". In April, when the freshwater overflow from the lagoon has largely drained into the ocean, high tides deposit sand on the beach, sealing off the passage until the following February. This natural sequence traps in the lagoon a large number of mature fish. The spawning season thus draws a concentration of fish to the lagoon and creates an opportunity for large catches.

Kin Groups, Collective Property Rights and User Group Institutional Arrangements

An individual fisherman first established a claim to the lagoon some centuries ago. His descendants have fished the lagoon ever since. According to members of that descent group, no one who is not a member of their kin group ever attempts to fish in the lagoon, apparently because of concerns that "the ancestors" would punish such behavior, i.e., exploiting a collective resource belonging to another kin group. Thus at present there are no humanly-monitored and -enforced controls on access to Bemalae.[13]

The original claimant of the Bemalae lagoon figures as the founding elder of the clan. Two sub-clans (*uma lisan* in Tetum, East Timor's *lingua franca*) descended from the founding elder: *Fatuklaren,* the "senior" sub-clan and *Pasalaren,* the "junior" sub-clan. Leaders of those two groups long ago worked out institutional arrangements to control harvesting of fish in Bemalae.

[13] Kin group members report that a crocodile inhabits Bemalae, and that this animal is to some extent subject to ritual control by clan elders. While it appears never to attack clan members, knowledge that it inhabits the lagoon might well inhibit other would be fishers from exploiting the resource and thus serve as a non-human, non-ritual control on access. But because clan members share a strong sense that only kinsmen are allowed to fish in Bemalae, informal monitoring would appear to be effective: kinsmen can easily identify strangers and assert clan property rights to Bemalae.

These include the annual establishment of a *tarabando* (ritual prohibition) on fishing in the lagoon until the elders ritually lifted it through another clan ceremony. In times past, when most East Timorese believed in the power of the ancestors to punish their living descendents who violated the ancestors' rules, this system seems to have functioned reasonably well to regulate harvesting of the fish in Bemalae.

Mobilizing Resources for Ritualized Rule Making

Traditionally, responsibility for *leading* the *tarabando* rituals alternated year by year between the "senior" Fatuklaren and the "junior" Pasalaren sub-clans. But elders from both *uma lisan* always participated in these ceremonies, lending their joint prestige to the gravity of the proceedings. This ritual both reinforced all clan members' awareness of their heritage and neatly solved a resource mobilization problem inherent in making and lifting the *tarabando* prohibition on fishing in the lagoon.

Establishing the *tarabando,* and lifting it, required the immolation of two domestic animals (a cow and a pig) in order, according to clan beliefs, to engage the attention of the ancestors and "seal" their support for the regulation (or for its relaxation). Involving Fatuklaren and Pasalaren elders jointly in mobilizing money to acquire the animals appears in practice to have achieved rough equity among all members of the group in meeting the "tax burden" required to finance this RGM activity. Elders responsible for acquiring animals to sacrifice assigned "contributions" to each family unit within the lineage, based on their detailed, rich knowledge of the wealth of and the income received by each of the family units *that year.*

Elders in a belief system based on ancestor worship would appear to have strong incentives to treat all members of their kinship group as fairly as possible, to ensure that "their legacy" would be one of good memories and that living members of the kinship group would have solid reason to celebrate their memory and their good works after they have died. Members of each sub-clan, in turn, would be subject to strong social pressure from their kinsmen to meet their obligations to help finance purchase of the *tarabando* animals.

A Kinship Group Split Causes Possibly Negative Consequences for Fisheries RGM

History unfortunately intervened to upset this productive institutional arrangement. Causes and details of events described below are cloaked in clan taboos but the broad outlines are clear. At some point in the not recent past all members of the senior Fatuklaren *uma lisan* voluntarily left the fishing trade and physically removed from the sea coast to the hills in what is now Balibo subdistrict, where today they make their living as farmers. This has, over time, led to a split within the clan, as junior Pasalaren sub-clan members have remained settled near Bemalae and continue to earn their livings as fishermen.

The problem can be summarized as follows: Fatuklaren members return to Bemalae only for the annual clan "fish-in", the festival that follows the elders' annual lifting of the fishing ban sometime between late July and the end of August. Pasalaren members use cast nets to fish both the stream to the ocean and deeper parts of the lagoon. Normally they catch enough fish to make it worthwhile for fishmongers to attend the festival to buy fish wholesale for retailing elsewhere in the country. When Fatuklaren members descend from the hills to attend the festival, however, they only fish with sticks that they use to stun and then hand catch fish they find in shallower parts of the lagoon.

The fisheries RGM problem thus concerns primarily members of the Pasalaren (fishing) sub-clan. While they spend most of their fishing time working the open ocean coastal fishery, they presumably have an interest in being able to catch fish in Bemalae at night after days when they have boated too few fish in the ocean.[14] This presumptive illicit fishing, in violation of the clan *tarabando,* had led over time to reduced catches during the annual clan fish-in. Pasalaren members explain the decline in catches by reference to a rupture in sub-clan relations that dates to 1997, when elders of the senior clan "arrogated" to themselves authority to open and close the Bemalae fishing season, presumably because they suspected that their Pasalaren kinsmen were routinely violating the jointly established *tarabando*. Since that time establishing and lifting the *tarabando* have become politically sensitive actions. 2002 was the last time the *tarabando* was established.

Pasalaren fishers assert that the ancestors have caused the fish "to go away" from Bemalae because they are upset by this break-down in clan unity. Once elders of both sub-clans return to the hallowed practice of jointly establishing and lifting the *tarabando*, the fish will return. This sophistic explanation of smaller catches during clan fish-in enables Pasalaren fishers to continue to fish Bemalae at will as a convenient fisheries resource that is open access as far as Pasalaren sub-clan members are concerned. (Perhaps they consider this reasonable since the Fatuklaren are all full-time farmers anyway.) Despite a decade of effort to jump-start a return to the old practices, including one intervention by a Fatuklaren member of the Fisheries Department of the Ministry of Agriculture, Forestry and Fisheries (MAFF), the disagreement persists.

---

[14] Note that no Pasalaren sub-clan member was willing to discuss this issue. This characterization of the situation represents the author's speculation about the dynamics of the current situation.

Institutional Fragility and Covert Over-Fishing

This situation raises several interesting points. First, over-fishing of Bemalae, formerly during the closed season before the sub-clans ceased establishing the *tarabando* ban on fishing, appears to be the most reasonable explanation for falling catches at the community fish-in.

Second, the major stakeholders (members of the two sub-clans) have at this point quite different stakes in Bemalae. For Fatuklaren members, their interest is almost entirely the ritual one associated with the annual fish-in. While residents of contemporary East Timor are largely Roman Catholic at this point, a generalized belief that might be characterized as "ancestor worship" persists. Thus Fatuklaren members' ritual interest may well be non-trivial at least in psychological terms. Pasalaren fishers, by contrast, have a material interest in Bemalae that must be at least as strong as the ritual interest they share with Fatuklaren members. Up to this point, Pasalaren fishers do not report themselves unduly upset by the over-fishing of Bemalae, presumably because they are the ones doing it and they are the ones who benefit from it.

Pasalaren sub-clan members are the only ones who might be able to control over-fishing through a tightened monitoring and enforcement system to uphold a new set of rules regulating both access and harvesting (see infra). Fatuklaren members, by contrast, all live too far away to participate effectively in any local monitoring and enforcement scheme, and the Fisheries Department has too few officials to assign any exclusively to Bemalae. It is for precisely this reason that the Government of Timor Leste has adopted a policy of promoting RGM by local groups of RNR users.

One can draw the following conclusions, admittedly speculative because of the censored nature of the interview data, from this case:

1. Pasalaren fishers in effect control Bemalae and, until *they* become concerned about overfishing, it will continue. In a country like East Timor this, in a nutshell, is the problem. The National Government lacks the institutional and human resources to govern and manage RNR like the Bemalae fishery. A national government can unilaterally assert "authority" over RGM problems but if that same Government is unable to mobilize the resources to make, monitor and enforce rules, its assertion of authority may, at most, render official the *de facto* "open access", i.e., unmanaged and ungoverned status, of the target RNR. Even worse, it may preclude concerned local stakeholders from asserting control over a threatened resource.

2. Under the circumstances, national government efforts to assert control over Bemalae would very likely involve a quixotic waste of resources (both fiscal resources and RNR), and simply put off the Pasalaren sub-clan's day of reckoning.
3. If Pasalaren fishers decided that they wanted to convert Bemalae from a sub-clan open access resource to a clan or sub-clan common property resource, they would have to work out a set of institutional arrangements that would bring (their) demand for Bemalae fish back into line with supply.
4. This could be done by establishing a set of harvesting rules, *e.g.*, daily catch limits, or by establishing controls on access, for example, by limiting the number of days in the nominally closed season that a Pasalaren fisher could work Bemalae.
5. The sub-clan would have, simultaneously, to establish a monitoring system to ensure that all fishers complied with these regulations and to provide for sanctions in cases where fishers were caught infringing such local access and harvesting rules.
6. One advantage of this approach would be to create a set of institutional arrangements that could be modified by sub-clan members, their kin group leaders or by elected (necessarily Pasalaren) local government leaders when the need arose. This would vest in the group authority to modify and fine-tune rules governing the Bemalae fishery in light of evolving conditions.
7. A second advantage would lie in the Government's ability to "burden shed" responsibility for Bemalae RGM to the set of individuals with the greatest incentive to ensure sustainability of that resource, once over-fishing reaches the point where Pasalaren fishers themselves became concerned. To this end the Government might consider enacting a law to create a *special district enabling framework*. Under cover of this legislation the Government could officially recognize the Pasalaren sub-clan's authority to regulate fishing in Bemalae within the context of a special district established specifically to govern and manage the Bemalae fishery. This approach would presumably have to incorporate some accommodation of the Fatuklaren ritual interest in the fishery, but that should not prove impossible.
8. The Bemalae case can, however, provide a cautionary counter to observations contained in Christopher Pala's *New York Times* article, "No-Fishing Zones in Tropics Yield Fast Payoffs for Reefs" (Pala: Iff; *cf.* also Fn. 8, supra). Community efforts in the Micronesian country of Palau to establish stints on selected reefs through elder-based monitoring and enforcement systems have proven so productive that other Micronesian countries, to say nothing of Indonesia and several Caribbean nations, are

now quite reasonably seeking to apply that approach to their own fisheries. Community-based fisheries RGM systems in other parts of the world have proven similarly effective (Thomson (in press): *passim)*. But these systems depend on solid entente among local notables, leaders and decision makers. The Fatuklaren and Pasalaren fisher clans at Bemalae clearly fail this criterion. Without a modicum of entente at the community level the best of state good faith efforts to empower locals and recognize their institutional arrangements are not likely to foster better stewardship.

V. Conclusions and Implications

The foregoing three cases highlight a critical characteristic of RGM in East Timor. Threats to or actual degradation of RNR in these cases, whether forests (and associated watersheds) or fisheries, result from incentive structures that exceed the capacity of local communities, acting on their own, to control and/or modify. Whether the threat to forests comes from cross-border timber poaching raids conducted by ex-East Timorese militiamen with the goal of harvesting trees on Suco Leohitu community lands in the far west of the country, or locally generated timber felling by former guerillas in Lore Reserved Forest in the far eastern section of the country, or illicit fishing conducted by Pasalaren in-shore ocean fishers in the north coast Bemalae lagoon fishery (to which their whole clan long ago established a property claim), local communities need economic or legal assistance to restructure incentives in ways that will support local initiatives and rules designed to maintain or improve RNR stewardship.

State interventions appear most useful when they succeed in modifying incentive structures so that RNR stewardship becomes, in resource users' eyes, highly desirable. The *art* of achieving such outcomes lies in using economic, legal, and policy interventions that locals *approve*.

As successful RNR stewardship must involve, by its nature, long-term, institutionalized practices, state interventions must seek to make it *feasible* for RNR users to allocate time and effort to RGM activities over the long term. That implies that those same users must have economic opportunities in the short term that will enable them to support their families other than by degrading or destroying target renewable resources. *Optimum* state (or donor, financing agency and NGO-assisted) interventions should create attractive RNR-based economic opportunities (*e.g.*, fishing, wood processing, enhanced agricultural potential) that depend for their sustainability on the continued existence of the target resource. If that can be achieved, RNR users and communities can often find ways to mobilize the human and other resources necessary to conduct monitoring and enforcement of locally-crafted rules governing access to and harvesting of RNR, to resolve disputes about those processes, disseminate information throughout the group/community in ways that both encourage rule-compliant behavior and fine-tuning rules to adapt them more effectively, over time, to (often evolving) local circumstances.

What approaches might communities and the Government of East Timor and its subordinate agencies adopt to promote RNR stewardship by users? Three mutually reinforcing strategies can be proposed that would arguably produce *intended* positive side benefits. The theme that would tie them together is *applied research to inform the crafting and fine-tuning of enabling frameworks for improved RGM and renewable resource stewardship*. A brief description follows of each of these activities before concluding comments on how the Government might seek to coordinate their interactions to benefit East Timorese, both primary users of selected RNR and the broader society that depends on various products derived from the country's RNR.

1. Conduct applied research to document existing institutional arrangements for RGM in high priority regions throughout the country. A number of social science professors, students and graduates from the national university in Dili (UNTL) participated in the USAID-sponsored "Land Law Project" in East Timor. They received training in both qualitative and quantitative applied research methods. This human capital, as well as the best of future generations of students, could play leading roles in documenting existing RGM institutional arrangements.
2. State agency-UNTL collaboration to develop and archive information about these locally developed RGM stewardship systems. As documented cases cumulated over time, East Timorese government officials and legislators could exploit this "database" – which could be designed to incorporate both qualitative and quantitative information – to familiarize themselves with on-the-ground realities of resource stewardship in the country prior to drafting enabling legislation that would officially recognize local RGI1-I institutional arrangements. Recognition would strengthen them not only by enhancing their credibility but also by making available back-up enforcement capacity when local leaders judge that some prohibited behavior exceeds their capacities to control (*e.g.*, village and hamlet leaders in Suco Leohitu when East Timorese militiamen now domiciled in West Timor mounted cross-border "timber poaching" expeditions to harvest trees on Suco Leohitu's land).
3. Cross-visits organized to permit RNR users from communities where RGAI institutional arrangements are either non-existent or not particularly successful to spend time with their counterparts in communities with "high performing" RGM systems. This would allow the former to learn from the

> latter, in a shared language and in circumstances quite similar to those that prevail in their home communities. Cross visits would give actors associated with "high performing" RGM systems, who would function as teachers explaining their own institutions to outsiders, periodic incentives to analyze their own institutional arrangements with care, to highlight in their own minds the strengths and weaknesses of these systems, the better to clarify them for outsiders (peers from other communities).

East Timor's RGM policies and initiatives as of 2005 were sufficiently progressive that it would not be unreasonable to envision on-going university and government agency involvement in efforts to document local RGM institutional arrangements in the country. Extension officers in the MAFF Departments of Agriculture, Fisheries and Forestry could participate in these efforts with UNTL colleagues and students, with both contributing critical elements to the applied research. MAFF extension officers could, in turn, organize and oversee cross-visits to help rural RNR stewards learn "best practices" from each other and apply them. An intermittent but ongoing program of applied research focused on RGM institutional arrangements and processes could, moreover, supply members of East Timor's Parliament with critical evaluations of the impact of their legislative texts in promoting improved RNR stewardship in the country. Availability of this kind of information would arguably take some of the guesswork out of drafting by simultaneously affording East Timorese legislators materials from which they could learn, in "on-the-job" situations, about how people in different parts of the country interact with RNR. Legislators (and, if the data base were made available to the broader public, local-level political officials, primary and secondary school teachers, staffs of government agencies [*e.g.*, MAFF departments], of NGOs, and donor and financing organizations) could all exploit a rich and growing body of information that would conceivably enable them, over time, to advocate for appropriate enabling frameworks, refinements in local institutional arrangements, and so support more disciplined and sustainable approaches to RGM and to RNR stewardship in East Timor. An approach along these lines would create opportunities for productive incremental amendment of existing national laws, and community (suco) by-laws and working rules, in light of the lessons of experience. This would enhance, over time, the capacity of rural East Timorese to build on human and institutional resources already present in their communities.

It should be possible to generate a highly productive applied research program that would allow the Government gradually to "shed" a substantial part of the RGM burden to those with the most direct personal incentives to engage in better stewardship of their forests, watersheds, irrigation systems and fisheries, i.e., the owners and regular users of those renewable resources. By reducing the transactions costs of collective action through appropriate enabling legislation, by heightening the authority and credibility of local RNR stewardship, by providing back-up enforcement when particular problems exceed local capacities, this system could lay the foundation for future productive collaboration among RNR users, state resource technicians (foresters, agronomists, fisheries specialists), university-based applied researchers and national (and potentially sub-national) legislators. It would help actors at all levels – not just university researchers, government technicians and legislators, but local government officials and local level users of RNR (fishers, loggers, farmers, livestock owners, those who harvest non-timber forest products in wooded areas of East Timor) – hone their analytic skills regarding appropriate institutional arrangements for RGM. Several brief examples will illustrate this point.

Special districts are single-purpose (often local-level) jurisdictions designed to correspond with the precise geographic boundaries of particular RNR systems such as watersheds, irrigation systems, specific forests, fresh-water and coastal fisheries, community pasture areas and the like. Such special districts create, in many countries in North and South America, in Europe and in Africa, opportunities for a group of actors concerned to support sustainable stewardship of an important local or regional renewable resource such as freshwater, ocean shell and coastal fisheries, parks, lakes and river systems. The almost 60-year-old Ohio River Sanitation Compact, involving sections of eight (8) states located in the Ohio River watershed, a major river system of the humid eastern section of the United States, demonstrates that special districts may be both large in scale and hugely effective as institutional frameworks for environmental stewardship.

The Ohio River, a heavily polluted watercourse in the 1930s, was rehabilitated under ORSANCO leadership by industry and citizen groups, riverside municipalities and the like to the point where it is no longer an open sewer used for indiscriminate disposition of a wide variety of wastes but the source of an on-going flow of values that span the gamut from industrial cooling to tourism and water sports, including a major fresh water fisheries where anglers can eat the fish they catch with little risk of contracting diseases or ingesting noxious chemicals.

The advantage of special districts in countries such as France, Great Britain, the United States, Botswana and Malawi (for the latter two, *cf.* Thomson *et al.*, 2004: Botswana and Malawi case studies) lies in the flexibility with which district boundaries can be drawn. They can, in fact, be drawn fully *congruent with the contours of a specific renewable resource* (for example, watershed, forest or pasture). This means that the set of actors who develop rules governing access to and harvesting of a specific RNR can be limited to those directly affected by or involved with that particular resource. This minimizes the transactions costs of resolving tenure and RGM collective action issues, and so reduces negative incentives that impede resource stewardship. As users experience the benefits of more disciplined exploitation of RNR, they often make stronger commitments to stewardship (Pala).

As living human beings establish controls on access to and harvesting of RNR, presumably fewer violations of local rules will occur. While the following assertion is speculative, it is possible that local belief systems will, to some extent, reassert themselves. Those who wish to respect and honor their ancestors may find an added measure of security in the belief that the spirits of the departed continue to play an active and protective role in the life of the community, ensuring survival of vital RNR. Local humanly-operated RGM systems can indirectly support those beliefs by providing those with an interest in improved RNR stewardship some security that they will not disadvantage themselves and theirs if they comply with a stint.

If this happens, then community mores should, over time, incorporate more emphasis on RNR stewardship. Such practices will likely be reflected in the teachings of parents concerned to educate their children in the local rules and forms of proper behavior. If local public opinion stigmatizes free-riding behavior as a result of these human interactions then, in a society such as East Timor where the population formerly believed that departed ancestors continue to manifest interest in the actions of their living descendants, it seems reasonable to assume that the living will effectively "come to the assistance of their ancestors" by providing the local monitoring and enforcement systems that create incentives to comply with the wishes of the ancestors concerning resource stewardship (for an example, see the Suco Leohito case study in Thomson *et al.*, 2005). What better way to honor the ancestors? What better way to ensure the continued survival of the living who depend on renewable resources for their survival? Over time, as people realize that orderly systems of RGM serve their very immediate as well as long-term interests, and that they have strong incentives to support stewardship of local RNR, a "new" environmental ethic that largely recycles and revives old mores of resource stewardship may be consolidated.

This need *not,* be it noted, happen everywhere in East Timor all at once. If some communities in each region succeed in developing (or redeveloping) reliable and effective RGM systems, in part by building on the remnants of former institutional arrangements, past practices and inherited beliefs, those instances may come to serve as compelling examples for neighboring groups whose members suffer personally and in real time from falling living standards occasioned by their own "RNR stewardship failures." Such failures, be it noted, are not often caused by the "moral depravity" of RNR users. The latter, when they find themselves with families to feed and growing competition for a pool of vital RNR, quite rationally struggle "to get while the getting is good", rather than stinting themselves while others rape remaining renewables. These negative dynamics erupt in situations where institutional arrangements for collective decision-making and collective action are moribund. But these outcomes are *not inevitable*. They can be reversed by astute "institutional engineering" conducted by alert government technicians and legislators with the support of a range of other actors. The *key* element in such efforts is sophisticated understanding of institutional architecture – what the constitutional, decision-making and operational rules are and the processes through which those formal rules are converted into working rules (Commons, 1959). Professor Elinor Ostrom, first president of the International Association for the Study of Common Property (IASCP) 1994) and a host of scholars and practitioners associated with the organization have demonstrated beyond a shadow of a doubt that one does not require advanced degrees to acquire a sophisticated sense of institutional architecture.

The Government of East Timor could arguably contribute to the welfare of its citizens at very low cost, simply by providing appropriate enabling legal frameworks to support RNR stewardship, and then taking measures to ensure that information about these frameworks is thoroughly disseminated among relevant populations. After that, it will be largely a matter of rural people deciding to help themselves, although the Government (and NGOs, and donor and financing agencies) should take seriously the need to support self-governance initiatives among resource users as occasions and circumstances demand. An on-going, university-based monitoring program of RNR stewardship practices could, over time, pay large dividends in this regard.

Bibliography

Cleary, Edward J. 1967. Printed for Resources for the Future. Baltimore, MD: The Johns Hopkins University Press. 335 pp.

Commons, John R. 1959. *Legal Foundations of Capitalism*. First published 1924: New York, Macmillan; Madison, WI: University of Wisconsin Press. 394 pp.

East Timor, 2007. Ministry of Agriculture, Forestry and Fisheries (MAFF). Web site

Klare, Michael T. 2002. *Resource Wars: The New Landscape of Global Conflict* (with a new introduction by the author). First published 2001: New York, Henry Holt. 289 pp.

Mydans, Seth. 2007. "Divided and Embattled East Timor to Elect a President," *New York Times,* April 9, p. A3.

Ostrom, Elinor. 1994. *Governing the Commons: The Evolution of Institutions for Collective Action*. Cambridge: Cambridge University Press. 280 pp.

Pala, Christopher. 2007. "No-Fishing Zones in Tropics Yield Fast Pay-offs for Reefs, *New York Times,* 17 April 2007. pp. Iff

Thomson, James T. (In press). "Malawi's Lake Chiuta Fisheries: Intelligent Burden Shedding That Favors Renewable Resources Stewardship." Lexington: University of Kentucky Press.

Thomson, James T., *et al.,* 2004. Mali, Botswana, Namibia and Malawi: Institutional Aspects of Renewable Natural Resources Governance and Management through Special Districts. Document prepared and submitted to USAID by the ARD BioFor IQC Consortium under USAID Contract No. LAG-I-00-99-00013-00, Biodiversity and Sustainable Forestry (BIOFOR) IQC, Task Order No. 3.

Thomson, James, *et al.,* 2005. "Initial Assessment – 'When the Ancestors Need Help:' Renewable Natural Resources and Institutional Design in Contemporary East Timor," Land Law Program in East Timor (Preliminary Assessment of Community Resources Governance and Management [RGM]). Prepared by ARD, Inc. for the USAID Timor-Leste Land Law Program through Task Order #808 under USAID Contract No. LAG-I-0098-00031-00 Broadening Access and Strengthening lnput Market Systems (BASIS) for USAID/East Timor. December. v., 8 pp., six appendices (case studies).

Urresta, Edwin, Rod Nixon, *et al*., 2004. "Report on Research Findings and Policy Recommendations for a Legal Framework for Land Dispute Mediation." Prepared by ARD, Inc. for the USAID Timor-Leste Land Law Program through Task Order #808 under USAID Contract No. LAG-I-00-98-00031-00 Broadening Access and Strengthening lnput Market Systems (BASIS) for USAID/East Timor. February. i, 59 pp.

USAID. First published 2002. Republished 2004. *Nature Wealth and Power: Emerging Best Practice for Revitalizing Rural Africa*.

PART II

The Indonesian Occupation and Its Aftermath

How Many Persons in East Timor Went 'Missing' During the Indonesian Occupation?: Results from Indirect Estimates

Sarah Staveteig

Introduction

East Timor, a nation barely larger than Montenegro, captured world attention in 1999 during its historic United Nations-sponsored referendum on independence. The lead-up to the vote was marred by violence for several months, as pro-Indonesian militia killed, threatened, and intimidated the East Timorese population in an effort to keep them from voting for independence. On 30 August of that year, the East Timorese electorate overwhelmingly voted in favor of independence from Indonesia. The vote ended 24 years of Indonesian annexation. Following the elections, in an apparent act of revenge, pro-Indonesian militias killed an estimated 1,000 supporters of independence. One-quarter of a million East Timorese fled to West Timor (Gunn 2000). Looting and ransacking were widespread, and the Indonesian "scorched earth" policy destroyed more than 70 percent of the housing stock in East Timor (Dolan *et al.*, 2004). The events of 1999 were perhaps best described as a "brutal finale" to 24 years of Indonesian occupation (Nixon 2004).

Although much has been written about East Timor since 1999, little is known about the full impact of Indonesian occupation which began in 1975, following more than 400 years of Portuguese colonial rule. Currently, in the wake of East Timorese independence and the establishment of the Commission for Reception, Truth and Reconciliation in East Timor (CAVR), there is an interest in determining the extent of human rights abuses during the Indonesian occupation. This paper focuses on population-level estimates of "missing persons" from 1975 to 2000.[1] A tally of missing persons includes our topic of interest: the *excess mortality* during the period, that is, the number of deaths above and beyond those that would have been expected under "normal" circumstances.

[1] Since population estimates are generally done during mid-year, and the violence in East Timor in 1999 went well into the last months of the year, the missing person count is computed for mid-year 2000.

Yet because these estimates of "missing persons" are based on indirect methods, it is impossible to discern whether missing persons died, were not born, emigrated, or were simply not enumerated in a later census. Hence, we cannot label these 204,000 persons "deaths"; we can only state with certainty that our best estimate suggests that they went "missing" between 1975 and 2000. Despite these disadvantages, indirect estimation is an important way to verify the reasonability of existing estimates of excess mortality and to provide a hypothetical upper bound on excess mortality during the period.

Estimates of excess mortality cannot, of course, tell the entire story: by definition such figures obscure the richness of individual histories and events. Yet mortality figures are an important way to summarise the experiences of a population, particularly when so many victims and their stories will forever remain unknown. The fact that each person has equal weight in such counts could also be thought of as a "democratic counterbalance" to *ex post* efforts to steer historical attention toward one particular version of events.

Wars and occupations tend to cause indirect mortality in the population above and beyond battlefield deaths (Li and Wen 2005; Ghobarah *et al*., 2003), particularly if medical systems break down; internal migration causes poor living and sanitary conditions, and food becomes scarce. Excess mortality is difficult to pin down, however, because "missing" persons (who are absent even above and beyond the expected number of deaths) may in fact have emigrated, gone into hiding and been missed by later censuses, or died due to disease or natural causes that would have occurred even in the absence of an armed invasion. Similarly, a large portion of the post-occupation population may well have arrived from outside East Timor – for example, via Indonesia's transmigration program – and thus disguise high levels of wartime mortality among the native population.[2]

Despite these challenges, indirect estimation of mortality is still a critical task for truth commissions, historians, and politicians. The casualties of war are certainly a subset of the number of "missing" persons. When combined with survivor testimonies and other historical evidence of military incursions, consistently high levels of "missing" people are strongly suggestive that Indonesian aggression in East Timor was responsible for a large number of deaths in the population.

---

[2] Fortunately post-occupation censuses in East Timor have gathered data on the nativity of the head of household, which allow us to distinguish between native Timorese households and other immigrants. To the extent that there were mixed marriages among natives and immigrants, however, the census data may be misleading.

In this particular case, robust statistical evidence gathered by the Human Rights Data Group (HRDAG) on behalf of the Commission for Reception, Truth, and Reconciliation in East Timor (Silva and Ball 2006) has estimated that at least 102,800 (± 12,000) East Timorese died of causes related to the Indonesian occupation from 1974 to 1999 [herein referred to as the Silva and Ball estimate]. This result was based on years of painstaking data collection and analysis using a retrospective mortality survey, a graveyard census, and narrative testimonies. Given this well-documented finding, why use indirect estimation at all? First, for a question that is as politically contentious as the number of Timorese who went "missing" during the Indonesian occupation, it is important to see what we can determine from official sources. Critics of the high Timor death toll counts are more likely to trust estimates obtained from the Indonesian's own data, than from non-official sources of information such as those collected by Silva and Ball – however statistically impressive the latter may be. Secondly, this case is a unique opportunity to compare the validity of indirect to direct methods, because it is one of few cases where both types of data exist. In many situations, it is too expensive, time-consuming, or politically inexpedient to conduct retrospective surveys and gather other forms of independent data. This is not to say that these sources are not important. Indeed, they may offer our greatest hope of producing accurate reports of the extent of human rights violations. But if we want to be able to quantify the death toll of historical wars and other difficult-to-access population figures, indirect methods are important to develop. Third and most important, indirect estimation provides a useful "upper bound" on the total number of East Timorese who died during the Indonesian occupation. This upper bound is a useful complement to the multiple systems estimation and survey methods used by Silva and Ball which provide a "lower bound" of the total number of persons who died of causes related to the occupation.

Why do I claim that Silva and Ball's estimates are a lower bound? Each of the methods that they used – narrative testimonies by witnesses and survivors, a graveyard census, and a retrospective mortality survey – are, in and of themselves, likely to underestimate the actual number who died during the occupation. Relying on narrative testimonies is problematic because in many cases massacres and deaths go unwitnessed or survivors refuse to testify about what happened.[3] Graveyard censuses omit deaths when victims are buried *en*

[3] The opposite bias is also possible: that many survivors will report the same incident and thus lead to an overcount of the number who died, but Silva and Ball take painstaking efforts to eliminate such duplicate reporting. They also estimated that after accounting for recall bias, the number who died in East Timor of conflict-related deaths could be as high as 180,000.

masse, buried without a marker, or not buried at all, which is often the case during violent crises and famines. Retrospective mortality surveys underestimate mortality when deaths are "clustered" in families and there are no survivors in the country to report what happened.[4] If estimates from these three methods were simply added up, there would of course be risk of overestimation – multiple counting of the same deaths among different sources. However, Silva and Ball took painstaking efforts to avoid double-counting across different methods of estimation by detecting and eliminating duplicates. Hence their final casualty count is extremely well-documented and robust to evidentiary challenges, yet also likely to be lower than the "true" total. Indirect estimation thus provides a useful complement to their estimation of excess mortality.

East Timor, a very small country, is also an important case study of excess mortality. If the most commonly cited figure of 200,000 casualties during the first five years of Indonesian occupation is reasonable, then the Indonesian invasion of East Timor could have produced one of the highest *proportionate* death tolls of any war or mass murder in recent history. According to Kiernan (2003), the proportion of initial population who died in East Timor from 1975–1980 is on a par with, if not slightly above, the proportion of the original population killed during the Khmer Rouge regime in Cambodia (21 to 26 percent).[5] Chomsky (1999) has claimed that a death toll of 200,000 would make it the highest proportionate death toll of any war since the Holocaust. Yet some experts estimate the casualty count to be as "low" as 60,000, or less than 10 percent of the original population (Hull 2004), thus it is important to consider the issue carefully.

The availability of Portuguese censuses prior to the Indonesian takeover gives us a unique estimate of the pre-invasion population, something largely unavailable in other historical cases of colonisation. Timor's isolation as an island means that out-migration was necessarily quite limited. By and large refugees displaced by the Indonesian invasion fled into East Timor's vast forests and mountains.[6] Crossing the border into West Timor or fleeing by boat to a nearby island generally meant arriving in Indonesian territory, not an

[4] Here again, the opposite is possible: multiple surviving family members could report the same death. However Silva and Ball have taken measures to guard against such overcounting.
[5] Note that this percentage is slightly misleading as deaths do not occur only among those who were alive in 1975, but also among those born afterward. However, this figure provides a rough estimate by which to compare the casualty count.
[6] Less than 5 percent of East Timor's land area is arable (CIA 2005).

enticing prospect. Australia was close enough to receive some refugees, but these arrivals are well-documented. Hence, East Timor offers a unique perspective on the demographic impact of political annexation.[7]

Quantitative representations of human rights violations, such as death counts, are inherently controversial, because perpetrators often desire to discount the importance of the event while advocates may be tempted to overestimate what happened in order to draw public attention. Scientific evaluations of the evidence thus provide an appealing alternative to political debate. This paper is one of only a handful of serious efforts to estimate excess mortality in East Timor during the period of Indonesian occupation. Most efforts have focused only on the first five years of occupation, when it is believed population losses were the most dramatic (*cf.* Kiernan 2003; Cribb 2001). The general literature on East Timor cites a near-ubiquitous figure of 200,000 casualties (*cf.* Amnesty International 1997; Pilger 1994a; U.S. Congress 2000; Huridocs 2005), though the derivation of this number has not been well-documented.

The remainder of the paper proceeds as follows. First, the salient features of East Timor's history are laid out to provide some background to the study. Secondly, crude estimates of excess mortality based on population growth rates are given. The third section estimates excess mortality using age-specific death rates and all available information about migration. There my results are presented and documented. The fourth section concludes with a discussion of sensitivity testing of the results and compares my findings to other estimates.

Background

East Timor lies on an island just north of Australia on the eastern edge of the Indonesian archipelago. Its population is a mixture of Melanesians, Malays, and Chinese. The Portuguese colonised East Timor in 1520. Over the following centuries, Spain, the Netherlands, Britain, and Japan attempted to wrest control of the country from Portugal, but only Japan was successful in occupying East Timor briefly during World War II. Portugal regained control of East Timor following World War II. After a 1974 coup in Lisbon, the newly-

[7] Several authors have suggested that what happened in East Timor was a genocide (East Timorese being a national group whom the Indonesians attempted to exterminate), while others strongly contest this definition, particularly because it has been difficult to establish clear evidence of "genocidal intent." This paper is not the correct forum for such a debate, and hence I simply refer to what happened in East Timor as "annexation" or "occupation." From a demographic standpoint, the importance of the occupation is that it involved a massive number of excess deaths, regardless of whether it meets the legal standards for "genocide" or not.

established Portuguese Junta de Salvação Nacional declared that Portugal would withdraw from its overseas territories. East Timorese independence appeared to be inevitable (Lawless 1976).

Even before the Indonesians invaded, the inevitability of independence was a contentious and ultimately violent issue inside East Timor (Huridocs 2005; Nichertlein 1977). Fretilin (Frente Revolucionaria Timor Leste Independente), a popular left-wing movement, wanted to declare full independence. A second group, UDT (Uniao Democratica Timorense) wanted to remain linked with Portugal. The least popular group, Apodeti (Associao Popular Democratica Timorense), wanted autonomous integration into Indonesia, though Indonesia made it clear that autonomous integration would not be possible (Lawless 1976; Houk 1978). Initially UDT and Fretilin were in alliance, but UDT later withdrew and the two groups clashed violently. On November 28, 1975, Fretilin unilaterally declared East Timorese independence. Nine days later Indonesian forces invaded.

On 7 December 1975, approximately 2,000 Indonesian paratroopers and marines and 20 warships began attacking Dili (the capital) and other coastal areas, causing at least 500 Timorese casualties (Lawless 1976). Fretilin is said to have put up a surprising amount of resistance given its technological inferiority, but Indonesians still conquered key strategic areas. The UN Security Council called on Indonesia to withdraw from East Timor two weeks later, but to no avail. Indonesia only stepped up its continued incursions into rebel-held areas under the veil of anti-communism. A second invasion took place on 25 December 25 1975.

In 1976, Indonesia officially incorporated East Timor as its 27th province (CIA 2005). The United Nations vocally condemned the annexation of East Timor, but other superpowers, particularly the United States and Australia, were silent on the issue. The United States never formally recognised Indonesia's annexation of East Timor, but also never publicly objected to it. Indonesia portrayed East Timor as an emerging communist nation, virtually guaranteeing US support (Nichertlein 1977; Crossette 1994). The Indonesian invasion into East Timor began a mere 12 hours after US President Ford left Jakarta, which is widely seen as evidence of American acceptance of Indonesia's conquest of East Timor (Zunes 2000; Monk 2001; Kohen and Taylor 1979). The United States supplied the arms used by the Indonesian military and continued its military support long after the annexation of East Timor (Sidell 1981).

For Australia, Indonesia was a crucial trading partner and consideration to diplomatic relations was given more weight than ethical concerns (Wheeler and Dunne 2001). In 1977, Australia formally recognised Indonesia's annexation of East Timor on the grounds of "realpolitik". However, in the last decade of Timorese occupation there was significant pressure within Australia by human rights organisations to raise the Timor issue (Kiernan 2002).

Indonesia publicly claimed that what happened in East Timor was not a military takeover; rather volunteers from its military went to assist a pro-Indonesian Timorese political group in a war with a Marxist-controlled group, Fretilin (Sharkey 1977). It also maintained that the Timorese had willingly accepted Indonesian involvement. For example, a letter to the editor in the *New York Times* written by the US counsellor at the Indonesian embassy stated:

> Indonesia will not take over Portuguese Timor but will accept integration, should the people of the area democratically, and without terrorists' guns pointed at their heads, choose this course. (Abdullah 1976)

Yet the evidence that Indonesian rule in East Timor was anything but voluntary is overwhelming. In the *Sydney Morning Herald* on 5 April 1977, the Indonesian foreign minister was quoted as saying: "Fifty thousand people or perhaps eighty thousand might have been killed during the war in East Timor ... It was war ... Then what is the big fuss?" (as cited in Kohen and Taylor 1979). Two joint Congressional hearings documented testimony from dozens of experts on East Timor on the impact of Indonesian violence toward Timor (US Congress 1999a, 1999b). Eyewitnesses and experts described extensive bombing in the mountains where many Timorese had gone to seek refuge following the 1975 attack. They also told of the killing of entire villages near where Fretilin guerillas were operating, and the killing of anyone suspected of having any association with Fretilin (Sharkey 1977). Survivors have corroborated in great detail the brutality of Indonesian occupation (Jardine 1995; Pilger 1994a or b??- here it's both, but I'm not sure whether to say 1994a, 1994b or 1994a-b).

Journalists and aid workers had only limited access to East Timor until 1989; hence knowledge of the extent of atrocities committed during the Indonesian annexation of East Timor is limited. Indirect estimation of excess mortality may be the best way to determine what happened in East Timor during Indonesian occupation. This paper first presents a crude growth-rate estimate of excess mortality to obtain a broad picture of what happened, and then presents more specific estimates by age and sex to determine excess mortality in East Timor during the Indonesian occupation.

Simplistic Estimates of Excess Mortality

In order to get a sense of excess mortality, it is useful to begin with a simplified model. We choose 31 December 1999 as a useful stopping point, as the violence after the August elections lasted for a few months. We can express the actual[8] population of East Timor on December 31, 1999, as:

$$P_{Act1999} = P_{Act1975} + B_{interim} - D_{interim} \pm M_{interim}$$

where:

$P_{Act1999}$ is East Timor's population on December 31, 1999
$P_{Act1975}$ is East Timor's population on December 6, 1975
$B_{interim}$ is the number of live births during the period
$D_{interim}$ is the total number of deaths that occurred during the period
$M_{interim}$ is the net number of international migrants from 1975 to 1999

We can define two types of death during the period: *expected* and *excess*, where:

$D_{expected}$ is the number of deaths that would have been expected during the period if mortality rates held constant[9]
D_{excess} is the number of deaths that are not explained by the mortality rates in the starting year, a portion of which are presumably related to the Indonesian occupation

It follows that:

$$D_{interim} = D_{expected} + D_{excess}$$

Similarly, births and mortality totals are comprised of expected values and unexpected values. In the case of migration we take into account reported totals during the period in order to reduce the value of unexpected migration:

$$B_{interim} = B_{expected} \pm B_{unexpected}$$
$$M_{interim} = M_{expected} \pm M_{reported} \pm M_{unexpected}$$

[8] For ease of notation, I am equating actual population with the officially recorded population, even though they are not necessarily the same thing. Problems with census data are discussed in the next section.

[9] In fact, this is a conservative estimate, as most developing countries have experienced a "mortality transition" in the past half century, whereby mortality rates have been steadily decreasing.

Using a growth rate or another formula, we can derive an estimated 1999 population:

$$P_{Est1999} = P_{Act1975} + B_{expected} - D_{expected} \pm M_{expected} \pm M_{reported}$$

If we then subtract the actual 1999 population from both sides of the equation above, we find that all terms on the right hand side cancel except the number of deaths:

$$P_{Est1999} - P_{Act1999} = \cancel{P_{Act1975}} - \cancel{P_{Act1975}} + (B_{expected} - B_{interim}) -$$
$$(D_{expected} + D_{interim}) + (\pm M_{expected} \pm M_{reported} \pm -M_{interim})$$
$$P_{Est1999} - P_{Act1999} = D_{excess} + (B_{unexpected} \pm M_{unexpected})$$

As $(B_{unexpected} \pm M_{unexpected})$ approach 0:

$$P_{Est1999} - P_{Act1999} \approx D_{excess}$$

In other words, since what we are really interested in is excess deaths, we will try our best to reduce the absolute value of unexpected births and unexpected migrants, so that the estimated minus actual population will primarily be comprised of excess deaths. If fertility or net migration were lower than expected, this would inflate our count of the excess deaths. Conversely, if fertility or net migration were higher than expected, or if "normal" mortality rates fell[10] over time, we would underestimate excess mortality.

We also face an additional problem: there are no official records for Timorese population on 6 December 1975, nor are there any for the population on 31 December 1999. Table 1 lists the population data sources that will be used in this paper. As it indicates, the last recorded population census prior to 1975 was Portugal's 1970 census of its overseas territories. However, Portugal updated its census count with records of births, deaths, and net migration in 1971 and 1972.[11] Most population data during the period of occupation comes from Indonesian sources. Some post-independence data are available, but detailed population counts by age and sex from the 2004 census have not yet been released.

---

[10] It is nearly impossible to imagine that natural mortality rates would have risen during the period, as this would be contrary to the experience of peaceful and unoccupied developing countries during this period.

[11] Portugal also published a 1973 update, but it did not contain births and deaths for East Timor.

Table 1. Sources of population data for East Timor, 1960–2004.

Applicable Year	Series Title	Institutional Author	Contains
1960 1970 1971 1972	*Anuario Estatístico Provincias Ultramarinas*	Portugal Instituto Nacional de Estatística	Official census; possible undercount due to poll tax Contains information on births and migration only
1970–1999 1972	*World Population Prospects*	United Nations	Historical estimates of population totals, fertility, migration, crude death rates
	Revista Do Centro de Estudos Demograficos	Portugal Instituto Nacional de Estatística	Estimated fertility and mortality rates from 1972
1980 1990	*Sensus Penduduk: Rumahtangga Dan Penduduk, Timor Timur*	Bagian Statistik Demografi *[Indonesian Demographic Statistics Division]*	Official census; possible undercount (internally displaced persons in remote areas); but a political incentive to overcount
1991 1994 1997	*Indonesia Demographic and Health Survey*	Central Bureau of Statistics Indonesia *et al.*,	Contains 3–year retrospective age-specific fertility rates and 10-year retrospective infant and child mortality rates for East Timor
2000	*International Data Base*	U.S. Census Bureau	Population counts
2001	*Suco Survey*	Asian Development Bank	Population total
2004	*2004 census*	Direcção Nacional de Estatística *[Timor-Leste]*	Population total; age and sex counts not yet released

Hence our "actual" population counts in 1975 and in 1999 will actually be estimates based on census data before and after the occupation, which adds another layer of potential error. Moreover, official counts done prior to the invasion are thought to be flawed. The Portuguese collected a poll tax on the East Timorese, so it is likely that their population numbers are an undercount (Cribb 2001). Yet Indonesian census-takers were unlikely to be warmly received by East Timorese during the occupation, so in a sense the rates of enumeration before and during the occupation may be fairly comparable.

When all the potential sources of error are considered, the cost of producing an estimated count of excess mortality may, to some, appear to outweigh the benefit of having a potentially flawed estimate. This opinion is perhaps understandable. We will never know the real number of East Timorese killed directly or indirectly by Indonesians, and it would be dishonest to claim otherwise. Yet if we are careful and responsible with our methods and consider the possible sources of error, we can produce a reasonable estimate of this figure. If our methods here are carefully documented, scholars and critics can replicate the results, judge the integrity of the estimate, and improve the estimate if new historical information later appears.

A simple way to estimate excess deaths is to apply East Timor's average annual growth rate from 1960 to 1972[12] to the period from 1972 to 2000. The "actual" 2000 total can be subtracted from this estimated total to obtain an estimate. The growth rate formula estimates East Timor's expected 1999 population at 1,065,531. We do not have a recorded total for 1999, but we know that the 2001 Suco survey counted 787,338 persons in East Timor (Asian Development Bank 2002). Projecting the average annual growth rate from 1972 to 2001 (0.72 percent)[13] back to 1999 implies a population of 781,684 in December of 1999. If we instead take the growth rate from the 2001 Suco survey to the 2004 census (5.36 percent) and project backward, this would imply a 1999 population of 746,263. These figures imply an excess mortality of approximately 284,000 to 320,000 during the period. An illustration of the growth rate method is given in Figure 1. As the figure illustrates, the dip in population from 1970 to the 1980 period and onward is quite dramatic.

[12] The average annual growth rate increased from the 1960–1970 period to the 1970–72 period. To err on the conservative side, I obtain an average annual growth rate from 1960–1972.

[13] The estimated growth rate is extraordinarily small because of the massive mortality and out-migration during the period; but using a smaller growth rate in a backward projection errs on the side of caution because it produces a larger estimate of the actual 2000 population.

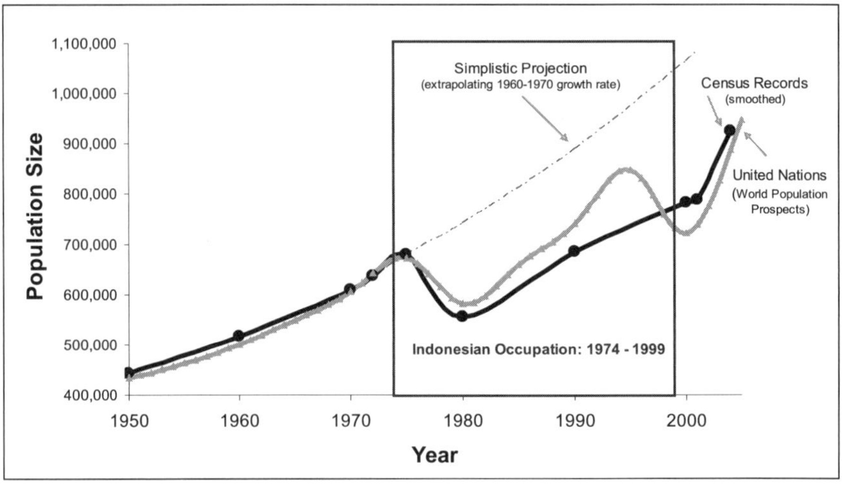

Figure 1. Recorded population compared with simplistic population projection: East Timor, 1950–2005. Sources: Census data from Portugal Instituto Nacional de Estatística (1970, 1972); Bagian Statistik Demografi [Indonesian Demographic Statistics Division] (1980, 1990); Asian Development Bank (2002); Direcção Nacional de Estatística de Timor-Leste (2005); United Nations (2005) and author's calculations.

A growth-rate calculation done for the entire period is obviously problematic, however. During the past half-century, hardly any human population has experienced a period of 24 years with an unchanging annual rate of growth. Constant population growth requires a stable age structure, constant levels of in- and out-migration during the period, and constant age-specific fertility and mortality rates. East Timor fits none of these assumptions.

Age-Specific Estimates of Excess Mortality

Initial crude estimates based on growth rates from 1975 to 1999 suggested a maximum of 284,000 to 320,000 missing persons during the period. These crude estimates based on growth rates provide a useful hypothetical maximum estimate of excess mortality in East Timor during the Indonesian occupation. But they do not account for the changing age structure of the population nor do they allow us to examine the age and sex composition of the "missing" population.

Fortunately we can achieve even more specific estimates of excess mortality by producing projections of population by age and sex. These age- and sex-specific projections have two major advantages over the simplistic total population estimates produced above. First, they take into account the ways in which changing age structure produces different composite fertility and mortality levels over the period, even when age-specific rates remain the same. Secondly, age- and sex-specific projections help us to distinguish between two types of excess mortality: deaths to the initial population alive on 6 December 1975 (who would be 25 years old or more if they survived to 31 December 1999) and deaths or non-births to children who would have been expected during the period. The former estimates are generally more reliable than the latter, because we know that "missing" persons aged 25 and above in 1999 either died, migrated outward, or were not enumerated in the second census. With the population of incoming births (those age 25 and below in 2000), however, it is impossible to distinguish between child deaths and children not born (due to reduced fertility rates) from census data alone.[14]

For these reasons, demographers prefer to use a Leslie Matrix to project populations. A Leslie Matrix employs age-specific mortality and fertility rates to provide a transition matrix that is more precise than a simple projection based on population growth rates (Wachter 2002). The R Programming language (R Development Core Team 2006) was used for all calculations. Appendix A provides detail about the computation and usage of Leslie matrices. Estimates of the current population (expressed as vectors) can be multiplied by the matrix to produce new population vectors.

To make use of all existing information, we break the calculation of excess deaths down into several time periods (as determined by the available data). Each time period can provide us with an estimate of excess deaths that we can sum to approximate the total excess deaths during the entire 1975–1999 period. First we establish the size of the baseline starting population. Then, using narrative historical information and Leslie matrices, we estimate excess mortality from 7 December 1975 to 1980; from 1981 to 1990; and from 1991 to December 31, 1999.

How Big was the Population of East Timor on 6 December 1975?

The population of East Timor on 6 December 1975, is one of the most important calculations in this estimation process. Error in the initial estimation

[14] The same would usually be true for immigrants as well: it would be difficult to distinguish whether they never arrived or whether they arrived and died before the census, except that in East Timor, the later surveys distinguish between household heads born in East Timor and those born elsewhere. This paper limits its mortality estimates to the native Timorese population wherever possible, so in-migrants are not a major concern.

will be further exacerbated over time by the application of population growth rates. Even though projecting the December 1970 population forward by five years seems relatively straightforward, there are questions about the reliability of the 1970 number. The Portuguese collected a poll tax during each census and hence all of their population counts were likely to have been understatements (Cribb 2001). What Cribb does not mention, however, is that undercounting the 1975 population will make excess mortality counts more *conservative* if later censuses are better enumerated. Hence we rely on the Portuguese numbers.[15]

Projecting forward from the June 1972 estimate to December 1975 with a Leslie matrix is problematic because Leslie matrices deal with whole years. Growth rates can easily be multiplied by fractions of a year, but it is not possible to multiply by fractions of a Leslie matrix. Therefore we produce a five-year Leslie Matrix from which to project the December 1970 population forward to December 1975.

The Portugal Instituto Nacional de Estatística (1985) provides age-specific mortality rates from 1972. Age-specific mortality rates are displayed as survival probabilities in Figure 2. Comparable survival probabilities for 1975, 1980, and 1990 were calculated from Coale-Demeny Model West Life Tables using Indonesian age-specific death rates. Why Indonesia? Here we want to understand the counterfactual: what East Timorese mortality might have looked like in the absence of the Indonesian invasion. East Timor's age-specific death rates would be problematic here because they already account for increases in deaths due to conflict, famine, and forced migration. Indonesian crude death rates are a convenient point of comparison to compute Coale-Demeny Model West age-specific mortality rates. Figure 2 shows that the pattern of death at younger ages is a different shape for the 1972 baseline Portuguese calculations as compared to the Coale-Demeny estimations. Thus half of all subsequent projection scenarios, even for later years, use the 1972 mortality rates while the other half use the Coale-Demeny period-specific mortality rates.

The Portugal Instituto Nacional de Estatística (1985) estimates that in 1972 East Timor's total fertility rate (TFR) was 5.1 births per woman over her lifetime. Unfortunately it does not provide any information on what the age-specific rates are. We relied on age-specific fertility rates from the East Timor

[15] There was a survey done by the Catholic Church in 1974 (Teixeira 1974) and one done in 1978 by the Indonesian army, but these population counts are also thought to be flawed (Hull 2003).

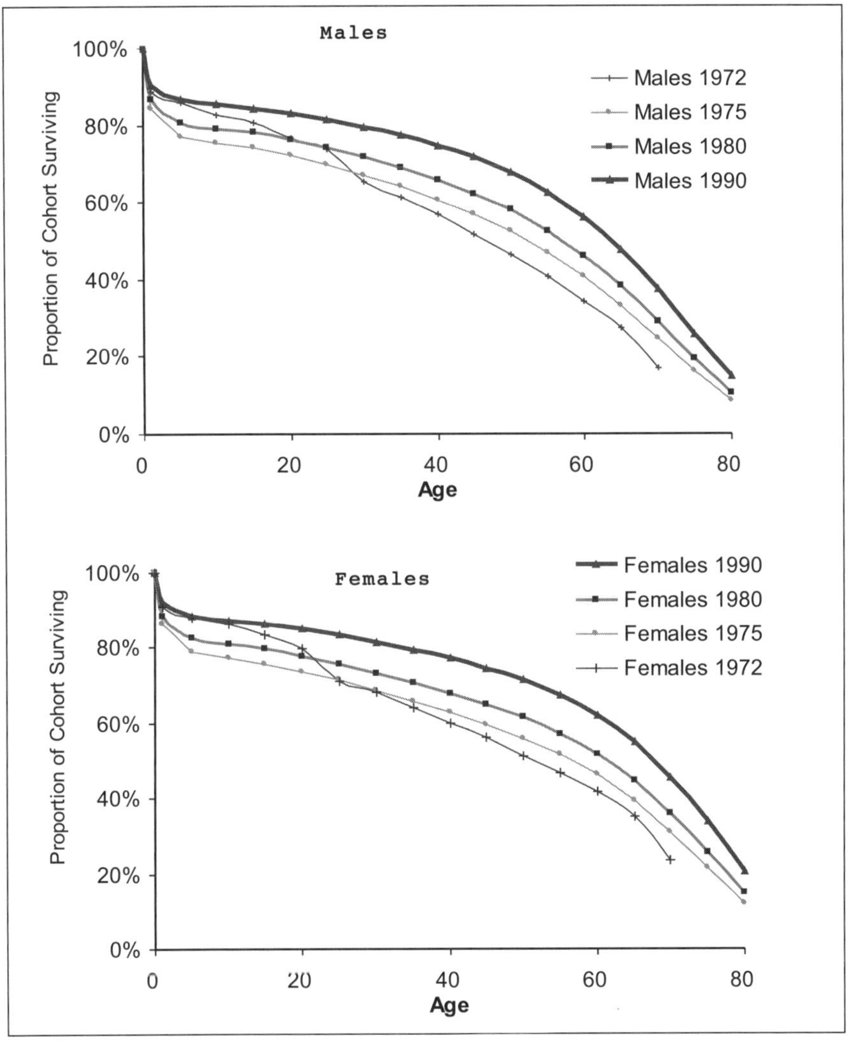

Figure 2. Cohort survivorship probabilities used for projections, 1972–1990. Sources: Portugal Instituto Nacional de Estatística (1985) and author's calculations using Coale-Demeny Model West Life Tables for Indonesia.

sample of the 1991 Demographic and Health Survey (DHS) (Central Bureau of Statistics Indonesia *et al.*, 1992) to obtain a proportionate distribution of age-specific fertility rates in 1972. We obviously cannot be certain that the distribution was the same in 1972, but the total fertility rates were quite close (5.1 in 1972 and 5.6 in the 1991 DHS), which suggests that there probably was *not* a dramatic shift in the age pattern of fertility from 1972 to 1991. Interestingly, these figures suggest that there was actually an *increase* in fertility during the period. It is not known whether this represents an actual increase or whether sampling, enumeration, and other methodological problems with the Portuguese statistics can explain the discrepancy. (The higher fertility rates are likely to be correct, as they were corroborated by even higher fertility rates for 2000–2005 from the United Nations.) Nonetheless, the higher fertility rate from the 1991 DHS indicates that the 1972 fertility rate of 5.1 is likely a conservative estimate. Figure 3 shows age-specific fertility rates $({}_{n}F_{x})$ for East Timor in 1972, as well as comparable DHS estimates from 1991, 1994, and 1997, and the United Nations estimate for 2000–2005.

In order to compute the starting (1975) population, age-specific fertility rates were combined with age-specific mortality rates to produce Leslie matrices for population projection (see Appendix A for a description of Leslie Matrices). For the period from 1970 to 1975, we had to take into account the thousands of refugees who fled from East to West Timor in early 1975 due to fighting between Fretilin and UDT. It is estimated that as many as 3,000 persons (largely former UDT combatants and their families) fled to Indonesian Timor before the Indonesian invasion, and that an additional 2,500 emigrated to Australia (Lawless 1976). The literature suggests that at least 1,500 (Kiernan 2003) and at most 13,000 (Hull 2003) were killed during the conflicts between

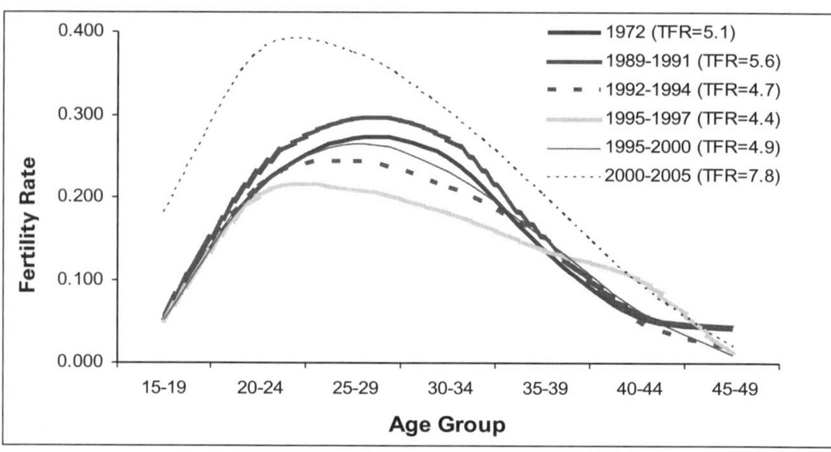

Figure 3. Age-specific fertility rates, East Timor, 1972–2005. Sources: Central Bureau of Statistics Indonesia *et al.*, (1992, 1995, 1998); Portugal Instituto Nacional de Estatística (1985); United Nations (2005). Note: 1972 fertility rates were assumed to follow the same age-specific pattern as fertility rates from 1989–1991.

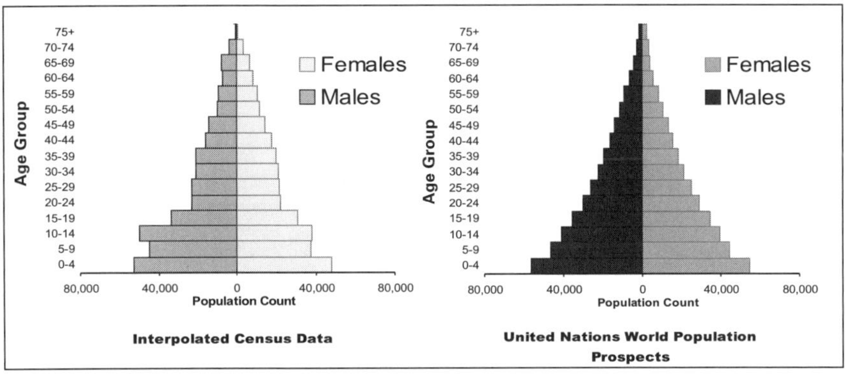

Figure 4. Age pyramid of East Timor, December 1975. Source: United Nations (2005) and author's calculations.

Fretilin and UDT. I approximate that from these sources the population lost an estimated 10,000 persons prior to the 1975 invasion. Thus my revised estimate of the 1975 population is 648,730. This estimate is near to Kiernan's (2003) suggested range of 652,250 to 707,500 persons alive immediately prior to the Indonesian invasion. We do not have any information on the age or sex of pre-invasion refugees, so we reduce our counts of all population age and sex groups proportionately. The resulting population pyramid for 1975 is shown in Figure 4, along with the smoothed version done by the United Nations (2005). Both baseline populations are used in projection scenarios for 1980.

The 1975–1980 Period

In 1980, the Indonesians conducted a census of East Timor and counted 554,721 persons. Using different combinations of age-specific fertility and mortality rates for the 1975–1980 period, we calculate 18 different projection scenarios.[16] We compute the expected 1980 population as the *median* estimate of the resulting 18 different projections. This helps reduce the sensitivity of our estimate to any particular combination of fertility and mortality rates. Figure 6 shows the United Nations estimate for 1980 compared to the median projected 1980 population. Given that the estimated population is much lower than the median projected population, it is clear that there was substantial out-migration, severe under-enumeration in 1980, or excess mortality during the

[16] In some scenarios fertility rates were revised downward for the period by 25 percent, as initial estimates produced an implausibly high number of missing infants.

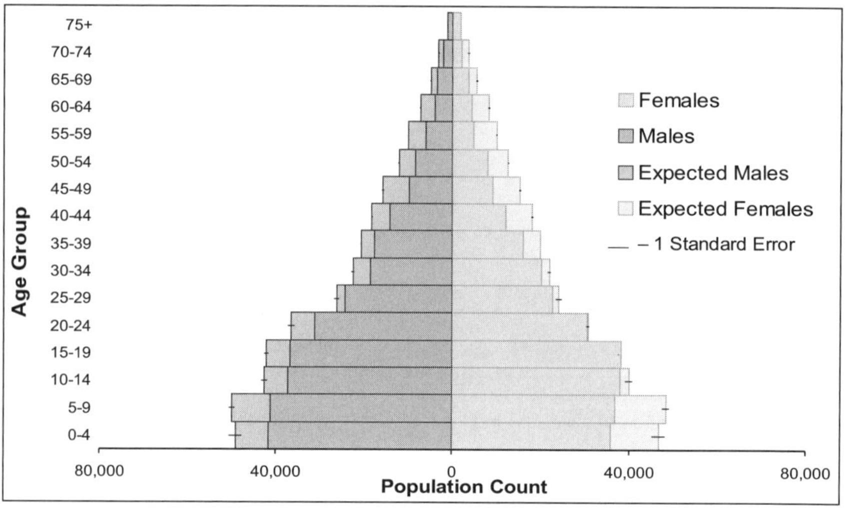

Figure 5. Expected versus reported population, East Timor, 1980. Source: United Nations (2005) and author's calculations. Note: Expected population refers to the median projection scenario and the standard error is computed from the set of alternative population projections.

time period. Standard errors from the sample of 18 different projection scenarios are also shown for purposes of comparing amongst different age groups. We have shied away from displaying standard deviations and confidence intervals throughout this report because our "population" of projection scenarios aims to be exhaustive (all possible combinations of baseline population, fertility, and mortality) rather than selective (favoring estimates that seem "most reasonable").

Our estimate produces a total "missing" population of 125,700 (with an inter-quartile range[17] of 28,000) from 1975 to 1980. How reliable is this figure? Cribb (2001) claims at most 50,000 were killed by Indonesian forces and an additional 50,000 died of starvation or disease brought about by the occupation. Kiernan (2003) puts the death toll at 120,000 during this period. Others have claimed that 200,000 is more appropriate (Crossette 1994; Amnesty International 1997). Given the large rates of internal displacement, it is possible that thousands of survivors were not enumerated during the 1980

[17] Absolute value of the difference between the 75th percentile and the 25th percentile.

census and United Nations estimates. Additionally, given the antagonistic relationship between East Timorese and Indonesians, many may have hid during census counting. Under-enumeration would artificially inflate our estimate of excess mortality. Yet at the same time, Indonesia also had a major incentive to inflate its population count of East Timor in order to cover up the real number killed. Moreover, since the Portuguese estimates are also thought to be undercounts, the Indonesian undercount would have to be quite severe to inflate the count of excess mortality.

It is estimated that 30,000 people left the territory between the 1975 invasion and 1979 (Anon. 1979). But by 1979, the majority of internally displaced people who had fled into the mountains and jungles reappeared. Additionally, there was a massive famine in the late 1970s (Sherlock 1996). Thus our estimate of 125,700 is on the high side but not out of the range of possibility.

Figure 6 shows the "missing" population by age and sex. Males have higher rates of excess mortality during the period, particularly those under the age of 25. Persons above age 45 also appear to have higher rates of excess mortality than middle-aged adults. Young children appear to be the most

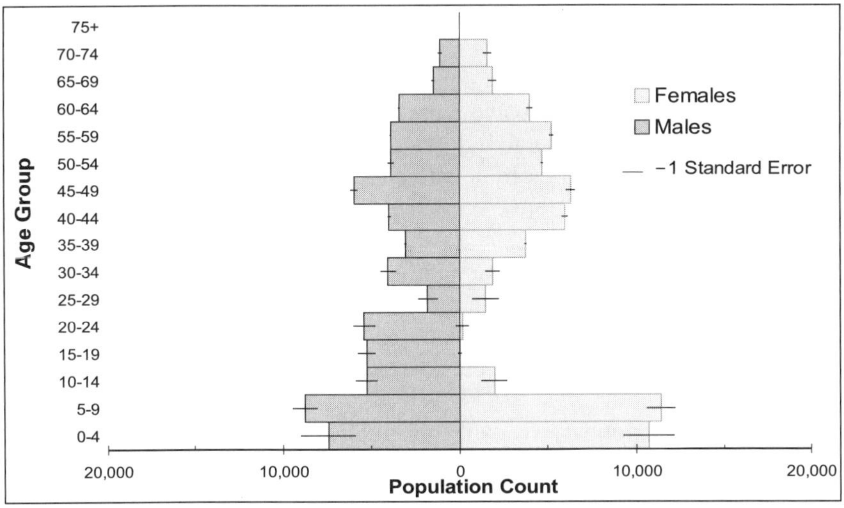

Figure 6. Age structure of "missing" population, 1980, East Timor. Source: United Nations (2005) and author's calculations. Note: "Missing" refers to the difference between the median projection scenario and the recorded United Nations (2005) total.

heavily affected group of all, accounting for nearly one-fourth of the estimated excess mortality from 1975 to 1980. Is this realistic? Infant mortality tends to be quite high during wartime (Urdinola 2004), so it is possible that this is a correct estimate of what actually happened. However as Cribb (2001) argues, the more likely scenario is that there was a drop in fertility from 1975 to 1980. It seems highly plausible that fertility would have declined during the 1975–1980 period, due to the high rates of internal displacement, the resulting breakup of families, food shortages, and lack of housing space. As noted previously, many of the projection scenarios reduced fertility by 25 percent to account for this decline.

Although it is possible that this excess mortality estimate is high due to an under-enumeration in the 1980 census, the age pattern is not suggestive of migration. The groups most impacted by mortality during the 1975–1980 period were the young and the old, the two groups least able to migrate on their own. These are also the two groups most vulnerable to disease and starvation. Hence one interpretation of Figure 6 is that the famine mortality from 1975 to 1980 was much higher than any combat-related mortality, an interpretation that is confirmed by much of the anecdotal literature.

The 1981–1990 Period

We can use similar techniques as above to estimate the excess mortality from 1981–1990. According to the Indonesian census, there were 747,557 persons in East Timor in 1990. However, due to the Indonesian trans-migration program, this total includes several thousand Indonesians. We need to exclude native Indonesians in order to avoid under-counting the number of "missing" persons. Other research has found that only 684,202 of these persons were living in households headed by a native of East Timor in 1990 (Hull 2003: 31).

We have very little information about the reliability of 1990 census data, and there are good reasons to believe that East Timorese may have avoided census enumerators, but also that Indonesians may have been tempted to overstate population totals in order to deflect attention to their annexation.

There was no new publicly available information on mortality rates from 1981 to 1990. Hence we use our results from the 1980 Coale-Demeny Model West Life Tables for Indonesia and the original 1972 mortality estimates from the Portugal Instituto Nacional de Estatística (1985). The former likely underestimate what Timorese mortality would have been in the absence of the Indonesian invasion, while the latter likely overestimate the same counterfactual. Fertility data was available from the 1991 DHS, but only for

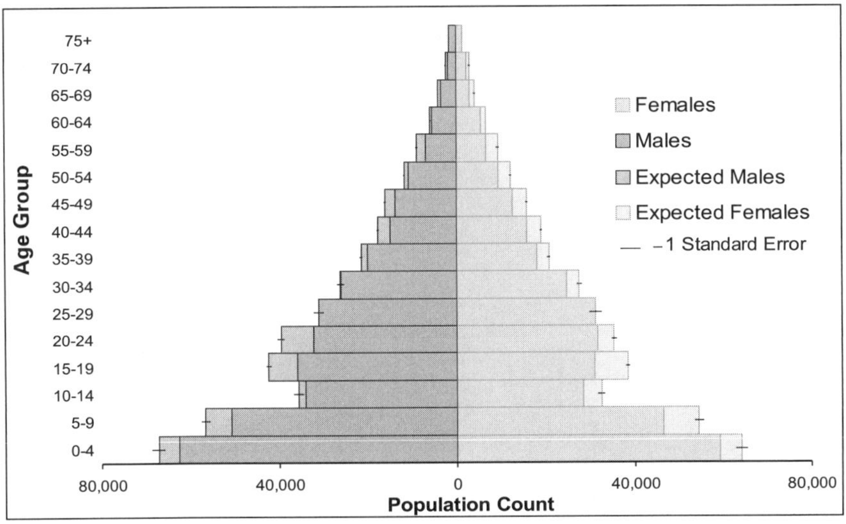

Figure 7. Expected versus reported population, East Timor, 1990. Source: United Nations (2005) and author's calculations. Note: Expected population refers to the median projection scenario and the standard error is computed from the set of alternative population projections.

the three-year period prior to the survey. Hence we divided our estimation into two five-year periods: 1981 to 1985 and 1986 to 1990. For the 1986 to 1990 period, we alternated between the DHS fertility and the United Nations fertility estimates, while for the 1981 to 1985 period we only used the United Nations 1980 fertility estimates. We computed a total of 16 different projection scenarios from 1980 to 1990. Figure 7 shows the median expected 1990 population versus the recorded 1990 population.

The median projection scenario suggests that 86,200 persons were "missing" from 1981 to 1990. The age structure of these missing persons is shown in Figure 8. The missing population is concentrated among persons under 24 and among persons aged 40 to 59. Interestingly, women were affected more than men. There was a massive Indonesian trans-migration program that brought thousands to East Timor, but this should not have had any substantial effect on the results shown above unless there was substantial intermarriage among Indonesians and East Timorese because we considered only persons in households headed by a native East Timorese. None of the literature indicates that intermarriage was common.

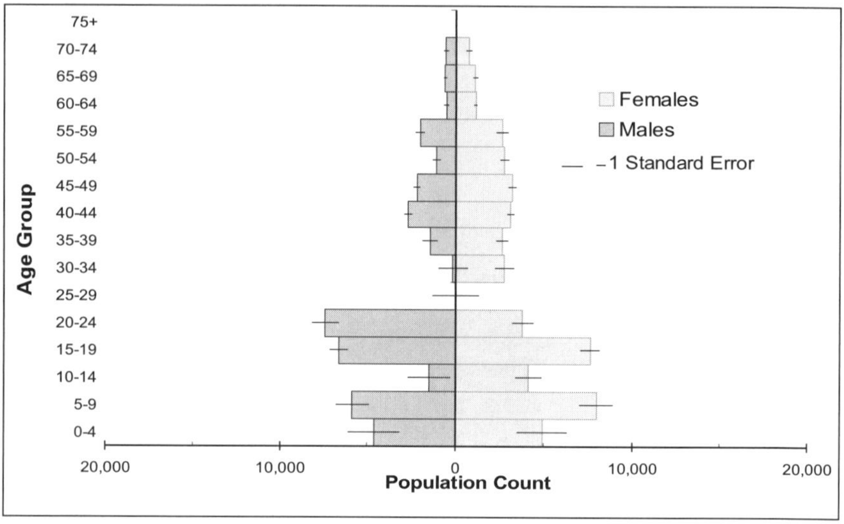

Figure 8. Age structure of "missing" population, East Timor, 1990. Source: United Nations (2005) and author's calculations. Note: "Missing" refers to the difference between the median projection scenario and the recorded United Nations (2005) total.

The 1991–2000 Period

Estimation of mortality during the 1991–2000[18] period is slightly more difficult due to the large-scale migrations which took place toward the end of the period. Following the August 1999 referendum and its subsequent violence, hundreds of thousands fled into West Timor (United Nations High Commissioner for Refugees 2000; Stahn 2001). Many returned in a short amount of time after the United Nations stabilised the situation. The United Nations estimates that eventually 90 percent of the 250,000 East Timorese who sought refuge in West Timor during 1999 were successfully repatriated into East Timor (Dolan *et al.*, 2004). By December 2000, at least 200,000 persons, or 80 percent of the refugees, had been successfully repatriated into East Timor. Therefore we need to incorporate what we know about excess emigration during the period in order to account for persons who were away in 2000 but would later return.

[18] The post-election violence subsided by January of 2000 but data were all from July of 2000. Because of the low levels of violence during 2000 it is assumed that these five months did not make much difference in the overall totals.

Based on a combination of fertility and mortality rates during the period, as well as assumptions about out-migration, 16 different projections for the 2000 population were computed. Half of the projection scenarios reduced their final total by 100,000 to account for the refugees who left, while the other half reduced their final count by 225,000. The results are shown compared to the reported 2000 population from the United Nations in Figure 9.

Without any knowledge of the age structure of refugees, I assumed they were evenly distributed across the existing age structure when I subtracted them from the estimated 2000 population. The resulting age structure of the median "missing" population in 2000, as shown in Figure 10, is heavily skewed toward persons aged 20–49 and toward younger children. It is also balanced in favour of women. This may indicate that young women of reproductive age were the most likely to migrate to West Timor during the post-election violence in 1999. Yet the age pattern of missing males is consistent with the targeting of working-age (and combat-age) young men by Indonesian forces and rebel groups. The total number of estimated "missing" persons from 1991 to 2000 (excluding returned refugees) is 34,000. Compared to totals from the previous decades, this is a rather "low" total.

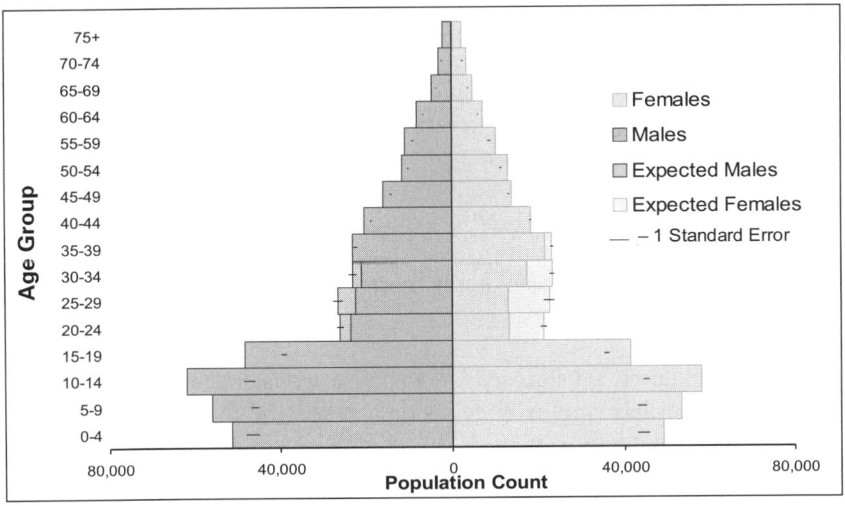

Figure 9. Expected versus recorded population, East Timor, 2000. Source: United Nations (2005) and author's calculations. Note: Expected population refers to the median projection scenario and the standard error is computed from the set of alternative population projections.

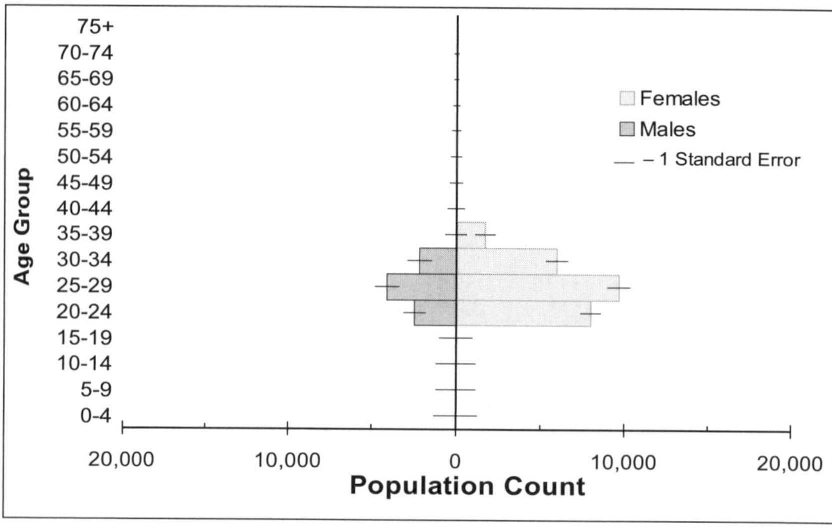

Figure 10. "Missing" population, excluding returned refugees, East Timor, 2000. Source: United Nations (2005) and author's calculations. Note: "Missing" refers to the difference between the median projection scenario and the recorded United Nations (2005) total.

Conclusions

There are two major ways to indirectly compute excess mortality in the absence of actual data on the number of casualties killed. The simplistic solution is to use a growth rate to estimate what the final population would have been, and then subtract the actual final population from that number. This is unsatisfactory, however. It does not account for the naturally-changing age structure of mortality and fertility during the period. Moreover, in a case like East Timor where a lot of persons died early on, a growth rate estimate would likely overstate excess mortality because it assumes these people would have gone on to bear children.

The second and more satisfactory way to indirectly calculate excess mortality, which this paper has employed, relies on age-specific fertility and mortality rates during intercensal periods to compare "actual" and "expected" population. However it is important to be clear that the result of such an exercise is not a total of excess mortality, but rather a total of "missing persons" – people who may have been missed in a later census, who may have moved out of the country, who might not have been born, or who might have prematurely died. From indirect data it is impossible to be conclusive about which of these sources caused the "missing" population, but experimenting with a variety of projection scenarios and examining qualitative evidence, as this paper has done, certainly helps.

My intercensal results found that there were likely 125,700 "missing" persons in 1980, 86,200 in 1990, and 34,000 in 2000. These three totals sum to 245,900 missing persons from the period 1975 to 2000. However after accounting for "excess" (unanticipated) population by birth cohort recorded in later years, the total estimated number of missing persons fell to 204,000. This is because during each period there were at least some age groups with apparent "excess" population, which I did not include in the total missing for that period. However in order to estimate the total number of "missing" persons from 1975 to 2000, I summed my estimates of missing persons in each intercensal period by *birth cohort* rather than by age. This ensures that some persons who left in one decade and returned in a different decade are correctly netted out from the total number of "missing." As they would likely be in a different age group by the time they returned, summing missing and excess persons by age alone would have had the unfortunate effect of showing a missing person in one age group and an "extra" person at another. That the total number of missing persons fell from 245,900 to 204,000 indicates that some of the population computed to be "missing" early on likely returned in later years, or that later population counts may have included Indonesian trans-migrants.

Using all possible combinations of my 18 different projection scenarios for 1980 with my 16 different projection scenarios for 1990 and 16 different scenarios for 2000 in this "birth cohort" method yielded a total of 18*16*16 = 4,608 different sums of "missing" persons throughout the entire period. Interestingly, the median net number of missing persons turned out to be 204,000 (±51,000),[19] quite close to what the literature has said about the total number who perished in East Timor. However, it should be noted that most of these estimates were intended to apply only to the pre-1980 or pre-1990 period, and hence may have been overestimates.

My best estimate of excess mortality in East Timor during the Indonesian occupation is 204,000 persons (± 51,000) either due to direct violence or else indirectly, perhaps as a result of hardships encountered when they were

[19] 51,000 refers to the standard deviation of the entire sample of 4,608 sums of "missing" persons. In this case it is not appropriate to provide a confidence interval over a "population" of estimates, since none were weighted by their perceived plausibility, but the sample standard deviation is included to offer a sense of the range of uncertainty.

forcibly displaced by the Indonesian army. This is likely a high estimate of deaths because the number of "missing" persons most certainly contains some non-deaths (migrants, non-births, and persons not enumerated in later censuses). I have tried to factor in lower fertility rates and high numbers of out-migrants wherever possible to err on the conservative side. The Indonesian trans-migration program that brought many non-native Timorese in the 1980s and 1990s may also be disguising an even greater number of casualties.

The median results by birth cohort, shown in Figure 11, also help distinguish among losses to the population existing in 1975 and to the population born during the invasion. Population in birth cohorts after 1975 that appears to be "missing" may in fact simply not have been born due to disruptions in fertility during the invasion period. Some slight downward adjustments in the fertility rate have been made in various projection scenarios to help account for this. As Figure 11 shows, missing persons came overwhelmingly from the population that was alive at the time of the invasion. As a reminder, expected mortality rates and known migration among this population has already been accounted for, so the "missing persons" shown in pre-1975 birth cohorts are likely – though not definitely – excess deaths.

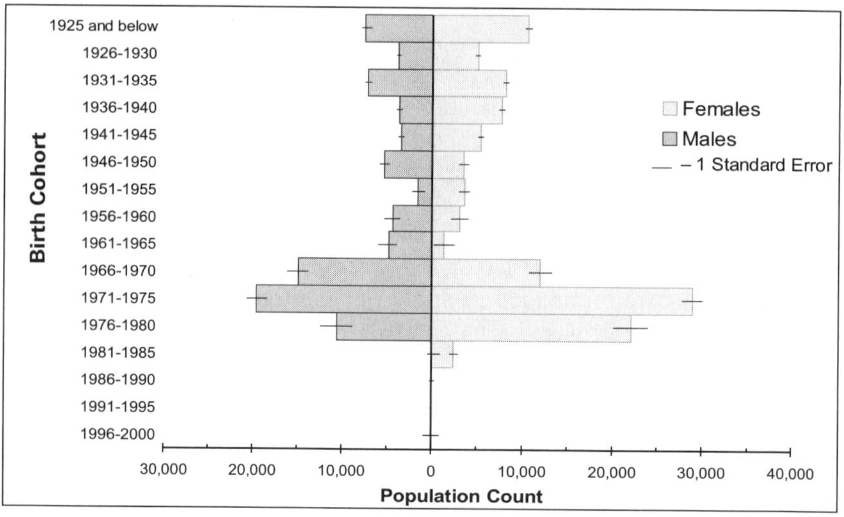

Figure 11. Median total "missing" population, 1975–2000, by birth cohort. Source: United Nations (2005) and author's calculations. Note: Birth cohort is used here instead of age in order to account for returned refugees, many of whom advanced age groups while out of the country.

Surprisingly, the birth cohorts from 1981–2000 appear to have fared quite well during the Indonesian occupation despite the fact that children are more susceptible than middle-aged persons to famine and disease due to forced migration. This may indicate that in fact fertility rates were higher during the invasion than previously thought, or that the Indonesian trans-migrant population was skewed toward adults with young children.

Interestingly, scholars and advocates who point to the massive financial investment Indonesia made in Timorese infrastructure and population (for example, Sherlock (1996) notes that Indonesians built far more schools during their 25 years of rule of East Timor than did the Portuguese during 400 years of colonialism) and the likely resulting decreases in "natural" mortality would actually have far more excess deaths to account for than others. This is because if Timorese mortality due to "normal" circumstances were in any way decreasing during the period, in keeping with the Coale-Demeny period estimates, then projected population totals would have been much higher, along with the counts of missing persons.

The data available for calculating estimates during this historical period were not ideal, and we cannot be certain of their precision. However, we do believe this to be the best approximation of deaths possible from census data alone. The estimates produced here were for "missing" persons, which could be deaths, emigrants, or the result of unexpected decreases in fertility. Estimates from Silva and Ball (2006) were for confirmed cases of mortality. Due to the survivor bias inherent in Silva and Ball's methods, it is likely that 102,800 is a lower-bound estimate. Silva and Ball also estimated that after accounting for recall bias, the number who died in East Timor of conflict-related deaths could be as high as 180,000. Due to the possibility that "missing" persons were not born, not enumerated, or had left, it is likely that 204,000 is a conservative upper-bound estimate on excess mortality. The "true" number of East Timorese who died because of the Indonesian occupation may never be known. This paper has, however, established the plausibility of a much higher excess death toll using only public data provided by the Portuguese, Indonesians, and the United Nations. Obvious ways to improve the estimates given here would be to incorporate information on the size and age structure of Indonesian trans-migrants and the age structure of emigrants who fled East Timor and did not return. As Waddingham (2003) suggests, it would be ideal to re-investigate original Portuguese and Indonesian census records or to more critically assess their accuracy, but this level of detail has not been made available.

Previous efforts to indirectly compute the "missing" population in East Timor simply extrapolated earlier-period population growth rates in order to surmise the number of missing persons. The estimates computed here are much more sophisticated: they indicate the age and sex distribution behind these totals, and account for changing migration, fertility, and baseline mortality during the period in order to help isolate the population that went missing due to excess mortality alone. Compared to the results published by Silva and Ball (2006), the most important advantage of these methods is that they are derived *entirely* from publicly-available data, much of it collected and published by the Indonesian government during the occupation. Hence it would be difficult for the Indonesians to claim that the large numbers of missing persons found here – especially those who went "missing" between 1975 and 1990, when the last official Indonesian census of East Timor was published – simply left or were undercounted.

References

Abdullah, Samsi. 1976. Letter to the Editor from U.S. Counselor of the Indonesian Embassy. *New York Times*, January 11, 1976.

Amnesty International. 1997. *Power and Impunity: Human Rights under the New Order*. New York: Amnesty International.

Anon. 1979. East Timor: The Next Cambodia. *The Economist* (November 10, 1979).

Asian Development Bank. 2002. *2001 Suco Survey*. Manila, Philippines: Asian Development Bank.

Bagian Statistik Demografi [Indonesian Demographic Statistics Division]. 1980. *Sensus Penduduk 1980: Rumahtangga Dan Penduduk, Timor Timur*. Vol. SP80-54.1. Jakarta, Indonesia: Biro Pusat Statistik (Central Bureau of Statistics).

Bagian Statistik Demografi [Indonesian Demographic Statistics Division]. 1990. *Sensus Penduduk 1990: Rumahtangga Dan Penduduk, Timor Timur*. Jakarta, Indonesia: Biro Pusat Statistik (Central Bureau of Statistics).

Central Bureau of Statistics Indonesia, State Ministry of Population, Ministry of Health, and Macro International. 1992. *Indonesia Demographic and Health Survey 1991*. Calverton, Maryland: Macro International.

Central Bureau of Statistics Indonesia, State Ministry of Population, Ministry of Health, and Macro International. 1995. *Indonesia Demographic and Health Survey 1994*. Calverton, Maryland: Macro International.

Central Bureau of Statistics Indonesia, State Ministry of Population, Ministry of Health, and Macro International. 1998. *Indonesia Demographic and Health Survey 1997*. Calverton, Maryland: Macro International.

Chomsky, Noam. 1999. Why Americans should care about East Timor. *Mother Jones,* August 26, 1999.

CIA. 2005. World Factbook. https://www.cia.gov/cia/publications/factbook/geos/tt.html

Cribb, Robert. 2001. How many deaths? Problems in the statistics of massacre in Indonesia (1965–1966) and Timor-Leste (1975–1980). Pages 82–95 in I.

Wessel and G. Wimhoefer (eds.), *Violence in Indonesia*. Hamburg: Abera-Verl.

Crossette, Barbara. 1994. Wave of migration is altering East Timor. *The New York Times*, October 30, 1994.

Defert, Gabriel. 1992. *Timor Est. Le Genocide Oublié. Droit d'un Peuple et Raisons d'États*. Paris: Éditions L'Harmattan.

Direcção Nacional de Estatística de Timor-Leste. 2005. Provisional Population Counts from 2004 Census. Dili: Ministry of Planning and Finance. http://dne.mopf.gov.tl/census/2004_census/2004_population_housing/provisional_counts.htm

Dolan, Chris, Judith Large, and Naoko Obi. 2004. *Evaluation of UNHCR's Repatriation and Reintegration Programme in East Timor, 1999–2003*. Geneva, Switzerland: United Nations High Commissioner for Refugees Evaluation and Policy Analysis Unit. http://www.unhcr.org/epau

Ghobarah, H.A., P. Huth, and B. Russett. 2003. Civil wars kill and maim people – Long after the shooting stops. *American Political Science Review* 97(2): 189–202.

Gunn, G.C. 2000. Showdown in Timor: Notes from the (battle) field. *Bulletin of Concerned Asian Scholars* 32(4): 52–54.

Houk, R.J. 1978. Drama of Portuguese Timor – Portuguese – Moreira, A. *Annals of the American Academy of Political and Social Science* 436(MAR): 163–164.

Hull, Terrence. 2003. From province to nation: The demographic revolution of a people. Pages 28–40 in J.J. Fox and D.B. Soares (eds.), *Out of the Ashes: Destruction and Reconstruction of East Timor*. Canberra: Australian National University Press.

Hull, Terrence. 2004. East Timor: Census shows fertility, population high, nutrition low. In *Interview with ABC Radio Australia*:
http://www.abc.net.au/ra/asiapac/programs/s1200019.htm.

Huridocs. 2005. *East Timor* 2003 [cited September 15 2005]. Available from http://www.qub.ac.uk/schools/SchoolofLaw/Research/HumanRightsCentre/Resources/html/Filetoupload,53218,en.htm

Jardine, Matthew. 1995. *East Timor: Genocide in Paradise*. Tuscon, Arizona: Odonian Press.

Kiernan, B. 2002. Cover-up and denial of genocide – Australia, the USA, East Timor, and the Aborigines. *Critical Asian Studies* 34(2): 163–192.

Kiernan, B. 2003. The demography of genocide in Southeast Asia – The death tolls in Cambodia, 1975–79, and East Timor, 1975–80. *Critical Asian Studies* 35(4): 585–597.

Kohen, Arnold and John Taylor. 1979. *An Act of Genocide: Indonesia's Invasion of East Timor*. London: TAPOL (the Indonesia Human Rights Campaign).

Lawless, R. 1976. The Indonesian takeover of East Timor. *Asian Survey* 16(10): 948–964.

Li, Q. and M. Wen. 2005. The immediate and lingering effects of armed conflict on adult mortality: A time-series cross-national analysis. *Journal of Peace Research* 42(4): 471–492.

Ministry of Health and National Statistics Office. 2004. [please complete; see Fig. 2] can delete - should be Direcção Nacional de Estatística de Timor-Leste. 2005.(above)

Monk, P.M. 2001. Secret intelligence and escape clauses – Australia and the Indonesian annexation of East Timor, 1963–76. *Critical Asian Studies* 33(2): 181–208.

Nichertlein, S. 1977. Struggle for East Timor – Prelude to invasion. *Journal of Contemporary Asia* 7(4): 486–496.

Nixon, Rod. 2004. Indonesian West Timor: The political economy of emerging ethno-nationalism. *Journal of Contemporary Asia* 34(2): 163–186.

Pilger, J. 1994a. Journey to East Timor – Land of the dead. *Nation* 258(16): 550–552.

Pilger, J. 1994b. A voice that shames those silent on Timor. *New Statesman & Society* 7(297): 16–17.

Portugal Instituto Nacional de Estatística. 1960. *Anuario Estatistico Provincias Ultramarinas 1960*. Lisbon: Portugal Instituto Nacional de Estatística. [I added – is this ref correct? In Table 1][Technically, I only had access to the 1970 and beyond editions, and these gave me the population counts from the 1950 and 1960 census. Do I need to state that somehow?]

Portugal Instituto Nacional de Estatística. 1970. *Anuario Estatistico Provincias Ultramarinas 1970*. Lisbon: Portugal Instituto Nacional de Estatística.

Portugal Instituto Nacional de Estatística. 1971. *Anuario Estatistico Provincias Ultramarinas 1971*. Lisbon: Portugal Instituto Nacional de Estatística.

Portugal Instituto Nacional de Estatística. 1972. *Anuario Estatistico Provincias Ultramarinas 1972*. Lisbon: Portugal Instituto Nacional de Estatística.

Portugal Instituto Nacional de Estatística. 1973. *Anuario Estatistico Provincias Ultramarinas 1973*. Lisbon: Portugal Instituto Nacional de Estatística.

Portugal Instituto Nacional de Estatística. 1985. *Revista Do Centro de Estudos Demograficos*. Lisbon: Portugal Instituto Nacional de Estatística.

R Development Core Team. 2006. *R: A Language and Environment for Statistical Computing*. Version 2.3.1. R Foundation for Statistical Computing, Vienna, Austria. http://www.R-project.org

Sharkey, John. 1977. House to probe charge Indonesians killed 100,000 on Timor. *The Washington Post*, March 13, 1977, A19.

Sherlock, Stephen. 1996. Political economy of the East Timor conflict. *Asian Survey* 36(9): 835–851.

Sidell, S. 1981. The United-States and Genocide in East Timor. *Journal of Contemporary Asia* 11(1): 44–61.

Silva, Romesh and Patrick Ball. 2006. The Profile of Human Rights Violations in Timor-Leste, 1974–1999. A Report by the Benetech Human Rights Data Analysis Group to the Commission on Reception, Truth and Reconciliation. February 9, 2006. http://www.hrdag.org/timor

Stahn, Carsten. 2001. Accommodating individual criminal responsibility and national reconciliation: The UN Truth Commission for East Timor. *The American Journal of International Law* 95(4): 952–966.

Teixeira, Manuel (Padre). 1974. *Macau e a sua Diocese. X. Missões de Timor.* Translated by K. Sherlock. Macau: Tipografia da Missão do Padroado.

U.S. Census Bureau. 2004. [Accessed 06-15–2005]. *International Data Base Summary Demographic Data for East Timor*. http://www.census.gov/cgi-bin/ipc/idbsum.pl?cty=TT

U.S. Congress. 1999a. *The Humanitarian Crisis in East Timor: Hearing before the Subcommittee on International Operations and Human Rights of the Committee on International Relations, House of Representatives, One Hundred Sixth Congress, first session, Thursday, September 30, 1999.* Washington, DC: U.S. Government Printing Office.

U.S. Congress. 1999b. *The Political Futures of Indonesia and East Timor: Joint hearing before the Subcommittee on Asia and the Pacific of the Committee on International Relations, House of Representatives, and the Subcommittee on East Asian and Pacific Affairs of the Committee on Foreign Relations, United States Senate, One Hundred Sixth Congress, first session, on September 9, 1999.* Washington: U.S. Government Printing Office.

U.S. Congress. 2000. *East Timor: A new beginning?: Joint hearing before the Subcommittee on Asia and the Pacific of the Committee on International Relations, House of Representatives, and the Subcommittee on East Asian and Pacific Affairs of the Committee on Foreign Relations, United States Senate, One Hundred Sixth Congress, second session, February 10, 2000.* [Corr. print.]. ed. Washington, D.C.: U.S. Government Printing Office.

United Nations. 2005. *World Population Prospects: The 2004 Revision.* New York: United Nations Population Division [CD-ROM].

United Nations High Commissioner for Refugees. 2000. *The State of the World's Refugees: Fifty Years of Humanitarian Action.* New York: Oxford University Press.

Urdinola, B. Piedad. 2004. *Could Political Violence Affect Infant Mortality? The Colombian Case*. Dissertation at the Department of Demography, University of California, Berkeley, USA.

Wachter, Kenneth. 2002. Essential Demographic Methods. Mimeo. University of California, Berkeley, USA.

Waddingham, John. 2003. East Timor Death Toll 1975–1999. *Submission to the East Timor Commission for Reception, Truth, & Reconciliation*. July 22. Mimeo copy.

Wheeler, Nicholas and Tim Dunne. 2001. East Timor and the New Humanitarian Interventionism. *International Affairs* 77(4) 805–827.

Zunes, Stephen. 2000. East Timor's tragedy and triumph. *Peace Review* 12(2): 329–335.

APPENDIX A: LESLIE MATRICES

A Leslie Matrix projects a population in steps that are equal to the width of its age intervals – for example, a population in five-year age groups can be projected five years ahead. We have five-year age groups and rates, but unfortunately because we want to project from 1972 to 1980 it will be necessary to convert our age groups and rates into age intervals that would allow us to project directly to 1980. In this analysis we employ five-year age intervals, which align perfectly with the dates of interest.

A Leslie Matrix is a transition matrix which is multiplied by a vector of single-sex population totals by age group to produce an age-disaggregated estimate of the single-sex population in the following period. The matrix uses single-sex mortality and fertility rates (usually for women) because fertility rates are very difficult to ascertain on a combined-sex basis. Using the ratio of women to men in the total population, this new estimate of the female population can be easily converted into a hypothetical total population estimate. The Leslie Matrix does not factor migration into account; it assumes a closed population. Migration rates can of course be added in later. According to the 1970, 1971, 1972, and 1973 Portuguese censuses, the migration in and out of East Timor was nearly equal. Hence, in the absence of additional information about migration, we assume that net migration was zero during the period.[20]

	0 to 1	*2 to 3*	*4 to 5*	*6 to 7*	......
0 to 1	*kids*	*kids*	*kids*	*kids*	......
2 to 3	*survivors*	0	0	0	
4 to 5	0	*survivors*	0	0	
6 to 7	0	0	*survivors*	0	
8 to 9	0	0	0	*survivors*	
......	......				

Figure A1. Leslie Matrix. Note: Because young girls cannot bear children, the entries in the top row of a Leslie Matrix will be zero until a column corresponding to a childbearing age group is reached. However for illustrative purposes we include "kids" (births) in the leftmost columns of the top row above.

[20] All available information suggests that the vast majority of displaced persons stayed in East Timor and hid in the mountainous areas.

A Leslie Matrix has a top row which projects fertility and a sub-diagonal which projects survivorship (Wachter 2002). The rest of the entries in the matrix are "structural zeroes", since transitions between these groups during the time interval are impossible. Each column corresponds to an age group in the current population, while each row corresponds to an age group in the projected population, as shown in Figure A1.

It is common to refer to $A_{i,j}$ as being the entry in the ith row and j^{th} column of our Leslie Matrix. As shown in Figure A1, all of the entries in the matrix will be structural zeros except for the first row and the subdiagonal. If we assume that ${}_nL_x$ is the female cohort person-years lived from age x to age x+n in a hypothetical life table computed using current period age-specific mortality rates and ${}_nF_x^{dau}$ is the female fertility rate from age x to x+n for daughters only,[21] then the formula for the jth column of the first row is given by the following formula:

$$A_{1,j} = \frac{{}_nL_0}{2l_0} \cdot \left({}_nF_x^{dau} + {}_nF_{x+n}^{dau} \cdot \frac{{}_nL_{x+n}}{{}_nL_x} \right)$$

This formula allows for the fact that some women in the current age group of interest will not survive through the four-year period to bear children, and that the older women in the current age group of interest will spend most of their four-years exposed to the next age group's fertility rate. The formula also accounts for the fact that some births will not survive until the end of the four-year period.

The sub-diagonal of the Leslie matrix (an entry in $A_{j+1,j}$) is more straightforward. It simply represents survivorship among women in the current age group as they transition to the next age group. Its formula is given as:

$$A_{j+1,j} = \frac{{}_nL_{x+n}}{{}_nL_x}$$

In this project, Leslie matrices were computed separately for women and for men due to the asymmetry of their mortality patterns. Male fertility was not estimated; instead births from the female Leslie matrix were converted into a likely number of male births during the same year and added into the male Leslie Matrix before the next projection step. This unique step was taken to increase the accuracy of overall results for both males and females.

---

[21] This is derived from the total female age-specific fertility rate multiplied by 0.4886, an internationally-used definition for the fraction of births which are female (Wachter 2002).

Appendix B: Data Tables

Table B1. World population prospects population counts, 1975. Source: United Nations (2005).

Age	Females	Males	Total
0–4	54900	56500	111400
5–9	44300	46200	90500
10–14	39400	41200	80600
15–19	34100	35200	69300
20–24	29100	30200	59300
25–29	24900	26000	50900
30–34	21000	22100	43100
35–39	18500	19300	37800
40–44	15500	16300	31800
45–49	13600	14200	27800
50–54	10700	11200	21900
55–59	8700	9000	17700
60–64	5900	6200	12100
65–69	4000	4300	8300
70–74	3300	2500	5800
75+	2500	1605	4105
Total	330400	342005	672405

Table B2. World population prospects population counts, 1980. Source: United Nations (2005).

Age	Females	Males	Total
0–4	36016	41541	77557
5–9	36889	41013	77902
10–14	38031	37179	75210
15–19	38157	36684	74841
20–24	30697	31038	61735
25–29	22726	24285	47011
30–34	20201	18436	38637
35–39	16223	17554	33777
40–44	12229	14175	26404
45–49	9168	9702	18870
50–54	8100	8202	16302
55–59	4943	6015	10958
60–64	4304	3837	8141
65–69	3627	3468	7095
70–74	2034	1986	4020
75+	1799	1121	2920
Total	285144	296236	581380

Table B3. Census data population counts, 1980. Source: Bagian Statistik Demografi (1980).

Age	Females	Males	Total
0–4	30579	32021	62600
5–9	40005	43436	83441
10–14	34731	42523	77254
15–19	28215	28078	56293
20–24	27063	25078	52141
25–29	20576	21651	42227
30–34	19880	19192	39072
35–39	17545	17700	35245
40–44	14270	12776	27046
45–49	11948	11784	23732
50–54	7700	7102	14802
55–59	6280	6247	12527
60–64	5872	5600	11472
65–69	3585	4478	8063
70–74	2304	2914	5218
75+	1517	2071	3588
Total	272070	282651	554721

Table B4. Median projection population counts, 1980. Source: Author's calculations.

Age	Females	Female SE	Males	Male SE
0–4	46763	1637	48945	1564
5–9	48333	754	49761	852
10–14	40002	641	42421	794
15–19	37659	529	41932	139
20–24	30854	670	36407	395
25–29	24189	604	26075	817
30–34	22083	463	22464	417
35–39	19989	65	20627	46
40–44	18199	89	18153	204
45–49	15484	207	15642	276
50–54	12783	170	12076	83
55–59	10140	52	9907	123
60–64	8273	64	7242	185
65–69	5504	105	4953	234
70–74	3619	126	3125	251
75+	538	22	452	6
Total	343307	2086	359623	2866

Table B5. World population prospects population counts, 1990[a]. Source: United Nations (2005).

Age	Females	Males	Total
0–4	64739	68330	133069
5–9	50744	55377	106121
10–14	30962	37165	68127
15–19	33708	39002	72710
20–24	34456	35006	69462
25–29	34036	33894	67930
30–34	27032	28268	55300
35–39	19775	21809	41584
40–44	17368	16223	33591
45–49	13773	15027	28800
50–54	10158	11683	21841
55–59	7305	7568	14873
60–64	6012	5894	11906
65–69	3276	3814	7090
70–74	2404	2020	4424
75+	1492	1872	3364
Total	357240	382952	740192

[a]. In actual calculations these figures were reduced by 8.47 percent so as to exclude non-native households from population totals. See Hull (2003:31) for further details.

Table B6. Census population counts, 1990[a]. Source: Bagian Statistik Demografi (1990).

Age	Females	Males	Total
0–4	65379	69010	134389
5–9	51244	55929	107173
10–14	31268	37535	68803
15–19	34041	39390	73431
20–24	34797	35354	70151
25–29	34373	34231	68604
30–34	27298	28549	55847
35–39	19971	22026	41997
40–44	17540	16384	33924
45–49	13909	15176	29085
50–54	10258	11799	22057
55–59	7377	7643	15020
60–64	6071	5953	12024
65–69	3309	3852	7161
70–74	2428	2040	4468
75+	1533	1890	3423
Total	360796	386761	747557

[a]. In actual calculations these figures were reduced by 8.47 percent so as to exclude non-native households from population totals. See Hull (2003:31) for further details.

Table B7. Median projection population counts, 1990. Source: Author's calculations.

Age	Females	Female SE	Males	Male SE
0–4	64181	1425	67176	1492
5–9	54437	953	56538	964
10–14	32470	750	35512	1234
15–19	38507	555	42317	528
20–24	35368	622	39449	798
25–29	31122	1322	30970	1139
30–34	27531	570	26030	843
35–39	20761	345	21428	443
40–44	19035	208	17546	228
45–49	15823	239	15968	209
50–54	12090	282	11803	221
55–59	9327	336	8955	254
60–64	6648	81	5933	134
65–69	4117	147	4101	88
70–74	2962	162	2405	159
75+	422	16	408	23
Total	375671	5272	387502	5716

Table B8. World population prospects population counts, 2000. Source: United Nations (2005).

Age	Females	Males	Total
0–4	49026	51086	100112
5–9	53342	55678	109020
10–14	57842	61701	119543
15–19	41478	48292	89770
20–24	13217	23512	36729
25–29	12829	22376	35205
30–34	17261	20916	38177
35–39	21395	23081	44476
40–44	18244	20219	38463
45–49	13764	15795	29559
50–54	12842	11633	24475
55–59	10213	10851	21064
60–64	7235	7970	15205
65–69	4771	4555	9326
70–74	3442	3011	6453
75+	2226	2029	4255
Total	339127	382705	721832

Table B9. Median projection population counts, 2000. Source: Author's calculations.

Age	Females	Female SE	Males	Male SE
0–4	44458	1236	46532	1293
5–9	44178	1120	45846	1176
10–14	45140	1124	47162	1189
15–19	35850	921	39098	1005
20–24	21236	595	25973	674
25–29	22520	685	26505	733
30–34	23261	653	23069	713
35–39	23131	617	22406	658
40–44	18192	488	18689	520
45–49	13126	356	14031	405
50–54	11256	313	10115	295
55–59	8687	238	8956	261
60–64	6097	166	6487	191
65–69	3861	129	3630	133
70–74	2555	130	2212	125
75+	275	14	285	16
Total	323823	8546	340997	9118

Table B10. Median estimate of "missing" population, 1975–2000, by cohort. Source: Author's calculations.

Birth Cohort	Females	Female SD	Males	Male SD
1996–2000	0	1024	0	1162
1991–1995	0	0	0	0
1986–1990	0	1532	0	1164
1981–1985	-2431	3810	0	1975
1976–1980	-22119	7124	-10603	7694
1971–1975	-28924	4759	-19534	4564
1966–1970	-12043	4664	-14925	4836
1961–1965	-1349	3890	-4798	4734
1956–1960	-3027	2850	-4300	4001
1951–1955	-3614	3322	-1606	2488
1946–1950	-3505	2129	-5328	2308
1941–1945	-5398	1318	-3452	1319
1936–1940	-7694	1496	-3665	1184
1931–1935	-8171	1761	-7149	1371
1926–1930	-5002	676	-3769	970
1925 and below	-10596	3311	-7539	1439
Total	-116496	25600	-88625	24490

Table B11. Sample female Leslie Matrix used in projections from 1975 to 1980. Source: Author's calculations.

	0–4	5–9	10–14	15–19	20–24	25–29	30–34	35–39	40–44	45–49	50–54	55–59	60–64	65–69	70–74	75+
0–4	0	0	0.0586	0.2759	0.5095	0.5611	0.4195	0.2122	0.104	0.0454	0	0	0	0	0	0
5–9	0.9621	0	0	0	0	0	0	0	0	0	0	0	0	0	0	0
10–14	0	0.9728	0	0	0	0	0	0	0	0	0	0	0	0	0	0
15–19	0	0	0.9623	0	0	0	0	0	0	0	0	0	0	0	0	0
20–24	0	0	0	0.9238	0	0	0	0	0	0	0	0	0	0	0	0
25–29	0	0	0	0	0.9217	0	0	0	0	0	0	0	0	0	0	0
30–34	0	0	0	0	0	0.9488	0	0	0	0	0	0	0	0	0	0
35–39	0	0	0	0	0	0	0.9392	0	0	0	0	0	0	0	0	0
40–44	0	0	0	0	0	0	0	0.938	0	0	0	0	0	0	0	0
45–49	0	0	0	0	0	0	0	0	0.9237	0	0	0	0	0	0	0
50–54	0	0	0	0	0	0	0	0	0	0.9112	0	0	0	0	0	0
55–59	0	0	0	0	0	0	0	0	0	0	0.9021	0	0	0	0	0
60–64	0	0	0	0	0	0	0	0	0	0	0	0.8682	0	0	0	0
65–69	0	0	0	0	0	0	0	0	0	0	0	0	0.7621	0	0	0
70–74	0	0	0	0	0	0	0	0	0	0	0	0	0	0.6406	0	0
75+	0	0	0	0	0	0	0	0	0	0	0	0	0	0	0.15	0

Table B12. Sample male Leslie Matrix used in projections from 1975 to 1980. Source: Author's calculations. Note: Male Leslie Matrix applies only to mortality; newborn males estimated as a fixed ratio of newborn females after using the female Leslie Matrix.

	0–4	**5–9**	**10–14**	**15–19**	**20–24**	**25–29**	**30–34**	**35–39**	**40–44**	**45–49**	**50–54**	**55–59**	**60–64**	**65–69**	**70–74**	**75+**
0–4	0	0	0	0	0	0	0	0	0	0	0	0	0	0	0	0
5–9	0.9494	0	0	0	0	0	0	0	0	0	0	0	0	0	0	0
10–14	0	0.9701	0	0	0	0	0	0	0	0	0	0	0	0	0	0
15–19	0	0	0.9642	0	0	0	0	0	0	0	0	0	0	0	0	0
20–24	0	0	0	0.9575	0	0	0	0	0	0	0	0	0	0	0	0
25–29	0	0	0	0	0.9226	0	0	0	0	0	0	0	0	0	0	0
30–34	0	0	0	0	0	0.9077	0	0	0	0	0	0	0	0	0	0
35–39	0	0	0	0	0	0	0.9346	0	0	0	0	0	0	0	0	0
40–44	0	0	0	0	0	0	0	0.9182	0	0	0	0	0	0	0	0
45–49	0	0	0	0	0	0	0	0	0.9025	0	0	0	0	0	0	0
50–54	0	0	0	0	0	0	0	0	0	0.8882	0	0	0	0	0	0
55–59	0	0	0	0	0	0	0	0	0	0	0.8624	0	0	0	0	0
60–64	0	0	0	0	0	0	0	0	0	0	0	0.8255	0	0	0	0
65–69	0	0	0	0	0	0	0	0	0	0	0	0	0.7151	0	0	0
70–74	0	0	0	0	0	0	0	0	0	0	0	0	0	0.5871	0	0
75+	0	0	0	0	0	0	0	0	0	0	0	0	0	0	0.1419	0

Building the Rule of Law after Conflict: UNTAET and Judicial Institution Building in East Timor[1]

Dominik Zaum

The establishment of the rule of law has become one of the key priorities of post-conflict peace-building missions, believed to be central to the promotion of security, democracy, and economic development.[2] The rule of law, described by one author as consisting of (1) government bound by law; (2) equality before the law; (3) law and order; (4) predictable and efficient government; and (5) human rights,[3] is essential for citizens' trust in the institutions of the state, guarding them against arbitrary use of state power. The rule of law and functioning judicial institutions are key elements of transitional justice to address war crimes and human rights violations that occurred during a conflict, and can therefore contribute to post-conflict reconciliation. More generally, a legal order is a constitutive element of modern states,[4] defining the locus and scope of political authority. In the absence of a legal order, the scope of the state's authority is unclear, and governance arbitrary and unaccountable.

For all these reasons, establishing the rule of law has become an essential element of state- and peace-building, reflected in the importance attached to the establishment of judicial institutions and the rule of law in the Brahimi Report on United Nations (UN) Peace Operations,[5] and the UN Secretary

---

[1] This chapter draws on excerpts from the author's previous publication, *The Sovereignty Paradox: The Norms and Politics of International Statebuilding* (Oxford, Oxford University Press, 2007).

[2] Kirsti Samuels, *Rule of Law Reform in Post-Conflict Countries: Operational Initiatives and Lessons Learned*, Conflict Prevention and Reconstruction, Paper No 37, World Bank (October 2006), 3.

[3] See Rachel Kleinfeld-Belton, *Competing Definitions of the Rule of Law: Implications for Practitioners*, Carnegie Endowment for International Peace, Rule of Law Series, No 55 (January 2005), 27.

[4] Elizabeth Heger Boyle and John Meyer, "Modern Law as a Secularized Global Model: Implications for the Sociology of Law", in Yves Dezalay and Bryant G. Garth (eds), *Global Prescriptions: The Production, Exportation, and Importation of a New Legal Orthodoxy* (Ann Arbor, University of Michigan Press, 2002), 68.

[5] Report of the Panel on United Nations Peace Operations (The Brahimi Report), UN doc. S/2001/42 of 21 August 2000, paras 79–83.

General's High Level Panel report.[6] Its importance was also emphasised by Paddy Ashdown, former High Representative in Bosnia and Herzegovina, when he stated that:

> We should have put the establishment of the rule of law first, for everything depends on it: a functioning economy, a free and fair political system, the development of civil society, public confidence in police and the courts.[7]

While promoting the rule of law is an important element of post-conflict peace-building, it is also one of the most difficult tasks. The provision of justice is different from other services, such as healthcare or education. In fragile, post-conflict states, the actors and institutions responsible for providing justice are often sources of injustice.[8] Furthermore, unlike other aspects of peace-building, such as reconstruction or strengthening public administration, rule of law promotion is not susceptible to technocratic solutions that can be applied, with minor variations, in the same way to institutions across the world, independent of their social, cultural, and historic context. Instead, the rule of law is deeply rooted in existing local customs, traditions, and values, and needs to reflect those to be effective. Conceptions of justice can differ, in particular in societies characterised by traditional authority structures, be they tribal or religious, often emphasising mediation and reconciliation to ensure the welfare of the community over individual rights. While there is now a greater recognition of the importance of traditional law, and the challenge of reconciling it with the authority of formal state institutions, this has proven to be difficult terrain for international actors.[9]

This chapter examines the efforts of the United Nations Transitional Administration in East Timor (UNTAET) to establish the rule of law in East Timor, from INTERFET's intervention in September 1999 until Timorese independence in May 2002. Promoting the rule of law was an essential part of UNTAET's mandate,[10] but has also been described as its "Achilles heel" by a

[6] Report of the High Level Panel on Threats, Challenges and Change, "A More Secure World: Our Shared Responsibility", UN doc. A/59/565 of 2 December 2004, paras 239–40.

[7] Paddy Ashdown, "What I learned in Bosnia", *New York Times*, 28 October 2002.

[8] OECD, *Enhancing the Delivery of Justice and Security in Fragile States*, Paris, July 2006, 3.

[9] There has been a growing literature on the relationship between traditional and formal judicial institutions in the context of intervention in societies with traditional authority structures, such as Afghanistan or East Timor. See for example Jarat Chopra and Tanja Hohe, "Participatory Intervention", (2005) 10 No 3, *Global Governance*, 289–306; Thomas Barfield, *Afghan Customary Law and Its Relationship to Formal Judicial Institutions*, United States Institute for Peace, June 2003.

[10] Report of the Secretary General, 4 October 1999, para 29(h).

senior member of the mission.[11] The challenges faced by UNTAET were succinctly summarised by two of its legal advisors: "How does that organisation [the UN], steeped in Northern European and Anglo-American values and dedicated to upholding the highest international legal standards, establish a cheap and effective legal system?".[12] Unfortunately, UNTAET failed to establish a judicial system that was effective in conducting trials speedily and in a procedurally appropriate manner observing international rule of law standards, and that was at the same time affordable for one of the world's poorest countries. Instead, it left a legacy of dysfunctional institutions.

One can identify four main reasons for this failure to establish the rule of law and functioning judicial institutions. First, the physical infrastructure of the justice system, such as courtrooms, penal facilities, court records, and legal libraries had been destroyed by pro-Indonesian militias, presenting UNTAET with a situation where elements of the system had to be built from scratch in a short period of time.[13] Second, the legacy of Indonesian occupation left East Timor ill-prepared to staff the formal institutions of the judiciary. Only a very limited number of Timorese legal professionals were available to work as judges, prosecutors, and defence counsel. Before the post-ballot violence, approximately 100 Timorese had completed a law degree in Indonesia, but when UNTAET arrived it was unclear how many of them were still in the territory. The World Bank's Joint Assessment Mission (JAM) in 1999 could only identify five lawyers who were licensed to practice law.[14] Under Indonesian rule, no Timorese had been judges or prosecutors, and all the Indonesian legal officials left after the ballot and the ensuing violence.[15] Third, UNTAET faced a conflict between the formal judicial system, characterized by international human rights standards, and traditional local law, prevailing in particular in rural areas. Even under Portuguese colonial rule and later under

---

[11] By Dennis McNamara, Deputy Special Representative of the UN Secretary General (DSRSG) in East Timor. Cited in Conflict, Security, and Development Group (CSDG), *A Review of Peace Operations: A Case for Change – East Timor Study* (London, King's College, 2003), para 214.

[12] Jonathan Morrow and Rachel White, "The United Nations in Transitional East Timor: International Standards and the Reality of Governance" (2002) 22 *Australian Yearbook of International Law*, 1–2.

[13] According to the World Bank, "over 70% of administrative buildings have been partially or completely destroyed, and almost all office equipment and consumable materials have been destroyed." World Bank, *Report of the Joint Assessment Mission to East Timor* (World Bank, Washington DC, 1999), 4.

[14] World Bank, *Joint Assessment Mission to East Timor - Governance Background Paper* (World Bank, Washington DC, 1999), para 21.

[15] Hansjörg Strohmeyer, "Policing the Peace: Post-Conflict Judicial System Reconstruction in East Timor" (2001) 24 *University of New South Wales Law Journal* 175.

Indonesian occupation, formal legal institutions, competing with traditional authority structures, had at best a shallow reach into Timorese society. The perception that Indonesian law had been an instrument of oppression,[16] and the destruction of the physical judicial infrastructure, made the competition between the two systems even more salient. Finally, UNTAET compounded these constraints by a lack of strategy when it came to building judicial institutions.

To examine UNTAET's efforts to promote the rule of law in East Timor, this chapter focuses on two key questions. First, it will look at attempts to rebuild formal judicial institutions, in particular the court system, to establish an independent, impartial, and effective judiciary. Secondly, it will examine the question of the applicable law and of the law not applicable but widely applied – traditional law. This highlights the tensions that existed between attempts by UNTAET on the one hand to maintain international human rights standards, but on the other hand to try to ensure local ownership of the legal system established in the country. The chapter concludes by assessing the implications of this analysis for East Timor, and for the promotion of the rule of law more generally.

Building Judicial Institutions

While under the 5 May Agreement, Indonesia formally remained responsible for maintaining law and order for a transitional period, the physical destruction of courts and prisons, and the exodus of Indonesian judges and police after the ballot meant that the international community had to take on not just the promotion of the rule of law, but also its provision. As UNTAET needed several months to establish its own mission structures, it was the Australian-led INTERFET troops that originally took responsibility for maintaining law and order, and building the first rudimentary institutions of the post-ballot justice system.

In anticipation that detainees arrested by international troops would be tried by a UN-led civilian authority, INTERFET did not establish military tribunals. Instead, it established a mechanism to review the detention of alleged criminals that it could for the time being not hand over to any civilian authority, to protect as far as possible the right of these detainees to be tried without undue delay.[17] This mechanism, the Detainee Management Unit (DMU) was created on 21 October 1999, four days before the Security

[16] CSDG, *East Timor Study*, para 219.

[17] *International Covenant on Civil and Political Rights*, 16 December 1966, Art 9(3).

Council decided to establish UNTAET.[18] By the time the DMU was disbanded on 12 January 2000, it had reviewed 60 cases of detention, but had not conducted any trials, which were left to the civilian judiciary to whom the detainees were handed over.[19] The establishment of the DMU thus bought some time for UNTAET to establish civilian judicial institutions to deal with the detainees.

Judicial Appointments

UNTAET moved quickly to select and appoint legal personnel, even before it had decided on the structure of the judicial system. As Timorese lawyers had been excluded from serving in the judiciary both under Portuguese and Indonesian rule, the appointment of the first Timorese judges and prosecutors was highly symbolic. To uphold the independence of the judiciary – a requirement under international law, but a requirement difficult to reconcile with UNTAET's potentially absolute powers over the judiciary[20] – the Transitional Administrator (Sergio Vieira de Mello, the head of UNTAET) established the Transitional Judicial Service Commission (TJSC) on 3 December 1999.[21] This body was responsible for selecting and recommending judicial personnel for appointment, for investigating complaints about the judiciary, and recommending disciplinary measures. It was composed of three Timorese and two internationals, all appointed by the Transitional Administrator. The Timorese members were representatives from the Catholic Church and from human rights NGOs, while the international representatives were a staff member from the judicial affairs department and the Cabinet member for justice.[22]

While the UN's planning document acknowledged that it might have to recruit some international legal personnel to help run the judiciary, it envisaged that as far as possible posts should be filled with Timorese legal professionals.[23] For three reasons, UNTAET originally went a step further and decided on a

[18] On the DMU, see Lt Col Michael Kelly, "INTERFET Detainee Management Unit in East Timor", paper presented at the Swiss Seminar on the Law of Armed Conflict, Geneva, 27 October 2000; Maj Bruce M Oswald, "The INTERFET Detainee Management Unit in East Timor" (2000) 3 *Yearbook of International Humanitarian Law* 347.

[19] Kelly, "INTERFET Detainee Management Unit in East Timor", *ibid.*, 9–10.

[20] UNTAET's mandate stated that it "will be endowed with overall responsibility for the administration of East Timor and will be empowered to exercise all legislative and executive authority, *including the administration of justice*". See SC Res 1272 of 25 October 1999, para 1 (emphasis added).

[21] UNTAET Regulation 1993/3, Establishment of a Transitional Judicial Service Commission, 3 December 1999.

[22] CSDG, *East Timor Study*, para 231.

[23] Report of the Secretary General, 4 October 1999, para 51.

purely Timorese judiciary.[24] The first two reasons were pragmatic. First, it would be expensive to deploy international judges and prosecutors, and the use of local personnel would make the transition after UNTAET's departure and the inevitable decline in donor funding easier. Secondly, it would take a long time to recruit the necessary number of international judges and prosecutors, who would also need time to acquaint themselves with Indonesian law. This would have led to further delays in addressing the backlog of cases that had arisen from INTERFET's arrests, and would seriously compromise UNTAET's human rights commitments. The final reason was local ownership: as the Timorese had been mostly excluded from senior positions in the judiciary under Portuguese and Indonesian rule, the decision underlined the commitment of UNTAET to Timorese self-determination. Some UNTAET officials, like the legal advisor who had previously served in the United Nations Interim Administration Mission in Kosovo (UNMIK), thought that local ownership would be necessary to sustain Timorese support for UNTAET, an assumption based on their experience with the early phases of judicial reform in Kosovo earlier in 1999.[25]

The decision to have a purely Timorese judiciary without any international judges and prosecutors was questioned by a range of Timorese lawyers and UNTAET officials. They argued that international personnel would be needed to deal in particular with the complex issues of war crimes, but also to allow for time to properly train Timorese legal professionals.[26] Their concerns were disregarded when the decision to appoint only Timorese legal professionals to the judiciary was made, and on 7 January 2000, the first judges, prosecutors, and defence lawyers, all Timorese, were sworn in by UNTAET.[27] By the end of June, 26 judges, eight prosecutors, and six defence lawyers had been appointed.[28]

---

[24] The official reasons for a fully "Timorised" judiciary are outlined in Strohmeyer, "Policing the Peace", above, n.15, at 176–77.

[25] See Hans-Jörg Strohmeyer, "Collapse and Reconstruction of a Judicial System: The United Nations Missions in Kosovo and East Timor" (2001) 95 *American Journal of International Law*.

[26] Phone interview with former UNTAET official, 7 September 2004. Interview with member of the Constitutional Assembly, New York, 9 April 2002.

[27] The decision to only appoint Timorese judges and prosecutors led to the resignation of the acting head of UNTAET's Legal Affairs section soon after their appointment. See Taina Järvinen, *Human Rights and Post-Conflict Transitional Justice in East Timor*, UPI Working Papers 47 (2004), Helsinki, Finnish Institute of International Affairs (UPI/FIIA), 26.

[28] Strohmeyer, "Policing the Peace", above, n.15; Report of the Secretary-General on the United Nations Transitional Administration in East Timor, UN Doc. S/2000/53, 26 January 2000, para 44; Report of the Secretary General, 26 July 2000, para 42.

It quickly became obvious that a purely Timorese judiciary was hardly sustainable. Of the 60 Timorese who had originally applied for positions in the judiciary, none had any experience as a judge or a prosecutor. Only a few of them had any practical legal experience, mostly in legal aid and paralegal organisations.[29] Thus, in March and June 2000, UNTAET finally decided to employ international judges and prosecutors for so-called "special panels", to deal with serious crimes committed in 1999 in the run-up to and after the ballot.[30]

In May 2002, when UNTAET handed over to its successor mission, the United Nations Mission in Support of East Timor (UNMISET), there were 22 trainee judges, nine trainee prosecutors, nine public defenders, and 35 support staff across all the courts.[31] In January 2005, all local judges were disqualified after failing professional examinations, and were given full-time training for up to three years.[32] In the meantime, the courts were operated entirely by internationals.[33] The decision to disqualify all local judges five years after they had first been appointed underlined UNTAET's lack of strategy with regard to the justice system.

Establishing Judicial Institutions

While UNTAET quite quickly created mechanisms to select judges and prosecutors, it took much longer to establish a legal framework for setting up courts and prosecutors' offices. Only in March 2000 a regulation on the organisation of the court system in East Timor was promulgated,[34] and it took a further three months to pass a regulation to establish a public prosecution service.[35] A public defender's office was not formally created until September 2001, even though the first defence lawyers had been recruited in January

[29] Strohmeyer, "Policing the Peace", above, n.15, at 175. The World Bank JAM identified a total of 29 persons in East Timor with experience in the judicial sector (list compiled on 4 November 1999). See World Bank, *Governance Background Paper*, 69.

[30] UNTAET Regulation 2000/11, On the Organization of Courts in East Timor, 6 March 2000, s 15. UNTAET Regulation 2000/16, On the Organization of the Public Prosecution Service in East Timor, 6 June 2000.

[31] Claudio Ximenes, "The Courts", in Civilian Support Group Advisors, *Timor Leste: A Strategy Foundation of Governance for Peace and Stability* (UNMISET Public Information Office, Dili, 2004), 44.

[32] Judicial System Monitoring Programme, *Overview of the Justice Sector: March 2005,* Dili, March 2005, 12.

[33] World Bank, *Strengthening the Institutions of Governance in Timor Leste*, Washington DC, April 2006, para 45.

[34] UNTAET Regulation 2000/11.

[35] UNTAET Regulation 2000/16.

2000.[36] While these delays were partly the result of the physical destruction and lack of human and financial resources, they also reflected a lack of strategy and planning by UNTAET.[37] This was particularly evident with regard to the court system.

The regulation on the organisation of the courts originally envisaged the establishment of eight District Courts of first instance (in Dili, Baucau, Los Palos, Viqueque, Same, Maliana, Ermera, and Oecussi),[38] and the Appeals Court in Dili.[39] In light of the limited Timorese human resources, and the inability to pay for a judiciary of this size, the number of District Courts was soon recognised as disproportionate, and after only two months the legislation was amended to reduce the number of courts by half, leaving only four District Courts (Dili, Bacau, Oecussi, and Suai), and the Appeals Court in Dili.[40] In addition, special panels were established at the Dili District Court, so-called "hybrid" panels with both international and local judges, to address transitional justice issues arising from the post-ballot violence in 1999.[41]

The Dili District Court heard its first case in May 2000, a month before an office of the Public Prosecutor formally existed. Bacau heard its first case in June of the same year.[42] Even though judges and prosecutors were appointed to the two courts in Oecussi and Suai as well, the court buildings were not finished by the end of UNTAET's mandate,[43] seriously undermining the functioning of the judiciary and the access of Timorese, in particular in rural areas, to the court system.

In addition to the lack of strategy and planning, three other factors contributed to the weakness of the judicial institutions. First, the lack of resources and

---

[36] UNTAET Regulation 2001/24, On the Establishment of a Legal Aid Service in East Timor, 5 September 2001.

[37] Samuels, *Rule of Law Reform in Post-Conflict Countries*, above, n.2, at 16.

[38] UNTAET Regulation 2000/11, s 7.1.

[39] *ibid.*, s 14.

[40] UNTAET Regulation 2000/14, Amending Regulation 2000/11, 10 May 2000.

[41] UNTAET Regulation 2000/15, On the Establishment of Panels with Exclusive Jurisdiction over Serious Criminal Offences, 6 June 2000. These "hybrid" tribunals addressing serious crimes and war crimes, which have also been established in Cambodia and Sierra Leone, present a middle way between international tribunals and local justice, and are a recent development in transitional justice. For a discussion, see Suzanne Katzenstein, "Hybrid Tribunals: Searching for Justice in East Timor" (2003) *The Harvard Human Rights Journal* 16; Suzannah Linton, "New Approaches to International Justice in Cambodia and East Timor" (2002) *International Review of the Red Cross* 845. The special panels were dissolved with the departure of UNMISET on 20 May 2005.

[42] Report of the Secretary General, 26 July 2000, para 42.

[43] CSDG, *East Timor Study*, n.238.

qualified administrators weakened the court administration, leading to long delays and a growing backlog of cases, thus compromising the human rights of detainees, such as the right to no undue delay of trial, or to access to case-related information.[44] Secondly, language problems and a lack of interpreters obstructed the effective functioning of the judiciary, as four languages – English, Bahasa Indonesian, Portuguese, and Tetum – were and are used in the courts. The language issue also affected the training of judges, which was conducted in Bahasa Indonesian under UNTAET, the language in which almost all Timorese judges had received their legal training; but which changed to Portuguese once the Timorese Minister of Justice assumed responsibility – even though only a very small minority of the judges spoke Portuguese fluently.[45] This language problem extended to the courts as well as to the ministries (thus also affecting the drafting of legislation), both during UNTAET's rule and after independence.[46] Finally, the training provided by UNTAET and various donors seriously interrupted the work of the judges, and was often perceived as irrelevant for their daily work. Thus, judges spent up to 10–15 days each month training in Dili. As all judges and prosecutors would train together on a regular basis, the court system would be shut down at such times.[47]

As a consequence of the lack of resources and a strategy for the building of judicial institutions, East Timor's judiciary was dysfunctional when UNTAET handed over authority to the nascent Timorese government. One year after independence, almost a quarter of detainees in East Timor's prisons were in jail under expired warrants.[48] The four District Courts still barely functioned, with the Prosecutor in Oecussi not having issued a single indictment by June 2003[49] and the Court of Appeal not sitting between October 2001 and June 2003 because of a lack of judges.[50] With continued international support, all courts were formally operational at the end of UNMISET's mandate in May

---

[44] See JSMP, *Justice in Practice: Human Rights in Court Administration* (JSMP, Dili, 2001).

[45] UNDP, *Support to the Judiciary in East Timor - Project Review, Final Report*, (UNDP, Dili, October 2001), 9.

[46] For an account of the language problem in the Ministry of Justice from 2002–2004, see João Nataf, 'The Legal and Legislative Unit', in Civilian Support Group Advisors, *Timor Leste: A Strategy Foundation of Governance for Peace and Stability* (UNMISET Public Information Office, Dili, 2004), 59. Nataf was a senior UN advisor to the Minister of Justice.

[47] Interview with former JSMP member, London, 17 March 2003.

[48] Report of the Secretary General on the United Nations Mission of Support in East Timor, UN Doc. S/2003/944, 6 October 2003, para 20.

[49] JSMP, "Background Paper on the Justice Sector", Dili, 4 June 2003.

[50] Report of the Secretary General, 6 October 2003, para 7.

2005, but at that time relied exclusively on international judges and prosecutors.[51] However, as judges and prosecutors are not in residence in the towns outside Dili, and rely on UN support for transport, the District Courts outside Dili function only sporadically.[52]

The events in April and May 2006 have underlined the ongoing weakness of the judiciary, and the challenges to the rule of law in East Timor: "neither citizens with grievances nor politicians have considered recourse within the justice sector a legitimate alternative to resolving disputes".[53] However, there have been some encouraging signs that judicial institutions are striving to fulfil their role. As soon as the international forces started to make arrests, the judiciary started to conduct pre-trial hearings, and prepared prosecutions of some of the key individuals involved, indicating their commitment to the rule of law, even if the institutional capacity was limited.[54]

Challenges to Judicial Independence

In addition to its weak capacity, a further challenge to the Timorese judicial institutions has been encroachments on their independence, both by UNTAET and the government. Regulation 99/3 which established the Transitional Judicial Service Commission, emphasised the independence and impartiality of the Commission, and of the appointment and disciplinary process. While its institutional independence was upheld until the end of the mission, UNTAET at times exercised a degree of control over the TJSC incompatible with international standards of judicial independence,[55] and generally sidelined the commission with regard to the appointment of international judges and prosecutors.[56]

From its establishment, one of the international expert members of the TJSC was also the Cabinet member for Judicial Affairs. In 2001, the Cabinet suggested that he should sit on the Commission *ex officio*, rather than as an

[51] JSMP, "Justice Update: Recent Developments in the Court", Dili, October 2005.

[52] World Bank, *Strengthening the Institutions of Governance in Timor Leste*, para 43.

[53] Rebecca Engel, *The Crisis in Timor-Leste: Restoring National Unity through State Institutions, Culture, and Civil Society*, FRIDE Working Paper No 25, Madrid, August 2006, 7.

[54] UNHCHR, *Report of the United Nations Independent Special Commission of Inquiry for Timor Leste*, Geneva, 2 October 2006, para 173.

[55] "Any method of judicial selection shall safeguard against judicial appointments for improper motives." UN, Basic Principles on the Independence of the Judiciary, UN Doc. A/40/32, 29 November 1985, Art 10.

[56] Frederick Egonda-Ntende, "Building a New Judiciary in East Timor" (2001) 14 *Commonwealth Judicial Journal* 26.

expert, and planned to amend Regulation 99/3 accordingly.[57] According to two of UNTAET's legal advisors, in that way the mission wanted to increase its control over the appointment and disciplinary processes to increase the quality and effectiveness of the judiciary by removing unqualified judges from office.[58] Amending the regulation in this way, however, violated international standards of judicial independence. The National Council, the purely Timorese quasi-legislature established under the ETTA structure,[59] rejected this when confronted with the proposal.[60] UNTAET subsequently amended the regulation so that it conformed to international standards.[61]

The presence of the Cabinet member for Judicial Affairs on the commission, even if not *ex officio*, set a bad precedent for the government after independence, which has continued to exert influence on the appointment and disciplinary procedures for judges and prosecutors. The Statute of Judicial Magistrates, promulgated on 9 September 2002, contains no reference to the independence of the Superior Council of the Judiciary, the successor of the TJSC.[62] Moreover, both local NGOs and the Special Rapporteur on the Independence of Judges and Lawyers have expressed concerns that the law might not adequately protect the independence of the judiciary.[63]

The Applicable Law and the Challenge of Traditional Law

The Applicable Law

In addition to the creation of a justice system, the decision as to what law should apply in a country, in particular after civil conflict, is an important

[57] Morrow and White, "The United Nations in Transitional East Timor", above, n.12, at 18–19.
[58] *ibid*., 19. This was confirmed in a phone interview with a former UNTAET official, 17 April 2003.
[59] UNTAET Regulation 2000/24, On the Establishment of a National Council, 14 July 2000.
[60] It was also suggested by UNTAET that the Prosecutor General should sit on the commission. For the National Council's position, see Yayasan HAK, "Serious Concerns Regarding the Independence of the Judiciary under United Nations Transitional Administration in East Timor", Dili, 24 July 2001.
[61] UNTAET Regulation 2001/26, On the Amendment of UNTAET Regulation No 1999/3 on the Establishment of a Transitional Judicial Service Commission and on the Amendment of UNTAET Regulation No 2000/16 on the Organization of the Public Prosecution Service in East Timor, 14 September 2001. See also UNHCHR, "Report of the United Nations High Commissioner for Human Rights on the Situation of Human Rights in East Timor", 1 March 2002, para 36.
[62] Democratic Republic of East Timor, *Statute of Judicial Magistrates*, unofficial translation from Portuguese, on file with the author.
[63] Judicial System Monitoring Project (JSMP), *Report on Statute of Judicial Magistrates: Law No. 8/2002 of 20 September 2002* (JSMP, Dili, 2003); Special Rapporteur on the Independence of Judges and Lawyers, 'Civil and Political Rights, Including the Questions of: Independence of the Judiciary, Administration of Justice, Impunity - Report of the Special Rapporteur on the independence of judges and lawyers', Addendum, 25 February 2003, para 202. See also Engel, *The Crisis in Timor Leste*, 8.

question for peace-building missions, and was a pertinent issue in East Timor. In the words of the Transitional Administrator in East Timor, "What law applies in countries that do not yet exist?".[64]

The first to face the problem of the applicable law in East Timor was not UNTAET but INTERFET, in the context of the DMU. For predominantly pragmatic reasons, it decided to apply Indonesian law, as this had been the *de facto* official legal regime in East Timor for the 24 years of occupation.[65] However, in particular with regard to criminal procedure, INTERFET relied on a framework of international humanitarian and human rights law, especially the Fourth Geneva Convention.[66] In its decision to apply Indonesian law, INTERFET was also guided by the Report of the UN Secretary General of 4 October 1999, which foresaw the continued application of Indonesian law in East Timor.[67]

UNTAET followed this path with regard to the applicable law. Its first regulation, "On the Authority of the Transitional Administration in East Timor", declared that the laws that applied until 25 October 1999, the day UNTAET was established, would be the applicable law until replaced by UNTAET regulations or laws passed by democratic Timorese institutions.[68] UNTAET qualified this by a range of international human rights standards,[69] abolished capital punishment, and declared certain laws, such as the laws on anti-subversion and on social organisations, which had previously limited the political activities of the East Timorese, as no longer applicable.[70]

---

[64] Sergio Vieira De Mello, "How Not to Run a Country: Lessons from Kosovo and East Timor", unpublished manuscript, 2000. On file with the author.
[65] Kelly, "INTERFET Detainee Management Unit", above, n.18, at 4.
[66] *ibid.*
[67] Report of the Secretary General, 4 October 1999, para 32. In 2000, the Brahimi Report recommended the creation of an interim criminal code by the UN that could – with regional variations – be applied by transitional administrations immediately after conflicts. However, this recommendation has yet to be implemented. See Brahimi Report, para 83.
[68] UNTAET Regulation 1999/1, On the Authority of the Transitional Administration in East Timor, 27 November 1999, Art 3.1.
[69] *ibid.*, para 2. The applicable human rights provisions include the Universal Declaration of Human Rights; the International Covenant on Civil and Political Rights and its Protocols; the International Covenant on Economic, Social, and Cultural Rights; the Convention on the Elimination of All Forms of Racial Discrimination; the Convention on the Elimination of All Forms of Discrimination Against Women; the Convention Against Torture and other Cruel, Inhuman or Degrading Treatment or Punishment; and the International Convention on the Rights of the Child.
[70] *ibid.*, Art 3.3.

On the one hand, the reasons for applying Indonesian law were largely pragmatic – to ensure a degree of legal continuity and stability,[71] and to avoid a situation where local lawyers, who were almost all trained in Indonesian law, would have to learn a new, foreign legal system.[72] While the decision was not very controversial, some Timorese complained about the continued use of a legal system that had served as an instrument of oppression for almost 25 years.[73] On the other hand, the qualifications to the law, and UNTAET's insistence on applying international human rights standards, highlight its commitment to these standards, often regardless of their effects on the sustainability of institutions in East Timor which is one of the poorest countries in the world. For example, the original plan to create eight District Courts, which East Timor could not have sustained, was a consequence of UNTAET's commitment to human rights standards that it could not fulfil given the circumstances the mission faced as a result of the scorched-earth tactics of the militias.

An envisaged full review of the applicable Indonesian law to ensure that it complied with international human rights norms was never undertaken by UNTAET. Indeed, it seems that originally not even a full translation of Indonesian law was available to the mission.[74] Laws were translated and reviewed in an uncoordinated, *ad hoc* fashion by different departments as the need arose.[75] As a consequence, it was left to the courts to assess whether laws were still applicable, thus shifting the responsibility for review to judges who were insufficiently trained in human rights law. This only increased the burden on the already weak judicial system.

A good example of the problems arising from uncertainty about the applicable law and possible conflicts with human rights standards was a case arising from defamation charges against Takeshi Kashiwagi, a Japanese journalist accused of having made slanderous remarks about Xanana Gusmão. Arrested on 22

---

[71] Report of the Secretary General, 4 October 1999, para 32.

[72] Strohmeyer, "Policing the Peace", above, n.15, at 174.

[73] *ibid.*, Among the critics of the decision was the leader of the conservative, pro-Portuguese União Democrãtica Timorense (Timorese Democratic Union), who suggested that Portuguese law continued to apply in East Timor, notwithstanding Regulation 99/1. See Morrow and White, "The United Nations in Transitional East Timor", above, n.12, at n.33. Members of the NGO community generally supported the application of Indonesian law, as it was known by the people.

[74] Phone interview with a former UNTAET official, 17 April 2003. The Judicial Affairs Office was originally mandated to conduct such a review. See Report of the Secretary General, 4 October 1999, para 50.

[75] CSDG, *East Timor Study*, para 226.

August 2000, he was held in prison on the basis of a provision in the Indonesian Criminal Code – the applicable law at the time – on charges of defamation. These were charges incompatible with rights of freedom of speech, but were punishable with up to nine months' imprisonment under the applicable law.[76] Two applications were made by Kashiwagi's defence counsel to the Dili District Court for his release, to no avail. Only when the Transitional Administrator passed an executive order decriminalising defamation[77] did the General Prosecutor order Kashiwagi's immediate and unconditional release.[78]

The lack of knowledge of Indonesian law also meant that UNTAET's legislative work did not proceed on the basis of existing law, but rather tried to import template legislation taken from other contexts, like the UN administration in Kosovo, thereby frequently failing to obtain adequate input from the Timorese. An example was the criminal procedure code, which UNTAET lawyers drafted in 2000.[79] Several Timorese lawyers recommended use of the Indonesian Criminal Procedure Code, modified by applicable human rights legislation. This law was known by Timorese legal personnel, and seemed sensible in the light of the applicable substantive criminal law – the Indonesian Criminal Code. The UNTAET legal advisor, however, who was charged with the drafting, did not accept these comments, and in the end the Transitional Administrator promulgated a law in the face of some protest by the Timorese legal community.[80]

Applied but not Applicable – UNTAET and Traditional Law

International human rights provisions not only clashed with elements of the existing formal applicable law, but more importantly also with traditional law. By declaring Indonesian law the applicable law in East Timor, UNTAET might have renounced a role for traditional law in the legal system in favour of a formal, European-style civil law regime. However, Indonesian law was far from being the law applied in most of the rural parts of East Timor, where the majority of the population lives. The rural population continued to predominantly employ traditional legal paradigms, which base their legitimacy on history and tradition, and emphasise the welfare and survival of

[76] Amnesty International, "East Timor: Justice past, present, and future", 27 July 2001, 23–24.
[77] UNTAET Executive Order 2000/2, On the Decriminalisation of Defamation, 7 September 2000.
[78] Amnesty International, "Justice past, present, and future", 24–25.
[79] UNTAET Regulation 2000/30 On Transitional Rules of Criminal Procedure, 25 September 2000.
[80] Morrow and White, "The United Nations in Transitional East Timor", above, n.12, at 10–11.

the community, rather than the rights of the individual.[81] Under Portuguese and Indonesian rule, the formal legal systems coexisted with, rather than superseded traditional law in East Timor.[82] Even though Indonesia had made a concerted attempt to establish its own legal and administrative system all over the island, the partiality of the Indonesian judiciary, and the perception that it was an instrument of Indonesian oppression rather than justice, led to widespread mistrust of the formal justice system and continued reliance on traditional justice.[83]

UNTAET was slow to establish a presence across East Timor's territory, especially in rural areas, and its authority for several months hardly extended beyond Dili. Consequently, former clandestine resistance structures and traditional leaders filled this vacuum and re-asserted their authority, not only maintaining law and order, but also mediating conflicts between villagers.[84] Today, traditional law, rather than the formal justice system established by UNTAET, is considered by many Timorese to be the most legitimate legal paradigm.[85]

Regulation 99/1 did not take any account of this *de facto* legal order for three reasons. First, little was known about traditional law by UNTAET, and it was often dismissed by international officials as local "folklore".[86] As one international official, who worked for UNTAET from the beginning argued, there had never been an assessment by UNTAET of how the East Timorese actually perceive justice and the rule of law, and how they access the system.[87] The first report on traditional justice was not published until 2001,[88] prior to

[81] It should be noted that there is no single traditional law in East Timor, but a wide range of different local systems. See Hohe, "The Clash of Paradigms"; Hohe and Nixon, "Reconciling Justice"; David Mearns, "Variations on a Theme: Coalitions of Authority in East Timor. A Report on the Local and National Justice Systems as a Basis for Dispute Resolution", Report prepared for Australian Legal Resources International, December 2001.

[82] Hohe, "The Clash of Paradigms", 573–79.

[83] CSDG, *East Timor Study*, para 219.

[84] Hohe and Nixon, "Reconciling Justice", 28–37.

[85] JSMP, "The Interaction of Traditional Dispute Resolution with the Formal Justice Sector in Timor-Leste", Dili, November 2005.

[86] Hohe, "The Clash of Paradigms", 570.

[87] Phone interview with former UNTAET official, 7 September 2004. The most comprehensive study on how the East Timorese population views and accesses the justice system was published in 2004, two years after the conclusion of UNTAET: The Asia Foundation, *Law and Justice in East Timor: A Survey of Citizen Awareness and Attitudes Regarding Law and Justice in East Timor* (Asia Foundation, Dili, 2004).

[88] The first published report seems to have been Mearns, "Variations on a Theme", above, n.81.

which evidence about the nature and content of traditional justice in East Timor was mostly anecdotal.[89] Some officials also seem to have feared that traditional law masked illegitimate power structures that arose out of the resistance struggle and the power vacuum that followed the post-ballot violence.[90]

The second reason that Regulation 1999/1 did not acknowledge traditional law was that this law was seen as an insufficient legal basis for a modern state, and could not regulate the complexities of a modern economy.[91] This argument certainly struck a chord with the Portuguese-educated political elite that had returned from exile, and which largely viewed traditional law as "uncivilised".

Finally, the main reason for the comprehensive shunting of traditional law was its incompatibility with international human rights standards. Unlike liberal, western formal legal systems which are based on the rights of the individual, traditional law in East Timor aims to protect a social order conceived of in terms of the traditional needs of the community. While formal legal systems emphasise accountability, and thus punishment for transgressions, traditional law focuses on compensation and reconciliation in addition to punishment.[92] Traditional law therefore raises a number of important human rights issues, both procedural and substantive. The traditional legal process is predominantly community based, and involves traditional authorities like household and village chiefs as well as the conflicting parties in the negotiations. It therefore does not necessarily fulfil standards of judicial independence or impartiality. As restoring social order within a community is an important aspect of traditional justice, and as "[t]here cannot be a winner and a loser left behind in the same village",[93] the rights of the individual risk being subordinated to the restoration of social order as interpreted by the traditional authorities, who might also use their authority to manipulate decisions to their own advantage. The latter is problematic in particular, because traditional law does not tend to have an appeals process.

A major concern has also been that the traditional law process appears insufficient to adequately protect women from domestic and sexual violence in a very patriarchal, conservative society. In the case of rape, for example, traditional law does not demand a prison sentence, but rather that the

---

[89] Phone interview with former UNTAET official, 19 August 2004.

[90] Strohmeyer, "Policing the Peace", above, n.15 at 179–80.

[91] Morrow and White, "The United Nations in Transitional East Timor", above, n.12, at 7.

[92] See Hohe and Nixon, "Reconciling Justice", 17–18.

[93] *ibid.*, 22.

perpetrator either marries the woman or pays compensation to the family, as her reputation has been damaged and she cannot find a husband.[94] Similarly, domestic violence is not always seen as a serious matter under traditional law, even by women in the countryside, who stopped reporting cases of domestic violence to UNTAET after they led to the detention of the perpetrators.[95] The socio-economic conditions, in particular in rural areas where imprisonment of violent husbands would deprive women of the family's breadwinner, undermined the acceptance of key institutions of the formal legal system – police and the courts – by a large part of the rural population of East Timor.

These aspects of traditional Timorese law are incompatible with a range of international human rights standards, in particular civil and political rights related to judicial procedure. This made it difficult for UNTAET to integrate traditional law in to the legal framework. This finding is supported by the research of Tanja Hohe and Rod Nixon on traditional law in East Timor, who observed that:

> [t]he requirements of those principles underlined in UN Security Council Resolution 1272/1999 relating to "international humanitarian, human rights and refugee law, including child and gender related provisions" … would have complicated any attempts to reconcile these two requirements [human rights obligations and relying on traditional justice mechanisms] in a formal policy development process.[96]

Both the Human Rights Unit and the Judicial Affairs Department in UNTAET were aware of the human rights problems posed by traditional law.[97] However, neither of them managed to develop an effective policy response. While the Human Rights Unit tried to facilitate access of parties and victims to the formal justice system on an *ad hoc* basis where it believed that their rights were violated by traditional law,[98] the Judicial Affairs Department focused solely on the strengthening of the formal justice system,[99] in particular trying to increase the effectiveness of the courts, as the best response to the problems posed by traditional law. No imaginative attempt was made to reconcile the two legal orders, for example by allowing the traditional law system to deal

---

[94] *ibid.*, 19. See also JSMP, 'Traditional Dispute Resolution'.

[95] Hohe and Nixon, 'Reconciling Justice', 49–50.

[96] *ibid.*, 38–39.

[97] Phone interview with former UNTAET official, 19 August 2004; phone interview with former UNTAET official, 7 September 2004.

[98] Phone interview with former UNTAET official, 19 August 2004.

[99] Phone interview with former UNTAET official, 7 September 2004.

with particular minor issues that would not have raised human rights implications.[100] This inclination to sideline traditional law has been continued by the Timorese government, dominated by politicians who have returned from exile in Mozambique. When the government adopted the Law on the Applicable Law in East Timor on the eve of independence in May 2002, it refrained from making any reference to traditional law.[101]

The Commission for Reception, Truth, and Reconciliation

The one exception to this lack of engagement with traditional law was the establishment of the Commission for Reception, Truth, and Reconciliation (CAVR[102]). The Commission had been a suggestion of the CNRT in June 2000, and UNTAET's Human Rights Unit and Judicial Affairs Department drafted a Regulation, which was promulgated in 13 July 2001, under extensive consultation with the CNRT, local NGOs, and international experts.[103]

The CAVR consisted of community-based panels to try perpetrators of human rights violations during the Indonesian occupation and the post-ballot violence, and to reconcile and receive them back in their communities. The panels could determine their own procedures, and include participation from traditional authorities, such as community leaders.[104] Interestingly, the Regulation foresaw a strong role for the General Prosecutor responsible for serious crimes, who could choose to end the truth and reconciliation process, undertake investigations, and bring to court cases of serious crimes.[105] Thus, the primacy of formal over traditional law was also reflected in the truth and reconciliation process; minor crimes were supposed to be predominantly dealt

[100] As Hohe and Nixon show in their analysis, many police officers in the districts tried to reconcile formal law requirements with the traditional justice mechanisms they encountered. However, they did not receive any guidance on how to proceed from the UN mission, and UNTAET never developed any policy guidelines for dealing with traditional law. See Hohe and Nixon, "Reconciling Justice".

[101] Democratic Republic of East Timor, *Law No.2/02 on the Interpretation of Applicable Law*, 19 May 2002. Unofficial translation from Portuguese, available at *www.eastimorlawjournal.org*.

[102] Comissão de Acolhimento, Verdade e Reconciliação de Timor Leste.

[103] UNTAET Regulation 2001/10, On the Establishment of a Commission for Reception, Truth and Reconciliation in East Timor, 13 July 2001. For a detailed account of the drafting of the regulation, see Piers Pigou, *The Community Reconciliation Process of the Commission for Reception, Truth and Reconciliation* (UNDP, Dili, 2004), 15–21.

[104] UNTAET Regulation 2001/10, s 26.1. On the relationship between the CAVR and the formal justice system, see also Patrick Burgess, "Justice and Reconciliation in East Timor. The Relationship Between the Commission for Reception, Truth and Reconciliation and the Courts" (2004) 15 *Criminal Law Forum*, 135.

[105] Regulation 2001/10, s 24.

with through traditional law in the commissions, and serious crimes through formal law in the courts.

However, the limited resources available to the Serious Crimes Unit, to whom the Office of the General Prosecutor delegated the review and investigation of cases from the Commission, constrained the attempts to bring perpetrators of serious crimes to justice through the formal legal system.[106] As a consequence of the growing backlog of cases, it appears that the Serious Crimes Unit and the Office of the General Prosecutor frequently allowed serious crimes to be processed through the truth and reconciliation process.[107] The priority of formal over traditional law has thus to some extent been compromised, but as the result of insufficient resources rather than deliberate policy.

Conclusion

Peace-building and international administrations have been likened to "transmission belts" that convey the norms and standards of the international community – such as democracy, respect for human rights, the rule of law, and a free market economy – to post-conflict societies.[108] The problems faced by UNTAET when trying to establish effective judicial institutions, and the weakness of the judiciary since independence, shows the limitations of peace-building as such a "transmission belt".

It would be easy to be very critical of UNTAET and its efforts at promoting the rule of law, and to explain its failures merely as its lack of a strategy for judicial reform. The disqualification of all local judges in January 2005 in particular raises doubts about a key decision by UNTAET in 1999 – to establish a purely Timorese judiciary. It might suggest that the six years from 1999 until the complete internationalisation of the judiciary in 2005 were lost years with regard to judicial reform. While it certainly highlights the fact that the problems faced by the justice system are not merely the result of material constraints and the legacy of Portuguese and Indonesian rule but also the consequence of UNTAET's lack of strategy, such an assessment would be very unbalanced. It is important to recognise the situation that UNTAET and the East Timorese population faced in late 1999, with most of the public physical infrastructure destroyed, and few experienced lawyers available to staff the justice system. It is also important to note that this situation was made

[106] Pigou, *The Community Reconciliation Process*, above, n.103, at 52–53.

[107] *ibid.*, 7.

[108] Roland Paris, "International Peacebuilding and the 'mission civilisatrice' (2004) 28 *Review of International Studies* 653.

even more difficult by the degree of uncertainty about the duration of the UN's commitment to East Timor, under which UNTAET had to operate. It was not clear in 1999 how much time UNTAET would have available to establish local institutions, as the appetite for expensive, long-term peace-building missions was limited among Security Council members and major donors in 1999, and there was a desire to limit the duration of the mission to two or three years.[109] In addition, soon after UNTAET's deployment the Timorese political elite began to push for a faster transition to local rule.[110] Given these pressures, it is to the UN's credit that it has continued its engagement in East Timor beyond the end of UNTAET's mandate to this day, through UNMISET (2002–2005), UNOTIL (2005–2006), and UNMIT (2006–present).

Finally, though, it highlights the difficulty of building institutions that reflect conceptions of justice and political authority that are held by most powerful members of the international community in societies that largely subscribe to alternative conceptions that might conflict with these international norms. If the norms these institutions embody fail to adequately reflect those of the wider society, institutions are likely to lack legitimacy, and are likely to be challenged by alternative arrangements. The challenge for international actors promoting the rule of law and human rights in such situations is to reconcile these alternative normative conceptions through innovative institutional design and relationships between traditional and formal institutions.

---

[109] Anthony Goldstone, "UNTAET with Hindsight: The Peculiarities of Politics in an Incomplete State", (2004) 10 *Global Governance* 87.

[110] Dominik Zaum, *The Sovereignty Paradox: The Norms and Politics of International Statebuilding* (Oxford, Oxford University Press, 2007), 188–193.

The Continuity of Australian Foreign Policy towards East Timor

Dr Clinton Fernandes

In September 1999, the Australian government took the lead in assembling a multinational peacekeeping force to guarantee East Timor's independence. It portrays its actions as a noble moment in Australia's history of foreign interventions. For instance, the Department of Foreign Affairs and Trade (DFAT) published *East Timor in Transition 1998–2000: An Australian Policy Challenge*. Foreign Minister Alexander Downer launched the book, which purported to be 'a full and balanced account of Australia's response to the extraordinary foreign policy challenge of East Timor' (DFAT 2001). Revealingly, the book was not produced by DFAT's Historical Documents Project, but by a team of departmental officers who had worked on East Timor over the period. In other words, those who had implemented policy were purporting to evaluate their own performances using material they had themselves selected.

This chapter analyses Australian foreign policy towards East Timor.[1] It explores the continuity that has characterized the policy, showing how – even in 1999 – the Australian government tried to hold the line but was forced into a policy reversal against its wishes.

The continuity of Australian foreign policy was obvious to Indonesian observers like Teuku Rezasyah, who pointed out that 'Australian foreign policy changes from one regime to another are largely incremental, not radical'. Rezasyah observed that both major political parties are 'willing to cultivate a cordial relationship with Indonesia, regardless of the latter's position on East Timor. They remain steadfast in their attitude even though local backbenchers and the media are pushing for tougher Australian measures against Indonesia' (Rezasyah 1996:432–446). Indeed, every Australian government has had to grapple with the problem of public opinion. The imperative of 'stability' and 'good relations' meant that Indonesia's occupation of East Timor could not be opposed; however, the need to contain public disquiet meant that governments had to give the impression of concern. However, governments have usually

[1] See Fernandes 2004 for an early account of the policy shift.

enjoyed the tacit support of parliamentary oppositions, thereby ensuring a margin of comfort necessary to neutralise public opinion.

The Australian Labor Party (ALP) under Prime Minister Gough Whitlam was in power at the time of Portugal's 1974 Carnation Revolution. Labor had come to power in the 1972 elections, and Australia-Indonesia relations were running smoothly at the official level by this time. Whitlam, an erudite and cosmopolitan figure who spoke of the need for Australia to be 'at home in Asia', nevertheless regarded a 'stable' Indonesia under the Suharto regime as vital to the Australian national interest. He therefore supported Indonesian claims to sovereignty over East Timor. He argued that an independent East Timor 'would be an unviable state and a potential threat to the area' (Meaney 1985:772).

The problem was the hostility of the Australian population to Indonesia's plans. Since public opinion was at odds with policy, public opinion would have to be neutralised. Accordingly, policy makers issued perfunctory statements supporting the East Timorese right to self-determination. These statements were no more than routine representations, with the understanding by both sides that no meaningful action would be taken to prevent the invasion or support the right of self-determination for East Timor. The government did identify opportunities that would give the East Timorese some diplomatic support – in order to neutralize them. In 1974, for example, then-Foreign Minister Willesee wrote to his Prime Minister arguing against the ALP's own proposal to organise a parliamentary delegation to East Timor. The problem was that any parliamentary delegation that went to East Timor would see immediately that the population supported independence under the leadership of Fretilin (*Frente Revolucionaria de Timor L'Este Independente* – Revolutionary Front for an Independent East Timor):

> On the return of the delegation to Australia we could expect public statements which could reflect the anti-Indonesian impressions members might have gained in Portuguese Timor. These will make the conduct of our relations with Indonesia more difficult than the problem of Portuguese Timor in itself might otherwise make them. ... A visit by a joint Parliamentary delegation would be the most substantial external incursion ... in recent years. Would it not encourage others? (Way 2000:144)

Although they knew that other political parties in East Timor (UDT – *União Democratica Timorense* or Timorese Democratic Union – and Apodeti – *Associaçao Popular Democratica Timorense* or Timorese Popular Democratic Association) were influenced by Indonesia, Australian diplomats tried to blame Fretilin for the problem, claiming that it had 'aggravated an already tense situation in Portuguese Timor' (Way 2000:595). Fretilin was accused of being unwilling to compromise with the other parties. Its 28 November 1975 declaration of independence was criticized as an act of intransigence. Privately, of course, Australian officials were not misled about the basic issues; they understood the problem very clearly. They acknowledged that 'Fretilin's claims ha[d] to be taken very seriously. Its credentials as the legitimate representative of the people of Portuguese Timor are potentially strong in an international debate; as indeed they are within Portuguese Timor' (Way 2000:464).

There were plenty of alternatives available: Australia could have lobbied internationally for a UN-supervised referendum at any time after the 1974 Carnation Revolution in Portugal. Furthermore, a de-colonisation process under the auspices of the UN would have obstructed the Indonesian invasion by internationalising the issue. Australia could have recognised Fretilin and UDT, and insisted on their legitimacy as representatives of the East Timorese in any de-colonisation process. Australia could also have informed the US that its preference was for an independent East Timor, even if under heavy Australian influence. None of these steps was taken because they may have led to a viable democratic alternative in the middle of Indonesia, then under the authoritarian rule of President Suharto. And this, ultimately, was the real issue – the Indonesian public must not see, in their geographical midst, a viable alternative to the New Order. In the words of a leading policy maker, Michael Curtin (Head of the Department's Indonesia Section from 1975–1976):

> If an independent and politically radicalised East Timor were to make a go of it, with political and economic help not to Indonesia's liking, it would certainly become something for discontented Indonesians to look to (Way 2000:465–6).

The Liberal-Country Party coalition led by Malcolm Fraser succeeded the Whitlam government in 1975. It was committed to the same policy as its predecessor on Indonesia and East Timor. As the killings mounted during the War of Pacification (1975–79), it moved to legitimise the Indonesian presence by extending *de facto* recognition of Indonesia's sovereignty in January 1978, followed by *de jure* recognition with the opening of negotiations on the seabed boundary in the Timor Gap in February 1979. The continuity of Australian foreign policy was illustrated starkly in 1980, when an attempt was made to publish a book called *Documents on Australian Defence and Foreign Policy 1968–75*. It contained classified documents outlining some of the written advice provided by senior Australian bureaucrats to the governments of John Gorton (1968–1971), William McMahon (1971–1972) and Gough Whitlam (1972–1975). Two newspapers, the *Sydney Morning Herald* and the *Age,* were scheduled to publish three series of extracts from the book on 8 September 1980. Hours before the first extract was due to hit the newsstands, the government obtained *ex parte* injunctions[2] against both newspapers in the High Court of Australia. The first instalment of the extracts made it into the first edition of the newspapers, but they were withdrawn from all subsequent editions. The next day, injunctions were obtained against the publishers. The day after that, further injunctions were obtained against the distributors. A proportion of the print run had already been sold to the book trade. Some of this was resold to the public. When the applications for injunctions were heard, the Commonwealth cited national security considerations and invoked section 79 of the *Crimes Act*, but it was unsuccessful. It then cited copyright (since the leaked materials were government property), invoking sections 41 and 42 of the *Copyright Act*. The injunction succeeded on these grounds and the book was withdrawn. All unsold copies held by the publishers were surrendered to the government and later destroyed, although some libraries do still have copies. Although the Fraser government had not been responsible for the diplomatic manoeuvres outlined in the book, it was nevertheless determined to prevent the public from knowing about them. In other words, the contours of Australian foreign policy did not change despite a change in government.

The ALP was in opposition during this time. It declared in 1979 that it condemned;

> 'in the strongest terms, the Australian government's recognition of Indonesia's annexation of East Timor and undertakes, on becoming the Government of Australia, to reverse the decision.

Three years later, while still in Opposition, it reiterated that it:

> 'recognises the inalienable right of the East Timorese to self-determination and independence and rejects the Australian government's recognition of the Indonesian annexation of East Timor

Upon winning government under the leadership of Bob Hawke (Prime Minister from 1983–1991), however, it reversed these policies very quickly.

---

[2] A temporary measure in which the defendant is not usually heard. It is given on a provisional basis to ensure that, if a judgment is eventually obtained, it will not be in vain.

Labor's former Defence Minister Bill Morrison led an Australian parliamentary delegation on a so-called 'fact-finding tour' of East Timor. On this tour, Fretilin representatives tried to make contact with Morrison on the road between Baucau and Los Palos but were rebuffed. They were later captured and killed by the Indonesian military (ABRI – *Angkatan Bersenjata Republik Indonesia*, or Armed Forces of the Republic of Indonesia). Morrison reported that 'the Indonesian government was acting in good faith in the territory' (Taylor 1999:140–2). On cue, Labor abandoned its former policy on East Timor. It continued the Fraser government's negotiations with Indonesia on the seabed boundary in the Timor Gap, eventually signing the Timor Gap Treaty in December 1989. Hawke's successor, Paul Keating (Prime Minister from 1991–1996), continued in this vein, pursuing closer ties with the Indonesian military. Keating and his foreign minister Gareth Evans accelerated Australia's links with the Suharto regime on the basis of maintaining 'order' and 'stability'. Nine months before the Dili massacre of 12 November 1991, Evans had stated that East Timor's 'human rights situation has, in our judgment, greatly improved under the present military arrangements'. When the Dili massacre occurred, Evans attempted to contain the widespread public outrage by calling the massacre 'an aberration, not an act of state policy' (Aarons and Domm 1992:66). On his return from Indonesia after the Dili massacre, Keating advised his fellow Labor members of parliament that 'President Suharto was the best thing in strategic terms that had happened to us; by bringing stability to the archipelago he has minimised the Australian defence budget' (Blewett 1999:101).

Implicit in Keating's call for 'reconciliation' was the long-standing (and propagandistic) assumption that the East Timorese were at war with themselves, not the widely known fact that the Indonesian military was an occupying power that was subjugating the population. It is significant that, despite the violence that gripped Dili in 2006, there are no calls by the East Timorese for a return of Indonesian rule. Indonesian authorities were able to legitimise their presence by going along with the fiction that they were merely 'keeping the warring factions apart'. Under Keating, Australia filled the void left by the US's decision, itself taken under Congressional pressure, to cut its military training program after the 1991 Dili massacre. During a visit to the US in September 1993, Keating lobbied President Clinton on the issue of military training for Indonesia, urging him to withdraw human rights considerations from the drafting of economic and defence contracts. Under Keating, Australia carried out more military exercises with Indonesia than with any other country. Indonesian foreign minister Ali Alatas received the award of the Order of Australia in 1995. In that year, the Australia-Indonesia Agreement on Maintaining Security was negotiated in secret. Keating tacitly acknowledged the public's opposition when he conceded that the Agreement might have been unachievable had its negotiation been preceded by public scrutiny:

> If there'd been a more public process, there probably wouldn't have been a treaty (*The Australian* 19 December 1995:1).

For its part, the Liberal-National opposition affirmed that Indonesia's annexation of East Timor was 'irreversible', and maintained its stance when it came to power in March 1996. At this time, the Asian financial crisis had not yet occurred and President Suharto was still in power in Indonesia. Two months before, in the dying moments of the Keating administration, two East Timorese women had entered the Australian embassy in Jakarta and sought refugee status. They were later joined by two more East Timorese women and seven East Timorese men, who climbed over the fence of the embassy and jumped in. All of them requested refugee status. When Alexander Downer became Foreign Minister, he continued his predecessor's practice of claiming that East Timorese asylum seekers were dual citizens of Indonesia and Portugal and that they did not meet the accepted definition of 'refugee'. It did not matter that the East Timorese did not accept Portuguese nationality, or that Portugal would not confer nationality on those unwilling to accept it, or, indeed, that Australia had recognised East Timor as a part of Indonesia.

Later that year, the Nobel Prize for Peace was awarded to José Ramos-Horta and Bishop Carlos Ximenes Belo. The result was a sharp rise in international awareness of East Timor. It was a shot in the arm for Australian activists because Ramos-Horta was a resident of Sydney. A leading activist triumphantly described it as 'an up-yours to Gareth Evans, Gough Whitlam, Malcolm Fraser, Hawke and Keating and Howard' (*Daily Telegraph* 12 October 1996:2). The Australian government did not send an ambassador to Oslo for the award ceremony, and Ramos-Horta could not secure a meeting with Howard. The public reacted very differently, attending standing-room-only meetings around Australia.

In November that year, several delegates from Australia travelled to Malaysia to attend an international conference on East Timor. The conference was disrupted when 200 thugs from the Malaysian ruling party's youth organisation (United Malays National Organisation Youth) stormed in and began attacking the delegates. Malaysian police stood by, allowing the delegates to be hit and jostled for about 20 minutes before intervening. Prime Minister John Howard's first response was to claim that the conference was banned and that the *delegates*, not the Malaysian government, had acted illegally by attending a banned conference: 'When you are in another country, if you are told that something is not permitted, well you have to take notice of that or expect certain consequences'. To his discomfort, however, it transpired that Melbourne's Catholic Bishop Hilton Deakin was one of the delegates. Deakin contradicted Howard's claims publicly by telling the media that he was 'advised, and advised constantly by the legal advisers attached to the conference, that we were observing all the laws' (Turner 12 November 1996). Howard's criticism of the pro-East Timor delegates, not the government-backed mob that attacked them, illustrates the continuity of Australian foreign policy. Furthermore, when the Suharto regime cracked down on pro-democracy demonstrators in 1996, there were no official expressions of criticism or even disapproval from the new Foreign Minister; Alexander Downer declared that the military crackdown was an 'internal affair' and hoped it would 'settle down quickly' (Hartcher 29 July 1996:14). Deputy Prime Minister Tim Fischer said that Suharto was perhaps the world's greatest figure in the latter half of the 20th century.

Australian governments could rest secure in the knowledge that no parliamentary opposition would argue seriously for self-determination for the East Timorese. This cozy bi-partisan consensus was fractured by the Labor Opposition's new foreign policy spokesman, Laurie Brereton. Brereton had a reputation as a tough political numbers man. He had been in Australian parliamentary politics since 1970 and had worked on many contentious issues over the years in a number of ministerial portfolios. With no background in foreign policy, and no political or emotional baggage invested in the Australia-Indonesia relationship or the East Timor question, he looked afresh at the developing situation in order to assess what might eventuate in five-six years' time, when Labor might realistically have a chance of getting back into government. In his view[3], it was highly likely that President Suharto would have departed, or be on the way out – if not for political reasons, then surely for biological ones. One way or another, Australia would have to deal with a post-Suharto era in the very near future, but there did not appear to be a definite succession plan. While there were a limited number of potential successors, the situation would probably be fluid. In these circumstances it was likely that Indonesian politics would bear a resemblance to the 1950s, with a range of competing parties, groups and interests.

[3] Interview with Laurie Brereton and his policy advisor Dr Philip Dorling.

He therefore argued publicly that Indonesia was beginning to go through a:

> process of political transition in which President Suharto's New Order government will sooner or later give way to a successor regime, the precise nature of which is at present highly uncertain.

He noted that the emergence of an indigenous democracy movement in Indonesia was 'a critical development of potentially far-reaching significance', and that unless a role were 'found for this movement in the political process ... further turmoil and conflict may follow'. According to Brereton, the likely fluidity of the post-Suharto era meant that Australian policy makers had to build a working relationship with the next group of Indonesian rulers. This meant that :

> Australia should not confuse any particular political group with [Indonesia] as a whole. Nor should we assume a necessary congruence between the interests of any group, including the Suharto government, with the interests of both Indonesia and Australia

He said that the government:

> should not hesitate to make clear the Australian community's concerns about respect for fundamental human rights in Indonesia, including the detention of opposition activists following the recent disturbances in Jakarta.

Brereton says that he was conscious of the rich imagery created in the public mind by the Labor Party's record on East Timor. This imagery was exemplified by former foreign minister Gareth Evans sipping champagne with his Indonesian counterpart Ali Alatas in an aircraft at 30,000 feet above the Timor Gap. Brereton knew that, for many people, these images 'were not just unforgettable – they were unforgivable'. This kind of imagery reinforced the impression in the electorate that Labor had developed an unseemly adaptation towards the Suharto regime. After Suharto departed, the residual effects of this impression would be a huge political liability for Labor. Brereton therefore took the lead in changing Labor's policy on East Timor. His draft expressed the:

> considered view that no lasting solution to the conflict in East Timor is likely in the absence of a process of negotiation through which the people of East Timor can exercise their right of self-determination

The ALP adopted the new policy on self-determination in January 1998.

A few months later, Suharto had resigned and all bets were suddenly off. The new President, Bacharuddin Jusuf Habibie, was under intense pressure to prove his democratic credentials. Habibie also had to cope with the deteriorating situation in East Timor and the increased international interest in the problem. He therefore offered the East Timorese what he called 'special status', predicated on its acceptance 'as an integrated part of the Republic of Indonesia' (Reuters 10 June 1998). While the Howard government signalled its approval, Brereton argued that the offer fell well short of what was required for a lasting solution. Realising that East Timor would be *the* big foreign policy issue from then on, Brereton began to exert maximum pressure on the Australian government, which was providing diplomatic support to the Indonesian government. He was ably assisted in his efforts by support from a re-energised transnational solidarity movement, which had sensed that a decisive victory was finally in sight. Accordingly, Brereton called for a permanent international presence to monitor military activity in East Timor:

> Real progress toward a lasting East Timor settlement is unlikely to be achieved amidst allegations of clandestine military action and arming of para-military squads. Establishment of an independent and effective international monitoring presence in East Timor would allow dialogue and negotiation to proceed in an environment characterised by transparency, improved confidence and trust (Brereton 30 October 1998).

This was the first time a major figure with real political clout and a platform to air his views had called for international monitors. Soon, another development unnerved the Indonesian and Australian foreign policy establishments. President Habibie had previously announced that many combat troops would be withdrawn from East Timor. Downer had praised this decision, calling it 'a step in the right direction' (Stewart 28 July 1998:7). However, Dr Andrew McNaughtan, a Sydney-based activist in the transnational solidarity movement, smuggled out the entire Indonesian army personnel records for East Timor. His action showed that Indonesia's claims of withdrawal and demilitarisation in East Timor were lies. The Indonesian military had not withdrawn combat troops but rotated them. The exposure of the personnel records led to a dramatic increase in the pressure on Habibie and the Indonesian foreign policy apparatus.

Meanwhile, the economic situation in Indonesia was plunging to new depths. Real GDP had shrunk, the exchange rate had fallen, inflation was sky-rocketing, the price of food was soaring and oil prices – a key source of government revenues – were stagnating at $10–12 per barrel. Domestic unrest was threatening to get out of control. In the midst of all this, international activism about East Timor was a problem that President Habibie simply did not need. He therefore announced a program of troop withdrawals, beginning with 1000 combat troops. He also said that more combat troops would gradually be replaced by troops devoted to civil improvement projects. In fact, combat troops were not withdrawn at all. A few hundred personnel left the port of Dili amidst much fanfare and then landed under cover of darkness north of Los Palos. Activists in Australia, who were in regular contact with the East Timorese, tried to draw attention to the deception, but the government dismissed their claims. Downer praised the decision to withdraw troops, calling them 'a step in the right direction'. He said he had been assured that more withdrawals would follow:

> 'I discussed this matter with Foreign Minister Alatas. He has confirmed media reports that troop numbers would be reduced. He has confirmed a figure of about a thousand and tells me that this is to be the first in a series of withdrawals' (Stewart 28 July 1998).

In November 1998, thousands of East Timorese commemorated the seventh anniversary of the Dili massacre by gathering at the Santa Cruz cemetery and demanding self-determination. The next month, major demonstrations brought Dili to a halt as pro-independence youth commemorated the anniversary of Indonesia's invasion with protests, roadblocks and scuffles with police. It was becoming increasingly clear that the status quo was untenable. Senior Australian opinion-leaders who were committed to the status quo were forced to look for an escape valve that would take the heat out of this rapid rise in pro-independence sentiment. Paul Kelly, an influential and long-time supporter of 'stability', with excellent access to the Foreign Minister and Prime Minister, explained in *The Australian* that Habibie's offer of autonomy, which had been supported by the Australian government, was no longer enough. The reality, he acknowledged, was that the 'weak Jakarta government can't now cut a permanent deal merely on greater autonomy. East Timor is heading towards a process, down the track, that involves some method of self-determination'. Kelly noted that while Australia backed the autonomy offer in public, 'in private Downer has told Indonesia it should go further; the formula must be autonomy now, with a review after a number of years on final status which may involve an act of self-determination'. The Howard Government remained committed to the Indonesian occupation of East Timor because its 'strategic view [was] that full independence for East Timor [would] represent a serious problem for Australia and Indonesia'. Since 'Indonesia's incorporation policy [had] not succeeded on the ground', the independence of East Timor was once again a live issue. Howard was trying to bury it by postponing any meaningful activity to a vague, undefined future. For Howard:

> [the] best feasible result [was] the "autonomy now, final determination later" formula, which may allow East Timor to remain under Indonesian sovereignty with Jakarta retaining responsibility only for defence and foreign affairs.

The Indonesian military's political and economic weaknesses were temporary; at some time in the future, it would once again be strong enough to crush East Timorese demands. Self-determination would have to be delayed until such a time. Howard therefore wrote to Habibie on 19 December 1998, suggesting that 'the East Timorese desire for an act of self-determination' could be addressed 'in a manner that avoids an early and final decision'. Howard approvingly cited the Matignon Accords[4], which 'enabled a compromise political solution to be implemented while deferring a referendum on the final status ... for many years'. Indonesia too could adopt the formula of 'a substantial period of autonomy' followed by 'an act of self-determination by the East Timorese at some future time'.

Howard's letter does not constitute evidence of his support for East Timorese self-determination, but the exact opposite. It was designed to defuse the issue and postpone self-determination indefinitely. The government reiterated months after the letter was sent that there had been no shift in policy:

> On all the evidence available, the Prime Minister has come to the conclusion that if the objective is economic and strategic stability then an autonomous East Timor within Indonesia, at least for the time being, would be the better option (Hill 11 February 1999:205).

DFAT's official submission to a parliamentary inquiry on East Timor confirmed that the government's 'declared preference remains for a long transition period before a decision is taken on East Timor's final status' (DFAT 1999:3–4). The Deputy Secretary of DFAT reiterated a year later that 'a very important part of our thinking at the time that the Prime Minister dispatched his letter was that Indonesia had only one last chance to keep East Timor as part of Indonesia' (Dauth 9 December 1999). Howard's letter was therefore an attempt to make the best of this 'one last chance' for Indonesia to contain the forces of independence.

---

[4] Only weeks before, Alexander Downer had celebrated the 10th anniversary of the Matignon Accords, which had been signed between the Government of France and constituencies in New Caledonia. These Accords had effectively deferred a decision on New Caledonia's final status for more than a decade.

An electronic copy of the letter was transmitted by cable to Australia's ambassador in Jakarta. The original would arrive later, via diplomatic bag. The ambassador presented the cable to President Habibie, who rejected it because of the colonial analogy with New Caledonia. Yet he realised that many of his colleagues in the new post-Suharto cabinet was bearing the burden of a policy for which they were not responsible, and from which they derived no benefit. Howard's letter arrived subsequently via diplomatic bag, but Habibie's thinking had moved past its central point – addressing the issue 'in a manner that avoids an early and final decision'. He suggested holding a referendum on independence or autonomy within Indonesia. The referendum idea was discussed at the 25 January meeting of cabinet's Political and Security Committee, and two days later by the full cabinet. Most cabinet members were of the view that Indonesia would win the referendum. The vote in East Timor for the ruling party Golkar had always been higher than the national average in previous elections[5].

Nor were senior Indonesian military figures opposed to such a referendum. According to Assistant Coordinating Minister for Home Affairs Major General Garnadi, the Indonesian government was optimistic that 'autonomy would be the people's choice'[6]. Other officers later confirmed Garnadi's view. In his biography, Lieutenant General Feisal Tanjung, the Coordinating Minister for Politics and Security, said that the military first estimated that about 75% of the electorate would reject independence in favour of autonomy within Indonesia. Later, Foreign Minister Ali Alatas confirmed that most members of cabinet 'were then very convinced we would win the referendum. Everything was painted with optimism' (Tempo 18–24 September 2000). He said: 'Up to the balloting, the reports we got from our people, of the pro-integration people, including Lopez da Cruz and so on, is that we were going to win' (Suryodiningrat and Purba 2 November 1999). The new policy was announced by Ali Alatas and Information Minister Yunus Yosfiah on 27 January 1999, and was the opposite of Howard's suggestion of 'a substantial period of autonomy before a decision is taken on East Timor's final status'.

In order to ensure a victory for the autonomy proposal, the Indonesian authorities began to intensify operations against the East Timorese population under the guise of proxy forces, known as 'militias'. These operations required

---

[5] For example, in 1987 Golkar won 73.1% nationally but 93.6% in East Timor. In 1992, Golkar won 68% nationally but 82.6% in East Timor. See the Centre for Southeast Asian Studies at Northern Illinois University http://www.seasite.niu.edu/indonesian/Indonesian_Elections/Election_text.htm

[6] Memo no M.53/Tim P4-OKTT/7/1999 dated 3 Jul 99. Cited in the Sydney Morning Herald, 20 Jul 99.

plausible denial, whereby the military posed as a force for peace between East Timor's 'warring factions'. Plausible denial required a foreign ally to provide diplomatic cover by arguing against international involvement. This ally would have to argue that the militias were somehow distinct from the military. The Howard government was this ally.

> The lead-up to the ballot was marked by a contest between the Australian government's diplomacy on the one hand and, on the other, a vigorous and re-energised transnational solidarity movement, a parliamentary opposition that kept the Howard government on the back foot, and a constant series of leaks of classified material that severely embarrassed the government.

Foreign Minister Downer downplayed claims that the Indonesian military was arming militias in East Timor: 'The Indonesian military are denying this ... It's obviously very hard for us to verify one way or another' (Downer 5 February 1999).

Only a few weeks before, however, Australia's Defence Intelligence Organisation (DIO) reported that:

> ABRI's decision to arm local militias has drawn its first blood. As long as ABRI continues to contract-out some of its security responsibilities, more clashes are likely... ABRI recognises that using force against pro-referendum groups will continue to attract international criticism. So using force against the referendum movement looks likely to continue to be subcontracted (Ball 2002:246).

On 9 February 1999, just four days after Downer said that it was 'obviously very hard for us to verify one way or another', Australia's Defence Signals Directorate (DSD) intercepted messages confirming that two Indonesian special forces units, codenamed Tribuana and Venus, had arrived in East Timor to join undercover operations. Five days later, DSD intercepted a telephone call from one of the militia figureheads to the Tribuana unit. This call concerned the condition of an injured member of the militia group called MAHIDI (*Mati Hidup Demi Integrasi*, or *Integration, Dead or Alive*). According to the intercept, the special forces unit informed the militia contact that 'Brigadier-General Simbolon is concerned that one of his crew is injured'(McDonald 14 March 2002). The reference was to Brigadier-General Mahidin Simbolon, Deputy Commander of the military command area responsible for East Timor. Simbolon was a covert operations expert who had served at least six tours of duty in East Timor. He had led the operation to capture Xanana Gusmao in 1992 and was a key actor in the Indonesian military's covert warfare strategy in 1999 (McDonald *et al.*, 2002).

Labor's Laurie Brereton began to call for a full-fledged international peacekeeping force. In response, Indonesia cancelled his planned visit to East Timor. Citing the 'unruly behaviour of the pro-referendum elements in East Timor', the Indonesian Ambassador refused entry 'until a later and more convenient date'[7]. Downer appeared on television in support of the Indonesian authorities, rejecting calls for a peacekeeping force and saying that the real need was for 'reconciliation between East Timor's factions' (Downer 21 February 1999). A peacekeeping force was counter-productive, he argued, because it would create the impression that efforts to achieve reconciliation wouldn't work.

Downer was asked at a press conference on 25 March 1999 whether he raised the militia issue in his meetings with the Indonesian government. He replied:

> Yes, with Ali Alatas [Indonesia's Foreign Minister] I did. I made it clear to him that we had heard reports that the Indonesians were providing arms, and that we were concerned about this. It wouldn't improve the environment. Obviously it wouldn't. And he explained to me that they weren't giving arms out to pro-integrationists.
>
> But what they were doing was what they were doing in all the provinces, or just about all the provinces. I think he might have said all the provinces of Indonesia, and that is that they do have some civilian people who help in a policing function.

No leaks had occurred at that stage, and the government's statements were at their most loquacious. Its utterances fit comfortably with the Indonesian government's own rhetoric, and followed clear themes. First, the facts are in dispute: '*if* it is happening/it's possible/it's hard to say for sure'. Second, the Indonesians have given assurances: 'the Indonesian government assures us it isn't their policy/we certainly aren't saying it is their policy'. Third, they may be the actions of 'rogue elements'. All themes are on display in the following statement by Downer:

> If it's happening at all and there is concern that it could be happening, if it's happening at all, it certainly isn't official Indonesian Government policy, it certainly isn't something that's been condoned by General

[7] Letter by Ambassador Wiryono Sastrohandoyo to the Hon Laurie Brereton dated 21 January 1999.

> Wiranto [the Minister for Defence and head of the armed forces]. But there may be some rogue elements within the armed forces who are providing arms of one kind or another to pro-integrationists who have been, you know, fighting for the cause of Indonesia. ...
>
> The Indonesian Government when we've raised it with them, including when I raised it with Ali Alatas the other day, have said that it certainly wasn't happening, that they weren't arming paramilitaries, there was some arming of the informal police support group who are civilians in East Timor but that applies in all of the provinces of Indonesia. There is nothing different or unusual about that, so I mean, I do accept the Indonesian Government's word for it, that it's not official Indonesian policy, but on the other hand it may be that some soldiers informally are doing this (Downer 7 March 1999).

Despite numerous reports to the contrary, Downer continued to repeat Indonesia's assertions that it was not engaged in a proxy war:

> Ali Alatas... told me that the Indonesian armed forces were not arming paramilitaries. Nevertheless whilst we accept that is not the official policy of ABRI or the Indonesian government, there is a risk that some rogue elements within ABRI may be or may have been providing arms to the so-called paramilitaries in East Timor (Downer 31 March 1999).
>
> Six days after this statement, a massacre occurred in Liquiça, a town in Liquiça district on the northern coast of East Timor. The circumstances of this massacre were unambiguous: on 6 April 1999, a number of militia went to Liquiça village accompanied by army and police. They surrounded a church where villagers were sheltering, dragged two priests out of the church compound and took them to the local military district headquarters. Once the priests were removed, Indonesian troops began to throw tear gas into the church. When the refugees ran out, blinded and trying to save themselves, the militia rushed towards them. Women and children were attacked with fists, sticks, rifle butts, stones, arrows and machetes. More than fifty people died and seven were injured during this attack. Afterwards, the militia forced the local people to hoist the Indonesian national flag.

The Howard government moved into damage control mode. Commenting on the massacre, Downer followed the established themes:

> Well, look, they [the military] were present, I understand, at the incident but there again, there's a debate about what part they played. They clearly

> didn't themselves kill people, but there is an argument, about whether they did try to stop the fighting or they didn't do enough to try to stop the fighting, and the trouble is it's very hard given we ourselves had no eye witnesses there, to be able to prove the case either way.
>
> The military give one story. Others give another story. Still others give a different story again. So our report is that you're getting very conflicting accounts, wildly different accounts of what actually happened, but what you can be sure of is that some people did die, some people were injured and it was a very violent and unfortunate incident and we hope that such an incident doesn't occur again (Downer 11 April 1999).

He later refused to release the report prepared by Australian diplomats into the massacre (Newman 22 March 1999). However, the call for peacekeepers had gained real traction in the public consciousness because of Brereton's demands and because of a well-timed leak of classified intelligence material that differed spectacularly from Downer's assurances. The Defence Intelligence Organisation's preliminary assessment of the massacre was contained in its Current Intelligence Brief dated 8 April 1999 (three days before Downer's comments absolving ABRI):

> ABRI had fired tear gas into the church and apparently did not intervene when the pro-independence activists were attacked. BRIMOB [Police Mobile Brigade] were allegedly standing behind the attacked at the church and firing into the air. ... ABRI is culpable whether it actively took part in the violence, or simply let it occur' (Ball 2002).

A clear difference had begun to appear between the government's private advice and its public assurances. Eleven days after the Liquiça massacre, militia groups in Dili attacked the houses of prominent independent supporters and the local newspaper office. Manuelito Carrascalao, the teenage son of a prominent East Timorese family, was killed along with at least twelve – and possibly twenty-five – others (Martinkus 2001:174–5). Tabloid newspapers in Australia displayed photographs of the photogenic young boy, and members of the Australian public began to express their anger at the mass murder. At that very moment, the Irish foreign minister David Andrews was in Dili on a scheduled visit. Andrews was accompanied by Tom Hyland of the East Timor Ireland Solidarity Campaign. Andrews ended his visit immediately and returned to Jakarta, where he raised the alarm about the mass murders. Hyland tapped into the solidarity movement, rapidly escalating the international pressure on Indonesia. As a result, Alexander Downer made a public call for the military to maintain security and disarm the militias. Howard telephoned

Habibie to express his concerns, and the two agreed to meet in Bali to discuss the situation.

After this meeting, the Howard government resumed its program of providing diplomatic cover. At a press conference on 25 April 1999, Howard spoke of the 'strong commitment made by the Indonesian government to the holding of an open and clean ballot. ... I have no reason to doubt the sincerity of the commitments that were made yesterday by both the President and also the other ministers who were present... the confidence I expressed was a confidence that things were infinitely better than they were a week or so ago'. Downer was effusive in his praise of the Indonesian authorities, saying that there wasn't 'any doubt that the Indonesians through this process are committed to the laying down of arms... we have no reason at all to doubt their goodwill' (Downer 27 April 1999). He declared his faith in the Peace and Stability Commission, itself established by Indonesia in April 1999 as a ploy to contain international outrage after the Liquiça massacre.

Brereton ridiculed Downer's faith in the Commission, describing it as a 'non-statutory, non legally binding talkfest' where the 'militias will have an effective veto':

> To think that this is going to give people a sense of security in going to the polls and expressing their view, this again is bordering on the surreal. To suggest that the police rather than ABRI are going to be responsible for security is equally surreal. I mean in East Timor for the last twenty-three years, the police have been ABRI and ABRI have been the police (Brereton 28 April 1999).

The combination of leaked intelligence material, increased visibility of events in East Timor and Brereton's outspoken advocacy of an international presence on the ground were having an effect on Downer's credibility.

The Howard government was keen to prevent or minimise international involvement, throwing the full weight of Australian diplomacy behind this aim. On 22 February 1999, the Secretary of DFAT, Ashton Calvert, met US Assistant Secretary of State Stanley Roth in Washington. Roth was of the view that a full-scale peacekeeping operation in East Timor would be unavoidable, and that in the absence of international action to push for peacekeepers, the territory would descend into violence. Calvert, stating the Australian government's position, made it clear that Australia wouldn't support peacekeepers, and continued to run the 'factions' line:

> One of the central themes to achieving a resolution was to convince the Timorese that they had to sort themselves out, and to dispel the idea that the UN was going to solve all their problems while they indulged in vendetta and bloodletting (Lyons 12 October 1999:25–9).

Roth described the Australian Government's position as 'defeatist' and stressed the importance of building an international coalition to persuade UN members and the US Congress that peacekeeping simply had to be done. His efforts were rebuffed by Calvert, who was clearly determined to prevent an international peacekeeping force (Lyons 12 October 1999:25–9). The transcript of the Calvert-Roth meeting was leaked to the media some months later. Caught red-handed, the government stumbled for words at first, then tried to downplay the significance of the meeting by saying that Roth had only been expressing a personal view (Daley 10 August 1999; DFAT 2001). However, astute observers understood the significance of the meeting clearly. Roth was the US's most influential regional bureaucrat. He had served as Principal Adviser on Foreign Policy to Stephen Solarz, Chair of the Asian and Pacific Affairs Subcommittee in the House of Representatives until 1993. Roth then moved to the Department of Defense as Deputy Assistant Secretary for East Asian and Pacific Affairs. He had also been Senior Director for Asia on the US National Security Council. Roth was meeting Australia's most senior foreign policy bureaucrat in order to discuss the possibility of an international peacekeeping presence because of the dangers in East Timor. Yet the official Australian response was to dismiss the prospect and maintain the fiction that the problem was to 'convince the Timorese that they had to sort themselves out'. Had the government been committed to an international peacekeeping presence, it would have leapt at the opportunity, not rejected it. For the Howard government, though, the objective was to minimise international involvement and give Indonesia a free hand in East Timor. It pursued this objective consistently. Had the transcript of the Calvert-Roth meeting not leaked, the Australian public would not have found out about the government's secret rejection of Roth's proposal until 2029, when the archives open up under the thirty year rule. By contrast, the real-time leak resulted in a swift escalation of political pressure.

On 5 May 1999, Indonesia and Portugal signed an agreement at the United Nations headquarters in New York. The 5th May Agreement, as it came to be known, provided for an autonomy proposal to be put to the East Timorese people. If they accepted this proposal, the East Timor issue would be considered solved once and for all. If they rejected it, authority would be transferred to the UN, allowing East Timor to begin its passage to independence. In order to ensure the result it wanted, Indonesia demanded – and received – complete responsibility for maintaining security. It could therefore continue to use its militia proxies to terrorise the East Timorese while keeping foreign security personnel at bay. Two days later, the Australian Defence Force began planning for logistic support to the ballot. This was known as *Operation Concord*. In parallel with this operation, planning was also begun for *Operation Faber*, which involved military observers who would serve with the United Nations Assistance Mission in East Timor (UNAMET). However, Defence planners began work on another plan on 11 May 1999. Known as *Operation Spitfire*, the aim of this plan was to evacuate foreign observers (ANAO 2002:28–9). Now that Indonesia had gained control over 'security', it would be in a position to destroy pro-independence supporters regardless of the result of the ballot. As discussed previously, the Indonesian military was of the view that it would win the ballot. However, just in case it didn't, it would need to move rapidly to reverse the result. Under these circumstances, foreign observers would impede any Indonesian action. They would have to be removed from the territory, just as they had been when Indonesia first invaded in 1975. *Operation Spitfire* – which was designed to evacuate personnel, not to send in a peacekeeping force (Wilson 2003:6–11) – fitted in with the Indonesian military strategy. It allowed the Indonesians to act without witnesses.

All the while, Downer continued to argue that the central problem wasn't Indonesian military terror but differences between East Timorese 'factions'. In a press conference on 14 March 1999, he argued that:

> … the problem in East Timor is the tension between the pro-integrationists, that is the people who support remaining with Indonesia, and the other East Timorese. And we've been encouraging as hard as we possibly can the pro-integrationists and the pro-independence people to get together and start to work through the resolution of their differences.

He kept deflecting calls for a stronger international presence, deriding those who called for peacekeeping forces as 'bunyip Napoleons' (Downer 25 May 1999). In doing so, he was not making an impromptu, off-the-cuff remark but was reading from a pre-written, planned speech at the launch of a book at Parliament House. His remarks were consistent with the rest of his arguments against the deployment of an international peacekeeping presence: after meeting UN Secretary General Kofi Annan on 14 March 1999, he said:

> We hope that there won't be a need for a peacekeeping force because if you need a peacekeeping force, you need a peace to keep and peace first has to be negotiated and we hope that when the peace is negotiated it will be a peaceful peace that won't require a peacekeeping force.

Downer sought to make his meaning clearer. The situation in East Timor didn't warrant the presence of peacekeepers. And peacekeepers should not be put in harm's way; rather, the 'factions' should negotiate 'a peaceful peace that won't require a peacekeeping force':

> [W]e're not passionately of a desire to send Australian troops into danger and it would only be a complete fool who would want to do that. They have lives, we don't want them to risk their lives or for them to lose their lives. We have a responsibility to them.

There was a curious illogic at the heart of the Australian government's position. On the one hand it was arguing that the violence was of a level that would cause peacekeepers to risk their lives ('they have lives, we don't want them to risk their lives or for them to lose their lives'). On the other hand, the violence was not that serious, because a small unarmed presence would suffice ('administrative assistance, observers, some technical assistance, perhaps some people to assist with policing functions and we hope it won't be more than that'). So East Timor was safe enough for the matter to be resolved peacefully, yet dangerous enough to cause the deaths of peacekeepers. If the Foreign Minister was of the view that troops should not be placed in harm's way, the obvious question arose: what exactly are troops for?

This conundrum could be resolved by only one explanation: the government would say and do anything to prevent an international peacekeeping presence.

The government's outlook was not shared by the US authorities, who were growing more and more concerned about the possibility of violence. In June, the US military's Hawaii-based Pacific Command raised the possibility of attaching Australian military officers to a possible US peace enforcement operation in East Timor (Daley 10 August 1999; 31 August 1999). The US request spoke of using 'overwhelming force to stop the killing' and was conveyed to the Commander Australian Theatre, Air Vice Marshal Treloar. Since Treloar commanded the headquarters that would oversee any deployment of troops to East Timor, the US military was deliberately addressing the Australian Defence Force officer best placed to advise the government that the proposal was feasible. Treloar undertook to refer the request to senior levels in the Australian government. The request was declined 'after lengthy, top-level consideration' because 'any discussion of possible UN peacekeeping involving the Marine Corps was "premature" and could be "damaging" to bilateral relations between Australia and Indonesia' (Daley 31 August 1999). When asked about the request during Question Time in Parliament, Downer initially claimed that he had neither seen the cable nor knew of the request, although he was an addressee, as were the Prime Minister, the Minister for Defence and the heads of their respective departments. Downer assured the House that he was 'completely unaware of any proposal by the United States defence force to mount a peace enforcement exercise in East Timor' (Downer 9 August 1999a).

A diplomatic cable containing a copy of the request was leaked to members of the press. Late that night, the government learnt that early editions of the next day's *Age* were carrying detailed excerpts of the cable. Downer rushed back to Parliament at 11:32 p.m. and made a 'clarification', saying that 'apparently' the issue 'was informally raised' by officials who 'asked hypothetically' about peace enforcement. But, he continued, this wasn't a 'formal United States government request' (Downer 9 August 1999b). A sceptical press gallery and many members of the public could see this for what it was – yet another attempt by the government to prevent international intervention in East Timor. It was Downer's third forced 'clarification' since become Foreign Minister. The government's fury at being exposed by leaks from inside the system led to the launching of the largest and most expensive leak investigation ever mounted in Australian history. Although the government claimed that the leaks were a matter of national security, the Australian Security Intelligence Organisation pulled out of the investigation on the grounds that national security was not an issue. No incriminating evidence was found and no charges were ever laid.

Australia refused a direct US request to hand over intelligence material detailing links between the Indonesian military and its militias. The requests were made on several occasions to Australia's Ambassador in Jakarta, John McCarthy, and to Australia's Ambassador to the US, Andrew Peacock. Both envoys refused to make the information available (Wilkinson 13 August 1999). The Australian intelligence liaison officer to the US, Merv Jenkins, was required to exchange intelligence as part of his normal duties (Ball 2002:254–5). The US intelligence community was particularly interested in material that tied the Indonesian military to the militias. When Jenkins passed on such intelligence to his US counterparts, Australian officials flew to the US and interrogated him. Jenkins later committed suicide. A senior officer of the US Embassy in Canberra contacted Brereton's policy adviser to convey 'the concern of the United States intelligence agencies that, notwithstanding public statements to the contrary, the Australian government had withheld or otherwise delayed the sharing with the US of important intelligence material relating to Indonesian military and militia activities' (Daley 4 May 2004).

The testimony of the Deputy Secretary of DFAT, Mr John Dauth, before the Senate Committee on Foreign Affairs, Defence and Trade also had the effect of providing diplomatic cover for the TNI's proxy war. Dauth was asked whether he agreed with DIO's assessment that 'the Indonesian military could apprehend or easily control the pro-integrationist militias but has chosen not to'. He replied:

> No, I would not agree with that at all. Controlling the security situation in East Timor is an extremely difficult task. It is the responsibility of the government of Indonesia, it is the responsibility of the Indonesian military and police, but it is a real tough ask, particularly since the militia has become better armed. It is very much more difficult. Frankly, the whole question of disarmament is a very difficult issue indeed (Dauth 5 May 1999).

What Dauth was claiming, of course, was that it was 'a real tough ask' for the military to control the militia, which had somehow 'become better armed'. In fact, the military itself had been arming, training and sustaining the militia, and could control them quite well. Asked about the presence of Kopassus (*Komando Pasukan Khusus* – Special Force Command) in East Timor, Dauth responded:

> Just precisely what the make-up of the Indonesian military in East Timor is I am not really able to say, not because I am hiding anything but because we do not have definitive information on that. I cannot offer a very clear answer… I simply do not know whether it is true (Dauth 13 August 1999).

During private discussions on East Timor between Australian and United States officials held in Washington just three days later, on 16 and 17 August 1999 it was noted as follows:

> There was agreement that fundamental security problems remained, including the presence of Kopassus forces and hence the presence of mischief, especially in western agencies[8].

Thus, even as Australian officials were saying privately that 'the presence of Kopassus forces' was one of the 'fundamental security problems', John Dauth was telling the Senate that he was 'not really able to say' whether Kopassus

---

[8] This is from a chronology of events provided by DFAT and used by Downer to brief selected members of the Parliament House press gallery, later obtained by me.

was operating in East Timor. The Howard government later rewarded John Dauth for his efforts with the sought-after posting of Australian ambassador to the United Nations, where he played a prominent role in arguing that Iraq had to be invaded because of the threat posed by its weapons of mass destruction.

In the lead-up to the ballot of 30 August 1999, the Howard government continued making public statements expressing confidence in the Indonesian military while privately making meaningless 'diplomatic representations'. By August 1999, the Howard government had made approximately 120 such representations (Wensley, 23 February 2000:5). The results of the ballot were announced on 4 September 1999. Despite the climate of terror and the presence of dubious voters from West Timor, 78.5% of registered voters opted for independence from Indonesia.

The Indonesian military were surprised, but moved quickly to reverse the result of the ballot by force. They commenced an ethnic cleansing campaign, driving many East Timorese from their homes in the central and western parts of the territory. The Australian government continued to make public statements that took the pressure off Indonesia. Downer, for instance, said, 'I get the impression that President Habibie, Mr Alatas, General Wiranto are all trying to do the right thing. And some of the commanders, clearly, are trying to do the right thing. But there have been and there still are some fairly wild elements within the Indonesian military' (Downer, 5 September 1999).

The ethnic cleansing campaign first sought to contain foreign observers and remove them from East Timor. Accordingly, foreigners were intimidated and corralled into confined areas where they could not provide eyewitness reports to the outside world, but they were generally not harmed. Ian Martin, the head of UNAMET, ordered the evacuation of UN staff, journalists and observers from the besieged compound on 8 September. This evacuation could have resulted in the rape or murder of the 1,500 refugees sheltering there. The international staff refused to leave until all the refugees had first been taken to safety (Martinkus 2002:24–5; Christalis 2002:236–248). As a consequence, the refugees were airlifted to the safety of Darwin. The Australian evacuation plan fitted in with the Indonesian strategy. Between 6th and 14th September, 2,478 foreign observers, journalists and international and local staff were evacuated by RAAF and RNZAF C130 Hercules transport aircraft to Darwin (Wilson 2003:6–11).

Once foreign witnesses had left, the East Timorese were driven out of their homes. Approximately 250,000 people are thought to have been driven across the border in a deliberate campaign by senior Indonesian generals, whose aim was to reverse the ballot and create new demographic facts on the ground (McDonald 14 March 2002). Approximately 70% of the buildings in East Timor had been destroyed. Vital infrastructure was crippled, leaving Dili and major towns without running water, electricity or telephones (KPP-HAM 2002:15–59). Indonesia also announced that East Timor would be placed under martial law from midnight on 6 September 1999. Under the terms of martial law, all power belonging to the civil administration passed to the military. Although this was a mere formality, it provided a legal basis to 'stop anyone and search them for weapons, arrest anyone suspected of creating disturbances for 20 days without a warrant, and shoot on sight anyone who breaks the curfew' (Sudrajat 7 September 1999).

Indonesia continued to insist that international intervention was unacceptable. It also talked up the violence and the dangers, knowing that Western governments were reluctant to accept casualties. Foreign Minister Ali Alatas warned that a foreign peacekeeping mission would sustain casualties, saying that 'any nations willing to send peacekeepers to the province would have to shoot their way in' (Johnstone 9 September 1999). The Indonesian military announced that additional troops were being deployed into East Timor; any foreign intervention would meet armed opposition. Indonesia's Air Force chief warned that his forces were 'ready to face any intruders from Australia' (Jenkins 11 September 1999).

The United States, which had failed to persuade the Howard government on the issue of peacekeepers, was not contemplating military intervention. At the regular Pentagon briefing on 7 September 1999, Defense spokesman Kenneth Bacon said that there were 'regrettable and unfortunate problems in East Timor' but that the US would 'continue to encourage the Indonesian authorities to provide security' (Ellis 7 September 1999). National Security Adviser Sandy Berger also signalled the Indonesians that, although they had to wind up operations quickly, the US would not intervene:

> My daughter has a very messy apartment up in college, maybe I shouldn't intervene to have that cleaned up. I don't think anybody ever articulated a doctrine which said that we ought to intervene wherever there's a humanitarian problem (Berger 8 September 1999).

Understandably, then, Indonesia's military leaders believed they could stave off international pressure long enough to create new facts on the ground. They could therefore afford to ignore UN officials like Mary Robinson, the High Commissioner for Human Rights, or the UN Security Council's five-man mission that arrived in Jakarta on 8 September, particularly in light of the remarks of the man who sent them, UN Security Council President Arnold Peter van Walsum of the Netherlands. Van Walsum made it clear that the Security Council would not authorise the deployment of foreign forces without the express consent of the Indonesian government (Aita 7 September 1999). Australia's Defence Minister concurred, saying that 'we're not going to go in there and invade Indonesia. That would be, you know, tantamount to creating a very substantial war, and that would I think result in a lot of unnecessary loss of life for both nations' (ABC Radio 9 September 1999).

By this stage, however, the Howard government's policy of support for the Indonesian military was thoroughly exposed. Tens of thousands of Australians had begun to demonstrate in support of peacekeepers. The demonstrations were escalating into even larger and angrier rallies, and were drawing in the trade unions. Crucially, the broader Australian public's support for the Australia-US alliance was in jeopardy; people were contrasting the feeble US response with Australia's own record of military deployments in support of US objectives. Policymakers in both countries were alarmed. Confronted by this kind of anger, the Australian government was finally forced to abandon its defence of the Indonesian military, pleading with the US to exert pressure on Indonesia to allow peacekeepers in. The problem was that, for the whole of 1999, the government had lobbied to keep peacekeepers *out*. It now worked frantically to allow international forces to enter East Timor in order to prevent a political crisis in Australia. On 7 September, when the burning of Dili was already underway, the government established an East Timor policy unit within Australian Defence Headquarters. So quickly was it set up that it did not have a room of its own to meet in; it was located in a temporary conference room, and required external infrastructure to function. The Australian ambassador to the UN, Penny Wensley, was instructed to lobby members of the Security Council. Howard held four telephone conversations with UN Secretary-General Kofi Annan during the course of the week, each more desperate than the one before. Defence minister John Moore was trying to get through to General Wiranto, the Minister for Defence and head of the armed forces, but Wiranto would not take his calls.

Realising that the Australia-US alliance was under threat, the Clinton administration acted swiftly. As a senior official said, 'We don't have a dog running in the East Timor race, but we have a very big dog running down there called Australia and we have to support it' (Hartcher 13 September 1999). At very senior levels of the US government, the overriding policy concern was how to design an appropriate response to Australian requests. US planners were concerned less about US–Indonesia relations than about US-Australia relations. They assumed that the Indonesian military would be angered but would give in without any threat to longer-term US interests in

Indonesia. The US delivered its message to the Indonesian military leadership in person. According to undersecretary of state Thomas Pickering, the commander-in-chief of the US forces in the Pacific informed General Wiranto in Jakarta on 8 September 1999 that the US would be suspending its military ties with Indonesia.

The Clinton cabinet's public pronouncements carried a hint of menace towards Indonesia. Defence secretary William Cohen warned that 'the international community has a number of levers we can pull on. There are serious economic consequences to be sure'. State Department spokesman James Rubin publicly informed Indonesia that its 'relations with the international community, including the United States, are at risk here ... we do spend tens of millions of dollars on economic development directly with the Indonesian Government and, obviously, the Indonesian government receives substantial billions of dollars in support pursuant to an agreement with the International Monetary Fund. The International Monetary Fund has indicated it is closely monitoring the situation in East Timor. Senior US officials began to impose deadlines on the sanctions, which were explained unambiguously to the Indonesian authorities. The chairman of the joint chiefs of staff, General Hugh Shelton, telephoned Wiranto several times during the week after the announcement of the referendum result. Jakarta remained adamant past the first deadline, triggering a suspension of all US military assistance. In the morning before he boarded Air Force One to attend an APEC summit in Auckland, President Clinton warned that 'if Indonesia does not end the violence, it must invite—*it must invite*—the international community to assist in restoring security ... it would be a pity if the Indonesian recovery were crashed by this'. Later, in a refueling stop in Hawaii, Clinton was briefed on the East Timor situation by Admiral Dennis Blair, who was fresh from his meeting with General Wiranto. Then, while on the final leg of his flight to Auckland, Clinton issued his strongest statement yet: 'It is clear the Indonesian military is aiding and abetting the militia violence ... This is simply unacceptable'. In an emergency debate in the UN Security Council on 12 September 1999, US envoy Richard Holbrooke finally warned Indonesia that it faced 'the point of no return in international relations' if it did not accept an international peacekeeping force' (Fernandes 2004:98–104).

The Indonesian military's resistance ended within hours. On 12 September 1999, Habibie and Wiranto emerged from a special cabinet meeting. Before the television cameras and microphones of the assembled international media, Habibie announced that his government had decided to allow a UN force into East Timor. Contrary to Howard and Downer's claims, it took only four days of diplomatic pressure for Indonesia to agree to foreign troops. So quickly were Australian strategic planners forced to move that they named the peacekeeping force IFET – International Force East Timor. When it was pointed out that IFET was an acronym for the International Federation for East Timor – a global coalition of activists and groups who had campaigned for East Timorese independence for years – the acronym was changed to InterFET.

The Australian National Audit Office later conducted a performance audit into the management of the InterFET operation, also known as *Operation Warden*. It concluded that the Department of Defence 'could not provide evidence that formal planning for [a multilateral operation] began until later in 1999... The nature and size of the ADF involvement in East Timor were not known until shortly before deployment [because] there was no government strategic requirement for the ADF to be able to form or lead an international peace-keeping coalition force'. According to information submitted by the Department of Defence to the Audit Office, 'the actual nature and size of the military operations to be undertaken were not clear until shortly before deployment. The number, size and force capability to be provided, and the support required, by the non-Australian troop contributing nations were not known until after the deployment had started' (ANAO 2002).

The government later claimed that it had acted effectively by announcing as early as 11 March 1999 that another brigade would be raised to 'high alert'. The fact, however, is that this brigade was an already existing formation that was told to be prepared to move on 28 days' notice. It was not a new brigade and it was not placed anywhere near high alert. The InterFET Post Operations Report puts this in perspective:

> As a consequence of the move to 28 days' notice, 80 new riflemen were posted to one of the major units in the brigade. This resulted in 'deficiences [which] profoundly affected [our] readiness and ultimately our capability on deployment'. It 'gave commanders little confidence in [these] soldier's abilities'. In fact, when the unit deployed to East Timor, these soldiers were withdrawn to the rear echelon and not used. In the hasty atmosphere preceding *Operation Warden*, this unit 'was offered new .50 calibre machine guns in mid September but declined due to lack of training time, confidence in the weapon system, etc'.

The brigade was a contingency plan to deal with Indonesia's June 1999 elections, during which there was a possibility that Australian and other nationals might need evacuation in case of unmanageable electoral violence.

The militias, of course, were little more than a creation of the Indonesian military and were no match for a professional fighting force. The Howard government's constant obfuscation of this basic fact served to take the pressure off the Indonesian military. We know from a few leaked documents that the Howard government and its diplomats worked energetically to prevent a peacekeeping force from entering East Timor. In doing so, it was acting within the contours of pre-existing Australian foreign policy towards East Timor. In maintaining the continuity of Australian foreign policy, all governments had previously been secure from the opposition of the public because no parliamentary opposition would argue seriously for self-determination for the East Timorese. The Australian Labor Party's foreign policy spokesman, Laurie Brereton, fractured this cozy bi-partisan consensus, thus removing a central pillar on which stood the continuity of Australian foreign policy. The transnational solidarity movement became the little wheel inside the bigger wheel of public opinion, causing a major policy reversal. The success of the transnational solidarity movement is best encapsulated by the following quote from one of its most important participants:

> To the great credit of the people of Australia, in 1999 they compelled their government to abandon this cynical stand. Australia led the international force (InterFET) that entered East Timor after the Indonesian generals were informed by Washington that the game was over in mid-September 1999, and immediately withdrew, quickly reversing their forceful insistence that they would never do so. The events teach a dramatic lesson as to how the crimes of a quarter-century could have been ended, at any time, without force, sanctions, or any threats at all beyond the withdrawal of participation – a lesson with far broader implications (Chomsky 2005:x).

SOURCES

Aarons M and Domm R 1992, *East Timor: A Western-made Tragedy*, Left Book Club, Sydney.

ABC Radio 9 September 1999, Defence Minister John Moore on Indonesia, AM.

Aita J 7 September 1999, '*UN mission will urge Indonesia to accept foreign peacekeepers on Timor*', USIS Washington File, US Information Agency.

ANAO 2002, *Management of Australian Defence Force Deployments to East Timor*, Audit Report No. 38, Australian National Audit Office, Canberra.

Ball D 2002, *Silent Witness: Australian Intelligence and East Timor,* in McDonald *et al*., 2002.

Berger S 8 September 1999, *Press Briefing by National Security Advisor and National Economic Advisor*, The Briefing Room, White House.

Blewett N 1999, *A Cabinet Diary: A personal record of the first Keating government*, Wakefield Press, Kent Town.
Brereton L 21 August 1996, 'Australia and Indonesia: A Labor Perspective', *Speech to the 2nd Indonesian Students' Conference*, University House, Australian National University.
Brereton L 30 October 1998, Press Release.
Brereton L 28 April 1999, *Speech to the New South Wales Young Labor Foreign Affairs Forum*, Randwick Labor Club, Sydney.
Chomsky N 2005, *Foreword*, in *Masters of Terror: Indonesia's military and violence in East Timor*, R. Tanter, D. Ball and G. van Klinken (eds) 2006, Rowman & Littlefield Oxford.
Christalis I 2002, *Bitter Dawn*, Zed Books, London.
Daily Telegraph 12 October 1996, p2.
Daley P 22 March 1992, *GALP confirms Lucy funding*, Sunday Age.
Daley P 10 August 1999, *US marines set for Dili*, The Age.
Daley P 31 August 1999, *We snub offer to send in the Marines*, Sunday Age.
Daley P 4 May 2004, *Timor: Envoy claims US kept in dark*, Bulletin Vol. 122, No. 6419.
Dauth J 5 May 1999, FADT Senate Committee.
Dauth 13 August 1999, FADT Senate Committee.
Dauth J 9 December 1999, FADT Senate Committee.
DFAT 1999, Submission to the FADT Senate Committee on East Timor.
Way 2000, *Indonesia and the Incorporation of Portuguese Timor*, Melbourne University Press, Canberra.
DFAT 2001, *East Timor in Transition: An Australian Policy Challenge*, Brown and Wilton, Canberra.
Downer A 5 February 1999, *Interview, ABC Radio*.
Downer 21 February 1999, *Face to Face*.
Downer A 25 February 1999, Press Conference.
Downer A 7 March 1999, *Interview on Sunday program*, Nine Network.
Downer 14 March 1999, Press Conference, APH, Canberra.
Downer A 31 March 1999, Speech to the National Press Club, Canberra.
Downer A 11 April 1999, Alexander Downer interviewed by Glen Milne, Face to Face, Channel Seven.
Downer A 27 April 1999, ABC Radio.
Downer 25 May 1999, *Speech at book launch of 'East Timor and Australia: AIIA Contributions to the Policy Debate'*, Parliament House, Canberra.
Downer 9 August 1999a, *Response to Question without Notice*, House of Representatives Hansard, APH, Canberra.
Downer 9 August 1999b, *Clarification of response to Question without Notice*, House of Representatives Hansard, APH, Canberra.
Downer 5 September 1999, *Interview on Meet the Press*, Channel Ten.

Ellis S 7 September 1999, '*US expects Indonesia to protect people of East Timor*', USIS Washington File, US Information Agency.

Fernandes C 2004, *Reluctant Saviour: Australia, Indonesia and the independence of East Timor, Scribe Publications, Melbourne.*

Hartcher P 29 July 1996, Howard's discomfort over Jakarta, Australian Financial Review, p 14.

Hartcher P 13 September 1999, '*The ABC of winning US support*', Australian Financial Review.

Hill R 11 February 1999, *Committee Hansard*, FADT Senate Committee.

Howard J 28 April 1999, *Press Conference.*

Jenkins D 11 September 1999, 'A general squeeze, and Habibie quickly succumbs', *Sydney Morning Herald.*

Johnstone C 9 September 1999, 'UN deserts East Timor', *Courier Mail.*

Kelly P 5 December 1998, 'The Timor tangle', *The Weekend Australian.*

KPP-HAM 2002, *Full Report of the Investigative Commission into Human Rights Violations in East Timor*, in McDonald *et al.*, 2002.

Lyons J 12 October 1999, *The secret Timor dossier, Vol 117, No 6195.*

Martinkus J 2001, *A Dirty Little War*, Random House, Sydney.

Martinkus 2002, *Review of 'Deliverance'*, Australian Book Review No 244.

McDonald H 14 March 2002, '*Australia's bloody East Timor secret' and 'Silence over a crime against humanity*', Sydney Morning Herald.

McDonald H, Ball D, Dunn J, van Klinken G, Bourchier D, Kammen D and Tanter R 2002, *Masters of Terror: Indonesia's Military and Violence in East Timor in 1999*, Canberra Paper #145, Strategic and Defence Studies Centre, Canberra.

Meaney N 1985, *Australia and the World: A Documentary History from 1870 to the 1970s*, Longman Cheshire, Melbourne.

Newman J 22 March 1999, Response to Question on Notice, Senate Hansard, APH, Canberra.

Reuters 10 June 1998, *Habibie interview with the BBC.*

Rezasyah T 1996, 'Uncovering Australian Foreign Policy Making: The Prevalence of a Dominant Bureaucracy', *The Indonesian Quarterly*, Vol XXIV No 4.

Robinson G 2002, *The fruitless search for a smoking gun*, in Colombijn F and Lindblad J (eds) 2002, *Roots of violence in Indonesia*, ISEAS, Singapore.

Stewart I 28 July 1998, 'Downer hails Timor troop withdrawal', *Australian.*

Sudrajat E 7 September 1999, *Statement by TNI chief spokesman*, Voice of America.

Suryodiningrat M and Purba K, 2 November 1999, *Ali Alatas looks back on 11 years of Indonesia's foreign policy*, Jakarta Post.

Taylor J 1999, *East Timor: The Price of Freedom*, Pluto Press, Annandale.

Tempo 18–24 September 2000, *Ali Alatas: Santa Cruz incident a turning point in our diplomacy.*

The Australian 19 December 1995, 'Leaders sign historic Indonesian treaty'.
Turner J 12 November 1996, *21 Tragic Years*, Advertiser.
Wensley P 23 February 2000, *East Timor and the United Nations*, Speech to the Australian Institute of International Affairs, Sydney.
Wilkinson M 13 August 1999, *Why we kept Timor secrets from the US*, Sydney Morning Herald.
Wilson D 2003, *Warden to Tanager*, Banner Books, Queensland.

Postcolonial Troubles: The Politics of Transitional Justice in Timor-Leste

Dr Simon Philpott

Introduction

Nearing the sixth anniversary of its independence, Timor Leste[1] is experiencing a host of problems that have precedent in other transitions from colonial rule to independence that took place during the latter half of the twentieth century. Its political elite is currently fractured and engaged in the manipulation of Timor Leste's fragile formal institutions. The Constitution has been tested and the rule of law repeatedly breached. Sadly, violence and death are an increasingly common part of political life and likely to remain so for the foreseeable future. In a pattern repeated throughout the former colonial world, the unity forged among Timorese nationalists by common opposition to colonial rule has given way to internal differences and alternate visions that are significantly harming the country's immediate prospects. Many of these divisions have their origins in unresolved struggles dating back to the period before the Indonesian invasion of late 1975. While these persisted throughout the Indonesian occupation, they were at least partly subsumed to the exigencies of resistance.

Moreover, in Xanana Gusmao, guerrilla leader and now STET President, and Jose Ramos Horta, roving ambassador and now Prime Minister, East Timor had two individuals that enjoyed a measured respect and legitimacy in the international domain. In East Timorese public life Bishop Carlos Belo became the most significant and visible advocate for justice and a cessation of Indonesian violence against the Timorese. Others of Timor Leste's political elite including former Prime Minister Mari Alkatiri and former Interior Minister, Rogerio Lobato,[2] spent the years of Indonesia's occupation in Portugal or former Portuguese colonies, particularly Mozambique and Angola. They acquired skills and attributes not available to those in the armed

---

[1] Independent East Timor is officially known as the Democratic Republic of Timor Leste. In this paper, I have used the shortened version Timor Leste when referring to independent Timor and East Timor when referring to the period of the Indonesian occupation.

[2] On 7 March 2007, Rogerio Lobato was convicted of manslaughter and illegally arming civilians for the purposes of intimidation of government opponents. He faces seven and a half years in prison. The effects that his conviction will have on Timor Leste's political dynamics are yet to be seen.

resistance or living ordinary lives in East Timor, and they saw first hand the experiences of other new nations. While the differing backgrounds of Timor Leste's elite are not alone the cause of friction, such differences are magnified by the distinctive political discourses and approaches to governance evident among some of the most influential figures in Timorese political life.

During the Indonesian occupation sympathisers and activists around the world easily overlooked the deep complexities of East Timorese politics in their campaigning for an independent nation. Falantil, the armed resistance, was small, limited, and stretched but could be seen as fulfilling the dictum that the guerrillas win the war if they do not lose. While the campaign of armed resistance was successful enough in drawing the Indonesian armed forces into painful and embarrassing skirmishes, it was conducted beyond the purview of the international media, activists, and other governments. Arguably, the resistance was more effective in its peaceful, mainly urban-based protests against the occupation – especially after East Timor was partially opened to outsiders in the later 1980s when Suharto tried to convince the world, and perhaps himself, that all was well there. However, the massacre in the Santa Cruz cemetery of 12 November 1991 finally brought the reality of Indonesian military policy into the living rooms of people around the world and decisively shifted the dynamic in favour of the East Timorese. While the massacre and independence ballot are separated by just under eight years, in a post-Cold War world shaped by discourses of the peace dividend, human rights, and humanitarian intervention, the Indonesian government never completely recovered from the effects of the Santa Cruz massacre.

Since the ballot, political life in Timor Leste has been complicated by a range of factors including the elite divisions that will be discussed in more detail below, the issue of official languages of state, perceptions of identity difference, the use and abuse of key institutions for individual political gain, the persistence of poverty, and, importantly, a sense of disappointment and frustration among many Timorese that human rights abusers have escaped justice.[3] In the absence of meaningful support from the UN and nations such as the US, Japan, Australia, and the UK, President Gusmao and Prime Minister Ramos Horta have argued that vigorous pursuit of human rights criminals in Indonesia and elsewhere will prove harmful to the interests of the new nation, and have instead opted for processes of reconciliation with Indonesia. Timor Leste is by no means the first country to have to decide on whether to pursue

---

[3] J Kingston, "Balancing Justice and Reconciliation in East Timor" (2006) 38 *Critical Asian Studies* 271.

human rights abusers in its transitional phase and the difficulties in doing so that face legislators, activists and judiciaries are well documented.[4]

In one sense, none of this is surprising: the small country has borne immense costs of every kind for decades. Its physical infrastructure was largely destroyed in 1999 amid a final, bitter rein of terror as the Indonesian military withdrew. The emerging country lost most of its administrative, professional, teaching, and medical personnel along with its institutional memory and archives. It has to a reasonable extent enjoyed the material support of the UN and international community in terms of financial and development aid, but it has been less successful in securing assistance and political support in pursuing those indicted for war crimes. Moreover, current political instability may contribute to the worsening of human rights abuses and other forms of political violence given growing concerns about the arming of different political factions.[5]

The Genesis of the East Timor's Political Troubles

The path of Timor Leste to independence is somewhat atypical. Unlike Indonesia for example, explicitly nationalist sentiment came relatively late to the Portuguese colony, despite a history of periodic resistance to colonial rule. When finally it did materialise in the early 1970s, its similarities with other anti-colonial nationalism in Southeast Asia is evident. That is, among the first to articulate a vision of an independent nation was a small group of literate young men including disaffected colonial bureaucrats and school teachers, some of whom were educated in the Jesuit seminary at Dare, just outside Dili. Their views took institutional shape in the Timorese Social Democratic Association (ASDT) which foreshadowed a ten-year path to independence. However, this approach was rapidly made implausible by events in Lisbon.

In April 1974, the so-called Carnation Revolution organised by leftists in the Portuguese military brought to an end the stultifying authoritarian dictatorship that had ruled over Portugal for nearly five decades. Part of the agenda of the revolutionaries was divestment of Portugal's (primarily African) colonies. While detailed comment is beyond the scope of this chapter, the decolonisation process was poorly coordinated and executed and in East Timor effectively required a population with a literacy rate of only 10 percent and

[4] P Hayner, Unspeakable Truths: Confronting State Terror and Atrocity (Routledge, London, 2001); G Di Palma, To Craft Democracies: An Essay on Democratic Transitions (University of California Press, Berkeley, 1990).

[5] Australian Associated Press, "Jakarta Closes Timor Borders After Raid", *Sydney Morning Herald*, 26 February 2007.

with little political education to very quickly take decisions about its future as an independent nation.[6] One consequence of the changes in Portugal was that the ASDT quickly morphed into the Revolutionary Front for an Independent East Timor (Fretilin) which emerged in September 1974. Fretilin sought immediate independence from Portugal. Its vision was partly shaped by radical African nationalism, its counterpart in Mozambique, Frelimo, and, to a lesser degree, by the ideas of Marx. It very quickly became the most popular political group in East Timor spreading its vision through literacy and political education campaigns. Its political organisation reached more deeply and into more areas of East Timor than any of its competitors. A new Portuguese administration seeking rapid divestment of its colonies and the emergent Fretilin appealing for immediate independence found some common cause.

However, its desire for rapid and complete independence and its call for a thoroughgoing social transformation quickly placed it at odds with another emergent party, the Timor Democratic Union (UDT). The UDT was comprised of wealthier and more socially conservative elements including coffee planters, the Portuguese oriented elite, and some Chinese-Timorese merchants. It flirted with continuing constitutional ties with Portugal but quickly realised this was untenable given the enthusiasm for independence that had been generated in the volatile political situation of 1974–75. Tensions between Fretilin and UDT, partly manipulated by the Indonesian government, became violent in the months before the Indonesian invasion and resulted in a brief civil war and some 3,000 combat deaths. The differences between key actors at that time spilled into the post-invasion period and continue to animate the politics of independent Timor Leste.[7] Moreover, sharp political differences were manifest in Fretilin and these simmered throughout the occupation period and beyond.

For example, in the lead up to the Indonesian invasion of December 1975, Fretilin's membership was expanded by an influx of East Timorese soldiers that had served with the Portuguese colonial garrison. These included Rogerio Lobato, the garrison's most senior indigenous soldier and who went on to lead Falantil, at that time Fretilin's armed wing, in the brief civil war.[8] These soldiers were more conservative in their social and political outlook than the earlier members of Fretilin mentioned above. The soldiery was more attracted to the vision of Nicolau Lobato, who became Prime Minister of the short-

[6] SG Simonsen, "The Authoritarian Temptation In East Timor" (2006) 46 *Asia Survey* 575.
[7] International Crisis Group, *Resolving Timor Leste's Crisis*. Asia Report No 120 (2006).
[8] *ibid*.

lived government unilaterally proclaimed on November 28 1975 by Fretilin, and who advocated a form of radical African nationalism, political pragmatism, and conservative self-reliance.[9]

Despite the Indonesian invasion, differences within Fretilin persisted and deepened leading to violence within its ranks when its Central Committee authorised intimidation and murder of opponents of its vision of a Leninist revolutionary front. This swiftly led to the alienation of Xanana Gusmao who throughout much of the occupation led the resistance politically, militarily and symbolically. Indeed, by the mid-1980s, Gusmao had withdrawn Falantil, the armed wing of the resistance, from Fretilin and declared his support for a broad, multi-party, inclusive, independent East Timor. The formation of the National Council of Maubere Resistance (CNRM) in 1987 is an important moment in the transformation of East Timorese resistance from leftist internationalist to nationalist discourse. That is, the term *maubere*, a common greeting among the Mambai but used by the Portuguese as a derogatory term, facilitated the "Timorisation" of the resistance through the authentication of ordinary rural life.[10] For its part, Fretilin bitterly resented Gusmao's taking control of Falantil and his view that Fretilin's was simply one of many potential legitimate voices in East Timorese politics.

From the late 1980s onwards, East Timor became an ever more complex problem for Suharto's Indonesian government. Journalists and activists took advantage of the opportunities to enter East Timor and began to report on conditions there. The Pope visited in October 1989 drawing the extensive global media coverage of an "event" and widespread, if brief, attention to East Timor's plight. Four months later the US ambassador to Indonesia, David Newsom, visited Dili only to be confronted by pro-independence activists who were violently dispersed by Indonesian authorities. In the following year, footage of the Santa Cruz massacre of November 1991 aired around the world, and the 1992 testimony of journalist Allan Nairn, who survived the massacre, before the US Senate Committee on Foreign Relations focused the minds of at least some US legislators on Indonesia's policies and practices in East Timor.

In 1996, East Timor's foreign minister in exile, Jose Ramos Horta shared the Nobel peace prize with the Catholic Bishop of East Timor, Carlos Belo, much

[9] S Philpott, "East Timor's double life: Smells like Westphalian spirit" (2006) 27 *Third World Quarterly* 135.
[10] *ibid*.

to the embarrassment and irritation of authorities in Jakarta. Finally, in 1997–98, Indonesia's economy collapsed in spectacular fashion shredding what was left of Suharto's legitimacy and leading to his resignation from office in May 1998, at which time he was replaced by the unpopular and unpredictable Vice President, BJ Habibie. It was Habibie who in January 1999 put East Timor on the road to independence with his decision to allow a plebiscite that offered the choices of special autonomy within Indonesia or outright independence. Thus, in 10 years, East Timor went from an integral part of the Indonesian state that, despite the best and impressive efforts of indigenous and international campaigners, showed no sign of willingness to renegotiate its relationship with the province it (effectively) annexed in 1976. While East Timor was always a more significant problem for Indonesia than Foreign Minister Ali Alatas' dismissal of it as gravel in Jakarta's shoe, it would have been a brave prediction in 1989 that the East Timorese would be voting in an internationally sanctioned plebiscite for their independence within a decade.

Meanwhile, the resistance in East Timor was also adapting to Indonesia's many setbacks and the CNRM was superseded by the National Council of Resistance of the People of East Timor (CNRT) in September 1998. The CNRM was comprised of the five political parties that existed at the time of Indonesia's invasion and was an attempt to overcome differences within the resistance. The formation of the CNRT is also indicative of the East Timorese leadership's recognition of the importance of a united front given the rapid and uncertain political changes in Indonesia.

However, over nine years after the formation of the CNRT it is clear that in independent East Timor the political divisions of the resistance period persist and are having a deleterious effect on the capacity of the young nation to establish its institutions.[11] Long remembered betrayals, slights, and other wounds are now playing out in full and are sharply magnified by the fact that the country's political elite is so small: the origins of and solutions to East Timor's political problems entail no more than about 10 people who have a shared history going back 30 years.[12] Beyond the personal antagonisms lies another problem and that is the weakness of the country's political institutions and the willingness of some in the elite to abandon the rule of law.

The Slow Slide into Political Crisis

Other factors have also contributed to the current political problems in Timor Leste. First, the demobilisation of Falantil troops during the period between

[11] Above, n.7.
[12] *ibid.*

the ballot and independence in May 2002 was poorly conceived and executed and has led to strong disaffection among some former guerrillas. Secondly, disillusionment among former fighters has been exacerbated by flaws in the recruitment policies and training of the East Timor Defence Force (F-FDTL) and the national police (PNTL). Specifically, there are perceptions among peoples from the western districts of Timor Leste that they are victims of discrimination on ethnic grounds. These tensions, which I will put into the context of the current political crisis shortly, have become the axes around which personal conflicts have taken shape. Both the army and police have been manipulated by some members of the political elite for personal aggrandisement and in the interests of consolidating their power. As such, perceptions of discrimination have become aligned with individual members of the elite and their ideological predispositions, further sharpening perceptions of identity differences.[13] It is, however, worth noting that in the thousands of statements collected during Timor Leste's truth and reconciliation process, no evidence emerged suggesting that regional tensions animate Timorese politics.[14]

Thirdly, fortuitously, several members of the elite were outside of East Timor at the time of the Indonesian invasion only returning in 1999. Some of these, including Mari Alkatiri (former Prime Minister), Rogerio Lobato (former Minister of the Interior) and the better known Jose Ramos Horta (currently Prime Minister) assumed positions of power and authority in independent East Timor. A perception exists among some of those who saw out the occupation in East Timor under difficult circumstances that returnees have snaffled political power without earning it. Muslim Mari Alkatiri, in particular, has been the subject of much criticism despite being leader of East Timor's dominant political party, Fretilin. Fourthly, and related to the previous point, the adoption of Portuguese and Tetum as official languages of state has angered many Timorese who perceived the use of Portuguese as a means of their political exclusion. This is a complex matter indeed.

The occupation confirmed Tetum as a language of national unity and also turned Portuguese from a language of colonial oppression to one of resistance. However, Indonesian became central to East Timorese life given the rapid expansion of education and literacy under Indonesian rule. At the time of the invasion the literacy rate was only 10 percent and there were only two lower

---

[13] Above, n.7.

[14] UNHCR, Report of the United Nations Independent Special Commission of Inquiry for Timor-Leste (Geneva, 2006).

secondary schools in Dili compared to 103 in 1994. Thus, by the end of the occupation, 90 percent of people under 30 understood Indonesian, falling to about 50 percent of people older than that.[15] The returning exiles, typically older, Portuguese speaking (having sought refuge in Portugal, Mozambique and Angola) and more worldly, have been able to use their linguistic talents to (partly) fulfil their political aspirations. For example, while some 27 percent of 35–50 year olds speak Portuguese, only about 11 percent of under 25s can.[16] Thus the decision of the government to phase out Indonesian, largely for political reasons, in favour of Portuguese and Tetum is potentially disenfranchising of many young East Timorese and has been understood as such. Moreover, despite perceptions among some Timorese that the Indonesian language is one element in attempts to "Indonesianise" them, the language also provided a window onto the archipelago in which they live through television soap operas and other entertainments. This has contributed to a benevolent view towards Indonesian society among many Timorese, and perhaps also serves to reinforce differences between returned exiles and those that lived out the occupation.

Settling upon a date which marks the institutionalisation of these various tensions is difficult but one could look to the election for a constituent assembly which took place on the second anniversary of the ballot for independence, August 30 2001. Fretilin won a handsome victory with 57 percent of the vote and 55 of 88 seats but its support was much stronger in the eastern parts of the country than the west, perhaps anticipating some of the problems now evident in Timorese politics.[17] Moreover, it may be that many people supported Fretilin believing it to be Xanana's party, something that it patently was not. Indeed, Xanana was disappointed by Fretilin's success.[18] The Constituent Assembly charged with drafting the Constitution for the new republic was dominated by Fretilin and it took full advantage of the opportunity to shape the new institutions in its own image. For example, it adopted 28 November (the anniversary of its unilateral declaration of independence in 1975) as the national day, and it adopted its flag as the national flag and its anthem, *Patria Patria*, as the national anthem. These moves were resented by opposition parties.

The parliament established with the coming of independence in May 2002 has been largely ineffective in the sense that there has been little debate or

[15] M Leach, "History on the Line: East Timorese History after Independence" (2006) 61 *History Journal Workshop* 223; Simonsen, above, n.6.

[16] *ibid*.

[17] Above, n.14.

[18] Simonsen, above, n.6.

amendment of Fretilin's legislation.[19] My own interviews and discussions with educated young Timorese in early 2005 revealed quite strong discontent with Fretilin's conduct, something remarked upon by at least one other scholar.[20] Other examples of Fretilin's heavy-handed political approach include a December 2004 law that prohibited demonstrations convened for the purposes of criticising the head of state and other government office-holders, a February 2005 government boycott of the largest newspaper, *Suara Timor Lorosae*, for reporting on famine deaths, and the politicisation of the bureaucracy with the appointment of 62 of 65 regional administrators from Fretilin ranks.[21] Fretilin also renamed the FDTL as Falantil-FDTL (F-FDTL) in attempt to link the future of the armed forces to Fretilin's past.[22] This is significant.

In late 2000 Xanana Gusmao managed to convince United Nations Transitional Administration in East Timor (UNTAET) authorities that the formation of the new army, the FDTL, should be an internal Falantil process. This excluded Fretilin from influence over the foundation of the armed forces that would ultimately come to be responsible for the security of the new nation. The FDTL came into being on February 1 2001 and consisted of two battalions totalling 1500.[23] The first recruitment of 650 was comprised almost exclusively of Xanana loyalists, creating immediate suspicion and resentment among Fretilin's leadership. It also quickly became clear to many former Falantil fighters that there would be no place for them in the new force. This added to a growing sense of grievance further exacerbated by a very high rate of unemployment: most lacked the skills to compete for jobs. Reintegration of the former guerrillas has thus proved difficult.[24] Discontent among former fighters was exploited by Rogerio Lobato who managed to use the loyalty of these malcontents to force his way into government where he became Interior Minister with responsibility for the police (PNTL).[25] Problems quickly arose as a result of his appointment.

Many members of the PNTL had a background in the Indonesian police. This was problematic for a number of reasons. Not least of these was trust, as many of those recruited had singularly failed to protect the East Timorese during the militia violence of 1999. Moreover, new recruits were somewhat

[19] *ibid.*
[20] *ibid.*
[21] *ibid.*
[22] UNHCR, above, n.14; Simonsen, above, n.6.
[23] UNHCR, above, n.14.
[24] International Crisis Group, above, n.7; Simonsen, above, n.6.
[25] International Crisis Group, above, n.7.

frightened of former Indonesian era police and did not respect them as professionals. This almost guaranteed internal problems and instability from the outset. UNTAET's decision to hastily create this new police force has been widely criticised.[26] Moreover, demobbed Falantil fighters still cantoned in the interior were overlooked once again.[27] Lobato encouraged public disaffection about the plight of former Falantil fighters and insisted upon diversifying recruitment policy. In practice this meant recruiting men loyal to him personally rather than the office he held. As a result, Xanana Gusmao called for his resignation on the grounds of incompetence on the first national day of the independence period, 28 November 2002.[28]

From the earliest days of the F-FDTL perceptions grew among those with origins in the western districts of Timor Leste that they were being discriminated against, particularly with respect to promotion to the officer's ranks. Falantil was stronger in the east than the west during the Indonesian occupation because eastern areas saw more combat action. This gave rise to sentiments among those from the west that their peers from the eastern districts were more highly admired and favoured due to their earlier combat exploits. Westerners also faced a disproportionate number of disciplinary measures arising from absenteeism because they had further to travel home to see family when on leave, given the stationing of Battalion I in Los Palos, located at the eastern end of Timor Leste.[29]

Discontent within the F-FDTL grew and continued until January 2006 when 159 troops of mostly western origin petitioned Xanana Gusmao about their grievances. Feeling that their problems were not being addressed, hundreds began deserting in the first week of February 2006. After extensive negotiations between commanders of the F-FDTL and the absentee soldiers failed to end the dispute, approximately 600 troops were dismissed from the army in mid-March 2006. Prime Minister and President were, on this issue as with many others, in disagreement, with the latter opposing the dismissals in an emotional televised address to the nation on 23 March. The speech infuriated the commanding officer of the F-FDTL, thus dividing two men who had been political allies for more than 20 years. Intentionally or not, Gusmao's speech also gave legitimacy to the grievances of westerners and provided impetus for attacks on easterners in Dili in late March.[30]

---

[26] Simonsen, above, n.6.

[27] International Crisis Group, above, n.7.

[28] *ibid.*

[29] *ibid.*

[30] *ibid.*

Uneasy calm then prevailed until late April when a demonstration of several days for which the so-called petitioners had been given permission turned violent on its final day, 28 April, with little doubt that politicised youth and other troublemakers infiltrated the demonstration. The police charged with keeping the peace melted away in the heat of the violence. The Prime Minister, Mari Alkatiri then took a decision, probably unconstitutional, to use the F-FDTL to quell the violence. Whether this was a desperate attempt to bring the situation under control or to inflict political defeat upon Xanana Gusmao and Jose Ramos Horta is unclear. Whatever the intent, it was disastrous and led to indiscriminate use of violence and a small number of deaths.[31]

The troops were understood by some protestors to be pro-eastern, emboldening westerners in their attacks on easterner neighbourhoods in Dili, and rapidly fuelling conspiracy theories. Events then spiralled out of control with the defection of the head of the military police, Major Alfredo Reinado, and 17 of his men. Reinado, remains at, claimed to have defected in protest at discrimination against westerners. Mari Alkatiri and other former exiles regarded the crisis as a full frontal assault on the authority of Fretilin, given their perception that Xanana Gusmao was politicising F-FDTL, and dug in at its second national congress beginning on 17 May.[32] Relations between PNTL and F-FDTL had completely broken down by 24 May and there was widespread clashes between various armed groups, in part calmed by the return of peacekeeping troops from Australia, New Zealand, Portugal and Malaysia.[33]

The troubles of April and May 2006 left 38 people dead and 69 injured, the majority of whom were civilians. In addition, 150,000 people were uprooted and 1650 houses were destroyed by early June 2006.[34] Mari Alkatiri resigned as Prime Minister on 26 June to try and halt the country's slide into chaos, but he was and remains bitter about the circumstances of his downfall.

In the wake of this crisis, Interior Minister Rogerio Lobato was sacked and later charged for providing weapons to civilian groups, armed as partisans to the conflict. Concerns about the sorts of weapons being procured and the ways in which they were being acquired were first aired in the Australian press in mid 2005. At that time Mari Alkatiri's brother had a monopoly on their procurement and sale to the government. Paramilitary style weapons were

---

31 *ibid.*
32 *ibid.*
33 UNHCR, above, n.14.
34 *ibid.*

being directed towards police special units including border police, counter-insurgency and riot police, and bodyguard units.[35] Lobato, tried by a panel of three international judges, was found guilty in March 2007 of manslaughter and unlawfully using weapons to disturb public order, and sentenced to seven and a half years jail.[36] Lobato did not deny the charges against him, but argued that weapons were distributed under the orders of then Prime Minister Mari Alkatiri who, Lobato claims, asked him to "eliminate" the government's political opponents. Alkatiri denies the allegations and no charges were brought against him due to of lack of evidence.

As of late 2006, 219 PNTL weapons remained unaccounted for. Of these, 190 were 9mm pistols but there were also 25 semi-automatic assault rifles among the missing weapons. Also missing from the F-FDTL inventory were at least 45 M16 weapons, and there were others in the FDTL armoury whose provenance could not be established.[37] Moreover, the vacuum of authority that is one consequence of the crisis has been partly filled by an expansion of dozens of youth gangs, some of which are drawn along the east-west divide and which recruit from the 50 percent and more young men unemployed across Timor Leste. These youths feel politically, economically, and socially excluded. A growing number are being drawn into violence. It is also possible that some of the groups are being used by members of the political elite and are being activated along the old clandestine networks.[38]

The crisis which has engulfed Timorese politics is highly complex but there are several points about it worth noting. First, it is deep rooted and reflects problems and tensions between certain groups and individuals that pre-date the Indonesian invasion of 1975. In late 2006, the International Crisis Group reported that it was impossible to get the key actors into the same room, and that resolution of these problems remained but a remote possibility. Secondly, the political stakes involved threaten to overwhelm the rule of law and the institutions of state. That is, Timor Leste's political institutions seem unable to contain the conflict, suggesting manipulation and abuse of key institutions and exploitation of pockets of discontent have become means by which certain politicians and their allies secure their own positions and harm the prospects of perceived opponents. Thirdly, the UN bears significant responsibility for the exacerbation of these tensions and problems, particularly for reasons of excessive haste and inadequate support in the multiple and complex processes

[35] Philpott, above, n.9.

[36] J Jolliffe, "Former minister guilty of arming Timor hit squads", *The Age*, 8 March 2007.

[37] UNHCR, above, n.14.

[38] J Scambary, A Survey of Gangs and Youth Groups in Dili, Timor-Leste AusAID, (Canberra, 2006).

of rehabilitation. Finally, it is possible that the rule of law has been seen to fail in so far as senior Indonesian military perpetrators of war crimes and crimes against humanity have escaped justice, encouraging individuals and groups to seek their own remedies to whatever grievances they may have.

An analysis of truth, reconciliation and justice processes forms the second part of this chapter and provides a broader context for understanding Timor Leste's tribulations. Arguably, given its failings, the international community must (once more) bear some responsibility for the current crisis.

TRUTH, RECONCILIATION AND JUSTICE IN TIMOR LESTE

Brief analysis of the legal frameworks, procedures, processes, and outputs of the Commission for Reception, Truth, and Reconciliation (CAVR); the Special Panels for Serious Crimes (SPSC); and the Commission of Truth and Friendship (CTF) will form the final component of this outline of Timor Leste's transitional state. Whatever the failings of these legal and other processes, it must be noted that when departing Indonesian troops laid waste to East Timor in 1999, its entire pre-existing legal infrastructure was lost: judicial facilities, archives, books and other judicial resources.[39] Thus, the challenge of delivering justice to Timor Leste's innumerable victims was, and remains, enormous.

It is no surprise that a small country that endured centuries of European colonial subjugation, a brief and violent political contest in the mid-1970s, nearly 25 years of Indonesian military occupation, a traumatic and violent transition from Indonesian rule to independence, and ever more frequent violent political intrigue should be engaged in complex processes of truth- and justice-seeking, rehabilitation, and reparation. Each of the processes has had weaknesses and problems, some generic to institutions such as truth commissions, some specific to circumstance in Timor Leste. The most significant successes have come at local community level, where minor crimes have been atoned for through symbolic and material means of rectification. Many thousands of ordinary people's experiences and views have been recorded, and a variety of forums have brought whole communities together in structured public gatherings to discuss the past. To the extent that such processes engender reconciliation and rehabilitation of perpetrators and victims of violence alike, community processes have been moderately successful.

[39] Kingston, above, n.3.

However, those who bear the greatest responsibility for crimes against humanity and war crimes have largely escaped justice. There are several reasons for this, which will be canvassed in more detail shortly. First, pursuit of Indonesian war criminals required strong political will on the part of the international community which may, in turn, have galvanised the governments of Timor Leste and Indonesia. This was not forthcoming. Secondly, the serious crimes process in Timor Leste has been grossly under-funded by the UN, undermining the quality of justice meted out to perpetrators of violence and, indeed, the integrity of the entire process. Thirdly, the failure of the Indonesian government to accept responsibility for the deeds of its military, police, and other government officials has led to deeply flawed judicial processes that have enabled impunity on the part of those that bear the greatest responsibility for the violence that characterised the Indonesian occupation. As a consequence, and fourthly, Timor Leste's government has been left with little option but to abandon, at least for the present, its pursuit of senior Indonesians who bear command responsibility for the violence of the Indonesian occupation and its aftermath.

Despite all that has now been revealed about the Indonesian occupation of East Timor and the events of 1999, the Indonesian administration remains the beneficiary of Western goodwill, primarily because of a belief among nations such as the US and Australia that Indonesia is vital to the prosecution of the war on terror.[40] As a direct consequence of the absence of pressure on Indonesia, Timor Leste's hybrid court has not been successful in enforcing its indictments against higher level Indonesian military officials. To date, no significant power has attempted to give force to any indictment issued against Indonesians charged with serious crimes. No significant power has suggested it intends to detain any Indonesian charged with serious crimes.[41] Indeed, President Gusmao and Prime Minister Ramos Horta have both been critical of the serious crimes process precisely because the indictments cannot be enforced, and as such they regard them as an unnecessary antagonism to Indonesia.[42] Both have strongly argued that reconciliation with Indonesia is a political necessity and Timor Leste's only realistic option given the state does not have the diplomatic, legal (personnel and jurisprudence), or economic resources to vigorously pursue alleged criminals.[43] One unfortunate

---

[40] *ibid.*

[41] CT Call, "Is Transitional Justice Really Just?" (2004) *Brown Journal of World Affairs,* XI (I), pp.101–113.

[42] K Lanegran "Truth Commissions, Human Rights Trials, and the Politics of Memory" (2005) 25 *Comparative Studies of South Asia, Africa and the Middle East* 111.

[43] P Pigou *Crying Without Tears: In Pursuit of Justice and Reconciliation in Timor-Leste: Community Perspectives and Expectations* (International Centre for Transitional Justice, New York, 2003).

manifestation of this political vision is widespread criticism of the Commission of Truth and Friendship for, among other things, its failure to comply with international standards with respect to its granting of amnesties.

As a result of these multiple failings, the dominant discourse of Timor Leste's transition from colonialism to statehood is currently one of reconciliation, but the failure of Indonesian political will and legal process make this a one-sided affair.[44] However, these various processes and institutions will contribute to the making of the popular and official memory of Timor Leste's past, and as such will shape its political future in direct ways. As Kimberly Lanegran argues, it is not just remembering, but selective forgetting of national tragedies that shapes collective memory.[45] Moreover, a perceived lack of credibility in the utterances of influential political figures in Timor Leste may enhance sentiments of injustice and resentment among Timorese people.[46] More importantly perhaps, many Timorese, academics, activists, and other commentators perceive the rule of law to have failed its first major challenge in the new nation. Arguably, this encourages aggrieved parties to take matters into their own hands. While it is difficult to form a reliable judgment, it is quite possible that the deepening crisis in Timor Leste is in part a consequence of the impunity with which the rule of law has been abandoned.

Commission for Reception, Truth, and Reconciliation (CAVR)

Truth commissions with their genealogy in the Nuremberg and Tokyo trials conducted after WWII have become central elements of the so-called third wave of democratisations, the start of which, coincidentally, Samuel Huntington dates to the coup in Lisbon in 1974.[47] Priscilla Hayner notes that truth commissions have several common features which, in the case of the CAVR, are all present:

> to discover, clarify, and formally acknowledge past injustices; to respond to specific needs of victims; to contribute to justice and accountability; to outline institutional responsibility and recommend reforms; and to promote reconciliation and reduce conflict over the past.[48]

---

[44] Kingston, above, n.3.
[45] Above, n.42.
[46] Kingston, above, n.3.
[47] E Stanley, "Truth Commissions and the Recognition of State Crime" (2005) 45(4) *British Journal of Criminology* 582; SP Huntington, *The Third Wave: Democratization in the Late Twentieth Century* (University of Oklahoma Press, Norman, 1991); CJM Safferling, "Can Criminal Prosecution be the Answer to Massive Human Rights Violations?" (2004) 5 *German Law Journal* 1469.
[48] Above, n.4, p.24.

Truth and reconciliation commissions are essentially political institutions whose budgets, mandates, time frames for reporting, processes, and structures are reflections of the wishes of significant national and international actors anxious to further their own interests through making best use of the past. There are common and recurrent problems with truth and reconciliation commissions, including politicisation, insufficient resources, and the impunity of powerful countries that may have a case to answer with respect to crimes against humanity.[49] Despite improvements in the more recent processes for Sierra Leone and Timor Leste, the CAVR is not free of these shortcomings.[50]

Moreover, the idea that "truth" is available to be discovered and recorded is hotly debated in literature on truth commissions precisely because "truth" is a product of political contest among powerful national and international elites. The entanglement of truth and power shape not only the structures of commissions such as the CAVR but also the construction of the public memory of violent histories. On this view, power produces both truth and collective memory.[51] Kimberly Lanegran asks a series of questions that are entirely pertinent to Timor Leste's present and future:

> By demanding to know 'the truth' about past atrocities, do societies risk over-simplifying their pasts? Should remembering the past always be privileged over forgetting? To what degree does collective memory of atrocities contribute to society's healing? To what degree does it maintain wounds? Can calls for justice ever be answered when the crimes are as horrendous as those of … the combatants … in … East Timor?[52]

These questions are at best half answered in Timor Leste's case. Over-simplification of national histories, violent or not, is an inherent problem in nationalist historiography which while contested in Timor Leste, is currently authored by Fretilin. Arguably, the scale of crimes against humanity in Timor Leste makes forgetting what happened implausible: it is probable that no family in Timor Leste is untouched by the violence of the Indonesian occupation. However, the decision of some among Timor Leste's governing elite to seek reconciliation with Indonesia suggests many wounds will not be salved. It remains an open question as to how this period of Timor Leste's history will be framed in official nationalist discourses.[53]

---

[49] *ibid.*

[50] Call, above, n.41.

[51] Lanegran, above, n.42.

[52] *ibid.*

[53] Pigou, above, n.43.

The CAVR was established by UNTAET (Regulation 2001/10) as an independent state-sanctioned entity in 2001. It was originally proposed by Timorese human rights activists and endorsed by the CNRT Congress of August 2000. It was composed of seven national commissioners (five men and two women of different backgrounds and interests) and 29 regional commissioners. Its primary objective was to "promote national reconciliation and healing following the year of political conflict in East Timor, and in particular, following the atrocities committed in 1999".[54] Its functions were to seek the truth about human rights violations, to promote community reconciliation, and to produce a report documenting human rights abuses and recommending strategies for protecting human rights and promoting reconciliation. It was able to investigate serious crimes (war crimes, crimes against humanity, murder, sexual crimes, and torture) but these were referred to the General Prosecutor's Office for indictments to be issued. The CAVR focused more on reconciliation through its Community Reconciliation Process (CRP) often given effect through Community Reconciliation Agreements that generally entailed practical and symbolic acts of restitution.[55]

The CAVR could not offer inducements to criminals to solicit full admissions of guilt. Nor could it offer amnesties to human rights abusers. It also had a limited budget and maximum time frame (two years plus extension of six months) in which to complete its work, but was unable to meet such a stringent deadline.[56] Ultimately, its major output was *Chega! (Enough!)*, a report of more than 2,000 pages produced in Indonesian, Portuguese, and English and submitted to the President in October 2005. Among other findings and recommendations, the report found between 102,800 and 200,000 to have been killed or to have died of causes directly attributable to the Indonesian occupation of east Timor.[57]

Demonstrating the powerful political interests that limit and condition the work of truth commissions, CAVR's powers to examine the role of international state and non-state actors in the perpetration of human rights abuses were little used. While it was mandated to seek information from victims, witnesses, and government officials in other countries and enter into

[54] BS Lyons, "Getting Untrapped, Struggling for Truths: The Commission for Reception, Truth and Reconciliation (CAVR) in East Timor", in C Romano, ed, *International Criminal Courts: Sierra Leone, East Timor, Kosovo, and Cambodia* (Oxford University Press: New York, 2004), at pp.99–124.

[55] *ibid.*

[56] Lanegran, above, n.42.

[57] Kingston, above, n.3; Commission for Truth, and Reconciliation, *Chega!* (Dili, 2005).

cooperative agreements with official bodies of other countries, it received little or no cooperation from other states. Beyond Indonesia, countries such as the US and Australia had little to gain from cooperating with the CAVR with respect to their roles in East Timor's occupation.[58]

Among its many recommendations, the report calls upon all who contributed to the occupation of East Timor, Indonesia, other governments, and arms dealers, to provide reparations to the people of Timor Leste. It emphasises the importance of educating Indonesians about this facet of its recent history in promoting reconciliation, and it calls upon Indonesia to prosecute its criminals.[59] However, President Gusmao, to general dismay and widespread criticism, attempted to suppress the report, referring to its "grandiose idealism", and expressing concerns about the lack of support for its recommendations in the UN Security Council and among other nations of the world.[60] Inevitably though, the report found its way into the public domain and was posted to the websites of NGOs and other organisations.

Special Panels of the Serious Crimes Unit (Dili Courts)

Serious crimes uncovered by the work of the CAVR or those which came to its attention in statements submitted by perpetrators of violence seeking reintegration through CAVR mechanisms were referred to the General Prosecutor's Office. In 2000, UNTAET established a hybrid court, the Special Panels to try Serious Crimes of the Dili District Court (SPSC), to handle murder and sexual offences during the period 1 January 1 to 25 October 1999 and crimes against humanity, war crimes, and genocide whenever they occurred.[61] The creation of a hybrid court of this type is in part a response to the strong opposition of the Indonesian government to the formation of a purely international tribunal to try those accused of war crimes.

The SPSC was made up of a Special Panel of international and Timorese judges and staff under UN oversight, a Serious Crimes Unit (SCU) of international investigators and prosecutors, and a Public Defenders Office staffed mainly by Timorese but with some internationals. These institutions operated alongside the CAVR which, as already mentioned, dealt with less serious crimes.[62] The SPSC was from the outset seriously under-resourced

58 Lyons, above, n.54.
59 Kingston, above, n.3.
60 *ibid.*
61 Pigou, above, n.43.
62 Call, above, n.41.

both materially and politically.[63] For example, while the International Criminal Tribunal for Rwanda (ICTR) attracted $178 million in UN funding in 2001 and the International Criminal Tribunal for Yugoslavia (ICTY) $223 million in 2002–03, the SPSC and the SCU attracted only $6.3 million in 2001.[64] This under-funding seriously undermined the work of these institutions and the quality of the justice delivered to victims and perpetrators alike.[65]

In establishing the SPSC, the UN had accepted the assurances of the Indonesian administration that it would bring human rights abusers to justice through the *ad hoc* Human Rights Court for Timor Leste established in Jakarta.[66] In this sense, the work of the SPSC was to be complemented with an equal commitment to investigation of serious crimes by the Indonesian Commission on the Violation of Human Rights in East Timor (established in 1999) and prosecution through the *ad hoc* court. However, then President Megawati Sukarnoputri empowered the court only to investigate crimes that occurred between April and September 1999 and in only three of East Timor's 13 districts. This limited mandate meant the vast majority of crimes fell outside of the *ad hoc* court's powers of investigation.[67] Indeed, according to one estimate, only one percent of Indonesian occupation-era killings in East Timor occurred in 1999.[68] No Indonesian national brought before this court for crimes against humanity was convicted.[69]

However lamentable, Indonesia's refusal to cooperate reflects a predictable lack of political will but just as worryingly, weaknesses in its jurisprudence and judicial institutions. The governments of other key nations including the US, Australia, the UK, and Japan failed to place Indonesia under meaningful pressure to establish credible legal processes to deal with war crimes and crimes against humanity.

In addition to problems between the governments of Timor Leste and Indonesia, the SPSC itself embodied certain limitations. These included; the provision of more and better lawyers and more generous funding for

[63] J Nevins, "Restitution over coffee: truth, reconciliation, and environmental violence in East Timor" (2003) 22(6) *Political Geography* 677; Kingston, above, n.3.
[64] Kingston, above, n.3.
[65] D Cohen, Indifference and Accountability: The United Nations and the Politics of International Justice in East Timor (East-West Center, Honolulu, 2006), 9.
[66] Lanegran, above, n.42; Nevins, above, n.63.
[67] Nevins, above, n.63.
[68] La'o Hamutuk, "The Special Panels for Serious Crimes: Justice for East Timor", (2004) 5(3–4) *La'o Hamutuk Bulletin* 1.
[69] Nevins, above, n.63; Stanley, above, n.47.

prosecutors than defenders received; UN problems recruiting sufficient numbers of adequately trained international judges; non-existent and/or inadequate appeals procedures; inadequate capacity-building with respect to Timorese judicial institutions and personnel; problems arising from the diverse legal and cultural backgrounds informing individual panels; poor and insufficient translation facilities leaving those on trial unable to follow proceedings and limiting public knowledge of SPSC activities; legally dubious detention practices; and weak jurisprudence.[70]

Nonetheless, the UN Commission of Experts that reviewed investigations of serious crimes and their judicial handling in Timor Leste and Indonesia, reported in May 2005 that it was satisfied with the performance of the Serious Crimes Unit and the Defence Lawyers Unit with respect to their jurisprudence and other procedures. The report acknowledged that the work of both was hampered by inadequate resources.[71] It was, though, highly critical of almost every element of the work of Indonesia's *ad hoc* Human Rights Court for Timor Leste citing a lack of commitment, training, expertise, and inadequate investigations on the part of the prosecutorial team.[72] However, it seems the UN Commission of Experts has held Indonesia to a higher standard of accountability than the processes funded and supported by the UN itself. As David Cohen argues, this is another manifestation of UN inadequacy in confronting its own many shortcomings.[73]

In February 2003, President Gusmao was publicly critical of the decision of the SCU to indict senior Indonesian military figures including General Wiranto, the Indonesian army's commanding officer from 1998, charged with crimes against humanity under the doctrine of command responsibility. Gusmao argued that Timor Leste had forged an amiable relationship with Indonesia and that prosperity, progress, stability and peace were dependent on sound relations with its neighbour. He also drew a clear distinction between what may for him have been desirable and what he believed was achievable in promoting reconciliation above justice.[74] The warrant was disavowed by the UN and later the government of Timor Leste itself.[75]

---

[70] Call, above, n.41; La'o Hamutuk, above, 68; Kingston, above, n.3; and Cohen, above, n.65.

[71] P Bhagwati, S Shameem, and Y Yokota, Report to the Secretary-General of the Commission of Experts to Review the Prosecution of Serious Violations of Human Rights in Timor-Leste (then East Timor) in 1999 (United Nations, New York, 2005).

[72] *ibid.*

[73] Above, n.65.

[74] Lanegran, above, n.42.

[75] Kingston, above, n.3.

On 20 May 2005, the SPSC mandate expired and trials were drawn to a close despite hundreds of files remaining open. In total, it recorded 84 convictions (mainly against lower level criminals) and three indictees were cleared of all charges.[76] In total, the SPSC issued 95 indictments against 391 individuals, but 339 indictees remain at large in Indonesia, beyond Timor Leste's jurisdiction. The failure of Indonesian political will and judicial process means many ordinary Timorese, NGOs, church representatives, and academic observers across a range of disciplines feel that the processes of justice have contributed little to a sense of healing in Timor Leste.[77] The Commission for Truth and Friendship will, arguably, only deepen this sense of disappointment and disillusion.

Not for a moment, though, should the political and legal challenges faced by the two countries be underestimated. Robust democracies with strong legal institutions and cultures such as the US, Canada, and Australia have themselves experienced profound legal and moral challenges in addressing crimes committed against their indigenous peoples and in seeking workable processes of reconciliation.

Commission for Truth and Friendship (CTF)

The CTF was established in an agreement between the governments of Timor Leste and Indonesia in December 2004 with its secretariat located in Denpasar, Bali.[78] The CTF is the practical manifestation of President Gusmao's willingness to effect reconciliation with Indonesia and the Indonesian administration's determination to avoid responsibility for its crimes in East Timor. The CTF has been widely criticised by human rights organisations, the church in Timor Leste, and individuals concerned that it will simply facilitate the avoidance of justice for those that bear primary responsibility for the violence perpetrated in East Timor.[79] The CTF is flawed in domestic and international law, is unable to compel testimony from those alleged to have committed crimes, and cannot recommend prosecution or other judicial measures. It can, though, offer amnesties to those who cooperate fully.[80] The status of the CTF is also in question because the Indonesian Constitutional Court recently overturned the law upon which is founded Indonesia's own Truth and Reconciliation Commission and of which the CTF is an outgrowth.[81]

---

76 Judicial System Monitoring Programme, Special Panels for Serious Crimes (2005), http://www.jsmp.minihub.org/Court%20Monitoring/spsc.htm.

77 Above, n.42.

78 Bhagwati *et al.*, above, n.71.

79 Kingston, above, n.3.

80 Bhagwati *et al.*, above, n.71.

81 East Timor Indonesia Action Network, Joint Commission Unlikely to Further Truth or Friendship Between Timor and Indonesia (2007), http://etan.org/news/2007/02ctf.htm.

The CTF also represents a joint attempt by the governments of Timor Leste and Indonesia to ameliorate the failure of the *ad hoc* Human Rights Court for Timor Leste that convicted only an East Timorese militia leader, Eurico Guterres, despite 15 of 18 people tried being from either the Indonesian military or police.[82] While the establishment of the CTF may have brought the two governments closer together, it did not satisfy many other interests.[83] For example, despite the lack of UN support for thoroughgoing, properly resourced and staffed processes of justice within Timor Leste itself, the failings of the *ad hoc* court prompted former UN Secretary-General Kofi Annan to appoint a Commission of Experts to review the prosecution of serious human rights violations that occurred during 1999. This suggests that the various limitations of the CTF were viewed with some concern in the Secretary-General's office, and its activities formed part of the review.

The UN's Commission of Experts criticised the CTF's failure to adequately distinguish between categories of perpetrators of violence (less and more serious crimes); its absence of specific mechanisms to address serious human rights violations; the apparent foreclosure on any further judicial and/or accountability processes with respect to human rights abuses; and, its inadequate sensitivity in the handling of confidential material and vulnerable witnesses.[84] Nonetheless, in January 2007, the CTF announced it will recommend full amnesties to the governments of Indonesia and Timor Leste for anyone that appears before it and makes a full confession and apology for their actions. This may well clear the way for many of Indonesia's most senior military commanders, including General Wiranto, to have indictments against them lifted.[85] However, the report of the UN Commission of Experts makes explicit the UN's opposition to the offering of amnesties for those accused of crimes against humanity, war crimes and genocide.[86]

The CTF's website is infrequently updated and free of any suggestion of the political and jurisprudential controversy that surrounds it. Given how central this institution now is to the reconciliation of Timor Leste and Indonesia, these are worrying signs. Moreover, one of its Indonesian representatives, Achmad Ali, has stressed the importance of avoiding any suggestion that the CTF "... merely corners Indonesia instead of seeking the truth".[87] It is remarkably

---

[82] Bhagwati *et al.*, above, n.71.
[83] *ibid.*
[84] *ibid.*
[85] L Murdoch, "Amnesty Offer Over East Timor", *The Age*, January 15 2007.
[86] Bhagwati *et al.*, above, n.71
[87] Murdoch, above, n.85.

difficult to imagine just how the truth might emerge while leaving Indonesia's reputation intact. Indeed, given the woeful record of successive Indonesian governments over human rights abuses in Timor Leste, there is little reason for confidence in the integrity of the CTF.

Conclusion

Timor Leste may now be in what Daan Bronkhorst calls the readjustment phase of its transition. In Bronkhorst's schema, readjustment is the last of three phases (genesis and transformation being the other two) and is generally a period of great uncertainty in transitional societies as there is no consistent pattern to which countries can look for guidance.[88] From the vantage point of early March 2007, Timor Leste appears to be staggering towards violent political convulsion. This would be a significant setback for the Timorese themselves but also for the UN and countries with an interest in Timor Leste's well being. For the Timorese, and despite the opportunity to have benefited from the experiences of other nations that have made transitions from colonialism to independence, a slide into political chaos will be a particularly bitter blow. For the UN, should Timor Leste lapse into prolonged political violence and instability, the legacy of one of its boldest and most significant humanitarian interventions would be gravely tarnished and perhaps enfeeble responses to future humanitarian crises. For Indonesia and Australia, ongoing political violence would be most unwelcome given the proximity of the two countries and given the potential for new tensions in a relationship noted for its periods of uneasiness and suspicion.

In the most direct ways, Timor Leste's problems are outgrowths of a prolonged international conspiracy to deny the violence of Indonesia's brutal invasion and occupation. The failure of countries with influence over Indonesia (the US, the UK, Japan, and Australia notable among them) to confront it over its policies and practices in East Timor has contributed significantly to the collective trauma of the Timorese. Despite significant efforts on the part of the UN and individual donor nations and other aid agencies to address this trauma, it is possible that the Timorese have been forced too quickly into the complex responsibilities of democratic statehood. Decisions made in haste and without proper understanding of the complexities of Timorese social, political and economic life have created a range of new tensions and problems. The establishment of key institutions such as the military and the police have been

---

[88] T Järvinen, *Human Rights and Post-Conflict Transitional Justice in East Timor* (The Finnish Institute of International Affairs, 2004).

badly handled by UN agencies and are at the centre of the current political crisis.

The failure of international political will on the question of war crimes and crimes against humanity will also have direct consequences with respect to official and collective, popular memory of the Indonesian occupation. Arguably, it is in this respect that the Timorese have been most comprehensively let down by the international community. President Xanana Gusmao and Prime Minister Jose Ramos Horta have been left with invidious decisions to make given the absence of explicit international political commitments to seek out and prosecute those responsible for war crimes and crimes against humanity. Their emphasis of reconciliation with Indonesia has created extensive disillusion on the part of many of the victims of the Indonesian occupation and has, arguably, gravely undermined their legitimacy. While the international community may be anxious to forget this particular conflict and move on, it may well be the Timorese that will long live with the consequences.

The Constitution of Timor Leste in Comparative Perspective

William Binchy

The Constitution of Timor Leste offers a fascinating range of themes for consideration from a comparative perspective.[1] It is the product of many minds, from within and outside the country. It has high aspirations, hard to achieve in a fragile democracy emerging from a history of colonial exploitation which had little respect for norms of constitutionalism and human rights.

This paper examines some of the aspects to the Constitution which are of particular interest from a comparative standpoint. It raises questions of interpretation on issues that have yet to be tested at the judicial level.

Constructing the Constitution

The process of constructing any constitution raises a range of issues. How broad a range of consultation should take place? Should political parties dominate? Should several drafts be proposed for consideration? Should the constitution come into effect by way of national referendum or by some less direct means? What should be the time framework?

The approach adopted in Timor Leste was controversial. It involved a national election in August 2001 of 88 representatives to a Constituent Assembly which was charged with the task of producing and adopting the Constitution within the very short period of six months – extended ultimately to seven months. Fretelin won 57.3% of the national vote and 55 of the 88 seats.[2]

Although five parties submitted draft texts, the draft that Fretelin had endorsed at its party congress in Melbourne in 1998 was the one that was adopted on

---

[1] Little has so far been written in English on the themes. Influential analyses include Charlesworth, "The Constitution of East Timor, May 20, 2002", 1 Int'l J. of Constitutional L. 325 (2003), Garrison, *The Role of Constitution-Building Processes in Democratization: Case Study – East Timor* (International Institute for Democracy and Electoral Assistance, 2005) and D. da Costa Babo Soares, M. Maley, J. Fox & A. Regan, *Elections and Constitution making in East Timor* (2003).

[2] Garrison, *op. cit.*, 18.

the basis for discussion.[3] Public consultation took place between 24 February and 2 March 2002.[4]

The Constitution was approved on 22 March 2002 by 72 votes to 14, with one abstention and one absence.[5] The Constitution is a complex document, "combining broad statements of principle with intricate regulation of some topics".[6] The influence of the Portuguese Constitution is obvious; also striking are the marks of the recent struggle for independence,[7] the cosmopolitanism of its reception of international human rights instruments, and its delicate accommodation with the Catholic Church.

Overview of the Structure of the Constitution

The Constitution has seven Parts, preceded by a strong, rhetorical Preamble. Part I sets out the fundamental principles relating to such matters as citizenship, the objectives of the State and the place of international law in the Constitution. Part II contains provisions relating to fundamental rights, duties, liberties and guarantees. These include personal rights, liberties and guarantees, in Title II, and economic, social and cultural rights and duties, in Title III. Part III deals with the organisation of political power, identifying the four organs of sovereignty – the President, parliament, government and courts – and prescribing their respective competencies. Part IV is concerned with economic and financial organisation; Part V, national defence and security. Part VI deals with the 'guarantee' of the Constitution – that is, judicial review of putatively unconstitutional measures – as well as constitutional amendment. Part VIII contains final and transitory provisions.

---

3 Garrison, *op. cit.*, 20.

4 See Nancy M. Lutz, "Constitutionalism as Public Culture in East Timor", Paper presented at the Law and Society Meetings, Pittsburgh, 7 June, 2003. *Cf.* Garrison, *op. cit.*, 20:

> "The Constituent Assembly's consultation process was marred by its tight time frame and by a lack of information for the public in advance of the meetings. A particular problem was that the draft constitution initially existed only in Portuguese. Tetum and Indonesian versions were completed late in the process and were generally not available in advance of the meetings. Often the supposed consultations were more about providing information about the context of the draft constitution than a process for hearing input."

5 Garrison, *op. cit.*, 22.

6 Charlesworth, *op. cit.*, at 329.

7 These manifest themselves in the Preamble, which gives a detailed recital of "the liberation of the Timorese People from colonization and illegal occupation of the Maubere Motherland by foreign powers"; section 11 (valorisation of "the historical resistance of the Maubere People against foreign colonization ...."); and section 15 (the National Flag).

International Law and Human Rights

Section 9 of the Constitution gives a privileged status to international law. It provides as follows:

> "1. The legal system of East Timor shall adopt the general or customary principles of international law.
> 2. Rules provided for in international conventions, treaties and agreements shall apply in the internal legal system of East Timor following their approval, ratification or accession by the respective competent organs and after publication in the official gazette.
> 3. All rules that are contrary to the provisions of international conventions, treaties and agreements applied in the internal legal system of East Timor shall be invalid."

Section 9 has been described as "adopt[ing] a radically unitary approach to international law."[8] There is no need for a process of domestic incorporation of the international instruments by way of legislation or otherwise: simple approval, ratification or accession followed by due publication will suffice.

When it is recalled that many of these instruments have a significant human rights component, the question arises as to the precise relationship between section 9 and the other provisions in the Constitution dealing with human rights,[9] notably those relating to civil, political, economic, socal and cultural rights. The process of reconciliation of these various rights is complicated further by section 23, which provides that fundamental rights enshrined in the Constitution "shall not exclude any other rights provided for by law and shall be interpreted in accordance with the Universal Declaration of Human Rights."

Let us consider a couple of difficulties that can arise. The first is where a specific provision of the Timorese Constitution is in contradiction to a provision in an international human rights treaty. Which is to prevail? The short answer might appear to be that this theoretical problem will never arise in practice because none of the provisions of the Timorese Constitution is so seriously out of harmony with international human rights culture as to be in actual opposition to an international human rights treaty. Undoubtedly, most of the provisions in the Timorese Constitution are in harmony with the treaties and susceptible more

[8] Charlesworth, *op. cit.*, at 330. Charlesworth goes on to observe (*ibid.*) that "[t]he practical effect of these provisions may be profound."

[9] Section 8 provides that, on matters of international relations, the Democratic Republic of East Timor is to govern itself by a number of specified principles, which include the protection of human rights.

to the criticism that in some respects they fall short of the plenitude of protection afforded by the treaties, but one cannot discount the possibility of a conflict. The issue must therefore be addressed. No doubt, the courts would treat this as a matter requiring resolution within the text of the Constitution rather than attempt to locate the *grundnorm* outside the Constitution. A close perusal of section 9 suggests that it does not give inevitable priority to duly approved international treaties over the other provisions of the Constitutions. In the event of an apparent conflict, a court would be required to make a contextual reconciliation within the terms of the Constitution perhaps by 'reading in' the norms of the international human rights instruments into some of the more modestly drafted provisions of the Constitution.

A second difficulty, relating to section 23, involves the challenge of interpreting the fundamental rights enshrined in the Timorese Consitution "in accordance with the Universal Declaration of Human Rights". The Universal Declaration has enoromous international prestige but it is not an international treaty; it has no authoritative forum for its interpretation. If a court were to follow slavishly the admonition contained in section 23, it would have to incorporate the terms of the Declaration into the Constitution as the primary text relating to fundamental rights. This cannot be correct. One should therefore read section 23 as being subject to the implied qualification that the interpretative process should be followed "so far as possible", or some similar proviso.

Dignity

Section 1 (1) proclaims that the Democratic Republic of East Timor is a democratic, sovereign, independent and unitary State based on the rule of law, the will of the people "and respect for the dignity of the human person"[10]. This echoes Article 2 of the Portuguese Constitution, which contains, however, considerably more references to aspects of dignity.[11] The Lusophone constitutions are

[10] See also section 40 (3) which requires the exercise of the right to freedom of speech and the right to inform and be informed impartially to be regulated by law "based on the imperative of respect for the Constitution and the dignity of the human person". For a magisterial analysis of the place of dignity in modern constitutions, see McCrudden, "Human Dignity and Judicial Interpretation of Human Rights", 19 European J. of Inter'l L. 655 (2008).

[11] Thus, Article 13 (1) of the Portuguese Constitution provides that every citizen "shall possess the same social dignity and shall be equal before the law"; Article 59 (6) provides that every worker shall possess the right "that work be organized in keeping with social dignity..."; Article 26 (2) requires the law to lay down effective guarantees against the procurement and misuse of information concerning persons and families and its use "contrary to human dignity"; Article 26 (3) requires the law to guarantee "the personal dignity" and genetic identity of the human person, particularly in the creation, development and use of technologies and in scientific experimentation; Article 67 (e) provides that, in order to protect the family, the state shall particularly be charged with regulating assisted conception "in such a way as to safeguard the dignity of the human person".

generally enthusiastic about dignity. Article 119 (3) of the Constitution of Mozambique provides that, "[i]n the context of the development of social relations based on respect for human dignity, the State shall guarantee the principle that marriage is based on free consent"[12]. Article 48 (3) mirrors section 40 (3) of the Timorese Constitution regarding freedom of speech and the right to information. Angola's Constitution contains an important provision, in Article 20, requiring the State "to respect and protect the human person and human dignity".[13] Cape Verde's Constitution contains in Article 23 the concept of social dignity that appears in Article 13 (1) of the Portuguese Constitution.[14]

Dignity has, of course, a place in many other post-war Constitutions. Article 1 (1) of Germany's Basic Law proclaims that:

> "[h]uman dignity shall be inviolable. To respect and protect it shall be the duty of all state authority."

Undoubtedly human dignity has such a central place in the German constitutional order as a result of the experience of the previous decades in which human dignity had been violated so profoundly.[15]

A similar transition from gross oppression explains the centrality of human dignity in the South African Constitution of 1996, section 10 of which provides that:

> "[e]veryone has inherent dignity and the right to have their dignity respected and protected."[16]

The concept of dignity is capable of transforming the judicial understanding of equality in a fundamental way that can breathe life into the constitutional

---

[12] See also Article 19 (1) which expresses Mozambique's solidarity with the struggle of the African peoples and States for "unity, freedom, dignity, and right to economic and social progress".

[13] See also Article 2, which mirrors section 1 (1) of the Timorese Constitution.

[14] See also Article 1 (1), mirroring section 1 (1) of the Timorese Constitution; Article 62 1(a) acknowledges that workers have the right to conditions of dignity in their work.

[15] See Andries, "On the German Constitution's Fiftieth Anniversary: Jacques Maritain and the 1949 Basic Law (Grundgesetz)", 13 Emory Int'l L. Rev. 1 (1999).

[16] This is not the only mention of human dignity in the South African Constitution. Section 1 (a) identifies dignity as a foundational value of the Republic. See further O'Connell, "The Role of Dignity in Equality Law: Lessons from Canada and South Africa", 6 Int'l J. of Constitutional L. 267 (2008).

provisions relating to social and economic rights. It can, moreover, encourage courts to interrogate ingrained social assumptions of inferiority and superiority and social prejudices against people whose sexual orientation is not shared by the majority.

Religion

The Constitution does not favour Catholicism or the Catholic Church.[17] The Preamble acknowledges that "[i]n its cultural and humane perspective, the Catholic Church in East Timor has always been able to take on the suffering of all the People with dignity, placing trust on their side in the defence of their most fundamental rights". In section 11 (2), the State acknowledges and values "the participation of the Catholic Church in the process of national liberation of East Timor". Both these acknowledgments go no further than recording with gratitude the past political and social activities of the Catholic Church in East Timor. They have no substantive constitutional implications.

The Preamble reaffirms the determination of the Timorese People to fight "all forms of … religious domination and segregation". The State undertakes to recognise and respect "the different religious denominations, which are free in their organisation and in the exercise of their own activities, to take place in due observation of the Constitution and the law".[18] The State also undertakes to "promote the cooperation with the different religious denominations that contribute to the well-being of the people of East Timor".[19]

Important questions of interpretation arise here. The first concerns the connotation of "the different religious denominations"; the second relates to the identity, and grounds for identification, of "the different religious denominations that contribute to the well-being of the people of East Timor". On one view, the phrase "the different religious denominations" refers to a specific group of such denominations rather than every religious denomination that exists now or may come to existence in the future. If this is so, then the question arises as to which denominations come within the group. A possible group consists of those that existed at the time the Constitution came into effect. The case in favour of this interpretation is that these denominations

---

[17] While this proposition is correct as a matter of simple textual analysis, the complex social environment of Timor Leste requires a more nuanced understanding. The Catholic Church, as a significant political force in Timor Leste, influenced the contents of a number of provisions in the Constitution, notably those relating to marriage, equality and the separation of church and state. See further Garrison, *op. cit.*, 20.

[18] Section 12 (1).

[19] Section 12 (2).

would have been known to the framers of the Constitution. An open-ended commitment to 'respect' all denominations in the world, even those with no existing connection to Timor-Leste, might seem imprudent. As against this, such an interpretation would discriminate sharply against religious denominations that might come into existence in Timor-Leste in the future. It is, of course, possible for a constitution to confer some recognition or advantage on a finite group of denominations in existence in the State at the time of the promulgation of the constitution, thereby placing future denominations at a potential disadvantage: the Irish Consitution of 1937, in its original manifestation, is an obvious example.[20] Whether such an approach is consonant with contemporary international human rights standards may be debated: that is, in effect, an argument against this interpretation in view of the prominence afforded to such standards by the Timorese Constitution. A further difficulty with this interpretation is that it requires an authoritative adjudication as to which religious denominations had sufficient connection with Timor Leste at the time of the promulgation of the Consitution to warrant their falling under the protection of section 12 (1). Is there some minimum number of believers necessary for such categorisaton? Should belief for this purpose need to have been manifested by practice?

The second question of interpretation, which is linked to the first, relates to the State's undertaking to "promote the cooperation with the different religious denominations that contribute to the well-being of the people of East Timor". Which are these denominations? Are they only that subset of "the different religious denominations" where the particular members of the subset, as an empirical fact, do actually contribute to the well-being of the people of East Timor? If the answer is in the affirmative, then the Court must adjudicate as between religious denominations, holding that some of them contribute to that well-being, and thus are constitutionally entitled to insist that the State promote "the cooperation" with them, and some other denominations do not contribute to the well-being of the people and thus are not entitled to such cooperation.[21]

One might have thought it inconveivable that a Court should be placed in the invidious position of having to interrogate particular denominations to assess their impact on the well-being of the people of East Timor. Yet there is a

[20] See J.M. Kelly, *The Irish Constitution* (4th ed., by G. Hogan & G. Whyte, 2003), 2034–2042.

[21] Whether in such latter instance the State is *obliged not to promote the cooperation* with the particular denomination rather than simply *not obliged to promote it* is debatable. Section 12 (2) in its express language goes no further than not obliging the State to promote the cooperation; it would, however, be odd if the State were entitled to promote cooperation with religious denominations that do not contribute to the well-being of the people.

precedent in the Mozambican Constitution of 1990 which is worth noting. Article 9 (3) provided that:

> "[t]he State recognises and values the activities of religious denominations which promote a climate of social understanding and tolerance and strengthen national unity."[22]

No doubt, it is considerably easier for a court to address the sociopolitical question of whether a particular denomination promotes social understanding and national unity than the far broader question of whether it contributes to 'the well-being' of a people. When interpreting the latter expression the Court would be prudent to give it just such a sociopolitical slant. The concept of the well-being of a people can, just about credibly, be so understood. For a court to range further into the realms of moral, psychological or even spiritual welfare would surely be dangerous. It is worth noting that we are dealing here, not with personal well-being, but with the far broader well-being of *the people of East Timor*. It does not therefore seem disingenuous to restrict the interpretation to the sociopolitical realm.

The substantive provision relating to freedom of religion in the Timorese Constitution is contained in section 45, which provides as follows:

> "1. Every person is guaranteed the freedom of conscience, religion and worship and the religious denominations are separated from the State.
> 2. No one shall be persecuted or discriminated against on the basis of his or her religious convictions.
> 3. The right to be a conscientious objector shall be guaranteed in accordance with the law.
> 4. Freedom to teach any religion in the framework of the respective religious denomination is guaranteed."

Section 45 is similar to, but not as extensive as, Article 18 of the International Covenant on Civil and Political Rights, which provides as follows:

> "1. Everyone shall have the right to freedom of thought, conscience and religion. This right shall include freedom to have or adopt a religion or

---

[22] The Constitution of 2004 has a radical transformation from empirical test to statement of generic purpose. Article 12 provides that:

> "[t]he State shall recognize and esteem the activities of religious denominations in order to promote a climate of understanding, tolerance and peace, the strengthening of national unity, the national and spiritual well being of citizens, and economic and social development."

belief of his choice, and freedom, either individually or in community with others and in public or private, to manifest his religion or belief in worship, observance, practice and teaching.

2. No one shall be subject to coercion which would impair his freedom to have or to adopt a religion or belief of his choice.
3. Freedom to manifest one's religion or beliefs may be subject only to such limitations as are prescribed by law and are necessary to protect public safety, order, health or morals or the fundamental rights and freedoms of others.
4. The States Parties to the present Covenant undertake to have respect for the liberty of parents and, where applicable, legal guardians to ensure the religious and moral education of their children in conformity with their own convictions."

Article 18 specifically recognises freedom of *thought* as well as freedom of conscience and religion. The Human Rights Committee has emphasised that Article 18 "protects theistic, non-theistic and atheistic beliefs, as well as the right not to profess any religion or belief".[23] Although Article 41 of the Portuguese Constitution, which was clearly the model for section 45 of the Timorese Constitution, does not articulate an express right of non-belief, some other Lusophone constitutions use clear language on this point. For example, Article 54 (1) of Mozambique's Constitution of 2004 provides that "[a]ll citizens shall have the freedom to practise or not to practise a religion".

It can scarcely be maintained that the Timorese Constitution does not protect freedom of non-belief. The incorporation of the International Covenant on Civil and Political Rights is surely sufficient to achieve this. Moreover, the language of section 45 seems susceptible to such an interpretation on account of the incorporation within section 45 (1) of an express guarantee of freedom of conscience, religion and worship with an express separation of church and state.

The principle of non-discrimination in relation to religion is clearly expressed by section 16 (2) of the Timorese Constitution. This is in harmony with Article 26 of the International Covenant on Civil and Political Rights.[24]

[23] Human Rights Committee, General Comment 22, Article 18 (U.N. Doc. HRI /GEN/ Rev. 1 at 35 (1994), para. 2. See also the Declaration on the Elimination of All Forms of Intolerance and of Discrimination Based on Religion or Belief (U.N. General Assembly Resolution 36/55, November 1981), Article 1 (1).

[24] See further The Human Rights Committee, General Comment 22, Article 18 (U.N. Doc. HRI/GEN/ Rev. 1, at 35 (1944), paras. 8-9; the Declaration on the Elimination of All Forms of Intolerance and of Discrimination Based on Religion or Belief (U.N. General Assembly Resolution 36/55, November 1981), Articles 2-4.

States of Emergency

Section 25 deals with states of exception. It provides that suspension of the exercise of fundamental rights, freedoms and guarantees is to take place only if a state of siege or a state of emergency has been declared as provided for by the Constitution.[25] The specified circumstances are "effective or impending aggression by a foreign force, ... serious disturbance or threat of serious disturbance to the democratic constitutional order, or .... public disaster."[26] A suspension may last for not more than thirty days "without prejudice of possible justified renewal, when strictly necessary, for equal periods of time."[27] Authorities are required to restore constitutional normality "as soon as possible".[28] In no case may a declaration of a state of siege affect the right to life, physical integrity, citizenship, non-retroactivity of the criminal law, defence in a criminal case and freedom of conscience and religion, the right not to be subjected to torture, slavery or servitude, the right not to be subjected to cruel, inhuman or degrading treatment or punishment, and the guarantee of non-discrimination.[29]

It is interesting to compare section 25 with Article 4 of the International Covenant on Civil and Political Rights, which permits States Parties to derogate from their obligations under the Covenant to the extent strictly required by the exigencies of the situation, in a time of public emergency which threatens the life of the nation. Official proclamation to that effect is required. Moreover, measures taken must not be inconsistent with States Parties' other obligations under international law or involve discrimination solely on the grounds of race, colour, sex, language, religion or social origin.[30]

[25] Section 25 (1).

[26] Section 25 (2). The declaration must be substantiated, specifying rights, freedoms and guarantees the exercise of which is to be suspended. Simon Chesterman notes that, in permitting a state of emergency to be declared on the basis of a threat, rather than actuality, of serious disturbance, section 25(2) is broader than Article 19 of the Portugese Constitution; he observes, however, that there would appear to be little question that the higher threshold had been reached on the two occasions, in May 2006 and February 2008, when a state of emergency was declared: "Unaccountable? The United Nations, Emergency Powers, and the Rule of Law in Asia", in V. Ramraj & A. Thiruvengadem eds., *Emergency Powers in Asia* (forthcoming).

[27] Section 25 (3).

[28] Section 25 (6).

[29] Section 25 (5).

[30] Section 16 of the Timorese Constitution goes somewhat further in outlawing discrimination on grounds of marital status, gender, ethnical origin, political or ideological convictions, education and physical or mental condition. The right to freedom of expression may be derogated from, both under the Timorese Constitution and the Covenant. The obligation not to discriminate on grounds of political or ideological convictions possibly raises a question as to whether the selective denial of freedom of expression on the basis of what is likely to be communicated is truly based on justified concerns regarding state security or the protection of human rights of targeted victims (in the light of the experience of the abuse of media in Rwanda, for example) or the unwillingness to permit certain political voices being heard.

Moreover, no derogation may be made from Articles 6 (right to life), 7 (torture, etc.), paragraphs 1 and 2 of Article 8 (slavery and servitude), 11 (imprisonment for inability to fulfil a contractual obligation), 15 (non-retroactivity of criminal law), 16 (recognition of a person before the law) and 17 (freedom of thought, conscience and religion).

Gender

One of ten fundamental objectives of the State is "to create, promote and guarantee the collective equality of opportunities between women and men".[31] Section 17 provides that "[w]omen and men shall have the same rights and duties in all areas of family, political, economic, social and cultural life". This specific provision follows the general assurance in section 16 that "[a]ll citizens are equal before the law, shall exercise the same rights and shall be subject to the same duties"[32] and the requirement that no one is to be discriminated against on the ground of gender.[33]

Marriage is required to be based upon free consent by the parties, "on terms of full equality of rights between spouses",[34] in accordance with the law. Special protection is guaranteed to women during pregnancy, and "for an adequate period before and after delivery" is assured.[35] Section 50 (1) provides that "[e]very citizen, regardless of gender, has the right and the duty to work and to choose freely his or her profession". Clearly this opens up the non-domestic workplace to women on an equal basis with men. It may be worth reflecting on the concept that a woman has "the duty to work". Where must that duty be discharged? It is unlikely that section 50 (1) would be interpreted as *requiring* women to work outside the home where this would conflict with the constitutional imperative that "[m]aternity shall be dignified".[36] There seems no basis, however, for interpreting the Timorese Constitution as endorsing the norm that a woman's place is in the home. It

---

[31] Section 6 ( ).

[32] Section 16 (1).

[33] Section 16 (2).

[34] Section 39 (3).

[35] Section 39 (4) provides as follows:

> "Maternity shall be dignified and protected, and special protection shall be guaranteed to all women during pregnancy and after delivery and working women shall have the right to be exempted from the workplace for an adequate period before and after delivery, without loss of remuneration and other benefits, in accordance with the law".

[36] Section 39 (4).

seems that the Constitution leaves it to the spouses to come to their own agreement as to the distribution of work within and outside the home[37].

Reverting to the text of section 50 (1), thus, the question of interpretation arises as to whether "the right and the duty to work" includes the right and duty to work within the chosen environment of the home and whether the right[37] to choose freely one's profession embraces the choice of a domestic role of houseparent. It is one thing for a constitution to permit spouses or partners work out their respective roles as workers in the non-domestic environment and in the home: it is quite another for the State to give an unqualified entitlement to every citizen to make the choice between work outside and inside the home. If every woman in Timor Leste and half the men chose to work within the home, to the severe detriment of the national economy, presumably the State could intervene without falling foul of the provisions of section 50 (1).

Section 63 is important in encouraging gender equality in political life. Section 63 (1) provides that:

> "[d]irect and active participation by men and women in political life is a requirement of, and a fundamental instrument for consolidating, the democratic system."

Section 63 (2) requires the law to provide equality in the exercise of civil and political rights and non-discrimination on the basis of gender for access to political positions.

It would be wrong to condemn the Timor Leste Constitution for completely failing the goals of gender equality. Many of the specific provisions just mentioned go a considerable distance in that direction. Moreover, the place given to international law is important: rules provided for in international treaties such as the Convention on the Elimination of All Forms of Discrimination Against Women apply in the internal legal system of East Timor following ratification and publication in the official gazette[38]; all rules within the domestic legal order that are contrary to the provisions of these treaties, thus applied, are invalid.[39]

---

[37] In Ireland, Article 41.2 of the Constitution has proved an embarrassment to judges in recent years. The apparent consignment of women to domestic duties in the house has been re-interpreted as a gender-neutral recognition of the benefit, to society and to children, of work in the home of a parent: *D.T. v C.T.* [2002] 3IR 334, at 406–407 (Supreme Ct., *per* Murray, J.).

[38] Section 9 (2). Timor-Leste ratified CEDAW on 16 April 2003.

[39] Section 9 (3).

The provisions relating to gender in the Constitution fall some way short of the ten Articles of the *Women's Charter of Rights in East Timor*, which a working group on Women and the Constitution, composed of several civil society organisations and supported by 8,000 signatures, presented to the Members of the Constituent Assembly.[40]

Missing from the Constitution is a general provision entitling the State to engage in affirmative action to promote equality between men and women. Article 2 of the *Charter of Rights* is arguably given effect by section 30 (1) of the Constitution, to the effect that "[e]very one has the right to personal freedom, security and integrity". The failure to mention women specifically or to identify the danger of domestic violence is a weakness. Secton 57 of the Constitution acknowledges that everyone has the right to health and medical

---

[40] See UNTAET Fact Sheet II (UNTAET Press Office, April 2002):

"*Article I Equality*. The Constitution must prohibit all forms of discrimination, including in all matters of law. The State may implement positive measures to promote equality between men and women.

Article 2 Right to Security of the Person. The Constitution must protect women's right to live free from any form of violence, both private and public.

Article 3 Political Rights. The Constitution must guarantee equal rights of women in political activities and public life, including the right to vote, to run for elected office, to participate in government policy decision making, and to participate in organizations concerned with communal and national politics.

Article 4 Right to Health. The Constitution must protect all people's right to basic health care of the same quality. The State must provide reproductive health care for women.

Article 5 Right to Education. The Constitution must guarantee equal rights to formal and non-formal education for men and women. Women must have equal opportunity to study, and have equal access to scholarship opportunities and literacy programs.

Article 6 Social Rights. The Constitution must guarantee the rights to livelihood, shelter, sanitation, electricity, water, transportation and communication, health and education, and social security in case of sickness, unemployment or incapacity to work. Women must participate in development programs at every level.

Article 7 Labor Rights. The Constitution must guarantee equal pay for equal work. Women must have a right to maternity leave without loss of salary, job, or position, and women's safety and health needs must have full protection in the workplace. Dismissal must be prohibited in cases of pregnancy or maternity leave.

Article 8 Tradition and Women's Rights. The Constitution must guarantee equal rights to inheritance, and regulate the dowry system to prevent violence against women. Women must be guaranteed participation in traditional decision-making processes.

Article 9 The Right to Freedom from Exploitation. The Constitution should prohibit prostitution and slavery.

Article 10 Children's Rights. The Constitution must protect children's basic rights, including the right to food, shelter and social services, the right to be cared for by parents and family, and the right not to carry out work beyond the child's age capacity.

The Constitution must provide an institutional mechanism to ensure the protection and realization of women's rights in East Timor."

care but does not refer explicitly to reproductive health care for women. Section 59 of the Constitution, guaranteeing to every citizen the right to education and imposing on the State the obligation to promote the establishment of a public system of universal, free and compulsory basic education, contains no special reference to women. Similarly, section 56, recognising the entitlement of every citizen to social assistance and security, is silent as to the particular needs of women. Section 50, which recognises the right (and duty) of every citizen to work, does not include an express guarantee of equal pay for equal work. Section 39 (4), as has been mentioned, delivers certain guarantees relating to maternity leave. It does not include an express prohibition on dismissal in cases of pregnancy or maternity leave. The latter is surely implicit in section 39 (4); the former less clearly so, though probably a necessary consequence of the ratification of the international human rights instruments, notably CEDAW.

The Constitution contains no prohibition on prostitution or slavery. Slavery is, of course, inconsistent with the guarantee to everyone of the right to personal freedom, security and integrity contained in section 30 (1). Moreover, section 18 (1) provides that children are entitled to special protection particularly from (*inter alia*) violence, oppression, sexual abuse and exploitation. As to the lack of explicit constitutional response to prostitution, this may reflect a wider internationally unresolved discourse, in which norms of gender discrimination, autonomy, privacy and dignity have been invoked to require the criminalisation of prostitution, or of recourse by men to prostitution, on the one hand, and its complete decriminalisation, on the other.[41]

EQUALITY

Section 16 provides as follows:

> "1. All citizens are equal before the law, shall exercise the same rights and shall be subject to the same duties.
>
> 2. No one shall be discriminated against on grounds of colour, race, marital status, gender, ethnical origin, langauge, social or economic status, political or ideological convictions, religion, education and physical or mental condition."

A few points are worth noting. Subsection (1) refers to citizens "exercis[ing]" the same rights and being "subject to" the same duties. It raises the question as

[41] For a perspective relating to Timor Leste, see the Asia Foundation and University of San Francisco Report, *Civil Society Workshop for Policy Development: Analysis in Relation to the Issue of Prostitution* (Dili, 16–24 June 2004).

to who might respect the exercise of such rights and who are the beneficiaries of such duties. The State is clearly so; but what other legal entities? What is in question here, of course, is the issue of horizontality. Constitutions adopt widely differing approaches to this question. The Irish Constitution is perhaps the most expansive in this regard in making no differentiation between State and citizen: all actors, whether the State or otherwise, must not infringe a person's constitutionally protected rights.

It is possible to read section 16 (1) as involving no horizontality and as merely prescribing rights and duties relative to the State. In support of this interpretation it may be argued that the subsection fails to make any reference to non-State holders of rights or duties and that there is no need even to raise a question as to whether the rights and duties to which it refers extend beyond the State.[42] As against this, the international trend of constitutional theory is towards embracing horizontality, either directly or indirectly.

The Right to Life

Section 29 deals succinctly with the right to life. It contains three propositions: that "[h]uman life is inviolable",[43] that the State shall recognise and guarantee the right to life[44] and that there shall be no death penalty in the Democratic Republic of East Timor.[45] This prohibition on the death penalty applies even in states of siege or states of emergency.[46] It remains to be seen whether a broad interpretation will be given by the Timorese courts to the right to life, as has been done most notably in India, so as to encompass basic entitlements to accommodation, food and education. The centrality of respect for dignity surely encourages this development.

Guarantees in Criminal Proceedings

Section 34 contains law guarantees in relation to criminal proceedings. The presumption of innocence continues from charge to conviction.[47] An accused person has the right to select, and be assisted by, a lawyer at all stages of the proceedings "and the law shall determine the circumstances for which the presence of the lawyer is mandatory".[48] Every individual is guaranteed "the

---

[42] It is noteworthy that, in contrast to the Timorese Constitution, Article 18 (1) of the Portuguese Constitution expressly provides that its provisions regarding rights, freedoms and guarantees "shall be directly applicable to and binding on public and private persons and bodies."
[43] Section 29 (1).
[44] Section 29 (2).
[45] Section 29 (3).
[46] *Cf.* Section 25 (5).
[47] Section 34 (1).
[48] Section 34 (2).

inviolable right of hearing and defence in criminal proceedings.[49] Evidence is of no effect if obtained by torture, coercion, infringement of the physical or moral integrity of the individual or wrongful interference with private life, the home, correspondence or other forms of communication."[50]

Article 32 of the Portuguese Constitution is far fuller. It contains a guarantee that criminal proceedings shall enshrine all necessary safeguards for the defence, including the right to appeal.[51] Every defendant must be brought to trial as quickly as is compatible with the safeguards of the defence.[52] Preliminary investigations must be conducted entirely under the responsibility of a judge, who may, however, subject to the terms of the law, delegate to others the practice of such investigative acts as do not directly concern fundamental rights.[53] Criminal proceedings must possess an accusatorial structure.[54]

The guarantees contained in the Mozambican Constitution of 2004 are broadly similar to those in Timor-Leste's Constitution.[55]

Arrest and Detention

The provisions on arrest and detention are somewhat disappointing. No one is to be arrested or detained "except under the terms clearly provided for by applicable law"[56] and the order of arrest or detention "should always be presented for consideration by the competent judge within the legal timeframe".[57] This deference to legislative discretion contrasts with Article 29 (1) of the Portuguese Constitution which requires that, within at most 48 hours, all detentions are to be submitted to judicial scrutiny with a view either to the detainee's release or to the imposition of an appropriate measure. The judge is required to become acquainted with the reasons for the detention and to inform the detainee of what they are, to question the detainee and to give the detainee the opportunity to present a defence. Moreover, Article 29 (2) of

---

49 Section 34 (3).
50 Section 34 (4).
51 Article 32 (1).
52 Article 32 (2).
53 Article 32 (4).
54 Article 32 (5). The law is to define the cases in which, subject to safeguarding the rights of the defence, the presence of the accused may be dispensed with: *ibid*. Victims are given the right to take part in proceedings, as laid down by law: Article 32 (4). (The Constitution uses the word 'victims' rather than 'complainants'.)
55 See Articles 59 to 65.
56 Section 30 (2).
57 Section 30 (2).

the Portuguese Constitution contains generous provisions relating to remand which are not mirrored in Timor-Leste's Constitution.[58]

Freedom of Expression

The constitutional provisions relating to freedom of expression have proved controversial. Section 40 entitled *Freedom of Speech and Information*, provides:

"1. Every person has the right to freedom of speech and the right to inform and be informed impartially.
2. The exercise of freedom of speech and information shall not be limited by any sort of censorship.
3. The exercise of rights and freedoms referred to in this Section shall be regulated by law based on the imperative of respect for the Constitution and the dignity of the human person."

Section 41, entitled *Freedom of the Press and Mass Media*, provides:

"1. Freedom of the press and other mass media is guaranteed.
2. Freedom of the press shall comprise, namely, the freedom of speech and creativity for journalists, the access to information sources, editorial freedom, protection of independence and professional confidentiality, and the right to create newspapers, publications and other means of broadcasting.
3. The monopoly on the mass media shall be prohibited.
4. The State shall guarantee the freedom and independence of the public mass media from political and economic powers.
5. The State shall guarantee the existence of a public radio and television service that is impartial in order to, *inter-alia*, protect and disseminate the culture and the traditional values of the Democratic Republic of Timor-Leste and guarantee opportunities for expression of different lines of opinion."

[58] Remand in custody "shall be exceptional in nature and shall not be ordered or maintained wherever it is possible to grant bail or apply another, more favourable measure provided for by law". Where a court makes an order instituting or maintaining a measure entailing the deprivation of a person's freedom, notice must immediately be given to the relative or other person.... whom the detainee nominates: Article 28 (3). The period of 48 hours within which a suspect must be brought before the Investigating Judge is specified in section 12.6 of UNTAET Regulation 2000/11, as amended by UNTAET Regulation 2000/14 and UNTAET Regulation 2001/18.

These rights and freedoms recognised in Sections 40 and 41 must be balanced with section 36, entitled *Right to Honour and Privacy*, which provides that:

> "[e]very individual has the right to honour, good name and reputation, protection of his or her public image and privacy of his or her personal and family life."

Indonesia's somewhat liberal Press Law of 1999 continues to apply.[59] This legislation was a product of the post-Soeharto *reformasi* movement.[60] It gives journalists the entitlement to form their own associations and it protects the confidentiality of sources of information. One potentially significant limitation is the requirement, in Article 5 (1), that the press, when reporting events and opinions, do so "with respect to public religious norms and moral norms."[61]

Considerable controversy was engendered by the provisions for criminal defamation contained in a Penal Code introduced by executive decree in 2005. This measure provided terms of up to three years' imprisonment for defaming those performing State, religious or political duties and six years where the defamation was made through the media. President Gusmao exercised his veto in 2006. The matter rests there with no further steps having been taken by the Government to revisit the subject.

As regards freedom of information, we have seen that section 40 of the Constitution recognises in subsection (1) "the *right* to inform and be informed impartially"[62] and goes on, somewhat inconsistently, in subsection (2), to the exercise of "*freedom* of ... information."[63] The scope of this right or freedom is somewhat narrower than Article 19 (2) of the International Covenant on Civil and Political Rights, which acknowledges that the right to freedom of expression includes "freedom to *seek, receive and impart information and ideas of all kinds* ..."[64] and which contains no requirement of impartiality.[65]

---

[59] See Article 19, *Freedom of Expression and the Media in Timor-Leste*, p.48 (December 2005).
[60] *ibid.*, p.49.
[61] For criticism of this limitation as "unduly vague and broad", in conflict with international norms on freedom of expression, see *ibid.*, p.53.
[62] Emphasis added.
[63] Emphasis added.
[64] Emphasis added.
[65] See Article 19, *Note on the Draft Constitution of the Democratic Republic of Timor-Leste of 9 February 2002: Focus on Provisions Affecting Freedom of Expression*, Article 19, *Freedom of Expression and the Media in Timor-Leste*, p.26 (December 2005).

As is the position under Article 4 of the International Covenant on Civil and Political Rights, freedom of expression is not considered under section 25 of the Constitution of Timor-Leste to be a non-derogable right in states of siege or emergency. This is scarcely surprising. Criticism has, however, been made[66] in this context of the negative impact on freedom of expression which may follow from the breadth of those states in the definition contained in section 25 (2). Article 4 (1) refers to a "public emergency which threatens the life of the nation"; section 25 (2) refers to a situation "of effective or impending aggression by a foreign force, of serious disturbance or a threat of serious disturbance to the democratic constitutional order, or of public disaster."

Freedom of Assembly

Section 42 (1) guarantees to everyone the freedom to assemble peacefully and unarmed, without a need for prior authorization. The right to demonstrate is recognised by section 42 (2) but this right, in contrast to freedom of peaceful and unarmed assembly, is subject to the requirement that it be in accordance with the law.

The Court of Appeal, in an anticipatory review of constitutionality,[67] held that certain provisions of a legislative measure[68] on freedom of assembly and demonstration were unconstitutional. The Bill prohibited demonstrations "with the intent of questioning the constitutional order, thus undermining the democratically elected organs and institutions". The Court observed that:

> "the right to question, by peaceful means, the democratically elected organs and institutions, as enshrined in section 42 of the Constitution, is inherent in democracy. By prohibiting any demonstrations that might undermine 'the democratically elected organs and institutions', the provision under scrutiny unjustifiably restricts that right, in contravention of subsection 24.1 of the fundamental law."

The Court also had a difficulty with a provision in the Bill prohibiting assemblies and demonstrations "whose objective constitutes contempt of the good reputation and respect due to ... office holders of the State organs". It considered that the protection of the right to reputation might be effectively secured by other means, "namely through the criminal law",[69] without the

---

66 Article 19, *Freedom of Expression and the Media in Timor-Leste*, pp.39–40.
67 Under Article 149.
68 Draft Law 29/1/3A. For a stringent critique of the Bill, see JSMP Report, *Draft Law 29/1/3A: Freedom of Assembly and Demonstration* (October, 2004).
69 This observation is likely to antagonize vocal opponents of the use of criminal libel, such as Article XIX.

need to resort to prohibition, which the court regarded as an undue restriction on the rights of assembly and demonstration, impinging on section 24 (1) of the Constitution:

> "It prohibits, for instance, a demonstration intended to ask for the resignation of the officeholder of an organ of sovereignty who is blatantly incompetent or has practised acts of corruption, as a denunciation of that personal quality or acts would always tarnish the good reputation and respect of the person being challenged. This provision deprives citizens of the right to challenge, by peaceful means, officeholders of the organs of sovereignty, precisely in those cases where the challenge is most justified."

The Court did not, however, have a difficulty with the Bill's prohibition of demonstrations between 6.30pm and 8am. This did not, in its view, impinge upon the essence of the right to demonstrate:

> "It limits itself to making the exercise of that right consistent with the prevalent social practice in order to guarantee the right of people to calm and rest during the period of the day normally destined for that purpose, and to avoid that people become concerned at a time when they are less prepared and carefree. In the current context of Timor-Leste where power blackouts are frequent, people usually stop their chores soon after dusk and unusual movements, like those that are likely to occur during a demonstration, would obviously be a cause for concern.
>
> On the other hand, the prohibition of holding nighttime demonstrations does not fully impede the exercise of the right to express an opinion, for such a right can always be exercised at night by way of an assembly."[70]

---

[70] Among the other provisions upheld by the Court was a restriction on assembly and demonstration within 100 metres of offices of organs of sovereignty and certain other premises such as diplomatic missions and airports. The Court considered this restriction not to be disproportionate. It provided clarity for police and demonstrators alike. The Court prudently observed:

> "Leaving to authorities the task of defining, on a case-by-case basis, the minimal distance might generate greater uncertainty, resulting from subjectivity, if not arbitrariness, on the part of those doing the job. In practice, this might also lead more easily to a restriction on the exercise of that right, especially if one takes into account the fact that the person determining it might be naturally tempted to increase the distance in those cases where he or she dislikes the demonstration being staged. To that extent, such a solution also entails the added risk of confrontation between demonstrators and authorities over the very decision regarding determination of the minimal distance; and this risk ceases to exist if such a distance is determined beforehand."

Protection of Personal Data

Section 38 contains generous provisions relating to the protection of personal data. Every citizen has the right to access personal data regarding him or her stored in a computer system or entwined into mechanical or manual records and also has the right to demand the purpose of such data.[71] The processing of personal data on private life, political and philosophical convictions, religious faith, party or trade union membership and ethnic origin, without the consent of the interested person, is prohibited.[72] The absoluteness of this latter protection is striking and goes so far as to render it susceptible to a somewhat narrow judicial interpretation in the interests of practicality. The equivalent protection in Article 35 (3) of the Portuguese Constitution contains the sensible rider permitting the use of computers to treat data of this kind where there is "authorisation provided by law and with guarantees of non-discrimination, or for the purpose of processing statistical data that cannot be individually identified".

Children

The Timor-Leste Constitution contains broadly articulated, but quite unspecific, guarantees in relation to what it characterises in section 18 as 'child protection'. Children are entitled to special protection by the family, the community and the State, particularly against all forms of abandonment, discrimination, violence, oppression, sexual abuse and exploitation.[73] Children 'shall enjoy all rights that are universally recognised, as well as those that are enshrined in international conventions commonly ratified or approved by the State'.[74] Every child born inside or outside wedlock is to enjoy 'the same rights and social protection'.[75]

Timor-Leste acceded, without reservations, to the U.N. Convention on the Rights of the Child[76], as well as its Optional Protocols. The effect of section 9 of the Constitution is that the provisions of this Convention apply in the internal legal system of Timor-Leste. Thus, a child is defined as every human being under the age of 18 years.[77] The minimum age for marriage for females

[71] Section 38 (1).
[72] Section 38 (3).
[73] Section 18 (1).
[74] Section 18 (2).
[75] Section 18 (3).
[76] The Convention has been criticized for its "Eurocentrism" and its failure fully to embrace cultural diversity: see Barsh, "The Draft Convention on the Rights of the Child: A Case of Eurocentrism in Standard-Setting", 58 Nordic J. of Int'l L. 24 (1989), Harris-Short, "Listening to the 'Other'? The Convention on the Rights of the Child", 2 Melbourne J. of Int'l L. 305 (2001).
[77] Convention on the Rights of the Child, Article 1.

is 15, subject to parental approval.[78] It appears that marriages can occur under this age.[79]

Corporal punishment of children in educational and domestic environments has not yet been rendered unlawful. The Committee on the Rights of the Child has expressed its concern at "reports that corporal punishment is a common phenomenon at home and is frequently used to discipline children at school and in other educational settings".[80] It recommends[81] that corporal punishment be prohibited in all settings, in line with its General Comment on the issue published in 2006.[82] The principle of the best interests of the child, which is central to the Convention on the Rights of the Child,[83] is, on the Government's admission, apparently not well understood or applied during judicial proceedings or administrative decisions.[84]

Economic, Social and Cultural Rights and Duties

Title III of Part II of the Constitution contains twelve provisions relating to economic, social and cultural rights and duties: the right to work,[85] the right to strike and a prohibition on lock-outs[86], trade union freedom[87], consumer rights[88], the right to private property[89], the duty of citizens to pay tax[90], the entitlement to social assistance and security[91], the right to health and the duty

[78] Indonesian Civil Code, Article 35. The minimum age for marriage for males is 18: *id.*, Article 29.
[79] *Cf.* the *Core Document Forming Part of the Reports of States Parties : Timor Leste* UN HRI/CORE/TLS/2007, 16 July 2007, para. 668:

> "Marriages [involving] girls as young as 13 or 14 years old have been reported in the districts [citing the results of group discussions, regional CEDAW treaty reporting workshops, 2005]. These are often marriages decided with a particular family before the birth of the marriage partner. In other cases, as a result of extreme poverty, families arrange child marriages in an attempt to obtain *barlake* [dowry], not informing potential suitors of the child's real age. Invariably, the child is not able to read or write and has never attended school. This practice seems to be more common in rural areas than the capital."

[80] Committee on the Rights of the Child, *Concluding Observations : Timor Leste*, CRC/C/TLS/CO/1, 1 February 2008, para. 42.
[81] *id.*, para. 43.
[82] Committee on the Rights of the Child, General Comment No. 8, *The Right of the child to protection from corporal punishment and other cruel or degrading forms of punishment,* CRC/C/GC/8 (2006).
[83] Convention on the Rights of the Child, Article 3.
[84] Committee of the Rights of the Child, *Initial report of Timor Leste*. CRC/C/TLS/1 (28 June 2007), para. 32.
[85] Section 50.
[86] Section 51.
[87] Section 52.
[88] Section 53.
[89] Section 54.
[90] Section 55.
[91] Section 56.

to protect it[92], the right to housing[93], the right to education and culture[94], the protection of intellectual property[95] and "the right to a humane, healthy, and ecologically balanced environment and the duty to protect it and improve it for the benefit of the future generations."[96]

Let us look more closely at some of these provisions.

Health

Section 57 contains a strongly articulated right to health, in the following terms:

> "1. Everyone has the right to health and medical care, and the duty to protect and promote them.
> 2. The State shall promote the establishment of a national health service that is universal and general. The national health service shall be free of charge in accordance with the possibilities of the State and in conformity with the law.
> 3. The national health service shall have, as much as possible, a decentralised participatory management."

This provision is very similar to Article 64 of the Portuguese Constitutioin and Articles 89 and 116 of the Constitution of Mozambique. In expressing a positive right to learn and medical care, section 57 goes further than the provisions of many other constitutions, which use aspirational or programmatic language.[97]

Consumer Rights

Section 53 of the Constitution contains a provision dealing specifically with consumer rights, as follows:

> "1. Consumers have the right to goods and services of good quality, to truthful information and protection of their health, safety and economic interests, and to reparation for damages.

---

[92] Section 57.
[93] Section 58.
[94] Section 59.
[95] Section 60.
[96] Section 61 (1).
[97] See Kinney & Clark, "Provisions for Health and Health Care in the Constitutions of the Countries of the World", 37 Cornell Int'l L.J. 285, at 290–291 (2004). See Further Den Exter & Hermans "Constitutional Rights to Health Care: The Consequences of Placing Limits on the Right to Health Care in Several Western and Eastern European Countries", 5 Eur. J. of Health L. 261 (1998), Hendriks, "The Right to Health in National and International Jurisprudence", 5 Eur. J. of Health L. 389 (1998).

2. Advertising shall be regulated by law, and all forms of concealed, indirect or misleading advertising are prohibited."

Similar provisions exist in a number of other constitutions, including those of Portugal, Spain, Switzerland, the Philippines and Japan.[98] The impact of Section 53 seems clearly horizontal: the composite right which it articulates would be a poor one if capable of being exercised only against the State.[99]

Questions on interpretation arise as to how to characterise the right: is it based on contract, on some delictual foundation, on the criminal law or independently on the Constitution? Certainly, it extends beyond the criminal law in that it explicitly provides for "reparation for damages". As regards the circumstances precipitating the entitlement to such reparation, clearly fraudulent misrepresentation is captured by the requirement that information be truthful; but what about cases where the goods or services are not of good quality through no fault of the provider? In short, does section 53 import a negligence or strict liability test for product or service liability? It may be suggested that the latter is the test. This is the requirement of contract law and of delictual responsibility in Europe and the United States of America, and is in harmony with a broad philosophy of accommodating reasonable consumer expectations. It is interesting to note that the Supreme Court of Appeal in South Africa rejected the argument that the South African Constitution's express protection of the right to bodily integrity required the imposition of strict product liability[99A]. In Timor-Leste, by way of contrast, the Constitution contains an express right of consumers to goods and services of good quality as well as the further express right to protection of their health and safety.

A few points of difficulty remain. It is one thing to have a strict product liability regime; it is quite another to impose strict liability on service provision, especially professional services, such as medical care. In many countries, all that is required of doctors is that they take reasonable care in their treatment of patients: to ask more of them would arguably inhibit medical treatment as well as imposing a standard impossible in practice to fulfil. Perhaps the language of section 53, in referring to "sources of good quality", goes no further than imposing a standard of reasonable care in this context, in contrast to that relating to products where the qualitative assessment is made

[98] See Deutch, "Are Consumer Rights Human Rights?" 32 Osgoode Hall L.J. 537, at 574–577 (1994).
[99] For consideration of the horizontal effects of a number of Constitutions in Europe, including Portugal's, in this context, see Ciacchi, "The Constitutionalization of European Contract Law: Judicial Convergence and Social Justice", 2 E.R.C.L. 167 (2006).
[99A] *Wagener v Pharmacare Ltd.*, 2003 (4) SA 285.

of the product rather than the conduct of the producer. Finally, one should note the uncertainty as to the range of potential defendants under section 53. It seems clear that those in a contractual relationship with the consumer fall under the obligation to respect the right in question. Beyond that, the position is less clear. It is not at all unreasonable to assume that section 53 extends its remit to producers; but what about others in the supply chain such as importers and wholesalers? And what is the position where a substandard product or service purchased by one person (the consumer) foreseeably injures or kills another? The language of section 53 seems to exclude a claim in this latter case. If so, the underlying values are controversial.

PROPERTY

Section 54, entitled "Right to Private Property", provides as follows:

> "1. Every individual has the right to private property and can transfer it during his or her lifetime or on death, in accordance with the law.
> 2. Private property should not be used to the detriment of its social purpose.
> 3. Requisitioning and expropriation of property for public purposes shall only take place following fair compensation in accordance with the law.
> 4. Only national citizens have the right to ownership of land."

This is a clear statement of the right of the individual to private property and an equally clear expression of the limits of that right: private property should not be used to the detriment of its social purpose.[100] What emerges here is a philosophical understanding of the right to private property, harmonising with Catholic natural law theory. It would appear that a property owner[101] who uses the property to the detriment of its social purpose would be acting in violation of the Constitution. Thus, for example, the destruction of a work of art in private ownership or the use of property in a way that damaged environmental or health policies could violate section 54 (2). Sections 57 and 61 reinforce such a conclusion.

The terms of section 54 (3) are worth noting. Most Constitutions contain provisions relating to the expropriation of property for public purposes.

---

[100] This contrasts with Article 62 of the Portuguese Constitution, sub-article (1) of which is similar to section 54 (1) of the Timorese Constitution but which contains no equivalent of section 54 (2); Article 82 (1) of the Constitution of Mozambique provides that the State "shall recognize and guarantee the right of ownership of property". There is no qualifying provision equivalent to section 54 (2). Article 82 (2) provides that expropriation may take place "only for reasons of public necessity, utility or interest, as defined in the terms of the laws, and subject to payment of fair compensation".

[101] Or other possessor of an interest in property.

Reference to requisitioning property for these purposes is somewhat less frequent, though it features in a number of Constitutions, including those of Portugal[102] and India[103].

As regards the requirement of compensation in the event of expropriation or requisitioning, this must be 'fair' and, it seems, must precede the expropriation or requisitioning. The concept of fairness is not elaborated upon. Comparative constitutional jurisprudence suggests that it is not the same as full economic value. Some circumstances may no doubt require full commercial compensation, but by no means all circumstances necessarily do.

Judicial Review

The courts are given an important role in ensuring that respect is paid by the organs of State to the provisions of the Constitution. Section 26 guarantees everyone access to courts for the defence of their legally protected rights and interests.[104] Section 48 gives every citizen the right to submit, individually or jointly with others, petitions, complaints and claims to organs of sovereignty[105] or any other authority for the purpose of defending his or her rights, the Constitution, the law or general interests. These two provisions are open-ended in their drafting but other provisions implicitly limit their potential scope.

Section 120, entitled *Review of Unconstitutionality*, requires courts not to apply rules that contravene the Constitution or the principles contained therein. There is, however, a difference between the judicial non-application of a rule considered by a court to be inconsistent with the Constitution, on the one hand, and a definitive determination of unconstitutionality by a court which renders the rule invalid *in futuro* and retrospectively, on the other. One has to look to Part VI of the Constitution to find the circumstances in which such definitive judgments may be handed down.

Four types of case are prescribed. All deal with the role of the Supreme Court of Justice, "the highest court of law and the guarantor of a uniform enforcement of the law..."[106]

---

[102] Portuguese Constitution, Article 62 (2).

[103] Indian Constitution, Article 31 (2).

[104] Section 26 goes on to provide that justice is not to be denied for insufficient economic means.

[105] Section 118 (1) identifies courts as organs of sovereignty with competencies to administer justice in the name of the People.

[106] Section 124 (1). Decisions of the Supreme Court of Justice are not appealable and have "a general binding effect on processes of abstract and concrete monitoring, when dealing with unconstitutionality": section 153. In this respect, the decisions differ from those of lower courts.

(I) Anticipatory Review of Constitutionality

The President has sole responsibility to request the Supreme Court of Justice to undertake an anticipatory review of the constitutionality of any statute submitted to him or her for promulgation.[107] The President has twenty days to act from the date he or she received the statute.[108] The Supreme Court of Justice is under a tight limitation of time: twenty-five days, or less if the President reduces the period for reasons of emergency.[109] If the Supreme Court of Justice rules that the statute is unconstitutional, the President must submit a copy of the ruling to the Government or the National Parliament and request the reformulation of the statute in accordance with the Court's ruling.[110] The National Parliament can circumvent the effect of the ruling by the procedure specified under section 88, the essence of which permits Parliament to confirm its vote by an absolute majority of its members in full exercise of their functions or, in respect of matters covered by section 95, by a two-thirds majority of members present, where that majority exceeds an absolute majority of the members in full exercise of their functions.[111] The idea that the National Parliament should be able to insist in the pormulgation of legislation already considered unconstitutional by the Supreme Court of Justice is alarming. What is the Court to do when the legislation comes into effect? It is no less unconstitutional then than it was at the time of the Court's original ruling. A Court, if it is to be faithful to the Constitution, must continue to insist on the unconstitutionality of the measure, if given an opportunity to do so.[112] When that happens, the legislative measure dies and cannot be revived by legislative reconfirmation.

---

[107] Section 149 (1).

[108] Section 149 (2).

[109] Section 149 (3). The period of twenty-five days seems far too short for legislation involving complex matters of social, scientific or economic policy where expert evidence of a contested empirical character is required. The Irish Supreme Court has evinced disquiet about a sixty-day limit, contained in Article 26 of the Constitution.

[110] Section 149 (3).

[111] Section 149 (4). The subsection is infelicitously drafted. It refers to "[t]he veto for unconstitutionality of a statute", yet no such words appear earlier in section 149, which refers to a Supreme Court "ruling". The power of veto attaches to the President and it must be exercised within thirty days after his or her receiving the statute from the National Parliament: section 88 (1). The periods of time specified in section 149 of up to twenty and twenty-five days, respectively, add up to forty-five days. Manifestly, a ruling by the Supreme Court of Justice could occur after the thirty day period specified in section 88.

[112] Under section 150 or 152. The President or Ombudsman would scarcely be acting inappropriately in sending the legislation to the Court; indeed, it may be argued that not to do so would fail to support the Court's Constitutional role.

(Ii) Abstract Review of Constitutionality

Six persons, or groups of persons, may request a declaration of unconstitutionality by the Supreme Court of Justice.[113] These are the President; the Speaker of the National Parliament; the Prosecutor-General, based on the refusal by the courts, in three concrete cases, to apply a statute deemed unconstitutional; the Prime Minister; one fifth of the Members of the National Parliament; and the Ombudsman.

(Iii) Unconstitutionality of Omission

The President, the Prosecutor-General and the Ombudsman may request the Supreme Court of Justice to review the unconstitutionality by omission of any legislative measure deemed necessary to enable the implementation of the constitutional provision.[114]

The concept of unconstitutionality by omission raises significant jurisprudential issues. It is, of course, possible to envisage situations where a legislative measure is so incompetently drafted as to reveal, on its face, an unconstitutional omission, but other situations can arise where arguably an unconstitutional omission is involved but, from another perspective, the position should not be so characterised. If, for example, two separate legislative provisions appear to contradict each other, is this an unconstitutional omission[115] or rather a situation calling for subtle constitutional rationalisation by referring to underlying constitutional norms? And what of a case where legislation addresses a policy area inadequately, revealing deficiencies and gaps that a court may be tempted to repair? Can the passage of time render particular legislation unconstitutional by omission where that omission emerges as a result of shifting constitutional norms? Must the omission have been foreseeable by the legislature at the time of enactment?

Clearly an important question relating to the separation of powers arises here.[116] If courts were to exercise their power to scrutinize unconstitutionality by omission too vigorously, they would undoubtedly trespass on the legislative domain. Conversely, if a judicial finding of unconstitutionality by omission had

[113] Section 150.
[114] Section 151.
[115] Portuguese Report for the XIVth Congress of the Conference of European Constitutional Courts, *Portuguese Constitutional Court: Problems of Legislative Omission in Constitutional Jurisprudence*, p.3 (Vilnius, June 2008).
[116] *Cf. ibid.*, p.10.

no practical impact on the legislature, the principle of the separation of powers would be compromised by legislative disrespect for the judicial function.[117]

(Iv) Appeals on Constitutionality

The Supreme Court of Justice has jurisdiction to hear appeals against court decisions *refusing to apply* a legal rule on the grounds of unconstitutionality or decisions *applying* a legal rule the constitutionality of which was challenged during the proceedings.[118] In the latter case, the appeal may be taken only by the party who raised the question of unconstitutionality.[119]

[117] The doctrine, as interpreted by the Portuguese Constitutional Court, enables the legislature to ignore the court's holding if it wishes since there is not "any serious enforcement mechanism": Mark Tushnet, *Weak Courts, Strong Rights: Judicial Review and Social Welfare Rights in Comparative Constitutional Law*, 156 (2007). Tushnet (*ibid*., at 167) acknowledges that "[c]onceptually, one could construct a doctrine under which an individual would be entitled to compensation from the government on the basis of harms caused by failure to enact required legislation, but the Portuguese Constitutional Court has not yet done so."

[118] Section 152 (1).

[119] Section 152 (2).

PART III

International Law and Human Rights

Current International Law Influences in the Government of Timor-Leste

Gernot Biehler

Introduction

From an international law perspective Timor-Leste's recent history is a great success story. The self determination expressed by its people in its declaration of independence brutally disregarded by Indonesia for a quarter of a century was eventually confirmed by the international community and made real by its co-operation. There is now a president and a full government exercising effective control in most of their territory, and some recurring border conflicts with Indonesia and Australia on land and sea appear about to be settled peacefully. The role of the United Nations, now culminating in the integrated mission UNMIT[1] with its office (UNOTIL) in Dili, a police force and military advisers seems to be uncontroversial and should be viewed in the context of the United Nations' peace-keeping operations. It appears that Timor-Leste has all the ingredients to be regarded as a textbook example of a people's right to self determination in a formerly unfriendly environment. A President and a Parliament have been elected April, May, and June 2007. The principle enunciated in Art 1, para 2 of the UN Charter seems rarely to have found a better application than in this case.

However, events did not allow everything to be accomplished according to schedule. The riots in Dili on 28–29 April 2006, just one month before the international community's role was due to terminate with the withdrawal of the United Nations office in Dili made it impossible to gently allow Timor-Leste to fade from the international agenda. The moment the question of effective control in the State seemed not to be settled the role of the international community's forces came into focus again. All international engagements with troops and governmental assistance must have the principle of non- interference in mind. Article 2, para 7 of the UN Charter prohibits the United Nations and its member states from intervening in matters which are

---

[1] The United Nations Mission in Timor-Leste (UNMIT) was established according to Security Council Resolution 1704 and succeeded the preceding missions UNAMET, UNTAET, UNMISET and UNOTIL.

essentially in the domestic jurisdiction of any state. Only strict adherence to this principle can guarantee that states acting under the auspices of the United Nations do not develop into a new kind of colonisation and domination adverse to the principles of international law and the UN Charter. Certainly, any informed and free request for assistance may justify international engagements. However, the involvement of foreign troops and advisers in Iraq, Afghanistan, Abchasia, Moldavia, Georgia, Uzbekistan and other places make's it clear what a fine line there is between a formally freely expressed request for assistance and foreign domination, even if blue helmets are sometimes worn.

It is to be borne in mind that UN missions create a potential conflict with the right to self determination as soon as they put structures in place which may neither be assessed nor changed by those concerned. As welcome and benevolent as it may seem to many, the deficit of democratic accountability of the UN requires an assessment of its activities. The current legitimising formula of "international community" action should not in itself obviate the principle of self determination and democratic accountability. From the British colonialist Lord Lugard's double mandate to the High Representative in Bosnia to Lord Ashdown dismissing prime ministers, lines may be drawn. Between the peace operations of today and the colonial activities of the past, a clear distinction is more than desirable. Therefore, the legitimacy and the challenges faced by UNMIT should be appraised.

The Legal Framework

The UN missions in Timor-Leste base themselves on Security Council resolutions.[2] However, these resolutions do not make clear on which Article of the UN Charter they are based. It is not Chapter Seven which gives the Security Council the power to authorise the use of force as an exception to Art 2.4. of the UN Charter in case of a threat to international peace and security. Nor is the resolution based on Chapter Six which is concerned with peaceful conciliation of international conflicts. Furthermore, there is no doubt that the issues currently to be addressed in Timor-Leste are of an internal not an international nature. No issue between Timor-Leste and, *e.g.*, Australia, Indonesia, or Portugal is at the heart of the UN measures any more. Therefore,

[2] See, *e.g.*, Security Council Resolution 1704 of 25 August 2006, declaring that UNMIT will consist of a civilian force including up to 1608 police personnel and 34 military liaison and staff officers and confirming the international security forces stationed in Timor-Leste.

taking up a well known term in international law the resolutions may be seen as based on "Chapter Six and a Half".[3] This term is extremely fitting as it signifies the somewhat mysterious legal character of the measures so readily accepted by most. They may be described as inherent powers, but there is no doubt that they are undefined in codified international law. To be more specific, these powers are actually self defined by those using and exercising them.

What is Actually Planned by the International Community after the Riots?

Despite the achievements of the past eight years, state institutions have been increasingly challenged in terms of addressing the grievances of various groups and the rising expectations of the people, as well as the potential risks associated with the first post-independence presidential and parliamentary policies of 2007. For this reason, the United Nations proposed to continue its military and police presence to reinforce support for governmental bodies and to help the armed forces develop managerial capacity. They would support the Ministry of Defence and the armed forces in developing policies, rules and regulations, procedures and principles governing all areas of defence. They would also assist the Ministry in developing statutory instruments governing military services. The continued presence of United Nations police may be essential to ensure that law and order, as well as respect for human right's is maintained. Training and advisory personnel would be required for training in electoral policing procedures and practices, including security responsibilities, during and immediately following the elections; to assist in monitoring and reporting on the conduct of the elections; and in the development and implementation of a comprehensive election security plan, thereby forestalling a volatile and possibly violent situation. What this means can be seen from the Timorese governmental website;[4] the UNMIT monitoring news of 8 August 2007, which states that the security situation in Timor-Leste remains volatile, there is rock throwing and burning of tyres and public disturbances. One hundred and fifty five tear gas shells were used on one day in an incident against people which are associated with the opposition Freitilin Party.

---

[3] See Biehler, *International Law in Practice* (Thomson Round Hall, Dublin, 2005), p.248 *et seq* with reference in footnote 10 to the former UN Secretary General's invention of the six and a half measures in *http://www.un.org/peace/bnote010101.pdf*.

[4] *www.timor-leste.gov.tl*.

The internal problems afflicting the Timorese armed forces were mirrored by the 2006 riots in Dili, and indicate an acute need to address them. In addition to the deaths and injuries, government offices were damaged and numerous properties destroyed during the riots. While the physical damage remained minuscule in comparison with the destruction in 1999, the psychological impact on the people has turned out to be immense. What is more alarming in the international context is that UN forces may be increasingly acting in an internal political struggle.

Legal Assessment of Security Council Resolutions

The relevant Security Council Resolutions themselves must be examined to determine the extent to which they may violate the principle of non interference in the internal affairs of Timor-Leste according to Art 2, para 7 of the United Nations Charter.

A more recent resolution is No 1677 (2006) determining that the Security Council extends the mandate of the United Nations Office in Timor-Leste (UNOTIL) as is done by subsequent resolutions, ultimately No. 1704 until March 2008. This continues a development which reflects the fact that Timor-Leste is a child of the international community. Through four successive missions (UNAMET, UNTAET, UNMISET and UNMIT with UNOTIL), the United Nations has played a key role in laying the foundation for Timor-Leste's democratic institutions and processes. Today, those institutions and processes stand exposed. The sad events of 28 April 2006, however, reflect shortcomings not only on the part of the Timorese leadership, but also on the part of the international community in adequately sustaining Timor-Leste's nation-building process. It must be acknowledged that the building of institutions on the basis of fundamental principles of democracy and the rule of law is not a simple process which can be completed within a few short years. However, it is not the usual task of the United Nations or other countries to assume any responsibility when riots or other challenges to internal policing arise. This generally remains an internal matter for each country. That this is not so in the case of Timor-Leste proves that her independence is not complete. The UN assumes responsibility for internal security and evaluates, criticises, and ameliorates the policing and border patrol activities. If this lack of domestic policing power becomes permanent or recurrent, we may label Timor-Leste on the model of Somalia as a failed state under international law which is not able to perform functions normally associated with states. There is still some way to go before such an assessment could be made, and many hopeful signs indicate that Timor-Leste will avoid such a dire fate in the future.

Resolution 1599 (2005) adopted by the Security Council on 28 April 2005, exactly one year prior to the riots, gives the best account of what the international community intends to do, although it has been partly overtaken by Resolution 1704. The text may be restated here:

> The Security Council, reaffirming its previous resolutions on the situation in Timor-Leste, in particular its resolutions 1543 (2004) of 14 May 2004 and 1573 (2004) of 16 November 2004, having considered the report of the Secretary-General of 18 February 2005 (S/2005/99), commending the people and the Government of Timor-Leste for the peace and stability they have achieved in the country, as well as for their continuing efforts towards consolidating democracy and strengthening State institutions, further commending the United Nations Mission of Support in Timor-Leste (UNMISET), under the leadership of the Special Representative of the Secretary-General, and welcoming the continuing progress made towards the completion of key tasks inscribed in its mandate, particularly during its consolidation phase, in accordance with Security Council resolutions 1543 (2004) and 1573 (2004), paying tribute to Timor-Leste's bilateral and multilateral partners for their invaluable assistance, particularly with regard to institutional capacity-building and social and economic development, expressing its appreciation to those Member States which have provided support to UNMISET, having considered the letter dated 20 January 2005, from the Prime Minister of Timor-Leste to the Secretary-General (S/2005/103), noting the Secretary-General's analysis of the need for a United Nations presence to remain in Timor-Leste after 20 May 2005, although at a reduced level, noting also that the emerging institutions in Timor-Leste are still in the process of consolidation and that further assistance is required to ensure sustained development and strengthening of key sectors, mainly rule of law, including justice, human rights, and support for the Timor-Leste police, and other public administration, acknowledging the excellent communication and good will that have characterized relations between Timor-Leste and Indonesia including the decision to establish a Truth and Friendship Commission, and their land border agreement signed in Dili 8 April 2005, which covers approximately 96 per cent of the land border, and encouraging continued efforts by both Governments towards resolving this and all pending bilateral issues, acknowledging the Secretary-General's decision outlined in his letter to the Security Council dated 11 January 2005 (S/2005/96) to send a Commission of Experts to Timor-Leste and Indonesia to review the serious crimes accountability processes, and recommend further measures as appropriate, remaining fully committed to the promotion of long-lasting stability in Timor-Leste,

The Resolution goes on to state that the Security Council:

1. Decides to establish a one-year follow-on special political mission in Timor-Leste, the United Nations Office in Timor-Leste (UNOTIL), which will remain in Timor-Leste until 20 May 2006;
2. Decides further that UNOTIL will have the following mandate:
   (i) to support the development of critical State institutions through provision of up to 45 civilian advisers;
   (ii) to support further development of the police through provision of up to 40 police advisers, and support for development of the Border Patrol Unit (BPU), through provision of up to 35 additional advisers, 15 of whom may be military advisers;
   (iii) to provide training in observance of democratic governance and human rights through provision of up to 10 human rights officers; and
   (iv) to monitor and review progress in (i) through (iii) above;
3. Requests that, when implementing its mandate, UNOTIL emphasise proper transfer of skills and knowledge in order to build the capacity of the public institutions of Timor-Leste to deliver their services in accordance with international principles of rule of law, justice, human rights, democratic governance, transparency, accountability and professionalism;
4. Requests further that UNOTIL be led by a Special Representative of the Secretary-General, who will direct the operations of the mission and coordinate all United Nations activities in Timor-Leste through his office, with due attention to safety of personnel, and facilitated by appropriate levels of logistics support, including transportation assets, such as air transport when necessary;
5. Requests that the Secretary-General deploy some of the advisers, authorised in paragraph 2 (ii) above, to assist the National Police of Timor-Leste in developing procedures for and in training the Border Patrol Unit (BPU) and to assist the Timor-Leste Government in coordinating contacts with the Indonesian military, with the objective of transferring skills to the BPU to assume full responsibility for such coordination as soon as possible;
6. Underlines that United Nations assistance to Timor-Leste should be coordinated with the efforts of bilateral and multilateral donors, regional mechanisms, non-governmental organizations, private sector organizations and other actors from within the international community, and encourages the Special Representative of the Secretary-General to establish and chair a consultative group, made up of these stakeholders in Timor-Leste, that will meet regularly for that purpose;

7. Urges the donor community as well as the United Nations agencies and multilateral financial institutions to continue providing resources and assistance for the implementation of projects towards sustainable and long-term development in Timor-Leste, and urges the donor community to actively participate in the donor's conference scheduled to be held in April 2005;
8. Encourages, in particular, the Government of Timor-Leste, UNOTIL, the United Nations Secretariat, United Nations development and humanitarian agencies, and multilateral financial institutions to start immediately planning for a smooth and rapid transition, in Timor-Leste, from a special political mission to a sustainable development assistance framework;
9. Reaffirms the need for credible accountability for the serious human rights violations committed in East Timor in 1999, and, in this regard, underlines the need for the United Nations Secretariat, in agreement with Timor-Leste authorities, to preserve a complete copy of all the records compiled by the Serious Crimes Unit, calls on all parties to cooperate fully with the work of the Secretary-General's Commission of Experts, and looks forward to the Commission's upcoming report exploring possible ways to address this issue, including ways of assisting the Truth and Friendship Commission, which Indonesia and Timor-Leste have agreed to establish;
10. Requests the Secretary-General to keep the Council closely and regularly informed of developments on the ground and of the implementation of the mandate of UNOTIL, and the planning for a transition to a sustainable development assistance framework, and to submit a report within four months of the date of adoption of the present resolution and every four months thereafter, with recommendations for any modifications such progress might allow to size, composition, mandate and duration of the UNOTIL presence;
11. Decides to remain actively seized of the matter.

The Significance of the Resolution

As outlined above, the resolutions despite addressing military and policing activity are not adopted under Arts 39 and 41, 42 of the Charter. They are not meant to counter threats to international peace and security, but rather threats to national peace and security. These measures are not intended to be coercive but rather to assist the Government. First and foremost in para 2(iii) it is stipulated that the UN will provide training in observance of democratic governance and human rights.

It may be noted that para 5 of Resolution 1677 provides for UN assistance in "coordinating contacts with the Indonesian military". The Indonesian military has for 25 years been the occupying force which has suppressed independence against international law. It may now be seen that the UN supports military involvement of Indonesia because international law wants to be effective and takes this power into consideration.

In Art 9 the UN reserves a full copy of the criminal files compiled by the Serious Crime Unit of Timor-Leste, giving the UN a say in the country's criminal procedure and her practice of leniency through the Truth and Friendship Commission, a commission which is broadly modelled on the South African model. Also, the judiciary is partly taken over by the international community by creating an internationalised so-called hybrid tribunal.[5]

What was indicated by the 2005 resolution is now confirmed by practice. The Special Representative of the Secretary General for Timor-Leste, Atul Khare, urged on 11 September 2007 that the UN Police be kept at its present strength which would enable UNMIT to reform the security sector "including the screening of the Timorese National Police"[6] "at least until the end of the current mandate in February 2008."[7] This cannot but be understood as a taking charge of the country's security by the UN authorities. Screening the national police by UN forces puts the national forces in a position in which they must feel subject to approval of the UN. It should not be denied that there may be very good reasons for this on the merits. However, the entire lack of democratic accountability of the international forces combined with the obvious limits they may set to the Timorese right to self determination must be noted by international law without diminishing the merits of the UN presence in the country.

Conclusion

Timor-Leste is the product of the international community. The government is still nurtured and supervised to grow into the functions of a modern independent state. Templates are drawn from many successful models including South Africa. What seems a great success story from a distant perspective must be recognised on closer inspection as a fragile state of affairs which has still to win the full trust and support of its people and the international community alike if it is to deal independently with its own

[5] Suzanne Katzenstein, "Hybrid Tribunals- Searching for Justice in East Timor", (2003) 16 Harvard Human Rights Journal 245.

[6] Brief of the UNMIT head to the Security Council from *www.unmit.org/unmisetwebsite.nsf*.

[7] See *www.unmit.org/unmisetwebsite.nsf/6032cf1262b2a349256f0a003ef7d8/0aa6*.

internal security challenges. A tension between the right to self determination in its internal affairs and the entitlement not to have its military and police scrutinised by anyone not democratically legitimised and authorised to do so by parliament and the obvious necessities met by the UN forces and police in Timor-Leste must be carefully balanced. Fortunately, all concerned seem prepared to co-operate to achieve this end.

East Timor's Tortured March to Statehood: The Triangle of Self-Determination, International Norms and Realpolitik

Jackson Nyamuya Maogoto

I. Introduction

Portuguese presence in Timor dates back to the fifteenth century. It officially became a Portuguese colony in the eighteenth century. Timor was a vestigial appendage of the Portuguese empire largely neglected and used mainly as a place to exile Portuguese political dissidents. In the course of the eighteenth century, the Dutch aggressively sought to create the Dutch East Indies by colonising the Timor Island and the surrounding archipelago. Repeated attacks led the Portuguese to move the capital of their Timor colony from Lifau to Dili (East Timor's present day capital). After decades of hostility, in the nineteenth century, Portugal and the Netherlands signed the Treaty of Lisbon which formally ceded the western part of the Timor Island to the Dutch with the Portuguese retaining the eastern part. By the twentieth century, East Timor's status as a colony of Portugal, its strong independent socio-political identity, and its physical separateness was well established.

In the course of World War II, Japan occupied the Indonesian Archipelago, but Australian and Dutch troops were deployed to East Timor to maintain a foothold. A year-long war with Australian and Dutch troops for the control of East Timor ensued. With the Allied Powers rapidly subduing the Axis Powers, Indonesian nationalists under Sukharno with the help of indigenous army units created by the departing Japanese declared independence on 17 August 1945, proclaiming the Republic of Indonesia. With the Netherlands still tottering after being freed from German occupation, the Republicans rapidly gained control of vast areas of the Archipelago. However, the Dutch were not giving up easily and were determined to foreclose Indonesia's declared independence and regain its vast colony. This resulted in dozens of military skirmishes and two major military campaigns with the Republicans. However, four years later, Republican determination and control of vast territory forced the reluctant Dutch to assent to Indonesian independence on 27 December 1949.

Meanwhile, East Timor had been handed back to the Portuguese. The Indonesian Republicans, occupied with wrestling with the Dutch for control of West Irian and New Guinea (which the Dutch tenuously held), left East Timor alone, and in fact Sukharno acknowledged it as a Portuguese colony. The status quo was to remain until 1974 when the Portuguese fascist regime fell. The new democratic regime in Lisbon wasted no time in encouraging East Timorese independence. A new Portuguese governor arrived in East Timor with the primary role of overseeing East Timor's transition to independence. Political parties were formed with three dominant ones emerging – Timorese Democratic Union (UDT), Revolutionary Front of Independent East Timor (Freitlin) and Timorese Popular Association (Apodeti).

In local elections in 1975, UDT and Freitlin emerged as the two largest parties and formed an alliance to campaign for independence. However, the Indonesian government was unhappy with the Marxist-leaning Freitlin and was concerned that it would act as an inspiration for some of its troublesome independent minded provinces, particularly Aceh and West Irian. On the other hand, the other chief regional player – Australia – saw East Timor as an unviable state that would only serve to undermine stability in the region. In any case, it was more interested in robust ties with the Indonesian government in charge of a vast, resource-rich archipelago. The powder keg was ignited on 28 November 28 1975 when Freitlin made a unilateral declaration of independence in the face of a UDT-engineered coup supported by Indonesia aimed at curbing Freitlin's growing popularity. Nine days later, despite the marginal economic value of East Timor in proportion to Indonesia's extant possessions,[1] Indonesian military forces invaded and subdued East Timor in the face of international condemnation.

Without effective local opposition, Indonesia absorbed and annexed East Timor in 1976 as its twenty-seventh province. The integration remained controversial at international level. It was never recognised by the United Nations (UN) which, following the invasion, called on Indonesia to withdraw from East Timor and to respect the East Timorese's right to self-determination,[2] with the UN naming Portugal the Administrator of the

[1] TD Grant, "East Timor, The U.N. System, And Enforcing Non-Recognition In International Law" (2000) 33 *Vanderbilt Journal of Transnational Law* 273, 297.
[2] See GA Res. 3485, UN GAOR, 30th Sess., Supp. No 34, at 118, UN Doc. A/10634 (1975); GA Res. 34/40, UN GAOR, 34th Sess., Supp. No 46, at 206, UN Doc. A/34/46 (1979); and GA Res 37/30, UN GAOR, 37th Sess., Supp. No 51, at 227, UN Doc. A/37/51 (1982); see also SC Res. 384, UN SCOR, 30th Sess., 1869th mtg, at 10, UN Doc. S/INF/31 (1975); and SC Res. 389, UN SCOR, 31st Sess., 1914th mtg, at 18, UN Doc. S/INF/32 (1976) [East Timorese Resolutions].

territory. In addition, the UN called upon Portugal to stop the violence and to effect an act of free choice in their former colony.[3] Recognition of Portugal's interest in East Timor was an attempt to move protection of East Timor from theory to action, despite Portugal's physical abandonment of the colony and disclaimer of responsibility. The supposed right of self-determination, well established in international legal theory and possessed by the people of East Timor in 1975,[4] was however functionally irrelevant to the Indonesians when they swept through the island to begin more than three decades of oppressive rule. The Indonesian action was certainly abetted by major powers in the West through their indifference. The indifference was the result of prevailing realpolitik, a factor that was to dominate East Timor's quest for self-determination, leading JC Beauvais to note that: "East Timor's accession to statehood bears an international significance disproportionate to its tiny size and severe poverty".[5]

In the course of the next three decades, and in the face of heavy-handed tactics by Indonesian forces keen to wipe out a guerrilla resistance and effectively "pacify" East Timor, thousands were killed. Indonesian police forces regularly detained and tortured innocent civilians and brutally suppressed peaceful protests.[6] Massive violence committed by Indonesian-backed militia forces on East Timor increasingly hardened the international community's support for East Timor's independence. The turning point was the Dili Massacre in 1991 in which over 250 unarmed youth were mowed down by Indonesian military personnel at the Santa Cruz Cemetery. This chapter has as its modest aim an exploration of the nexus of the principle of self-determination and the geopolitics that contributed to East Timor's tortured march to independence. In particular, the chapter will seek to examine the tenets of self-determination and its practical dynamics which yielded little protection to the aspirations of the East Timorese.

---

[3] *ibid.*
[4] *ibid.*
[5] JC Beauvais, "Benevolent Despotism: A Critique of U.N. State-Building in East Timor", (2001) 33 *New York University Journal of International Law and Politics* 1101, 1102.
[6] See P Carey, "East Timor: Third World Colonialism and the Struggle for National Identity" (1996) 293/294 *Conflict Studies* 1 (1996) (describing effects of Indonesian invasion); B de Magalhães, "East Timor: A People Shattered By Lies and Silence", (17 July, 1996), *http://www.uc.pt/timor/silence.htm*, sec. 1; "East Timor Independence Issue Raised", *Boston Globe*, 28 January 1999, at A10, available at *http:// www.boston.com/dailyglobe2/028/nation/East _Timor_independence_issue_raised+. shtml.*

II. Self-Determination: A Legal Right on a Slippery Slope

There is some uncertainty about the origins of the principle of self-determination. Some scholars trace the concept to the time of the Greek city states,[7] while others attribute the principle of self-determination to the French and American revolutions.[8] However, the maturation of the principle dates to the twentieth century in the immediate aftermath of World War I which redrew the map of Europe.[9] There is little controversy that in the aftermath of World War I, US President Wilson "elevated the principle of self-determination to an international level"[10] through his Fourteen Points, recognising "that every people has a right to choose the sovereignty under which they shall live ...".[11] The idea underlying "respect for the ... self-determination of peoples,"[12] by drawing international borders around them, was a hope that it would be possible to create inherently peaceful nations. The League of Nations implicitly accepted the principle of self-determination through articulation of a mandate system that granted states guardianship rather than sovereignty over territories. After World War II the principle was explicitly incorporated into the United Nations Charter under its trusteeship system.[13]

In the post-World War II period, the principle of self-determination was invoked by colonial territories in the process of separating from their colonisers. This fell solidly in the external spectrum of the principle of self-determination, considering that inhabitants of colonised territories constituted separate communities from their overlords and were internally "made up of individuals freely associated on the basis of a social contract" prepared to

---

[7] See J Falkowski, "Secessionary Self-Determination: A Jeffersonian Perspective", (1991) 9 *Boston University of International Law Journal* 209, 212.

[8] See C Saladin, "Self-Determination, Minority Rights and Constitutional Accommodation: The Example of the Czech and Slovak Federal Republic", (1991) 13 *Michigan Journal of International Law* 172, 173.

[9] Antonio Cassese A *Self-Determination of Peoples: A Legal Reappraisal* (1995) pp.14–27.

[10] H Morris, "Self-Determination: An Affirmative Right or Mere Rhetoric?", (1997) 4 *ILSA Journal of International & Comparative Law* 201, 203.

[11] President Woodrow Wilson, 'Address before the League to Enforce Peace' (27 May 1916), reprinted in 53 *Congressional Records* 8854 (29 May 1916).

[12] UN Charter, Art 1, para 2.

[13] The UN Charter calls on member states "to develop friendly relations among nations based on respect for the principle of equal rights and self-determination of peoples ....", UN Charter, Art 1, para 2. It also creates a trusteeship system designed to "promote the progressive development of the inhabitants of the trust territories toward self-government or independence, taking into account the freely expressed wishes of the peoples concerned," and requiring members to become the administering powers and protect the interests of those countries whose people had not yet attained self-government. UN Charter, Art 76.

determine their own future in the international community. Despite the UN Charter's explicit recognition of the principle of self-determination, controversy erupted with some scholars feeling the right extends only to colonies or areas subject to foreign control.[14] This so called "external self-determination" gives people subject to colonisation or foreign occupation the right to govern their own affairs free from outside interference.[15] Others disagreed, saying that the right to self-determination belongs to all peoples, including minorities and indigenous people living within existing countries.

The two dimensions regarding self-determination mentioned above led to a cleavage of the principle of self determination into two spectrums in international law: internal and external.[16] Internal self-determination "regulates relations between rulers and ruled within the community which inhabits a defined territory".[17] External self-determination "regulates relations between a self-defined community and the outside world".[18] Against this backdrop the principle of self-determination acquired a dichotomous role – a vehicle for justice that satisfies the aspirations for independence for colonial and oppressed peoples but also a threat to the extant world order's preservation of the approved political and legal order in the case of statehood for national minorities in light of the *uti posseditis* principle that militates against fragmentation of sovereignty.[19] In essence, there is and continues to be a significant tension underlying United Nations' doctrines concerning self-determination and international concern over the secession of ethnic minorities from existing sovereign states.

Commencing in 1960 against the backdrop of numerous colonial territories increasingly casting off the shackles of colonisation or agitating for independence, the evolution and maturation of the principle of self-determination in international law was cemented by three General Assembly resolutions. On 14 December 1960, the General Assembly adopted Resolution 1514 (XV) – Declaration on the Granting of Independence to Colonial

---

[14] See S Blay, "Self-Determination: A Reassessment in the Post Communist Era", (1994) *Denver Journal of International Law & Policy* 275; GH Fox, "Self-Determination in the Post Cold War Era: A New International Focus?" (1995) 16 *Michigan Journal of International Law* 733.

[15] H Hannum, *Autonomy, Sovereignty, and Self-Determination: The Accommodation of Conflicting Rights* (1990) 49.

[16] See KS Shehadi, "Ethnic Self-Determination and the Break-up of States", *The Adelphi Papers*, No 283, December 1993, 4.

[17] *ibid.*

[18] *ibid.*

[19] A Cassese, *Self-Determination of Peoples: A Legal Reappraisal* (1995), 165–204.

Countries and Peoples – by a vote of 90 to none, with nine abstentions.[20] The resolution stated that all people have the right to self-determination and, with decolonisation considered fundamental, it called on administering powers of trust and non-self-governing territories to take immediate steps to transfer without reservation all powers to the peoples of such territories "in accordance with their freely expressed will and desire".[21] The resolution did not stop at rhetoric. Art 6 provided that member states:

> ... continue to wage a vigorous and sustained campaign against activities and practices of foreign economic, financial and other interests operating in colonial Territories which are detrimental to the interests of the population.[22]

On the day following the adoption of Resolution 1514, the General Assembly in Resolution 1541 outlining principles for determining whether a territory was a non-self-governing territory.[23]

A decade after Resolutions 1514 and 1541, the principle of self-determination within territories was entrenched and cemented as a principle of international law with the passage of General Assembly Resolution 2625 (XXV), entitled Declaration on Principles of International Law Concerning Friendly Relations and Cooperation Among States.[24] The enumerated goals of the Declaration on Principles included the need to bring a speedy end to colonialism, having due regard to the freely expressed will of the peoples concerned.[25]

In the author's opinion, however, the three resolutions passed by the General Assembly articulating the principle of self-determination were biased towards the then prevalent climate of decolonisation. The resolutions seem to possess

[20] See Declaration on the Granting of Independence to Colonial Countries and Peoples, GA Res. 1514, UN GAOR, 15th Sess., Supp. No 16, at 66, UN Doc. A/4684 (14 December 1960) proclaiming the need to solemnly bring to a speedy and unconditional end colonialism in all its forms and manifestations.
[21] *ibid.*
[22] S Rabitt Roff, "The Contemporary International Law of Territorial Rights of Nations and Peoples", in JR Jacobson, ed, *The Territorial Rights of Nations and Peoples* (1989), 5.
[23] Principles Which Should Guide Members in Determining Whether or Not an Obligation Exists to Transmit the Information Called for Under Article 73e of the Charter, GA Res. 1541, UN GAOR, 15th Sess., Supp. No 16, at 29, UN Doc A/4684 (1960).
[24] Declaration on Principles of International Law Concerning Friendly Relations and Cooperation among States in Accordance with the Charter of the United Nations, GA Res. 2625 (XXV), UN GAOR, 25th Sess., Supp. No 28, UN Doc. A/8028 (1970) [Declaration on Principles].
[25] *ibid.*

an underlying philosophy and assumption that colonial western powers were the main danger to self-determination. Thus, they implicitly incline towards "external" self-determination. This dynamic inevitably sidelined "internal" self-determination which gives minorities and indigenous people control over their own destinies. East Timor would soon provide a novel scenario that would subsequently hobble its ability to derive the benefits of the three explicit resolutions, primarily due to confusion around the scope and character of self-determination, and in particular the cleavage identified above between "internal" and "external" self-determination.[26]

In the case of East Timor, its right to self-determination as a Portuguese colony was clear-cut, especially considering that it had held the status of a non-self-governing territory according to the UN,[27] and Portugal was recognised as the administering power.[28] However, Portugal's abandonment of East Timor and the subsequent invasion and annexation by Indonesia in 1975 muddied the clear-cut path to external self-determination. Portugal was rendered neither a physical occupier nor governor of East Timor since 1975 when that role had been usurped by Indonesia's invasion and proclamation of sovereignty over East Timor, and its subsequent entrenchment of control and authority. Essentially then, the East Timorese were hard to catergorise under either of the two recognised approaches mentioned above,of defining a "people" in the context of nationalism and self-determination: ethnic and territorial.[29] Bolstering Indonesia's sovereignty claim was the reality that the inhabitants of East Timor were culturally indistinct from the inhabitants of West Timor; theirs was not a culture specific to the artificial territorial boundaries imposed by Dutch and Portuguese authorities.[30] This served to undermine the protective mechanisms of international law available to East Timor.

In the face of international opposition (but with tacit support of the West), Indonesia claimed that no process of self-determination was required in the territory, apart from that already coordinated by the Indonesian government

[26] EA Laing, "The Norm of Self-Determination, 1941–1991", (1992) 22 *California Western International Law Journal* 209, 248.

[27] See GA Res. 1542, UN GAOR, 15th Sess., Supp. No 16, at 30, UN Doc. A/4684 (1960) (naming Timor and dependencies as Portuguese territory); GA Res. 36/50, at para 3 (naming Portugal administering authority); *East Timor*, 1995 I.C.J. at 90 (declaring East Timor remains non-self-governing territory).

[28] SC Res. 384, above, n.2 (referring to Portugal as administering power of East Timor); GA Res. 3485, above, n.2 (recognising Portugal's responsibilities as administering power over East Timor); SC Res. 389, above, n.2 (calling on Indonesian withdrawal from Timor).

[29] See Shehadi, above, n.16, at pp.4–5.

[30] R Cribb and C Brown, *Modern Indonesia: A History Since 1945* (1995) 5.

and its forces of occupation. Self-determination of the East Timorese, Indonesia claimed, was achieved through incorporation of their territory into Indonesia.[31] Indonesia persisted in this claim, even though the advent of Indonesian rule in East Timor was condemned as an illegal use of force[32] and the continuation of that rule was criticised as a violation of the rights of the inhabitants of the territory.[33] However, the annexation of East Timor through use of force added another dimension to the issue of East Timorese self-determination.

The Nexus of "Aggressive" Use of Force and Self-Determination

In the aftermath of Indonesia's invasion of East Timor, General Assembly and Security Council resolutions repeatedly called upon member states not to recognise Indonesia's claim, and to respect the territorial integrity of East Timor. Commencing in 1975, UN General Assembly Resolution 3485 (XXX) affirmed Portugal as the "administering Power" for East Timor[34] (the first of eight UN General Assembly Resolutions to call for Indonesian withdrawal from the territory[35]). The UN Security Council shared the same view as the General Assembly. Resolution 384 of 22 December 1975 also called for "all States to respect the territorial integrity of East Timor as well as the inalienable right of its people to self-determination".[36] The following year, Security Council Resolution 389 unanimously condemned the Indonesian invasion.[37]

---

[31] See A Alatas, "East Timor: De-Bunking the Myths Around a Process of Decolonization", *Indonesia News*, 20 March 1992, at 1, 4, cited in GJ Simpson, "The Diffusion of Sovereignty: Self-Determination in the Postcolonial Age" (1996) 32 *Stanford Journal of International Law* 255, at 339, n.74.

[32] See GA Res. 3485, UN GAOR, 30th Sess., Supp. No 34, paras 4–5, UN Doc. A/10034 (1976) ("strongly deplor[ing] the military intervention of the armed forces of Indonesia in Portuguese Timor" and "[c]all[ing] upon the Government of Indonesia to desist from further violations of the territorial integrity of Portuguese Timor and to withdraw without delay its armed forces from the Territory in order to enable the people of the Territory freely to exercise their right to self-determination and independence"); SC Res. 384, UN SCOR, 30th Sess., 1869th mtg (1976).

[33] See Situation of Human Rights in East Timor, UN Commission on Human Rights, Res. 1997/63, UN Doc. E/CN.4/RES/1997/63 (1997). See also GA Res. 35/27, UN GAOR, 35th Sess., Supp. 48, para 4, UN Doc. A/35/48 (1981) (expressing "deepest concern at the continued suffering of the people of East Timor as a result of the situation still prevailing in the Territory"); GA Res. 37/30, UN GAOR, 37th Sess., Supp. 51, at 228, UN Doc. A/37/51 (1983) (expressing concern "at the humanitarian situation prevailing in the Territory").

[34] GA Res. 3485, above, n.2.

[35] See East Timorese Resolutions, above, n.2; For a crisp incisive analysis of East Timor's march to statehood, see RS Clark, "The "Decolonisation" of East Timor and the United Nations Norms on Self-Determination and Aggression", in *International Law and the Question of East Timor* (Catholic Inst. for Int'l Relations & Int'l Platform of Jurists for East Timor eds., 1995) 65.

[36] SC Res. 384, above, n.2, para 1.

[37] See SC Res. 389, UN SCOR, 31st Sess., 1914th mtg (1997).

Despite a raft of UN resolutions that were critical of Indonesian action, condemnation of the occupation became progressively weaker over the years, mainly because Western powers saw Indonesia as a bulwark against communist influence. As a result the West maintained a studious policy of silence which extended to Indonesia's own bloody domestic purge of thousand's of suspected communists and sympathisers. Abandoned by the Portuguese, and East Timor's claims for self-determination largely deemed by major Western powers as subordinate to geopolitics, East Timorese resistance movements took to arms and were to maintain a guerrilla campaign against the Indonesian army throughout the long occupation, during which much of the civilian population lived in an atmosphere of repression and violence.[38]

In the face of Indonesia's continued assertion of sovereignty over East Timor, the matter of the use of force which had delivered East Timor to Indonesia continued to be a thorny issue. Indonesia's military occupation remained politically and legally unacceptable, with the repressive rule of Indonesia failing to attract significant support. Politically this was clear from the UN resolutions calling upon all member states to respect the territorial integrity of East Timor by denying recognition to Indonesia.[39] In addition, through the long occupation, East Timor continued to feature annually on the United Nations General Assembly agenda, as well as in the list of non-self-governing territories within the meaning of Chapter XI of the UN Charter.[40] On the legal front, In the *Case Concerning East Timor*, the ICJ effectively stated that, if a non-self-governing territory is entitled to the right of self-determination, that right is not extinguished due to forcible intervention by a third party, by the passage of time, or by failed attempts at decolonisation.[41] The strongest statement was offered by Judge Weeramantry in his dissenting opinion. He stated that the Friendly Relations Doctrine, contained in the annex to UN Resolution 2625 (XXV), mandates that *no territorial acquisition resulting from the threat or use of force shall be recognized as legal*.[42] In effect, if the

[38] The most prominent resistance organisation was Freitlin, along with its military wing, Falantil.
[39] See for example United Nations Resolutions 348 (1975) and 389 (1976), above, n.2; see also United Nations Resolution 3485 (1975), above, n.2, where the General Assembly called upon all countries to respect East Timor's territorial integrity.
[40] East Timor had been declared a non-self-governing territory. See GA Res. 1542, UN GAOR, 15th Sess., Supp. No 16, para 1, UN Doc. A/4684 (1961).
[41] See *Case Concerning East Timor (Portugal v Australia)* (judgment) [1995] ICJ 90, (30 June), 97 (holding East Timor remains non-self-governing territory with right to self-determination). See further *infra*.
[42] Declaration on Principles, above, n.24, at 125.

use of force is not recognised as legal, any consequences flowing from the illegal use of force would also necessarily be illegal.

As noted in this section, the political and legal dimensions of Indonesia's invasion and its continued denial of East Timor's right to self-determination under international law was clear-cut. However, despite a flurry of subsequent resolutions calling for non-recognition passed with the approval of the majority of states, East Timor continued to labour under the oppressive and bloody rule of Indonesia. While self-determination cannot legitimately be imposed by force, Indonesia's cultural ties and undeniable geographic proximity to the territory of East Timor made integration the most sensible political outcome in the eyes of many onlookers. East Timor was reduced to a pawn in a complex game of political and economic chess.

III. Self-Determination in the Shadow of Realpolitik

While international realpolitik played a key role in the seeming tacit acquiescence of Indonesia's invasion,, regional geopolitics sealed East Timor's fate for close to three decades. Effective control of the territory served as a basis for international acceptance of Indonesia's actions.[43] Though the international community widely held the view that Indonesia held East Timor illegally,[44] few concrete measures were taken to sanction the delinquency. With the Cold War in full force, and Communism advancing steadily in Indochina:[45]

> Western nations served their best interests at that time by supporting Indonesian annexation of East Timor, rather than allowing East Timor to fall prey to even the most remote possibility of Communist or Marxist control.[46]

Western support and the adoption of a policy of silence bolstered Indonesia's confidence, with the government publicly announcing that it would not tolerate the possibility of East Timor's independence.[47] Western support was

[43] See S Carlson, *Indonesia's Oil* (1977); see also NS Klein, "Multilateral Disputes and the Doctrine of Necessary Parties in the East Timor Case" (1996) 21 *Yale Journal of International Law* 305.
[44] See Clark, above, n.35, at 71, n.29.
[45] See Carey, "East Timor: Third World Colonialism and the Struggle for National Identity", above, n.6; de Magalhães, above, n.6, at sec. 2.
[46] JM Sforza, "The Timor Gap Dispute: The Validity Of The Timor Gap Treaty, Self-Determination, And Decolonization" (1999) 22 *Suffolk Transnational Law Review* 481, 488.
[47] See de Magalhães, 'East Timor: A People Shattered by Lies and Silence', above n.6 at sec. 5.

not limited to silent approval, but backed up with a supply of planes and war equipment to fight Timorese resistance to Indonesian annexation. In the poisonous political climate created by Soviet expansionism, Indonesia now had a perfect excuse both for the military invasion and subsequent annexation in the name of regional stability and defence of the free world.[48] It was not lost on observers that Indonesia commenced a full-blown invasion of East Timor the day after United States President Gerald Ford and his Secretary of State Henry Kissinger met with Suharto in Indonesia.[49]

Prevailing realpolitik created fertile ground for States in the region to adopt a hard-nosed pragmatic approach that neutered the illegality of the situation and inhibited East Timor's quest for self-determination. Considering the size of Indonesia and its wealth of resources, economics pushed the law to the backseat. This meant that "no countries in the region were prepared to accept any shifts in the balance of power or a breaking of economic ties with Indonesia over the fate of East Timor".[50] The influence of realpolitik is symptomatic in Robert Pringle's observation regarding the position of the United States' position. Writing four years after the annexation of East Timor, he noted that despite the existence of acrimonious debate between human rights and regional bureaux in the State Department, human rights considerations had not had any specific negative impact on dealings with Indonesia.[51]

The fate of East Timor was further sealed by the decision of Australia, a key regional power, to acquiesce Indonesia's occupation of East Timor in a self-serving measure driven by economic considerations. Though Australia had voted in favour of General Assembly Resolution 3485 of 12 December 1975, it abstained from the vote on Resolution 31/53 of 1 December 1976 and Resolution 32/34 of 28 November 1977. With General Assembly Resolution 33/39 of 13 December 1978, Australia shifted further from its earlier participation in the censure of Indonesian conduct in voting against Resolution 33/39. In connection with its vote, the Australian Department of Foreign Affairs stated: "The text of the Resolution did not reflect a realistic appreciation of the situation in East Timor and no practical purpose was served by the Resolution".[52]

---

[48] *ibid*, at sec. 2.

[49] See Carey, "East Timor: Third World Colonialism and the Struggle for National Identity", above, n.6, at 5.

[50] SA Paulk, "Determination of Self in A Decolonized Territory: The Dutch, The Indonesians, and The East Timorese", (2001) 15 *Emory International Law Review* 267, 288.

[51] See R Pringle, *Indonesia and the Philippines* (1980) 116.

[52] Australian Department of Foreign Affairs, *Annual Report 1978* (1979) 30, quoted in CM Chinkin, "East Timor Moves to the World Court" (1993) 4 *European Journal of International Law* 206, 207 n.5.

At the beginning of 1978, Australia granted Indonesia de facto recognition.[53] In August of 1985, about ten years after Indonesia's invasion, Australia's then Prime Minister, Bob Hawke, formally recognised Indonesian sovereignty over East Timor.[54] In justifying the move, Hawke's comments were clearly based on practical rather than legal considerations. In his words it was a reality that Australia had to come to terms with. He went on to note that, accordingly, the Australian government had decided, despite being "critical of the means by which integration was brought about, it would be unrealistic to continue to refuse to recognize de facto that East Timor [was] part of Indonesia".[55] This recognition made Australia the only country officially to recognise Indonesia's sovereignty over East Timor.[56] With all of these initiatives, Australia was positioning itself for a more sinister national interest issue – the resources in the Timor Gap. By the end of 1989, the government of Australia had concluded a maritime delimitation treaty with Indonesia entitled Treaty on the Zone of Cooperation in an Area between the Indonesian Province of East Timor and Northern Australia.[57] Under the bilateral treaty, the two countries agreed on seabed boundaries between Australia and East Timor and established a Zone of Cooperation for joint exploration and exploitation of the oil and gas resources in the waters.[58] Two years later the "Timor Gap Treaty" between Australia and Indonesia came into force.[59]

After many years of indifference, the recognition of Indonesia's sovereignty over East Timor by Australia and the joint initiatives to exploit resources in the Timor Gap goaded Portugal, the former colonial power which had abandoned East Timor,into a more proactive position. In the same year that the Timor Gap Treaty came into force, Portugal, viewing the treaty as a delict, instituted

[53] See *Case Concerning East Timor*, above, n.41, at 97 (quoting the then Australian Minister for Foreign Affairs).
[54] See "Key Dates in Australia Indonesia Relations", AAP Newsfeed, 21 May 21, available in LEXIS, Intlaw Library, News File [Key Dates].
[55] See *Case Concerning East Timor*, above n.41, at 97.
[56] 'Background to the Timor Gap Treaty', AAP Newsfeed, August 20, 1998, available in LEXIS, Intlaw Library, News File [Background].
[57] Thomas D Grant, 'East Timor, The U.N. System, And Enforcing Non-Recognition In International Law', (2000) 33 *Vanderbilt Journal of Transnational Law* 273, 299.
[58] MS French-Merrill, 'The Role of the United Nations and Recognition in Sovereignty Determinations: How Australia Breached its International Obligations in Ratifying the Timor Gap Treaty', (2000) 8 *Cardozo Journal of International & Comparative Law* 285, 288–89; J Aubrey, "Canberra: Jakarta's Trojan Horse in East Timor", in P Hainsworth and S McCloskey, eds, *The East Timor Question: The Struggle for Independence from Indonesia* (2000) 133, 142.
[59] Treaty between Australia and the Republic of Indonesia on the Zone of Cooperation in an Area Between the Indonesian Province of East Timor and Northern Australia, 11 December 1989, Australia-Indonesia, 1991 *Australia treaty Series* No 9.

proceedings against Australia and Indonesia before the International Court of Justice (ICJ).[60] The proceedings claimed in part that Australia, by entering into the Timor Gap Treaty with Indonesia, infringed East Timor's right to self-determination and permanent sovereignty over its natural resources, and infringed upon Portugal's rights as the administering power of the territory.[61] The chapter now turns to consider these proceedings.

IV. The Judicial Dimension: The ICJ Gets Blind-Sided by Realpolitik

The Portuguese proceedings commenced before the ICJ in 1991 sought a declaration from the Court that Portugal's status with respect to East Timor and the rights of the people of East Timor to self-determination, territorial integrity and unity, and permanent sovereignty over its wealth and natural resources opposed Australia's treaty with Indonesia on the Timor Gap.[62] Four years later, on 30 June 30 1995, the ICJ ruled in a 14–2 decision that it could not exercise jurisdiction over the case because it would require the Court to determine the lawfulness of Indonesia's presence in, and occupation of East Timor, as well as Indonesia's treaty-making power over East Timor.[63] In light of Indonesia's failure to submit to the Court's jurisdiction, the ICJ declined to exercise jurisdiction based on the absence of Indonesia, a necessary party, whose legal interest would have been implicated upon adjudication on the merits. The majority decided it was unable to adjudicate the issue since the violations Australia allegedly perpetrated by entering into the treaty with Indonesia were linked with the question of the legitimacy of Indonesia's signing of the Timor Gap Treaty.[64]

Though the ICJ did not decide the issue, disturbingly the majority of judges supported the notion that "Indonesia had manifested its sovereignty and was,

---

[60] For initial motions in the case, see *Case Concerning East Timor (Portugal v. Australia) (Initial Motions)*, 1993 ICJ 32 (19 May); *Case Concerning East Timor (Portugal v Australia)*, 1992 ICJ 228 (19 June); *Case Concerning East Timor (Portugal v Australia)* 1991 ICJ 9 (3 May).

[61] See Treaty between Australia and the Republic of Indonesia on the Zone of Cooperation in an Area Between the Indonesian Province of East Timor and Northern Australia, 11 December 1989, Australia-Indonesia, 29 ILM 475 (1990); *East Timor*, 1995 ICJ 90 at 98; GA Res. 1803, U.N. GAOR, 17th Sess., Supp. No 17, at 15, UN Doc. A/ 5217 (1962) [GA Res. 1803].

[62] See *Case Concerning East Timor* (judgment), above, n.41 at 92.

[63] *ibid*, 100; see also Bello & Bekker, "Treaty of 1989 Between Australia and Indonesia Concerning the Gap-Existence of Legal Dispute Between Portugal and Australia-Objections to Jurisdiction-Effect of Court Ruling on Absent Third Parties—Right to Determination as Right Erga Omnes—Status of East Timor as Non-Self-Governing Territory" (1996) 90 *American Journal of International Law* 94.

[64] See BF Fitzgerald, "Portugal v. Australia: Deploying the Missiles of Sovereign Autonomy and Sovereign Community" (1996) 37 *Harvard International Law Journal* 260, 264.

through *animus occupandi*, the sovereign power of East Timor".[65] The ICJ majority went further by embracing the argument advanced by Australia that Portugal no longer exclusively controlled East Timor and that the power over East Timor had passed, under general international law, to Indonesia.[66] In the words of Michael S Merill-French:

> The crux of Australia's argument, therefore, was that sovereignty is a factual determination. By invading East Timor and occupying all the political and economic centers of the island for over 20 years, Indonesia had exercised enough dominion to be regarded as the sovereign power of East Timor. Australia, while not approving the means by which this sovereignty was brought about, declared that it would be unreasonable not to consider Indonesia as the sovereign power given the facts of the situation.[67]

However, it was the dissenting opinions by Judges Weeramantry and Skubiszewski which grappled with the hard legal issues. The judges asserted that recognition of the territorial changes effectuated by Indonesia's invasion was an international delict, arguing that Australia violated a general duty to the international community by recognising Indonesia's claim of sovereignty.[68] Their major criticism was that no nation outside of Australia recognised Indonesia's illegal annexation. Since the Indonesian invasion violated international law, depriving the East Timorese of the right of self-determination, Indonesia could not be regarded as sovereign of East Timor as a matter of law. Their net conclusion was that Australia violated obligations due to the international community by recognising Indonesia's actions. Judge Skubiszewski further noted that, in light of Australia's membership of the UN and the corresponding duty to respect Portugal's claim as administering power in East Timor, as well as the right of the East Timorese to self-determination, it had breached its duties under international law.

Three years after the ICJ judgment, the political machine that had been slowly coming to life finally clinched a breakthrough. In August 1998, the Indonesian and Portuguese governments agreed in UN-brokered talks to work towards

---

[65] French-Merrill, "The Role of the United Nations and Recognition in Sovereignty Determinations" above, n.58 at 292.
[66] *Case Concerning East Timor* (judgment), above, n.41, at 101–103.
[67] French-Merrill, "'The Role of the United Nations and Recognition in Sovereignty Determinations" above, n.58, at 293.
[68] *Case Concerning East Timor* (judgment), above, n.41, at 172.

autonomy for East Timor.[69] This was followed on 5 January 1999 by Australia's recognition of the right of the East Timorese to self-determination.[70] Five months later, Indonesia and Portugal signed an agreement requesting the UN to conduct a ballot in East Timor enabling the East Timorese to choose between autonomy and independence.[71] On 30 August 1999, after further UN-brokered negotiations between Indonesia and Portugal,[72] a popular referendum on East Timor's future status was held under the auspices of the UN Mission to East Timor (UNAMET).[73] An overwhelming majority voted for independence from Indonesia. On 20 May 2002:

> after more than four centuries of Portuguese colonial rule, followed by twenty-four years of brutal occupation by Indonesia, and finally a two-year period of UN interim administration, the people of East Timor celebrated their long-awaited independence.[74]

V. Conclusion

Despite some debate regarding the principle of self-determination, the author avers that authority from most of the sources of international law supports the conclusion that self-determination is a norm of *jus cogens* imposing binding obligations on all nation states.[75] Considering that self-determination

---

[69] Report of the Secretary-General, UN GAOR, 53d Sess., UN Doc. A/53/349 (1998); Human Rights Watch, World Report (1999).

[70] J Aubrey, above, n.58, at 146.

[71] See generally Agreement Between Indonesia and Portugal on the Question of East Timor, UN SCOR, 53d Sess., Annex I, at 4, U.N. Doc. S/1999/513 (1999); Agreement Between the United Nations and the Governments of Indonesia and Portugal Regarding the Modalities for the Popular Consultation Through a Direct Ballot, UN SCOR 53d Sess., Annex II, at 24, U.N. Doc. S/1999/513 (1999); Agreement Between the United Nations and the Governments of Indonesia and Portugal Regarding Security Arrangements, U.N. SCOR, 53d Sess., Annex III at 29, U.N. Doc. S/1999/513 (1999).

[72] A Downer, "East Timor—Looking Back on 1999" (2000) 54 *Australia Journal of International Affairs* 5, 5–6; J Cotton, "The Emergence of an Independent East Timor: National and Regional Challenges" (2000) 22 *Contemporary Southeast Asia* 1, 2–6.

[73] UNAMET was authorised on 11 June 1999, under UN Security Council Resolution 1246. UN SC, 4013th mtg., UN Doc. S/RES/1246 (1999), available at *http://0-www.un.org.library.newcastle.edu.au:80/Docs/scres/1999/99sc1246.htm*. For an account of the challenges faced by the mission, see Martin, above, n.4, at 21–54. See also Report of the Secretary-General on the Question of East Timor, UN SC, UN Doc. S/1999/803 (20 July 1999); Report of the Secretary-General on the Question of East Timor, UN SC, UN Doc. S/1999/862 (9 August 1999) [SG Report of 9 August 1999].

[74] JC Beauvais, "Benevolent Despotism: A Critique Of U.N. State-Building In East Timor" (2001) 33 *New York University Journal of International Law and Politics* 1101, 1102.

[75] H Morris, "Self-Determination: An Affirmative Right or Mere Rhetoric?" (1997) 4 *ILSA Journal of International & Comparative Law* 201, 204.

is a norm of customary international law,[76] the East Timorese should be seen in many ways as a people betrayed by the international community in light of the realpolitik factors identified above. As MS French-Merill notes:

> Indonesia's illegal use of force and its interference with the self-determination of the East Timorese were regarded as violations of general international law as well as violations of UN resolutions. As a consequence, the United Nations called upon member states not to recognize the Indonesian annexation.[77]

The schism between external and internal self-determination is a worry but should be shorn of geopolitics. While the principle of *uti posseditis* has a real role in international law, it should not be a basis for inaction and deliberate subversion. When the Wilsonian principles elevated the matter to the international law agenda and the UN Charter outlawed aggressive use of force, the hope was that brute force was no longer an accepted avenue to either acquire territory by force's or snuff out the aspirations of a people to self-determination. East Timor, as one of the latest entrant into the community of nations, despite its small size and poverty, should be a lesson and a reminder that self-determination is a right that should be both adequately protected and safeguarded where the circumstances call for it.

[76] R Higgins, *Problems and Process: International Law and How We Use It* (1994) 114–128; 113; J Klabbers and and R Lefeber, "Africa: Lost Between Self-Determination and *Uti Possidetis*" in C Brolmann *Peoples and Minorities in International Law* (1993), 39–41; M Lachs, "The law in and of the United Nations" (1960-61) 1 *Indian Journal of International Law* 429.

[77] French-Merrill, "'The Role of the United Nations and Recognition in Sovereignty Determinations", above, n.58 at 300.

Denial of Self-Determination and Utilisation of Natural Resources by an Illegal Occupier of Territory: the Role of Non-Recognition in such Instances in the Light of the *East Timor* Case and the Situation in Western Sahara

*Clive R. Symmons**

INTRODUCTION

The situations in East Timor (now Timor Leste) and Western Sahara are similar in several respects. Firstly in the fact that both these territories were in the latter part of 1975 (within a few weeks of each other) invaded by a neighbouring Third World State with neo-colonialist ambitions (Indonesia through its armed forces in the case of the former and Morocco through the so-called "Green March" of some 350,000 Moroccans across the border in the case of Western Sahara). Secondly in the fact that in both cases the Security Council called upon both sets of invading forces to withdraw (which was initially ignored in the former case and is still being ignored in the latter case). Both territories thus shared the unenviable situation where "colonial rule was not ended peacefully or in consultation with the indigenous population as required by international law".[1]

Thirdly, there is the fact that the UN prescribed self-determination for the peoples of both respective territories which for many years previously had been

*I have earlier addressed aspects of this subject in chapter 6 ("The Role of Recognition in Instances of Denial of Self-Determination in the Light of the East Timor Case") and chapter 11 ("The International Recognition Position Regarding the Purported Incorporation of East Timor into Indonesia") in the book published by IPJET in 1998 entitled The East Timor Problem and the Role of Europe, ed. P. Pinto Leite, pp.107–142 & 211–221. I am grateful to Pedro Pinto Leite for his permission to use these researches when preparing this chapter.

[1] See S. Zunes, "East Timor and Western Sahara: A Comparative Analysis on Prospects for Self-Determination": paper prepared for the Conference on "International Law and the Question of Western Sahara": Institute for Social Studies, The Hague, 27 and 28 October, 2006, at p.1.

on the UN list of Non-Self-Governing Territories[2] (in the case of Western Sahara it was included on the list in 1963, with an affirmation of the right to self-determination in 1966). Indeed, in the case of Western Sahara this was backed up by an Advisory Opinion from the ICJ which in 1975 found that there were "no legal ties of such a nature as might affect the application of resolution 1514 (XV) in the decolonization of Western Sahara and, in particular, the principle of self-determination through the free and genuine expression of the will of the peoples of the Territory".[3] As part of this realisation the UN has since 1991 been engaged in the Territory through MINURSO (the UN Mission for the Referendum in Western Sahara), though a referendum there has still not taken place due largely to intransigence on the part of Morocco.[4]

Thirdly, there has been the linkage of *economic* interest being in the background of both situations, most obviously in the case of Western Sahara. In the case of East Timor, one of the main potential resources was to be maritime-based (hydrocarbons); and this indeed led to the treaty between Indonesia and Australia over the delimitation of the continental shelf in the so-called Timor Gap area (hereafter the 'Timor Gap treaty'). In the case of Western Sahara there was the land-based resource of the potash deposits at Bou Craa which had been exploited by Spain prior to its departure, but also the maritime-based resources of fisheries off the territory which have been subject to a recent controversial treaty between Morocco and the EU (discussed below), as well as potential hydrocarbon resources, as will be seen, in the seabed thereof, which have in more recent times been subject to contract between Morocco and third parties.[5] This factor raises the whole issue of the principle of *economic* self-determination and its inter-relationship with political self-determination, a matter which will be repeatedly referred to below. Indeed the UN-based "Corell opinion" mentioned below describes the legal nature of the core principle of sovereignty over natural resources as a "corollary" to the principle of self-determination.[6] Breach of this interconnected right received frequent mention in the Portuguese pleadings in the *East Timor* case: to the effect that a dependant people have a right to

[2] See P. Pinto Leite, "International Legality Versus Realpolitik — The Cases of Western Sahara and East Timor", in *The Western Sahara Conflict: The Role of Natural Resources in Decolonisation*, ed. C. Olsson, Current African Issues No.33, Norddiska Afrikainstitutet, Uppsala, Sweden (2006), 11. On analogies between the East Timor situation and Western Sahara generally, see, F. Rigaux, "East Timor and Western Sahara: a Comparative view", *op.cit., infra* n.10 at p.166.

[3] ICJ Rep.(1975) at p.68.

[4] See Pinto Leite, *infra* n.42.

[5] See T. Shelley "Natural Resources of the Western Sahara" *op.cit.*, ed Olsson, *supra* n.2, at p.17.

[6] See *infra* n.18.

permanent sovereignty over their natural resources. Accordingly, the latter right was often mentioned *interchangeably* with that of self-determination in the pleadings in the case where it was to be described by Portuguese counsel in the case as "also an integral part of the law of self-determination".[7]

In other ways, however, differences appear between the two situations. For example, in the case of Western Sahara, Spain signed a 'partition agreement' with both Morocco and Mauritania on November 14th, 1975, whereby it ceded the territory, and under the terms of which tripartite agreement Spain, in 1976, withdrew from the territory in return for 35 percent of the phosphate mines and fishing rights in Saharan waters for 10 years.[8] It was this latter concession that was indirectly to lead to problems within the EU, analogous to those concerning recognition, in recent years. In the case of East Timor, the treaty of alleged economic exploitation was the bilateral one referred to above — the Timor Gap treaty of 1989 — between Indonesia and Australia. In both cases there were seemingly no protests (except in the latter instance by Portugal)[9] on the basis that such treaties might be not only depriving the inhabitants of each territory of the right to self-determination, but also their right to permanent sovereignty over their natural resources.

Another difference between the two situations is that in the case of East Timor (now Timor Leste), the former colonial sovereign, Portugal, was formally designated as "administering Power" under UN resolutions;[10] whereas, as seen, Spain, in the case of Western Sahara abandoned its former colony in 1976 and had (arguably) no such official designation thereafter.[11] For this reason when issues of recognition are looked at in the latter instance, there is no clear issue of what this writer has dubbed a 'positive recognition duty' of its status as 'administering Power'.

It is also arguable, however, that any such positive recognition duty cannot be directly linked with the administering Power's rights. For example, Judge Oda

---

7 See CR 95/4.

8 See Pinto Leite, *supra* n.2, at p.13.

9 See the Australian Counter-Memorial in the *East Timor* case at p.77, para 174 where Australia alleged that even Portugal had not protested against earlier Indonesian treaty negotiations.

10 See C. R. Symmons, "The Role of Recognition in Instances of Denial of Self-Determination in the Light of the *East Timor* Case", *in the East Timor Problem and the Role of Europe* ed. P. Pinto Leite, IPJET, The Netherlands (1998), 107, 120–121.

11 But see the recent EU Legal Opinion (*infra* n.66) prepared by R. Passos, G. Mazzini & G. Clariana (SJ-0085/06,D (2006)7352, at p.3 ("Spain is still reported on the list of *de jure* administering powers"). It also pointed out that Morocco never had effective control over the whole territory in the last three decades, part of the Territory being under the *de facto* administration of POLISARIO .

in his Separate Opinion in the *East Timor* case stated[12] that in the UN, Indonesia's claim that East Timor should be integrated into its territory was "rejected solely in order to uphold the rights of the people of East Timor, but not to protect the rights and duties of Portugal in relation to East Timor or the status of Portugal as the administering Power". In its majority judgment, the ICJ left the matter unresolved, whilst noting that it could not be inferred from the sole fact that certain UN resolutions referred to Portugal as "administering Power" that it was "intended to establish an obligation on third states to deal exclusively with Portugal as regards the continental shelf of East Timor".[13]

Economic Self-Determination

In UN resolutions under the agenda item entitled "Implementation of the Declaration on the Granting of Independence to Colonial Countries and Peoples" in October 2003, the UN Fourth Committee approved a two-part draft resolution[14] whereby the GA affirmed the inalienable right of the peoples of Non-Self-Governing Territories to self determination and re-affirmed (in a draft resolution on economic and other activities that affect the interests of peoples of such Territories) that the damaging exploitation and plundering of the marine and other natural resources of the Territories, in violation of relevant UN resolutions, were a threat to the integrity and prosperity of those Territories. It thus urged that the administering Powers concerned should take effective measures to safeguard the inalienable right of the peoples to their natural resources.

It seems from such UN moves that a State without a legal right to occupy a territory has no right *as purported sovereign there* to utilize or dispose of the natural resources for it own purposes, though it may have some temporary rights as an "occupying power".[15] Indeed the UN legal opinion given at UN Security Council (hereafter 'SC') request by Hans Corell (hereafter the 'Corell opinion'),[16] in indicating that Morocco may not dispose of resources of the

[12] Separate Opinion, at para 15, p.16 (emphasis added), noting that in 1976 the SC did not refer to Portugal, nor did the General Assembly in 1977. *Cf.* by way of analogy the Australian argument in the *East Timor* case (CR 93/7 at p.21), that "Chapter XI [of the Charter] is concerned with the rights of non-self governing peoples and not the rights of states administering them".

[13] *Case Concerning East Timor* (1995) ICJ Reports, 90, at para 32. See I. Scobbie & C. Drew, "Self-Determination Undetermined: The Case of East Timor", (1996) 9 Leiden Journal of International Law, 185, 203.

[14] See Pinto Leite *supra* n.2 at p.16.

[15] See M. Scholdtz & P. Wrange, "Swedish Foreign Policy on the Western Sahara Conflict" in The Western Sahara Conflict – The Role of Natural Resources in Decolonisation, ed. C. Olsson, Current African Issues, Nordic Africa Institute (2006), 22.

[16] S/2002/161: Letter dated 29 January 2002 from the Under-Secretary-General for Legal Affairs, addressed to the President of the Security Council, set out as Appendix 1 in *op.cit.* at n.15.

Western Sahara for its own benefit, was that *any agreement entered into by Morocco in its own name does not cover Western Sahara*. This has some relevance in interpreting the recent controversial renewal of a fisheries agreement between the EU and Morocco in 2007 as discussed below.[17]

It is relevant to note that the abovementioned Corell opinion[18] considered that the legality of "réconnaissance agreements" with Morocco (see below) for evaluation of hydrocarbon resources off Western Sahara involved "an analysis of the status of the Territory ..... and the status of Morocco in relation to the Territory", as well as "an analysis of the principles of international law governing mineral resource activities in Non-Self-Governing Territories",[19] as contained in the UN Charter and UN General Assembly ('GA') resolutions "pertaining to decolonization in general and economic activities in Non-Self-Governing Territories, in particular".[20] The opinion went on to stress that any exploitation of the natural resources of a Non-Self-Governing Territory should be for the benefit of the people of the Territory.[21] One of the oil companies concerned (Kerr McGee) has emphasised in the past that it believes it is acting within the terms of the Corell opinion.[22] This opinion was, as will be seen, to be much relied upon in a Legal Opinion given within the EU in 2006 on the international legality of the Fisheries Partnership Agreement between the EU and Morocco.[23]

Self-Determination and East Timor

In its judgment in the *East Timor* case[24] of 30 June 1995, the International Court of justice (hereafter the ICJ) endorsed the second preliminary objection argument to its jurisdiction by Australia, namely that any judgment given on the merits of the case would effectively breach the rule endorsed in the *Monetary Gold* case[25] *i.e.*, involve the potential liability of a State (in this case Indonesia) which was not a party to the proceedings.[26]

---

[17] See n.136, and accompanying text.

[18] See Appendix 1 to *op.cit. supra* n.15, para 3 at p.25.

[19] *ibid.*, at para 3.

[20] *ibid.*, at para 4.

[21] *ibid.*, at para 25

[22] See *supra*, n.16 and T. Shelley, "Natural Resources of the Western Sahara" in Pinto Leite, *op.cit. supra* n.14, 17, at p.19.

[23] See P. San Martin below n.67.

[24] *Case concerning East Timor* (1995) ICJ Reports, 90.

[25] (1954) ICJ Reports, 19, 32.

[26] *Supra* at para 34.

The Court therefore laconically concluded that it could not "rule on Portugal's claims on the merits, whatever the importance of the questions raised by those claims and of the rules of international law which they bring into play".[27] This was an unfortunate, if inevitable, result of the proceedings".[28] However; this was mitigated by three factors in the case:

(i) The ICJ had "taken note" in the judgment (that for the two Parties) the territory of East Timor "remain[ed] a non-self-governing territory, and its people ha[d] the right to self-determination"; and in conjunction with this,[29] it described Portugal's assertion that the right of peoples to self-determination, as it evolved from the Charter and United Nations practice, having an "*erga omnes* character" as "irreproachable".[30] Indeed even Australia (in the case) did not dispute this latter principle.[31]

(ii) The two *Dissenting Opinions* in the case — those of Judges Weeramantry and Skubiszewski — supply an impressive discussion of what the Court *might* have decided had it been able to deal with the merits of the case. It is the latter two Opinions which form the basis of this chapter insofar as they touch on questions of recognition and denial of self-determination, as supplemented by the Australian and Portuguese pleadings in the *East Timor* case. These Opinions — together with the statements of the majority judgment mentioned above — have at least important symbolic value.

(iii) As the arguments on admissibility and the merits were joined, the "ICJ received extensive written and oral pleadings on the *substantive issues* of the case".[32] The material on the merits from these pleadings thus constitutes a large part of the present chapter.

It may be noted parenthetically that it has been alleged in connection with self-determination and the *East Timor* case that the ICJ "explicitly asserted both [the right of the people of East Timor to self-determination] and its

---

[27] Judgment, para 36.

[28] As one commentator graphically put it: "In this case; the shadows cast by the actions of Indonesia against the people of East Timor deflected attention from the claims and arguments of those actually-before the ICJ: Portugal and Australia"; and accordingly, "in its outcome the interests of Indonesia took priority": see note by C. Chinkin (1996) 45 ICLQ 712, 713.

[29] *Supra* n.24 at para 31.

[30] *Id.*, at para 29.

[31] Rejoinder, at p.32.

[32] C. Chinkin, *supra* n.28 at p.716 (emphasis added).

continued status as a non-self-self-governing territory in a number of separate paragraphs".[33] However this is perhaps to somewhat overstate the case; as although it is true that the ICJ concluded that "the territory of East Timor remain[ed] a non-self-governing territory, and its people has the right to self-determination", this has been well-described as being "a carefully-worded" *obiter dictum*.[34] Thus the Court was otherwise careful to preface such "findings" as "for the two parties"; or that the Court was simply "noting Portugal's claim", as *e.g.*, in the case of it claiming to be the "administering Power of East Timor as a non-self-governing territory".[35] In other words, the Court seemed reluctant to make objective findings on such vital substantive issues.[36]

This matter was well brought out by Judge Skubiszewski, who pointed out in the case that the Court's statements on the status of East Timor and on self-determination "might have been elaborated on"; and that there was nothing in the judgment "on the application of the right to self-determination to the present situation of the East Timorese people and on the view of each Party regarding the implementation of that right".[37] One of the legal ramifications of this "application" might be possible *duties of non-recognition* vis-à-vis the illegal occupant of the territory, as will be seen below. And in fact Judge Skubiszewski did go on to more specifically decry[38] the Judgment's failure to address some "uncertainties" regarding a non-self-governing territory which has been incorporated into a State "without the consent of the United Nations".

Self-Determination and Western Sahara

In similar fashion to what occurred in the case of East Timor, Western Sahara was (in 1963) listed by the UN as a Non-Self-Governing Territory under Chapter XI of the Charter, after which Spain, as administering Power, transmitted to the UN the necessary information on the territory under Art. 73e of the UN Charter. This was followed by a series of UN resolutions in the

---

33 *ibid.*, at p.173.

34 See G. Simpson, "A Stone in Each Shoe: Australia Foreign Policy and East Timor" in Leite *op.cit. supra* n.10, 143, at p.149.

35 *Supra*, n.13, at para 31. Judge Skubiszwuski accordingly regretted (Dissenting Opinion, at para 113) that the Court's "important affirmation" regarding the non-self-governing status of East Timor "did not find its place in the dispositif". Since 1960 (Res. 1342, 1960), East Timor had been mentioned in the UN list of non-self-governing territories.

36 But see Simpson, *supra* n.34 at p.149 who notes the reference to "East Timorese rights" in the final paragraph of the judgment.

37 *ibid.,* at para 53.

38 *ibid.,* at para 103.

UN GA on the question of Western Sahara, affirming the applicability of the UN Declaration in GA Res. 1514 to the Territory;[39] and as early as 1966, the UN adopted a resolution urging Spain to organize a referendum as soon as possible, under UN supervision (as detailed in 1991) on the Territory's right to self-determination.[40] Thus UN resolutions since[41] have confirmed the right of the peoples of Western Sahara to self-determination; and since 1966 the UN has clearly established that the future of the Western Sahara should be determined by way of a UN-supervised self-determination referendum, though to date this has not occurred, largely due to Moroccan intransigence.[42]

Issues Involving Aspects of Recognition arising from the *East Timor* Case and the Situation in Western Sahara

(a) East Timor

Australia, in its pleadings in the *East Timor* case, was to point out that, in its opinion, the case was not concerned with the existence of the rights to self-determination, but with the "corresponding obligations arising for third States".[43] The hope, however, of some international lawyers that the ICJ might clarify obligations of third States and the "specific rights and duties of third parties towards groups possessing the right to self-determination and the effect of unilateral recognition" in the event of illegal suppression of the right[44] was not, as seen above, to be realized in the case, despite the broad potential impact and importance of such obligations involving a far wider State spectrum than Australia in the East Timor situation itself.

As Judge Weeramantry pointed out in his Dissenting Opinion[45] (albeit in the jurisdictional context) the "Court's determinations on matters pertaining to Australia's obligations and actions [might] indeed have consequences not only

---

39 See the Corell opinion, *supra*, n.16, at para 5.

40 See M. Scholdtz & P. Wrange, *op.cit. supra* n.15, at p.22.

41 Such as UN SC res.S/RES/1598.

42 See further, *e.g.*, P. Pinto Leite, "International Lergality versus realpolitik: the Cases of Sahara, East Timor and West Papua", an up-dated and extended paper of that presented at a seminar in Stockholm on 24 November 2005, at p.9.

43 Rejoinder, at p.82, para 171.

44 See G. Simpson, "The Politics of Self-Determination in the Case Concerning East Timor", in *International Law and the Question of East Timor*, (1995) CIIR/IPJET, 251, 252. As Judge Skubiszewski pointed out in the case (Dissenting Opinion, para 96), "non-administrators [of non-self-governing territories] also have some duties".

45 Dissenting Opinion, at p.157.

for Indonesia, but for other countries as well" as, according to information from Australia, several other countries "ha[d] dealt with Indonesia in respect of East Timor". So that, for example, if the Court had found for Portugal, "this finding would have repercussions on many other States which may or may not have acted in accordance with their individual obligations to recognise the rights of East Timor".[46] These repercussions might have involved third States having to *withdraw recognition* of Indonesian sovereignty over East Timor and possibly termination or suspension of treaties with Indonesia which could apply to East Timor.[47] In the light of this broader perspective, at times the Australian pleadings in the *East Timor* case lapsed into reliance on the weakest of all excuses based on 'safety in numbers' — namely that Australia was not the only State to have entered into relationships with Indonesia over East Timor.[48]

In a broad sense, perhaps one of the most interesting features of the case — at least in so far as the Dissenting Opinions are concerned — is how far such a principle of (objectively acknowledged) political and *economic* self-determination[49] for a particular territory may lead to both negative (and positive) duties *for the world community* (and not just the illegal occupant and former colonial Power) in terms of non-recognition *or a similar concept*.[50] Unfortunately, in this respect the language of the Portuguese pleadings in the *East Timor* case became quite semantic; so that, as Australia pointed out in its Rejoinder,[51] Portugal did "not rely on a duty of non-recognition of Indonesia's sovereignty [in East Timor], but on a duty not to misrecognise Portugal's status" (a so-called duty of 'non-méconnaissance'). Australia was surely right[52] in implying that the word "méconnaissance" was used for tactical reasons: namely, to avoid direct invocation of Indonesia's responsibility; and

---

[46] *ibid*., at p.173.

[47] See Australian argument in CR 95/11 at pp. 63/64.

[48] See Counter-Memorial, p.132, para 300 ("...the underlying issues in this case concern the political relationships of many States, of which Australia is but one....").

[49] As seen, this right intrinsically interrelates with that of the sovereign right of a people to their natural resources, an aspect very relevant to the subject matter of the Timor Gap treaty. See *infra* n.190.

[50] For example, the separable issue, much discussed in the Corell opinion (see *infra* n.82 relating to Western Sahara, of the duty of third States to respect the right of peoples denied the right to self-determination to the benefits of any of their natural resources in any dealings with a neo-colonial occupier of their territory.

[51] At p.5, para 5.

[52] *ibid*., at p.8. See also *id*., at p.47, para 92 ("[e]ven Portugal itself concedes that, because Indonesia is not a party to the proceeding, the *Monetary Gold* principle, prevents it from alleging that Indonesia's use of force gave rise to a duty of non-recognition") (emphasis added).

that, as terminology involving a double negative, it led to an "illusory" distinction.[53]

Unfortunately also (as lamented by Judge Skubiszewski in the case),[54] the operative judgment of the Court had no word on the relevance of non-recognition (the relevant negative duty as described in this chapter in respect of denial of self-determination), nor (as the other side of the coin, as it were), the positive duty of States "to recognise the status of an entity denied self-determination", and, consequentially, the status of the appropriate administering State in that situation.[55] This contrast was well summarised by Australia as involving "affirmative attitude recognition" as opposed to the "negative aspect" (*i.e.*, non recognition) — both essentially being described as "two sides of the same coin".[56]

The more nebulous 'positive' duty mentioned here to respect a people's right to self-determination in appropriate circumstances (or, inter-connectedly, a former colonial Power's continuing formal status in respect of that territory) has been dealt with elsewhere by the present writer.[57] Hence this chapter concentrates on the matter of *third State attitudes* in the *negative* aspect, which essentially involves obligations of non-recognition in respect of actions of a State *de facto* illegally administering or exercising sovereignty in such a territory.[58] Furthermore, as the convoluted Portuguese pleadings in the *East Timor* case stated (but without using the word "recognition"), "the duties, powers and rights of Portugal as the administering Power of the Territory of East Timor are opposable to Australia which is under an obligation not to disregard them, but to respect them". For the word "respect" one can justifiably substitute "recognise". It is arguable *a contrario* from this that to accord *de jure* (rather than *de facto)* recognition to a State in wrongful possession of a non-self-governing territory, could, by implication, be a further (or more serious) breach of international law.

[53] *ibid.*, at p.8.

[54] Dissenting Opinion at para 157.

[55] See C.R. Symmons, *supra* n.10 at pp.115–121.

[56] See CR 95/8 at pp.7 & 8.

[57] See above n.55. Arguably, a consequential positive ('affirmative') duty may also arise as to the status (and rights) of a former (now dispossessed) State which claims powers in a territory pending a proper exercise of the peoples right there is self-determination; that is to say, recognition of a status which may be dubbed as that of the "*de jure* administering Power". *Cf.* Australia's complaint on this in its Rejoinder, at p.83 fn. 215; also *ibid.*, at paras 264–67.

[58] See CR 95/2 at p.55.

(b) Western Sahara

On 14 November 1975, a 'Declaration of Principles' was concluded between Spain, Morocco and Mauritania (the "Madrid Accords") whereunder Spain's powers were transferred to a temporary tripartite administration, but falling short of transfer of sovereignty or according the two other parties any status as administering Powers[59]; so this agreement did not directly affect the Territory's existing international status.[60] However, on 26 February 1976, Spain informed the UN S-G that as of that date it had terminated its presence in Western Sahara and had relinquished its responsibilities in the Territory, so leaving the Territory in fact under the administration of both Morocco and Mauritania in their respectively controlled areas.[61] Accordingly Spain then unilaterally withdrew from the Territory without UN sanction and without consultation of the peoples of the Territory.

(i) Fishery agreements with Morocco covering Western Saharan Waters

As regards fisheries off Western Sahara, under the above-mentioned "Madrid Accords", Spain retained treaty-based fishing rights off Western Sahara which, on joining the EU, were provisionally incorporated into EU practice; though it is important to note that the Accords did not refer specifically to the waters of "Western Sahara" as such.[62] EU policy towards the Territory has in fact been to the effect that the UN has the central role in dealing with the Western Sahara problem.[63] Nonetheless, there was a fishery protocol drawn up between Morocco and the EU covering the period 1 December 1995 to 30 November 1999, after which date it was not renewed. In 2005, however, the European

---

[59] A status which Spain alone could not confer. A recent EU opinion (see below n.66) expressly acknowledges Morocco as the *de facto* administering Power in Western Sahara (at p.7).

[60] See the Corell opinion, *supra*, n.16 at para 6.

[61] In fact thereafter Morocco administered Western Sahara, but not as administering Power and without any commitment to send relevant information under Art.73e of the UN Charter. See the Corell opinion, at para 7. Unlike Spain in the Western Sahara, Portugal never intended to relinquish its administrative power responsibilities in East Timor. It seems, though, to be not to be absolutely clear whether Spain did officially lose its status after its withdrawal: see, *e.g.*, CR 95/3 at p.62 and the Australian Rejoinder in the *East Timor* case, nn.335 & 336 at pp.115 and 117.

[62] See T. Shelley, *supra* n.22, at p.18.

[63] See, *e.g.*, recently the "Summary of Meeting of the Ad Hoc Delegation to Western Sahara on 21 June 2006, Brussels": Council of the EU Doc.10971/06 (26 June, 2006); and the "Statement by the EU" at the Sixth Meeting of the EU-Morocco Association Council (23 July 2007) (12062/07 (Press 178) at p.7 ("The EU welcomes the negotiations which have been launched under the aegis of the [UN] and on the basis of [SC] Resolution 1754 of 30 April 2007 on the future status of Western Sahara" and hopes that "these negotiations will result in a solution which is politically fair, lasting, and mutually acceptable and which allows for the *self-determination of the people of the Western Sahara*, as recommended in [UN] resolutions") (emphasis added).

Commission began negotiating a renewed fishing agreement to accord fish quotas to vessels of several EU nations in 'Moroccan' waters.

The new Agreement — the Fisheries Partnership Agreement between the European Communities and the Kingdom of Morocco — came into force on March 6th, 2007, following Moroccan ratification at that date, for a period of four years. However, from the start the Agreement caused difficulties within the EU as it "explicitly include[d] waters controlled by Morocco but not under its recognised sovereignty".[64] Thus the Agreement makes repeated reference to the area of fishing waters covered as being the "Moroccan fishing zone" (*e.g.*, Arts. 4 and 6). This vital phase is defined in Art. 2(a) as meaning "the waters falling *within the sovereignty or jurisdiction* of Morocco" (emphasis added), a meaning which implicitly takes in not just Moroccan waters *per se* but also those under Moroccan occupation in Western Sahara, thus amounting to what one commentator has branded as "back-door recognition of the *status quo* in Western Sahara".[65] It was preluded by a Legal Opinion on the draft Agreement given in 2006 by EU legal advisers. They opined that an agreement could be legal if based on the following elements: namely, the acknowledgment of Morocco as the *de facto* administering power of the Western Sahara; the understanding (based on the UN Corell opinion) that "the exploitation activities in Non-Self-Governing Territories violate the principles of international law if they disregard the interests and wishes of the people" therein; that the *de facto* administration of Morocco in Western Sahara is therefore under an obligation "to comply with the rights of the people of Western Sahara"; and that this does not mean that the Agreement, as such, is contrary to the principles of international law, as at that stage it could not be prejudged that "Morocco [would] not comply with its obligations under international law vis-à-vis the people of Western Sahara".[66]

One critic[67] of this legal opinion has rightly commented that the opinion attempts to introduce into the policy practice of the EU the "highly dangerous concept" of a "*de facto* administering power" (an aspect which, interestingly, has analogies with the East Timor situation in the past) as opposed to a *de jure* administering Power as recognized in UN practice. He views such a so-called "*de facto* administering Power" as merely being an "occupying power" with

[64] Shelley, *supra*, n.22, at p.18.

[65] *ibid*.

[66] See opinion at pp.7, 8.

[67] See P. San Martin, "EU-Morocco Fisheries Agreement: the Unforeseen Consequences of a Very Dangerous Turn": http://www.gees.org.articulo/2601, at p.2.

no rights over the occupied territory[68]. The basic drift of such a critique thus seems to be to the effect that entering into such a multilateral treaty with an illegal occupant of a non-self-governing entity comes close to according it *de jure* recognition there despite the above-acknowledged reference to Western Sahara being a non-self-governing territory. Thus this critic opines that that the Agreement's formal endorsement by the EU may set a bad precedent for the future: as it implies that the EU may recognize "all non-sovereign and non *de jure* actors ... as legitimate parties with which to negotiate and sign agreements for the exploitation of natural resources in the areas that fall under the control of such non-sovereign and non-*de jure* but *de facto* administrators".

Such legal concerns were reflected in certain sectors of the EU at the time of the treaty negotiations and its conclusion. Several MEPs, for example, were troubled by the *implicit inclusion* of Western Saharan waters within the Agreement on the basis that the grant to the EU fishing fleet of access to waters south of the 27.4° line would break international commitments. Such fears are justified on a close reading of the 2007 Agreement, as in Appendix 4 the "Limits of the Moroccan Fishing Zones" have their various co-ordinates spelt out; and several of them apply generally below (*i.e.*, "south of") 30° 40', or of 29° 00' taking in *Western Sahara* waters. Because of this, POLISARIO launched an international campaign opposing the Agreement.[69] Even the EU Fisheries Committee of the EU Parliament in May 2006, whilst approving the Agreement, proposed several amendments; including:

- an insistence that any EU financial contribution under the treaty "should also be used for the development of coastal populations living on fishing in Morocco *and Western Sahara*";[70]
- "an annual report on the implementation of the Agreement";[71]

[68] *ibid.*, Note that this reference to "occupying power" reflects the basic emphasis also of the UN Corell opinion, *supra* n.16.

[69] Thus a Spanish Law professor, Carlos Ruiz Miguel, published a critique entitled "Is the EU-Morocco fishing agreement an attempt by Spain to legalise Moroccan occupation of the Western Sahara?" cited in the "EU-Morocco Fisheries Agreement: The Unforeseen Consequences of a Very Dangerous Turn" by Pablo San Martin, 13 June 2006 (available on http://www.gees.org/articulo/2601)(emphasis added). *Cf.* Irish concerns as expressed in the Dáil in 2006 "about the possible implications for the overall issue of the status of Western Sahara and regarding the exploitation of the resources of the Saharan people", in response to which the EU Commission "undertook to ensure that the [partnership] Agreement would not compromise the issue of status, and would reflect exactly the terms in relation to territorial extent contained in previous Fisheries Agreements between the EU and Morocco": *Dáil Debates*, Vol. 620, Col. 1259.

[70] Amendment 1, May 16th, 2006. See hhp:www.europarl.europa.eu/sides/getDoc.do?pubRef. (emphasis added).

[71] Amendment 3a.

- approval of the Agreement "subject to its implementation in accordance with international law";[72]
- that in the event of evidence that the use to which the Agreement is being put "is in contravention of international obligations, the Commission shall take immediate steps to suspend the Agreement" — an obvious reference to the relationship between Morocco and its control over the waters of Western Sahara.[73]

Despite such *caveats*, on 22 May 2006, the Agreement was duly endorsed by the EU Fisheries Ministers and ratified by the EU on 29 May 2006.

Significantly, the draft Agreement upset some EU *Member States*. Sweden was in particular of the view that waters off Western Sahara should not be included in the EU agreement.[74] As a Swedish EU Delegation statement said at the time "Western Sahara is not part of the territory of Morocco under international law and a process is under way to find a just, lasting and mutually accepted political solution to the conflict".[75] The agreement also caused similar concern to others such as Ireland (which, as will be seen, ultimately made a Declaration before the EU Council), Finland and the Netherlands, all of which asked for close scrutiny to be kept on the Agreement. As a past backdrop to this, reportedly POLISARIO and its supporters had been seeking to counter Moroccan exploitation of the waters of Western Sahara by including the threat of legal action against the EU if the fishery agreement was implemented.[76]

The Irish "Declaration" was, according to statements in the Dail, "made to the [EU]Council".[77] It indicated that Ireland supported the conclusion of the Agreement "on the basis that it does not prejudice the long-standing position of the EU on the status of Western Sahara"(*i.e.*, the right to self-determination); that it saw as important the Joint Committee set up under the treaty (Art. 10) as supposedly ensuring that "the Agreement is implemented to the benefit of all the people concerned and in accordance with the principles

[72] Amendment 3 to Art.1, para 1.
[73] Amendment 6 to Art.3(1)(b).
[74] See Scholdtz & Wrange, *supra* n.15, at p.23.
[75] See "Western Sahara is not a part of the territory of Morocco": BBC News: 22/5/06 (http://news.bbc.co.uk/go/pr/fr/-2/hi/europe/50006562).
[76] Shelley, *supra* n.22, at p.20.
[77] Accordingly it was seemingly not appended to the treaty itself. See *Dáil Debates*, Vol.620, Col.1259.

of international law".[78] Lastly, Ireland interpreted the advice of the EU's legal service as being "that the agreement does not entail a *de jure* recognition of Morocco's legal rights in respect of the [Western Sahara] area". Aspects of this Irish view will be analysed in the conclusion below.

(b) Oil and Hydrocarbons Contracts

In 2001, Morocco announced that it had granted so-called "réconnaissance licences" to French company Total and US company Kerr McGee du Maroc Ltd[79] for evaluation activities off-shore from Western Sahara, with standard options for continuation beyond 12 months and an option for future oil contracts. Total dropped out of the picture largely due, it seems, to external pressures.[80] So it remains to be seen whether the remaining contractor, Kerr McGee, will graduate from a 'réconnaissance' licence to a full exploration licence. It was the conclusion of agreements between these two contractors and Morocco that prompted the request of the UN legal opinion mentioned above[81] — the Corell opinion. This was requested by the UN SC in November 2001 on the question of the "legality in the context of international law, including relevant resolutions of the [SC and the GA of the UN], and agreements concerning Western Sahara of actions allegedly taken by the Moroccan authorities consisting in the offering and signing of contracts with foreign companies for the exploration of mineral resources in Western Sahara".[82]

Worldwide Recognition Policy regarding East Timor and Western Sahara

Australia

In the case of East Timor, the most interesting "third State" situation was respecting Australia. In its pleadings in the *East Timor* case, Australia had

78 In fact an analysis of Art.10 of the Agreement makes no direct reference to such *international legal* concerns, referring, for example, more broadly, as in para 1(a) and (d) (respectively) to supervision of the implementation, interpretation and smooth operation of the application of the Agreement and acting as a forum for "settlement of any disputes". It is noteworthy that under the Agreement, Irish vessels were allocated 2,500 tonnes of pelagic fish *per annum* (*Dáil Debates*, Vol.621, Col.1766). In the Dail, an official reply at the time expressed the pious hope that it was "essential that the Joint Committee make use of all instruments under the Agreement to ensure that the Agreement is implemented to the benefit of all the people concerned and in accordance with the principles of international law: *Dáil Debates*, Vol.621, Col.1766.

79 Shelley, *ibid.*, at p.18.

80 See generally *ibid.*, at p.19 ("would concern about a concerted campaign in Europe and beyond keep oil companies away from [the waters of the Western Sahara]?").

81 See para 2 of the Corell opinion, *supra* n.16.

82 *ibid.*

constantly reiterated the *reality* of the Indonesian take over of East Timor; so that in 1978, Australia *de facto* recognised the incorporation.[83] In so doing it claimed that Australian "*policy* has done no more than recognise the continuing reality of Indonesia's control of East Timor [being *de facto* part of Indonesia]"; although it remained "critical of the means by which was brought about it".[84] This reflected a constant theme in the Australian pleadings in that case that it nonetheless recognised the right of the East Timorese to self-determination. Furthermore, Australia admitted that as it perceived that by 1978 "more states recognised that East Timor had become part of Indonesia", it had "joined those voting against the resolution"[85] of the General Assembly.[86]

As is well known, Australian recognition policy went still further the shortly after grant of the *de facto* recognition. For, in 1979, *de jure* recognition to the Indonesian takeover was given by Australia when entering into negotiations for the Timor Gap delimitation treaty. This was confirmed in 1985.[87] In so doing Australia appeared at the time to have gone further than any other State.[88] It may be asked why Australia felt it necessary to take this further step, which as the Portuguese pleadings emphasized in the *East Timor* case, seemed to be a contradiction in terms to its claimed recognition of the right of East Timor to self-determination. Could not at least a minimalist recognition procedure have been used in such a situation, such as mere *de facto* recognition?[89] Herein lies the nub of the Australian legal dilemma, which allegedly was never satisfactorily explained away in the pleading (though see further below), as indeed Judge Weeramantry pointed out in his Dissenting Opinion.[90] The Australian attitude here has been aptly likened to saying when shooting someone, that you "recognise their right to live".[91]

Additionally, the repeated Australian argument in the case that its recognition of Indonesian sovereignty over East Timor did not involve denial of its status as a "non-self-governing territory", ill fitted with its UN voting record on GA

---

[83] See the statement of the Australian Minister for Foreign Affairs on 20 January 1978 (set out in Counter-Memorial; Annex 221 at p.A69).

[84] See Counter-Memorial, at p.29, para 68.

[85] *ibid.*, at p.53, para 123.

[86] Res.33/ 39, 13 December 1978.

[87] See *e.g.*, Australian Hansard, 11 December 1991.

[88] See Judge Weeramantry in the *East Timor* case, Dissenting Opinion, at p.51.

[89] See Portuguese argument in CR 95/12 at p.27.

[90] At p.201. He noted the "[t]he inconsistency between Australia's stated position and its practical actions over self-determination for East Timor".

[91] Quoted by Portugal's counsel in CR 95/12 at p.11.

resolutions on East Timor, *i.e.*, its voting *against* resolutions which; *inter alia,* recognised the East Timorese right to self-determination.[92]

In fact there is only isolated evidence in the pleadings in the *East Timor* case which seems to explain the possible reason for Australian progression to *de jure* recognition; namely, that without this acknowledgment (*i.e.*, of the reality of power in East Timor), Australia would not have been in a position to make the arrangements contained in the treaty and that as a practical matter it could not "have avoided the decision to recognise Indonesia" if it were to secure its economic rights in the Timor Gap.[93] It seems, therefore, that *de jure* recognition was the price demanded by Indonesia for agreeing to the delimitation treaty.

This situation has a precedent in the Western Saharan situation, as in a draft 1977 fisheries agreement between Spain and Morocco, Morocco seemingly decided not to ratify the treaty[94] because Spain was unwilling to state explicitly "that the treaty fishery waters covered those off the disputed territory of Western Sahara".[95] The Portuguese pleadings in the *East Timor* case acknowledged that a maritime delimitation agreement deals with what is effectively a vital sovereign right — namely title to resources — as opposed to more day-to-day issues *i.e.,* "human necessities", which may be given cognisance to without the full panoply of recognition — *e.g.*, recognition of divorces or matters of taxation.[96] However, Portugal seemed rightly to have argued in the case that the conduct of Australia was distinguishable from that of *many other States, which had entered into treaties with Indonesia*, because, as seen, Australia had recognised *de jure* the incorporation of East Timor into Indonesia, whereas other States, while dealing with Indonesia in respect of the territory of East Timor, had *not* used the phrase "*de jure*" in their agreements.[97]

The Australian riposte[98] to this at the time was weak and controversial in law: namely that in international law, recognition produces the same effect, whether

---

[92] See CR 95 /2 at p.30.

[93] Counter-Memorial, at p.158, para 354. This was also the Portuguese assessment of the situation: see CR 95/4 at p.72. The justification offered by Australia was based on geographical proximity: see Rejoinder, p.28, para 51; and *infra*, n.287 and accompanying text.

[94] See CR 95/10 at p.8

[95] See *ibid.*, at pp.9/10 where three reasons are given for this; and where Australia claimed, the possible illegality of recognition was stronger in that situation than in the case of East Timor.

[96] See CR 95/5 at p.13.

[97] Rejoinder, p.127, para 226. See also CR 95/5 at p.10.

[98] Rejoinder, para 226, p.127.

expressed as *de jure* or *de facto*, or merely implied. Such a contention is highly disputable. For to accord *de jure* recognition usually implies the ultimate seal of approval on a state of affairs — as Judge Weerarnantry put it in the *East Timor* case, the "highest level" of recognition:[99] as it indicates in the eyes of the bestower that no other entity has better title to the territory.[100] Despite this, Australia argued weakly in the case that "use of the expression *de jure* recognition ... certainly does not imply that the recognising State considers that the means by which the situation was originally brought about was legal, nor that it approves of the present situation"[101] and that it would only have recognised the "legitimacy of the means" if that was its "express or implied intention".[102] This attitude has shades of what has more recently happened through the 2007 EU fisheries agreement with Morocco.

The Australian argument in the *East Timor* case sought, then, to downgrade the difference between *de facto* and *de jure* recognition. For example, in its Rejoinder[103] Australia alleged that whether the large number of states recognising the reality of Indonesian control was "expressed as a situation existing *de jure de facto* or only implicitly", did " not matter"; and that the "distinction in the nature of the recognition [was] irrelevant for present purposes". However, as indicated above, *de jure* recognition (as opposed to *de facto* recognition) implies legitimacy of means. This was seemingly the opinion of Judge Weeramantry in the case,[104] who stressed that the delimitation treaty "expressly" described East Timor as an "Indonesian province".[105] As he pointed out[106] Australia had "gone beyond that [*i.e.*, granting *de facto* recognition] to what appears to be an unreserved *de jure* recognition of Indonesia's rights over East Timor", added to which the preamble to the treaty recited that Australia and Indonesia were "[d]etermined to cooperate further for the mutual benefit of their peoples in the development of the resources

---

99 Dissenting Opinion, at p.204.

100 *Cf. e.g.*, the past recognition practice in respect of the Baltic states, where many countries seem to have expressly withheld *de jure* recognition of the USSR takeover in 1939 as a sign of their disapproval of the forcible incorporation, but still, in some cases at least, accorded *de facto* recognition.

101 Rejoinder, p.128, para 226.

102 *ibid.*, at p.129, para 226. See the Portuguese observation in CR 95/4 at p.59 that *de jure* recognition was obviously an "embarrassment to Australia" which referred to it only twice in its Counter-Memorial "as though in passing"; and (at p.60) that in its Rejoinder, it had seemingly sought to "transform retrospectively the *de jure* recognition into .... a *de facto* recognition".

103 *ibid.*, at p.28, para 50.

104 *Supra* fn.13, at p.199.

105 See also *ibid.*, at p.202.

106 *ibid.*, at p.200.

…".[107] He even implied there may be gradations of *de jure* recognition by adding that "[s]uch an unreserved recognition of Indonesia s sovereignty over East Timor in an important treaty is perhaps one of the highest forms of *de jure* recognition".[108]

Viewpoint on Recognition of Other States Respecting East Timor

The pleadings and Dissenting Opinions in the *East Timor* case contained interesting discussion over the extent to which third States may have previously recognized the Indonesian take-over in East Timor. By 1982 Indonesia had alleged at the UN that "[o]nly about 30 *per cent* of all [UN] members continue[d] to question East Timor's integration with Indonesia" and that the numbers of same supporting the UN resolutions on East Timor had "steadily diminished".[109] In its Counter Memorial and Rejoinder in the case, Australia made great play of the extent of recognition in this regard, even implying that many States had tried in their statements to disguise their intent to recognize Indonesian sovereignty there. There is no doubt that, on close analysis, many of such statements make no explicit reference to "recognition" of the situation by the State concerned, as has been detailed elsewhere by this writer.[110] For example, a number of States claimed to have simply accepted the "reality of the incorporation of East Timor, but without expressing any view whether the people of East Timor have already exercised their right to self-determination".[111]

Only Judge Skubiszewski was to address the recognition problem in the *East Timor* case in any detail, as he was sceptical about the Australian assessment of world recognition of the Indonesian take-over, finding the group of supposedly recognizing States was small (in fact consisting of mostly third world States or States proximate to Indonesia). He thus referred to alleged recognition by the phrase "in one way or another". As he explained, the reason he had not endorsed all the States referred to by Australia as "accepting the incorporation" or recognizing "the reality of Indonesian control" was because he doubted on proper examination that the statements "could be classified under the rubric of recognition".[112]

---

[107] *ibid.*, at p.201. See also *ibid.*, at p.202.
[108] *ibid.*, at p.204.
[109] Cited in the Australian Counter-Memorial, at p.61, para 140.
[110] "The International Recognition Position regarding the Purported Incorporation of East Timor into Indonesia" in the book published by IPJET in 1998 entitled *The East Timor Problem and the Role of Europe*, ed. P. Pinto Leite, pp.211–221.
[111] *ibid.*, at p.214.
[112] See his Dissenting Opinion, *supra* n.13 at para 26.

Recognition and Western Sahara

In the case of Western Sahara, the UN S-G has, in the past, stated that "no member of the [UN] has recognized [Moroccan] sovereignty "over Western Sahara.[113] An analysis of the reaction of third States to the status of the territory shows that some like Ireland and the UK effectively recognize no authority there[114] or others recognize Morocco's administration rather than sovereignty over Western Sahara, such as the USA,[115] which has nonetheless taken some positive steps to avoid implied recognition, such as its refusal to include Western Sahara in its free trade agreement with Morocco.[116]

The UN itself, whilst, as seen, recognizing Morocco and POLISARIO as the two parties involved in the dispute, has never (beyond *de facto* dealings through MINURSO there) recognized the sovereignty of either the Saharawi Republic (although recognized by the OAU) or Morocco over the whole territory. It is interesting in this somewhat analogous situation that the UN did use somewhat differing terminology to that in the case of East Timor; *e.g.*, stating that Morocco and Polisario alone were the "two parties to the conflict".[117] Additionally, there have been no situations arising here analogous to those in the case of East Timor where several States — particularly those nearest Indonesia — were to announce that the East Timorese had exercised self-determination: conduct which Australia claimed in the *East Timor* case amounted to an "unqualified recognition of Indonesian sovereignty",[118] and amounting to *de jure* recognition of Indonesian sovereignty there (which allegedly went beyond the recognition accorded by itself[119]).

It has been validly pointed out that ironically Indonesia had greater success diplomatically regarding its territorial expansion than has Morocco; for 75 countries have recognized an independent Western Sahara ('Saharwi Arab Democratic Republic'); and it has obtained full membership of the OAU[120]

---

[113] See UN Doc.S/2006/249.

[114] See (for Ireland) 373 *Dáil Debates*, Cols.915–916 and for the UK, see *Hansard* (H.C.). Vol.119, Col.415; and R. White, "Recognition of States and Diplomatic Relations" (1988) 37 I.C.L.Q. 983 at p.985 ("The UK ... does not recognize the "Sahara Arab Republic" or Moroccan claims to sovereignty...").

[115] See *supra* n.1 at p.6 where S. Zunes contrasts this with the US recognition of "Indonesia's incorporation of East Timor into Indonesia" albeit the US noted that the inhabitants' wishes had not been taken into account.

[116] Cited by Shelley, *supra*, n.22, at p.19.

[117] See the Australian Rejoinder in the *East Timor* case, at p.118, para 212.

[118] Rejoinder, p.25, para 52 and Counter-Memorial, at p.71 *et seq*.

[119] *ibid.*, at pp.125/7, para 225. See also CR95/7, at pp.17/18.

[120] As a result of OAU recognition of the entity, Morocco withdrew from the Organisation in 1982.

(mainly because the Moroccan invasion conflicted with the *uti possideti*s doctrine which has usually held sway to preserve colonial boundaries at all costs). Whereas, by contrast, allegedly only 15 countries recognized an independent East Timor.[121] Despite this, it has been stated in the case of both the purported incorporations of East Timor and Western Sahara that "despite some level of acquiescence by some foreign governments", in both situations the incorporating States "were unable to establish real legitimacy in the eyes of the international community".[122]

Treaties as Evidence of Recognition of Territorial Sovereignty

In the *East Timor* case, Australia relied on treaties, both bilateral or multilateral, made between Indonesia and other States, to show at least implicit recognition of Indonesian sovereignty in East Timor,[123] some of which, unlike in the case of those negotiated with Morocco such as the EU Partnership Agreement of 2007, did make specific reference to the subjugated territory (here East Timor) as such in them.[124] Certainly, in these treaties with Indonesia, there was no accompanying declaration of "non-recognition" stated at the time of their conclusion, as, for example, has recently happened in the case of Ireland and the EU Fisheries Partnership treaty with Morocco.[125]

In the *East Timor* case, the ICJ mentioned in general terms "treaties capable of application to East Timor, but which do not include any reservation in regard to that Territory".[126] Such judicial reference hints at the possibility of *implied recognition* of territorial aggrandisement by such means. Certainly Australia in the case made the valid point that several bilateral treaties were "significant evidence" of recognition of Indonesian sovereignty in East Timor,[127] especially as such States had then accepted a provision in such treaties d*efining the territory of Indonesia in a way which included East Timor*.[128] Australia particularly

[121] See Zunes, *supra*, n.1 at p.6.
[122] *ibid.*, at pp.32, 33.
[123] See its Rejoinder, at p.25, para 46.
[124] See above n.105. See also, *e.g.*, the Australian Counter Memorial at p.72, para 64.
[125] See above n.77; and *cf.* Australia's Counter-Memorial in the *East Timor* case at p.86, para 176 ("no State that has diplomatic or consular relations with Indonesia has qualified the terms of its diplomatic recognition in any way to take account of the dispute … over East Timor"). See generally C.R. Symmons, "The International Recognition Position regarding the Purported Incorporation of East Timor into Indonesia" in P. Pinto Leite (ed.) *The East Timor Problem and the Role of Europe*, pp.211–218.
[126] Judgment, *supra* n.13, at para 32.
[127] See Counter-Memorial, at p.73.
[128] Rejoinder, at p.72, para 174.

referred to bilateral double taxation treaties in this context entered into by some 31 States with Indonesia *since 1976* (the date of the Indonesian invasion of East Timor), most of which had a territorial application clause which allegedly "necessarily incorporate[d] the territory of East Timor as part of Indonesia" (referring to the "territory .... of Indonesia *as defined in its law*"[129]). By way of contrast, tax treaties negotiated *before 1976* had simply referred to "the Territory of Indonesia".[130]

Portugal argued in the case that such revised wording was adopted to avoid any effect on the international plane;[131] but more realistically it seems that insertion of the italicised wording was insisted on by Indonesia in a standardised form: so that third States were forced to accept the formulation as the price for conclusion of such treaties. Even more territorially specific was, of course, the preamble in the Timor Gap treaty which Australia admitted it was forced to accept as a from of *de jure* recognition of the East Timor's incorporation[132] ("Indonesian Province of East Timor"). Indeed Judge Skubiszewski in his *Dissenting Opinion* in the *East Timor* case expressly downplayed the abovementioned standardized wording in the double taxation treaties on the basis that they were not referring "explicitly to East Timor", so having no effect on the matter of recognition.[133] The latter interpretation is reinforced by the fact that several States making such double taxation agreements, particularly from the EU (such as Sweden), explicitly asserted that they had given no implied recognition of such Indonesian sovereignty, even on a *de facto* basis.[134] As will be later concluded, this may be a very different situation to, for example, a fisheries agreement which *by its very nature* takes in the waters of a territory denied self-determination, as appears to be the case, as seen, of the recent EU fisheries agreement with Morocco where indeed the treaty was *intended* to so apply to Western Saharan waters.

Australia was also in its pleadings in the *East Timor* case to allege implied recognition from several *multilateral* treaties to which Indonesia was a party since 1976 (some 41 in all). These *might* have provoked States which had not

[129] See Counter-Memorial, at p.72, para 165 (emphasis added).
[130] Emphasis added. See Counter-Memorial, at p.72, para 165.
[131] Rejoinder, at p.29, para 54. *Cf.* the more specific treaty with Canada (see Counter-Memorial, p.73, para 165) which contained the words "the territory of Indonesia *as defined in its laws* and parts of the continental shelf and adjacent seas, *over which .... Indonesia has sovereignty, sovereign rights, or other rights in accordance with international law*" (emphasis added).
[132] See Counter Memorial, at p.158, para 354.
[133] Dissenting Opinion, at para 122.
[134] See CR 95/4 at p.64.

recognized the Indonesian take-over of East Timor to lodge some protest insofar as they "purport[ed] to include East Timor in the area of territorial application".[135] However, implied recognition from negotiation of a *bilateral* treaty may be more easily found in international law. It is interesting that Portugal in the case did proffer the analogous but differing situation of the *earlier* EU fisheries agreement with Morocco[136] which might, on one view, have implied Moroccan sovereignty in Western Sahara, but which *allegedly* did not do so because the treaty wording did not expressly mention "Western Sahara"; nor did it qualify the territory as a "Moroccan Province" in a situation where the EU is on record as not recognizing integration of that territory into Morocco.[137] Interestingly, Australia in the case sought to prove that such a multilateral agreement *did* imply EU recognition of Moroccan expanded sovereignty as it was in fact *intended*, as seen, to also apply to Western Saharan waters.[138] As will be later concluded, this seems to be a necessary legal interpretation of the latter situation.

Duties of Non-Recognition respecting Denial of Self-Determination to a Peoples or of Benefits thereto of Natural Resources in their Territory

(a) Where Territory is Acquired by Forcible Means

Where a state has, through an act of aggression or illegal force, annexed a piece of territory, it is now well-established in international law that there is a duty on other States not to recognise such illegal territorial aggrandisement. Such a doctrine dates back to the famous Stimson doctrine under the League of Nations and has been strengthened by certain UN resolutions (see below). Some of the past academic legal comment in respect of the East Timor situation has concentrated on duties of non-recognition in such circumstances.[139] Though in the case of the Western Sahara situation the legal emphasis seems to have been on a narrower issue than that of recognition as such: namely on ensuring that international efforts deny an illegal occupier's

[135] Counter-Memorial, at p.73, para 167. However, Australia put forward this aspect with some hesitation: see its Rejoinder, p.29, para 53.

[136] See above n.64.

[137] See Portuguese oral argument pleadings in the case: CR 95/12 at p.78.

[138] See *ibid.*, CR 95/9 at pp.86/87.

[139] See, *e.g.*, L. Hannikainen, "The Case of East Timor from A Perspective of *Jus Cogens*", *International Law and the Question of East Timor,* IPJET/Catholic Institute for International Relations, UK, 103, at pp.112/3, who argues that "[m]ost States *de facto* acquiescing in Indonesia's annexation without protests [had] avoided giving official recognition".

rights to the natural resources of the occupied territory.[140] In more recent times, the United Nations itself has through the General Assembly — or more importantly through the Security Council — prescribed such a duty of non-recognition in unambiguous terms in particular cases.[141] Furthermore, the weapon of non-recognition may be implicitly contained in the sanctions article, Article 41, in such circumstances, which is not exhaustive in its stated measures not involving armed force.[142]

In its pleadings in the *East Timor* case, Portugal did list, as one of several reasons why Australia's recognition was unlawful, not only "military action" by Indonesia which the UN had "deplored",[143] but also the principle that non-recognition in such circumstances was confirmed by State practice.[144] Judge Skubiszewski it was who there related the history of the "policy" of non-recognition in such instances. He concluded with the following important viewpoint:[145]

> [The rule or principle of non-recognition] may be said to be at present in the course of possibly reaching a stage where it would share in the nature of the principle of which it is a corollary, *i.e.*, the principle of the non-use of force. In that hypothesis non-recognition would acquire the rank of a peremptory norm of that law (*ius cogens*). But that is a future development which is uncertain and has still to happen.
> The Friendly Relations Declaration correctly states the law on the subject: 'No territorial acquisition resulting from the threat or use of force shall be recognised as legal'... The rule is self-executory.

The reference here to the "non-use" of force[146] — including, it seems, its corollary as to non-recognition of the fruits of the use of force (particularly relevant to the question of the natural resources of the occupied territory) — as a possible rule of *ius cogens* may, as will be seen, be interpreted as further developing a rule of non-recognition in customary international law in favour of peoples denied self-determination through use of force.[147]

---

[140] See below nn.147 and 279 and *supra,* n.14 and accompanying texts.
[141] See Australia's Counter-Memorial in the *East Timor* case, at p.155, contrasting the situations of Rhodesia etc.
[142] See Portuguese oral argument: CR 95/4, at para 40.
[143] See Reply, at p.172.
[144] See CR 95/12 at pp.50/51.
[145] Dissenting Opinion, at para 125.
[146] *Cf. Nicaragua v US* (1986) ICJ Rep.14, at para 190.
[147] See L. Hannikainen, *supra* n.139, at p.112, where he argues that *ius cogens* can apply beyond the realm of treaty law to invalidate, *e.g.*, an unlawful title gained by aggressive force or even obstruction of a people's right to self-determination; and below.

Some academic commentators might, however, argue, like Australia in the *East Timor* case,[148] that neither the SC nor the GA even specifically condemned the use of force by Indonesia in the East Timor situation. The same can be said of the Moroccan take-over of Western Sahara. As has been pertinently pointed out, for political reasons in both cases, the Security Council could only pass "relatively weak" resolutions deploring the invasions and calling for withdrawal of invading forces,[149] whilst in both cases reaffirming the right of self-determination, as seen.

Objectively viewed, however, the Indonesian annexation of East Timor did constitute a conquest *manu militari i.e.*, by use of force.[150] And the UN resolutions — both of the GA and SC — seemed to impliedly confirm this;[151] for example, the illegality of the use of force may have been assumed by the international calls therein for withdrawal of Indonesian forces.[152]

Unfortunately because of the way the Portuguese pleadings were drafted in the *East Timor* case (in an attempt to eliminate any direct consideration by the Court of the conduct of Indonesia — as seen using the terminology of "disregard" rather than non-recognition as such),[153] the Portuguese case did not stand "upon the obligation of non-recognition of situations resulting from the unlawful use of force as such".[154] Accordingly, the Court's majority finding (as mentioned above applying the *Monetary Gold* case) led to no substantive discussion in the Court's judgment on the legality of Indonesia's initial take-over in East Timor — which most legal observers[155] and indeed even Australia[156] — have viewed as being forcibly carried out contrary to international law.

---

148 See *e.g.*, Counter-Memorial, at para 332, p.149; also *ibid.*, at p.151 para 338; and Rejoinder, at p.88 and *id*, at p.143, para 255 (though Australia admitted that there was the preamble "deploring the intervention of the armed forces").

149 See Zunes *supra* n.1 at p.24.

150 *Cf. e.g.*, C. Chinkin, "Australia and East Timor in International Law", *op.cit. supra* n.110, at pp. 269, 280. *Cf.* the Portuguese argument (referred to in Rejoinder, at p.143, para 255) that the SC had "already established the illegality" in its resolutions.

151 See Portuguese oral argument in the *East Timor* case: CR 95/4 at p.18.

152 See C. Chinkin, *supra* n.150, at p.282.

153 See *supra* n.52 and accompanying text.

154 Reply, at p.146, para 6.30.

155 See, *e.g.*, R. Clark, "The De-Colonisation of East Timor and the UN Norms on Determination and Aggression", *op.cit. supra* n.110, at p.65.

156 See, *e.g.*, CR 95/9, at p.49, para 59 ("In 1975 the people of East Timor involuntarily exchanged Portuguese 'dominatio.... for the control of Indonesia"). However, Australia constantly emphasised the fact that its position as a "third State" was very different from that of Indonesia (Rejoinder, at p.51, para 103); and that it was not accused of any illegality in relation to Indonesia's intervention in East Timor (Counter-Memorial, at p.7, para 15).

However, there were some signs that even the majority judgment of the ICJ in the case may have implicitly confirmed the illegality of the Indonesian action.[157] Had the case proceeded on the merits,[158] no doubt this illegality would have been confirmed by the Court as well as a concomitant duty on third States not to recognise such a neo-colonialist incorporation. As Judge Skubiszewski commented:[159] "... [T]he Court preferred not to consider the problem of the non-recognition of a situation, treaty or arrangement which came into being by means contrary to 'the threat or use of force against the territorial integrity or political independence of any State ...' ".

Undoubtedly, in regard to a forcible annexation of territory, where the Security Council has (as in several instances) prescribed *non-recognition* of the annexation in a mandatory resolution,[160] all States would be bound to adopt such a policy vis-á-vis that territory, a matter which even Australia appears to have conceded in its pleadings in the *East Timor* case.[161] For at the very least, the normally discretionary nature of recognition as regards legality of territorial possession would here be subject to the law of the Charter. However, Australia's denial in the case that any non-recognition duty could arise *independently* of this[162] seems to have constituted special pleading of a very specious kind, although it is plainly the case that no special recommendation relating to non-recognition was made either by the Security Council[163] *or the General Assembly*[164] concerning East Timor. This point, emphasised at the very beginning of the Australian pleadings in the *East Timor* case,[165] was constantly repeated thereafter: and it undoubtedly helped Australia's attempt to justify its progressive recognition of Indonesian sovereignty in East Timor from *de facto* to *de jure*.[166]

---

157 See the Dissenting Opinion of Judge Skubiszewski (at para 73) who referred to the ICJ's judgment on this in paras 13 & 14.
158 See, *e.g.*, the Separate Opinion of Judge Shahabuddeen, who opined (at p.123) that had the case gone to the merits, the Court might have had to decide whether "Indonesia engaged international responsibility which disqualified it from acquiring that power under general international law".
159 At para 124, p.29.
160 See, *e.g.*, note by C. Chinkin in (1996) 45 I.C.L.Q., 712, at pp.713/714, fn. 11.
161 See Counter-Memorial, p.158, para 353.
162 See, *e.g.*, Judge Skubiszewski, Dissenting Opinion, at para 127.
163 See C. Chinkin, *supra* n.150 at p.275.
164 See *e.g.*, L. Hannikainen, *supra* n.139, at p.112.
165 See, *e.g.*, Counter-Memorial, at p.8. para 19.
166 See C. Chinkin, *op.cit. supra* n.150, at p.279.

Many international lawyers take the view that a UN prescription is unnecessary for a non-recognition duty to arise in such circumstances:[167] and this viewpoint receives a further boost in the *East Timor* case where Judge Skubiszewski, having firmly ruled out practical considerations as relieving a State of a non-recognition duty, made the following important statement:[168]

> While recognition of States or Governments is still a free act, it is not so with regard to the irregular acquisition of territory: here the discretionary nature of the act [relating to recognition] has been changed by the rule on the prohibition of the threat or use of force. As indicated above (para 125) the rule of non-recognition operates in a self-executory way. To be operative it does not need to be repeated by the United Nations or other international organisations. Consequently, the absence of such a direction on the part of an international organisation does not relieve any State from the duty of non-recognition. Nor does the absence of 'collective sanction' have that effect.

It may be comparatively noted that in the case of Western Sahara there is again no background of SC mandatory resolution relating to the take-over of the Territory by Morocco nor, of course, any decree of sanctions.[169]

Undoubtedly, then, the trend of customary international law may have been strengthened by such judicial analysis in developing an independent and self-executing non-recognition rule as regards territorial gains resulting from an obvious act of aggression or use of force, if only as a necessary interpretation of the UN Charter[170] and it makes no difference that the territory acquired was still in the throes of self-determination rather than fully sovereign.[171] It is an unfortunate fact, however, that where an already-independent State is annexed (*e.g.*, Kuwait), such action is more likely to be branded as aggression or a

---

167 See, *e.g.*, S. Marks, "Kuwait and East Timor: a Brief Study in Contrast" *op.cit supra* n.110, at pp.174, 178; C. Chinkin, *supra* n.150 at p.281; also R. Clark, "The Substance of the *East Timor* Case" in *op.cit. supra* n.110, at pp.243, 249 (the duty of non-recognition "simply arises from the general law").

168 At paras 129, 130 (emphasis added).

169 See above n.39.

170 Such an obligation may be implicit in the more general UN prescriptions against the use of force, most particularly Article 2(4) of the UN Charter: see C. Chinkin, *op.cit. supra*, n.150, at p.280.

171 Compare the Iraqi invasion of independent Kuwait, though in neither case was the use of force "internal to one State": see S. Marks, *op.cit. supra*, n.167, at pp.175 & 176. It was, as Professor R. Clark puts it, a use of force "against another territorial entity": *op.cit. supra* n.167, at p.93. Australia, incidentally, never recognised FRETILIN's unilateral declaration of independence at the end of 1970: see Counter-Memorial, at p.26, para 59.

breach of the peace by the UN[172]: whereas the "language of decolonization" rather than prohibition of use of force, may be seen as more appropriate in the case on a non-self-governing territory.[173]

Even Australia appears, in the *East Timor* case, to have accepted in principle[174] — in its later pleading, at any rate — that "recognition must not be exercised in a way that contravenes" an international obligation; and it cited Res. 2625 of the GA — which famously states that "[n]o territorial acquisition resulting from the threat or use of force shall be recognised as legal" — as "[o]ne such obligation under *customary international law*". However, it queried the content insofar as dealing with the "factual consequences" of such territorial acquisition were concerned;[175] and produced a semantic argument that the customary rule did not refer to this ("it does not follow that States are under a duty in perpetuity never to recognise the consequences of that illegal acquisition").[176] Hence came Australian emphasis again on the necessity of *binding* SC resolutions on recognition as this allegedly answered the question as to what attitude States are to "adopt".[177]

It is arguable, however, that just as there can be no 'historical consolidation' of such illegal title[178] (even where, as in the case of East Timor, the UN organs might have remained silent on an issue for a considerable time — in that case effectively since 1982), so also there can be no relaxation of the non-recognition rule on this basis; particularly where there has been no intended abandonment, as in the case of East Timor at least, by the former sovereign.[179] Australia argued otherwise in the *East Timor* case,[180] maintaining that "response from the international community" was allegedly relevant to such recognition issues.[181] Goa, for example, was there cited as an example where ultimately the Indian incorporation of the former Portuguese colony was recognised by the international community, albeit at different times.[182] And

[172] See the Portuguese oral argument in the *East Timor* case: CR 95/4, at p.29, para 37, and at p.41 ("military intervention" rather than "aggression").
[173] See the Portuguese argument, *ibid.*, at p.31, para 44.
[174] Rejoinder, at p.121, para 217 (emphasis added).
[175] Rejoinder, at p.122, para 218.
[176] *ibid.*, at para 219.
[177] See Rejoinder para 221, at p.124.
[178] See C. Chinkin, *op.cit. supra*, n.150, at pp.282–284.
[179] See CR 95/5 at p.15.
[180] See Counter-Memorial. pp.159-1G1
[181] *ibid.*, at p.159.
[182] Rejoinder, at p.125

even Judge Skubiszewski admitted that "the attitude of non-recognition may undergo a change by virtue of a collective decision of the international community".[183] The epithet "collective" here may be seen as important in this regard. In other words, in some circumstances, so many acts of recognition, quite independently of any UN recommendation or decision, may accrue as to effectively legalise the previously illegal situation. However, the same judge was careful to add that "up to [then] nothing of the sort ha[d] happened with regard to East Timor".[184]

(b) Where Territory is Acquired or Retained in Defiance of the Principle of Self-Determination, but where No Obvious Use of Force is Involved

The issue arising here is whether an independent (or related) rule of non-recognition covers broader situations than those considered in (a) above; so as to take in those situations which involve simply an international illegality of some sort[185] — what Portugal might have dubbed in its Reply[186] in the *East Timor* case as situations or actions "which are incompatible with the most basic principles of international law". These situations might, for example, include the breach of a mandate (or trusteeship) obligation as in the Namibian situation[187] (albeit here a UN 'decision' did result from the Security Council) where the ICJ, in the advisory opinion thereon, did in fact use the phrase "an internationally unlawful situation";[188] or, most particularly, as in the East Timor and Western Sahara contexts, a denial of self-determination in a particular territory[189] or abuse of the inhabitants' related right of permanent sovereignty to their natural resources therein[190] by the controlling State of a territory in circumstances that *may not point clearly to an illegal use of force*.

---

[183] Dissenting Opinion, at para 132.

[184] *ibid.*

[185] See, *e.g.*, C. Chinkin; *op.cit. supra* n.150, at p.281 (some "prior illegality under international law").

[186] At p.176, para 6.37. See also, *e.g.*, R. Clark, *supra* n.167, at p.248 who says "Southern Rhodesia, the Bantustans of South Africa and Namibia were all objectionable situations and 'illegal' in different ways". Before the UN, Portugal treated the illegalities arising in East Timor from use of force, on the one hand, and denial of self-determination, on the other, as separable issues; see *e.g.*, its statement to the UN 'Committee of 24' on 8 August, 1991.

[187] See, *e.g.*, G. Simpson, "The Politics of Self Determination in the Case concerning East Timor", *op.cit. supra* n.110, 251, at p.265.

[188] ICI Reports (1971), 16, at p.52, para 112; referred to in the *East Timor* case pleadings: see CR 95/9 at p.53.

[189] See, for example, in the *East Timor* case pleadings, the Australian statement in CR 97/9 at p.36 ("Portugal said that a permanent, imprescriptible obligation of non-recognition arises automatically. for the whole world from a breach of self-determination by any State").

[190] See above n.14 and accompanying text.

For example, there may have been a spurious manipulation of events in a territory to produce an alleged option by that territory for incorporation with an existing State through reliance by the incorporating State on an invitation to intervene[191] and/or a situation similar to a purportedly *civilian* takeover or "green march" (as happened in the case of Western Sahara) where the armed forces of the illegally-acting State are not directly involved, at least initially. Or where, in an existing long-standing colonial situation, the administering State refuses to accede to self-determination (*cf.* South Africa in Namibia[192]); or more controversially still, in the context of a unitary state, where part of its territory opts for secession (insofar as international law may allow) and is denied it — a situation which may loom larger in the future with the wind-down of traditional colonies.

In all these instances, of course, the denial of self-determination leads to an involuntary status which arguably could be caught by the vague phrase in the latter part of Art. 2(4) of the UN Charter concerning at least a "threat of force" in a manner "inconsistent with the purposes of the United Nations". More specifically in the East Timor context, it is also arguable that, in terms of the relevant UN resolutions alone, the SC's call for "all States to co-operate in the realisation of self determination for East Timor", may have contained the implicit requirement not to recognise the rights of a State denying such self-determination.[193]

It is noteworthy that even Judge Skubiszewski in his Dissenting Opinion in the *East Timor* case used the vague phrase "irregular acquisition" of territory rather than a more forthright expression;[194] and, indeed, he tended to mention use of force and denial of self-determination in the same breath.[195]

---

[191] See, *e.g.*, the Indonesian argument that in East Timor a valid act of self-determination favouring Indonesia did take place, *inter alia,* for such a reason.

[192] See, in the *East Timor* case pleadings, CR 95/4 at p.34 (the presence of South Africa in Namibia was "initially legal"). Where there is a strained UN perception of the continuing colonial presence (as, *e.g.*, in Mayotte where the UN has affirmed the sovereignty of the Comoros Republic), the duty is less clear. See the Australian argument in the *East Timor* case pleadings (CR 95/10 at pp.ll/12) alleging that even the EU (in OJ No.L263/1) had listed Mayotte as a "collectivité territoriale" of France – allegedly a "decision no less than recognition contrary to the UN position" (*id.*, at p.12). However, this situation was in one important way not truly analogous to that in East Timor or Western Sahara, as there what the UN had prescribed was not 'pure' self-determination, as the Mayotte island peoples themselves wished to maintain the UN-condemned colonial link.

[193] See the pleadings in the *East Timor* case: CR 95/4 at p.24.

[194] Dissenting Opinion, at para 129.

[195] *E.g.*, *ibid.*, at para 133 ("matters pertaining to military invasion, decolonisation and self-determination").

Several academic commentators have in the past argued that a duty of non-recognition may arise *independently*[196] in the more general type of circumstances described above, even where an unlawful use of force is not obviously involved, if only because any other rule would drain the principle of self-determination of all content. However, during the oral pleadings in the *East Timor* case, Australia belatedly referred to the work of the International Law Commission on State Crimes as being (allegedly) the "only international authority for an automatic obligation of recognition in the context of breach of self-determination".[197]

The Australian pleadings in the *East Timor* case understandably played on such uncertainty of international law in this regard, alleging that there is "much that is complex about issues of decolonization";[198] and argued that the international community was not yet agreed even as to basic matters, including the extent to which Indonesia's sovereignty should then be recognised. Nonetheless, even Australia seemed to have accepted there is *some* duty owed by third States towards a territory validly claiming self-determination, even if this falls short of an automatic non-recognition rule as to its illegal occupier. For it admitted that "general principles of international law", including those "concerning recognition" would be relevant here.[199] Australia, however, made much of the fact that in this context Portugal had mentioned "breach of a duty not to disregard or fail to respect .... the right of the people of East Timor" — *i.e.*, a duty (as seen) of alleged "non-méconnaissance" — stressing the vagueness of the content of any such rule; so that, allegedly, without mention

[196] Such as Professor Chinkin. She has argued that "the right of the East Timorese to self-determination...[did] not exist in a vacuum but entail[ed] certain legal consequences for other members of the international community, including the obligation not to act so as to undermine that right" (see *op.cit. supra* n.150, at p.282); see also R. Clark, *supra* n.110, at pp.243, 246; and B. Bowring, "Self-Determination and the Jurisprudence of the ICJ", *op.cit. supra* n.139 at p.158, citing the ICJ's statement relating to Namibia und the illegality of South Africa's presence being opposable to "all states". See also the Dissenting Opinion of Judge Weeramantry, *supra* n.13 at p.194.

[197] See CR 95/9 at p.55.

[198] See Counter-Memorial, at pp.131/2, para 298; and see more generally, *ibid.*, at pp.143–147.

[199] See Rejoinder, at p.120, para 214 (emphasis added). Australia also appears to have conceded that it was "probably true" that a third State which fails to respect the right of a particular peoples to self-determination (at least as specified by UN resolution) might "incur State responsibility": CR 95/8 at p.24. Though note that Australia also argued that there was no express obligation in the UN Charter on individual third States to "promote self-determination in relation to territories over which they individually have no control": CR 95/9 at p.64. *Cf.* Counter-Memorial, at p.146, para 324 (States are "under no more than a general obligation to 'respect' the right of a particular people to self-determination"; and "[t]his does not mean that States are prevented from *dealing with the administering or occupying Power* in relation to the territory" (emphasis added).

of any more "specific obligation", the obligation to respect the right to self-determination would need to be defined in far more detail before it could be "determined in a concrete case whether or not there had been a failure to fulfil that obligation".[200] However, it may be argued that in essence the contents of any such rule lie in the sphere of the over-arching idea of *non-recognition* (as in (a) above), the practical implications of which should be obvious in terms of extent of dealings with the illegal occupant of a territory.

Unfortunately, the terminology used by the dissenting judges supporting the Portuguese case in the *East Timor* case was also somewhat vague on this issue. For example, Judge Weeramantry seemed to stress *positive recognition* duties for third States of a peoples' self-determination rights *rather than duties of non-recognition of the illegal incumbent State*.[201] However, on closer analysis, he seems to have imposed a parallel duty on third States going beyond simple non-recognition. See, for example, his *dictum* that "... in regard to rights so important to contemporary international law, the duty of respect for them [*i.e.*, rights to self-determination and permanent sovereignty over natural resources] extends beyond mere recognition [*sic*], to a duty to abstain from any state action which is incompatible with those rights or which would impair or nullify them"; and a duty above the "level of non-recognition".[202]

Judge Skubiszewski seems to make a similar analysis without direct reference to a situation involving use of force, indicating that international law only "might" protect rights of self-determination *via* a non-recognition duty. He also implied in the case that an act of recognition made in these circumstances will not even necessarily be illegal; merely that it will be invalid and so have no force. As he said:[203]

> Non-recognition might protect, or indeed does protect, the rights of self-determination and to permanent sovereignty over natural resources. Any country has the corresponding duty to respect these rights and no act of recognition can release it from that duty.

It is noteworthy that in this rather cumbersome analysis of third-State duties – influenced no doubt, by the ever-lurking background consideration in the

---

200 Rejoinder, at p.83, para 172. See also *ibid.*, para 171, ("Portugal's analysis of the content of the corresponding duties [to the right of self-determination].... is cursory").

201 See, *e.g.*, his Dissenting Opinion, *supra* n.13, at pp.197 & 208, 209; also L. Scobbie and C. Drew, *supra* n.13, at p.203, fn.˙72.

202 *ibid.*, at p.204 & 209.

203 *ibid.*, at para 131.

case (namely the admission that the Court had not been asked to adjudicate or make a declaration on non-recognition in regard to Indonesian control over East Timor[204]) — he directly refers to a non-recognition duty in respect of rights to permanent sovereignty over natural resources, a matter of particular contemporary relevance to the situation (as seen) in the case of the Western Sahara.

Both Dissenting Opinions in the *East Timor* case may thus be interpreted as laying down third State's duty *via non-recognition* in general terms to keep alive a right of self-determination and indigenous rights to natural resources, quite irrespective of considerations of lack of illegal force; this duty arising in general international law, *even without specific UN prescription*. Indeed, Judge Weeramantry seemed to view the existence of Security Council resolutions on self-determination for East Timor as simply *further obliging* States not to "*de jure*" recognise the "annexation of a non-self-governing territory".[205] As seen above, he spelt out, in the circumstances of the *East Timor* case, how the "act of being party to the Timor Gap Treaty would appear incompatible with recognition of, and respect for, the principle of East Timor's rights to self-determination...", as, *inter alia,* that treaty "expressly recognize[d] East Timor as a province of Indonesia without its people exercising their right".[206]

In this context of self-determination, as mentioned above,[207] even Australia seems to have accepted in the case that, under UN auspices at least (see further below), there may be created "an obligation opposable to all States to refrain from dealing with, or recognising the authorities of a State in control of a territory, whether on account of a denial of self-determination there, or on account of some other illegality",[208] even if this obligation might be less clear-cut than in a situation where obvious illegal use of force has occurred.[209] In the *East Timor* case Australia cited here the 1985 GA resolution on *Western Sahara* as an example of where the GA had "not necessarily prohibited other States from dealing with the State in control of [a] territory" where self-determination has been decreed by the UN[210]: and it instanced this (supposedly

---

[204] *Cf.* above n.24, and accompanying text.
[205] Dissenting Opinion, at p.206.
[206] *ibid.,* at p.212.
[207] See n.199.
[208] Counter-Memorial, at p.159, para 355 (emphasis added).
[209] See, *e.g.*, the regular Australian complaint in the case (*e.g.*, in its Rejoinder, at p.6) that the Portuguese Memorial only spoke of a duty of non-recognition of "situations resulting from the illegal use of force" (emphasis added); also *ibid.*, at p.87, para 179.
[210] *ibid.,* at p.147.

somewhat analogous) situation[211] in an attempt to prove that even EU States have entered into treaty relationships with Morocco in matters which apply to this (illegally) annexed territory.[212]

In this context Australia pointed out[213] that "even though the United Nations rejected the Moroccan claim that the people of Western Sahara had decided in favour of incorporation with Morocco, even though the UN ha[d] been critical of Morocco's presence in the territory, and even though a large number of States have recognised the Saharan Republic, this has *not prevented certain States from having dealings with Morocco as the State in effective control of the territory, in respect of the natural resources of the territory*". Australia cited *e.g.*,[214] the abovementioned 1988 Fisheries Agreement between the EU and Morocco which defined Morocco's fishing zone as the waters over which Morocco had "sovereignty or jurisdiction" — in fact the very same wording which is repeated in the latest EU/Morocco fisheries treaty of 2007. However, it has been argued, as seen, that this geographical reference was more vague than that in the East Timor treaty between Indonesia and Australia, where there was *de jure* recognition of Indonesian sovereignty actually and specifically in respect of *East Timorese territory*. As seen, the EU/Morocco treaty did not refer specifically *to the waters off the Spanish Sahara* (though this is, as seen, necessarily implicit in the wording); and Portugal stressed this purported difference in the *East Timor* case, pointing out that the "[EU] Commission has always refused to accept any geographical determination of those waters".[215]

Vaguer and more controversial as the concept of a mandatory non-recognition duty may be in the case of *denial of self-determination as such*, two principles seem to have been be relied on in the Dissenting Opinions in the *East Timor* case, and elsewhere, to underpin such a possible non-recognition duty; namely that every right should have a duty; and that the principle of self-determination is a part of *ius cogens* law. It must, however, be remembered that the unlawful use of force was in evidence, in addition to the denial of a proper process of self-determination, in *both* the instances of East Timor and the Western Sahara; and this, of course, could, *in its own right*, give rise to a non-recognition duty.[216]

---

[211] See the Australian comment in CR 95/9 at p.82 ("the closest analogy to East Timor among other self-determination territories").
[212] See above n.62 and accompanying text.
[213] See its Rejoinder, at p.118, para 212 (emphasis added).
[214] *ibid*.
[215] CR 95/4, at p.65.
[216] See, *e.g.*, R. Clark, *supra* n.167. In the case of Western Sahara, after the Moroccan so-called 'Green March' into the territory on 6 November 1975, Moroccan and Mauritanian troops entered the territory.

(i) Every Right should have a Reciprocal Duty

It was Judge Weeramantry who stressed the Hohfeldian idea[217] — which has found some academic expression before in the self-determination context[218] — that the duty generated by the "fundamental norm"[219] of self-determination has implicit in its positive aspect (to "recognise and respect" those rights) *a corresponding negative aspect* — "the duty not to act in any manner that will in effect deny those rights or impair their exercise". As he said:

> "Corresponding to the rights so generated ... there are corresponding duties lying upon the community of nations ... for a right without a corresponding duty is no right at all."

These rights, he maintained, Australia would be "obliged to recognise".[220] And, indeed, as seen in the *East Timor* case, to a limited extent in its pleadings Australia did seem to accept that such a reciprocal duty may emerge to complement the right of self-determination.[221] However, it may be justifiably contended that it was too simplistic to view reciprocal duties of third States in this way divorced from the source of Indonesia's obligation there (as the actual State denying self-determination).[222] Having rightly pointed out in the case that "[w]hile the right to self-determination has attracted much attention in international law, the notion of duties corresponding to that right has not received the same degree of analysis",[223] Judge Weeramantry implied, as seen[224] at the minimum, a *full* non-recognition duty amongst these when he stated that the accompanying duties could not be kept at a level of "semi-recognition".

(ii) The Principle of Self-Determination is of a Jus Cogens Character

Several commentators have in the past viewed Indonesia's title to East Timor as being void as a violation of *ius cogens,*[225] though Portugal did not directly

---

[217] *Supra* n.13, at pp.51, 65.
[218] See, *e.g.*, A. Whelan, "Wilsonian Self-Determination and the Versailles Settlement (1994) 43 I.C.L.Q. 99; at 100; but he uses this idea essentially in the context of imposing a duty on the "administering State" (at p.110), without any reference to a non-recognition duty on third States.
[219] See, *e.g.*, his Dissenting Opinion, at p.60 ("the need is manifest for a recognition that the right, like all rights, begets corresponding duties").
[220] At p.51.
[221] See *e.g.*, *supra*, nn.174 and 197.
[222] Counter-Memorial, at p.162, para 364.
[223] Dissenting Opinion, at p.208.
[224] *Supra*, n.206.
[225] *E.g.*, L. Hannikainen, *supra* n.139, at p.114.

rely on this principle in the *East Timor* case,[226] presumably because, as Australia speculated,[227] to do so would necessarily invoke the invalidity of the Australia/Indonesia treaty (and therefore Indonesia's responsibility). And the two Dissenting Opinions in the case hinted at a similar viewpoint.[228]

Although, as seen, the Court in the case characterised the principle of self-determination as being "one of the essential principles of international law"[229] it did not directly categorise it as coming within the ambit of *ius cogens,* though, of course, the epithet "essential" might imply such a categorisation. The importance of the principle coming into *this* international legal category is that it helps bolster a *customary rule of mandatory non-recognition* in cases of denial of self-determination.[230]

Australia seems to have argued in the *East Timor* case that self-determination did not come into this category[231] and addressed the matter in terms of potential treaty invalidity rather than affecting recognition.[232] So that, allegedly, unless Portugal could prove that the duties Australia owed formed part of *ius cogens* (so that the abovementioned Timor Gap treaty was rendered invalid under Art. 53 of the Vienna Convention on Treaties), there was allegedly "no relevant basis upon which the Court [could] enjoin Australia from enforcing the treaty".[233]

A Non-Recognition Duty is Universal because of the '*Erga Omnes*' Character of Self-determination

The Portuguese pleadings in the *East Timor* case laid heavy emphasis on self-determination being a principle of an *"erga omnes"* character; and even Australia accepted this categorisation.[234] This was not surprising as a tactical ploy, because it more clearly highlighted a right "opposable to Australia" in

[226] See Reply, at para 4.71. But *cf.* the Rejoinder, at p.48, para 92.
[227] Rejoinder, at p.12.
[228] See, *e.g.*, Judge Weeramantry, *supra,* n.13, at p.43 who noted the "central nature of this right in contemporary international law"; and Judge Skubiszeski, *ibid.,* at paras 134, 135.
[229] At p.102, para 29. See also Judge Skubiszewski, Dissenting Opinion, *ibid.,* at para 134.
[230] See Judge Skubiszewski, *ibid.,* at para 135. Even if it does not come into a '*ius cogens*' category, Judge Weeramantry noted (Dissenting Opinion, at p.194) that it was "important to note... the central nature of this right in contemporary international law... and the wide acceptance it has commanded internationally".
[231] See Counter Memorial, at p.104, para 223.
[232] *ibid.*
[233] Counter-Memorial, at p.176, para 409.
[234] Rejoinder, at p.42, para 78.

its specificity; and therefore involved "individual action" on the latter's part.[235]

Importantly, as seen, this *erga omnes* quality was endorsed by the ICJ in the case,[236] including being contained in the Separate Opinion of Judge Ranjeva, who pointed out than both parties recognised in principle "an objective right [of self-determination] *erga omnes"*.[237] Judge Skubiszewski referred to the Court's affirmation of this, but pointed out that it was not repeated "in the operative clause of the judgment".[238] The importance of this now-confirmed feature of self-determination is that it may consequentially affect — and so universalise — a concomitant duty not to recognise any State's retention of territory in denial of the principle.[239] So, as was pointed out in the *East Timor* case, the multilateral dimension of the principles of self-determination may reflect on any accompanying duty of non-recognition in respect of a denial of the principle by an occupying State, thus affecting responsibility "beyond those who are directly concerned" *i.e.*, beyond that of the officially administering authority (*e.g.*, Portugal and the *de facto* controlling State (Indonesia) in the East Timor situation). The alleged effect of this would be to lead to a "series of rights *erga singulum"*.[240]

Judge Skubiszewski found that because of this factor — which is bolstered by the UN Friendly Relations Declaration[241] — the issue was "not restricted to a quadrilateral relationship" (which at the time found expression in the UN-sponsored negotiations over East Timor — *i.e.*, "the people of East Timor, the United Nations, Portugal and Indonesia"); and that the duty to comply with the principle of self-determination did "not rest with Portugal and Indonesia alone", as "[d]epending on circumstances, other States may or will also have some obligations in this respect".[242]

---

235 See Dissenting Opinion of Judge Weeramantry, *supra* n.13, at p.202.
236 See *supra*, n.30.
237 At p.131.
238 Dissenting Opinion, at para 134.
239 See Judge Weeramantry, Dissenting Opinion, at p.215.
240 See Judge Weeramantry, *ibid.*, at p.172.
241 Dissenting Opinion, at para 138. This states: "Every State has the duty to promote, through joint and separate action, realisation of the principle of equal rights and self-determination of peoples, in accordance with the provisions of the Charter, and to render assistance to the United Nations in carrying out [these responsibilities]…".
242 *ibid.*, at para 137.

Are Specific UN Non-Recognition Resolutions Vital to any Compulsory Non-Recognition Duty in the Above Matters? And if so, Need they be to Mandatory Effect?

In the *East Timor* case, Australia repeatedly argued along the lines that[243] "[t]he right to self-determination gives rise to consequential obligations for third States only where there has been a collective decision by the international community to that effect". This raises the question, therefore, whether consequential obligations of non-recognition in the context of denial of self-determination — as discussed above — can arise independently of UN assessment.[244] Accordingly, it was one of the major arguments, as seen, in the Australian pleadings in the case that legal obligations other than for Indonesia[245] could not arise *per se* for other States.[246] This factor assumed greater importance because Portugal had emphasised the UN perspective to show the independent duties on Australia as opposed to Indonesia.[247] For example, there Australia stated that in all the UN debates from 1975 to 1982, "[n]o delegation suggested at any time the insertion of a paragraph calling for the non-recognition of Indonesia's incorporation of East Timor",[248] in contrast with "resolutions dealing with other situations". And that not only had there been "no decision" by the General Assembly which directed that States should not have dealings with Indonesia with respect to East Timor,[249] but that such resolutions were in any event purely "recommendatory";[250] also that the Security Council had "failed to give any direction [sic] to States not to deal with Indonesia".[251] (This UN omission was possibly because at the time the UN realized that the "sanction of non-recognition" would not be sufficiently supported by UN, Members[252]).

As Judge Weeramantry put it:[253] "[i]t [was] pointed out that in this [self-determination] connection, that there [were] no UN resolutions prohibiting or

---

243 Counter-Memorial, at p.119, para 263.
244 See Judge Weeramantry, Dissenting Opinion, at p.194.
245 Australia never having, of course, been an "administering authority" in East Timor: Counter-Memorial, at p.164, para 366.
246 *E.g.*, Counter-Memorial, at p.163, para 365.
247 See Rejoinder, at p.8; also *id*, at p.49, para 95; and at p.87, para 178. This was dealt with in most detail in Pt III of the Counter-Memorial.
248 Counter-Memorial, at p.62, para 142 (set out in Appendix A).
249 Counter-Memorial, at p.155, para 347.
250 See Counter-Memorial, p.48, para 112.
251 Rejoinder, at p.77, para 169.
252 See Australian argument in CR 95/10 at p.27.
253 Dissenting Opinion, at p.197.

criticising the recognition of East Timor as a province of Indonesia". Surprisingly he was to be the only member of the Court who examined in detail[254] the issue of the legal effects of the relevant UN resolutions in this connection.[255] As far as the General Assembly was concerned, he was forced to admit that "many" resolutions thereof are of an "entirely hortatory character";[256] but added that:[257]

> "When ... the General Assembly determines that a particular dependent territory has not exercised the right to self-determination ..., the Assembly is making a determination within the area of its competence; and upon a review of a vast range of material available to it. Legal consequences follow from [such] determinations."

He viewed, therefore, the several General Assembly resolutions citing particular territories as "non-self-governing", as having "dispositive force and effect"[258] under the principle stated in the Advisory Opinion on *Certain Expenses of the UN*[259] *and* that in the case of Security Council resolutions on East Timor — Resolutions 34/80, 34/40, 35/27 and 37/30 — these were, in his view, resolutions "productive of legal effects".[260] And, in a more general way (because of the importance of the right of self-determination) he found it difficult to accept that the duty of States rested only at a level of "assistance to the United Nations" in such specific actions as they may take, but lay "dormant otherwise".[261]

In its pleadings, Australia had argued that the "language" of the main Security Council resolutions on East Timor — resolutions 384 and 389 — was "entirely recommendatory", as those resolutions merely "called upon", but did not "demand", "insist" or "order" Indonesia to "withdraw from the Territory"; added to which the resolutions did not make a "specific finding" of unlawful force (under Chapter VII of the UN Charter).[262] As it concluded, the

254 *Cf.* Judge Skubiszewski's more perfunctory analysis, Dissenting Opinion, at paras 71–78.
255 Dissenting Opinion, at p.185 *et seq.*
256 *ibid.*, at p.186.
257 *ibid.*
258 *ibid.*, at p.187.
259 (1962) ICJ Rep. at p.163. *Cf.* the Australian argument (CR 95/9 at p.60) that in effect the General Assembly only had important "dispositive powers" in respect of "mandates and trust territories".
260 Dissenting Opinion, at p.186.
261 *ibid.*, at p.45.
262 Counter-Memorial, at p.37, para 88. See also Rejoinder, at p.139, para 243 & p.141, para 250. Note that Judge Weeramantry, in his Dissenting Opinion, found to the contrary. He analysed the SC resolutions on East Timor (at p.206), concluding (*ibid.*) that "[w]ords such as urges and calls upon are not necessarily of a hortatory character".

phraseology in certain GA resolutions indicating that it regarded the situation as "one likely to endanger international peace and security" showed that "it sought only to engage the recommendatory powers of the Security Council" under Chapter VI of the Charter[263] and so there was no "decision" under Chapter VII such as to bind third States under Article 25 of the Charter.[264]

Australia predictably cited the *dictum* from the *Advisory Opinion on Namibia* regarding Article 25; namely that "the question whether a resolution of the Security Council is intended to give rise to binding obligations, under Article 25 of the Charter, depends on the terms of the resolution; the Charter provisions invoked, and in general, all circumstances that might assist in determining the legal consequences of the resolution ...";[265] and it argued that the Security Council resolution on Namibia could be distinguished from other previous situations because in the case of East Timor the Security Council did not order member States to refuse recognition of the Indonesian authorities there.[266] By way of contrast, it cited the situation of Rhodesia, Namibia, Transkei, the Turkish Republic of Cyprus, Iraq's annexation of Kuwait and Israel's claim to Jerusalem, as examples where duties "not to recognise or have dealings with the occupying State" had been so imposed.[267]

However, it should be noted that in the case of Namibia, the Security Council did not call for *non-recognition* as such, stressing simply the "illegality" of the presence of South Africa there.[268] It seems arguable that in the East Timor situation there was at least the equivalent of condemnation of an "illegal situation" (which was also citied as a distinguishing factor),[269] insofar as, *e.g.*, there was mention of the right to self-determination, the denial of which might have been implicitly viewed, in the case of East Timor, as an "illegal situation".[270]

What, then, can one conclude on this UN-oriented issue? Unless the rule of non-recognition arises independently — which it seems in current international law

263 See *e.g.*, Counter-Memorial, p.150, para 333; and S. Marks *supra* n.167, at p.177.
264 See Rejoinder, at p.139, para 243
265 See Rejoinder, at p.139, para 244. *Cf.* Portuguese argument (CR95/3 at p.25) making analogous references to the UN Council for Namibia's Decree No.1 to protect the natural resources of the territory which had '*erga omnes*' implications for all States not to so deal with South Africa.
266 Rejoinder, at p.140, para 245.
267 See Rejoinder, at p.140, para 245.
268 See Portuguese argument in CR95/4 at pp.22, 23.
269 See Rejoinder, at p.140, para 245.
270 See above n.188, and accompanying text.

it only *clearly* may if forcible means are used to deny self-determination to a territory[271] — it would seem generally necessary for the UN to have made what amounts to a *mandatory* determination to this effect. In this context the subsequent practice and actions of the UN in respect of the territory in question would appear to be of vital evidentiary importance. From this perspective, in the East Timor scenario, as well as that in the case of Western Sahara, the evidence seems to be against any mandatory 'non-recognition' obligation in terms of UN law; though, of course, this in no way affects a binding duty to this effect arising in customary international law. In the *East Timor* case, a telling point made by Australia was that *if* the Security Council resolutions had been binding in 1976, surely it was "unthinkable that a binding decision would be allowed to go unremarked upon or unenforced by the Security Council ..."; or that States making such acts of recognition should not be condemned by the UN as a body.[272] It seems from the ICJ's judgment in the *East Timor* case that the majority of the Court also saw this as a decisive factor.[273]

Interrelated with this is the additional fact that UN may, in any event, have effectively acquiesced on the question of relationships by third States with the unlawfu1 claimant of a territory entitled to self-determination. As Australia stated in its pleadings:[274] "[p]rior to 1989 when the [Timor Gap treaty] was made, the United Nations had done nothing through its political organs to preclude any State from entering into an agreement with Indonesia with respect to East Timor". Nor, allegedly, had the international community generally. As it later stated in the case:[275] "[t]here ha[d] been no criticism by the international community, or from competent United Nations bodies[276] of Australia or of any of the other States" which had then "recognised Indonesian sovereignty over East Timor ..."; and since when no international steps had been taken to censure the action of States in entering into, and implementing, arrangements with Indonesia involving East Timor. Surely this could not simply be attributed (as Portugal alleged in the case) to the UN having an "over-loaded agenda" and being unable to watch "every single matter occurring in every single non-self-governing territory"?[277]

---

[271] See *supra*, section 5(a).

[272] Rejoinder, chap.2, at p.137, para 241. Thus Australia cited other situations of express UN criticism of States which in the past had failed to co-operate: see Rejoinder, at p.144, para 259.

[273] See *supra* n.13, at para 32 ("no responsive action" was taken either by the GA or SC).

[274] Counter-Memorial, para 285, at p.127.

[275] Rejoinder, at p.126, para 224.

[276] Including the 'Committee of 24': see, *e.g.*, CR 95/7 at p.53.

[277] See CR 95/5 at p.31.

In contrast, as seen above, the UN SC *has* taken an interest in the matter of contracts or treaties between Morocco and other States which might impinge on the status, as determined, of Western Sahara: in this instance expressly commissioning a legal opinion by Hans Corell in respect of the "reconnaissance licences" applying to Western Sahara waters.[278] No such action happened in the case of East Timor.

Conclusion

It has been seen above that although the ICJ had no need to address the 'non-recognition' problem in its judgment in the *East Timor* case, the Dissenting Opinions there point the way to development of a rule in current international law that any acquisition (or even holding) of territory in circumstances which denies the right to self-determination to a particular people — a seemingly "peremptory norm of international law" — may lead, perhaps even independently of any UN prescription, to a duty on all third States not to recognise the illegal situation.

Despite, however, these useful opinions, it still remains arguable whether general international law automatically brings in, independently of UN action, a rule of non-recognition to protect a self-determination right (or the associated right of peoples to their natural resources) *simpliciter*.[279] For example, the UN Declaration on Friendly Relations which calls on each State to "promote, through joint and separate action, realisation of the principle of equal rights and the self-determination of peoples" — is perhaps in itself too vague and generalised to bring in such an obligation in a situation where there is seemingly no previous precedent.[280] By contrast, as seen above, where denial of self-determination and use of force go hand-in-hand, such an independently-generated rule seems now to be part of general international law. Similarly, as seen above, even where a non-recognition duty does arise, it is doubtful in the present state of international law — despite what was said in the Dissenting Opinions in the *East Timor* case — whether a positive duty to recognise a (UN-designated) "administering Power" does arise for third States (a matter as seen which was relevant to East Timor but not (seemingly) to Western Sahara). However, it is submitted that any such latter duty is not of the same importance as the former in terms of protecting the right to self-determination; for the simple reason that a duty of non-recognition is normally *sufficient in its own right* to bar third State dealings with the illegal occupier

278 See above n.16, and accompanying text.
279 See *e.g.*, CR 95/9 at p.65 in the pleadings in the *East Timor* case.
280 See CR 95/12 at p.50.

of a particular territory. Accordingly, the duty on third States to recognise, and only deal with, the true administrator will, in most circumstances, be only of academic interest, being the 'flip-side' of the recognition coin; except in exceptional circumstances where the *Monetary Gold*-type consideration interposes as in the *East Timor* case itself. Thus, provided at the very minimum, that a third State recognises no authority in the disputed territory,[281] it may still be complying with international law.

If such a rule of non-recognition applied in the past to the East Timor situation in a self-executory way, the same should hold true in the analogous case of the Western Sahara, based at least on the limited substantive case law contained in the Dissenting Opinions in the *East Timor* case as analysed above. A curious feature to the latter situation, though, is that the legal opinions expressed in relation to the opening up of contract or treaty relationships with Morocco which apply to the waters of Western Sahara — both the UN Corell opinion and, more recently, the EU legal advice[282] — is that *none of these seems to take the broader approach of looking at third State relationships of this nature as involving non-recognition duties as such*, but rather as involving narrower issues such as duties on such States to ensure that the inhabitants of the territory in question *solely* benefit from revenue gained from exploitation of natural resources in their territory; on the basis that, for example, the *East Timor* case did not entail that mineral resource exploitation in such a non-self-governing territory was "illegal *per se*";[283] or, as the Corell opinion also put the matter whether "by analogy as part of the more general question of whether mineral resource activities in a Non-Self-Governing Territory by an administering Power are illegal as such or only if conducted in disregard of the needs and interests of the people of that Territory".[284] The Corell opinion decided that the latter principle was supported by a legal analysis of sources.[285] However, this seems to be an unfortunate precedent in the light of the legal analysis of the Dissenting Opinions in the *East Timor* case, as analysed above, which are not referred to as such in the analysis. As one commentator has stated recently, the Corell opinion "controversially" equated the powers of an Administering Power with those of an illegally occupying power".[286]

[281] See, *e.g.*, past British policy: *Hansard* (HC), vol.975, col.214 (WAs, 5 December, 1979).
[282] See above n.66.
[283] See the Corell opinion, *supra* n.16, at para 23.
[284] *ibid.*, at para 21.
[285] *ibid.*
[286] P. Pinto Leite, *supra* n.2, at p.13.

The critical problem here seems to be that such an analysis — by according even *de facto* recognition of the usurped territory as being controlled by the illegal occupier which, for example the mineral and fisheries agreements in relation to Western Saharan waters seem to do — is to grant respectability to the occupier in this regard. Thus even a declaration contemporaneous with the treaty in question (as the Irish one in response to the EU/Morocco Fisheries Partnership Agreement 2007) relative to such an agreement, or an expressed third State understanding, that the agreement is not intended to benefit the occupier, but only the people entitled to self-determination, seems to be to little legal effect insofar as what is given by one hand (a 'non-benefit' to the occupier clause) is more than taken away by the other (the entering into the agreement with the occupier in the first place). Thus the reference in the Irish 'Declaration', announced unilaterally in the EU Council only as seen, that the advice of the EU Council's legal service that the "agreement does not entail a *de jure* recognition of Morocco's legal rights in respect of the [Western Sahara] area" seems to be an unfortunate analysis of the precedent value of this whole matter, implying as it does at least *de facto* EU recognition of the Moroccan take-over of Western Sahara. Furthermore, in fact, the financial Protocol to the 2007 Agreement in Art. 2(6) states quite clearly that (subject to Art. 6 of the Protocol which is only ostensibly concerned with technical matters such as conservation) the Moroccan authorities shall have "full discretion" regarding the use to which the EU financial contribution is put, thus not dictating *in terms* that such fishing revenues shall, in respect of Western Saharan waters, only benefit the inhabitants of Western Sahara.

This is especially unfortunate as the latter situation does not approximate to that in the East Timor where a neighbouring State of the usurper — a "front line State"[287] such as Australia in that instance — feels forced to take practical action to protect its essential economic interests, even though there may allegedly be "doubt or disagreement as to the precise legal position":[288] for example, for such a front-line State to negotiate an maritime boundary[289] with the neighbouring coastal State *possessing adjacent illegal territory,* on pain of otherwise leaving its off-shore resources unclaimed.[290] Since 1978, the alleged principal Australian motivation in relation to its policy on East Timor had

[287] As was pleaded in Rejoinder in the *East Timor* case, para 224, at p.126.
[288] Counter Memorial, at p.173, para 402.
[289] See Rejoinder, at p.21.
[290] See CR 95/10 at p.43.

been to take "account of realities". Thus, a State bordering the illegally-occupied territory in question may be the "first State to recognise the new situation" as it "simply cannot ignore the new reality indefinitely but is forced to deal with it".[291] The idealistic answer to the dilemma in such an instance may be that international law requires action which falls short of recognition to overcome such problems. Even Judge Skubiszewski acknowledged this to be a relevant factor in the *East Timor* case,[292] though, as he suggested, at the very least any contacts with the occupying power should be preluded by "the obligation to consult the administering Power and the legitimate representatives of the Territory".[293] In the case of the EU Partnership Fisheries Agreement of 2007 with Morocco, a less compelling situation of necessity and immediate geographical adjacency with the occupied territory was in evidence.

Following on from this, then, it may be argued that the type of recognition accorded by any third-party agreement with the illegal occupier of territory cannot be left out of the legal equation: for example, by reference to pious hopes, as in the EU/Morocco treaty of 2007, that somehow one State treaty partner will be able to monitor whether the other — the illegal incumbent of territory and its off-shore waters included in the treaty — *is actually* benefiting the inhabitants of that territory with revenues earned thereunder. Certainly the bestowal of *de jure* recognition by a State on the occupier of an involuntarily incorporated territory — with a people determined by the UN to be entitled to self-determination — would appear to be a breach of international law, if only by logical necessity,[294] as reinforced by *dicta* in the *East Timor* case[295] and, indeed to be an intrinsic denial that such a territory has non-self-governing status.[296] However, even bestowal of *de facto* recognition to a State denying self-determination — as in the Western Saharan situation — may arguably be in breach of the consequent

[291] Rejoinder, para 222 at p.125. Indeed, Art.83 (4) of the LOSC may force such a State to come to "provisional arrangements" in such situations; see Australian argument in CR 95/11 at p.42.
[292] Dissenting Opinion, *supra* n.13, at para 163.
[293] *ibid.*, Towards the end of his judgment he did attempt to spell out the "duties of the States" which are "independent of, and do not concern, the bilateral relationship of the parties to the Timor Gap Treaty" (*ibid.*, at p.41). Some such duties (*ibid.*, at para 163) may be dictated by various considerations, including the fact that the "third State is part of the same region". This seems to imply that a neighbouring State, such as Australia, might, for example, be granted greater latitude than other States in its relationships with the then *de facto* illegal occupier of East Timor.
[294] See CR 95/2 at p.36.
[295] See, *e.g.*, Judge Weeramantry, Dissenting Opinion, at p.206.
[296] See the Portuguese comment in CR 95 /12 at p.10.

international obligation.[297] The point has been well put in the past by Professor R. Clark:[298]

> ".... an obligation not to recognise might mean an obligation not to deal with an aggressor in any manner at all. It might mean an obligation to deal with the aggressor only on the understanding that an express reservation of the position is made. It might mean an obligation not to grant *de* facto recognition. It might mean an obligation not to grant *de jure* recognition. Total non-dealing is probably too much to expect from a close neighbour .... I believe that international law means at least that neither *de facto* nor *de jure* recognition should be expressly given."

---

[297] See the Portuguese statement in CR 95/4 at p.60 ("Portugal.... does not admit that any, recognition whatsoever, even a *de facto* one, is lawful").

[298] See *supra op.cit.* n.166, at pp.247/248. Judge Weeramantry in the *East Timor* case similarly emphasised the different gradations of "recognition" (at p.204 of his Dissenting Opinion) (a "range of options stretching all the way from *de facto* recognition through many variations to the highest level of recognition", as did Judge Skubiszewski who also stressed the variety of 'recognition' responses (*e.g.*, "sometimes *de facto* only") (Dissenting Opinion, at paras 26 and 39).

Timor-Leste's Language Policy: Does it Breach International Law?

Dr Fernand de Varennes

Introduction

> Education for all means a quality education for all. In today's world this means including consideration of the many varied cultural and linguistic contexts that exist in contemporary societies.[1]

Criticisms of Timor-Leste's language policy have come from two main sources: outside observers, particularly from Australia, who decry the apparent prominence of Portuguese as one of the country's official languages, and East Timorese who feel either Bahasa Indonesia or English should have a much higher status in the new country's legal and political order.

In both cases the unstated reaction appears at least partially to assume that the current language policies are inappropriate given the position of the respective populations involved, or perhaps even discriminatory. The latter argument involves a still currently relatively unexplored and controversial topic in international law circles: can international human rights be used a state's official language policies? This chapter considers the significance of such a possible approach to the language policies in Timor-Leste and its potential impact, if any, on the debate and tensions surrounding the status of Portuguese, Bahasa Indonesia, and other languages.

The Current Language Situation in East Timor

Perhaps, contrary to what some outside people may assume, the people of Timor-Leste do not speak "Timorese", since there is no such language. The complex linguistic landscape of Timor-Leste's population of about one million is best described as involving a number of layers: first, a layer of some 16 indigenous languages, over which comes a very small coating of Portuguese, then another of Bahasa Indonesia, and finally one more for English. These layers are not all of the same importance or weight: indeed, the number of native speakers of some of these languages is actually quite small, but they may have a role and significance which far outstrips their actual numbers. To

[1] Education in a Multilingual World, UNESCO Education Position Paper, 2003.

better understand this, one must go back to Timor-Leste's long and sometimes tragic past.

A History of Diversity

Timor-Leste's one million people are made up of a large number of ethnic groups, speaking some 16 indigenous languages (Bekais, Bunak, Dawan, Fataluku, Galoli, Habun, Idalaka, Kawaimina, Kemak, Lovaia, Makalero, Makasai, Mambai, Tetum, Tokodede and Wetarese),[2] as well as non-indigenous languages such as Portuguese and Bahasa Indonesia. Most of these indigenous languages are of Austronesian origin, and four are of predominantly Melanesian-Papuan origin. Among the country's largest linguistic groups are the Tetum with about 10 percent of the population: it is one of the country's two official languages (the other being Portuguese). They live mainly around Dili and on the neighbouring northern coast. The Mambae, who may constitute around eight percent, live mainly in the central mountains. Some of the other main groups are the Tukudede, Galoli, and the Baikeno.

The presence of these indigenous languages on the island of Timor goes back thousands of years, as other contributors to this book have already noted. The presence and prominence of non-native languages such as Portuguese, Bahasa Indonesia, and perhaps to a lesser extent English, is the result of the vagaries of history and world politics, and of invaders from the outside imposing their rule and authority over the eastern parts of the Timor island. In a way, the current linguistic dilemma is the result of the arrival on the shores of Timor of the first Portuguese ship almost 500 years ago. By the close of that century, Portuguese outposts were established, mainly as a means of accessing the sandalwood trade. The Dutch quickly followed the Portuguese in the race for spices in this part of the globe, and the next 300 years would see the Dutch and the Portuguese competing with, and sometimes fighting over, this part of the archipelago.

Eventually by the mid-nineteenth century, Portuguese presence in this part of the world was limited to the eastern part of Timor Island, and the Portuguese settled their headquarters for Indonesia in Dili, retaining their part of the island which they shared with the Dutch as a colony until 1975.

---

[2] There are additionally a large number of dialects, as many as 35 by some counts. The dividing line between a language and a dialect is however often a difficult one, and there is no absolute agreement on any clear way of distinguishing them. For this reason, the 16 indigenous languages identified here are those which appear to be currently the most agreed upon, though there are others who propose that the number of languages spoken in Timor-Leste should be increased substantially.

It is this 300 years of political dominance which explains the particular position and significance of Portuguese in Timor-Leste's linguistic mosaic, and its prominence as an official language. While its roots in Timor are not as deep as those of indigenous languages, Portuguese was – and still is – the language of a small percentage of the country's population. Indeed, this has "traditionally" been the language of Timor-Leste's elite:

> Prior to 1975, Portuguese was the official government language in East Timor, and as such, was primarily the language of Church and State. (And it should be noted that Church and State have had a very close association throughout Portuguese colonial history.) The ability to read and write Portuguese was a prerequisite for Portuguese citizenship, and Portugal's *assimilado* policy encouraged cultural and linguistic assimilation. Only a small percentage of Timorese were "*assimilados*" or "*civilizados*"....[3]

Though by 1950 less than one percent of Timor-Leste's population was Portuguese-speaking, the language was in effect the main language of government, schooling, and to a large extent the Catholic Church, though in many of these areas it shared this role with Tetum. Until the Indonesian invasion of 1975 and the subsequent rule by Jakarta, Tetum was the most widely spoken language in Timor-Leste.

Invasion and Incorporation: The Post-1975 Imposition of Bahasa Indonesia

1975 thus becomes in many respects a pivotal point. Until then, the *de jure* language of government, and the language of instruction in most schools (mostly run by the Catholic Church) was Portuguese, though Tetum played an occasional auxiliary role, was used in Church services in many parts of the former colony, and was a *de facto* lingua franca for many of the indigenous Timorese, divided as they were between more than 16 languages (when one adds Portuguese). None of the indigenous languages, and this is also true of Tetum, were actually used as a medium of instruction nor even taught in the school system prior to 1975, despite Tetum's relative high profile.

The brief period of freedom before the Indonesian invasion suggested that the status of Portuguese was intended to be maintained by the emerging political leadership of the not-yet independent Timor-Leste. Fretilin,[4] for example, was

[3] Nancy Melissa Lutz, "Colonization, Decolonization and Integration: Language Policies in East Timor, Indonesia", 5 April, 1995. *www.uc.pt/timor/language.htm#Nancy*.

[4] The *Frente Revolucionària do Timor Leste Independente* (Revolutionary Front for an Independent East Timor) which was to lead the movement towards independence.

apparently willing to maintain "for a time" Portuguese's status as an official language, though also encouraging local literacy efforts in Tetum.[5] It is to be noted that at that time, many among the most prominent leaders within Fretilin, and indeed among the current top political leaders of Timor-Leste, were educated in Portuguese or even members of the "*assimilados*" or "*civilizados*" community – including the President and Prime Minister of Timor-Leste, Xanana Gusmão and José Ramos-Horta.

While previously Portuguese had been the almost exclusive language of government and education, the situation was overturned completely and dramatically upon Indonesia's invasion of the former colony in 1975, with the newly arrived authorities replacing Portuguese with Bahasa Indonesia as the new, exclusive language of government,

Bahasa Indonesia was perceived as an important pillar in uniting all of Indonesia, and its role was seen as particularly important in what was then known as East Timor. In addition to state authorities banning the official use of Portuguese, Indonesia quickly sought to replace the impact and prominence of the Portuguese language among the Timorese by quickly expanding the number of schools in the province, and requiring all students to learn exclusively in Bahasa Indonesia. Thus, as many observers have pointed out, Indonesia built more schools in East Timor between 1975 and 1980 than Portugal did in the 100 years before the arrival of the Indonesians.

The efforts of the Indonesian authorities did not cease with its own language preferences: there were attempts in 1981 to have the Catholic Church abandon the use of Portuguese during Mass services. Instead, Church authorities in East Timor switched to Tetum, after receiving the authorisation of the Vatican. This, by the way, illustrates the role that Portuguese continued to play during the period of Indonesian occupation until independence in 2002 and the Indonesians' efforts to stamp it out. As it was understood by very few Indonesians, Portuguese was perceived by Timorese and Indonesians alike as a visible sign of rejection, opposition, and even resistance to Indonesia's rule. As one author eloquently points out:

> Not only does [Portuguese] represent a challenge to Indonesian governmentality, it also represents a "secret" language, opaque to the Indonesian administration. Portuguese, therefore, is much more highly suspected – more analogous, perhaps, to the use of Dutch in Indonesia

[5] Lutz, above, n.3.

> during the Japanese Occupation. From an East Timorese point of view, in fact, the analogy is quite fitting, as many people in East Timor feel they are under a military occupation. The Indonesian military, for their part, also act like agents of a military occupation. Despite ostensibly "nationalist" rhetoric, "development" in East Timor is not a "nationalist" or a "citizenship" type program of development. Rather, it is a program of "development" through and for "governmentality", and language policy is an integral part of that program.[6]

Indigenous languages until 2002 fared somewhat better than Portuguese, in the sense that they were not being suppressed actively by Indonesian authorities. The drive to implant Bahasa Indonesia in the local population in effect also mandated that no other languages be promoted or used, especially for purposes of education. Thus, except for occasional and limited presence of Tetum for some broadcasting of radio programmes by Indonesian authorities, and despite a form of recognition of these languages as indigenous to the region and having some kind of "right to exist", no official use or recognition of any of these languages could be said to be in place in the almost three decades of Indonesian presence.

This period did however add a new language to the linguistic scene of Timor-Leste: the arrival en masse of Bahasa Indonesia. The thousands of teachers in the newly built schools were initially almost all from other parts of Indonesia, as were the many thousands of soldiers, government employees and settlers, the latter arriving as part of Indonesia's *transmigrasi* programme.[7] By the 1990s, as Timorese school children had for a couple of decades been exposed to and formed by education using exclusively Bahasa Indonesia as medium of instruction, and given the presence of a large number of mainly speakers of Bahasa Indonesia (soldiers, police officers, doctors, government employees, etc), that language had probably become the most commonly used language in the province. Though exact figures are difficult to verify, it is thought that by 1999, Muslims (most of whom could be considered to be users of Bahasa Indonesia, if not necessarily native speakers) were thought to represent perhaps 18 percent of the population, to which should be added also the many Timorese who as a result of more than two decades of exclusively Bahasa

[6] *ibid*.

[7] Indonesia's "transmigration" programme was possibly the world's largest resettlement programme and seems to have led to the resettlement of millions of people to various parts of the country. Critics point out that it tended to favour ethnic Javanese and other Muslim groups, and usually involved the loss of land and eventual overwhelming of mainly indigenous and non-Muslim minorities.

Indonesia education policies were more comfortable with that language than any other.

The fate of Bahasa Indonesia – and the future status of Timor-Leste's other languages – was to change dramatically after 1999. The departure of President Suharto and the movement towards democracy in Indonesia, combined with increasing international pressure, led in that year to a UN-sponsored agreement between Indonesia, Portugal and the United States for a UN-supervised popular referendum to determine the future status of the province. Without recounting the terrible events which followed, there ensued violent clashes and riots after the East Timorese had voted massively for independence, events generally seen by most outside observers as having been instigated by the Indonesian military and aided by Timorese pro-Indonesia militias.

Eventually an international peacekeeping force intervened, but by that time most Muslims and others sympathetic to Indonesia had left East Timor, with the result that only a few percent of Timor-Leste's population today is made up of Muslims, and many of these are in fact part of a previously existing population that predates the 1975 Indonesian presence. This population shift at the same time had a dramatic – though not fatal – consequence for the size of the Bahasa-speaking community.

By independence in 2002, Timor-Leste had to deal with the presence of a large, for the most part youthful, proportion of its population which had grown used to using Bahasa Indonesia in their daily life, especially in official and educational matters. Most of the younger generation is thus educated in Bahasa Indonesia and fluent in that language. It is that legacy of almost three decades which adds another dimension to Timor-Leste's already rather rich linguistic mosaic, one which some critics feel has not been handled properly.

This linguistic tapestry does not end there however, as another late player was to enter the scene much more recently to complicate the picture even more.

To the destruction after 1999 of much of Timor-Leste's physical infrastructure must be added the disappearance of almost all of its lawyers, teachers, doctors, and civil servants. Though some of these professionals were ethnic Timorese, it appears that even in 1999 many were Indonesians from other parts of the country. Their departure meant an incredibly difficult task lay ahead for Timor-Leste's leaders, a reconstruction challenge which the new country could not meet without massive help from the international community, through the United Nations and countries such as Australia and the United States. While

Portugal still was to play a non-negligible role in these efforts, the truth of the matter is that these efforts in the main brought a relatively new language on the shores of Timor: English.

The Current Language Policy

History thus explains the rather difficult choices made by the government of newly independent Timor-Leste in 2002: Portuguese and Tetum were in a sense the languages of resistance to the Indonesian occupier. Tetum bound the people as a *lingua franca*, while Portuguese was historically and politically prominent before the arrival of Bahasa Indonesia, especially for the traditional elites. At the same time, Indonesian was widespread among the population, as the language associated in the minds of many Timorese with education and the civil service. Finally, English was seen by many, especially by the youth, as an important international language. Perhaps more controversially, it was associated with the large presence of numerous international agencies all seeming to require some knowledge of English in order to be employed.

The compromise between these four main linguistic actors (and disregarding for a moment the status of the other indigenous languages) resulted in a constitution which outlines the new country's language policies: Portuguese and Tetum would have the status of official languages; Indonesian and English would become working languages:

> Section 13
> 1. Tetum and Portuguese shall be the official languages in the Democratic Republic of East Timor.
> 2. Tetum and the other national languages shall be valued and developed by the State.
>
> Section 159
> Indonesian and English shall be working languages within civil service side by side with official languages as long as deemed necessary.[8]

At first glance, this apparent higher priority afforded to both Tetum and Portuguese might be seen as not reflecting the reality on the ground. One survey conducted by the Asia Foundation confirmed that Tetum is by far the most widely understood language in the country (91 percent), followed by Bahasa Indonesia

[8] See the Constitution of the Democratic Republic of Timor-Leste, *www.geocities.com/alextilman/download/constfnen.pdf*.

(63 percent), Mambae (24 percent) and Portuguese (17 percent).[9] English was not part of the survey, and at the time would probably not have been a significant language. There is also a generational gap in the survey's results:

> 83% of those under 25 can speak Indonesian, as opposed to only 27% of those over 50. 27% of East Timorese between the ages of 35 and SO can speak Portuguese, as opposed to only 11% of those under 25.[10]

While there are conflicting views as to the language preferences the Constitution of Timor-Leste should contain, some of the loudest calls for change appear to be seeking the replacement of Portuguese as an official language with English,[11] to increase the latter's use as a school subject, and even to add Bahasa Indonesia as one of the country's official languages.

From the point of view of international law however, it is more than doubtful that the current positions of Tetum and Portuguese as official languages could be challenged successfully, though there may be issues of discrimination on the ground of language that may be raised in relation to the level of use of languages such as Tetum and Bahasa Indonesia. Before examining whether or not this is possible and how exactly the current language policy in Timor-Leste may – or may not – be in violation of international human rights standards, an explanation as to how these standards operate in relation to language preferences by government could be useful.

International Law and Language Policies: A Growing Understanding

The relationship between religion and international law is one that has long been recognised: not only was freedom of religion an international principle which eventually emerged in opposition to the concept of *Cuius regio, eius religio* (a ruler may decide the faith of his or her people), it began to crystallise after the Treaties of Westphalia in the mid-seventeenth century provided for a measure of religious freedom, eventually becoming a well-established rule of international law.

Eventually, it came to be realised that neither freedom of religion nor the right to equality without discrimination prevented a state from having a designated

---

[9] East Timor National Survey of Voter Knowledge (Preliminary Findings), Asia Foundation, May 2001, *www.asiafoundation.org/pdf/EastTimorVoterEd.pdf*.
[10] *ibid*.
[11] See Portuguese in East Timor, Lingua Franca, ABC Radio, 24 March 2000, *www.abc.net.au/rn/arts/ling/stories/s113139.htm*.

official religion, though such a status did not entitle a government to breach this, or any other, human rights:

> 9. The fact that a religion is recognized as a state religion or that it is established as official or traditional or that its followers comprise the majority of the population, shall not result in any impairment of the enjoyment of any of the rights under the Covenant, including articles 18 and 27, nor in any discrimination against adherents to other religions or non-believers. In particular, certain measures discriminating against the latter, such as measures restricting eligibility for government service to members of the predominant religion or giving economic privileges to them or imposing special restrictions on the practice of other faiths, are not in accordance with the prohibition of discrimination based on religion or belief and the guarantee of equal protection under article 26.[12]

It is clear from various international decisions and opinions in the last few decades that freedom of religion thus protects an individual's freedom in matters of beliefs that are private in nature. Situations involving a state's "religious preferences", such as government support or advantages attributed only to a particular religion, would more likely involve potential issues of discrimination.

If a state can therefore choose an official religion, and that this in itself is not prohibited in international law (unless it breaches freedom of religion or non-discrimination), what of an official language?

Freedom of Expression includes Language, but what of Official Languages?

Perhaps surprisingly, only in 1993 was it clearly established in international law that freedom of expression includes the protection of an individual's choice of language in private activities. In *Ballantyne, Davidson and McIntyre v Canada*,[13] the authors claimed that the prohibition against using any language other than French on outdoor commercial signs or in a firm's name infringed upon their freedom of expression, guaranteed by Art 19 of the International Covenant on Civil and Political Rights.

The UN Human Rights Committee stated that Art 19(2) of the Covenant applies not only to ideas and subjective opinions which can be transmitted to

[12] General Comment No 22: The right to freedom of thought, conscience and religion (Art 18) CCPR/C/21/Rev.1/Add.4

[13] *John Ballantyne, Elizabeth Davidson, and Gordon McIntyre v Canada*, Communications No 359/1989 and 385/1989, UN Doc. CCPR/C/47/D1359/1989 and 385/1989/Rev.1 (1993).

others, but also to any news or information, any expression, any commercial publicity or signs, and to any work of art. In other words, to restrict the private use of a language would be a restriction of a form of expression, and cannot be done under the guise of an official language policy.

It is worth pointing out that the UN Human Rights Committee's comments emphasised that freedom of expression only applies to private language choices and usage, not to the use of a language by state authorities which belongs to the sphere of public life:

> A State may choose one or more official languages, but it may not exclude, outside the spheres of public life, the freedom to express oneself in a language of one's choice.

Though very brief, the UN Human Rights Committee appears to suggest, albeit implicitly, that individuals may be excluded from using the language of their choice "in the sphere of public life" by a state's determination of the language or languages that are official.

As the situation and controversies surrounding Tetum, Portuguese, Bahasa Indonesia and English involve the use of languages in the public sphere (i.e. by state authorities), and thus would appear to be outside the scope of freedom of expression, other international human rights need to be considered to determine if the language policy of Timor-Leste breaches any other international standards.

Official Languages and Non-discrimination: A New Understanding of an Old Right

While non-discrimination on the grounds of religion has long been acknowledged to be an obvious potential restriction on any official or national religious preference, the same reasoning has not until very recently been considered closely in international law. Only in 2000 did an international body, the UN Human Rights Committee once again, consider directly whether non-discrimination on the grounds of language could be used to affect a state's official language policy. The answer – yes – surprised quite a few observers, though not without causing a rift within the UN Human Rights Committee itself.

In *Diergaardt v Namibia*,[14] the UN Human Rights Committee considered whether individuals of an Afrikaans-speaking minority in Namibia were the

[14] *JGA Diergaardt (late Captain of the Rehoboth Baster Community) et al., v. Namibia*, Communication No 760/1997, UN Doc. CCPR/C/69/D/760/1997 (2000).

subjects of discrimination because of the refusal of authorities to respond to telephone calls and other contacts in their language. English is Namibia's only official language under the Constitution, and a government circular specifically prohibited the use of Afrikaans by Government officials in official phone calls and correspondence. By excluding the use of Afrikaans, a majority of the members of the UN Human Rights Committee observed that Namibian authorities were in fact denying them a benefit or advantage (a response from authorities in their own language) which users of English automatically receive:

> 10.10 The authors have also claimed that the lack of language legislation in Namibia has had as a consequence that they have been denied the use of their mother tongue in administration, justice, education and public life. The Committee notes that the authors have shown that the State party has instructed civil servants not to reply to the authors' written or oral communications with the authorities in the Afrikaans language, even when they are perfectly capable of doing so. These instructions barring the use of Afrikaans do not relate merely to the issuing of public documents but even to telephone conversations. In the absence of any response from the State party the Committee must give due weight to the allegation of the authors that the circular in question is intentionally targeted against the possibility to use Afrikaans when dealing with public authorities. Consequently, the Committee finds that the authors, as Afrikaans speakers, are victims of a violation of article 26 of the Covenant.[15]

Using only one language – even if it is a country's official language – creates a distinction based on language which may be intended to, or result in an individual being excluded or disadvantaged. Once such a distinction or "linguistic preference" is established, it is for authorities to demonstrate that such a distinction is justified – and non-discriminatory. Whether or not the threshold for such a justification is very high remains unanswered, but the

[15] Some members of the Committee, opposed to the conclusion of the majority, were of the opinion that non-discrimination could not be applied to an official language, despite nothing in the International Covenant on Civil and Political Rights to support this point of view: "7. (...) It is significant to note that it is nowhere alleged in the communication that the action of the State in declaring English as the official language and not allowing the use of other languages was directed only against the use of Afrikaans while permitting the other languages to be used. The action of the State in declaring English as the official language and not allowing the use of other languages by enacting appropriate legislation was clearly not violative of article 26 because all languages other than English were treated on the same footing and were not allowed to be used for official purposes and there was no discrimination against Afrikaans vis-à-vis other languages."

main point to bear in mind is that regardless of a state's official language or languages, it may be discriminatory for state authorities not to use other languages in the public sphere.

International Human Rights and Language Policy: The Current Situation

Though still in a state of flux and subject to some debate among legal experts, it would seem that, as in the case of religion, a state is free to choose whichever language it wishes as an official language, since such a designation does not automatically breach any right.

An official language is neither necessarily exclusive nor even privileged: the exact impact and importance of an official language will vary according to what the relevant legislation and practices in a specific country provide for. Thus, in some countries such as New Zealand where there are two official languages, English and Maori, the former is generally used at all levels by state authorities, while the latter is used to a much smaller, almost insignificant, degree in comparison.

In other words, there is nothing in international human rights law – neither freedom of expression nor non-discrimination on the ground of language – which provides a basis for having other languages declared official. It would appear therefore that the ultimate decision of designating a language as official remains entirely within the prerogative of the state.[16]

A state's choice of official language(s) can however also raise issues of discrimination, if the impact of not using additional languages is unreasonable or unjustified in the circumstances. Thus, while international law will not interfere in the official choice of which language is designated as official, non-discrimination may in some situations require state authorities to modify language policies that are discriminatory. This would probably require the additional use of other languages, even if they are not designated as official if it is unreasonable and unjustified for authorities not to use these languages, as the UN Human Rights Committee concluded in *Diergaardt v Namibia*.

Once again, the exact parameters in determining how one can qualify a government's language restriction or preference as unreasonable or unjustified has not yet emerged clearly from the very few cases at the international (or

---

[16] See what appears to be implied by the European Court of Human Rights in *Podkolzina v Latvia*, European Court of Human Rights 46726/99 [2002] ECHR 405 (9 April 2002).

European) level which touch on this issue. Factors that may be considered in determining the appropriate scale of use of a minority language by state authorities, or as to what is a sufficient number or is reasonable and justified in a particular case, will depend on a wide range of factors. Prominent among these would be the number of speakers of a minority language, the level of demand for the use of a minority language, the territorial concentration of the minority, a state's available resources, and the type of service being requested in the minority language, and the relative ease or level of difficulty in responding to the demand. There may also be other relevant considerations.[17]

Where public authorities at the national, regional or local levels face a sufficiently large number of individuals who use a minority language, the authorities must provide an appropriate level of service in this language. For example, in the case of the administration of districts where minorities are concentrated, local authorities should generally provide for an increasing level of services in their language as the number of speakers of a particular language increases. Not to provide an appropriate, i.e. "slidingscale", response could be deemed to be unreasonable or unjustified, and therefore a form of discrimination. Individuals whose fluency in a state's official language is generally lower than that of a native user of the language favoured by public authorities would therefore in many cases experience a disadvantage. In some situations, especially where it is relatively simple for public authorities to accommodate to some degree the language of a large minority, not to use their language as is "appropriate" in the circumstances could be deemed to be unreasonable or arbitrary in light of the disadvantages caused, and therefore discriminatory.

There is an increasing level of legal and political support for this interpretation. Recent treaties and international instruments often embody this concept of a sliding-scale as a proper response to the use of the language of minorities by state authorities, and this has been most visibly incorporated in a number of treaties in Europe. The Central European Initiative Instrument for the Protection of Minority Rights[18] (Art 13: "whenever in an area the number of persons ... reaches...a significant level"); the Framework Convention for the Protection of National Minorities[19] (Art 10: "in areas inhabited by persons

---

[17] See in particular the list in Femand de Varennes, *Language, Minorities and Human Rights* (Martinus Nijhoff, The Hague, 1996), s 4.5.

[18] CEI Instrument for the Protection of Minority Rights, Turin, 19 November 1994. *www.ceinet.org/download/minority_rights.pdf*.

[19] Framework Convention for the Protection of National Minorities, Council of Europe, ETS No 157, Strasbourg, 1 February 1995, *www.conventions.coe.int/Treaty/en/Treaties/Word/157.doc*.

belonging to minorities traditionally or in substantial numbers, if those persons so request and where such a request corresponds to a real need, the Parties shall endeavour to ensure, as far as possible ..."); and the European Charter for Minority or Regional Languages[20] (Art 10: "within the administrative districts ... in which the number of residents ... justifies the measures specified below and according to the situation of each language"), to name but a few, all recognise that there is a gradation that must be respected as to the degree to which public authorities should use a minority language.

While not necessarily warranting a dramatic change in the overall language policy adopted by the Government of Timor-Leste, it does suggest that a number of aspects of this policy may run foul of the international human rights standards that are relevant in terms of state language preferences.

Applying International Standards to the Timor-Leste Language Policy

The Choice of Tetum and Portuguese as Official Languages; the Omission of Bahasa Indonesia and English

Despite some criticisms of the status of Portuguese as an official language, since the percentage of the population of Timor-Leste who can speak it fluently is relatively low when compared to other languages, it is clear that there is no violation of any international human right (such as freedom of expression or non-discrimination) in such a choice *per se*. Nor is there automatically a breach of any international right by not adding Bahasa Indonesia or English as official languages.

The few international decisions or views dealing with official language issues – and those which have touched upon official religion choices – are fairly consistent in suggesting that any decision in relation to the choice of an official language (and religion) remains the prerogative of the state involved. No human rights treaty contains a provision which explicitly or implicitly creates any kind of "right to an official language". There may however be a right to a "reasonable and justified" use of a language by state authorities.

Greater Use of Other Languages?

As outlined in *Diergaardt v Namibia*, while there is nothing in international law to create an actual right to an official language, the refusal of state

[20] European Charter for Regional or Minority Languages, Council of Europe, ETS No 148, Strasbourg, 5 November 1992, *www.conventions.coe.int/treaty/en/Treaties/Html/148.htm*.

authorities to provide for a greater use of other languages could possibly constitute discrimination if the refusal or denial of such use is deemed to be unreasonable and unjustified in the circumstances.

From the few existing cases and comments written in this area, it would appear that one of the main determinants would be whether, given the legitimate objective of having a unifying official language (or in this case languages), not having state authorities use English, Bahasa Indonesia or other indigenous languages more is unreasonable and unjustified. In order to answer that question, it must be shown how, on the one hand, the preference or prominence given to those who use one language is in effect so disproportionate, in light of the objective sought, that it can be deemed to be a breach of the prohibition of non-discrimination. It requires therefore an examination of the benefits attributed on the basis of the official languages, and denied to others.

Claims in Relation to English

Among the more vocal demands, at least from some of the youth in Timor-Leste, is for English to be taught more extensively in schools than Portuguese. As explained by one observer:

> Students receive Portuguese lessons as part of the new regular curriculum, however, both teachers and students expressed the view that they need to learn English since that is the *true international language* [their phrasing] and if they are to have future opportunities in education or jobs Portuguese will not help them much. At times an extremely strong anti-Portuguese language sentiment was expressed which reflected the general attitudes of the Atsabe Kemak who were vociferous in their critique of the national language choice with reference to future opportunities for participating in a global arena.[21]

Despite the obvious strength of the feelings expressed in the above example, it is doubtful that the privileged position of Portuguese in the school curriculum could be deemed discriminatory when compared with the use of English. As indicated earlier, in order to satisfy the criteria for determining whether a language preference is unreasonable and unjustified, there must first be a situation involving a language preference or some kind of restriction

[21] Andrea Molnar, "East Timor: An Introduction to the History, Politics and Culture of Southeast Asia's Youngest Nation", Northern Illinois University, Department of Anthropology and Center for Southeast Asian Studies, May 2005, *www.seasite.niu.edu/EastTimor/language.htm*.

which has the aim or effect of disadvantaging or excluding individuals in their enjoyment of a particular right or benefit. If English were the mother tongue of the students involved, such a requirement would be fairly obvious: they would be denied a benefit enjoyed by students for whom Portuguese is their own language, namely the benefit of learning their own language. It would then have to be determined whether this benefit only enjoyed by some is reasonable and justified in the circumstances.

While many students may feel it more beneficial to have English instead of Portuguese in school, the current situation in state schools does not involve any individuals receiving a greater benefit or advantage than others on account of their language: in the particular case of English not being taught to a greater degree, all students receive the same advantage (or disadvantage in the eyes of some): the teaching of Portuguese as part of the school curriculum instead of English. Given that English is not the language of a significant number of pupils, it would be difficult to maintain that there is any type of unreasonable or unjustified denial of an advantage of the kind which occurred in *Diergaardt v Namibia*.

Claims in Relation to Bahasa Indonesia

While English and Bahasa Indonesia are both "working languages", Bahasa Indonesia is still much more frequently used in daily life by many Timorese, a language of instruction used at some levels in state schools (though this is diminishing) and is also prominent in the local media. In many respects, it is in fact used much more extensively than Portuguese, despite the latter's "exalted" position as an official language.

In other words, there does not at first glance appear to be many areas where there could be said to be a discriminatory language policy in relation to Bahasa Indonesia, since by and large the language is still favoured extensively in many areas of public life. Were this to change, however, for example by the government of Timor-Leste forbidding all teaching in Bahasa Indonesia or in any official transaction in the language by state authorities, the huge disruption and disadvantage this could entail for many might be so unreasonable and unjustified as to constitute discrimination.

One important qualification to the above theoretical scenario would be that of the reaction of the Timorese population. Surveys such as the Asia Foundation's 2001 *East Timor National Survey of Voter Knowledge* suggest that while Bahasa Indonesia is the country's most widespread language, it is at the same time also widely rejected or at least not strongly held in esteem by many Timorese, especially the older generations. If therefore, despite their knowledge of the language, only small numbers of Timorese were to request or insist on the use of Bahasa Indonesia, then it would possibly not be discriminatory for state authorities to decrease their own use of the language in the public sphere.

Claims in Relation to Tetum

Ironically, Tetum as an official language seems to be in a slightly less prominent position than Bahasa Indonesia, a working language (with Portuguese), at least in areas such as schooling, the media, and public administration. This relative weaker prominence of Tetum is of course in a way understandable: Bahasa Indonesia having for decades been the exclusive language of government and education, its vocabulary well-known and its usage in these areas quite well established and therefore accepted by large segments of the population.

Portuguese is gradually replacing Bahasa Indonesia as the medium of instruction, while Tetum's poorly developed technical vocabulary and lack of written materials are usually identified as reasons for not using the latter for schooling purposes.[22]

Yet demands to increase Tetum's actual use and prominence within the operations of state authorities, including public education, could still validly be based on arguments relying on the discriminatory impact of a mainly Bahasa Indonesia language preference in the country's administration and schooling, and especially if a significant portion of the population of Timor-Leste were to make such a demand.

Whether this would be enough to demonstrate that the continued prominent role and use of Bahasa Indonesia is so unreasonable and unjustified as to constitute discrimination in international law is perhaps more difficult to demonstrate conclusively. Many teachers have been trained in Bahasa Indonesia (and to a lesser extent Portuguese). Curriculum materials are widely available in Bahasa Indonesia and Portuguese but simply non-existent in Tetum. The latter language's vocabulary may not yet have developed the scientific and other technical terms that are required in a modern school setting. All of these factors could combine together to make it reasonable to maintain the current language policy: at least for a time.

22 *Timor-Leste: Education Since Independence: From Reconstruction to Sustainable Improvement, Human Development Sector Unit East Asia and Pacific Region*, World Bank, December 2004.

Nevertheless, if a significant proportion of parents were to demand that at least part of the state schools' curriculum be taught in Tetum, and that Bahasa Indonesia and/or Portuguese be mainly used in the more scientific and technical fields, then it could be possible to conclude that such an arrangement would in the circumstances be reasonable and justified, and thus in compliance with the right to equality and the prohibition of discrimination on the ground of language as guaranteed in human rights treaties. This is certainly a valid argument, especially when one is reminded that at least one third of Timor-Leste's population does not speak Bahasa Indonesia, and even less are fluent in Portuguese, whereas close to 100 percent can speak Tetum.

While such a change in its language policy would certainly impose new demands on the Government of Timor-Leste, it would probably not be too onerous given that Tetum is in fact the country's most widely spoken language. Though it has been until recently a mainly oral language, it could easily be adapted to be used in primary levels of education, if such a direction were in fact to be demanded by the population. It would additionally not preclude students from acquiring fluency in Bahasa Indonesia or Portuguese – or English for that matter.

Conclusion

> Language is certain to be a controversial issue in East Timor over the coming years. Because of a turbulent recent history and the general neglect of Timorese studies to date, restoring Portuguese, developing Tetum, providing the people with linguistic and educational resources in all their languages, and controlling the presence of the two ancillary/utilitarian languages (Malay-Indonesian and English) will be among the nation's many challenges of the twenty-first century.[23]

This chapter has not attempted to exhaustively examine the above prediction made in 2000 which correctly saw the pending challenges of Timor-Leste's linguistic diversity and, perhaps most importantly, the legacy of almost three decades of Indonesian occupation. Its objectives were much more modest: whether or not there are principles in international human rights law that might affect in any way the country's sometimes controversial language policy.

The answer is both a clear no and a tentative maybe. Partially because of the still nascent international jurisprudence in areas affecting a state's language

[23] Geoffrey Hull, "Current Language Issues in East Timor, University of Adelaide", 29 March 2000, *www.asianlang.mq.edu.au/INL/speech1.html*.

preferences, many aspects of the impact of the most relevant human rights standards such as freedom of expression and non-discrimination are either still to be determined, or have only been elucidated to any extent quite recently. There is therefore still a fair amount of uncertainty as to the exact significance and impact of these rights as they may affect language policies.

It remains clear, however, that the actual status of official language which has been awarded to both Tetum and Portuguese cannot be considered to breach either freedom of expression or non-discrimination provisions, as both these rules leave such a designation entirely at the discretion of state authorities – just as freedom of religion and non-discrimination do in the case of an official religion.

At the same time, however, both freedom of expression and non-discrimination can impact significantly on the effects of a state's language policy, regardless of whether or not it involves an official language. As the private use of a language is protected under freedom of expression, any attempt by a state to prohibit private language expression would thus breach one of the most fundamental human rights in international law.

Additionally, any language preference or restriction by state authorities, including in their own use of an official or any other language, may run foul of the prohibition of discrimination on the ground of language if it is not in pursuit of a legitimate objective, proportionate in the pursuit of this objective, and therefore reasonable and justified in the circumstances.

The official language position of both Tetum and Portuguese thus does not appear to be threatened, nor can any of the relevant human rights standards be used as a basis for requiring that other languages also be recognised as official. It is possible nevertheless that the relatively low level of use of Tetum as medium of instruction, particularly at the primary levels of education, and in some local government offices, could be deemed to be an unreasonable and unjustified benefit (instruction in one's mother tongue; ability to use one's language in contacts with government employees) that is denied to too many individuals. Despite the low level of technical vocabulary and syllabus in Tetum, this difference of treatment could be deemed to be unreasonable and unjustified, especially if it can be demonstrated that part of teaching or local government offices could easily be conducted in Tetum.

PART IV

Gender

Time to get Serious about Women's Rights in Timor-Leste: Wrestling Change from the Grassroots Up

Carolyn Graydon

Introduction

Fulfilling the human rights of Timor-Leste's women is not the only imperative driving the need to address entrenched gender inequality in the world's newest nation. The stability, security and development prospects for Timor-Leste depend in part upon its ability to remove barriers to women's participation by moving beyond gender equality rhetoric and drawing upon female insights, energy and intelligence to make progress on the nation's extensive challenges. The ongoing political and social crisis in Timor-Leste which erupted in April/May 2006, has highlighted the disenfranchisement of many, including women. Despite state efforts to comply with international standards and the presence of women in some important positions, the political culture, agendas, main protagonists, participants, and efforts to orienteer towards peace, are almost exclusively commandeered by men.

A gendered perspective must be an essential part of the soul-searching processes going on in Timor-Leste as the nation struggles to come to terms with what has gone wrong in its short life to date, and wrestles with finding durable solutions to both old and new cleavages so dramatically dividing Timor-Leste today. It also presents a critical opportunity to re-assess how all of Timor-Leste's citizens can contribute to developing Timor-Leste's people, economy, and institutions, as they are able. Such a gendered analysis must go well beyond the immediate issues of political leadership and the liberal strategy of ensuring female representation, a necessary, but insufficient path to tackling gender inequality. In addition to existing strategies, key to unlocking the huge potential that genuine and substantive female participation in Timor-Leste's nation-building offers, is deconstruction of rigidly defined gender roles and targeted, long term culturally transformative approaches grounded in indigenous understandings of culture and human rights; processes necessarily designed and directed by Timor-Leste nationals.

This paper aims to contribute to the broader project of enhancing knowledge of how achieving greater gender equality not only underpins the fulfillment of women's rights, but also the prospects for peace and development in Timor-

Leste. This journey begins with an examination of the impacts and processes involved in constructions of gender during the Indonesian occupation and its aftermath.[1] Aside from highlighting the value of women's contributions and experiences, such probing illuminates the lessons learnt and provides instructive insight into how Timorese women could more effectively re-assert and defend spaces for themselves in the context of the current political instability. Given the limited advances made by Timorese women since independence, and the substantial retreat in women's rights underscored particularly in recent months, Part II of this paper urges human rights practitioners to develop a new focus and strategy to dismantle gender inequality. The approach suggested is the gradual transformation of cultural norms and practices which discriminate against women, as a means of entrenching more widespread and sustainable advances in women's rights. Five strategies as to how Timorese social actors might tackle this are then posited and debated in Part III.

Part I: Scrutinising the Scorecard: Timorese Women under Occupation, in Transition and since Independence

Setting the scene

A powerful trinity of forces combines to fix prevailing ascribed gender roles in Timorese society today. I identify them as dominant cultural mores, processes involved in post-occupation patriarchal backlash, and the conservative doctrine and values of the Catholic Church. The impact of these factors is symbiotic. For example, dominant cultural values which relegate women to the home are consistent with Church values and reinforced by the patent lack of security for women in public spaces during occupation and the 2006 crisis. The Catholic prohibition on divorce combines with dominant patrilineal kinship systems and economic marginalisation of separated and divorced women, to compel women to remain in violent relationships. An undeveloped economy creating high unemployment combines with traditional and Church-supported family structures entrenching male control over economic means and domestic decision making.

While a detailed historical account of how Timorese women have fared under the various phases of violence in Timor-Leste is well beyond the scope of this

[1] The notion of "aftermath" or a "post conflict" environment is problematic given that many women experience a continuum of violence, from the war frontier to the home. "For women there is no aftermath." S Meintjes, A Pillay, M Turshen, *The Aftermath: Women in Post-Conflict Transformation* (Zed Books, London and New York, 2001), p.8.

paper, it is worth bearing in mind the breadth and length of Timor-Leste's tumultuous past and present. This history spans from pre-colonial indigenous wars, to more than 400 years of neglectful and exploitative Portuguese colonisation, to four years of cruel occupation by Japan during World War II, to hastily effected decolonization by Portugal resulting in a short but vicious civil war culminating in an all-out invasion and brutal occupation by Indonesia lasting for 24 years. It is also worth considering how resistance to occupation drove the population to Catholicism and the impact the revered status enjoyed by the Church, has had upon the construction and maintenance of gender roles. An internationally supervised referendum, in which more than two thirds of voters supported independence, culminated in a total breakdown of law and order in 1999 when Indonesian army-backed militias exacted their revenge. They killed more than 1,500 people, forcibly deported hundreds of thousands to West Timor and destroyed most houses, livelihoods and infrastructure throughout the country. Following the installation of a United Nations transitional government tasked with re-building the state, power was peacefully transferred to a national government in May 2002. However, only four years later, internecine fighting saw state institutions dramatically collapse into violence and instability, rapidly silencing those who had prematurely heralded Timor-Leste's transition to, and post-Independence record as a UN success story and template for "gender mainstreaming" in post-conflict reconstruction efforts.

Women and War

The past decade has seen a growing awareness of the gendered nature of war, conflict and reconstruction. The vastly different experiences, contributions, and needs of men and women in situations of conflict has highlighted the importance of their equal participation in peace-making, reconstruction, and development, to sustaining peace, and entrenching greater gender equity within a society. While entire communities suffer the consequences of war and occupation, women and girls are particularly victimized for a range of reasons including their reduced access to resources, decision-making power, information, mobility, their fundamental roles in maintaining their families and communities, and their sex, rendering them vulnerable to particular human rights abuses such as rape. The suffering of Timorese women, especially under Indonesian occupation, while particular in its detail, is consistent with women's experiences of loss elsewhere. While it is estimated that women (and children) make up around 80 percent of civilian casualties and displaced persons globally, they are stuck in a cruel paradox, being conflict's primary victims, yet often denied a seat at the peace negotiating table, and marginalised in processes of reconstruction, further entrenching their disadvantage in the post-occupation era.

However the dominant discourse of casting women primarily as victims of conflict does them the double disservice of denying their agency, perpetuating inaccurate assumptions about their contributions in times of war and peace, and undermining their potential as future participants in peace-building.[2] It also ignores that the devastating dimensions of war and occupation can open up "ambivalent spaces for women's agency, through loss",[3] and re-write fundamental aspects of societal make-up such as underlying norms that define gender relations and power dynamics. Due to the exigencies of war and occupation, women commonly step outside of their socially ascribed roles and occupy new extended roles to ensure family and community survival. Ironically, conflict can be transformative in empowering some women and catalyse a challenge to the grip of entrenched gender roles. The critical issue is how to achieve consolidation of those gains in the aftermath of conflict and whether, if carefully harnessed and nurtured, they might create the impetus for longer term processes of transforming gender norms to bring about more equitable gender relations.[4] Whether or not war-time empowerment can be capitalised upon to achieve longer term processes of gender norm transformation very much depends upon conscious and sustained effort to create the spaces and opportunities for women's participation in peace-making, peace-building and development. The alternative trajectory, which unfortunately is the most common, is that as peace is ushered in, women are subordinated to a powerful backlash which compels their reversion to more traditional pre-conflict roles and status.

Feminist interrogation and critical analysis of the processes involved in women's regression after conflict are helping to develop an understanding of why post-conflict societies' default mode commonly appears set to re-establishing the gender *status quo ante*. In times of upheaval and insecurity, when the desire for a return to normalcy is strong and there is a need for a post-war healing process, "the certainties of patriarchal institutions and tradition seem therapeutic".[5] Like women's achievements generally, the achievements of women in managing survival, supporting families and sustaining community during war or occupation, are quickly forgotten as the

[2] B Sorensen, "Women and Post-Conflict Reconstruction: Issues and Sources." WSP Occasional Paper No 3, June 1998, *http://wsp.dataweb.ch/wsp_publication/op3-09.htm*, accessed on 23 February 2006.
[3] R Manchanda, "Ambivalent Gains in South Asian Conflicts", Meintjes, Pillay and Turshen, above, n.1, at p.100.
[4] R Strickland and N Duvvury, "Gender Equity and Peacebuilding: From Rhetoric to Reality: Finding the Way. A Discussion Paper", *International Centre for Research on Women* (ICRW) (2003).
[5] B Sorensen, above, n.2.

political project of reconstruction becomes more structured and hierarchical.[6] Manchanda argues that the shake-up of gender identities during war or occupation is permitted to occur only because it fits the contours of the broader nationalist struggle, which once resolved, relegates women to "purveyors of tradition and community identity",[7] a reversion which is part and parcel of what is meant by and expected of "peace".

The under-representation and marginalisation of women in nationalist independence movements has increasingly been the subject of academic scrutiny, especially in the context of the status of women in emerging new states:

> … nationalisms are, from the outset, constituted in gender power but, as the lessons of international history portend, women who are not empowered to organise during the struggle, will not be empowered to organise after the struggle. If nationalism is not transformed by an analysis of gender power, the nation-state will remain a repository of male hopes, male aspirations and male privilege.[8]

An alternative perspective contends that women may appear to be marginalised if analysis of their roles is limited to the forum of formal, nationalist organisations. However through their centrality and dominance in "matrifocal" family structures, women are clearly empowered participants in the struggle.[9] Frequently, women's contributions to national struggles are not recognised in either respect, through formal nationalist movements and their roles as resisters and supporters as mothers, sisters and grandmothers, and the nationalist debate is dominated by men, who then marginalise women from power in the post-conflict period.

How well do these conceptions of the losses and ambivalent gains of conflict fit the experience of Timor-Leste's women? In what ways have they resisted and assumed non-traditional roles? Have those women mobilised through their

---

[6] Meintjes, Pillay, and Turshen, above, n.1, at p.8.

[7] R Manchanda, "Ambivalent Gains in South Asian Conflicts", in Meintjes, Pillay, and Turshen, above, n.1, at p.103.

[8] A McClintock, 1995 "No Longer in a Future Heaven: Nationalism, Gender and Race" in *Imperial Leather: Race, Gender and Sexuality in the Colonial Contest* (Routledge, New York and London, 1995), at p.385.

[9] J Siapno, "Gender, National and the Ambiguity of Female Agency", in M Waller and J Rycenga, eds, *Frontline Feminisms: Women, War and Resistance* (Garland Publishing Inc, New York and London, 2000) chap 21.

experience of war and occupation succeeded in bedding down sustainable challenges to traditional gender constructions or been overwhelmed by the common pattern of backlash, driven by the re-assertion of patriarchal "traditional" and religious values which ignore established female competence and achievement in non-traditional roles? How can Timorese women carve out a more powerful and permanent stake in the current processes involved in piecing together what is now a deeply divided people and restoring some of the fragile post-independence confidence and optimism shattered by the 2006 re-implosion of State?

Timorese Women as Fighters and Victims under Indonesian Occupation

In illuminating Timorese women's experiences as resisters and victims, I focus primarily upon the period of the Indonesian occupation (1975–1999), as it has the greatest lasting impact upon the living memory of Timorese people and fundamentally re-wrote the features of Timor-Leste's basic social demographic, religious, and gender characteristics.

To place this analysis of the occupation in some context, it is estimated that up to 200,000 people[10] or around one third of the original population were killed, or perished during this period. Following a brief but bloody civil war between hastily established political parties which emerged in anticipation of independence from Portugal,[11] the Revolutionary Front for an Independent Timor-Leste (FRETILIN), a left-leaning and popular party, declared independence. Nine days later, after months of orchestrated border incursions and skirmishes, the Indonesian army, claiming FRETILIN to be a communist threat, commenced a full-scale military sea, land, and air attack upon Dili aimed at quickly integrating the territory. Rather than gaining control of Timor-Leste in a matter of days as expected, Indonesia faced a tenacious and determined local resistance supported by a large majority of the population. Shortly after the invasion, the Security Council of the United Nations repeatedly called for the withdrawal of the Indonesian occupying forces and

---

[10] *Chega! (Enough!)* Final Report of the Comissão de Acolhimento, Verdade e Reconciliação de Timor Leste, Commission for Reception, Truth and Reconciliation in East Timor (CAVR), accessed on 15 December 2006 at *www.etan.org/news/2006/cavr.htm*. Up to 183,000 died as a result of famine and displacement (p 143) and 18,600 civilians killed or disappeared. (p 294). An alternative estimate of 200,000 is provided by G Robinson, "With UNAMET in East Timor-An Historian's Personal View", in R Tanter, M Selden, and S Shalom, *Bitter Flowers, Sweet Flowers: East Timor, Indonesia and the World Community* (Pluto Press, Sydney, 2001) at p.56.

[11] Estimated by the CAVR to have claimed around 3,000 lives. *Chega! (Enough!)*, above, n.10.

recognised the East Timorese peoples' right of self determination.[12] However these resolutions were ignored. No follow-up or enforcement action was taken against Indonesia and hence the occupation dragged on largely out of sight of the international community for the next 24 years.

The Suffering of Women

The suffering of Timorese women during the occupation came in almost every imaginable form. Especially in the early years of occupation, enormous numbers of women and children starved due to displacement and interruption of normal food cycles. Women suspected of supporting the resistance were detained, tortured, raped, and often killed. Women detainees were considered by the military as trophies and threatened with sale between different parts of the military for the opportunity to rape them.[13] Those related to male resistance leaders were used as leverage over male FALINTIL[14] guerillas and FRETILIN leaders, and were killed, threatened, raped, or otherwise tortured in efforts to extract information from them regarding their husbands' or relatives' whereabouts and activities, or to effect surrender.[15] The scale of killings, especially of men, resulted in a huge swell of female-headed households. Such women were vulnerable on a range of levels, first because they were perceived as "available" for abuse by Indonesian military members. Secondly, many widows faced even greater economic uncertainty than the rest of the population and with the collapse of family support systems, fended for themselves and their families, often surviving in camps in extremely poor conditions. The scarcity of other employment forced larger numbers of East Timorese women into prostitution, for many who were already rape victims,

---

[12] See UN Security Council Resolution 384 recognizing the "inalienable right of the people of Timor-Leste to self-determination and independence in accordance with the principle of the Charter of the UN ..." and calling upon Indonesia to withdraw its forces from the territory (para 2) and on the government of Portugal to cooperate fully with the UN "so as to enable the people of Timor-Leste to exercise freely their right of self-determination" (para 3). In 1976, Resolution 389 of the Security Council once again reaffirmed this position.

[13] See the story of "Kaikei" in R Winters, *Buibere: Voices of East Timorese women vol. 1* (East Timor International Support Centre, 1999) at p.41.

[14] Forças Armadas de Libertação Nacional de Timor-Leste (Armed Forces for the National Liberation of East Timor).

[15] For example, in 1992 the youngest sister of Xanana Gusmao, Amandina dos Santos, was detained for more than six weeks with other family members and harassed and raped by Kopassus Indonesian Special forces. Xanana Gusmao's wife, Emilia Baptista Gusmao, was also detained on several occasions, forced at gun point to write letters to her husband urging him to surrender. G Aditjondro, "The Silent Suffering of Our Timorese Sisters" report prepared for the *UN Special Rapporteur on Violence Against Women* reproduced in J Aubrey, ed, *Free East Timor: Australia's Culpability in East Timor's Genocide* (Random House, 1998) at p.257.

continuing a cycle of abuse[16] and leading to many other undesirable consequences such as unwanted pregnancy, high incidence of STDs, and ostracism from other members of the community.

The occupation of Timor-Leste has been characterised as genocide, not only due to the sheer number of fatalities but also due to the evident intent to dilute the indigenous population as a means of overcoming the resistance and render East Timorese people strangers in their own land. No doubt this motive was part of the rape strategy. However there was also the much-resented transmigration policy, where incentives such as jobs and accommodation were provided for people from throughout the Indonesian archipelago to re-settle in Timor-Leste. The third prong to this strategy was to limit the indigenous birth rate by introducing a vigorous family planning programme. While after years of allegations of covert contraception and sterilization,[17] the CAVR final report concluded that no such systematic programme existed,[18] the family planning programme was "coercive",[19] and fear of abuses undermined women's confidence to access health services, especially during pregnancy and birth, leading to high levels of infant and maternal mortality and leaving a legacy of mistrust of health professionals, still obstructing access to health services today.

While there were particular categories of women especially vulnerable to gender based persecution,[20] as the Indonesian military became more desperate to eradicate the resistance, tactics were extended to demoralise and destroy the cultural fabric of the entire population. Foremost in this strategy was to attack those most central to the maintenance and survival of families and the community, and any woman or girl became a legitimate target. While men in war are more likely to be killed, disappeared, or seek refuge, women play key roles as stabilisers in preserving order and normalcy in the midst of chaos, and often assume the burden of ensuring family livelihood.[21] These critical

---

[16] *ibid.*, at p.261.

[17] M Sissons, "From One Day to Another: Violations of Women's Reproductive and Sexual Rights in East Timor", East Timor Human Rights Centre, 1997.

[18] Although the Commission did find that the coercive dimensions of the Indonesian family planning programmes in East Timor were particularly pronounced compared to other parts of Indonesia. *Final Report of the Comissão de Acolhimento, Verdade e Reconciliação de Timor Leste, Commission for Reception, Truth and Reconciliation in East Timor* (CAVR), chap 7.9, at pp.33 and 37.

[19] *ibid.*, p.33.

[20] i.e. political activists, political party members, relatives of the former, women without "male protection".

[21] B Sorensen, above, n.2.

community anchorage roles also make them targets. Rape, sexual assault, forced "marriage" or concubinage to members of the Indonesian military, and establishment of military rape camps, became key tools in prising open the tight knit cohesion and loyalty within the Timorese family unit, terrorising the female population, and "biologically 'de-purifying' their ethnic constituency".[22] These violations were designed to cause maximum damage to the woman and her community, being especially potent through the doubly damaging effect of causing the victim to internalise shame associated with such abuse, and having the invidious consequence of isolating those women from the rest of the community who were often judged as prostitutes for the Indonesians.[23] Unfortunately adverse consequences continue to flow for some brave women who have disclosed sexual abuse, finding themselves stigmatised in a community which commonly fails to distinguish between rape and sex, or abandoned by husbands unable to cope with the perceived damage to their honour, or suspicions that the victim cooperated with the abuse.[24] Hence many women carry the double burden of the abuse and a lack of support and recognition of their suffering for very long periods. Some of these women only recently began to relate their experiences through processes such as those undertaken by the CAVR, aimed at providing an environment where women felt safe and confident to add their experiences to the documented human rights history of the occupation.[25] In the words of one Timorese woman "If men are hurt they can recover and forget what happened but for women, if they are raped or tortured, they cannot forget. Their life is destroyed forever".[26]

Women Take Up the Challenges

The flip side of this very heavy coin, is that many Timorese women rose to the new and often bitter challenges presented by war and occupation and proved themselves tough and canny survivors, adapting by stepping outside of their

---

[22] G Aditjondro, above, n.15 reproduced in J Aubrey, ed, *Free East Timor: Australia's Culpability in East Timor's Genocide* (Random House, 1998) at p.247 from R Seifert, "War and rape: a preliminary analysis", in A Stigmayer, ed, *Mass Rape: the war against women in Bosnia-Herzegovina* (University of Nebraska Press, Lincoln, 1994) at pp.62–64.

[23] *ibid.*, at p.260, and see for example the story of "Bialex", R Winters, *Buibere Voices of East Timorese women vol. 1* (East Timor International Support Centre, 1999), at p.28.

[24] In my experience as a lawyer for many East Timorese women seeking asylum in Australia between 1993 and 1998, a number of clients related the experience of abandonment by spouses following disclosure of prior sexual assault.

[25] The CAVR conducted a public hearing in April 2003 titled "Women in Conflict" specifically on the human rights abuses faced by women during the period of its mandate being from 1974 to 1999.

[26] Amnesty International, *Women in Indonesia and East Timor: Standing Against Repression*, AI Index ASA 21/51/1995, 13 December 1995 at p.14.

traditional roles and learning new skills associated with their roles in the resistance and political activism. They demonstrated themselves to be competent militants, activists, organisers, and supporters of resistance activities, shouldering heavy responsibilities and taking huge risks. They became household heads in great numbers, no longer the subjects of male guardianship. They demonstrated their strength and ingenuity in finding means of support for themselves and their families, providing sustenance both physically and emotionally. They cooperated with other women to create new meanings and communities. They asserted for themselves new public roles, whether in demanding to know the whereabouts of missing loved ones, or in undertaking public roles of leadership at a community level. Others able to persist with education succeeded in securing employment in the Indonesian public service and managed for years to live double lives, using their positions to procure or deliver supplies or other benefits to the resistance.[27] Some of those fortunate to escape overseas were able to undertake high quality education and were exposed to modern feminist movements in western countries, causing them to challenge many assumptions regarding the roles of men and women in their home country. Natércia Godinho-Adams' address in 2001 to the UN Security Council, highlighted the incidental gains and identity transformation that many Timorese women experienced during the Occupation.

> … while crisis creates serious problems for women it also creates opportunities. Men's and women's roles changed substantially during the years of conflict and social disruption since 1974. A significant number of women assumed active roles in the clandestine liberation front and the armed resistance. They were soldiers, they smuggled medication, food, armament, and information to the resistance movement hiding in the mountains. … In the absence of the male household head, women assumed new responsibilities in traditional male income generation. East Timorese women want to build a society that will respect their newly acquired post-conflict roles, and will not force them to return to traditional powerless roles.[28]

Women's experiences during the Indonesian occupation changed many of them irreversibly, and with the opportunities presented by the transition to

---

[27] I Cristalis and C Scott, C *Independent Women: The story of women's activism in East Timor* (Catholic Institute for International Relations, London, 2005), at pp.34–35.
[28] "East Timorese woman addresses UN Security Council," 30 October 2001, *www.etan.org/et2001c/november/01-3/0etwoman.htm*, accessed on 14 July 2006.

independence, some steadfastly refused to fit neatly back into the gendered roles expected of them by men. However many more women did revert to the gender status quo. Perhaps the element distinguishing the two groups of women is whether they consciously internalised the changes in their roles and themselves, both individually and collectively:

> ... without a conscious translation, there can be no concerted effort to defend women's opportunities and gains in peacetime. If women do not transform their sense of themselves during conflict, they cannot defend themselves when, in the wake of war, men reassert their claims.[29]

The story of the wife of a FALINTIL fighter who in reflecting on how that experience had indelibly changed her, stated:

> This experience has given me a new perception of my womanhood and my power. I know that almost every other woman in my village has had a similar experience of violence. I am determined to fight for the life of other women. Men may fight with guns, but as a woman I will fight with the power that I have gained out of my suffering, by raising my voice.[30]

Women as Resisters

East Timorese women contributed to all aspects of the resistance. Like men, they paid a very high price. A minority of women joined FALINTIL and fought alongside the men in addition to undertaking a range of other important roles such as recovering Indonesian weapons and military uniforms, cooking and providing food to fighters, providing medical assistance to the injured, and organising FALINTIL camps including providing security. Aside from joining the combatant aspect of FALINTIL, women directly supported the resistance in a range of other ways. Indonesian gender stereotyping frequently enabled women to undertake roles too dangerous for men, virtually all of whom were assumed to be FALINTIL sympathisers. Essential and sensitive roles including smuggling information, providing food and other supplies, and maintaining a reliable communication network between FALINTIL units were entrusted to women and children who generally attracted less suspicion and hence were able to enjoy greater freedom of movement. Despite their substantial contribution, no women ever entered the command structure of

---

29 Meintjes, Pillay, and Turshen, above, n.1, at p.9.

30 World Council of Church WCC) and Christian Conference of Asia (CCA) 1999. Women to women: A solidarity visit to Indonesia and East Timor. 23 June–1 July 1999, *www.wwc-coe.org/wcc/what/international/indon.html*.

FALINTIL and the failure to recognise women's contribution to FALINTIL remains an ongoing issue in Timor-Leste.[31] While many former FALINTIL guerrillas were recruited into the first battalion of the country's new defence forces, the F-FDTL,[32] no female former FALINTIL members were amongst them.[33]

Many girls and women were members of FRETILIN and the women's branch of FRETILIN, OPMT[34] which succeeded in organising a national support network for FALINTIL and were active in promoting the voices of women in the political struggles going on both in rural and urban areas. Political party membership often came at a high price, and women were persecuted specifically due to their membership of OPMT. For example in 1978 in Viqueque, the local Indonesian military command would select an OPMT member each night who would be taken by the troops and raped.[35] The clandestine planned around the rare opportunities when international media or organisers of the resistance would be present to capture international attention, such as the Pope's visit[36] to Timor-Leste in 1989, the UN/Portuguese Parliamentary Human Rights Delegation visit planned for 1991[37] and a UN Representative visit in 1997, which gave rise to a demonstration at the Makhota Hotel. Women and girls participated as organisers and activists of the resistance protest movement. However, while Timorese women played crucial and sensitive roles in supporting the resistance inside Timor-Leste, Timorese women both in and outside of the country were excluded from participation in key decision-making roles and bodies.

---

[31] To celebrate international women's day in 2002, the Office of Gender Equality produced a booklet, for the first time recognising the contribution of women to the resistance. The President established a Veterans' Commission, the Comissão para os Assuntos dos Antigos Combatentes (Commission for Matters of Former Combatants/CAAC) was established by the President in 2002 which commenced a process of public registration to identify those entitled to pensions or other benefits. No women were included in the final veterans register. A second Commission, the Commission of Former Members of the Resistance/Comissão para os Assuntos dos Quadros da Resistencia /CAQR of non-combatant veterans was created to identify those eligible for at least public recognition of their roles and 9,796 women were listed – close to one third of the total number. Independent Evaluation of the CAQR, May 2006.

[32] F-FDTL: FALINTIL – Forças Armadas de Defesa de Timor-Leste.

[33] While a small number of women were recruited, "In December 2002, 27 women, the first female cadets, were amongst the 260 graduates from the F-FDTL training centre", p10 Commission on Human Rights, 59th Session, 4 March 2003, E/CN.4/2003/37, *Situation on Human Rights in Timor-Leste, Report of the High Commissioner for Human Rights,* p.10.

[34] OPMT: Organisação Populár da Mulher de Timor.

[35] G Aditjondro, above, n.15, at p.249.

[36] The first major international visitor to the province since the invasion.

[37] Which was cancelled, however the media was still present and captured the Dili Massacre on film.

Throughout the years of the lack-lustre "All-inclusive intra-East Timorese dialogue" process, East Timorese women struggled for representation. The sum of these efforts over the six-year period, resulted in a modest increase in female representation from one in 30, to four. When the National Council of Timorese Resistance (CNRT) was established in April 1998, creating a non-partisan unified resistance organisation for the first time under the leadership of Xanana Gusmao, women activists were disappointed that women and women's issues were sidelined in this and future CNRT processes. However they were not deterred and grouped to transform the OPMT into the OMT,[38] a non-partisan women's branch of the CNRT involving women from all political parties.

Especially in the lead-up to Suharto's demise, East Timorese women activists defied the pattern of male domination of East Timorese politics and proliferated a new generation of women's organisations outside of the Fretilin party structure, within the student movement, and through the establishment of non-partisan NGOs such as FOKUPERS[39] and *Gertak*.[40] New student organisations established both in Timor-Leste[41] and by Timorese students studying in Indonesia[42] were typically male dominated, and so women met the challenge of either organising in women's only branches within the broader organisation,[43] or by establishing independent women's organisations. With the onset of *Reformasi*,[44] the resistance movement enjoyed greater liberty to organise openly and women were quick to seize this opportunity. In November 1998 a coalition comprised of the East Timor Student Solidarity Council[45] and its girls' branch the GFFTL,[46] Fokupers and OMT organised a

---

[38] *Organisação de Mulher Timor,* the Organisation of Timorese Women. established in 1997 to focus on women victims of human rights violations. In 1998, In line with this change, OPMT, the women's branch of Fretilin became OMT and included women from other political parties. Following liberation in 1999, OPMT revived and OMT continued also.

[39] *Forum Komunikasi Untuk Perempuan Loro Sae*, Timorese Women's Communication Forum.

[40] Established in November 1998 to provide protection and advocate for equal rights for women and children. Later Gertak changed its name to ETWAVE, East Timorese Women Against Violence.

[41] East Timorese Student Solidarity Council was created in 1998 and included a women's branch GFFTL.

[42] RENETIL and IMPETTU.

[43] *e.g.*, the GFFTL *Grupo Feto Foinsa'e Timor Lorosa'e,* Young Women of East Timor, was created within the Student Solidarity Council.

[44] Following 32 years of rule, the fall of President Suharto in 1998 spawned by the Asian currency and financial crisis, created a new environment of political liberalisation known as *Reformasi* which spread across the whole of Indonesia, including the harshly repressed Timor-Leste.

[45] *Dewan Mahasiswa Solidaritas.*

[46] *Grupo Feto Foinsa'e Timor Lorosa'e,* Young Women of East Timor.

public women's conference involving hundreds of women from all over the country[47] where they spoke publicly of their abuse by the Indonesian military for the first time.[48] Women throughout the diaspora were also very active, beginning to use UN mechanisms to draw attention to the plight of Timor-Leste, especially its women, and challenging male assumptions of dominance within the political party structures.

Women in the Transition

Immediately following the dramatic events of the ballot and its violent aftermath, Timorese women achieved a major victory when the CNRT agreed upon a transitional structure for governance which included a gender equity commission. In many senses events overtook the Timorese leadership when the UN belatedly began planning for a follow-on mission from UNAMET largely in a vacuum from the Timorese leadership, which was presumed defunct. The United Nations Transitional Administration in East Timor (UNTAET) was given a mandate unprecedented in ambition and, in keeping with the UN's commitment to "mainstream" gender issues in peace-keeping missions,[49] the resolution emphasised "the importance of including in UNTAET personnel with appropriate training in international humanitarian, human rights and refugee law, including child and gender-related provisions".[50] This was the first time that a UN mandate explicitly recognised gender dimensions in its composition.[51]

While significant gains were made in promoting the advancement of women during the UNTAET period, these can be attributed more to the tenacity of the women activists involved than any planned and coordinated approach taken to gender mainstreaming by the UN. For example, in June 2000, women activists initiated the first national women's congress, a two-day meeting involving women from all over Timor-Leste at a which a national plan of action for women's rights was developed.[52] The rhetoric emanating from

[47] In a dialogue titled "Today's Conference is on the Image of the East Timorese Women (Conferencia Loron Rua Kona Sa Laloek Feto Timor Loro Sae), R Winters, *Buibere: Voices of East Timorese women vol. 1* (East Timor International Support Centre, 1999), at p.ix.

[48] *ibid.*, some were emboldened to have their stories recorded in the book of personal testimonies *Buibere*: *Voice of East Timorese women volume I.*

[49] See S/RES/1325 calling for the inclusion of women in peace building, expressing concern at the adverse effect of conflict on women and urging specialised gender-sensitive training for all UN peacekeepers.

[50] See S/RES/1272.

[51] H Charlesworth and M Wood, "Women and Human Rights in the Rebuilding of East Timor" (2002) 71 *Nordic Journal of International Law* 325, at p.329.

[52] Cristalis and Scott, above, n.27, at p.77.

UNTAET recognised the differential impact of conflict upon Timor-Leste's women but did not tally with the overall "master" plan and was not matched with the allocation of resources or the institutional machinery necessary to achieve gender mainstreaming. Successes in the area of gender equity were largely haphazard and uncoordinated due to the lack of priority given to promoting women, and the failure to properly resource and give voice to the initiatives of women's NGOs and advocacy groups. The axing, and then delayed reinstatement of an emasculated Gender Affairs Unit,[53] the perceived failure to adequately deal with victims of sexual assault during the 1999 crisis and aftermath,[54] and the active opposition of senior UN staff in Electoral Affairs to the campaign to entrench in law a requirement that parties field in the 2001 Constituent Assembly elections a 30 percent quota of female candidates, are examples of how for many in the Timorese women's movement, the UN represented a whole new world of gender-insensitive bureaucrats and unfamiliar red tape to be overcome. This was quite in addition to the continuing challenge of persuading Timorese men that women must be included and permitted to secure a foot-hold in the reconstruction agenda. That said, important milestones were achieved such as Constitutional inclusion of protection of the principle of equality between the sexes[55] and the incorporation of international legal norms into domestic law.[56] While the female candidate quota proposal was defeated at the National Council in March 2001, FRETILIN who won an overwhelming majority of seats was persuaded[57] to field 30 percent female candidates, and as a consequence, 24 women (27 percent) were elected to the Constituent Assembly, a percentage that would rival or surpass most legislatures' efforts of the past century to promote female inclusion.

Women of Independence

With the transformation from UN administration to independence, further important gains were made for women at high levels of the State. Timorese

---

53 Charlesworth and Wood, above, n.51, and C Scott, "Are women included or excluded in Post-Conflict Reconstruction?: A Case study from East Timor, *Catholic Institute for International Relations*, 30 June 2003, at *www.peacewomen.org/resources/Timor-Leste/CIIRWomens Part03.html*.

54 See S Harris Rimmer, "Untold numbers: East Timorese women and transitional justice", in C Lambert, S Pickering, eds, *Global Issues, Women and Justice,* Sydney Institute of Criminology Series No 19, Sydney, 2004.

55 See s 17 of the Constitution. It is worth noting however that the wording does suggest that "equality" may be limited to formal equality, as opposed to substantive equality.

56 See s 9 of the Constitution which adopts into domestic law the general or customary principles of international law and the rules provided for in international conventions and treaties.

57 Women activists sought the support of the SRSG who refused air-time to political parties unless they could demonstrate their commitment to gender equity. C Scott, above, n.53.

women activists succeeded in securing an Office for the Promotion of Equality ("OPE") reporting directly to the prime minister in the new government with responsibility to coordinate gender mainstreaming, promote the participation of women in development, and to inject gender-sensitive perspectives into policy and law reform programme.[58] Five ministerial appointments in the government were women, and more than 20 percent of initial recruits into the new police force were women.[59] Considerable leaps forward were made in improving female participation in local governance, often an impenetrable male bastion, with the reservation of three seats for women within all local councils,[60] and in local elections in 2004/2005, a modest number of women succeeded in being elected to the positions of Suco (village) and Aldeia (hamlet) chiefs, previously almost exclusively the preserve of men.[61]

On paper, Timor-Leste would appear to be an excellent place to be a woman. Timor-Leste is a signatory to CEDAW without reservation and the East Timorese Constitution automatically incorporates the provisions of CEDAW into domestic law.[62] Moreover the Constitution contains provisions relating directly to the equality of women in all areas of family, political, economic, social, and cultural life.[63] Despite several years of delays and re-drafts, the government remains committed to enacting a series of laws specifically addressing domestic violence. In addition, there is (relatively speaking) excellent representation of women in parliament.[64] A specialist unit[65] within

---

[58] "Gender and Nation Building in Timor-Leste: Country Gender Assessment", *Asia Development Bank/ UNIFEM*, November 2005, p.12.

[59] *ibid.*, at p.28, data from UNTAET 2001 F-FDTL, although efforts lag in relation to female civil servants, *www.adb.org/Documents/Reports/Country-Gender-Assessments/cga-timor-leste.pdf.*

[60] See "Law on the Election of Suco Chiefs and Suco Councils", 2/2004, Art 3 accessed on 10 December at *www.eastimorlawjournal.org/LAWSINDEPENDENCE/2of2004sucoelections.html.*

[61] From across Timor-Leste, 22 women were elected as Aldeia chiefs, seven as Suco Chiefs and two as Lia Nain or indigenous justice leaders. Prosesu Eleitoral iha Timor-leste 2004–2005, Secretariado Tecnico de Administração Eleitoral (STAE), Dili, Timor-Leste 2006, p.129.

[62] See s 9 of the Constitution which provides that "The legal system of East Timor shall adopt the general or customary principles of international law. Rules provided for in international conventions, treaties and agreements shall apply in the internal legal system of East Timor following their approval, ratification or accession by the respective competent organs and after publication in the official gazette. All rules that are contrary to the provisions of international conventions, treaties and agreements applied in the internal legal system of East Timor shall be invalid."

[63] See ss 17 and 39(3) which further provide that "marriage shall be based upon free consent by the parties and on terms of full equality of rights between spouses, in accordance with the law".

[64] Twenty seven percent of the current seats in Parliament are occupied by women. Women hold two senior cabinet positions, Minister of State and Minister of Finance and Planning, and three vice minister positions. One of the three judges on the Appeals Court is a woman.

[65] The Vulnerable Persons Unit (VPU).

the police has been established to deal with domestic violence and other gender-based cases and operates at national,[66] district, and sub-district levels.

Closer examination of women's actual positioning and power within these roles serves as a reminder that effective gender mainstreaming requires more than women positioned in decision-making and non-traditional occupational roles.[67] For example, to date, women parliamentarians (like all parliamentarians) have received little ongoing support or capacity building in their roles, and have not succeeded in forming alliances across party lines, hence their impact generally and on gender issues has been muted. In addition, they are part of an institution which since independence has been increasingly sidelined by ballooning executive power.[68] Women in the police force are largely constrained to junior "female" roles, in politically marginalised parts of the police force such as working within the Vulnerable Persons Unit, and complain of criminal conduct and discrimination by male colleagues.[69] Whether women in local governance roles are able to wield effective power and are accepted as legitimate, authentic community leaders are perhaps the greatest challenges.

Implosion of the Independence Dream: A Man-Made Mess

The crisis that commenced in April/May 2006 provided a sobering updated assessment of the continuing crushing effect of patriarchy upon female participation and empowerment in public life, even in the capital where women's gains had clearly been the strongest. A whole spectrum of male players, from incompetent and criminal male political leaders, to splintering factions of male soldiers and police, to marauding gangs of male youths,

---

[66] Although all national level policing has been interrupted by the 2006 crisis and at the time of writing around 200 individually screened police, had returned to active service. Press conference 3, SRSG UNMIT, January 2007.

[67] Especially where many of those women have had limited opportunities for education, training and capacity building.

[68] Most legislative measures, including some constitutionally required to be passed by the parliament, have been passed by the Executive as Decree Law, bypassing parliamentary scrutiny. In relation to the Penal Code, the National Parliament contributed to its own marginalisation by passing a law (Law No 16/2005) delegating its Constitutional law making powers to the Executive.

[69] Several cases of criminal assault by male officers upon female colleagues have emerged, for example in May 2006, a senior police officer who had previously been disciplined for sexually harassing a number of female colleagues, was charged with the rape of a female colleague. In relation to discrimination, while I was in Oecussi, a group of female police officers complained to their commander that male officer demanded they clean their boots for them every morning, and when functions were held, undertake the catering and cleaning. Another example is documented in JSMP's report *Police Treatment of Women in Timor-Leste*, Dili, Timor-Leste January 2005 accessed on 15 December 2006 at *www.jsmp.minihub.org/Reports/jsmpreports/01jan05_wju_police%20report/Police%20report(e).pdf*, at p.14.

essentially caused the collapse of the fragile peace and institutions which had provided a modicum of security since independence. Analysis of these events purporting to unpackage the origins of the violence, has focused primarily on political, historical, and social explanations, glossing over the clearly gendered nature of the conflict and the salient fact that virtually all of the protagonists were men.[70]

Since independence, a continuous theme running throughout the Timorese political landscape, has been the obsessive pursuit of competing and cross-cutting assertions of who can rightfully claim credit for Timor-Leste achieving independence. This divisive theme which has enslaved the country to its tragic history, boils down to the testosterone-charged question of "Who is the biggest hero?" The 2001 Constituent Assembly and 2002 Presidential campaigns predictably revolved around the backward-looking issue of candidates' ability to garner support on the basis of their war credentials, rather than a debate around how to best meet the country's current and future challenges. Unfortunately this has set the tone for the past five years. The key reason underlining the desertion of almost half the national army was an alleged continuous pattern of discrimination and insult by senior "Lorosae"[71] commanders against more junior "Loromono"[72] soldiers, the imputation being that they had been Indonesian collaborators and had not contributed to the independence struggle. This is what remains at the heart of the "Loromono/Lorosae" division which so dramatically and violently rose to prominence in Dili in 2006. The clashing and jockeying of male egos, whether they be ambitious politicians, disgruntled veterans, youths, or police/army members, overwhelmed by gun-induced rushes of power, have dominated the political debate in Timor-Leste since independence. This effect is magnified by a strong cult of personality, the smallness of the political elite, and the fact that the handful of leaders "running" Timor-Leste have been unable to rise above unresolved betrayals and battles of the past. Ironically, through the "competition of heroes", the value of the independence secured has been demeaned and devalued.

---

[70] See for example the findings of the UN Independent Special Commission of Inquiry for Timor-Leste accessed on 8 December 2006 at *www.ohchr.org/english/docs/ColReport-English.pdf*, accessed on 15 December 2006.

[71] In the 2006 conflict, Lorosae people are defined as originating from the three eastern-most districts, Lautem, Viqueque and Baucau.

[72] Loromono is the label affixed in the 2006 conflict to people originating from the remaining nine districts, including most controversially, Manatutu, the District from which the president Xanana Gusmao originates.

As this paper has sought to illuminate, the women of Timor-Leste also have an important war history to be told, and have also contributed and suffered enormously during the occupation. Yet their voices, for those who seek them out, carry quite different messages. This a sample of the words of some ordinary women I met who were struggling to look after their families in three of the IDP camps in September 2006.[73] I asked them who and what were responsible for the current political and security crisis.

> "Our leaders need to grow up. It's time we let some of our heroes go before they drag us all down with them."

> "These men argue about who won the war for Timor while the fruits of all our struggle lie in ashes at our feet."

> "I don't care about Loromono and Lorosae, I want my family back in our house, my children at school and able to go to the hospital."

> "All those men who want to chain us to our history just play into the hands of Indonesia who want to see us weak and poor forever. They should just go and fight it out on Atauro [an island just north of Dili] and let the rest of us get on with the important things, like giving our children a chance at a better life than we had."

Women talked about the problem of the Timorese "male character", their "hot headedness", "lack of discipline" and "intense pride" being common triggers for insult-trading. They also lamented the lack of cooperation between the key leaders at the top of the political hierarchy and wished that they could overlook their differences for the sake of the country. While of course not all women subscribe to these views, and the situation is no doubt far more complex than represented in these quotes, I found it interesting that amongst a small sample, so many identified the roles of the male leadership collectively, as the root cause of the difficulties faced.

Aside from being portrayed as refugee victims, women were notably absent, both as protagonists in the various emerging conflicts and as stakeholders in the conflict resolution processes. The invisibility of women as active players is evident in the report of the UN's Independent Special Commission of Inquiry for Timor-Leste tasked to "establish the facts and circumstances" and

[73] I spoke to 15 women in four IDP camps, in Caicoli, at the airport, at the Port and at Metinaro, most of whom were "Lorosae" or easterners.

"related events or issues" that contributed to the crisis, in which no female suspect is named in any of the events investigated, and few women are mentioned in the narrative of events[74] or were interviewed by the Commission.[75]Acknowledgement that any solution or reconciliation between the parties should also address the undeniable gender dimensions of the eruption, seems a long way off.[76] Sword-Gusmao, writer, activist and wife to the Timorese President noted poignantly:

> ... it is sad and disturbing to note that, in a time of crisis and conflict such as East Timor is presently experiencing, the platforms that women have managed to acquire seem to come crashing down, their voices drowned out by the din of the political clamourings of male leaders and the roar of the machinery of a peace-keeping operation directed and driven by men.. It is telling that not a single East Timorese woman has solicited an audience with my husband nor has had her views sought on solutions to the crisis over the past few weeks. It has not been a deliberate act of exclusion, it just hasn't occurred to anyone in this intensely patriarchal society that women may have something important and useful to contribute to the delicate and vital processes of disarmament, reconciliation and peace-building.[77]

Part II: Tackling Reality by Harnessing Cultural Change to Support Women's Rights

Taking Stock and Taking the Next Step

So why, despite the existence of female political leadership and reasonable representation in parliament and government, have Timorese women been rendered largely irrelevant to these recent major national events such that they have no place at the negotiating table? Some can be attributed to the dominant "big man" political culture, which is both hierarchical and masculine, and the common perception that authentic, credible political leadership and exercise

[74] The report mentions the presence of Ana Pessoa, Minister of State Administration at a key meeting, (p 27), but doesn't state the gender of other players including a female police officer who received a tip-off that the F-FDTL planned to attack the PNTL Headquarters (p 33), and four girls or women who were burnt to death in an attack on their house (p 37).

[75] I was a member of the Secretariat of the Commission and can confirm that less than a handful of women were individually interviewed, although the Commission convened at least one group meeting at which women's groups were represented.

[76] Although with one notable exception, the International Crisis Group which has urged that particular attention be given to the role of women in reconciliation initiatives. International Crisis Group, Resolving Timor-Leste's Crisis, Asia Report No 120, 10 October 2006, p.ii.

[77] K Sword-Gusmao, "Women suffering in silence", *The Australian*, 7 July 2006.

of "real" power remain male terrain. The saying "the hen may know how to crow but that is not her business!"[78] appears to have currency in Timor-Leste. Hence:

> the solution is not as simple as proving that women are in fact effective decision-makers or leaders. The challenge is a more difficult one of making women's competence count; making women's authority acceptable and legitimate.[79]

In addition, as is a common pattern and flaw of the "women representation" model as a stand-alone strategy, having women in positions of power does not mean that addressing gender inequality will necessarily be a priority for them, or that women bound to working within dominant masculine frameworks and political culture will be able to "work the system" for positive effect for women overall. A further contributing factor to the relative ineffectiveness of Timorese female political leadership in highlighting and acting upon the plight of women generally relates less to gender and more to the marked concentration and centralisation of power in Timor-Leste into very few hands, hence the drastic reduction overall in the number of places available at the figurative negotiating table.

Of course like women elsewhere, women in Timor-Leste are not an homogenous group. Amongst Timorese women there are many cleavages which cut across sex, such as socio-economic, class, educational, and rural versus urban backgrounds. The cavernous divide between the usually-educated women elites in the capital and other district centres and women who make up the rural backbone of the country, presents huge challenges for "women's" emancipation. However, women from all backgrounds share in the main problem underpinning their marginalisation: entrenched gender inequality.

I argue that entrenched gender equality can only be dismantled effectively through the hard task of longer term processes of cultural transformation at the grassroots level, rather than through a primary focus on state institutions and international protection frameworks. The existence of formal equality before the law or Timor-Leste's accession to CEDAW and its Optional Protocol have so far done little to advance the cause of equality for Timorese women due to

---

[78] C Nyamu-Musembi, "Are local Norms and Practices Fences or Pathways? The Example of Women's Property Rights", in A An-Na'im, *Cultural Transformation and Human Rights in Africa* (Zed Books, New York, 2002) at p.142.
[79] *ibid.*, at p.142.

the disconnection between state-based law and ordinary custom and practice, or the "living law" of Timor-Leste. This gap is demonstrative of the acute limitations of formal rights protections where the state is new, weak, and poor. The standards embodied in the Constitution and laws have been adopted by a small urban elite, without achieving a deeper consensus in Timor's rural heartland, where tribal dictates determine that different law and standards are regularly applied.

The effectiveness of liberal feminist strategies that focus on the representation of women and improvements in the formal law, will remain limited unless the deeper structural gender divisions in society are addressed. To that end, there will be always be local resistance to perceived externally-initiated change or the imposition of values or standards that do not resonate with local communities. The issue of women's rights commonly strikes fear into those often powerful and male members of communities who feel their culture, identity and way of life is acutely threatened by the prospect of a re-writing of the gender landscape. Some women feel similarly threatened by the prospect of the fundamental change involved in challenging entrenched gender constructions. Change will only be effected and sustained to the extent that it is internalised or legitimised by the communities concerned.[80]

The lack of traction of formal protections of gender equality throughout Timorese society leads to the inescapable conclusion that a much broader range of strategies than the typical state-focused, top-down human rights toolkit need to be developed, strategies with the potential to achieve a lasting transformation of attitudes regarding women's rights and roles. Of course gains secured by women activists in developing and using international human rights instruments are valuable and necessary. But they are insufficient to the mammoth task of achieving lasting equality and suggestive that the international feminist agenda should be more grounded in the day-to-day experiences and struggles of women. To achieve lasting transformation, human rights advocates should not overlook the importance of engaging custodians of culture and communities in ongoing relationships rather than pitching most effort towards state responsibility as the primary vehicle for social change, especially in countries like Timor-Leste where the reach of the state is weak. What is needed now are not further legal abstractions and debates about rights, but concrete measures and the "vernacularization of

[80] A An-Na'im, and J Hammond, "Cultural Transformation and Human Rights in African Societies", in An-Na'im, *ibid.*, p.14.

human rights",[81] for situating rights within local contexts of meaning and power, and for translating those rights into the realities of the lives of individuals and communities. This is not easy given that human rights ideas replete with their own assumptions are not easily transplanted from one context to another. Relatively little is known about how people and communities in different cultural contexts, develop, integrate or reject understandings of human rights. Certain general conundrums become evident, however, when applying human rights to particular local settings. One of these tensions is that human rights are more readily accepted and persuasive if they are packaged in familiar terms, yet only effective where they challenge particular existing power structures and practices.[82] Traditional assumptions about the roles of men and women can and must be challenged within communities, and by members of those communities, for change to be effective and sustainable. But how could this be tackled in Timor-Leste?

Playing the "Culture" Card

As explored earlier, "culture" is not the only ingredient transfixing unequal gender relations in Timor-Leste. Continuing processes associated with occupation, conflict, and the influence of the Roman Catholic Church and its doctrine, also play important roles and should equally be the focus of engagement and transformative approaches to encourage and support opportunities for advancing women. However "culture" is probably the most seemingly amorphous yet intransient and determinative factor of gender inequality and hence the processes involved in changing cultural values and practices are a particular focus in this paper. In addition, a process of long-term cultural transformation creates new opportunities to creatively expand the field of human rights practice and is likely to produce more durable and sustained results, as the change achieved will have been achieved internal to the indigenous culture. A precondition to changing cultural mores is the gaining of an understanding of the processes involved in the creation, maintenance, and reproduction of culture. By better understanding processes of cultural transformation and the factors that determine both the direction and quality of change, human rights actors can more effectively steer those processes to enhance the protection of the rights of women.

As elsewhere, in Timor-Leste the violation of women's human rights is commonly justified by use of "cultural" arguments. Globally, there is arguably no group which has been more victimised than women, in the name of

---

[81] SE Merry, *Human Rights and Gender Violence, Translating International Law into Local Justice* (University of Chicago Press, 2006), at p.1.

[82] *ibid.*, at p.5.

"culture".[83] In Timor-Leste women are commonly cast as central to the maintenance of culture on several bases; as custodians of culture, as representatives of fertility and reproduction in their communities and due to their common role as primary caregivers and hence as inculcators of culture to children. Their behaviour and dress are perceived as the embodiment of cultural markers and expectations, as is their consignment to "private sphere" activities (and conversely men's to the "public sphere").[84] This particular casting of women as purveyors of culture and community identity presents some values at odds with the pursuit of their human rights, and thus given the high stakes involved for all parties, the unsurprising historical antagonism between "culture" and women's human rights. This oppositional relationship, combined with uncritical adoption of patriarchal articulations of culture, have blinded many feminist thinkers to the potential and possibilities of strategically engaging and harnessing cultural processes of reproduction. Rather than casting culture as the enemy of gender equality and hence automatically distancing the feminist human rights enterprise from its critical locus of action at the grassroots, it is time to engage with the opportunities for reform through developing alliances with those positioned as key shapers and defenders of cultural norms and practice.

Sensitivity to cultural diversity is important, especially given arrogant assumptions of cultural homogeneity and consensus underpinning the genesis and development of debates around the universality of human rights. Equally, however, one must remain mindful of the existence of minority voices within communities, the existence of intra-societal gender oppression and the great danger of uncritically accepting assertions of difference as defences of violations of women's human rights. When faced with such a cultural defence, Rao postulates a series of interrogative questions to probe the politics of cultural defences of rights violations and to assist in assessing their credibility:

> First, what is the status of the speaker? Second, in whose name is the argument in culture advanced? Third, what is the degree of participation in culture formation of the social groups primarily affected by the cultural practices in question? Fourth, what is culture anyway?[85]

---

[83] A Rao, "The Politics of Gender and Culture in International Human Rights Discourse", *Women's Rights, Human Rights-International Feminist Perspectives,* Peters, J. Wolper, A.(eds), Routledge, New York London, 1995, p.169.

[84] *ibid.*

[85] *ibid.,* at p.168.

Defining the parameters of culture could be an infinite undertaking. For the purposes of this paper, "culture" is the learned and shared behaviours or patterns of meanings which manifest a people's, or rather a group's way of life. Culture is transmitted historically and provides a template of beliefs, assumptions and expectations which can be projected onto others to systemise the way people do things. "It is the cement that holds societies together by vastly simplifying interaction and cooperation."[86] Culture does not exist as a stand-alone, static, unchanging fixed body of knowledge, but rather the establishment and maintenance of cultural norms is a dynamic process and is in a constant state of flux. Cultural practices "are reproduced and transformed only through the activities of individuals, and are suspended or discontinued when the upholders of a given tradition entertain viable alternatives to it".[87] This process has been described as "the ambivalence and contestability of cultural norms and institutions".[88] Human agency propels all sides of any culture debate, both the proponents of change and those who resist it.

Culture is subjective in that it is subject to different interpretations by both those within and outside of it. Hence it does not exist as an objective homogenous entity, but is always mediated by the positioning of the speaker. Certain voices are privileged to speak and be heard in any society, and in Timor-Leste those voices are usually male. Within the powerful customary law system, there are particular persons, again usually male, who are assigned responsibility to preserve cultural traditions, the environment, or resolve disputes and hence their articulations of culture wield particular weight and influence. It is also no accident that their interpretations are commonly strongly patriarchal. Dominant articulations of culture may therefore easily become entrenched and the nuances and irregularities of actual cultural practice are easily lost.

Thus, a key strategy for addressing cultural arguments is to present a diversity of articulations of culture from within it, to amplify minority understandings of culture, so that culture is perceived as the textured, diverse, and varied phenomenon that it actually is, rather than received as an essentialist, one dimensional or rhetorically rigid articulation. If these latter descriptions of culture are permitted to go unchallenged and the dominant patriarchal

---

86 An-Na'im and Hammond, above, n.78, at p.22.

87 *ibid.*, at p.23.

88 An-Na'im, "State Responsibility Under International Human Rights Law to Change Religious and Customary Laws", in R Cook, ed, *Human Rights of Women: national and international perspectives*, (University of Pennsylvania Press, 1994), at p.173.

accounts of culture are uncritically adopted, then they can become self-fulfilling.

Part III: Possible Approaches to Cultural Transformation in Timor-Leste

People Make Things Happen: Human Agency and Social Change

What follows are some suggestions or thoughts based on what I have learnt in my research and work experiences in the human rights field in Timor-Leste[89] directed to the enterprise of re-orientating or harnessing aspects of Timorese cultures towards bolstering rather than undermining women's human rights. In addressing the key challenge of how to internally critically examine and test some Timorese cultural values or practices which discriminate against women, an initial and important question is what Timorese agents of social change have the internal cultural legitimacy and consciousness of gender inequality to drive such a sensitive, yet important, process?

It is critical for social change agents to, as far as possible, be from the local area or have an affinity such as a shared local language with the community in order to enhance internal legitimacy and authority of the process. Both men and women including Timorese scholars, activists, local leaders, and ordinary village men and women folk, are ideally positioned to provide the impetus and expertise for such a change process. The existence of actors on a range of levels in Timor-Leste who are motivated and committed to working towards gender equality presents positive possibilities for reform of cultural mores and attitudes which inhibit the realisation of women's human rights. Often this difficult work is left to women's organisations and women leaders, as it is seen as women's business and a necessary part of the emancipation project that women do it alone. It is critical that any change process be empowering to women, directed by women and firmly grounded in women's experiences. But it is also necessary that the process for change is based on current realities and pragmatic, savvy choices about what is likely to work best in any given community, and that a strong sense of partnership between like-minded men and women is fostered.

While people of both sexes may feel threatened by the prospect of gender recalibration within their communities, those who have the greatest interest in maintaining the *status quo*, and are most likely to be implacably resistant to change, are generally male. In maximising their receptivity to change

[89] See biographical information at end of chapter.

messages, careful selection of the messenger is critical. Bearing in mind that the objective is to change cultural practices which violate women's rights, then the importance of recruiting social actors who are likely to have maximum influence over the attitudes of key resisters such as some indigenous justice leaders tasked with preserving their notion of culture, should be identified and enlisted to participate with women in the change process. In the case of Timor-Leste, the main opinion-formers of men, are generally other men, namely community leaders from a range of backgrounds including elders and traditional leaders, resistance leaders, church leaders, civil servants, politicians, teachers, businessmen, youth leaders and non-government organisation leaders, ideally from within the relevant community. Hence any such men who support the emancipation of women should be recruited as a "vanguard" to participate in the change process alongside Timorese women. This strategy is already being implemented by an East Timorese men's group, Mane Kontra Violencia, founded by men in 2002 to challenge the social conditioning and attitudes of other men on gender-based violence.[90]

Women "socialisers" can play an especially effective role in developing consciousness, gender analysis, and the possibilities for change amongst women. Women leaders can be effective role models and supporters to other women. Elderly women, especially those from powerful Timorese family groupings, often enjoy a higher status. Hence greater weight is given to their voices. Additionally, they often have more discretionary time than women caring for children, and may therefore be well positioned to persuade and inspire other women and men. "Ordinary" women have power to set agendas, initiate discussions and take action in their homes and through their daily interactions or workings with each other and men, whether it be at the market, church, the well, or through micro-credit and other cooperative enterprises.

A whole range of ongoing possible activities could form the basis for the cultural change process. Discussion, persuasion, trials, and evaluations of alternative ways of doing things, graded change, incentive-based activities or, where resisters prove to be unreceptive, direct political grassroots action, are all the kinds of activities envisaged under a long-term campaign for gender justice. It is important that communities understand the very real economic and social dividends that can flow to all if women are given greater opportunities. Hence it is a discussion not about men losing ground and women gaining it,

---

[90] Headed by Marito Araujo, interviewed by Catherine Scott in Cristalis and Scott, above, n.27, at p.102. I was involved in supporting a local NGO piloting a men's group in Oecussi District in 2002–2003 which undertook a range of educational and counseling activities targeting other men.

but how women and all other communities members – including men – also gain ground. Concrete examples should be presented of how communities in comparable situations have achieved fast-tracked development, improved economic prosperity, and greater happiness, satisfaction and stability by supporting the enhanced participation of women in education and economic ventures especially.

Venues for engagement on the issue of gender justice in Timor-Leste could include but are not limited to forums, meetings, informal gatherings, individual "fire-side" chats, family consultations, focus groups, and cultural and community events. Both "men to men" and "women to women" forums are necessary in Timor-Leste,[91] complimented by mixed forums where "report-backs" on the single-sex discussions are presented so that the perspectives from both groups are shared and discussed together.[92] Such an approach heads off any potential sense of secrecy or conspiracy from developing between the men and women of a community, and strengthens the sense of common engagement and partnership between the sexes. A graded approach to change may be one option chosen. Where some level of consensus can be achieved on the consequences and impact of gender inequality upon a community, then some communities may choose to trial and evaluate alternative approaches collectively. For example, for each family to have some negotiation over the delegation of domestic tasks for a period, trial the redistribution of work, and then to re-gather as a community to share perspectives and to evaluate the trial. Communities may decide that their men or women need assistance in developing particular skills, such as negotiation skills for everyone, or cooking skills for men, or numeracy programmes for women, and then find ways of supporting each other or finding external resources to make identified programmes happen.

Internal Critical Evaluation Strategies

Culture and Human Rights: Identifying Common Ground

So what are some practical suggestions as to how indigenous agents of social change could engage in critical re-examination of cultural practices which discriminate against women? The first is to utilise what I term an "existent" approach to popular human rights education. It involves the logical and obvious, but often overlooked, starting point that communities will be much more receptive to discussing and reaching understandings of human rights if

[91] In my experience women are far more forthcoming and participatory in group discussions in female-only forums, hence such opportunities are critical if the aim is to elicit the views of women.

[92] Carefully facilitated to ensure equal "airtime" for women participants.

such notions are grounded in values of human rights which already exist and are understood and practiced within the cultures of that community. Aside from providing strong points of anchorage for more difficult human rights discussions down the track, such an approach also draws out positive aspects of cultural practice which support and bolster human rights, an important recognition, given that many human rights approaches tend to fix on violations and fail to give credit for positive human rights practices.

By at least starting with human rights principles which are an embedded part of local cultural practices, any discussion of human rights begins where it should, in terms of their direct and concrete relevance to the lives of real people, rather than as theoretical concepts floating around somewhere "out there". Human rights presented as an external parallel system or package of values and standards to those that exist within the receiving community, rather than the fulfillment and extension of values already evident and part and parcel of everyday life, are likely to create anxiety and confusion and undermine community ownership of human rights. As summed up in the question of one Timorese woman, "What is this human rights belief system and are we being asked to convert to it and leave our own culture and religion behind?"[93]

Once some values common to both the community in question and human rights principles have been identified, then they can be built or extrapolated upon as examples of why, for example, that value should be extended or applied consistently towards a discriminated-against segment of the community. While it still clearly requires long-term work to bring about basic attitudinal changes such as, for example, the right of women to live free from family violence or participate equally in the work force, such an approach does at least provide some immediate challenge to an indigenous value such as "equality and dignity of the individual" which is not consistently applied to women. It also ensures a point of traction or resonance with some known point of reference and understanding for the basis of that value. An important initial activity may be to explore with communities key values underpinning cultural life and analyse how they correlate with international human rights standards. While the values or aspirations distilled through such a process may not always be consistently applied, there being always internal contradictions between the values and practices of the people in any culture, the existence of individual lapses does not invalidate the value systems themselves.[94] The

---

[93] Woman speaking in community forum in Mahata, Oecussi District, October 2002.

[94] Law Commission of New Zealand, *Converging Currents: Custom and Human Rights in the Pacific*, Study Paper 17, September 2006, Wellington, at p.49.

greater challenge arises where there is a clash between the values or norms themselves, for example, agreement that everyone is to be treated with respect, but that some believe they are entitled to "teach" others in that society through the use of violence. In such situations it might be helpful to engage communities in ranking or prioritising which values are more important, or which should be dominant in habitual practice.

While as a non-indigenous player I recognise the limitations of research I have undertaken myself, I tentatively identified through 50 discussions with indigenous justice leaders and representatives from human rights and women's organizations in four districts,[95] a number of very broad values commonly underpinning a number of Timorese cultures that resonate with human rights principles and then, more particularly, those that might assist in further efforts to reduce the incidence of wife beating in Timor-Leste.[96] My methodology was based on semi-structured in-depth individual interviews. Participants were asked to explain their understandings of core human rights values, core cultural values and then to identify overlapping values. The responses of earlier participants to this exercise were put to or tested upon later participants along with a number of common values which had been tentatively identified by myself. Then participants were asked to rank those common values identified through this process in order of most to least central to their understanding of their culture. A similar process was undertaken in relation to values imbedded within culture which could be used to develop campaigns against wife-beating. Surprisingly, the suggestions and priorities of both participant groups were markedly similar, suggesting scope for the development of common approaches across a broad range of social actors.

The first issue tested was whether the approach of identifying indigenous notions of human rights was a useful starting point to grassroots discussions on human rights. All of those interviewed agreed that it would be, especially in light of the view articulated by several local justice leaders that previous efforts to socialise human rights concepts in their communities had had limited effect, as they were considered to be alien or foreign concepts pitted in a competitive relationship with aspects of Timorese culture.

---

[95] The research was conducted in Dili, Liquica, Oecussi and Ermera Districts and involved a total of 50 in-depth interviews.

[96] Domestic violence, more specifically wife beating, is the focus of my current research and hence the theme around which this exercise in identifying indigenous human rights values, was undertaken.

General values in Timorese cultures found to share common ground with human rights principles included the following:

1. Individual dignity: A fundamental respect for individual dignity arising primarily from the notion that all people are children of God and endowed with unique spirits, value and potential. All people are entitled to equal treatment and respect. Everyone has a right to speak and be heard and should not be interrupted. Everyone should be treated the way that they would like to be treated. All children are entitled to be loved and cared for. Children are particularly cherished. They must be taught to show respect to other people from a young age.
2. Love and care, especially for family members. Filial obligations and love bind together to form the primary cement of Timorese society.
3. Reciprocity: This value stresses the importance of maintaining harmony and balance in all relationships and the need to resolve transgressions to restore such harmony. Such reciprocity is often acted out through the exchange of gifts.
4. Consensus: The search for consensus runs through many facets of Timorese life, and can be seen especially in local dispute resolution practice which places a high value on the peaceful resolution of disputes, the reconciliation of the parties, and disparages those who resort to violence.
5. Sharing of resources: All people are entitled to equal treatment in access to, and allocation of resources necessary for basic livelihood.

In terms of values which could be emphasised in campaigning specifically to reduce the incidence of wife-beating, indigenous justice leaders strongly believed that emphasising the damage done to the well-being and development of children if they are exposed to domestic violence, would be the value with the strongest persuasive value over Timorese men. Human rights and women's organisation representatives concurred that an emphasis on the well-being of children and the damage inflicted upon them by domestic violence, would be an effective "angle".

Indigenous justice leaders believed that the second most compelling human rights concepts embedded in Timorese culture (92 per cent) were those reflected in the local justice system. Put in simplest terms, just as local justice requires the parties to a dispute to be disciplined and not resort to physical violence, but rather to sit, listen to each other, and negotiate a resolution, so too with disputes between husbands and wives, a similar approach should be adopted, rather than husbands using violence. Indigenous justice leaders thought that this would have a good prospect of success, as all men understood and respected the local justice system, and could clearly understand the analogy for its use to be extended to the realm of the home. Similarly, representatives of human rights and women's organisations suggested that non-violent "talking based" local justice conflict resolution methods should be used as an analogy and extended to the realm of the domestic household.

Another strategy suggested by indigenous justice leaders and endorsed by human rights and women's organisation representatives was highlighting the gap between the Timorese value of acknowledging human dignity and respect, and the treatment of many wives who are beaten by their husbands, emphasising that this is not the imposition of external values but rather that ending wife beating is the implementation of existent Timorese values. Concepts of respect and basic Christian values such as "do unto others" commonly acted out in the "public" realm should equally be extended to the "private", and it was suggested by some indigenous leaders that priests should more vigorously pursue this line from the pulpit.

A further suggested value basis for changing attitudes towards domestic violence included the extension of democratic principles, including the right to speak freely and to actively participate, to the family. Most leaders were supportive of this concept but some expressed concern that if children were permitted to say anything they wanted to, parental control and discipline over children would be compromised. Two representatives from human rights and women's organizations thought that this strategy would be less successful than others, as to many Timorese "democracy" is a concept firmly grounded in the realm of state politics. Applying it to domestic settings is likely to be resisted, especially by men, as different "cultural rules" apply there which benefit them.

In summary, the initial brief survey undertaken of traditional leaders and representatives from human rights and women's organisations indicated that a thoroughly researched and well implemented "existent" approach to popular human rights education might well provide a fruitful means for both recognising the human rights strengths of Timorese cultural values and providing traction points for successfully internally critiquing those which compromise the human rights of some community members, including women.

Illuminating Diversity in Local Cultural Practice

While acknowledging that the broad parameters of culture may condition the range of alternative courses of action available to individuals within it, there is frequently more complexity, live debate, dissent and flexibility concerning the actual social practice of indigenous justice systems approaches to gender, than that represented in dominant articulations of them. Culture represents an amalgam of both ideology and local practice, and incongruity between the two is characteristic of social life generally.[97]

As noted earlier, articulations of Timor-Leste which are presented as rigid patriarchal ideology, can become self fulfilling. This may be because those commonly articulating such custom may be those who have the greatest interests at stake, hence resulting in a version which privileges a particular patriarchal perspective. Statements of custom that are inconsistent with human rights standards and the goal of gender equality, should be challenged and tested to determine whether they reflect actual social practice. Producing and disseminating empirical evidence of alternative local cultural practices might be effective in diluting dominant interpretations of culture that entrench gender hierarchy.[98] By making visible the exceptions to general cultural rules which discriminate against women, and examples of women's leadership and power within traditional society, trenchant resistance to change might be overcome and interpretations of culture that accommodate human rights principles such as gender equality, might take their place.

For example, Timorese women's rights to inherit property are usually described as being determined by them either falling under the dominant patrilineal system, in which case women are entitled to nothing, as they are to all intents and purposes the responsibility of their husband's family and therefore have no need of property; or the minority matrilineal system, in which case the inheritance of family property follows the female lineage.[99] While this characterisation may well be accurate for the majority of cases, in my research which focused on women's rights under patrilineal systems, a not insignificant minority (33 percent) of local justice leaders (who frequently preside over such decisions), stated that, even if married, a woman would still receive at least some portion of inheritance.

Some of the variations include the following. Where a woman's parents die and she is unmarried, practices vary. Some 36 percent of local leaders stated that unmarried women enjoy the same rights as their brothers and should receive an equal share, although some stated that, if she subsequently married, her share should then be refunded to her brothers. A large minority (46

---

[97] Nyamu-Musembi, above, n.78, at p.132.

[98] *ibid.*, at p.126.

[99] See for example M Sumardjono, *Report on Research into Adat Land Law in East Timor, 1994/5* (2004) ETLJ 7, at p.27 accessed on 8 December 2006 at *www.eastimorlawjournal.org/Articles/sumardjononadatineastimor.html* or D Hicks, *Tetum Ghosts and Kin: Gender and Fertility in East Timor* (2nd ed, Waveland Press Inc, Illinois, 2004), at p.74.

percent) stated that she would be entitled to the family home and kitchen garden, but not to any share of other land. Others (18 percent) stated that it depended upon what provision the parents had made for the woman upon their death, and, if none was made, then it was up to the charity of her brothers to provide for her. A small minority (three percent) stated that irrespective of the woman's marital status, she was entitled to an equal portion as her brothers.

Further research into these rich and complex issues would no doubt uncover further diversity of practices. By making visible and sharing with local justice leaders and community members exceptions to dominant rules which discriminate against women, prevailing articulations of cultural practice (which may not accurately represent more equitable realities of actual social practice) may be broken down. Versions more amenable to negotiation, argument, and the exercise of discretion about what is just in the circumstances, might be given opportunity to flourish, and over time, take their place.

Scrutinising the Bona Fides of "Traditional" Practice

It should also be recognised that there is enormous scope for the abuse or manipulation of "culture" or, most especially, "tradition" (that is, those practices or beliefs which draw their legitimacy from having been transmitted between generations) to sanction illegitimate behaviour. One means of tackling the problem of traditional defences to such behaviour may be to engage a "retraditionalisation"[100] strategy. Historical research might reveal that original practices which were relatively benign in terms of gender equality, have been adopted and distorted over time. For example, where a husband asserts his right to beat his wife on the basis that because he has fully acquitted the *barlake*[101] to his wife's family, he can therefore treat her as he pleases, an investigation of the historical practice and meaning of *barlake* might reveal such assertions to be distortions of the traditional purpose and meaning of the practice; that *barlake* is paid in respect of the woman and her family, rather than the commodification of the woman to licence her abuse, or that payments of equal economic value are made also from the bride's family.

> Since the original practice derives its authority from religious or customary sanction, any effort to discredit it (and to substitute another where

[100] G Valencia-Weber and C Zuni, "Domestic Violence and Tribal Protection of Indigenous Women in the United States" (1995) 69 *St. John Law Review*, at p.134.
[101] Bride price or bride wealth.

appropriate) must draw its authority from the same source on which the original practice was founded.[102]

Through undertaking and publicising historical research which rejects the roots or origins of a practice which offends gender equality, erroneous customary defences might be exposed as such, and over time, more equitable practices could take their place.[103]

Unearthing the Powerful Women: Female power in Myth, Ritual and Politics

Another potential source for internal critique of entrenched gender inequality is the study of women's status in Timorese ritual, myth, and history. This may reveal examples of the exercise of female power which are indigenous to Timorese culture and by illuminating these roles and examples, demonstrate that rather than being a threat to Timorese culture, female empowerment is already a fundamental aspect of Timorese life.

Unearthing stories of Timorese powerful female role models should reach deep into Timor's historical and mythological roots: women who have occupied non-traditional occupations or positions, such as queens, female warriors, village or hamlet chiefs; the importance of the role of women in particular rituals or ceremonies, female forces existent in creation stories; the powerful symbolism of the feminine which runs right throughout Timorese ritual and mythological life. All of these and other examples of female power could be illuminated through Timor-Leste's powerful oral history. Poetry and the oration of stories and myths continue to be widely practiced and a key means of transmitting Timorese culture and identity within and between the generations. Engaging traditional leaders and encouraging them to also give "airtime" and profile to the contributions made by women could give the whole community a deeper sense and acceptance of the possibilities and potential currently locked up in its female population. This process could be further reinforced by ensuring the inclusion of a feminised version of Timorese history in the national school curriculum, over time fostering the development of strong models of female identity, which may inspire girls, and inculcate acceptance in boys of re-shaped gender relations in future generations.

---

[102] A An-Na'im, "State Responsibility Under International Human Rights Law to Change Religious and Customary Laws", in Cook, ed, above, n.88, at p.178.

[103] See for example A Swaine, *Traditional Justice and Gender Based Violence*, International Rescue Committee, August 2003, at p.30 where distortion of the traditional understanding of bride wealth is discussed as well as traditional law's historical rejection of domestic violence whatever its cause.

While I have not studied in depth the representation of women in Timorese mythology, ritual and history, for such would be an enormous undertaking, given the diversity of Timorese ethnic groups and the need to undertake primary research to document oral histories.[104] However, in investigating the viability of the strategy of drawing on Timorese mythology, ritual and history to advocate for the elevation of women's status, a number of key examples emerged which are interesting in themselves and could be useful starting points in this approach.

The first resolves around the centrality in East Timorese societies of imagery and religious symbolism of gender in classificatory thought. It should be noted that the following observations are limited to the Tetum ethnic group, the largest in Timor-Leste.[105] Women dominate men in ritual and mythological life, evident in the high feminine status prevalent in rituals, oral poems and narratives.[106] The cosmology of the Tetum is divided into the "underworld" and the "upperworld". Significantly, the underworld is also known as "the womb of the earth", the "earth mother" (*rai inan*) and the "sacred world". According to a common myth of origin,[107] following the surfacing of the land from the sea, two "vaginas" emerged and out of them from the underworld climbed the first three ancestors, the founders of the aristocratic classes in the upperworld. Another myth of origin concerns the sacred queen (*liurai feto lulik*) who, one day, was weaving the sea as an ordinary woman may weave cloth, when she became irritated by one of her children who kept playing around her and interrupting her work, so she threw her shuttle in the direction of the child, missed and inadvertently cut the cloth into two parts which is how the single sea became divided into two, the female sea in the north and the male sea to the south, with the island of Timor between them.[108] Another sacred queen (Cassa Sonek, one of the

---

[104] While feminist critiques across many social science disciplines have had significant impact over the last three decades and make the central demand that the lives and experiences of women also be valued and recorded, the main anthropological works which study Timor generally pre-date the feminist renaissance era which may explain why in the body of work examined, the roles and status of women are, with some notable exceptions such as Hicks, largely passed over.

[105] The Tetum (approx 100,000) inhabit the areas bordered by Western East Timor on the south coast from Suai to Viqueque. East of Atoni, west of Bunak (in Batagude) around Batibo, in from the south coast around Viqueque and Soibada, Dili and the northern coastline, source Ethnologue Report for Timor-Leste, *www.ethnologue.com/show_country.asp?name=TL*, accessed on 9 December 2006.

[106] See Hicks, above, n.99. Hicks acknowledges that consistent with the complementarity of symbolic dualism, male characters also feature in such myths, he notes that they usually capitulate or are subject to female power.

[107] *ibid.*, at p.31.

[108] *ibid.*, at p.30.

three original ancestors from the first myth of origin) is attributed with special and original knowledge of fire.[109]

Maintenance of the human life cycle is achieved through a process of uniting the under and upper worlds in an ordered fashion. All souls or spirits of future human beings live in the underworld and are then born into humans in the upper world, where they live, then upon death, return to the underworld ready to be "recycled" in future humans. "And so, human existence in the upperworld is a transitory episode in a cycle which begins and ends in the underworld."[110] The underworld is dominated by the female. The ultimate sources of female power are derived from the female-assigned quality of fertility which originates from the Earth Mother. Female fertility is considered the root of all life which is often represented in fertility statues which feature prominent female sexual organs and are common items in sacred houses which are dominated by female iconry. It is the woman's red fertile blood which mixes with the necessary, but less important, man's "white" sperm that recreates human life. All spirits are associated with femininity, even those of male ghosts appear as females. Witches and shamans are generally (although not always), female as well. The sacred or underworld is associated with night time, when the spirits sometimes leave the underworld to visit the upperworld. In this structure, women have the exclusive power to transform and mediate between spiritual and material agnates representing the crucial link between the "upper" secular world and the "lower" sacred world.

The upper or secular world by contrast is governed by a massive masculine divinity also known as "heavenly father" (*maromak*) who lives in the sky (and is sometimes conceived of as the sun), whose sole active one-off role was to impregnate the earth mother with his semen (in the form of rain), enabling her to conceive the ancestors of humanity who emerged in accordance with the first earlier described origin myth. While women dominate the sacred world and hence are considered superior in sacred rituals,[111] men and masculine symbolism feature more heavily in the secular world and hence dominate political, jural and economic offices and responsibilities. This system of cosmic classification where the human secular world is dominated by men, provides a strong cultural basis for men's domination over women in these areas.

---

[109] *ibid.*, at p.42.

[110] *ibid.*, at p.111.

[111] E Traube, "Mambai Rituals of Black and White" in J Fox, ed, *The Flow of Life* (Harvard University Press, 1980), at p.306 and D Hicks D, *Tetum Ghosts and Kin* (Mayfield Publishing Company, 1976), at p.54.

And so emerges a key challenge; Can Timorese women draw upon their powers as governors of the sacred world to achieve a greater level of equity in the secular male dominated world? There are important connections between the worlds which could assist. One is that the womb of the Earth Mother and the human mother are considered symbolically to be the same thing. In that way, women inherit the Earth Mother's power. Another is that unlike men who remain tethered to the secular world in any given situation, women performing ritual roles of importance can transcend their secular existence and exercise functions relating to the sacred world. They can even shift between the two worlds within a single ceremony.[112] Women's ability to move between the worlds may offer potential for women to bring to the secular world their higher divine world status. At least amongst the Tetum, however, there are also clear boundaries about the circumstances in which the upper and under worlds can permissibly come together, which may in practice limit the usefulness of this strategy.[113]

In addition, the feminine plays very powerful roles across all major rituals, except interestingly, for birth rituals. Even the very structure of traditional Timorese houses is conceived of as a metaphor for woman,[114] featuring a preponderance of female anatomical imagery such as the rear entrance being "the vagina" and the main room "the womb" the space used mainly by women and where they give birth. In marriage rituals, the bride's mother officiates over the rituals prior to bridewealth negotiations, taking on the role of "priestess" to mediate between the two lineages represented by the bride's and groom's respective families, and between the under and upper worlds to induce ancestral ghosts to ensure the marriage is a success. Women and feminine associations play key ritual roles in each stage of the death rites, as the corpse and soul are returned to the earth mother. Other practices revealing the clout of female ritual power include the important role of the "priestess" in fertility rites, carrying out the rituals associated with the fertility of buffalo, corn, and rice whose "souls" are believed to be empowered to give or withhold human fecundity.[115] Women, in ritual matters, are the head of the household responsible for conducting household rituals to placate ancestral ghosts and purge them from the husband's side. What is common in all of these rituals is

[112] Hicks, *ibid.*, at pp.20–21.

[113] Transgression of the rules concerning the coming together of the two worlds except in birth, marriage and death rituals can result in retribution from spirits such as infertility, sickness or death: Cristalis and Scott, above, n.27 at p.21.

[114] Traube, Elizabeth, "Mambai Rituals of Black and White" in *The Flow of Life* ed. Fox, J, 1980 Harvard University Press p.306.

[115] Hicks, above, n.99, at p.40.

the role of women in bringing together according to the requisite order a union between the sacred and secular worlds through their power to transform themselves and mediate between the two worlds, and by tapping into the generative powers of each agency, secure abundance and life for the community. It is through the transformative powers of women to move between the worlds that women can potentially challenge relegation to reification in the divine world.

In relation to the exercise of public power, women have not by definition been excluded from holding political office[116] and although far fewer in numbers than men, numerous instances have been uncovered in this research where women have held offices of political authority, usually as *Feto Ferik* or Queens, particularly in the west of the country and in matrilineal pockets (and occasionally in other areas, albeit usually only where there is an absence of male descendants, in which case the right of inheritance can pass to women). Two Queens of the Oecussi District have been documented in the context of their conversion to Catholicism. The first has been documented in descriptions of the arrival of Friar Antonio Taveira, a Portuguese Dominican priest in 1556 at Lifau. According to this description, many kings, warriors and indigenous priests were gathered in the Queen of Lifau's house to conduct a big ritual when they saw a large ship arrive. The Queen sent emissaries to the beach and ordered a counsellor to ask the stranger what he wanted. Upon receiving his explanation that he came to bring word of God, the queen and kings replied that that God was unknown to them and refused to give him permission to land. The stranger had dropped the ship's anchor and then proceeded to sail off, dragging the land of Timor with it. The queen and kings tried to cut the chains of the anchor without success and hence begged the stranger to leave them in their land. Amazed by his special powers, the stranger was welcomed back to shore and upon explaining the doctrine of Lord God to the Queen of Lifau, she and many of her subjects became Christians.[117] Another Oecussi Queen was Queen of Mena, who rose to power following the death of her husband and was baptised by Antonio de Sao Jacinto, the Dominican friar and Vicar-General of Solor in 1641.[118]

Queens also emerge as important political figures in a number of the Portuguese "pacification" wars, most particularly, the Cova Lima rebellion of 1868 and more; famous still, the revolt of Don Boaventura of Manufahi in

---

[116] Cristalis and Scott, above, n.27, at p.19.

[117] Hicks, above, n.99, at pp.4–6.

[118] *History of Timor*, *http://pascal.iseg.utl.pt/~cesa/History_of_Timor.pdf*, at p.29, accessed on 12 September 2006.

1911–1912. Following defeat of the indigenous rebel forces in May 1871, the Portuguese Governor of the colony, Joao Climaco de Carvalho attended to receive the official surrenders or "submissions" from the Queens of Cova and Balibo. Following the massacre of more than 3,000 men, women, and children at Leo-Laco mountain, and the surrender of the famous warrior Don Boaventura the following month, Don Boaventura's wife Queen Maria de Manufahi continued the rebellion triggering a further crackdown by Portuguese authorities resulting in them eventually encircling Boaventura and taking thousands of prisoners-of-war and bombarding the residence of the Queen of Betano as she was convening a meeting of local chiefs, resulting in around another 1,000 Timorese deaths.[119] The courage and agency of Queen Maria de Manufahi was remembered by Jose Ramos Horta speaking before the United Nations Security Council on 12 April 1976 when he "observed with pride that Queen Maria de Manufahi, Boaventura's widow, then 80 years old, was 'a militant' of the political party he represented".[120]

There was also the legendary Queen Hare-Manek of Bibiluto kingdom "a woman famous in Viqueque history for her bravery, extraordinary energy, great beauty and long hair which was about fourteen yards in length".[121] As the head of the army, Queen Hare-Manek was renown for her bravery and her special bamboo spear throwing powers, which aside from killing many aggressors also created bamboo forests as her spears could not be removed once they entered the earth. She was ultimately tricked by male soldiers who upon attempting to cut her with their swords discovered that her body was made of iron. In surrendering to her own death, she invited the aggressors to use her own machete against her, and they succeeded in killing her. Her legend continued to provide inspiration and protection to all subsequent warriors who would gather to receive ritual protection from her prior to engaging in any battle. There are also examples of where women have fought as warriors alongside men, against foreign invaders and in tribal wars, such as two sisters, Leonia Pires and Ravu Letok who became legendary for their courage and were believed to be bullet-proof when they fought against Indonesians infiltrating the border areas.[122] A further example of a woman occupying a traditional male role in customary law occurred in the district of Oecussi, when a female Tobe was appointed. Tobes are responsible for carrying out ritual

---

[119] *ibid.*, pp.95–96.

[120] H Xiieger, ed, *East Timor and the International Community: Basic Documents* (Cambridge, University Press, Melbourne, 1997), at p.97.

[121] Hicks, above, n.99, at p.8.

[122] Cristalis and Scott, above, n.27, at p.20.

ceremonies associated with the environment and agriculture. The position also requires abstinence from sexual intercourse, a restriction that on this occasion no male was willing to adhere to, hence the appointment of a female Tobe.[123] Once could facetiously suggest that perhaps the answer to the empowerment of women is to require abstinence in all powerful positions!

Direct Action: Crude, Rude but Sometimes Necessary

A fifth and final strategy remains an important card to hold or to play where the proponents of change determine that a blunter approach with shorter term impact is necessary. Direct political action can provide a transfusion of energy and focus which can empower its participants to take an unmediated stand against gender inequality at the same time as increasing the stakes and pressure upon its resisters to relent. For example, one collective direct action strategy used for intervening in, and preventing domestic violence in some communities in Papua New Guinea is for women to surround a house where domestic violence is occurring, beating pots, pans and drums, shaming the perpetrator to stop and then delivering him to police or traditional justice leaders for justice and providing support and assistance to the victim. Another strategy commonly used by women is to withdraw their labour or go on "strike" by refusing to undertake domestic work or have sex with their husbands for a set period. When undertaken collectively, such action could be quite effective in persuading all men to take responsibility for using their influence to stop other men from beating their wives. There are of course also risks attached to such actions where the stakes are heightened by their collectivity, such as men taking stronger reprisals against protesting women, or such actions resulting in all-out conflict between the men and women within a community. Timorese women already engage in a range of forms of protest and resistance against their mistreatment, actions limited only by the imagination. For example, one woman explained that if her husband mistreats her, she refuses to cook and serves rocks on the table in the place of food. When her children question where their dinner is, she directs them to ask their father and shame him into apologising. Another woman explained how if a man beats his wife in her village a group of powerful women will summons the man and make him eat dry coconut in front of his house, an apparently distasteful and humiliating punishment.

Tying the Pieces Together

This section has explored five possible strategies for developing grassroots-based processes for internally challenging gender inequality by grounding

[123] Conversation with Meitzner Yoder, L.S. February 2004, author of *Custom, Codification, Collaboration: Integrating the Legacies of Land and Forest Authorities in Oecusse Enclave, East Timor*, PhD Thesis, Yale University, May 2005.

such critiques in human rights notions already firmly anchored in the cultural norms and practices of that community; by making visible the diversity of cultural practice as a means of challenging and diluting the impact of dominant and often patriarchal articulations of culture; by scrutinising the authenticity of purported "traditional" cultural practices which discriminate against women and investigating whether more progressive origins of the practice have been lost or distorted over time; and by excavating and disseminating through both traditional and modern education systems examples of the exercise of female power in mythology, ritual, and history. All of these strategies are pre-supposed on the notion that cultural norms and practices are in a state of flux and can, over time, be influenced, moulded, and directed through targeted interventions and by engaging, rather than ignoring or excluding custodians of culture in the change process to bring about long-term sustainable cultural transformation of attitudes to gender in Timorese communities.

Ultimately, the important key elements are that the reform process be one of internal dialogue which includes strategically selected people, and empowering women within their own communities. Intra-community Timorese actors are clearly best positioned to decide how to pitch gender equality campaigns and thereby to ensure that this exercise does not repeat the mistake of cultural imperialism, which aside from being highly damaging, is also demonstrably counterproductive. There is a role for non-indigenous human rights actors, but it is necessarily a limited and background one of supporting indigenous players with ideas and suggestions, or to mobilise resources so as not to undermine the critical process of cultural legitimisation necessary to gain community acceptance of gender attitude reform.

Conclusion: Getting Smart about Making a Difference

This paper argues that during and after the Indonesian occupation, East Timorese women both gained and then, in the context of the post-conflict backlash, lost ground in their quest to be treated as equal citizens to men. The Indonesian occupation did cause a re-writing of gender relations to a degree and some spaces did emerge for women in the transitional period for consolidating gains based on these changes. Some of these, however, closed over before many realised they had even been there. While some women who had been mobilised by accepting the transformation of themselves caused by these stretched gender relations, did convert their occupation-period "gains" into ongoing opportunities to participate in state rebuilding, their effectiveness was limited by the strong resurgence of patriarchal patterns in public life and male monopoly over "legitimate" leadership. In these circumstances most women reverted to the gender roles *status quo ante*. The continuing crisis in

Timor-Leste now represents a further period of loss, as many of the tentative gains made by some women since independence have been swept aside in the rancor of unresolved male tensions, egos, and ambitions at the core of the current instability. It is timely to reflect on how lessons learnt following the Indonesian occupation could be applied in the current context to more effectively bed down gains for women. It is also worth reflecting upon how handicapped Timor-Leste is in fulfilling its aspirations as a nation, while the potential of half its adult population remains largely untapped. In the words of one Timorese woman:[124] "only half the Timorese population secured their independence and freedom in 2002. The women still have a long fight ahead of them".

The lessons of recent history portend that the propulsion of women into positions of influence in state-based institutions are an important but insufficient strategy for creating and securing gains by women in Timor-Leste. The current conflict is not a transitory crisis but rather has delivered an ongoing and fast-changing political and cultural landscape, one in which women from all walks of life and on national and local scales, must rapidly re-group to assert and entrench their role in, before it settles into a less malleable and receptive form. Additionally, the conflict has seen the Church reverting to its occupation role as protector and aid provider to those displaced, further expanding the influence achieved through its post-independence re-positioning as a key political opposition to the government. It is therefore critical that efforts be made to shape the direction of this influence towards enhancing women's rights through, for example, amplifying the grassroots work of individual feminist nuns who internally challenge attitudes and doctrines which damage women. The imperative is greater now than ever to develop broader and firmly rooted efforts to dismantle entrenched gender inequality in Timor-Leste. Tackling aspects of the cultural and religious norms and daily practices of Timorese communities is a formidable but essential "front" in the battle to bring about greater gender justice. Such change needs time, but time itself will not deliver such change. While the Timorese have a remarkable facility to incorporate outside influences, targeted, long-term interventions initiated from within communities are most likely to succeed in bringing about this transformative process.

A number of key ingredients make me optimistic that this can occur: the adaptability of Timorese cultures and ability to absorb a range of influences; the greater political fluidity in the context of the ongoing instability and the

[124] Staff member, women's NGO, April 2005, Dili.

range and quality of social actors in Timor-Leste, both men and women, with the commitment and drive to challenge local practices which discriminate against women. These features, combined with some of the potential strategies I have outlined, could effectively create processes to internally re-examine values and practices concerning gender. Provided the implementation of such strategies is pursued with sensitivity, patience and persistence, I believe that the Timorese political and cultural environment is ripe for the gradual transformation of gender constructions which underpin gender inequality in Timor-Leste.

Biographical Note

Between 1994 and 1998 I worked with East Timorese asylum seekers in Australia including many women who mounted claims of gender-based persecution. Between 2001 and 2003 I worked in Timor-Leste as a Human Rights Officer under UN missions based in the Oecussi Enclave, Ermera and Dili Districts. This involved monitoring and, where appropriate, intervening in human rights violations, including gender-based claims such as underage and forced marriage, domestic violence, and rape and sexual assault. It also involved working closely with international and local human rights NGOs in sustainable organisational practice, programme development and implementation, including programmes establishing safe-house and support services for victims of domestic violence; establishing hamlet-based women's cooperatives and economic activities; and establishing a district programme engaging influential local men as advocates against domestic violence and gender-focused human rights training for police, amongst others. Since 2003 I have regularly undertaken human rights work in Timor-Leste including building capacity of national human rights monitors, undertaking human rights programme design, and participating as an investigator in the secretariat of the UN Independent Special Commission of Inquiry to investigate responsibility for key incidents in the 2006 crisis. I have also conducted field research for my PhD, some of which is drawn upon in this paper, which focuses on the potential of indigenous justice systems to adapt so they are better capable of delivering justice to victims of domestic violence.

Beloved Madam: The Indonesian ad hoc Human Rights Court

Susan Harris Rimmer

> War, which produces large-scale destruction of visible objects, does so even more with humans. Only some individuals, and only gradually, become aware of this type of destruction. It takes off from our faces the last mask of humanity, turns us inside out and brings to the surface some unexpectedly qualities, radically different from what others believed us to be and what we believed we were. Moreover, it transforms the family system and produces changes of the sanctified rules and relations, including those deemed eternal and immutable, such as gender relations.
>
> *Ivo Andrić*

Introduction

Dominggas dos Santos Mouzinho was a survivor of the Suai massacre who testified on 28 May 2002 in the trial of Lieutenant Colonel Herman Sedyono and four others in the Suai case. During cross-examination by the defence counsel she was subjected to a diatribe couched in elaborate courtesy:

> Thank you, if you don't want to respond, I won't force you. But follow the conscience of your heart, my most beloved madam, were your daughters raped or about to be raped or wanting to be raped (*diperkosa atau mau diperkosa*). It's up to you if you don't want to answer, I am only talking about the pure inner self. Beloved madam.[1]

Dominggas dos Santos Mouzinho was questioned in a similar manner for five hours without a break – she was not even offered a glass of water.[2]

Trials dealing with the international crimes committed in East Timor were held concurrently in East Timor and in Indonesia. In Indonesia, Law 26/2000 on Human Rights Courts was adopted by the Indonesian legislature in November 2000. The law provided for the establishment of four permanent Human Rights Courts and, for cases which took place prior to the adoption of

[1] Amnesty International and JSMP, "Justice for Timor-Leste – the way forward", April 2004, pp. 42–43. From unofficial transcripts compiled by JSMP's trial observer.
[2] *ibid.*, p.43.

the legislation, the possibility of establishing *ad hoc* Human Rights Courts. The new courts were to have jurisdiction over crimes against humanity and genocide, crimes which until then had not been included in Indonesian domestic law. Presidential Decree No 96/2001 was issued by the newly installed President Megawati Sukarnoputri in August 2001 establishing an *ad hoc* Human Rights Court on East Timor. The jurisdiction was limited to only those crimes occurring in the districts of Liquiça, Dili and Suai, and only within the two months of April and September 1999. The trials were completed in 2004, and the appeal process in May 2006.

The Special Panels within Dili District Court were set up by the United Nations Transitional Administration in East Timor (UNTAET) by Regulation 2000/15.[3] The Panels had exclusive jurisdiction over genocide, crimes against humanity, war crimes wherever and whenever they occurred; and over murder, sexual offences and torture that occurred in Timor-Leste between 1 January and 25 October 1999. In addition, in order to establish the truth regarding the human rights violations that occurred between 1974 and 1999 and to promote justice, reconciliation and human rights, UNTAET in 2001 established the Commission for Reception, Truth and Reconciliation (CAVR), under its regulation 2001/10.

The UN withdrew its support for the serious crimes process on 20 May 2005 in accordance with Security Council resolution 1543 (2004), in the context of its overall withdrawal from Timor, although the Government of East Timor has tried to continue the process. After riots in Dili in April/May 2006, the UN Integrated Mission in Timor-Leste (UNMIT) was established with a focus on strengthening the legal system.

This chapter will provide a gender analysis of the role, operation and jurisprudence of the Jakarta Court, the most controversial of the transitional justice mechanisms established to date to deal with international crimes in East Timor.

The first section presents an analysis of the political circumstances in which the Court came to be established. My analysis shows that the obligation to punish under international law may be realised in such a fashion as to render it meaningless.

Analysis of the trials raises many questions about the domestic prosecution of war crimes, but none more pertinent to a global legal system which now

---

[3] UN Doc. UNTAET/REG/2000/15, 6 June 2000.

features the International Criminal Court than this: how will the UN determine when a state is unwilling or unable to prosecute international crimes? What will be the criteria to be applied where trials have been held that are perceived to be inadequate? What will be the resulting action if the state is in breach?

The second section provides an overview of the investigation process, legislative framework, and funding and staffing issues of the court, the indictments issued by the Court, and the eventual results and convictions.

In the third section I ask, as have many other legal commentators, whether the trials were a sham. There were three main problems with the Court that can be clearly identified from observing the trials: inherent procedural flaws in the legislative foundation of the court; possible conspiracy between the prosecution and the military, and the lack of training of prosecutors and judges. The cumulative effect of these factors has meant that the Court was unable to provide even the basic measure of justice in the cases before it.

There were some positive elements to the trials. The UN's decision to allow domestic prosecution was correct by all principles of international law and did produce some benefits. The Komnas HAM investigation was brave and well-executed. Overall, the mechanisms of a Human Rights Court and the Joint Truth and Friendship Commission may yet prove to be extremely important in establishing the rule of law in Indonesia and diminishing the impunity of the military. On the other hand, they could prove to be what Indonesian NGOs termed a "whitewash machine".[4]

In a similar manner to the Dili serious crimes process but in a much starker fashion, lack of political support from the international community and the Indonesian government sealed the Court's fate as a failure.[5] I then note the report of the UN Commission of Experts in 2005 and the resultant pressure on Indonesia and East Timor to set up a Joint Truth and Friendship Commission to stymie any UN momentums towards an international tribunal.

Usually this is where academic inquiry about the trials has ended. Within this overall failure of the Court, the consequences for women have been buried. This fourth section of this chapter focuses on the official silence in the

---

[4] MS Saraswati, Commission could be "whitewash machine" *The Jakarta Post,* 9 September, 2004.

[5] See further, Susan Harris Rimmer, "Untold Numbers: East Timorese Women and Transitional Justice" in Caroline Lambert and Sharon Pickering, eds, *Global Issues, Women and Justice*, (Federation Press, 2004).

indictments on gender-persecution, the intimidating court-room atmosphere, treatment of female witnesses and judges, and the reaction of Timorese women's groups to the trials.

Research Context

This chapter is part of a wider research project which examines theoretical arguments about whether there is a role for international law at all in transitional justice choices for modern post-conflict states. If so, how could or should international law be incorporated into transitional justice processes?

If international law has a role, what might be its impact on women involved in the relevant transitional justice processes? Is international law benign, detrimental, or beneficial in its impact on women in an immediate post-conflict setting in this context? What questions could be posed to discover this impact?

I posit that at present, international law can be said to impact on transitional justice mechanisms in three primary ways. The first impact is normative, in that international law seeks to *categorise* what behaviour can be considered a crime under international law. The second impact, consequent on the categorisation of certain behaviours into crimes, is that international law places an *obligation* to prosecute and punish certain crimes and designates individual responsibility for those crimes, although the site of where that obligation falls is contested. The third impact, again consequential, is that the categorisation of offences influences what is tried and with what priority, or *prosecution* strategies.

Analysis relating to transitional justice studies from the perspective of international law has, in the main, been limited to those conflicts where international criminal trials have been held. For example, the Nuremberg and Tokyo trials held after World War II, and the *ad hoc* tribunals set up by the UN Security Council to deal with international crimes committed in the former Yugoslavia, and in Rwanda have been closely examined.[6] The scholarship tends to deal with the conduct of the trials, the development of jurisprudence, or the content of international criminal law, and the creation of the International Criminal Court. In other words, legal scholarship in the transitional justice field has been almost exclusively trials-focused. The overwhelming majority of international law academics both presume and

[6] The exception to this is the important collection *Post-Conflict Justice,* M Cherif Bassiouni, ed, (Transnational Publishers, New York, 2002).

advocate the holding of trials as the preferred accountability option for post-conflict settings.[7]

Whilst there has been analytical focus on gender and international law, and on gender persecution within the framework of international law, there has not yet been a systematic investigation of gender and transitional justice. Various writings have focused on women's experiences in post-conflict reconstruction and peace-building,[8] and their input into truth commission processes,[9] but the theoretical framework of transitional justice has so far proven resistant to feminist analysis, or has perhaps seemed benign and gender neutral.

Feminist legal scholarship has mainly focused narrowly on the first and third impacts of international law identified above, namely the categorisation and prosecution of crimes as they have featured in international criminal trials. The aim of feminist scholars has been the global acceptance of gender-persecution as crimes under international humanitarian law, a project which many feminist scholars now consider finished with the advances made by the Rome Statute.[10] Another strategy has been to hold alternate tribunals such as the Women's International War Crimes Tribunal.[11] In relation to prosecution strategies at the current tribunals, the focus has been primarily on the inclusion of women in judicial institutions,[12] investigating, bringing indictments and

---

[7] See generally J Snyder and Lesley Vinjamuri, "Advocacy and Scholarship in the Study of International War Crime Tribunals and Transitional Justice" (2004) 7 *Annual Review of Political Science* 345.

[8] The most comprehensive is by B Sorensen "Women and post-conflict reconstruction: issues and sources" in Mazurana and S McKay, eds, *Women and peacebuilding: essays on human rights and democratic development*, (Montreal, International Center for Human Rights and Development, 1999).

[9] See in particular Beth Goldblatt and Sheila Meintjes, *Gender and the Truth and Reconciliation Commission: A Submission to the Truth and Reconciliation Commission* (South African Truth and Reconciliation Commission, Johannesburg, 1996); H Millar, "Facilitating Women's Voices in Truth Recovery: An assessment of women's participation and the integration of a gender perspective in truth commissions", in H Durham and T Gurd, eds, *Listening to the Silences: Women and War* (Martinus Nijhoff, Boston, Leiden, 2005), at pp. 171–222; and J Schirmer, "The Seeking of Truth and the Gendering of Consciousness: the Co-Madres of El Salvador and the CONAVIGUA Widows of Guatemala" in SA Radcliffe and S Westwood, eds, *VIVA, Women and Popular Protest in Latin America* (London, Routledge, 1993).

[10] See further H Durham, "International humanitarian law and the protection of women", in H Durham and T Gurd, eds, *Listening to the Silences: Women and War* (Martinus Nijhoff, Boston, Leiden, 2005).

[11] See further Fleming Terrell, "Unofficial Accountability: A Proposal for the Permanent Women's Tribunal on Sexual Violence in Armed Conflict" (2005) *Texas International Law Journal* 107.

[12] See further H Charlesworth and C Chinkin, *The Boundaries of International Law: A Feminist Analysis* (Manchester University Press, Manchester, 2000), chap 6.

bringing to trial those alleged to have committed gender persecution, and better treatment of female witnesses.[13]

This is a dangerous strategy, partly because it ascribes a central role to international law in a post-conflict context which may simply not exist or be marginal at best. Even then, I argue that the project of categorisation of crimes should not be considered closed, that international humanitarian law does not adequately address the protection needs of women in armed conflict as it currently stands despite the admitted advances made, especially in the area of forced maternity and post-conflict domestic violence.[14] An examination of the theoretical debates regarding the role for international law in transitional justice choices for modern post-conflict states show that the role of law is often controversial, and estimations of any impact by international lawyers are usually lacking an evidentiary basis. By analysing the trials in Dili and Jakarta, I seek to assess whether international law is capable of benefiting East Timorese women involved in these transitional justice processes. I limit my inquiry to an analysis of the treatment of gender-based violence experienced by East Timorese women in the period from 1975 to 2005 as highlighted within the formal transitional justice processes[15] that occurred between 1999 and 2006. Rather than finding tensions between retributive and restorative justice, it seems that the combination of mechanisms used in relation to East Timor has only prevented survivors' access to any type of justice at all. However, the overall failure of justice for the Timorese may have different impacts on women survivors in the transitional society, facing the lowest economic status, health standards, political representation, and greatly increased levels of domestic violence.

By taking this holistic view, the fissures between international law and transitional justice processes become more apparent, between what claims are made for the processes and what they can actually achieve. I advocate a "guardian" approach, which is predicated on the idea that international interventions should seek to at least do no harm, a proposition derived from

[13] See further V Nikolic-Ristanovic, "Sexual violence, international law and restorative justice" in Buss and A Manji, eds, *International Law: Modern Feminist Approaches* (Hart Publishing, Oxford and Portland Oregon, 2005).
[14] See further J Gardam, "Women and Armed Conflict: The response of international law", in H Durham and T Gurd, eds, *Listening to the Silences: Women and War* (Martinus Nijhoff, Boston, Leiden, 2005).
[15] The impact of informal mechanisms and non-State actors on justice outcomes for women, such as the Catholic Church, civil society groups, cultural/artistic programs and economic actors such as donor governments, the World Bank, IMF, corporations and development NGOs is very important and deserves further research but is outside the bounds of this chapter.

the Hippocratic oath and increasingly applied to humanitarian interventions. Put simply, at best transitional justice interventions should seek to be inclusive of women's experiences of the conflict and post-conflict periods and not undermine any progress for women. This forms the basis of my critical analysis of the Indonesian trials.

The effectiveness of the trials is judged according to four main criteria as applied to women. The first criteria is whether victims of serious violations and their relatives obtain any measure of restorative justice; for example do they receive reparations, including compensation, restitution, rehabilitation, satisfaction, and guarantees of non-repetition. Second, in the wider interests of reconciliation and ending impunity, does the process provide a full and truthful account of the events that took place in Timor-Leste from 1975 to 1999? Third, are perpetrators of serious crimes, including crimes against humanity held to account for their actions in accordance with international law according to the principles of retributive justice? Finally, is there an effective justice process that contributes to preventing such crimes from occurring in the future?

I aim to show that trials under certain circumstances can arguably make things worse for women, even if improvements were made on current practice. I agree with scholars such as Julie Mertus who argue that better prosecution strategies may not solve the inherent problems facing women involved in international trials, that we should be critical of claims that international adjudication of wartime rape cases necessarily advances the interests of female survivors.[16]

Focusing on the Timor experience shows us that a feminist analysis and reinvention is therefore needed of the second and fundamental impact of international law within the emerging field of transitional justice studies, the obligation to punish itself. With better understandings of women's experience of war and more analysis of the gendered impact of international law, there should be the ability to imagine transitional justice processes which better meet the needs of women, a focus that goes beyond an analysis of jurisprudence.

FOUNDATIONS: THE OBLIGATION TO PUNISH

The UN found that prosecutions were warranted as a result of the investigations into the 1999 violence. In a letter of 31 January 2000

[16] See further J Mertus, "Shouting from the Bottom of the Well The Impact of International Trials for Wartime Rape on Women's Agency" (2004) 6 *International Feminist Journal of Politics* 110.

accompanying the International Commission of Inquiry (ICIET) report, Kofi Annan wrote of the violence in 1999:

> ... the actions violating human and international humanitarian law were directed against a decision of the Security Council and were contrary to the agreements reached by Indonesia with the United Nations to carry out the decision of the Security Council. This fact reinforces the need to hold the perpetrators accountable for their actions .... The International Commission of Inquiry found that the United Nations and the international community had a particular responsibility to the people of East Timor in connection with investigating the violations, establishing responsibilities, punishing those responsible and promoting reconciliation. I believe the United Nations has an important role to play in this process in order to help safeguard the rights of the people of East Timor, promote reconciliation, ensure future social and political stability and protect the integrity of Security Council actions.[17]

Once the UN had reached this conclusion, the pressing issue was where and how the trials would take place. The ICIET Report of January 2000 recommended, at point 153, that the UN should form an international human rights tribunal. The UNCHR Special Rapporteurs also concluded in their December 1999 report that:

> Unless, in a matter of months, the steps taken by the Government of Indonesia to investigate TNI involvement in the past year's atrocities bear fruit ... the Security Council should consider the establishment of an international criminal tribunal for the purpose .... This should preferably be done with the consent of the Government, but such consent should not be a prerequisite.[18]

Indonesia's opposition to an international tribunal was clear from the outset. Dr Alwi Shihab, the then Indonesian Foreign Minister, stated to the Parliamentary Defence and Foreign Affairs Commission, "We will try not to deliver the generals to an international tribunal".[19]

---

[17] Identical letters dated 31 January 2000 from the Secretary-General, Kofi Annan to the President of the General Assembly, the President of the Security Council and the Chairperson of the Commission on Human Rights, UN Doc. A/54/726.

[18] Report on the joint mission to East Timor undertaken by the Special Rapporteur on extrajudicial, summary or arbitrary executions, the Special Rapporteur on the question of torture, and the Special Rapporteur on violence against women, its causes and consequences, *Situation of Human Rights in East Timor*, UN Doc. A/54/660, 10 December 1999.

[19] "Indonesia vows to avoid war crimes court", *Jakarta Post*, 8 December 1999.

The *Indonesian Observer* reported that on 19 January 2000, Shihab met UN Secretary-General Kofi Annan and explained Indonesia's opposition to an international tribunal on East Timor. He told Annan that the KPP HAM must be given the authority with no interference from any institutions, "including the UN", to handle the question of accountability for the crimes committed in East Timor.[20]

At the UN Headquarters in New York, Shihab also met with several members of the Security Council and UN representatives of some 20 members, including China, Russia, Portugal, Middle East and Asian countries. He then stated publicly that "We are trying to halt the international tribunal at all costs because it will lead to a bad name for Indonesia", and stated that there was a secret agreement among members of the UN Security Council (UNSC) to give Indonesia a chance to settle the case in Indonesia. He added that "If there is voting [at the UNSC] we will win a veto".[21]

Finally, in a letter to the UN Secretary-General dated 26 January 2000, Dr Shihab confirmed Indonesia's rejection of the recommendation of the ICIET for an international tribunal. He insisted that:

> "Indonesian laws are the only applicable laws to those violations and the Indonesian judicial mechanism is the exclusive mechanism for bringing the perpetrators of the violations of human rights to justice".[22]

The UN therefore allowed Indonesia to undertake its own investigations and domestic prosecutions of those responsible for violations in East Timor, noting that an inadequate response would bring the prospect of an international tribunal back on to the agenda of the Security Council.

It was clear this international threat of a tribunal had an immediate effect on Indonesia. Several confidence-building measures were taken to allay the concerns of the international community. In January 2000, the Indonesian investigation was turned over to Attorney-General Marzuki Darusman, the former head of the Indonesian Human Rights Commission, KPP HAM. Most importantly, President Abdurrahman Wahid suspended General Wiranto from his post of Security and Political Affairs Minister in February 2000, against muttered threats of a military coup reported in the press.

---

20 *Indonesian Observer*, 26 January 2000.

21 *ibid*.

22 Letter dated 26 January 2000 from the Minister for Foreign Affairs of Indonesia to the Secretary-General, UN Doc A/54/727 and S/2000/65, January 2000.

Secretary-General Kofi Annan then visited Indonesia in mid-February 2000 to assess the prospect of a credible domestic response from Indonesia. He said:

> I'm personally very pleased that the Indonesian government has taken on the responsibility of ensuring that those accountable for the atrocities in – and those responsible for the atrocities in East Timor will be made accountable and will be brought to trial.[23]

CNN reported that Annan, upon meeting with Indonesia's Attorney-General, then investigating Wiranto, said again that only a credible effort by the Indonesian government would deter the need for an international tribunal. The criteria for exactly what would constitute a credible effort were obviously a source of tension and confusion from the outset. According to CNN, the Secretary-General "bristled" when the Attorney-General asked for his definition of justice, and replied "What is yours?"[24]

Foreign Minister Alwi Shihab, at the time of the February 2000 visit, urged the Komnas HAM as well as the Attorney General's office to perform well in handling post-ballot atrocities in East Timor. He stated clearly that Indonesia's measures were designed to avoid a tribunal:

> Those institutions have to show the international community that Indonesia is able to set up a credible and transparent trial, so that there is no need for an international tribunal .... If those parties do not seem serious in carrying out their duties, the Security Council could actually favour an international tribunal to settle the case.[25]

Annan then visited Dili and told thousands of East Timorese at a news conference that an international court could be established if Indonesia failed to prosecute those responsible for the mass violence in the region in 1999. He said:

> If the trial does not go forward as planned, they (the UN Security Council) may revert to an international tribunal .... It is essential that those who committed the atrocities be brought to justice .... We will also never forget

[23] "Indonesia and East Timor Welcome Kofi Annan", CNN International Diplomatic License, February 19, 2000, *http://www.cnn.com/TRANSCRIPTS/0002/19/i_dl.00.html*.
[24] *ibid*.
[25] Antara, February 16, 2000, RI Needs to Remain Alert About Possibility Of International Tribunal.

the extreme violence that erupted. I wish we could have prevented or contained it.[26]

The US ambassador at the UN, Richard Holbrooke, said he expected pressure for an international tribunal would "continually and dramatically increase" if the Indonesian Government did not produce what the UN expected of it.[27]

Despite these remarks by the UN and international community, it was widely reported at the time, confirming the Foreign Minister Shihab's secret veto comments, that the Security Council – especially China and Russia – would not sanction an international tribunal because of the precedent it could set for conflicts with certain similarities such as Chechnya or Tibet.[28]

Leading NGO commentators were sceptical about the prospects of successful trials. Sidney Jones, at that time the head of UNTAET´S human rights division and now with the International Crisis Group, said "I am worried that waiting for Indonesian justice to run its course may mean waiting for something to happen, that may never happen".[29] Sonia Picado, leader of the UN International Commission of Inquiry, said that holding trials before an Indonesian court would "simply amount to the denial of justice".[30]

I have set out the political context of the foundations of the court in detail as it is pertinent to what quality of trials the UN was able to demand of Indonesia.

The Role and Operation of the Court

This section outlines the investigation process, legislative framework, and funding and staffing issues. The prosecution strategy and indictments are presented in brief, as well as the eventual outcomes of the trials.

Investigations

On 22 September 1999, along with the decree setting up the *ad hoc* human rights court for East Timor, the Habibie Government gave approval to Komnas HAM to form a Commission on Inquiry into Human Rights Violations in East

26 "U.N. chief says international court possible for East Timor", CNN, 18 February 2000, *http://edition.cnn.com/2000/ASIANOW/southeast/02/18/etimor.annan/*.

27 M Riley, "UN Scorn at Jakarta Justice for Timor", *Sydney Morning Herald*, 2 February 2000.

28 This was confirmed by comments from China foreign ministry spokesperson Zhu Bangzao – see "East Timor inquiry impresses global community," *Jakarta Post*, 2 February 2000.

29 "Senior U.N. official fears Indonesian human rights commission will not work", Deutsche Presse-Agentur, 3 February 2000.

30 Mark Riley, above, n.27.

Timor (KPP HAM) to investigate crimes committed between January and October 1999. This Commission consisted of five members of Komnas HAM and four independent human rights advocates.

A few days later a resolution was adopted by a special session of the UN's Commission for Human Rights (UNCHR) to set up an international commission of inquiry (ICIET) into the referendum violence beginning 30 August 1999. The UNCHR resolution therefore stipulated that the international commission of inquiry should work:

> in cooperation with the Indonesian National Commission on Human Rights … to gather and compile systematically information on possible violations of human rights and acts which may constitute breaches of international humanitarian law committed in East Timor since … January 1999.

The resolution also affirmed that "the primary responsibility for bringing perpetrators to justice rests with national judicial systems". The scene was thus set for two parallel investigations, one domestic and one international.

The UN's commission of inquiry came into being in late October, with a mandate to investigate human rights violations in East Timor since the beginning of 1999 and to complete its work and report to the UN Secretary-General by 31 December 1999. The five-member commission headed by Sonia Picado of Costa Rica, with members from Nigeria, India, Papua New Guinea, and Germany, visited East Timor for two weeks in late November and early December.[31] Both the ICIET and the KPP HAM reports were handed down on 31 January 2000 after consultation with each other.

The UNCHR resolution also provided for three UN Special Rapporteurs – dealing with extra-judicial killings, torture, and violence against women – and the UN Working Group on Disappearances to conduct investigations in East Timor. Indonesia denied the Rapporteurs entry to West Timor. Their report was handed down in December 2000.[32]

---

[31] Report of the International Commission of Inquiry on East Timor to the Secretary-General, January 2000, UN Doc A/54/726 and S/2000/59, 31 January 2000.

[32] Report on the joint mission on East Timor undertaken by the Special Rapporteur of the Commission on Human Rights on extrajudicial, summary or arbitrary executions, the Special Rapporteur of the Commission on the question of torture and the Special Rapporteur of the Commission on violence against women, its causes and consequences, in accordance with Commission resolution 1999/S-4/1 of 27 September 1999, UN Document A/54/60, 10 December 1999.

KPP HAM found that the army, police, and civilian government in East Timor had provided pro-Indonesian militia with arms, finance and training. It stated that individual TNI personnel had been implicated directly or indirectly in the mass killing, torture, disappearances, forced evacuations, and destruction that followed the September 4 announcement of the ballot result supporting East Timor independence. Finally it recommended that the Attorney commence a formal investigation of at least 33 people, and named some of the highest ranking generals in Indonesia as responsible, including Wiranto, who was interviewed by a KPP HAM team for three hours on 24 December 1999.[33] The report was initially secret but was obtained by the *Sydney Morning Herald* and published on its website on 30 April 2001.

All three reports contained hard-hitting evidence of systematic sexual violence. The KPP HAM report found:

> III.4 Violence based on gender
> 77. Cases of violence towards women identified by the Investigative Commission included torture and public sexual humiliation by the militia and the TNI, forcing under age females to serve the sexual needs of the militia, enforced prostitution and rape.[34]

The report went on to outline three specific cases of sexual enslavement.

The ICIET report concluded:

> 3. Gender Violence
> 126. Because the men fled to the mountains, the women were targeted for sexual assault in a cruel and systematic way.
> 127. There is evidence of actual sexual abuse and rape of women. While in general, the militia refrained from killing women, they were subjected to humiliation and different forms of harassment that includes, stripping and sexual slavery. Women and children were also victims of forced displacement into exile.[35]

---

[33] Indonesian KPP-HAM *Report*, 31 January 2000. *Masters of Terror: Indonesia's Military and Violence in East Timor in 1999* Paper 3. Full Report of the Investigative Commission into Human Rights Violations in East Timor KPP-HAM (pp.15–59, 262–264), Canberra Papers on Strategy and Defence No 145, Strategic and Defence Studies Centre, Australian National University, Canberra, 2002.
[34] KPP HAM Report.
[35] ICIET Report.

The most thorough examination of gender violence is contained in the Special Rapporteurs report. The Special Rapporteur on Violence against Women, during a joint fact-finding mission in November 1999 together with the Special Rapporteur on extrajudicial, summary, or arbitrary executions and the Special Rapporteur on the question of torture, found evidence of widespread violence against women in East Timor during the period [from January 1999] and concluded that "the highest level of the military command in East Timor knew, or had reason to know, that there was widespread violence against women in East Timor".[36] She reported that:

> Rape was used by the military as a form of revenge, or to force the relatives out of hiding. Much of the violence against women in East Timor was perpetrated in the context of these areas being treated as military zones ... rape by soldiers in these areas is tried in military tribunals, and not before an ordinary court of law. Under Indonesian law, for a rape to be prosecuted it required corroboration – including the testimony of two witnesses. Women lived in a realm of private terror, for any victims or witnesses who dared to take action were intimidated with death threats.

> Many of the women who were raped as virgins are single mothers who have suffered stigma in their communities after giving birth to children of Indonesian soldiers.... Some of these children are the result of rapes, others are the product of a situation that resembles sexual slavery and some are the result of consensual sex ... the women are having a very difficult time, not only because of poverty, but because the sight of these children often reminds them of rape.[37]

These reports and the investigative process formed a solid basis for any legal interventions. The processes had other benefits as well in preventing impunity. UK-based NGO Tapol reported the impact of the KPP HAM investigations within Indonesia:

> When three army generals were publicly grilled in November by members of Indonesia's newly elected Parliament, the DPR, about atrocities in Aceh, the whole nation was transfixed by the three-hour spectacle on their television screens. Now, at last, after more than three decades of impunity, men with the blood of many victims on their hands were being called to

---

[36] Report of UN Special Rapporteurs: Situation of human rights in East Timor. Based on visit between 4–10 November 1999. UN Document A/54/660, 10 December 1999.
[37] *ibid*.

> account. Then on 24 December, General Wiranto, former commander-in-chief of the Indonesian armed forces, TNI, was summoned to appear before a civilian commission investigating crimes against humanity in East Timor. That he agreed to appear signalled that the once all-powerful armed forces have been forced to acknowledge that they will have to account for their crimes to civilian authorities. They can no longer hide behind the smokescreen of "officer honour councils" to exonerate the top brass as they did in 1992 following the Santa Cruz Massacre in East Timor in November 1991, or military courts to hand down derisory sentences to low-ranking officers.
>
> However, the senior officers have treated the commission with contempt; they have used their appearances before the commission to spin lies, refute irrefutable evidence and prolong the commission's proceedings. They have shown that they will do everything in their power to protect themselves from possible prosecution.[38]

Tapol also reported that top generals attempted to discredit the activities of KPP-HAM, accusing it of pursuing an anti- Indonesia agenda, of being funded by money from abroad, and of basing its evidence on information from INTERFET – "[t]hey are seeking to portray KPP HAM as serving foreign interests. Some of its members have even been threatened with physical violence".[39]

General Wiranto, the highest ranking public figure implicated by the KPP HAM report, said it was biased, and did not constitute an accusation: the report "was raw material which should be evaluated by the attorney-general judiciously".[40]

Notably, Indonesia has had positive experiences of fact-finding committees in the post-Suharto era to investigate past crimes. There have been five such official committees that have investigated the following incidents: the violence in Aceh during the period when the province was called a Military Operation Area (1989–1998); the Jakarta riots of 13–15 May 1998; the massacre in Tanjung Priok in 1984; the violence in East Timor during the referendum process in 1999; and the killing of students during demonstrations in Jakarta

---

38 Tapol, *Ending the Cycle of Impunity: Can the East Timor Investigations Pave the Way?* (Tapol, the Indonesia Human Rights Campaign, Surrey, 2000).
39 *ibid.*
40 Business Times, Singapore, 2 February 2000.

at Trisakti University and the Semanggi cloverleaf in 1998–1999. The government established the first two commissions while the latter three were formed by Komnas HAM.

Legislative Framework

Indonesia's criminal code (KUHP – *Kitab Undang-Undang Hukum Pidana*) covers such crimes as murder, assault, torture, kidnapping, rape, and destruction of property. Gross human rights offences can technically be prosecuted under this code. However, as confirmed by the Serious Crimes Court's early experiences in Dili, the code has a number of inadequacies for dealing with gross human rights offences, especially in relation to dealing with those who plan the systematic nature of crimes, and military personnel acting under orders.[41] Legislation to deal with human rights violations was already put in train by the Indonesian government before the referendum violence in Timor, but was drastically sped up as a result of international pressure.

President Habibie issued a Presidential decree in September 1999 (Perpu 1/1999) providing for the creation of a human rights court to be considered by the parliament, just days before the UN Commission on Human Rights met in special session to discuss East Timor. An *ad hoc* Human Rights Court can be established by a presidential decree on the recommendation of the lower house of parliament, the People's Representative Assembly (Dewan Perwakilan Rakyat, hereafter referred to as the DPR). In the case of Timor-Leste, the DPR recommended the establishment of such a court. After 11 drafts, Law 26/2000 on Human Rights Courts was adopted by the Indonesian legislature on 23 November 2000. The law provided for the establishment of four permanent Human Rights Courts and, for cases which took place prior to the adoption of the legislation, the possibility of establishing *ad hoc* Human Rights Courts. The new courts were to have jurisdiction over crimes against humanity and genocide, crimes which until then had not been included in Indonesian domestic law. War crimes are not included in the jurisdiction of the Human Rights Courts.

The new law also introduced the concept of "crime of omission" alongside "crime of commission". The law specifically made military commanders responsible for gross violations committed by their troops where they knew "or under the prevailing circumstances ought to have known" that they were perpetrating or had

[41] See further, Susan Harris Rimmer, "Untold Numbers: East Timorese Women and Transitional Justice" in C Lambert and S Pickering, eds, *Global Issues, Women and Justice* (Federation Press, 2004).

recently perpetrated gross violations of human rights and where they failed to take action to prevent or stop such actions. Police and civil leaders were also made responsible for failure to control subordinates (clause 42).

The provision for retrospective application of the new law on human rights courts proved to be very controversial, which explains why the East Timor trials were undertaken in an *ad hoc* rather than a permanent court. Retroactive prosecution conflicts with Indonesian statutes (Clause 1 of the Criminal Code stating that an offence can be tried only if illegal at the time of the crime, and Clauses 4 and 18 of the Law on Human Rights adopted in 1999), as well as general principles of the rule of law. The International Crisis Group reports that when the Human Rights Courts Bill was taken to the DPR in June 2000, the retroactive principle was criticised particularly by the military and Golkar representatives who had been most identified with the New Order regime. The majority, however, accepted that without retroactive prosecution of "crimes of omission", it would be at least extremely difficult to convict those most responsible for human rights violations in East Timor and elsewhere and to persuade the international community that Indonesia was making a serious effort to hold those responsible for gross violations accountable.[42]

The final version of the law reflects compromise on this issue and was unanimously adopted. It provides for special *ad hoc* human rights courts to try gross violations of human rights that occurred before the new law came into force. However, as a safeguard, such courts can only be established to try specific cases through a special procedure. The President may establish an *ad hoc* court by decree only on the explicit recommendation of the DPR (clause 43). Provision is also made for the resolution of gross violations through a Truth and Reconciliation Commission to be established by a later law (clause 47), which finally passed into law in September 2004.

This compromise was quickly overtaken by a constitutional amendment in August 2000. An *ad hoc* Committee of the MPR's Working Committee had been preparing a detailed set of alternative constitutional amendments to the chapter of the constitution dealing with human rights. Among the 26 sub-clauses on human rights that were eventually adopted unanimously by the MPR, the new Clause 28.i read:

> The right to life, the right not to be tortured, the right to freedom of thought and conscience, the right to religion, the right not to be enslaved, the right

[42] *Indonesia: Impunity versus Accountability for Gross Human Rights Violations* (International Crisis Group, Brussels, 2001), 15, quoting Kompas, 16 June 2000.

to be recognised as a person before the law, and the right not to be prosecuted on the basis of a retroactive law are human rights that cannot be diminished under any circumstances.

The MPR claimed not to have been aware of the possible implications especially of the last right for the Timor trials, but the Minister of Foreign Affairs, Alwi Shihab, stated that "The Ministry of Foreign Affairs will certainly find it very difficult to explain the article to the world in the midst of our effort to avoid an international tribunal".[43]

Further, serious geographic and temporal restraints were placed on the East Timor trials. The then President, Abdurrahman Wahid, decreed in Presidential Decree 53/2001 that strict limits should be placed on its jurisdiction – specifically that it could only hear cases of violations that took place in the period after the 30 August 1999 referendum, thus excluding many hundreds of crimes committed throughout the year.

After strong protests the jurisdiction was later amended by a second decree, Presidential Decree 96/2001, issued by the newly installed President Megawati Sukarnoputri in August 2001. Nevertheless, the jurisdiction remained unacceptably limited. In contrast to the mandate of the KPP HAM which covered the whole of East Timor for the period from 1 January to 25 October 1999, the *ad hoc* Human Rights Court on East Timor was authorised only to hear cases that took place in April and September 1999. The jurisdiction was also further limited on the basis of locality, so that only cases that occurred within three of Timor-Leste's 13 districts would be heard. Thus, all prosecutions were based on events occurring in the districts of Liquiça, Dili, and Suai in only the two months of April and September 1999.

Limiting the temporal and geographical jurisdiction of the court in this way compounded the problem resulting from the selection of the cases that made it unlikely that the trials would uncover the full extent of human rights violations in Timor-Leste in 1999, and the full extent of the involvement of military, police and government officials.

The inadequacy of the foundational legislation was the first warning given to the international community that the process was under pressure.

---

[43] *ibid.*

The Defence

There was considerable fire-power on the defence team in stark contrast to the trials in Dili. The team of defence lawyers was led by Adnan Buyung Nasution, a well-known human rights lawyer. Former justice minister Professor Muladi was the defence team's senior legal adviser. Their defence strategy was simple and never wavered throughout the trials. The defence alleged that the human rights violations in the aftermath of the ballot "were a manifestation of society's disappointment with the conduct of the ballot which had been unfair and dishonest".[44] It was also alleged and continually repeated that Interfet, the international peace-keeping force which took control of security in East Timor on 20 September, had itself been responsible for 20 killings.

The Prosecution

A report released in late 2004 titled *Unfulfilled Promises: Justice in East Timor* by the Justice Initiative and the Coalition for International Justice confirmed the general view of court observers that the Attorney General's office exerted "little capacity and political will to pursue prosecutions vigorously".[45]

The report decided that the indictments and evidence introduced at trial revealed that the prosecutors were either "unfamiliar with – or else wilfully disregarded – basic international law concepts that are essential to proving a case of crimes against humanity",[46] even taking into account the jurisdictional and temporal limits upon the charges. The report authors also found that the prosecutors were similarly not only unfamiliar with, but also reluctant to pursue individual and superior responsibility for the crimes, expressed by judicial reform expert Greg Churchill as a "resistance to concepts of command responsibility".[47] This was linked to a fundamental lack of political will by the Attorney General's office to charge high-level military officers.

By focusing primarily on what can be described as middle-level perpetrators with operational responsibilities and by drafting the indictments in terms which omit any charges that the accused themselves were responsible for acts of violence committed in Timor-Leste in 1999, the prosecutors created for

---

44 Tapol, *Ending the Cycle of Impunity: Can the East Timor Investigations Pave the Way?* (Tapol, the Indonesia Human Rights Campaign, Surrey, 2000).

45 The Justice Initiative and the Coalition for International Justice, *Unfulfilled Promises: Justice in East Timor,* November 2004, p.22.

46 *ibid.*

47 *ibid.*

themselves multiple burdens of proof: that there was a chain of command linking the accused to certain persons who committed crimes; that those persons committed crimes against humanity; and that the accused were criminally responsible for failing to exercise proper command responsibility of those subordinates. None of the defendants were accused of planning or ordering the alleged crimes to be committed. Nor were they accused of any form of direct participation, even by way of aiding and abetting. Rather, the indictments alleged that the defendants were either accomplices to the commission of such crimes committed by others or, on the basis of command responsibility, had failed to prevent, stop, or take steps to investigate and prosecute the commission of crimes against humanity committed by persons under their command or authority.

However, there is some evidence that the prosecution faced genuine difficulties in building a case. Ketut Murtika, Abilio Soares' prosecutor and the Indonesian Attorney General's director of human rights says the "big fish" like General Wiranto and the then chief of territorial affairs, Susilo Bambang Yudhoyono were not prosecuted, because not a single witness could be found to testify against them.

When we investigated these defendants, the witnesses seemed to have their mouths locked. No one was willing to say who was behind the violence. They weren't prepared to go any further than the regional commander.

He added that:

> If there's sufficient evidence from the regional commander and his subordinates pointing the finger at these people, suggesting they were involved as planners, then of course we would want to look again at this matter.[48]

Or as HS Dillon, a former member of the National Commission on Human Rights, put it: "When you are a prosecutor, why would you really want to prosecute the army generals? The only thing you might get is a bullet in your head".[49]

---

[48] M MacGregor, East Timor: Last Indonesian governor is first jailed over violence. Asia Pacific/Radio Australia, 2004.

[49] Laksamana. Net. 18 Tried, 16 Acquitted. 9 August 2004, *http://www.laksamana.net/vnews.cfm?ncat=45&news_id=7365*.

The report also identified as a problem the lack of trial skills and preparation on the part of the lawyers, including those who argued the cases at trial. This was acknowledged as a problem that pervades the Indonesian court system generally, but was an acute problem in these difficult cases based on new laws.

The Judges

Law 26/2000 on Human Rights Courts provides that the human rights courts will consist of five judges, two of whom will be career, and three *ad hoc* from outside the present judiciary who will be appointed for five-year terms. In January 2002, Presidential Decree 6/2002 appointed 18 judges for the *ad hoc* human rights tribunal dealing with East Timor in 1999 and the Tanjung Priok riot in 1984. All 18 judges appointed by the President were recommended by the Supreme Court. Twelve judges served as first degree judges and six others served as appeals judges. They received a salary of Rp 1 million per month (about US$100) in addition to a fee of Rp 4 million for every case they handle. The 18 *ad hoc* judges worked together with 12 career judges appointed by Chief Justice Bagir Manan in December 2001.

Concerns were expressed at the appointment of the judges by rights activists, doubting the credibility and capability of judges for the *ad hoc* tribunal. Caretaker of the Indonesian Legal Aid Institute Foundation (YLBHI), Irianto Subiyakto, said it would be hard to put faith in the judges because their recruitment itself was not transparent, but "considering that the *ad hoc* judges have solid academic qualifications, we expect them to produce credible rulings". He expressed fears that the rights cases could be twisted into petty criminal cases during the trial due to a lack of experience by prosecutors and judges. Legal expert Achmad Ali of the Hasanuddin University in Makassar, South Sulawesi also doubted whether "The judges have the courage to try those powerful persons who can control many things, including law".[50]

There were three female First Degree Justice Non-Career *ad hoc* Judges: Seyfulina Faruddin (retired judge of the Jakarta State Administrative Court (PT TUN)); Komariah Emong Sapardjaja (academic) and Sanwani Nasution (academic). There were two women appointed as Appeal Court judges: Marni Emmy (Central Jakarta District Court) and Adriani Nurdin (Cibinong District Court).

[50] T Siboro, and TZ Simanjuntak, "Indonesian Government unveils names of rights tribunal judges", *The Jakarta Post,* 15 January, 2002.

Indictments

KPP HAM publicly identified 32 persons who fell into one of three categories of perpetrators: those responsible for specific crimes of violence on the ground; those with field responsibility for such crimes; and those with ultimate command responsibility. It recommended that these categories of perpetrators should be charged with a far broader range of crimes against humanity than the two, murder (Art 9(a)) and persecution or assault (Art 9(h)) that formed the basis of the charges in the Indonesian indictments. In the event, indictments were issued against only 18 people – 10 military and five police officers, two civilian government officials, and a militia leader. The most senior official to be indicted was the Regional Military Commander, Major-General Adam Damiri. The Indonesian authorities never explained why others named in the KPP HAM report were not indicted.

Excluded were some of the higher ranking members of the armed forces that KPP HAM had recommended should be investigated. Among them were the most senior military officials of the time, including, General Wiranto (former Commander of the Armed Forces and Defence Minister) and Major-General Zacky Anwar Makarim (the Security Advisor to the Indonesian Task Force for the Implementation of the Popular Consultation on the Special Autonomy on East Timor). As already noted, both have since been indicted by East Timor's General Prosecutor.[51]

This was the second and clear sign that the trials would be flawed. It was also at this point that it should have been clear to the international community that the trials would ignore completely the findings on gender violence contained in the UN and KPP HAM reports.

Outcomes of the trials

In total, six out of the eighteen defendants indicted by the *ad hoc* Human Rights Court were found guilty of crimes against humanity. Those convicted and sentenced to three years' imprisonment were the Regional Military Commander, Major General Adam Damiri; the former Governor, Abilio Jose Osorio Soares; and the former Police Chief for Dili District, Lieutenant Colonel Hulman Gultom. The Military Commander for East Timor, Brigadier General Mohammad Noer Muis and the District Military Commander for Dili, Lieutenant Colonel Soedjarwo, were sentenced to five years' imprisonment

[51] See *The Deputy General Prosecutor against Wiranto, Zacky Anwar Makarim, Kiki Syahnakri, Adam*, from unofficial transcripts compiled by JSMP's trial observer, Suhartono Suratman, Mohammad Noer Muis, Yayat Sudrajat and Abilio Jose Osorio Soares, 22 February 2003.

each. Eurico Gutteres, the Deputy Commander of the PPI and commander of the Aitarak militia received the longest sentence of 10 years.

All but Eurico Guterres were sentenced to terms of imprisonment below the specified minimum legal limit for these crimes. Both of the Articles under Law 26/2000 with which all the defendants were charged, murder as a crime against humanity (Art 9a), and assault/persecution as a crime against humanity (Art 9h) carry a minimum prison sentence of 10 years. It is unclear on what legal basis the judges were able to ignore these provisions.

All those convicted remained at liberty pending the outcome of their appeals. In some cases, including that of Major General Adam Damiri, the defendants remained in active service in the military or police.

Guterres was the eighth of 18 suspects to be tried by the Indonesian court and the second to be found guilty. Six police and military officers were acquitted on charges similar to those faced by Guterres. The province's former governor, Abilio Soares, was found guilty by the Court on 14 August 2002 and jailed for three years, but released after four months.

On 29 November 2004, the tribunal acquitted four military and police officers being tried for crimes against humanity, bringing the number of officers found not guilty in the case to nine. A panel of five judges from Indonesia's Human Rights Court dismissed all charges against Liquica's army commander, Lieutenant Colonel Asep Kuswandi; its police chief, Lieutenant Colonel Adios Salova; and Mr Martins of the same offence in connection with a massacre of up to 60 people in the Liquiça church on April 6, 1999. Prosecutors put the death toll at 22:[52] "It is true there have been human rights abuses but they were carried out by the Red and White Iron group, which has no relation with the defendants", chief judge Sutiarso said.[53]

Those who had already been cleared included the former provincial police chief, Brigadier-General Timbul Silaen, as well as eight military personnel including the former district chief, Colonel Herman Sedyono, charged over the specific case of the Suai church ground massacre of 6 September 1999. Lieutenant-Colonel Endar Priyanto, the former military commander in Dili,

52 At least three pieces of evidence which could have been used by the judges to secure a conviction in the Liquiça trial, including a priest eyewitness, an Indonesian military investigator and an Australian embassy report: see D Greenlees, "Smiles, but still no justice", *The Australian*. Sydney, 2002, at p.12.
53 *ibid*.

who is a member of the army's Kopassus special forces, was acquitted of charges that he failed to intervene to prevent the Carrascalao massacre.

In March 2005, the Supreme Court then upheld the acquittal by the human rights tribunal of Brigadier General Tono Suratman, who was the chief of the now defunct Wiradharma military command in Dili. The team of prosecutors led by Gabrial Simangunsong had previously asked for a ten-year sentence but then failed to submit legal arguments to the Supreme Court within the two-year deadline. Human rights actors in Indonesia said the Attorney-General's Office should explain their negligence and called on the new President Susilo Bambang Yudhoyono to summon Attorney General Abdul Rahman Saleh for an explanation.[54] None was forthcoming. However, Saleh had stated in November 2004 that there was still a chance that prosecutors could build new cases and name new suspects for crimes against humanity in East Timor.[55]

Former Governor of East Timor, Timorese civilian Abilio Soares received a jail term of five years for crimes against humanity and entered Cipinang prison in August 2004 where he spent only a few weeks before being released on appeal.

After appeals regarding his sentence finally failed on May 2006, Timorese militia leader Eurico Guterres became the only person, from the 18 individuals indicted by the Indonesian authorities for acts of violence committed in East Timor in 1999, whose trial ended in a conviction. Guterres was imprisoned in Cipinang prison centre in Jakarta on 4 May 2006.[56]

Some TNI officers named in the KPP HAM report or acquitted in the trials have been promoted. Major General Sjafrie Sjamsoeddin was appointed as the chief military spokesman. Brigadier General Mahidin Simbolon was the chief of staff of the Udayana regional command in Bali, which oversaw the military operations in Timor. Simbolon has subsequently been promoted to the rank of Major General and is now the military commander for Papua.

---

[54] T Siboro, "SBY told to summon AG over general's East Timor acquittal", *The Jakarta Post,* 10 March, 2005.

[55] M Taufiqurrahman, "Reopening East Timor cases possible, says AGO", *The Jakarta Post*, 10 November 2004.

[56] "Observing three main cases of Adam Damiri, Tono Suratman and Eurico Gutteres", Institute For Policy Research and Advocacy (ELSAM) Monitoring Report on *ad hoc* Human Rights Court Against Gross Human Rights Violations in East Timor Jakarta, Indonesia Report No. 6, 2002.

Timbul Silaen, who was acquitted of crimes against humanity, is now the Security Assistant, Inspector General to the National Police Chief, Da'i Bachtiar.[57]

Reactions

Reactions to the verdict from various sources offer evidence that the outcome of Guterres trial, coupled with the acquittal of senior military figures did not satisfy the basic expectations of stakeholders – the defendant himself, the victim, the Timorese government, Indonesian civil society, or international public opinion.

Mario Carrascalao, who now heads East Timor's Social Democracy Party, was asked whether the verdict had restored credibility to the Court. He responded that Guterres should "stay in jail forever" and said:

> We really don't trust it. We don't believe that the court is serious. This is just something to show to the international community that they did something. Justice should be equal to everybody whether he is East Timorese or he is Indonesian, he's military or he's a civilian. It should be the same for everybody. But this is not the case you know. For me, this is normal, it is normal, this happens in Indonesia, it is normal.[58]

At the political level, East Timor's foreign minister, Jose Ramos Horta, reacted angrily. He described the acquittal of the former Indonesian military commander in Dili, Lieutenant-Colonel Endar Priyanto as "scandalous". He also said that Eurico Guterres "deserved the maximum penalty [death] both under Timorese law and Indonesian law".[59]

Within Indonesia, NGOs and international media correspondents in Jakarta judged the Court harshly. Their reaction makes it clear that the proper operation of the Court is as significant to Indonesian civil society as to Timorese victims. Hendardi, an Indonesian human rights activist, told

---

[57] H McDonald, "Australia's bloody East Timor secret", *Sydney Morning Herald*, 14 March, 2002; "Silence over a crime against humanity" *Sydney Morning Herald*, 14 March, 2002.

[58] L LoPresti, "Critics say Guterres sentence is meaningless" (*Radio Australia*. Sydney, 2002).

[59] Lusa (2002), Jakarta court acquittals "scandalous": Ramos Horta. Jakarta. Notably, the Australian Foreign Minister, Alexander Downer, however, still expressed faith in the process. He said the Guterres sentence was "welcome and appropriate", and "shows that the *ad hoc* tribunal process in Indonesia is now starting to work and work well." Hamish McDonald (2002) November 30. "Guterres: the one that didn't get away," *The Age*, p.3.

Associated Press on November 28 that Guterres had been "sacrificed" to protect the top military. "They are untouchable by law".[60]

Solahuddin Wahid of the National Commission on human rights (Komnas HAM) also expressed scepticism about the Court because it only sentenced two East Timorese civilians, but acquitted Indonesian military and police officers. "Why only East Timorese. Are they the most responsible ones?" he asked.[61]

The judgment of Indonesian human rights commentators should be respected. The Court was then at the point where the UN should have resumed responsibility for justice. However the situation was made even worse by the jailing (albeit only briefly) of Abilio Soares.

Adam Ereli, deputy spokesman for the US State Department stated after the November 2004 acquittals:

> We are dismayed by this decision, and we are profoundly disappointed with the performance and record of the Indonesian *ad hoc* tribunal. In our view, as a result of this appeals decision, only two of the eighteen defendants have been convicted, and both individuals are ethnic Timorese and received sentences below the ten-year minimum set by law. We think that the overall process was seriously flawed and lacked credibility.[62]

The European Union, in a Declaration by the Presidency, stated that the trials "have failed to deliver justice and did not result in a substantiated account of the violence".[63].

The response from Indonesia was fierce. Acting senior security minister Hari Sabarno said "This is a court verdict ... America should better take care of its own self". Justice Minister Yusril Ihza Mahendra added:

> "We are not satisfied with America's actions in Vietnam, which have yet to be investigated ...[64] If we are talking about dissatisfaction, I am also not

[60] Djuhari, East Timor leader gets 10 Years, Associated Press, 27 November 2002.
[61] M.N. Kurniawan, *No hope of punishment [of] military [or] police in rights cases,* Jakarta Post, 2 December 2002.
[62] Voice of America Editorial, *Radio Scripts - EDITORIAL 0-11521* (2004).
[63] Declaration by the Presidency on behalf of the European Union on the *ad hoc* Human Rights Tribunal for crimes committed in East Timor, 6 August 2003.
[64] Associated Press, "Indonesian stung over US criticism of Timor acquittals" (13 August, 2004).

> satisfied with what America is doing and its invasion of Iraq, but we are powerless against America".[65]

New Zealand was also outspoken about the acquittals.

In September 2004, Indonesia announced that a truth commission would be set up, as had always been envisaged by the legislation, amidst civil society fears it could turn into a "whitewash machine".[66]

The leadership of the National Resistance Council of East Timor (CNRT) has made clear that it will not press for a thorough investigation, trial and punishment of the Indonesian generals. Speaking from Singapore in response to the release of the KPP HAM report, CNRT leader Xanana Gusmão expressed considerable sympathy for Wiranto: "I can't say if I am happy or unhappy. I am not seeking revenge. I know him and he knows me. I just want the truth to be revealed".

East Timor's then Foreign Minister, now Prime Minister Jose Ramos Horta reaffirmed his opposition to an international rights tribunal, telling Parliament that the country's economic future depended on good relations with its former occupier.

> Almost everything for our daily needs comes from Indonesia. Therefore, if we have a bad relationship with Indonesia it will effect the living standard of the people of East Timor. The past is history now ... the future is more important.[67]

PART III: WERE THE TRIALS A SHAM?

It seems clear that on most measures the trials were a failure. A more difficult question is whether they were a sham from the beginning, and whether the reasons for the failure can be pinpointed to a conspiracy or basic inadequacy. An even more difficult question is the responsibility the UN, representing the will of the international community, bears for the failure of the trials and what the consequences of the failure will be. The question that has not even been asked is that given the complete absence of any prosecution of sexual violence or offences against women, should the trials have been considered fair even if more convictions had been recorded?

---

[65] Agence France Presse, "Indonesian ministers tell Washington to keep quiet on Timor verdicts" (Jakarta, 12 August, 2004).

[66] MS Saraswati, "Commission could be 'whitewash machine'", *Jakarta Post,* 9 September, 2004.

[67] Associated Press, "East Timor's foreign minister opposes rights tribunal" (Jakarta, 8 September, 2004).

There were four main problems with the Court that can be clearly identified from observing the trials: inherent procedural flaws in the legislative foundation of the Court; intimidation of the judges and witnesses; possible conspiracy between the prosecution and the military, and the lack of training of prosecutors and judges. The cumulative effect of these factors has meant that the Court was unable to provide even the basic measure of justice in the cases before it.

Flaws in the Legislative Foundation

As noted above, there were serious human rights concerns expressed since the legislation setting up the Court was passed – the time frames were considered too narrow, the upcoming appeals were to be completed within six months, the witness protection scheme was completely inadequate and certain names were removed from the original indictment list provided to the Attorney-General by the Komnas HAM investigation team, such as General Wiranto.

The beginning of the trials did not alleviate these fears. As Sidney Jones, Indonesia director of ICG and leading commentator on the Court stated ominously in 2001:

> Unfortunately, the government's commitment to justice remains in doubt. The judges were poorly chosen, the prosecutors have shown no interest in accountability, the defense is likely to take advantage of an array of legal loopholes – and the suspects haven't even been detained.[68]

As the trials were in progress, the UN High Commissioner for Human Rights Sergio de Mello reported to the 59th session of the Human Rights Commission in April 2003 his concern that:

> the limited geographical and temporal jurisdiction of the Court; the lack of experienced prosecutors and judges; the intimidating and, at times, hostile, courtroom treatment of Timorese witnesses by some judges, prosecutors and defense counsel; the causes and consequences of non-attendance of Timorese witnesses at the proceedings; and the lightness of the sentences imposed, which bear no reasonable relationship to the gravity of the offences committed … the failure to put before the court evidence that portrays the killings and other human rights violations as part of a

[68] International Crisis Group, *Indonesia: Impunity versus accountability for gross human rights violations* (International Crisis Group, Jakarta/Brussels, 2001), at p.32.

> widespread or systematic pattern of violence seriously undermines the strength of the prosecution's case and jeopardizes the integrity and credibility of the trial process.[69]

Problems with the Court identified by JSMP/Amnesty include: the independence of the prosecution; the selection of judges; witness and victim protection; quality of indictments; the courtroom atmosphere; the selection of witnesses by the prosecution; the hostile treatment of witnesses; hostile prosecution witnesses; failure to challenge inconsistent statements; failure by prosecution to use documentary evidence; mixed performance of judges; and questionable verdicts and sentencing.

Allegations of Conspiracy/Bias

There has been a lack of testimony from East Timorese witnesses due to the inability of the Court to reassure witnesses of their safety. However, Indonesian judges have the ability to interrogate prosecution witnesses under the civil law system, and have so far failed to examine available witnesses effectively. ELSAM has noted that:

> The judges restricted themselves to the weak charges built by prosecutors who perceived the East Timor mayhem as a mere communal conflict. The court has allowed anyone connected to a state institution to be exonerated and cleared of any involvement.[70]

Most allegations of bias however, focus on the prosecution. Commentators note that although the Attorney-General's office had been provided with comprehensive evidence by Komnas-HAM, as well as UN prosecutors, that proved that the militia were created, trained and backed by the TNI, prosecutors used little of it. The government, through the Attorney General's Office, also failed to bring strong witnesses to the trial, which made it easy for the judges to acquit the officers. Finally, instead of constructing a case to prove that the massacres, and the forced removal of 250,000 people into West Timor, were orchestrated by the military, the prosecution has only tried to charge the police and military with the failure to stop violence.[71] This has led to speculation that a "deal" has been struck by the prosecution and the military.[72]

---

[69] Commission on Human Rights, Situation of Human Rights in Timor Leste, Report of the United Nations High Commissioner for Human Rights, UN Doc. E/CN.4/2003/37, 4 March 2003, para 52.

[70] T Siboro, "Rights abusers should be executed: East Timor leader", Jakarta Post, 29 November, 2002.

[71] P Lloyd, "Militia leader sentenced", Radio Australia. Sydney, 28 November, 2002.

[72] M Moore, "Militia leader Guterres gets 10 years", *The Age,* 28 November, 2002, at p.17.

Overall, Indonesian human rights commentators blamed prosecutors for the failure of the human rights tribunal in both the Timor and 1984 Tanjung Priok incident, but were reluctant to give it up altogether in the hope it may one day provide a measure of justice.

Hikmahanto Juwana, dean of the School of Law at the University of Indonesia stated that "We can't deny the fact that the court is being used to serve the interest of the military. This will more or less discourage people to bring their cases to the court". However he added that, "It is a process of learning. We will ultimately achieve a healthy process after several (more) cases are handled".

While the Tanjung Priok rights tribunal sent to jail 12 low-ranking military personnel implicated in the incident, it acquitted two officers – Maj. Gen. (ret) Pranowo and Maj. Gen. Sriyanto, the current commander of the Army's Special Forces (Kopassus).

Enny said Komnas HAM had done all it could to assemble convincing evidence against the generals: "We couldn't do anything after we submitted the case file to the prosecutors. If the generals are free then there is something wrong with the prosecutors' indictments".[73]

Lack of Training of Prosecutors and Judges

Amid conspiracy claims, the basic lack of competence of the court has been less analysed than it should be. It should be noted that the international *ad hoc* tribunal for Rwanda faces similar allegations of bias and mismanagement, as did Yugoslavia to a lesser extent. Prosecutor Mohammed Yusuf has defended the court's record and pleaded for patience: "This is a new area for prosecutors and judges in Indonesia. We have never had a Human Rights Court before".[74] There is evidence that international opinion has had an effect on some judges – Judge Rocky Panjaitan has been quoted as being "embarrassed" over the public criticism of earlier acquittals of soldiers and police.[75]

Ifdhal Kasim of the Institute for Policy Research and Advocacy (ELSAM) has acknowledged that unknowledgeable and poorly trained judges and prosecutors made for very poor performance.

> The judges and prosecutors are not even given appropriate literature to learn about other human rights cases in other countries, although the

[73] A Khalik, "Indictment of soldiers who murder civilians weak: Experts", *Jakarta Post*, 23 August 2004.
[74] D Greenlees, "Human rights are on trial, and so is the court", *Australian*, 25 November, 2002, at p.12.
[75] *ibid*.

information is very important to help them to take action. So only the creative prosecutors or judges, who will spend extra time and money to get the information can understand human rights.[76]

UN Commission of Experts and the Joint Truth and Friendship Commission

A Commission of Experts was appointed by Kofi Annan in January 2005 to investigate why a 1999 Security Council resolution calling for the trial of those accused of atrocities in Timor during its independence referendum had not been implemented. The three experts, Justice Prafullachandra Bhagwati of India, Professor Yozo Yokota of Japan and Shaista Shameem of Fiji, visited Indonesia and East Timor in early 2005.

The UN Security Council, as mentioned in Resolution 1599 (2005), called on all parties (including Indonesia) to cooperate fully with the work of the Commission of Experts. Despite this, in May 2005 Indonesia initially refuse their visas. The Security Council, in the same resolution, acknowledges the improvement of relations between Indonesia and Timor Leste, including the agreement to establish the CTF. The Council also slightly softened its position on the judicial process regarding serious human rights violations in East Timor in 1999, by only reaffirming the need for *credible accountability*, instead of reaffirming the *fight against impunity* mentioned in the Resolution 1573 adopted in 2004.

The Experts' 160-page report to UN Secretary-General Kofi Annan which was debated in the Security Council found that Indonesia should retry accused war criminals acquitted by a special court in Jakarta because the process was a sham. It says the trials were "manifestly inadequate" with "scant respect for relevant international standards". Prosecutors were "not committed to justice", and the court had been hostile to defence witnesses but lenient on the accused.[77]

The report recommended that Indonesia be given six months to prepare credible trials. If it does not comply, the experts argued, the UN should invoke its charter to set up an international war crimes court for East Timor. In direct response, in March 2005 the Governments of Indonesia and East Timor agreed to establish a bilateral Truth and Friendship Commission, set up to "resolve

[76] MN Kurniawan, above, n.61.

[77] J Jolliffe, "Jakarta's Timor trials 'a sham'", *The Age*, 19 June, 2005.

once and for all the events of 1999". The process will not lead to prosecutions and appears to be aimed at preventing all future national investigations and prosecution of senior Indonesian officials alleged to bear primary responsibility for the crimes against humanity committed in East Timor before and during 1999.

Even with its flexible mandate, the Joint Truth and Friendship Commission commenced in August 2005 but has not produced any tangible result or reports as yet. The mandate has been extended until August 2007. On 28 August 2006, disillusioned human rights groups within Indonesia called for the Commission to be disbanded.[78] The six month deadline given by the UN Commission of Experts has long since expired.

Part III: Gender Issues

Within the overall failure of the trials, the consequences for women have been buried. This section focuses on the official silence in the indictments on gender-persecution, the intimidating court-room atmosphere, treatment of female witnesses and judges, and the reaction of Timorese women's groups to the trials.

Official Silence on Gender Persecution

It is of particular concern that no cases of rape and other crimes of sexual violence were brought to trial in Jakarta despite the findings of the KPP HAM and UN reports. The full extent of such crimes is not known, but rape and other crimes of sexual violence were a feature of the human rights violations committed in Timor-Leste both before and during 1999.[79] Indonesia's record on addressing such allegations has been poor, not only in Timor-Leste, but also in other areas where military operations have taken place, notably in the provinces of Nanggroe Aceh Darussalam and Papua.

The reports focus only on the events of the 1999 referendum violence. Prior to 1999, an unverifiable number of Timorese women were abducted, raped, and impregnated by Indonesian solders, often kept captive under slavery-like conditions, and later rejected by their families. A more acute form of gender-based violence occurred during the post-referendum violence during 1999:

---

[78] M Rizal Maslan, "Rights activists want Truth and Reconciliation Commission disbanded", *Detik.com*, Jakarta, 28 August, 2006.

[79] See further Susan Harris Rimmer, "East Timorese Women and the Catholic Church", in C Evan and A Whiting, eds, *Mixed Blessing: Women, Religion and the Law in South East Asia* (Brill Press, 2005).

the systematic rape of East Timorese women in the context of the forced deportation of over 250,000 people into camps in West Timor.[80]

There are no accurate statistics on sexual violence during the occupation until 1999, and consequently during the period of forced deportation and internment in West Timor. However, a wealth of anecdotal evidence shows that gender-based international crimes in Timor have been widespread since 1975 and were rife in the 1999 violence. Testimonies to this effect have been collected by the United Nations,[81] human rights NGOs such as Amnesty International,[82] the Indonesian Human Rights Commission KPP HAM,[83] Australian journalists,[84] and most importantly, East Timorese NGOs themselves.[85]

The most comprehensive overview of sexual violence in Timor appears in Chapter 7.7 of the report by the CAVR entitled *Chega!* The CAVR recorded 853 cases of sexual violence but concluded:

> The Commission notes the inevitable conclusion that many victims of sexual violations did not come forward to report them to the Commission. Reasons for under-reporting include death of victims and witnesses (especially for earlier periods of the conflict), victims who may be outside Timor-Leste (especially in West Timor), the painful and very personal

80 Primary materials on the experience of women in the East Timor conflict were collated from primarily from witness testimony given to the UN investigative teams and KPP HAM, trials and CAVR hearings. Other important sources included reports issued by various UN organs including the Commission on Human Rights and Special Rapporteurs, the UN missions in East Timor, East Timorese and international NGOs and government records from the United States, Portugal, Indonesia, and Australia. The material is informed by the author's background visit to East Timor in 2001 and informal interviews with East Timorese women and NGOs.

81 See especially the *Report of the International Commission of Inquiry on East Timor to the Secretary-General*. UN Document A/54/726. 31 January, 2000; *Report of the Security Council Mission to Jakarta and Dili*, S/1999/976, 14 September 1999; *Report of UN Special Rapporteurs: Situation of human rights in East Timor*. Based on visit between 4–10 November 1999. UN Document A/54/660, 10 December 1999.

82 Amnesty International, *East Timor Justice – past, present and future* (27 July 2001) AI Index ASA 57/001/2001.

83 Indonesian KPP-HAM Report, 31 January 2000, *www.jsmp.minihub.org*.

84 H McDonald, D Ball, J Dunn, G van Klinken, D Bourchier, D Kammen, and R Tanter, *Masters of Terror: Indonesia's Military and Violence in East Timor in 1999* (Strategic and Defence Studies Centre, Australian National University (Canberra Paper #145), 2002).

85 See generally N Godinho, UN Security Council "Arria formula" meeting on the implementation of Security Council Resolution 1325, 30 October 2001; and Fokupers, *Gender-based Human Rights Abuses during the Pre and Post-Ballot Violence in East Timor* (2000). In September 1999, the office of FOKUPERS in Dili was attacked by militia, resulting in looting and burning of the premises and the staff of the organisation having to flee to save their lives.

> nature of the experiences, and the fear of social or family humiliation or rejection if their experiences are known publicly. These strong reasons for under-reporting and the fact that 853 cases of rape and sexual slavery, along with evidence from about another 200 interviews were recorded lead the Commission to the finding that the total number of sexual violations is likely to be several times higher than the number of cases reported. The Commission estimates that the number of women who were subjected to serious sexual violations by members of the Indonesian security forces numbers in the thousands, rather than hundreds.[86]

The reality of the suffering of Timorese women was therefore clear. The evidence was presented in the KPP Ham and UN reports on the 1999 violence which formed the impetus for the trials. Although a theoretical question now, as the trials have failed to provide any measure of justice: what if some of the cursory prosecutions had succeeded? Would the complete absence of all gender-based violence allegations have rendered the trials unjust?

This is particularly important because at the time the Jakarta trials were commencing, the UN serious crimes process in Dili had singularly failed to provide justice for women who had been forcibly deported to West Timor. In the camps in West Timor where tens of thousands of women were forcibly deported, a fact-finding team in one study alone found 163 different cases of violence against 119 women, and noted serious impacts of sexual violence on women's health.[87] There is still a serious campaign by activists, including the new First Lady of East Timor, Australian Kirsty Sword Gusmão, to obtain the release of several young women in the refugee camps of West Timor who are thought to be held against their will as "war trophies" by militia leaders.[88]

Elsewhere I have analysed the Serious Crimes cases of the *Leonardus Kasa* and *Lolotae* cases, and conclude that justice for women during the period of Indonesian occupation was not achieved through the Dili court. *The Prosecutor v Leonardus Kasa*[89] (the *Kasa case*) was decided by the Special

---

[86] *Chega!* Final Report of the CAVR, 2005, p.109.

[87] "Violence against IDP/refugee women – Report of TKTB (Tim Kemanusiaan Timor Barat) findings in IDP/Refugee Camps in West Timor", August 2000.

[88] D Farsetta, "East Timorese Refugees in Militia-Controlled Camps" in MHC Pus, ed, *The Devastating Impact of Small Arms & Light Weapons on the Lives of Women: A Collection of Testimonies* (WILPF for International Action Network on Small Arms (IANSA) Women's Caucus, 2001). Note the case of 15-year-old Juliana dos Santos in particular.

[89] *The General Prosecutor of the United Nations Transitional Administration in East Timor v Leonardus Kasa,* Dili District Court Special Panel for Serious Crimes Case no. 11/CG/2000, 9 May 2001.

Panel for Serious Crimes in May 2001. In the *Kasa* case, the Special Panel of the Dili District Court declared that it held no jurisdiction on the case as the rape had been perpetrated in West Timor, in spite of the principle of universal jurisdiction, thereby precluding all further cases of women who had been forcibly removed from East to West Timor from being tried. Due to lack of cooperation from Indonesia in handing over suspects still in Indonesian territory, both the Special Panels and the CAVR were focused on Timorese nationals who participated in violent acts, either as guerrillas in Falintil or as collaborators with the Indonesian forces.

Given this fact, the Jakarta trials were the only real chance to put the suffering of Timorese women on the record, even if only in indictment form, in the only jurisdiction which mattered. Why did the UN not insist on the inclusion of such offences at the beginning when it clearly had influence over Indonesia's response?

Gendered Discourse in the Jakarta Trials

The court room in Jakarta may be one of the clearest examples of Australian academic Hilary Charlesworth's belief that "sex and gender are deeply implicated in international law". She notes that society codes certain attributes as masculine or feminine, and cites rhetoric surrounding the Iraq War – urging tough leadership, taking action and military security – as coded "masculine" traits. In contrast conciliation, negotiation and human security, associated with "feminine traits", are seen as weak, and belittled.[90] Gendered discourse has been defined as "the phenomenon of symbolically organizing the world in these gender-associated opposites" or binary oppositions.[91] Gendered discourse then becomes a means through which certain kinds of thought and action get effectively pre-empted.

With this framework in mind, the gendered atmosphere of the Jakarta trials was obvious. Military figures routinely turned up in court to intimidate the judges and witnesses, often wearing matching t-shirts which read in Bahasa "Victims of UN Deception". More than 30 supporters of Timbul Silaen stood silently outside the courtroom during his trial with placards which read "Don't Make Us Angry".[92] The judges lacked the most basic court management techniques and did not have independent court security.

---

90 A Morgan, "The state and international law", interview with Professor Hilary Charlesworth (Canberra, 2003), *http://info.anu.edu.au/mac/Media/Research_Review/_articles/_Charlesworth.asp*.

91 C Cohn, "War, Wimps, and Women: Talking Gender and Thinking War" in M Cooke and A Woollacott, *Gendering War Talk* (Princeton University Press, Princeton, 1993), at p.230.

92 I Timberlake, "We did all we could to keep peace – Wiranto", *Sydney Morning Herald*, 5 April, 2002, at p.9.

The threat was quite real – the original chair of the committee charged with setting up the Court, Judge Syafuiuddin Kartasasmita, was gunned down in daylight in late July 2001 by unknown assassins.[93] The independence of the Indonesian *ad hoc* judges must therefore be at least questionable. The atmosphere for female judges and witnesses, as well as non-military men, must have been quite frightening.

Treatment of Female Witnesses

Amnesty and JSMP highlighted the situation for female witness, noting "the exposed position they found themselves in as a result of imperfect arrangements".[94] In the report *Justice for Timor-Leste*, the NGOs list the lack of security at airports; lack of secure accommodation; and lack of security in and around the Central Jakarta District Court as serious breaches of witness protection.

> Witnesses were forced to walk through public areas to enter the courtroom. Witness waiting areas were also insecure enabling members of the public, members of the defence teams and, on one occasion, the defendant and former militia leader Eurico Guterres himself to enter unchallenged. The witnesses from Timor-Leste were also subjected to intimidating and at times humiliating treatment by the Court.[95]

Amnesty and JSMP chronicle the treatment of one female witness in particular, based on unofficial transcripts compiled by a JSMP trial observer. As noted in the beginning to this chapter, Dominggas dos Santos Mouzinho, a survivor of the Suai massacre, and an uneducated villager from a remote part of Timor-Leste, testified on 28 May 2002 in the trial of Lieutenant Colonel Herman Sedyono and four others in the Suai case. Before the start of proceedings, she had asked the prosecution through UNTAET not to have to testify in the presence of the accused, as provided for under Section III, Article 5 of the Government Regulation on Victim and Witness Protection. It appears that this request was not conveyed to the Court. The presence of an interpreter, provided by UNTAET, had previously been agreed between UNTAET and

---

93 C Munro, "East Timor atrocities set for human rights court", *Canberra Times*, 2001, at p.10.

94 Amnesty International and JSMP, "Justice for Timor-Leste – the way forward", April 2004, pp. 42–43.

95 *ibid.*, p.42. See further East Timor Massacre Survivors Shun Jakarta Trial Over Safety Fears," AFP, 4 June, 2002. At least 13 witnesses have told UN officials they are too scared to come to Jakarta; "E. Timor Trial Verdicts Expected; Will Justice Be Done?" AP, 11 August, 2002. Human Rights Watch interview with ELSAM trial monitor, Jakarta, November 12, 2002, *http://www.hrw.org/backgrounder/asia/timor/etimor1202bg.htm#_ftn38*.

the Attorney General's Office. However, at the hearing the judge refused to allow the interpreter to appear on the grounds that he did not have "official accreditation" and because, in his view, the witness was fluent in Bahasa Indonesia and an interpreter was therefore not required.

Amnesty and JSMP comment that it quickly became apparent that Dominggas dos Santos Mouzinho was far from fluent in Bahasa Indonesia and was unable to understand many of the questions. The NGOs report that the:

> combined effect of the intimidating manner in which questions were asked and her inability to fully understand what was being said was to undermine the credibility of the witnesses who often remained silent or gave confused and contradictory answers to questions.[96]

The prosecution, who had called her as a witness, did not at any point raise an objection with the judge about the lack of interpretation. Nor did the prosecution object to what the NGOs termed "intimidating and frequently mocking manner" in which she was questioned by lawyers for the defence.[97] The judges also failed to exercise their responsibilities under Art 153 of KUHAP which requires them to "to see that nothing shall be done or that no question shall be asked that will cause the defendant or witness not to be free in giving his answer". The following exchange is cited as "typical" between the defence counsel and Dominggas dos Santos Mouzinho.

> Q: Your children, did they actively follow as officials in the Referendum, were there children of yours who followed?
> A: Followed.
> Q: Oo, so your children were with UNAMET? True madam? True madam, yes your children were chummy with UNAMET?
> A: No answer.
> Q: Fatimah was working when you were examined two years ago, or before you became a witness? Do you remember before you became a witness or after you became a witness, do your remember madam? Witness first or Fatimah worked first?
> A: No answer.
> Q: Madam can choose not to reply. This really is a "sham court" (pengadilan abu abu), political court. False testimony, madam, in Indonesia, is punishable by seven years, to give false testimony. Sorry, but

---

96 Amnesty International and JSMP, above, n.94, p. 43.
97 *ibid.*

> this concerns four TNI officers and police, their fate is to be accused. Beloved madam, I beg your honesty, Fatimah worked before you became a witness or after you became a witness? Don't look at the bule [white foreigner] on your right, I know he has been coaching you, don't look. Look at me if you need to, look at the judge, just listen no need for coaching. Beloved madam, was Fatimah working after you became a witness or before you became a witness?
> A: No answer.
> Q: Thank you, if you don't want to respond, I won't force you. But follow the conscience of your heart, my most beloved madam, were your daughters raped or about to be raped or wanting to be raped (*diperkosa atau mau diperkosa*) It's up to you if you don't want to answer, I am only talking about the pure inner self. Beloved madam.

As noted in the introduction above, Dominggas dos Santos Mouzinho was questioned in a similar manner for five hours without a break or any refreshment.[98] The intimidation of witnesses and the gendered language is clear even from the extract in translation.

Reactions from Timorese Women

The Jakarta trials seemed to make women's groups within Timor even more adamant about the need for an international tribunal. An East Timorese widows' organisation Liquiça-named *Rate Laek* (Tetum for "without graves") met with the UN High Commissioner for Human Rights Mary Robinson in mid-2002.

> We are women who have been interrogated and violated, women who have lost our family members, and women who carry great burdens from the loss of our husbands who were killed and disappeared. We are still waiting to know when will we see justice? At times, "justice" seems to be moving farther and farther away from us and we wonder what can help us heal from our deep wounds.
>
> The *ad hoc* Tribunal in Jakarta has not given us anything; in fact, it has only increased our suffering. We feel sick to hear that military and police officers who were part of the planning and even directly involved in killing our family members are free without any sentence and without any accountability. From the beginning, we rejected the establishment of the

[98] *ibid.*, pp.42–43.

> Indonesian *ad hoc* Tribunal because we knew that the decision would not give justice or truth to us, victims and families of victims. For 25 years, we have experienced the Indonesian justice system, and we do not believe that the Indonesian tribunal is credible unless there is a complete reformation.
>
> We continue to be committed to our demand for an international tribunal.[99]

Conclusion

Topo Susanto of the University of Indonesia stated that the implementation of Law No. 26/1999 on Human Rights Tribunal has so far reflected the "brotherhood among security personnel and the courts", instead of efforts to uphold human rights, and added that any effort to review the law in the current political climate would be fruitless.

> Looking back to the past, the law was born under international pressure and the demand for reform. All of these, of course, made political motives dominate the whole process at the House of Representatives, but failed to provide grounds that the gross human rights violations in East Timor had a strong relation with the government policy at that time.[100]

Were the trials worth holding? The Amnesty/JSMP report on justice for East Timor decides with considerable insight that the Indonesian court process was significant for two key reasons:

> First, the trials in Indonesia, however imperfect, represent a first attempt by the Indonesian authorities in what is intended to be an ongoing process of bringing to trial persons charged with crimes against humanity in a range of different cases. Second, the shortcomings of the process in Indonesia to bring to account those regarded as bearing final responsibility for crimes committed in Timor-Leste during 1999, together with the uncertainties surrounding the future of the process in Timor-Leste, throw the spotlight back on the international community and its responsibilities in such situations.[101]

The most thorough examination of the Jakarta trials has been undertaken by Professor David Cohen in late 2003 on behalf of the International Centre for

[99] Rate Laek, "Widows" group demands international tribunal", 24 August 2002.
[100] T Siboro, and TZ Simanjuntak, "Indonesian Government unveils names of rights tribunal judges", *Jakarta Post,* 15 January, 2002.
[101] Amnesty International and JSMP, above n.94, AI Index: ASA 21/006/2004.

Transitional Justice, entitled provocatively *Intended to Fail*. Ian Martin in his preface to this excellent analysis summarises Cohen's conclusions in the following manner:

> The inescapable conclusion of this report is that the trials as a whole must be regarded as a failure on every level, from technical competence to institutional integrity and political will. Some may point to the fact that six individuals, including high-ranking officials, have been convicted. However the report shows that this is more due to the notable bravery of a few individual judges than to a credible system of justice.[102]

While I agree whole-heartedly with Cohen's conclusions about the complete trials and the reasons for their failure, and even the premise that the Jakarta trials were intended to fail by the Indonesian authorities, I do not accept that this failure was inevitable. International pressure from the UN and international community was the first condition necessary to produce the political imperative for a fair and full investigation of the violence by KPP Ham. It was clear what level of pressure would be required to produce fair trials, and that level of international pressure was noticeably absent thereafter.

Part of the problem is the tendency of international lawyers to make two assumptions – that any trials are better than no trials, and that an international tribunal is always better.[103]

There are several advantages to an international tribunal. Being part of the Security Council gives an *ad hoc* tribunal financial security as they are funded through assessed funds rather than voluntary contributions. This allows for a longer time-frame in which to run trials. The use of international tribunals underscores the international nature of the crimes committed, in that it acknowledges that all people and states have a responsibility to ensure justice is served for such crimes, rather than just the state in which they were committed. An international tribunal can therefore avoid the appearance of victor's justice. The political and diplomatic weight of the Security Council may be the only way to pressure a State to hand over senior indicted officials.

---

[102] D Cohen, *Intended to Fail: The Trials before the Ad Hoc Human Rights Court in Jakarta,* (International Center for Transitional Justice ed, 2003), preface by Ian Martin p.iii.

[103] Vinjamuri & Snyder, "Advocacy and Scholarship in the Study of International War Crime Tribunals and Transitional Justice" (2004) 7 *Annual Review of Political Science* 345, at pp347–350. The International Criminal Court is unable to deal with the crimes committed in East Timor because the court cannot hear cases of crimes that were committed before its inception, and the Rome Statute entered into force in July 2002.

Threat of an international tribunal can also pressure a state into holding their own trials, an issue which has been explored here in relation to the setting up of the Jakarta *ad hoc* Human Rights Court.

Finally, an international tribunal can take pressure for justice issues off fragile states. As President Gusmão enunciated:

> What is the mandate of an international tribunal? It is to punish and to prevent atrocities. I say, don't force East Timor to punish. Have an international tribunal. The international community should deal with punishment of crimes, not East Timor. We also committed crimes before 1975; if we wanted to start to punish ourselves, we wouldn't exist as a community. If we talk about prevention: Indonesia will not invade us again. Also, there was a process of justice in Indonesia. Look at its size and population and how many challenges they have to face today. We ask ourselves to be patient with us and with Indonesia. They are dealing with their past. We don't want to undermine the democratization process in Indonesia in which they do very well.[104]

A post-conflict state often holds its own domestic trials. Under international law, and now incorporated into the Rome Statute, responsibility for providing justice for serious crimes falls upon the State first and then the international community only if the State is unwilling or unable to provide fair trials. In a weak democracy with little or no judicial infrastructure, this can be a significant problem, as Gusmão's words above attest.

There are two issues here – the first is that knowing how likely it was even in 1999 that the trials would fail, was it right for the UN to allow Indonesia to proceed with domestic prosecutions? There may not have been any real political alternative given the likelihood of a veto in the Security Council, but without this Realpolitik consideration, was it legally and ethically correct? The very hard answer in my opinion is yes – even the slightest chance that Indonesia might itself move to limit the impunity of its military through the rule of law was a chance that had to be taken, for the sake of the future of both countries. The question is what the UN had up its sleeve if the gamble failed.

This was a judgment call that had to be made fairly and wisely by the UN. As Cohen notes, it would not be fair to conduct a "trial of the trials" in Jakarta,

[104] *Watch Indonesia*. Notes on comments by Xanana Gusmão and Jose Ramos-Horta on dealing with past human rights violations made during a panel discussion. Paper read at German Council on Foreign Relations (Deutsche Gesellschaft für Auswaertige Politik, DGAP), 20 October 2004, Berlin.

without taking the totality of an extremely complicated process into account, and without comparison to the inordinately difficult task of transitional justice in other jurisdictions – Yugoslavia, Rwanda, Sierra Leone, and Cambodia to name a few. Numbers of convictions are not a proper guide, just as indictments do not give a proper picture of the trials in Dili. The core issue is justice for the wrongs that have been committed in East Timor. The substantive problem is that the international political process has led to a mixed approach consisting of entrusting the justice process to two national jurisdictions, neither of which had the slightest chance of carrying out their mandate for a myriad of reasons, of which most were foreseeable, even inevitable.

The second condition is that of practicality. In Indonesia, the promulgation of Law 26/2000 by Indonesia setting up Human Rights Tribunals, which provides also for *ad hoc* Tribunals to take up cases occurring in the past, the appointment of the judges and of the prosecutors, and generally, the organisation of the trials, were all done in a situation where there was no experience or precedent. The law is largely modelled on the Rome Statute, which is yet to be implemented. The ICTY and ICTR experience showed the complications and considerable resources needed to carry out the investigations and trials. There was – and still is – no other similar institution at the national level in any other country.

Unlike the ICTR, the ICTY and the ICC, the Indonesian Human Rights Tribunal does not have its own rules of evidence and procedure, but applies the Code of Criminal Procedure used in ordinary criminal trials. Thus, among other differences with the international tribunals, there is no provision for pre-trial procedures, putting the judges in a situation of "fait accompli" in regard to the indictments that they have to test. Regulation 2/2002, providing for witness protection, is no substitute for the arrangements for victim and witness protection provided in the international tribunals. These, and other considerations, reduce the scope of the trial considerably, since they affect the availability of witnesses, their testimony, and generally the validity of the process. It is these practical aspects that affect the conduct of the trials.

The Indonesian *ad hoc* Human Rights Court as a mechanism may not be completely ill-conceived and may still hold some value for the future. Certainly Indonesia should be encouraged by the international community to try their own violators of human rights. Under international law a sovereign nation must be given the opportunity to demonstrate accountability in its own courts before any international war crimes tribunal may be convened.

East Timor and Indonesia have opted for a Joint Truth and Friendship Commission. Clearly, this Commission cannot be invoked to try crimes against humanity, but it might make a significant contribution to creating a culture in which the prosecution of such crimes is made less of a challenge. The early signs for the Commission, however, are not promising.

Specific to the Timor trials, the KPP HAM investigations and report were excellent both as blueprints for prosecutions and as a historical record. The recommendations for indictment included senior military figures up to General Wiranto and Damiri themselves. The report dealt thoroughly with systematic gender persecution, as well as displaying a good analysis of apportioning accountability for the violence in accordance with international law. Some of the judges in the trials showed bravery and a commitment to humanitarian law that is to be commended in a fledgling institution, given the levels of intimidation in the court. Finally the facts that there were indictments of senior military figures at all, and Wiranto was initially forced to step aside is a breakthrough that should not be underestimated given Indonesia's history. The indictment and judgement of Damiri was extremely significant in this light.

However, these small gains pale next to the serious inadequacies of the trials and the legacy the court has left. In terms of gender analysis, there was no reflection of sexual offences in the indictments at all, and there was serious harassment of female witnesses and judges. The overall court environment was extremely distressing to all but military participants. Like the Serious Crimes Court in Dili, basic fair trial standards were not met, but this time the weakness lay squarely with the prosecution.

Overall, the acquittals on appeal of all but one Timorese non-military personnel send out a strong message of continued impunity for the Indonesian armed forces. This sets a disastrous precedent for West Papuan and Acehnese citizens facing continued military occupation, especially women.

It is important to note that implications of the Law on Human Rights Courts goes far beyond the Timor trials. As an International Crisis Group Report on Indonesia noted, gross violations in Indonesia have taken many different forms and affected different parts of society:

> … communists and communist sympathisers who were massacred or imprisoned in large numbers at the beginning of the New Order era in 1965–66; Muslim political opponents imprisoned in their hundreds in the 1980s; Muslim protestors at Tanjung Priok (Jakarta) in 1984 and Lampung in 1989 who were killed by government forces; and thousands of petty criminals who were systematically murdered during the early 1980s. Gross violations occurred during military operations in provinces where

> separatist or independence movements are or were active, including Aceh and Irian Jaya, as well as the special case of East Timor.[105]

The goal of transitional justice mechanisms to create an accurate historical record of the events in question has totally failed. The trials have produced a result worse than doing nothing. Coupled with the convictions in the Dili court, the trials have confirmed on the public record the military's distorted view that the Timorese themselves were responsible for the atrocities while the Indonesian army, entrusted with security, were entirely unable to prevent their civil savagery, and that the UN and Interfet were the real villains of the piece.

The East Timorese government has been placed in an extraordinarily difficult diplomatic position as a result of the trials, and arguably simply not been in a strong position to criticise the outcomes – as seen by the changing reaction to trial outcomes over time. This has led to the weakening of public support for the current Ministry and President by Timorese citizens, as well as undermining the faith of Timorese civil society in the UN.

The UN is also a victim of these trials, in terms of its credibility within Indonesia and the proper record of the role it played in East Timor, and also because of its inability to set clear standards for when the trials would be considered a failure. What is at stake in these trials is not only justice in individual cases but also the rewriting of history. Ian Martin, who supervised the UN-organised independence ballot, has said that the court was accepting a "mythical version" of events – that troops and police were powerless to halt violence between pro-integration and pro-independence East Timorese factions. In reality, Martin said, the army had created the militias, which waged a campaign of terror and coercion against pro-independence leaders and supporters.[106]

The lack of a definite and credible threat to Indonesia posed by an international tribunal at the outset, a threat which only dwindled as time went on, meant that the failure of the trials was in some ways pre-determined. This also has demoralising consequences for the civilian Indonesian leadership in relying on international community support in countering the political force of the military.

In the wake of the war against terrorism, the US has restored the International Military Education and Training (IMET) program for TNI officers, which had

---

105 *Indonesia: Impunity versus accountability for gross human rights violations* (International Crisis Group, Brussels, 2001), at p.1.
106 "Rights court acquits former Dili military chief", *Agence France Presse*, 29 November 2002.

been suspended following a series of rights violations blamed on the military in East Timor. The US revived military ties with Indonesia on the grounds that it needs local military partners to fight terrorism. Sidney Jones said the chances of the Congress rejecting renewed IMET funding are now fairly slim. "I think there will be a collective shrugging of shoulders".[107]

On the day that East Timor joined the UN, Portuguese Prime Minister Jose Durao Barroso said there were those who said East Timor would never be free of Indonesian rule, and the ceremony in New York showed they were wrong.

> It shows that the United Nations when it is properly backed by UN members, can make a difference and can work, for the application of international law. So it's a great success. I remember some years ago when I was foreign minister people were telling me that East Timor will never be independent, and we can see now that it was possible.[108]

In the final analysis, the UN took on the responsibility to push for justice for such blatant human rights violations in Timor and it has not yet fulfilled that responsibility. The Indonesian and Dili Courts have been given an appropriate period of time in which to prove their worth, and that time ran out. As the *South China Morning Post* editorialised:

> The international community is the only hope East Timorese have of winning retribution for the crimes committed by Indonesia during its 24 years of occupation. Until this happens, justice will remain a mirage for the tens of thousands of people who lost relatives and property.
>
> Indonesia was entrusted by the United Nations with bringing to trial those responsible for the violence that shattered East Timor as it pushed for independence three years ago. President Megawati Sukarnoputri promised justice and the arrest and trial of the alleged ring-leaders. She has not kept her word.[109]

This chapter has attempted to explain why, even if formal justice outcomes are lacking for all Timorese, women in that society may receive no overall benefit from independence compared to men, despite their contribution to achieving that independence. This then begs the crucial question – transitional justice

---

[107] *ibid*.
[108] ABC, 2002.
[109] South China Morning Post, 29 November, 2002.

rests on the assumption that there has been a transition from a state of conflict to a state of peace, however uneasy. If women are still experiencing serious levels of violence, commensurate with their experience of violence during the proclaimed conflict, have they entered a state of transition at all? If we ask the question – transition to what? – then the next logical question is therefore – justice for whom?

Those feminist international lawyers who accept a role for international law in post-conflict societies may need to move beyond improving the content and application of international criminal law in trials to a broader quest for justice for women in post-conflict States. The development of jurisprudence is an important endeavour, but it may not be the sole, or even the primary endeavour in a context where the trials themselves are badly designed or executed. For the reasons noted above, holding trials in the wrong circumstances may be worse for women that doing nothing at all in the early periods of transition. It may be better in the short term to "guard" the legal position of women, focusing on gaining the full participation of women in decisions about transitional justice processes, preserving evidence and acquiring data in relation to international crimes for the day when fair trials can be held, and focusing on keeping women safe from post-conflict spikes in domestic violence.

Given the absence of political will towards executing the transitional justice mechanisms properly, and the vulnerability of Timorese women to violence in the independence period, I advocated a guardian theory of transitional justice. Unless accountability mechanisms can be gender-sensitive, it may be better to funnel resources into the judicial sector and wait for the opportunity for a process that can meet the needs of women.

It is clear that where gender-based violence has been dealt with in the Dili and Jakarta trials, it has received minimal attention and been badly handled. After examination of women's experience of prosecuting sexual violence and assaults under the new legal system and traditional justice processes, I argue that the manner in which international crimes against women have been handled has contributed to the legal silences which perpetuate the post-conflict violence against women.[110]

---

[110] Susan Harris Rimmer, "'Orphans' or Veterans? Justice for Children Born of War in East Timor" in R Charli Carpenter, ed, *Born of War* (Kumarian Press, forthcoming). A shorter version of this paper won the 2006 Audre Rapoport Prize for Scholarship on the Human Rights of Women held by the Bernard and Audre Rapoport Center for Human Rights and Justice at The University of Texas School of Law.

The requirement of international law to punish by way of trials must take place in a manner designed to be inclusive of women and cognisant of their post-conflict needs. If not, trials may undermine the establishment of the rule of law and women's ability to trust in the new legal system.

This chapter opens with a quotation from Yugoslav Nobel-Prize winning author Ivo Andrić. Andrić notes both the destructive force of war and its transformative potential for gender relations once the "last mask of humanity" has been stripped away. However, unless international law can confront and make itself relevant to that potential for gender justice in a post-conflict setting, not only may opportunities for the betterment of women's situation be lost, but the interventions may be capable of worsening their situation.

PART V

Impunity, Truth and Reconciliation

Impunity, Truth and the Rule of Law: The Political Compromise of Accountability and Justice for Human Rights Atrocities in East Timor

Guy Cumes

The culture of impunity is a phenomenon of international law. It is entrenched by the history of inter-state relations and underpinned by the doctrine of national sovereignty and its corollary of domestic jurisdiction.[1] Impunity is premised on the law of sovereign immunity and the non-observance of international humanitarian law and human rights law.

The culture of impunity refers to the systematic absence of the application of the rule of law by the state and its institutions. As the UN Principles on Impunity[2] put it, impunity is "the impossibility of bringing perpetrators of violations to account … since they are not subject to any inquiry that might lead to their being accused, arrested and tried." It is a situation in which coercive power, not rules, regulations or law is the organising principle.[3]

Impunity is sinister because it actively erodes the foundational principles of liberal democracy, particularly the separation of powers and the application of the rule of law by an independent judiciary. These doctrines are founded on conventions that include a robust, independent police and prosecution service. When these services are manipulated by members of the executive through arbitrary interference in prosecutorial and judicial processes the effect is the corruption of the state and its institutions, and of public values.

A culture of accountability represents the antithesis of impunity. In its strict sense, it is the actualisation of the rule of law within and against the state, its

[1] Paul G Lauren, "From impunity to accountability: Forces of transformation and the changing international human rights context", in R Thakur and P Malcontent, eds *From sovereign impunity to international accountability: The search for justice in a world of states* (United Nations University Press, Tokyo, 2004), pp.15–17.

[2] Updated Set of principles for the protection and promotion of human rights through action to combat impunity. UNCHR, Economic and Social Council, E/CN.4/2005/102/Add.1, 8 February 2005.

[3] KC Moghalu, "Reconciling fractured societies: An African perspective on the role of judicial prosecutions", in Thakur and Malcontent eds, above, n.1, at p.198.

institutions, and its agents so that each of these entities, along with private individuals and institutions, are responsible in law for their acts. Whereas accountability connotes justice, impunity profanes justice through the abandonment and denial of truth and the manipulation of processes of justice to actively distort reality.

A requirement that the state and its individual actors are accountable to law allows a broader sense of accountability to emerge. Accountability ensures that victims are provided with a sense of justice and closure. Especially in post-conflict societies, accountability helps to promote national reconciliation as communities come to terms with reasons why the law was violated. Additionally, accountability aims to deter future violations because, apart from punishing offenders and operating as a deterrent, it promotes the rehabilitation of the offender and the restoration of society.[4]

Notwithstanding the entrenched position of impunity in international law, the Nuremberg and Tokyo trials, following Justice Jackson's prescription that "the ultimate step … is to make statesmen responsible to law",[5] gave momentum to a shift of emphasis in international law away from the doctrine of national sovereignty to a focus on individual liability. The ensuing years have established that in committing the act of an international crime, as opposed to merely an international wrong, an individual does not act as an organ of the state, and is therefore unable to claim immunity for those acts whether in international courts or in foreign domestic courts.[6]

It is this enhancement of the quality of international law,[7] supported in the 1990s with the creation of international tribunals and the institutionalisation of international accountability for serious violation of international humanitarian law and human rights law, that has done most to limit the culture of impunity and create a culture of accountability based on an international

---

[4] See SD Roper and LA Barria, *Designing criminal tribunals: Sovereignty and international concerns in the protection of human rights* (Ashgate Publishing Ltd, 2006) esp. Chapter 4 (hereafter Roper & Barria, 2006), p.4

[5] Lauren, above, n.1, at p.26.

[6] Y Simbeye, *Immunity and International Criminal Law* (Ashgate Publishing, 2004), esp. pp.127–131. However, critically, Simbeye distinguishes for the purposes of liability in domestic courts, immunity *ratione materiae* and immunity *ratione personae*. Except in international courts the latter is absolute while a head of state or high ranking government official is in office, noting *Democratic Republic of Congo v Belgium* (ICJ, 14/2/2002). See esp. pp.2, 4, 110 & 159

[7] Lauren, above, n.1, at p.31.

rule of law.[8] The existence of international tribunals is based on states foregoing some of their sovereignty and subjugating it to the tribunal in a process that amounts to an "orderly transfer of state sovereignty to international authorities".[9] This consensual process undermines the concept of sovereign impunity and the general trend of international law to immunity of certain individuals.[10]

The result of this development has been that international law now contains norms that posit a "serious challenge" to the doctrine of national sovereignty and enhance the acceptance of universal standards of law and human rights, justice in regional and global governance, and the concept of universal jurisdiction.[11] The question has become not "whether to pursue justice and accountability, but rather when and how".[12]

These developments in international law therefore offer as a minimum, a "glimmer of hope" in ending the culture of impunity.[13] However this trend is far from secure. It is in "real danger of being reversed" unless the world's leading democracies actively support the international rule of law and its "most powerful democracy ... respect(s) its international treaty obligations".[14] This requires effectively that they model good international citizenship so that other states, such as Indonesia, are less able to claim a

---

[8] The Rule of Law and Transitional Justice in Conflict and Post-conflict Societies, Report of the Secretary-General, 23 August 2004, S/2004/616, p.14 (hereafter UN Rule of Law Report, 2004). International courts and tribunals in this sense "might be the foundations of a coherent international order based on justice ... where all participants ... can be held accountable for their actions ... Thus conceptualised they might be depicted as a move away from a world where only states count and the mighty rule to an order where certain fundamental common values are shared, protected and enforceable by all members of a wider society..." CPR Romano, "The price of international justice", (2004) 4 *The law and practice of international courts and tribunals: a practitioner's journal,* at p.283.

[9] DP Forsythe, "International criminal justice and the United States: Law, culture, power, in Thakur and Malcontent eds, above, n.2, at p.75.

[10] Simbeye, above n.6, at pp.90–91.

[11] RJ Goldstone, "Foreword – The role of law and justice in governance: Regional and Global" in Thakur and Malcontent eds, above, n.1, at p.viii.

[12] UN Rule of Law Report, 2004, p.8. See also LE Fletcher and HM Weinstein, "A world unto itself? The application of international justice in the former Yugoslavia", in E Stover and HM Weinstein eds, *My Neighbor, My Enemy: Justice and Community in the Aftermath of Mass Atrocity* (Cambridge University Press, 2004), p.29.

[13] M Ahtisaari, "Preface – Justice and Accountability: Local or International?", in Thakur and Malcontent eds, above n.1, at p.xvi.

[14] Goldstone, above, n.11, at p.xi.

form of "exceptionalism" with respect to compliance with international obligations.[15]

This chapter examines issues of impunity and accountability that arise out of egregious human rights violations that were committed in East Timor during the period of the Indonesian occupation. It focuses on the criminal justice models that were established after 1999 to deal with crimes against international law committed during this time.

Dealing with international human rights violations is a complex matter and criminal trials have a critical role in this process. Although the creation of the International Criminal Court (ICC) ideally should have eliminated the need for further ad hoc international criminal tribunals, their continued existence requires that the problems inherent in establishing and running them need to be very carefully assessed. There is a substantial risk in endemic failure of the criminal justice model if its operations are contaminated by a culture of impunity. This is what has happened in the trials in Indonesia and East Timor and this essay explores how this has occurred.

Part of the reason for this failure is that criminal justice systems established to deal with massive human rights violations are essentially political processes. Decisions made about the nature, powers, structure and financing of international criminal tribunals reflect political compromises. It is questionable whether they can determine the truth of events, and indeed arguably, it is beyond their mandate to do so. As criminal trials conducted according to an adversarial model, their quintessential role is to determine culpability in law of particular accused who are arraigned before them. The "truth" is always a contested domain.

But "truth" is a critical element in understanding the reasons and complexity of human rights violations, and in rebuilding societies that are torn apart by them. These matters require that there be an exhaustive exploration of the events that is not necessarily tied to establishing culpability. There is a need to "know" which calls for something more than criminal trials can offer and here lies the rationale for independent truth commissions and other methods of accountability.

---

[15] I am referring here to the concept of US "exceptionalism", the US view of itself as "a good and great people divinely inspired to lead the world … to greater respect for personal freedom" with the effect that US law and practice is not to be trumped by international law. See DP Forsythe, above n.9, at pp.62–67.

It is accordingly necessary, in understanding the events of East Timor and how they may be dealt with by the communities who suffered from them, to have regard to the role of the truth commission that was established in East Timor – the Commission for Reception, Truth and Reconciliation (CAVR). If, as it appears to be the case, that leading perpetrators of atrocities will not be held to account in law for their crimes, the process of how affected victims and communities deal with them and the harm done to them must be addressed as part of the rebuilding of their society. In this sense some form of accountability is not an option, but is part of the broader framework of finding solutions to rehabilitating post-conflict states.

This chapter proposes that accountability for events that constitute the "truth" is central to the process of the restoration of post-conflict East Timor. This may be achieved by a multi-disciplinary approach. However, critical within this will be the institutionalisation of the rule of law and justice in the domestic legal system. It is this grounding of accountability that provides the foundation for addressing impunity. If there is to be any prospect of fairness, respect, and tolerance in contemporary East Timorese society, a government and institutions that are bound by the rule of law must be established as part of the framework by which restoration is achieved and impunity is defeated.

Invasion, Occupation and Violation of East Timor

In December 1975 Indonesia invaded the former Portuguese territory of East Timor and maintained its unlawful occupation until August 1999. During this period Indonesia executed a pattern of violence against a mainly unarmed civilian population that was deliberate, planned, widespread, systematic, and methodically executed.[16] Egregious human rights violations were committed

[16] These matters, and aspects of them in the following material and other sections of this essay, are based on the exhaustive examination of these issues contained in several excellent, comprehensive works. But for particular references, and with a view to footnote length, these principal references are noted here only. Detailed references for any material can be furnished. The works are: Final Report of the Commission for Reception, Truth and Reconciliation in East Timor (CAVR), 2006, accessed at *http://etan.org/news/2006/cavr.htm*. (hereafter CAVR), D Cohen *Indifference and Accountability: the United Nations and the Politics of International Justice in East Timor,* East-West Center Special Reports, No. 9. East-West Center, Honolulu, 2006, *www.eastwestcenter.org*. (hereafter Cohen, 2006), Open Justice Initiative and the Coalition for International Justice, 2004, *Unfulfilled Promises: Achieving justice for Crimes against Humanity in East Timor,* (hereafter OJI & CIJ, 2004), D Cohen, *Intended to Fail: The Trials before the ad hoc Human Rights Court in Jakarta,* International Center for Transitional Justice, 2003 (hereafter Cohen, 2003), MC Othman, *Accountability for international humanitarian violations: The case of Rwanda and East Timor* (Springer, Berlin-Heidelberg, 2005), SD Roper and LA Barria, above, n.4.

by Indonesian military and security forces and their proxies, militia groups which operated under their command and which were recruited, trained, and supplied by them.[17] The atrocities were institutionally and individually sanctioned at the highest levels of the Indonesian security apparatus and civil administration.

The invasion and occupation caused intense suffering for the people of East Timor. During the period 1975-1999, violations against citizens committed by agents of the Indonesian state included killings, torture, detention, rape, and sexual violations, as well as the forced displacement of people in the late 1970s and early 1980s which led to famine and death by deprivation.[18] The invasion had the tacit consent and acquiescence of the major international and regional powers. Their complicity in it, and the international community's tolerance of the Indonesian government's excesses, contributed both to the absence of accountability for the aggression and its human rights violations, as well as the climate of impunity that prevailed during the occupation.[19]

However, even by the extraordinarily indulgent, indeed complicit, standards of the international community towards Indonesia, it was forced to act after the Popular Consultancy on 30 August 1999 voted against autonomy within Indonesia.[20] With the announcement of the results on 4 September 1999, an orchestrated campaign of violence was unleashed which resulted in massive destruction of buildings and dwellings, widespread rape, torture, looting, and

[17] The relationship between the military (the TNI) and militia is not elaborated in this essay. See for detailed analysis Othman, 2005, and CAVR, especially on the role of senior military personnel, including General Wiranto, in the planning, formation and recruitment of the militias, and the coordination and sanctioning of their activities.

[18] See especially CAVR. The report sets out other human rights violations that were committed by other groups, but, as extensive as they were, notes that these were insignificant compared with those committed by the military. The CAVR details crimes committed by Fretilin/Felantil, the Timorese Democratic Union (UDT), the Apodeti party and others. However this was mainly in the years immediately following the invasion (1975–1979). It notes Fretilin "exercised genuine restraint" up to and following the 1999 ballot, in stark contrast to the TNI and militia. They and the other groups were responsible for "a small proportion of violations" (less than five percent). Of the total violations committed in the period 1974–1999, the CAVR finds that 84.4 percent were committed by the Indonesian military, police and their Timorese auxiliaries. For 1999 alone they were responsible for 95.2 percent of all violations. Part 6 CAVR sets out the Commission's statistical analysis and methods in formulating its findings.

[19] CAVR Part 11 p.2., OJI & CIJ, 2004, p.15

[20] This are matters of public record. See generally, references at n.16 above. I have elaborated on these matters in G Cumes, "Murder as a crime against humanity: Choice of law and the prosecution of murder in East Timor" (2003) 11/1 *European Journal of Crime, Criminal Law and Criminal Justice* 40–66.

approximately 1,400–1,500 cases of murder.[21] Some 240,000–250,000 East Timorese civilians were forcibly deported to Indonesian West Timor. These violations "were committed in execution of a systematic plan approved, conducted and controlled by Indonesian military commanders up to the highest level",[22] and were facilitated by members of the Indonesian police force and sanctioned by "the civil administration in East Timor and national-level government officials including ministers".[23]

Although this violence was the culmination of a programme of widespread, systematic intimidation, threats and violence against pro-independence supporters that had commenced in at least January 1999, its brutality shocked the international community into action. The UN Commission on Human Rights (UNCHR) called on the Secretary-General to establish an International Commission of Inquiry on East Timor (ICI) to investigate the atrocities and advise on whether an international tribunal should be set up. Its report,[24] presented to the Security Council on 31 January 2000 found that the TNI[25] had a specific role in engineering the violence and concluded that:

> ultimately the Indonesian army was responsible for the intimidation, terror, killings and other acts of violence experienced by the people of East Timor before and after the popular consultation.[26]

It recommended the establishment of an international tribunal for the perpetrators of the violence.

The findings of this report have been endorsed by reports of the UN Special Rapporteurs and the UNCHR. These in turn are corroborated by comprehensive investigations by international civil society.[27] The unanimous findings of these reports may be summarised in the following findings of the CAVR:

> the leadership of the Indonesian security forces at the highest levels (is) responsible and accountable for their role in planning and executing a

---

[21] D Cohen, 2006, notes 1,400 killed. The numbers killed range up to 2000. See Roper & Barria, 2006, p.50.
[22] CAVR Part 8, p.8.
[23] CAVR Part 8, pp.8, 25.
[24] Report of the International Commission of Inquiry on East Timor, UN Doc. A/54/726, S/2000/59
[25] Indonesian National Army (Tentara Nasional Indonesia – TNI), otherwise referred to as the Indonesian Armed Forces. The terms "TNI" and "military" forces are used interchangeably throughout this chapter.
[26] Quoted in Othman above, n.16, p.48.
[27] See reports and references noted at n.16 above.

> strategy of which violations of human rights were an integral part, for failing to prevent or punish perpetrators under their command, and for creating a climate of impunity in which military personnel were encouraged to commit abhorrent acts against civilians known or perceived to be supporters of East Timorese independence.[28]

The culpability of the military as agents of the state means that, according to principles of international law, the state of Indonesia is responsible and accountable for the atrocities committed both up to, and during 1999. This includes liability for "tens of thousands of serious human rights violations, and overall responsibility for the deaths of at least 120,000 East Timorese ...".[29] This is in addition to criminal liability for the invasion itself for which Suharto and others bear principal responsibility.

Post Violence: Institutional Responses and Compromise

Despite the findings of the ICI, other enquiries, and the direct knowledge of the international community of Indonesian sponsored atrocities, the UN Security Council decided against an international tribunal modelled on its then existing ICTY and ICTR templates. Instead it decided that domestic prosecutions and criminal trials would be conducted in both East Timor and Indonesia. This "dual track of accountability" was thought to be the most pragmatic way forward.[30] It supported both the process of transitional justice arrangements for East Timor and the new model for dealing with international crimes emerging from the ICC, namely that the presumptive forum for the trial of international crimes is the national courts of the state where the violence occurred.[31]

However in addition, the UN, through its authority in East Timor, the UN Transitional Authority in East Timor (UNTAET),[32] established a "truth commission" whose mandate ran concurrently with the tribunals. This commission, the CAVR, was established with the promulgation of UNTAET Regulation No 2001/10 on 13 July 2001. Its mandate, consistent with the rationale and purpose of truth commissions in post-conflict states, was "to establish the truth about the human rights violations which occurred in Timor-

---

[28] CAVR Part 8, p.8.

[29] *ibid.*, p.88.

[30] Othman above, n.16, p.149

[31] *ibid.*, pp.129–130

[32] UNTAET was established by Security Council Resolution 1272 (1999) of 25 October 1999 to oversee East Timor's transition to independence.

Leste" in the period 1974–1999.[33] It was not established as a "court of law" but rather to make recommendations that would form a foundation for legal, political and administrative measures and reforms that would "prevent the repetition of human rights violations and to respond to the needs of victims".[34] In this sense the CAVR was established to complement the tribunals and serve a justice and reconciliation function with the aim of finding a path to the "mutually reinforcing imperatives" of "justice, peace and democracy"[35] for East Timor.

With respect to the criminal tribunals in East Timor, UNTAET took responsibility for the design of the structure and procedures of the tribunal, the Special Panel for Serious Crimes (SPSC). It established a body, the National Consultative Council (NCC) which included 11 East Timorese representatives which was to oversee decision-making about the tribunal's structure and operation. However, most of the negotiation about these matters excluded the NCC.[36] The SPSC was established as part of the East Timor legal system, the applicable law of which was deemed to be Indonesian,[37] and was located within the District Court in Dili. It was given exclusive jurisdiction at original and appellate level over serious crimes including genocide, war crimes, crimes against humanity, murder, torture and sexual offences committed between 1 January 1999 and 25 October 1999.[38] This incorporation of international law meant that the applicable law to be applied by the SPSC was both international and domestic. Like the other international tribunals established during the same period, the Special Court for Sierra Leone (SCSL) and the Extraordinary Chambers for Cambodia (ECC), the SPSC was composed of national and international judges and a domestic and international prosecution team. These aspects of its institutional framework characterise it as a "mixed" or "hybrid" tribunal[39] with the advantage that, to some extent at least, it could be seen as part of a national system of administration of justice rather than one which was distant to the events it investigated.

---

[33] CAVR Part 1, p.8. This central purpose of truth commissions is supported by the Principle 6 of the Updated Set of principles for the protection and promotion of human rights through action to combat impunity.

[34] CAVR Part 11, p.2.

[35] UN Rule of Law Report, 2004, summary.

[36] Roper & Barria, above, n.4, p.51.

[37] UNTAET Regulation 1999/1 on the application of laws in East Timor, promulgated on 27 November 1999.

[38] UNTAET Regulation 2000/15 on the establishment of panels with exclusive jurisdiction over serious criminal offences, promulgated 6 June 2000.

[39] In addition to references noted at n.16 above, see also S Linton, "New Approaches to International Justice in Cambodia and East Timor" (2002) *International Review of the Red Cross,* vol. 84, no. 845, pp.93–119.

Indonesia came under considerable international pressure to participate effectively in dealing with the perpetrators of the East Timor violations from a number of sources.[40] Undertaking not to allow impunity for those responsible, and asserting the doctrine of national sovereignty, Indonesia succeeded in persuading the UN that it should be allowed to investigate and prosecute those responsible for the atrocities in a domestic tribunal which it would establish. On 6 November 2000, it enacted legislation to establish permanent human rights courts as well as ad hoc courts which were to have retroactive jurisdiction.[41] The East Timor cases were to be heard in such a court, the Ad Hoc Human Rights Court for East Timor in Jakarta (hereafter referred to as the Indonesian Human Rights Court (IHRC)). After a protracted Attorney-General's enquiry and presidential amendments, both of which demonstrated Indonesia's reluctance to comply with its undertakings,[42] the final form of the court's powers were settled. Prosecutions were restricted to human rights violations in the districts of Dili, Liquica and Suai in April and September 1999 only.[43] This had the effect that the court was not given jurisdiction to deal with atrocities highlighted in the reports of the ICI or Indonesia's own National Human Rights Commission (the KPP HAM report).[44] Of the 33 names listed in the KPP HAM report, only 18 individuals were indicted to answer charges before the IHRC. This comprised three army generals, military and police personnel and two civilians, but excluded the highest ranking officers and particularly General Wiranto, the former Defence Minister and Commander of the Armed Forces of Indonesia, whom the Human Rights Commission considered to be the "party that must be asked to bear responsibility".[45]

In the result, the SPSC and the IHRC, were established to exercise concurrent but independent jurisdiction over the human rights crimes committed in East Timor. The effect was that the same crimes could be dealt with in an international hybrid tribunal, the SPSC, and a purely domestic tribunal, the IHRC.

---

[40] These are not elaborated here. Apart from international pressure, the government was embarrassed into action by the enquiry and report of the National Human Rights Commission of Indonesia which appointed a special commission of enquiry into the violence and identified 33 individuals responsible for crimes against humanity (the "KPP HAM report"). The commission report was issued on 31 January 2000.

[41] For analysis of this legislation see Amnesty International's Comments on the Law on Human Rights Courts (Law No.26/2000) AI Index: ASA 21/005/2001, 9 February 2001. See also Comments on the draft law on Human Rights Tribunals AI Index: ASA 21/025/2000, 2 June 2000.

[42] See *inter alia* Roper & Barria, above, n.4, p.52

[43] See especially Othman, above, n.16, p.133.

[44] Above, n.40.

[45] Othman above, n.16, p.169.

The decision to establish a dual system of criminal tribunals to deal with human rights violations located in one territory, was driven by the then contemporary political and economic forces within the international community.[46] Prior to the creation of these tribunals, the international community had established the ICTY in 1993 and the ICTR in 1994. The ICC was established in 1998, although it became operational only on 1 July 2002. Contemporaneously with the establishment of the SPSC the international community was in the process of considering the establishment of tribunals dealing with the conflicts in Cambodia and Sierra Leone. The ICTY and the ICTR were international tribunals authorised under Chapter VII of the UN Charter and received funding as an assessed share of the UN budget. The substantial financial and logistical costs of running these tribunals[47] caused the international community to reflect on other alternative tribunal mechanisms.[48]

By October 1999, when Security Council members were under pressure to put into place effective tribunal mechanisms for the East Timor atrocities, a sense of "donor fatigue" had set in, which created resistance to establishing tribunals financed in the same way as the ICTY and the ICTR.[49] National courts were viewed as a more cost effective means for dealing with international crimes. The movement toward a purely national process was "seen as a logical next step in reducing the international financial burden."[50] It had the advantage that trials within states where atrocities occurred could bring home to domestic populations the offences that have been committed in their name and help to establish and embed democratic structures of governance and the rule of law.[51] The establishment and design of the SPSC and the IHRC were moulded by this experience.

These considerations suggest that the evolution of international tribunals reflects a changing political consensus and that they are crafted to exist within the then dominant political and legal culture. As the experiences noted briefly above demonstrate, they "represent an attempt by the international community and host states to balance financial needs and the protection of state sovereignty with the need to prosecute individuals ...".[52] As Roper & Barria

---

[46] Roper & Barria, above, n.4, p.51

[47] $4.5 billion by 2006: *ibid.*, pp.17, 29.

[48] UN Rule of Law Report, 2004, p.14.

[49] Roper and Barria, above, n.4, p.61. See also CPR Romano, above, n.8, p.300.

[50] Roper and Barria, above, n.4, p.72.

[51] R Thakur, "Dealing with guilt beyond crime: The strained quality of universal justice", in Thakur and Malcontent eds, above, n.1, at p.280. See also UN Rule of Law Report, 2004, p.15.

[52] Roper & Barria, above, n.4, p.93.

argue, "there is no international template (for tribunals) that works in all situations."[53] As "institutions of justice" they must be crafted to reflect the particular post-conflict domestic environment in which they are to operate. Differences between their institutional design, nature, and powers are therefore based on political and financial concerns and not necessarily on considerations of how best to provide justice to victims.

Seen within this framework, the SPSC and the IHRC, like the SCSL and ECC, represent a compromise between the international community and the individual states in which they are established with regard to their organisational structure, and legal and investigative powers. The compromise represented by the IHRC was to move the design and responsibility for determination of international criminal offences away from an international or hybrid model, to a purely domestic model, and thereby restore prominence to the doctrine of national sovereignty.[54] This has happened, it has transpired, at the flagrant cost of justice to victims.

This analysis of the establishment of the SPSC and IHRC suggests that even before the commencement of their core duties, they were compromised institutions. Their establishment however, contemporaneously with a "truth commission", demonstrates the broad duality of the international community's response to mass human rights violations. There is a general consensus in international civil society that the goal of justice – a broad, nuanced term[55] – in post conflict states necessitates a broad approach. Retributive justice which focuses on the culpability of offenders as a key to addressing impunity and ensuring accountability, and which is manifested through internationally created tribunals and the criminal justice model, is not the only road to peace, stability and the protection of human rights.[56] Restorative justice systems may offer a better solution to fractured societies. Such systems promote "an essentially communitarian vision of the proper relationship between the individual and society" and deal with offenders within the framework of this relationship.[57] They underpin, but are not necessarily limited, to truth commission models.

---

[53] *ibid*., p.84.

[54] *ibid*., p.13.

[55] See for example HM Weinstein and E Stover, "Introduction: conflict, justice and reclamation", in Stover and Weinstein, eds, above, n.12, at p.4 *et seq*, and E Stover, "Witnesses and the promise of justice in The Hague", in Stover and Weinstein, eds, above, n.12, at p.114. See also the definition of "justice" in UN Rule of Law Report, 2004, p.4.

[56] P Malcontent, "Introduction – Human rights and Peace: Two sides of the Same Coin", in Thakur and Malcontent, eds, above, n.1, at p.12. Weinstein and Stover, *ibid*., p.5.

[57] Thakur, above, n.51, at p.286.

Where both of these approaches have been adopted and their processes completed, the question becomes what is the next step for the international community, and the state and peoples where the violations occurred? This depends significantly on the outcomes of each process. In the case of the tribunal method of dealing with the East Timor atrocities, their widely acknowledged failings suggest that if peace, stability, and democracy is to be established in East Timor, serious regard now has to be given to the CAVR approach to eliciting the truth, and its proposals, both retributive and restorative, for a just and peaceful reckoning with the past.

The Failings of the SPSC and the IHRC: The Entrenchment of Impunity

The trials processes established in East Timor and Indonesia have been the subject of comprehensive critical examination.[58] Every analysis of the processes has concluded that, as one report puts it, they have "failed fundamentally to bring to account those most responsible for the atrocities in East Timor".[59] The result is that the commitment of the international community to punish the perpetrators of the 1999 violence has not been fulfilled and the "dual tract" system of accountability has concluded in an "incorrigible impunity gap".[60] Given these detailed analyses this part briefly addresses the core failings of the processes.

Although the reasons for establishing international tribunals are complex, the grounds for establishing any of the tribunals founded since the 1990s can be found in the UN resolutions that created them. These point generally to at least three factors that underpin the tribunal's goals. First, the tribunals are to act as organs of peace and security. Secondly, they are established to ensure that violations are halted and effectively addressed, and thirdly, they are intended to be processes that lead to national reconciliation as a precondition for permanent peace.[61] The extent to which any of these purposes is achieved depends on many factors. However, critical in this is the extent to which they have diminished the scourge of impunity which forms a leitmotif of attempts to impose accountability and justice for mass atrocities.

---

[58] See references at n.16. These are in addition to the reports of the international community noted briefly above. See also the *Report to the Secretary-General of the Commission of Experts to Review the Prosecution of Serious Violations of Human Rights in Timor-Leste (then East Timor) in 1999* (dated 26 May 2005) (S/2005/458), submitted to the Security Council on 27 June 2005 (hereafter Commission of Experts, 2005).

[59] OJI & CIJ, 2004, Executive summary, p.1.

[60] Othman, above, n.16, p.137.

[61] Roper & Barria, above, n.4, p.84.

The SPSC

With the INTERFET intercession in East Timor, investigation of human rights violations was placed with the UN Civilian Police (CIVPOL). A Serious Crimes Investigation Unit (SCU) was created within the national prosecution service pursuant to Regulation 2000/16 promulgated on 6 June 2000. Although it is argued that the establishment of this office led to "the birth of serious crimes litigation" in East Timor,[62] severe institutional deficiencies within UNTAET had the result that it was not until shortly before the trials process was closed down that it could optimistically be stated that "it had reached a point where it could meet appropriate standards".[63]

With the creation of the SCU, a prosecution strategy was adopted which sought to identify what became known as "priority cases" with a view to holding those with the greatest responsibility accountable for the violations.[64] These cases were to focus on major incidents of atrocities that occurred in 1999 where there were identifiable perpetrators ascertained particularly by evidence of co-perpetration. However the strategy also contained broader elements directed toward maximizing investigation results so that accountability was targeted toward the broadest level of perpetration and the direct execution of orders. It sought full accountability for all levels of perpetrators including a case load of "low-level perpetrators" inherited from INTERFET and CIVPOL. The breadth of this strategy has been criticised as being simultaneously both "over- and under-inclusive".[65] It reflects to some extent the history of indictments in the ICTY which in its early years disproportionately allocated resources to the investigation of low-ranking perpetrators involved in the direct commission of crimes such as murder.[66]

The core components of this strategy were affirmed but refocused in 2002 in accordance with the report of the UN Secretary-General of 17 April 2002, stating that the SCU was to focus its investigations on persons who organised, ordered, instigated or otherwise aided in the planning, preparation, and

---

[62] Othman, above, n.16, p.149.
[63] Cohen 2006, p.6.
[64] This is not elaborated here. The SCU made a policy decision to focus on crimes that took place in 1999, and identified 10 "priority case indictments". These included the Liquica church attack, the Suai Church massacre, the attack on the compound of Bishop Belo, the Maliana police station attack and the "TNI Battalion 745 killings". For the full list see Othman, above, n.16, pp.122–123. The final indictment of these "priority" cases was not filed until July 2003.
[65] OJI & CIJ, 2004, p.35.
[66] Roper and Barria, above, n.4, p.87.

execution of atrocities.[67] A direct result of this report was to focus investigations on high-level suspects in Indonesia. This led to the apparent embarrassment of the UN[68], and the East Timor President and Foreign Minister,[69] to the filing of an indictment against General Wiranto and seven others, on 24 February 2003.[70] However, at the same time many low-level Timorese continued to be prosecuted, severely diminishing already depleted resources, and allowing the focus to be shifted from the core strategy of getting the most culpable perpetrators before the SPSC.

During the whole of this process, the UNTEAT mandate was beset by significant problems with respect to financial support and resources, proper staff recruitment and training, proper case management, transcription and witness protection systems, and evidence-gathering. These hampered the whole investigation, prosecution, trial and appeal process, and seriously affected its overall legitimacy as a "successful" process in which there has been "meaningful accountability".[71]

These problems, such as the inequality of resources and support provided to defence teams compared to prosecution services, can be ascribed to a failure by the UN to adopt a "holistic approach" to the process of accountability for atrocity crimes.[72] Othman argues that effective accountability for human rights violations is not a "piggy bank affair" and requires appropriate expertise and adequate resources.[73] It requires approaching accountability as a "combined

---

[67] Secretary-General's report of 17 April 2002 to the Security Council (UN SCOR, S/2002/432). See also Office of the Deputy General Prosecutor for Serious Crimes Timor Leste, Information Release from the Serious Crimes Unit, Crimes against humanity charges for former Indonesian Minister of Defence, top Indonesian military commanders and East Timor Governor, 25 February 2003. This followed the experience of the ICTY in the issuance of the "super-indictment" (Roper and Barria, above, n.4, p.87).

[68] OJI & CIJ, 2004, pp.38 and 40.

[69] OJI & CIJ, 2004, p.40. Both continue to express opposition to the pursuit of justice for the East Timor crimes, p.46. See also on the background to this, S Linton, "Putting things into perspective: The realities of accountability in East Timor, Indonesia and Cambodia" (2005) *Maryland Series in Contemporary Asian Studies*, No 3, p.11.

[70] Called the "National Indictment". See Office of the Deputy General Prosecutor for Serious Crimes Timor Leste, Serious Crimes Unit Update, 4 February 2005.

[71] See references at n.16, especially Cohen 2006, who notes that the UN's insistence that the justice process was a success is "unconvincing", and its endorsement by the Commission of Experts, 2005, "calls into the question the impartiality of this report". See also CPR Romano, above, n.8, at pp.300–301. The relatively low cost and number of cases before the SPSC might suggest that this was an efficient institution. However as Romano argues, "(u)nfortunately, (it) is only cheap. Savings are made at the expense of the most vulnerable: the defendants and victims of crimes".

[72] Othman, above, n.16, p.103.

[73] *ibid.*, p.149.

process" with equal roles and resources allocated to both prosecution and defence services, as well as to the administrative arms of the trials process.[74] Only in this way can there be overall transparency and fairness in the process.

This analysis supports Cohen's assessment that, at the "root" of all the problems was "the failure by the UN to ensure proper leadership, a clear mandate, political will, and clear 'ownership' of the process from the very beginning".[75] This amounted, according to Cohen, to a "massive institutional failure of the UN and government of East Timor to create a judicial enterprise worthy of the values and standards that the UN represents".[76]

The failure to provide proper resources to defence teams exacerbated a general situation of inadequate defence representation which continued even after the commencement of the Defence Lawyers Unit (DLU). This was one of a number of significant problems which seriously called into question the quality and fairness of the trials in the SPSC and its Court of Appeal, and whether justice according to law has been effected. In a thorough examination of the trial and appeal proceedings, Cohen concludes that a significant majority of the judgments do not reflect international standards prescribed by the ICTY or the UNTAET (2000/30) Transitional Rules of Criminal Procedure (TRCP).[77] There are a "significant number of cases in which the rights of the accused appear to have been compromised" including extraordinarily, cases where there were convictions of individuals (confirmed on appeal) based on crimes they were not charged with and had no opportunity to defend. Further, there was very little uniformity in the articulation of judgments, indicating a "serious lack of consistency in their quality" and proper application of the law. The result is that there are a number of flawed judgments which, compounded by defence inadequacies, "call into question the legitimacy of a significant number of convictions."[78]

---

[74] *ibid.*, p.103.
[75] Cohen 2006, Summary, p.3.
[76] *ibid.*, p.6.
[77] See for this and the following material, Cohen 2006, pp.43–46, 89–90. This includes failure to satisfy international standards of judgement writing and presentation including failure to weigh versions of facts and legal arguments, to give adequate regard to the defence case (where it was presented!), adequately enumerate the elements of offences, and to have meaningful regard to the jurisprudence of the ICTY and ICTR.
[78] Cohen 2006, p.107; Roper and Barria, above, n.4, pp.55–56, note that from the beginning there was a shortage of qualified judicial personnel, which together with bureaucratic and managerial inefficiency and other systemic problems, led to poor decision-making and delays in trials.

The mandate of the SCU, and with it that of the SPSC, ended on 20 May 2005, without adequate explanation from the Security Council. At this time only 572 of the 1,400–1,500 murders committed in 1999 were subject to indictment and 500 investigative files remained open. Fifty five trials were completed before the SPSC in which 87 defendants were tried; after appeals, eighty four were convicted of crimes against humanity or other charges and three were acquitted.[79] The convicted consisted of relatively low level defendants including Timorese militia and low to middle level Indonesian military. However, they were "mostly impoverished illiterate, (Timorese) farmers who perpetrated single acts of violence ... under orders of the militias and the TNI".[80] No high level Indonesian military leaders were taken into custody or dealt with by trial.

These numbers do not reflect the large number of persons actually indicted, but against whom charges are still pending. At least 391 persons were charged in 95 indictments. However, of these, it has not been possible to bring 309 suspects before the SPSC because they were, and remain, outside East Timor.[81] This includes General Wiranto who is at large in Indonesia despite an arrest warrant having been issued.[82] Most of the indictees enjoy impunity in West Timor and this absence from the jurisdiction of the SPSC has been the "most glaring and debilitating problem with the serious crimes process".[83]

[79] See Cohen 2006, p.11. The statistics vary marginally. For example, the Report of the Secretary-General on justice and reconciliation for Timor-Leste, S/2006/580, 26 July 2006, p.3 notes that 85 of the 87 defendants were found guilty.

[80] See especially for this material, Cohen 2006, p.108.

[81] Cohen 2006, p.13. The Office of the Deputy General Prosecutor for Serious Crimes Timor-Leste, Serious Crimes Unit Update, 4 February 2005 notes that those outside of East Timor and subject to arrest warrants on which the Indonesian government has refused to act, include General Wiranto and 37 Indonesian TNI military commanders and officers, four Indonesian chiefs of police, 60 East Timorese TNI officers and soldiers, the former Governor of East Timor (Abilio Soares) and five former District Administrators. Of the 202 persons indicted in the "10 Priority case indictments" 183 are at large in Indonesia. See also Roper and Barria, above, n.4, p.55.

[82] The arrest warrant against Wiranto was issued on 10 May 2004, but nothing has come of it. Indeed Cohen 2006 notes, p.13, that following the issue of this arrest warrant the "almost complete breakdown of cooperation between the SCU and the Prosecutor General … sealed the fate of the attempt to exert international pressure against indictees ...". See "Brief in support of the application for the issuance of an arrest warrant for Wiranto" (undated), in which the allegations and evidence against Wiranto and his co-accused are fully set out. Indonesia stated it would ignore the warrant as it is "degrading and offensive" to the Indonesian state, Y Beigbeder, *International justice against impunity: progress and new challenges* (Martinus Nijhoff Publishers, Boston/Leiden, 2005), p.140.

[83] OJI & CIJ 2004, p.39.

Some cases are still being dealt with in the Dili District Court[84] by some international judges and prosecutors.[85] However, this is at odds with the stated wish of the East Timorese government that there will be no further trial process, by (presumably) a continued SPSC or otherwise.[86] The government's "hostility" toward the SPSC process was amply demonstrated by the conduct of the Prosecutor General and particularly former President Gusmao after the issue of the arrest warrant against General Wiranto.[87] Gusmao's view is that the SPSC has undermined the prospects of reconciliation between East Timor and Indonesia.[88]

This position of the government's leaders reflects a serious misunderstanding of the distinction between a criminal tribunal process, which is a retributive, legal process culminating in acquittal or punishment, and the social process of reconciliation which is properly ascribed to restorative processes such as a truth and reconciliation commission. It also contravenes its duties under the UN Principles on Impunity.[89] Principles 19, 20 and 21 impose an active duty on the government to conduct thorough and impartial investigations of violations of human rights and take measures with respect to perpetrators by ensuring that those responsible for serious crimes under international law are prosecuted. Principle 24 states that even if it is intended to promote a peace agreement or foster national reconciliation, an amnesty or other measures of clemency is to be subject to the obligation to deal with perpetrators as required by Principle 19.[90] Finally and critically, it does not reflect the expectations of

---

[84] JSMP Press Release, Dili, 6/2/2006, "Serious crimes suspects continue to be arrested", Cohen 2006, p.94.

[85] The extraordinary background to this is not elaborated in this chapter. See Cohen 2006, pp.93, 103–106. There are no Timorese judges, prosecutors or public defenders in office as they have all "failed" an examination of basic competency. However the circumstances of the disqualification amount, on investigation, to deliberate manipulation of the results in order to implement a policy of entrenching Portuguese as the sole language of the justice system. This is to be achieved through "the enforced production of a Portuguese-speaking cadre of judges, lawyers and public defenders". This deliberate policy is acquiesced to by both the East Timor government and the UN who have financed the capacity building programmes for the East Timor judiciary. The result, taken together with the performance of the SPSC and particularly its Court of Appeal, is that there must be serious questions about the role of UN agencies in the capacity-building programme and serious concerns for the future of the courts and the rule of law in Timor-Leste.

[86] See comments of the then Foreign Minister Jose Ramos Horta, quoted in Othman 2005, p.148: "There will be no further trial process, but the process will be closed; these are the politics of our President and our government".

[87] S Linton, above, n.69, p.11. Linton notes that although the East Timor government has "become a party to many international treaties on human rights … (it) has openly disassociated itself from the Serious Crimes project ...".

[88] Roper and Barria, above, n.4, p.95.

[89] Updated Set of principles for the protection and promotion of human rights through action to combat impunity. See above, n.2.

[90] See the affirmation of this aspect of these Principles in UN Rule of Law Report, 2004, pp.5, 11, 21.

the East Timorese population that justice would be done through a criminal trial process. The closure of the process has given rise to "widespread anger", frustration, and resentment that the trials were shut down prematurely, just at a time when the SPSC was "beginning to function at an acceptable level of international practice".[91]

Despite the government's ambivalence, and the background and circumstances in which the SPSC was developed, it had commendable but relatively insignificant results. As one report notes, although the SPSC process was not "intended to fail" as the Indonesian process was, "it has largely failed nonetheless".[92] This assessment however is kinder than Cohen's who concludes that "the process was so deeply flawed from the beginning that, despite important and successful efforts of key individuals ... egregious problems remained until the very end."[93]

The IHRC

The effect of the limited temporal, territorial, and personal jurisdiction of the IHRC noted above amounted to a "half-baked" and incomplete framework for accountability[94] and the results have borne this out. The trials began in March 2002 and were completed with the conviction of Major-General Adam Damiri in August 2003. Including Damiri, the court convicted six of the 18 accused, comprising three army officers, a former Dili police chief, a militia leader (Eurico Guterres) and the former Jakarta-appointed East Timor governor Abilio Soares. However, the convicted defendants appealed to the appeals division of the court, the Court of Appeals, and to the Indonesian Supreme Court. In a series of decisions up to November 2004, these courts overturned each of the convictions. Only on 13 March 2006, the Supreme Court confirmed the conviction of Eurico Guterres and he was sentenced to 10 years imprisonment for crimes against humanity. This decision means that only one of 18 defendants who were brought before the IHRC was convicted. More particularly, the court process has not resulted in the successful prosecution of any Indonesian national of military or police background. Guterres, although a senior militia leader and under Indonesian military command, is a civilian and ethnic Timorese.[95]

---

91 Cohen 2006, pp.107–108.

92 OJI & CIJ 2004, p.35

93 Cohen 2006, pp.1, 6. Despite his criticism, Cohen emphasises that "many outstandingly capable individuals struggled to improve" the credibility and legitimacy of the SPSC process, pp.108–109.

94 Othman, above, n.16, p.150.

95 See generally OJI & CIJ 2004, p.21. See also JSMP Press Release 17 March 2006, "One step towards justice, a long way to go".

The reasons for this outcome are associated with political, institutional and cultural norms embedded within the Indonesian justice and political system.[96]

The principal failing of the trials, exacerbated in the appeal process, was the inadequate and disinterested prosecution effort to secure convictions. Although particular judgments are not without criticism, in the end, at least at the trial level, judges could maintain that they had to base their decisions on the evidence before them, and this was manifestly inadequate. This insufficient execution of prosecutorial duties commenced with non-comprehensive investigations by the Attorney-General's office and its failure to use information from the KPP HAM report and the SCU. This led to a failure to produce material evidence of criminal culpability and weak indictments which did not properly articulate relevant facts and allegations. This conduct, which amounted to a "complete lack of prosecutorial diligence", was exacerbated by the absence of other core prosecutorial functions such as suitable witness protection measures.[97]

In particular, the prosecutions failed to allege an organised or coordinated effort by the Indonesian security forces or civil administration authorities to commit serious human rights violations. Apart from Guterres, all the accused were charged with either accomplice offences or on the basis of a theory of command responsibility which was based only on individual responsibility instead of being directed toward establishing command responsibility at the institutional level.[98] This critical failure in the presentation of the trials led to the acquittal of some TNI officers and the conviction of others "in a pattern that cannot be convincingly explained with reference solely to the merits of the individual's cases".[99]

The underlying reason for this approach can be located in a number of factors.[100] The first is the fundamental bias of the prosecution, and some judges and defence lawyers. This is reflected in the commonly adopted view that the violence in East Timor arose from actions of the pro-independence forces, corroborated by UN deceit,[101] which gave rise to a civil war in which the

---

[96] See references at n.16 above generally for the material that follows. See also S Linton, "Unravelling the first three trials at Indonesia's Ad Hoc Court for Human Rights violations in East Timor" (2004) 17 *Leiden Journal of International Law* 303.
[97] Othman, above, n.16, p.151
[98] *ibid*., p.146.
[99] Cohen 2003, p.54.
[100] See for this material especially Cohen 2003.
[101] A view propounded by General Wiranto. See OJI & CIJ 2004, p.24.

military responded appropriately. According to this revisionist version of the violence, spontaneous, random clashes led to a conflict between opposing armed, but unorganised groups, in which the military played no particular organising role. This reflected a widely held view in Indonesia that no extraordinary crimes were committed in East Timor, and of a perception of the violence which is at distinct odds not only with the findings of international enquiries, but also the KPP HAM report. This approach however, directly influenced the motivation of prosecutors and some judges, and the way in which cases were framed and presented. It also meant that the trials failed to fulfil any "truth function", to provide a basis for informing the Indonesian public of the accountability of its institutions, or to provide a foundation for reconciliation and justice with the East Timorese. Finally, it also helps to explain why no officers were made accountable by the military hierarchy for their participation in atrocities, and indeed that several of the most culpable such as Damiri, Suratman and Surajat won promotion after 1999. These officers were not punished because, in participating in the violence, they had been not merely acting in accordance with their orders,[102] but in a capacity that was endorsed by the Indonesian body politic.

The explanation for this attitudinal approach to prosecutorial and legal responsibilities is linked to the role of the military in Indonesian political and social life. The military represents an elevated, powerful institution in Indonesian society and enjoys a culture of impunity that permeates the entire judicial process.[103] This has historical roots. The military was politicised during Soeharto's regime with key cabinet posts, including particularly the Attorney-General (A-G) and Minister of Defence, being allocated to the military. Soeharto's political party, Golkar, was composed of military officers and military support was "paramount to maintaining political power".[104]

The militarisation of government portfolios contributes to a culture that permeates legal institutions.[105] The A-G's office and the public prosecution service are founded and operate on the basis of a military culture which inculcates military values of loyalty and discipline to the state above technical, legal preparation, and prosecutorial work. The values and goals of state policy are given greater precedence than values of the law and justice, with the result that the role of these offices is to enforce government policy rather than independently uphold the law. The effect is that there is a general absence of

---

102 CAVR Part 8, p.110.
103 OJI & CIJ 2004, pp.30–32.
104 Roper and Barria, above, n.4, pp.50, 56.
105 See for this material especially Cohen 2003.

any culture of an independent and binding entity of law. Instead there is a deference to military demands, resulting in a system of hierarchical control and an absence of independent accountability.

This culture helps to explain why indictments were framed as they were. Human rights cases which challenge the political and military order are not given any priority, and the lack of institutional will is reflected in the absence of commitment and motivation by prosecutors who are assigned to such cases. There is no moral conviction in the prosecution of such cases because there is no institutional sense of prosecuting "real crimes". Responsibility for this system lies in the highest levels of the A-G's office and a failure of political will, and this translates into systemic corruption within the Indonesian judicial hierarchy.

The effect of this institutional culture is that the IHRC *could not* provide an independent adjudication of human rights cases.[106] It underpins the "deepest underlying problem" of the cases: the lack of political will to prosecute and accept the outcome of the legal process; that is, the lack of a political context in which the administration of justice can function with legitimacy and independence. Accordingly, ultimate responsibility lies with the Indonesian government and its "lack of commitment … to encourage or permit a process that could lead to genuine accountability".[107]

The result is that the process of the trial of perpetrators by the specially established Indonesian court system has resulted in complete impunity for the Indonesian authorities and their highest ranking proxies. The trials "have failed to establish accountability and to undermine the culture of impunity that was responsible for the violence in the first place".[108] The process has been universally criticised.[109] Cohen's comprehensive analysis of the trials draws the "inescapable conclusion … that the trials as a whole must be regarded as a failure on every level, from technical competence to institutional integrity and political will."[110]

---

[106] Cohen 2003, p.54.
[107] *ibid.*, p.55.
[108] *ibid.*, p.54.
[109] See OJI & CIJ 2004, Executive summary p.2, "... the trials and appeals have been thoroughly flawed ...", and p.21, "... the consensus of informed observers is that the process has been a failure ...". See for detailed analysis of the trials and the flaws in their processes esp pp.22–33. According to Linton the trials process "has been used as an opportunity to whitewash Indonesia's role in East Timor and to cement impunity for those who believe in the absolute sanctity of nationalism and territorial integrity over the rights of human beings", Linton, above, n.96, at p.361.
[110] Cohen 2003, p.iii. The trials were "fundamentally flawed from the moment the attorney general's office took over the investigation ...". Accordingly in the end "overall responsibility" for the failure of the trials lies with the A-Gs office and the Government of Indonesia, p.54.

Added to all of this is Indonesia's refusal to assist the UN in its attempts to provide accountability through the SPSC. The dual structure that was established to deal with the violence and Indonesia's agreement with the UN, based on Resolution 1272 of 1999, required, if there was to be real accountability, that it was essential that Indonesia contribute meaningfully to bringing those with the greatest responsibility to justice. These arrangements were formalised by a memorandum of understanding (MOU) regarding cooperation in legal, judicial and human rights issues between UNTAET and Indonesia signed on 6 April 2000.[111] Based on this, a number of requests were made to Indonesia on various matters including questioning of witnesses, issue of arrest warrants, and to open investigations into particular matters. However, none of these requests were honoured by Indonesia. As a result, 80 percent of East Timorese accused indicted in East Timor of serious crimes by the SPSC remain in Indonesia. It has simply not cooperated with the UN in their return for trial.[112] Given these matters, the reality is that "there are no prospects for the transfer of any serious crime suspect or accused from Indonesia to East Timor"[113] whether they are Indonesian or East Timor nationals.

In the end, the result of the SPSC and IHRC processes is that the Security Council's framework for ensuring accountability for those responsible for the East Timor atrocities has failed. In spite of some successful prosecutions in the SPSC, Indonesia's unwillingness and inability to prosecute the leading perpetrators or to transfer them to East Timor for prosecution, and the latter's lack of political will and support for the SPSC process, has led to the complete impunity of those with the greatest responsibility. The "top leadership echelon", like the overwhelming majority of those allegedly responsible for the violence, will not, in fact, face justice in either East Timor or Indonesia despite the SPSC indictments against them.[114] This includes most notably General Wiranto. Although he has been indicted by the SPSC on the basis of superior responsibility, and a warrant for his arrest has been issued, Indonesia has refused to take any action against him and East Timor lacks the political will to do so.

Accountability, Justice and the Rule of Law in Post-conflict East Timor: A Restoration Model

International tribunals are "legal institutions embedded within a political environment..".[115] The experience of the creation and operation of the SPSC

[111] Othman, above, n.16, p.133.
[112] *ibid.*, p.128–135 .
[113] *ibid.*, p.136.
[114] *ibid.*, p.151.
[115] Roper and Barria, above, n.4, p.12.

and IHRC strongly supports the proposition that, as judicial institutions, they represent a "political compromise" within the international community about issues of sovereignty, finance and authority.[116] It is abundantly clear that, with respect to the prosecution of human rights violations in East Timor, this political compromise has resulted in the failure of the delivery of justice for victims.

States must cooperate to give effect to successful accountability for international crimes. The experience of the SPSC and the IHRC demonstrates that the need for political consensus reflects a "constant struggle between justice for individuals, society, and the international community of states".[117] In the end, the compromises involved in achieving this consensus can undermine the judicial effectiveness of tribunals as a tool of accountability, and ultimately the quest for justice under international law. This is particularly so, as demonstrated by the material addressed above, where offenders retain political power within the host state or remain outside the reach of international prosecution because of the host state's refusal to uphold its international obligations.

It is clear that the success of tribunals depends on the extent to which the host state and the international community are genuinely committed to addressing violations of international law through the creation of a tribunal. If, as the East Timor and Indonesian experience demonstrates, there is an absence in the host state of a legal culture that promotes and sustains the rule of law, this process will inevitably be flawed. Such a process fails to serve the purposes of justice and reconciliation, alienates society, and calls into question the commitment of the international community.[118] The existence of such a legal culture is a therefore a prerequisite for the establishment of a tribunal which is set up to address human rights violations in a host state.

At a broader level, the use of criminal trials as a method of accountability through an international criminal tribunal, despite positive features,[119] contains aspects that are not attuned to the complex reality of restoring peace and justice in post-conflict societies.

Although criminal law has a critical role in the development of a model of accountability through an international criminal justice system, it is not

[116] *ibid.*, p.2.
[117] *ibid.*, p.26. The material that follows is based on Roper & Barria, above, n.4.
[118] *ibid.*, p.94.
[119] See *e.g.*, amongst many sources UN Rule of Law Report, 2004, p.13.

established to explore or resolve core issues that contribute to crime. The social problems of poverty, deprivation, and social injustice which give rise to crime and human rights violations at a domestic or international level cannot be addressed by a criminal justice model alone. As a minimum, the model should be "accompanied by efficient domestic or international policies and structures" that address these issues.[120] Thus the need for a functioning international legal and social order in which the community of nations works towards common social and public justice goals is critical.

Further, criminal law and legal interventions are not of themselves necessarily the best means of recording past injustices or creating the conditions of justice which may foster national reconciliation.[121] The criminal trial is not always the best instrument for memory and healing. It cannot assist victims to trace their loved ones.[122] It may not properly deal with the "nuanced morality" of confronting and overcoming the past. These aspects of achieving justice for victims of mass atrocities suggest a need for a "principled mix of justice and high politics"[123] which is beyond the scope of a criminal trial and requires a broader focus on reconciliation of fractured communities and their 'enemies'.

These considerations suggest that the creation of legal institutions based on a criminal trial model is not, of itself, a "panacea" for resolving the manifold issues confronting conflict and post-conflict societies, such as East Timor.[124] Other processes for achieving accountability need to be considered.[125]

Post-conflict states need to have a process of "re-building of institutions and national identity"[126] which is based on "integrated, holistic and long-term approaches to intervention".[127] The UN has learnt from the experience of East

---

[120] Ahtisaari, above, n.13, p. xv.

[121] *ibid.*, p.xvi. See also KC Moghalu, above, n.3, pp.214–219 generally on the limitations of criminal trials. This includes the concern that resources are disproportionately put into reactive strategies of the international criminal justice model, rather than proactive strategies geared towards prevention of atrocities by addressing structural causes of human rights violations.

[122] UN Rule of Law Report 2004, p.16.

[123] Thakur, above, n.51, p.284.

[124] Roper & Barria, above, n.4, p.96, Stover and Weinstein, above, n.12, p.5.

[125] See generally, L Sebba, "Formal and informal conflict resolution methods in international criminal justice", in HJ Albrecht *et al.*, *Conflicts and conflict resolution in Middle Eastern societies – between tradition and modernity* (Max Planck Institute and Duncker & Humblot, Berlin, 2006), pp.25–43.

[126] Roper & Barria, above, n.4, p.95.

[127] A Bryden, "Shaping the security governance agenda in post-conflict peacebuilding", in A Bryden and H Hänggi, eds *Security governance in post-conflict peacebuilding* (Lit Verlag, Münster, 2005), at p.267.

Timor and other societies torn apart by conflict that the restoration of peace requires "legitimate structures for the peaceful settlement of disputes and the fair administration of justice" and that this can not be achieved by "approaches focussing on only one or another institution, or ignoring civil society or victims".[128]

Reconstruction of post-conflict societies can only be achieved by a focused strategic plan that aims to build "domestic justice capacities" through the application of transitional justice and entrenching the rule of law. The restoration of post-conflict societies to a condition of justice, peace, and democracy requires a broad approach that excludes "one-size-fits-all formulas and the importation of foreign models" in preference to national assessments of needs, capacities, and aspirations. This should be carried out by domestic stake-holders through local consultation at all levels of the public, including victims, with a view to a better understanding of the dynamics of the past conflict and domestic reform initiatives. The role of the UN and international community in this process is one of solidarity and facilitation, not as the main actor.[129]

This localisation of design means that the formulae and proper balance for transitional justice may go beyond international tribunals or truth commissions and embrace holistic strategies including reparations, truth-seeking, institutional reform, individual domestic prosecutions, vetting of the public service,[130] or a combination of all these.[131] All this recognises the role and contributions of different domestic institutions, and incorporates them into a strategic plan for the rehabilitation of society through integrated, complementary and comprehensive rule of law and justice strategies. The aim is to address the "rule of law vacuum" of post-conflict societies and strengthen national systems for administration of justice in accordance with international standards to ensure that no one is above the law.

These considerations illustrate that responses in post-conflict societies to flagrant violence, such as that which engulfed East Timor since the Indonesian

---

[128] UN Rule of Law Report 2004, Summary. See this report for the material that follows.

[129] See also S Vité, "Re-establishing the rule of law under transitional administration", in Bryden and Hänggi, eds, above, n.127 pp.187–208, at p.203 and P van Zyl, "Promoting transitional justice in post-conflict societies", in Bryden and Hänggi, eds, above, n.127, at *pp*.223–225, "local ownership and consultation are essential if transitional justice institutions are to be effective and lead to sustainable results" which address needs and develop local capacities.

[130] Also referred to as "lustration", Fletcher and Weinstein, above, n.12, p.29.

[131] The idea of complementary strategies is 'now almost universally recognised', van Zyl, P. above, n.129, p.226.

occupation, must incorporate a wide range of social processes of which the rule of law is a critical component. The rule of law is a vital security governance issue that underpins notions of transitional justice and frameworks for post-conflict peacebuilding.[132] It constitutes the foundation for a broader framework of strategies based on a multi-disciplinary approach to achieving justice. Ultimately justice is most effective when it works with other processes of social reconstruction and reflects the needs and wishes of communities affected by mass violence.[133] This is done by grounding justice in local conditions and practices. In this way post-conflict societies define and take ownership of the processes of justice and reconciliation with a view to incorporating broad processes in the social reconstruction and "reclamation" of their societies.[134]

Therefore, methods for achieving justice and accountability, as a response to impunity for crimes committed in the 24 years of occupation and conflict in East Timor, should incorporate a broad range of elements.[135] These will reflect and require choices between post-conflict systems of retribution and restoration or a mix of them.[136] The complexity and difficulty of crafting responses for this impunity means that these elements and any process developed to give effect to them will necessarily reflect compromises.[137] But this pragmatic sense of compromise is preferable to the compromise of credibility that follows if meaningful justice of some kind is not achieved for the victims of the East Timor atrocities.[138]

---

[132] A Bryden, above, n.127, pp.257–258.

[133] Weinstein, and Stover, above, n.12, p.11.

[134] *ibid.*, p.18. Weinstein and Stover propose an "ecological paradigm of social reconstruction". A strategic element of this paradigm is the concept of reclamation, a process of "post-war social repair" which embraces the elements of "identity, culture, memory and history", p.15. The components of these processes are articulated in Stover and Weinstein, "Conclusion: a common objective, a universe of alternatives", in Stover and Weinstein, eds, above, n.12, esp. at pp.327 *et seq*.

[135] See CAVR, Part 11. See also OJI & CIJ 2004, exec. summary pp.5–7, and pp.49–58.

[136] C Stahn, "The geometry of transitional justice: choices of institutional design" (2005) 18 *Leiden Journal of International Law* 425–466, at p.457 opines that the complementary operation of the international criminal tribunals and the CAVR in East Timor provide the foundation of a "justice and reconciliation formula … (which) presents overall a promising mechanism for the restoration of peace and justice in a post-war society". Notwithstanding this he cautions (p 458) that state practice with respect to transitional justice is "moving towards a holistic conception of post-conflict justice (in which) neither trials, nor alternative forms of justice deliver conclusive answers to the challenges of post-conflict justice".

[137] OJI & CIJ 2004, pp.5, 47.

[138] OJI & CIJ 2004, pp.9, 58. The assumption that individuals or groups who have been victims of human rights violations will simply forget them without "'some form of accounting, some semblance of justice, is to leave in place the seeds of future conflict", N Kritz, "Coming to terms with atrocities: a review of accountability mechanisms for mass violations of human rights" (1996) *Law and Contemporary Problems,* 59, pp.127–152, noted in R Alley *Internal conflict and the international community: wars without end?* (2004, Ashgate), pp.90–91 where these issues are addressed.

In the end however, these are "profoundly political choices that ... involve complex trade-offs, not primarily and simply legal decisions".[139] Therefore they are extremely difficult, and bitter divisions will be created, whichever emphasis is given. Understanding this helps to explain Gusmao's decision to subordinate justice for victims through criminal trials of perpetrators to the need for development and social justice, and to his support for the Joint Commission on Truth and Friendship between East Timor and Indonesia. It also explains why there is such extreme disquiet and opposition to this position.[140]

Conclusion

Human rights atrocities were committed in East Timor in the period 1975–1999 by agents of the state of Indonesia. It, as an entity, and its leading agent-perpetrators, therefore bear primary liability, responsibility and punishment for them. To date this has not happened.

The crimes of 1999, as vicious and unpardonable as they are, are "far outweighed by those committed in the previous 24 years of occupation" by Indonesia.[141] The 1,400–1,500 lives lost in 1999 represent less than one percent of the death toll of the Indonesian occupation. However, the international community has given scant regard to the heinousness of the invasion, the occupation, or its apparent strategic objective of deliberately creating chaos and suffering with the intention of setting civilians against each other.[142]

Ideally, prevention from human rights violations committed by the state should be focused on ensuring that state agents who commit international crimes – the military, police, intelligence services, and civil authorities; or who foster the impunity of those who do – politicians, government officials, the judiciary, prosecutorial services, and "defence" lawyers; are strictly accountable to the

[139] R Thakur, above, n.51, pp.288–289. Thakur argues that for this reason, and taking into account the divisions created by such trade-offs, these choices have to be made by the country concerned, "on a case-by-case basis, rather than according to a rigid formula".

[140] On 9 March 2005 the terms of reference of the joint Commission on Truth and Friendship (CTF) were signed, the main objective of which is to establish the "conclusive truth" of the 1999 events. The CTF is proceeding despite the absence of a social consensus (Roper & Barria, above, n.4, p.59) and trenchant international criticism. For example S Linton, above, n.96, p.11 describes it as "... what promises to be the most bogus truth commission ever established ...". See the CTF website at *www.ctf-ri-tl.org/ctfl*.

[141] CAVR, Part 11, pp.23–24

[142] The concept here is borrowed from J Maxted, "The International Criminal Court and the prohibition of the use of children in armed conflict", in Thakur and Malcontent, eds, above, n.1, p.254. Whilst Maxted refers to a different situation in proposing this assessment of offences against international humanitarian law, the description is apt for the nature of the violations committed in East Timor

people, the law, and internationally agreed standards. The international community should insist that these standards are complied with, and the national state should have the confidence to ensure compliance with them as part of the proper safeguards of a democratic state.[143]

Roper and Barria remind us however that "legal concerns are embedded within a political process ... in which rights and obligations are re-defined based on political necessity".[144] The "political necessity" of the processes of dealing with the East Timor atrocities has resulted in a legacy in which, in both East Timor and Indonesia, a culture of impunity has become entrenched. Those responsible for the atrocities have not, and in the "real-world" political climate, will not be brought to legal, criminal account.[145] Whilst this remains the case, respect for the rule of law and organs of the state responsible for its administration in East Timor will remain "extremely fragile".[146] This means that the prospects for the social reconstruction of East Timorese society are very marginal.

But the victims of the atrocities demand justice and accountability.[147] Justice is broader than legal responsibility and embraces both retribution and restoration. Restoration includes both personal and societal rehabilitation, both of which are embraced within the concept of "reclamation". This requires, amongst other things, social and economic redistribution for those who are impoverished by years of brutality and suffering. It is the responsibility of domestic government to provide this expanded form of justice. However, East Timor needs the strong, consistent assistance of the international community to put policies of restoration into place, otherwise the process, and with it, the state, will fail.[148] Critical amongst these are those which the UN itself recognises are fundamental in post-conflict societies, namely policies that assist the domestic state to construct a society that is based on the rule of law.

---

143 CAVR Part 11, p.3.

144 Roper & Barria, above, n.4, p.2.

145 As S. de Bertodano, "Current developments in internationalized courts: East Timor – justice denied" (2004) 2 *Journal of International Criminal Justice* 910, at p.926 puts it, "The unpalatable truth remains that ... the law seems to be applied only to those who are defeated, disgraced or politically unimportant. Those in positions of international political influence are still able not only to escape justice, but to hold power".

146 CAVR Part 11, p.24.

147 *ibid.*, p.23. See also OJI & CIJ 2004 p.48; S Linton, above, n.86, p.11.

148 See L Polman, "Only the trappings of a legitimate state", *Guardian Weekly*, 9–15 June 2006, p.15; and L Polman, *We Did Nothing: Why the Truth Doesn't Always Come Out when the UN Goes In* (Penguin Books Ltd, 2004).

The former UN Secretary-General Kofi Annan has said:

> "There can be no healing without peace; there can be no peace without justice; and there can be no justice without respect for human rights and the rule of law".[149]

But there can be none of these without truth. Truth tells the story of the reality. It reveals the human condition. It requires going and listening to ordinary people and hearing their stories of suffering, grief, loss and anger. Truth restores dignity to victims and gives foundation to an understanding of national identity and purpose. It dispels the lies of the past and of the powerful. In the case of East Timor it demonstrates the treachery and deceit of a quarter-century of misinformation, indifference, and hostility tantamount to criminal complicity by the international community. It provides the foundation for reconciliation and a process of moving forward in directions articulated by the people.

Truth confronts impunity because it reveals its insidiousness. Without truth there cannot be justice. Without justice there cannot be accountability. Without both of these there cannot be conclusion, and without conclusion there cannot be peace and security.

The truth of the East Timor atrocities has been told, repeated and forced into the consciousness of the guilty. Yet impunity thrives. For East Timor and Indonesia, as well as the international community, it is time that the scourge of impunity is finally and meaningfully admitted, addressed, and defeated. Otherwise, it seems that as human beings we are all subject to "ethicide" – the destruction and extinction of "set after set of our human priorities" which are "systematically sprayed, not with pesticides, but with ethicides, agents that kill ethics and therefore any notion of history and justice".[150]

---

[149] Quoted in Lauren, above, n.1, p.33.

[150] J Berger, "An Angel's Rage", *Le Monde Diplomatique*, November 2006, p.16. The word "ethicide" is taken from this article.

Truth, Justice and Reconciliation for East Timor in a World of Lions and Mice

Joseph Nevins

In the 1989 film, *A Dry White Season*, Marlon Brando plays a human rights lawyer in apartheid-era South Africa who tells a client, "Justice and law could be described as distant cousins, and here ... they're not even on speaking terms". These words could have easily been spoken simultaneously on the other side of the world in East Timor. From December 1975, when the Indonesian military (TNI) launched a full-scale invasion of the former Portuguese colony, to September 1999, when the TNI finally withdrew, the East Timorese people endured a brutal occupation, one that resulted in many tens of thousands of deaths and one backed by the majority of the world's most powerful countries.

Such support helps explain why UN action on the matter of East Timor was effectively stymied until 1999. It also sheds light on the reasons why the now-independent country continues to experience the veracity of the film character's observation – there has been no accountability for East Timor's plight – and to endure the profound socio-economic dispossession borne in no small part of its subjugation.

East Timor's experience is neither surprising, nor accidental. Impunity for the powerful and their friends is built into the architecture of international peace, security, and justice mechanisms. As the Mexican delegate to the United Nations' founding convention in 1945 opined, the UN Charter ensured that "the mice would be disciplined, but the lions would be free".[1]

Despite this founding flaw of the UN system, advocates of human rights and international law have endeavoured to ensure that those guilty of committing and overseeing gross crimes are held accountable. What many refer to as transitional justice – a collection of judicial and non-judicial approaches aimed at seeking accountability for mass atrocities and systematic human rights

[1] Quoted in Abba Eban, "The UN Idea Revisited" (1995) 74(5) *Foreign Affairs* 43.

abuses, and at reconstructing damaged social bonds and fabric – reflects that effort. A key component of that process is official truth-telling, usually by some sort of national or international commission that researches and publicises the extent of, and actors behind, past episodes of horror. The assumption behind such initiatives – South Africa's perhaps being the most well-known example – is that the "truth" can contribute to justice as well as facilitate conditions that allow former adversaries to live together in relative peace in the same society.

East Timor's Commission on Reception, Truth, and Reconciliation (CAVR) was charged with establishing the truth about human rights violations that occurred in the last quarter of the twentieth century. More precisely, the CAVR covered the period between 25 April 1974 – when the fascist Caetano government in Portugal was overthrown and the decolonisation of Portuguese Timor began – and 25 October 1999, when the United Nations assumed control over the ravaged territory following the ignominious withdrawal of Indonesian forces. Central to the CAVR's mandate was the identification of state and non-state actors – individuals, organisations, authorities, and institutions – involved in perpetrating gross human rights violations, such as unlawful killings, torture, arbitrary arrest, rape and sexual slavery, and the deprivation of and social and economic rights. The Commission had to determine who was responsible for the violations and to assess their level of responsibility. The commission also had to issue recommendations on how the various actors responsible for the violations were to be held accountable. The assumption was that findings on responsibility and follow-through procedures for accountability were crucial to promoting reconciliation between former adversaries. As *Chega!* states, "All aspects of the Commission's work were designed and implemented as part of a coordinated and integrated approach aimed at promoting reconciliation".[2]

"Truth commissions," historian Greg Grandin writes, "are curious, contradictory bodies" that:

> often raise hope of justice symbolized by the Nuremberg Trials yet operate within the of impoverished political possibilities that exist throughout much of the post-Cold War world.[3]

---

[2] *Chega!*, Final Report of the Commission for Truth, Reception, and Reconciliation (CAVR) in East Timor, 2005: part 1:32, *http://www.etan.org/news/2006/cavr.htm*.

[3] G Grandin, "The Instruction of Great Catastrophe: Truth Commissions, National History, and State Formation in Argentina, Chile, and Guatemala" (2005) 110 *The American Historical Review* 46.

East Timor, as one of the world's poorest and smallest (at about one million people) countries,[4] suffers from these "impoverished political possibilities" more than most. Its hard-fought-for independence has come about at a time when the United States exists as the world's sole superpower, one that doggedly insists on impunity not only for its own international crimes, but also for those committed by its allies.

The CAVR wrote a massive report full of documentation about terrible crimes and analyses of the actors responsible, but the East Timorese government has few resources, and little political space on the international scale to take any action on this information. It does not have the funds to hold an adequate number of trials of suspects. More important, all of the high-level suspects in the Indonesian military who are accused of crimes against humanity are living in Indonesia. East Timor does not have the clout to force Indonesia to extradite them and receives no support from the powerful countries of the world for putting those suspects on trial – to say nothing about East Timor's ability to hold accountable those same powerful countries for their complicity in Indonesia's crimes. As such, there has been almost no follow-through on the commission's work.

That said, the CAVR should not be dismissed as a pointless exercise. It had significant moral authority and left behind a detailed and comprehensive report that sets the ideals to which the East Timorese government and the international community should aspire. The report deserves careful consideration. While the report contains a lot that is valuable, much of which I discuss herein, this chapter highlights its limitations, as the CAVR did not go as far as it could and should have in analysing responsibility for atrocities and recommending amends. It thus limits our collective understanding of what transpired in and around East Timor during the period in question, and our imagination of how we might go about rectifying the damage done by Indonesia's war and occupation. In making this argument, this chapter moves beyond relatively conventional analyses of reconciliation that focus on

[4] According to the January 2006 report from the United Nations Development Programme, Timor-Leste is "chained by poverty." The manifestations are multiple: 90 out of 1,000 children there die before their first birthday: half the population is illiterate; 64 percent suffers from food insecurity; half lack access to safe drinking water; and 40 percent live below the official poverty line of 55 cents a day. See United Nations Development Programme, "The Path out of Poverty" (Timor-Leste Human Development Report 2006), (Dili, 2006), *http://content.undp.org/go/cms-service/stream/asset/?asset_id=420912*.

individuals and their attitudes, values, and beliefs, and overlook collective and material forms of violence and injustice.[5]

Responsibility

Chega! (Portuguese for Enough! or Stop!) provides chilling detail of many of the worst atrocities committed during Jakarta's reign of terror in Timor-Leste. These include torture, sexual violence, extrajudicial killings, "disappearances", human-induced famine, indiscriminate bombing, and the use of chemical and biological weapons.[6]

The CAVR established that there were *at minimum* 102,800 East Timorese civilian deaths – 84,200 of whom perished due to conflict-induced "displacement-related hunger and illness" (7.3: 5) – while advancing a figure of 201,900 as the *maximum* number of possible conflict-related civilian deaths. Whichever of the two figures is more accurate, both constitute a huge percentage of the country's population, one estimated to be less than 700,000 in 1975. The CAVR also estimates that Indonesian forces committed "thousands" of acts of sexual violence[7] – such as torture and mutilation of women, gang rapes, and sexual enslavement – acts that were "widespread and systematic", "widely accepted" within the military hierarchy, and "covered by almost total impunity".[8]

The Commission finds that the Government of Indonesia and Indonesian security forces were "primarily responsible" for the "death from hunger and illness of between 100,000 and 180,000 East Timorese civilians" that took place as a "direct result" of the TNI's invasion and occupation.[9] In terms of illegal killings and sexual violence, the Commission also finds Indonesian forces responsible for the vast majority of them. According to *Chega!*, Indonesian troops and police, and East Timorese auxiliaries (i.e. militia members or paramilitaries), were responsible for 89.9 percent of the killings and disappearances,[10] meaning that non-Indonesia-affiliated East Timorese forces (*e.g.*, Falintil, and parties involved with the August–September 1975

---

[5] For an example of this relatively conventional approach, see JL Gibson, *Overcoming Apartheid: Can Truth Reconcile a Divided Nation?* (Russell Sage Foundation, New York, 2004).

[6] *Chega!*, part 7, chapter 5: 27 & 128.

[7] *Chega!*, part 7, chapter 7: 109.

[8] *Chega!*, part 7, chapter 7: 3.

[9] *Chega!*, part 8: 6.

[10] *Chega!*, part 6: 3.

civil war), were responsible for approximately 10 percent of them.[11] As for incidences of sexual violence, Indonesian forces committed 93.3 percent of the documented atrocities.[12] In addition, the Commission established that all the major crimes committed by Indonesian forces against adults were also perpetrated against children. As *Chega!* reports:

> Children (persons under 18 years of age) were systematically killed, detained, tortured, raped, and otherwise violated on a widespread scale by members of the Indonesian security forces inside military facilities and at other official locations (8: 7).

What is unique about *Chega!* vis-à-vis other truth commission reports is the extent to which it focuses on international actors – beyond the conflict's immediate protagonists – in assessing responsibility. In a number of ways, the very nature of the invasion and occupation of East Timor necessitated it: Indonesia's blatant violations of international law were aided and abetted by a variety of powerful actors abroad. As the Commission's report makes clear, Western governments provided Jakarta with many billions of dollars worth of weapons, military equipment and training, and economic aid, as well as invaluable diplomatic cover.[13] Indeed, the collective assistance of the West was decisive in allowing the 1975 invasion to go forth and for the occupation to continue until late-1999.[14] Declassified government documents, many of them referred to in the Commission's report, reveal that Jakarta was sufficiently worried about how Western countries would react to its aggression that Suharto, Indonesia's dictator, vetoed earlier plans to invade East Timor.

---

[11] Given the very real possibility that the actual number of conflicted-related civilian deaths – especially those brought about by unlawful killings – might be significantly higher than the minimum estimate put forth by the CAVR, this might very well exaggerate the level of East Timorese responsibility for unlawful killings, as it is far more likely that Indonesian forces would have perpetrated the types of killings that are unknown (*e.g.*, mass deaths in particular areas that led to no witnesses who survived until 2002–2003 or did not result in marked graves with durable headstones).

[12] *Chega!*, part 7, chapter 7: 2.

[13] As *Chega!* explains, such assistance violates international law as it undermined East Timor's right to self-determination (part 7, chapter 1: 5).

[14] For a substantiation of this argument, see J Nevins, *A Not-so-distant Horror: Mass Violence in East Timor* (Cornell University Press, Ithaca NY, 2005). In using the term "the West," I mean an entity centered on the states of western Europe, Australia, New Zealand, Canada, the United States, and Japan. (See, for example, M Shaw, "The State of Globalization: Towards a Theory of State Transformation" (1997) 4 *Review of International Political Economy* 497. These states are almost synonymous with the member-states of the Organization for Economic Co-operation and Development (OECD), an entity made of 30 countries that, according to the OECD website, share "a commitment to democratic government and the market economy".

Only after consulting Australia, Britain, and the United States did Suharto launch the invasion.[15]

The Washington-DC-based National Security Archive supplied many of the documents detailing the United States and British roles. The non-governmental research institute issued two edited electronic "briefing books" of select, mostly formerly classified documents on 28 November 2005, the same day that East Timor's president, Xanana Gusmão, handed over the report to the country's parliament.[16]

The documents show that Washington – as well as London – had decided to effectively sacrifice East Timor well before the invasion. In March 1975, the US ambassador in Jakarta recommended to his superiors a "general policy of silence" on the Suharto regime's planned use of force to take over what was then Portuguese Timor.[17] He explained that Washington had "considerable interests" in Indonesia – what Richard Nixon once described as "by far the greatest prize in the Southeast Asian area"[18] – but had "none" in East Timor.[19]

President Gerald Ford and Secretary of State Henry Kissinger, well aware of the pending invasion, met with Suharto in Jakarta on 6 Decenber 1975. Ford assured his Indonesian counterpart that with regard to East Timor, "[We] will not press you on the issue. We understand . . . the intentions you have", while Kissinger expressed worry that "the use of US-made arms could create problems." The US had supplied about 90 percent of Indonesia's military equipment on the condition that it not be used for offensive purposes. Kissinger promised Suharto that the US would not regard the invasion as an aggression, while expressing understanding for Indonesia's "need to move quickly" and advising "that it would be better if it were done after we [he and Ford] returned [to the United States]".[20] About 14 hours after their departure, Indonesian forces invaded.

---

[15] See Nevins, above, n.14, chapter 3.

[16] B Simpson, ed., "A Quarter Century of U.S. Support for Occupation", National Security Archive Briefing Book, 28 November 2005, *http://www.gwu.edu/~nsarchiv/*; and H Dowson, ed., "Declassified British Documents Reveal U.K. Support for Indonesian Invasion and Occupation of East Timor, Recognition of Denial of Self-Determination, 1975–76"; National Security Archive Briefing Book, 28 November 2005, *http://www.gwu.edu/~nsarchiv/*.

[17] *Chega!*, part 7, chapter 1: 54.

[18] Richard Nixon, "Asia After Viet Nam", *Foreign Affairs*, October 1967: 111.

[19] Simpson, above, n.16.

[20] *Chega!*, part 7, chapter 1: 55 and 56.

The support continued, with few interruptions, until September 1999. Even during the administration of Nobel Peace Prize laureate Jimmy Carter, who once described human rights as the "cause that has been closest to my own heart",[21] US weaponry continued to flow to Jakarta. Carter's administration, in late 1977, when Indonesia was running short of military equipment, authorised $112 million worth of arms sales for fiscal year 1978 to Jakarta, up from $13 million the previous year.[22] The administration also approved the sale of 16 F-5 fighter jets and a squadron of A-4 ground-attack bombers, all while making clear to Jakarta that it did not question its takeover of East Timor.[23]

Although US assistance became more contested during the Clinton years, largely due to grassroots and congressional pressure, the essence of US policy continued, a fact that the CAVR report glosses over and distorts.[24] Indeed, it gives the false impression that there was something fundamentally different about the Clinton administration, which provided over $500 million in economic assistance, sold and licensed the sales of hundreds of millions of dollars in weaponry, engaged in joint military manoeuvres, and trained TNI members (in Indonesia) by ignoring and sidestepping the intent of Congress which had imposed a ban on such training in the United States.[25]

While the Commission correctly emphasises the role of the United States government, whose support the report characterises as "fundamental" to Indonesia's crimes,[26] it puts a heavy emphasis on Cold War-related factors in explaining the behaviour of Washington, and the West as a whole. *Chega!* states, for example, that Washington's support for Jakarta grew out of:

> a strategically-motivated desire to maintain a good relationship with Indonesia, whose anti-communist regime was seen as an essential bastion against the spread of communism in South-East Asia.[27]

---

21 US Department of State, *American Foreign Policy Basic Documents, 1977–1980* (United States Government Printing Office, Washington, DC, 1983), 1315.

22 G McArthur, "Indonesia Anxious to Replace Decrepit Arms," *International Herald Tribune*, 5 December 1977.

23 See T Smith, "Mondale Is a Nonexpert Who Matters," *The New York Times*, 14 May 1978: Chapter 4; Tapol, "Bartering Human Rights," *The Tapol Bulletin*, No. 27, June 1978: 1. Dunn 1983, p.298 and Taylor 1991, pp.73–74.

24 See *Chega!*, part 8: 92; and part 7, chapter 1: 60–61.

25 A Nairn, "Indonesia's Killers," *The Nation*, 30 March 1998, 6–7. The programme under which the Pentagon conducted the training is known as Joint Combined Exchange Training (JCET). For information on and analysis of the origins and nature of JCET, see C Johnson, *Blowback: The Costs and Consequences of American Empire* (Henry Holt and Company, New York, 2000).

26 *Chega!*, part 8, annex 1: 91.

27 *Chega!*, part 8, annex 1: 91; see also part 7, chapter 1: 52.

The report argues that US administrations:

> were driven by hard-nosed realism in the policy towards Timor-Leste: they all consistently stressed the overriding importance of the relationship with Indonesia and the supposed irreversibility of the Indonesian takeover.[28]

Yet it never explains what exactly the overall strategy was, the one suggested by phrases such as "a strategically-motivated desire" and "hard-nosed realism." By emphasising East-West tensions, the commission downplays North–South dynamics. These dynamics and the interests underlying them resulted in the West's essentially sacrificing the well-being of East Timor to ensure continued good relations with resource-rich Indonesia and favourable access to the country's large market and low-wage workforce. These factors were far more important than Cold War anti-communism in explaining the West's conduct in 1975 and in the 24 year period of the Indonesian occupation. As a US State Department spokesman explained in 1976 in justifying Washington's condoning of Jakarta's actions in East Timor: "We regard Indonesia as a friendly, non-aligned nation – a nation we do a lot of business with".[29]

The CAVR report does state that the East–West conflict was not only an ideological one, but also had commercial (as well as military) aspects to it. Yet, the overall effect of its framing of Western complicity makes it seem as if the East Timor conflict was largely a proxy war in "an ideological contest between the capitalist and communist systems".[30] As such, the report helps to obscure the fact that political-economic calculations by Western governments, ones rooted in the perceived need to maintain the unequal power relations between the global North and South, were the key factors in driving their alliance with Suharto's Indonesia.

What's curious about this is that information contained within the report itself contradicts the CAVR's framing. The report cites the British ambassador John Ford's opinion, for example, expressed in a 14 July 1975 letter to the Foreign Office that "the people of East Timor are in no condition to exercise the right to self-determination". The letter made clear that Cold War considerations were of little concern. Even "without the Soviets or Chinese intervention", Ford

---

[28] *Chega!*, part 8, annex 1: 92.

[29] R Waby, "Aid to Indonesia Doubled as U.S. Shrugs Off Timor," *The Australian*, 22 January 1976. A significant component of that "business" involved oil. Formerly classified documents show that Indonesia's oil wealth was an underlying reason for American support for Jakarta. See Simpson, above, n.16.

[30] *Chega!*, part 7, chapter 1: 5.

contended, East Timor would probably become the region's "problem child". He argued that "it is in Britain's interest that Indonesia absorb the territory", and that if "there is a row in the United Nations we should keep our heads down and avoid siding against the Indonesian Government".[31] The motivation for such a position, *Chega!* contends, was "largely dictated by the importance [Britain] attached to its long-standing commercial interests in Indonesia".[32]

Similarly, the report cites the Australian government's February 1975 letter to Suharto that expressed the belief that neither China nor the Soviet Union had any designs on Portuguese Timor.[33] As for Canberra's motivations for supporting Indonesia's invasion and occupation, the Commission offers nothing that suggests that Cold War ideologies were involved. The report contends that Canberra's acquiescence to Indonesia's plans was born of, among other factors, its:

> assessment that it would achieve a more favourable outcome to the negotiations on the maritime boundary in the Timor [Sea] [involving the dividing up of control over lucrative deposits of oil and natural gas] if it was dealing with Indonesia rather than with Portugal or an independent Timor-Leste on the issue.[34]

If the report's analysis is confused about international responsibility for the beginning of the Indonesian occupation, it is also confused about international responsibility for the ending: the post-ballot violence that engulfed East Timor in 1999. The report correctly points out that the Clinton administration's pressuring of Jakarta in September 1999 to accept foreign intervention demonstrated "the considerable leverage that it could have exerted earlier had

---

31 *Chega!*, part 7, chapter 1: 47.

32 *Chega!*, part 7, chapter 1: 48. According to a 26 September 1975, Foreign and Commonwealth Office "Briefing Paper", the reasons for London's favorable predisposition toward Jakarta were multiple. The key ones included the Suharto regime's "moderate" politics in international fora, and the fact that Indonesia was a "growing market" for British goods (including, potentially, military hardware) and a "fruitful area for British investment". See Dowson, above, n.16.

33 *Chega!*, part 7, chapter 1: 39. This analysis, according to the Commission, was shared by other Western governments and communicated to Jakarta (*Chega!*, part 7, chapter 1: 40; see also part 7, chapter 1: 45). Whatever sympathies the Soviet Union and China might have had for East Timor's self-determination struggle, the CAVR suggests that they were tempered by the perceived need to not damage relations with Indonesia.

34 *Chega!*, part 8, annex 1: 91. See also J Nevins, "Contesting the Boundaries of International Justice: State Countermapping and Offshore Resource Struggles Between Australia and East Timor" (2004) 80 *Economic Geography* 1; as well as various issues of the *La'o Hamutuk Bulletin*, *http://www.laohamutuk.org/bulletin.html*.

the will been there".[35] Yet it praises both Australia and Britain (Indonesia's second largest foreign investor after Japan) for their support for the holding of the referendum in 1999 without mentioning that both countries were following the same policy as the United States.[36] Like the United States government, both refused to use the leverage they had to pressure Jakarta to stop the TNI and militia terror and ensure that the referendum was held under peaceful conditions. The report states that Britain was supplying most of Jakarta's military equipment in the late 1990s,[37] but fails to note that senior TNI officials were receiving training in British military establishments at the same time. The United States, Britain, Australia, and Japan (which provided the lion's share of economic assistance to Jakarta during the occupation) prioritised their economic and military ties to Indonesia in 1999, even as it was clear that the TNI was responsible for terrorising the East Timorese. In a glaring omission, the CAVR report does not discuss how the West's refusal to seriously pressure Jakarta in the run-up to the referendum provided Indonesian troops and their "militia" proxies the space needed to unleash their final wave of killing and destruction in September 1999 following the announcement of the result of the vote.[38]

Despite significant flaws in its overall framing of Western responsibility, *Chega!* does provide a good deal of detail on the motivations and actions of various Western governments – especially Australia, Britain, and the United States.[39] It

[35] *Chega!*, part 8, annex 1: 92.

[36] *Chega!*, part 7, chapter 1: 33 and 51.

[37] *Chega!*, part 7, chapter 1: 50.

[38] It was one week into the scorched earth campaign, ironically on 11 September 1999, that Bill Clinton, under considerable domestic pressure, finally suspended US military sales to Jakarta. Hours later, London followed suit and announced a suspension of the sale and delivery of Hawk aircraft, in addition to support for a European Union arms embargo and a willingness to contribute to an international military force. Three days earlier, as reported in the *Financial Times*, an unnamed Jakarta-based diplomat explained why powerful countries were hitherto reluctant to support a suspension of aid or forcefully push for an international intervention in East Timor: "The dilemma is that Indonesia matters and East Timor doesn't". (The source of the quote turned out to be US ambassador Stapleton Roy, who, soon after making the statement, became the managing director of Kissinger Associates, Inc., Henry Kissinger's international consulting firm.)

[39] The CAVR prioritised the United Kingdom and the United States – along with China, France, and the Soviet Union/Russia – because they are permanent members of the UN Security Council (the UN body charged with maintaining international peace and security). While it makes sense to include an overview of Australian policy, the CAVR inexplicably categorises Australia as one of the conflict's "three main external stakeholders" (the other two being Indonesia and Portugal). Of all the Western countries, Australia was perhaps the one whose support for Indonesia's occupation was most steadfast. But that of the United States (especially) and Britain – and perhaps even Japan – was arguably more important in terms of facilitating and sustaining Indonesia's crimes in East Timor. The Commission does include an analysis of Japan's role given that country's (elected) membership of the Security Council in the "crucial years" of 1975–1976 and because it was "Indonesia's principal regional economic partner" (Executive Summary: 47).

says nothing, however, about numerous "lesser" Western powers that were also complicit. It is understandable that the Commission – given its limited time and resources – focused on the major countries, but it could have at least briefly mentioned how, for instance, Canada and Germany significantly enabled Jakarta's war and occupation in East Timor.[40] Instead, the Commission devoted three pages to the role of China[41] – simply because it is a permanent member of the UN Security Council – a country that supported East Timor's struggle for the first several years, and then gradually moved closer to Indonesia, but never provided support for the war and occupation.

Accountability

The Commission includes the matter of accountability as part of its mandate, but what it means by "accountability" is unclear. Often, *Chega!* uses the term when it speaks of "responsibility". It thus implies that those guilty of committing, or aiding and abetting the atrocities (responsibility) should be held liable (accountability). Yet, the report actually says little about how those most responsible for the crimes committed against the East Timorese people should be held accountable – whether by means of some sort of juridical process or other means – except in the recommendations section of the report (Part 11).

There, the Commission recommends that the United Nations renew the mandates for, and provide sufficient resources to, the Special Crimes Unit (SCU) and the "Special Panel for Serious Crimes" so that they can research and try cases from throughout the 1975–1999 period.[42] Established by the United Nations during its post-occupation administration of the territory, the SCU was an investigative body that prepares indictments, while the panels were internationally mandated "hybrid" courts made up of East Timorese and international judges. While in existence through mid-2005, they prosecuted and convicted a number of individuals for gross crimes committed in 1999

---

[40] Regarding Canadian policy, see S Scharfe, *Complicity: Human Rights and Canadian Foreign Policy: The Case of East Timor* (Black Rose Books, Montreal, 1996); J Klaehn, "Canadian Complicity in the East Timor Near-Genocide: A Case Study in the Sociology of Human Rights," (2003) 11(1) *Portuguese Studies Review* 49; and the Canadian documentary (circa 1997) *Bitter Paradise: The Sell-Out of East Timor*, produced and directed by Elaine Brière. As for the complicity of Germany, Sweden, Denmark and other European countries, see G Defert, *Timor Est: Le Génocide Oublié – Droit d'un people et raisons d'État* (Éditions L'Harmattan, Paris, 1992); T Retbøll, ed., *East Timor, Indonesia and the Western Democracies*, (International Work Group for Indigenous Affairs, Copenhagen, 1980); T Retbøll, ed., *East Timor: The Struggle Continues* (International Work Group for Indigenous Affairs, Copenhagen, 1984); and J Taylor, *East Timor: The Price of Freedom* (Zed Books, London, 1999).

[41] *Chega!*, part 7, chapter 1: 39–42.

[42] *Chega!*, part 11: 24–25.

(and only that year), but all of them were low-level East Timorese, typically members of TNI-organised and TNI-directed militia, as Jakarta refused to extradite persons indicted by the courts despite having promised to do so.[43] These shortcomings almost had the effect of reducing the Serious Crimes process to irrelevance. Yet, by issuing indictments, the Serious Crimes process established a judicial trail that could serve as a foundation for a more effective process in the future. It is the hope of the Commission that Indonesia will cooperate with the renewed Special Panels, and that the international community ensures such cooperation by, among other steps, linking aid to Jakarta to its willingness to provide said cooperation. Should such measures fail to bring about sufficient accountability, the report recommends that the UN Security Council be prepared to establish an international tribunal to try those parties responsible for the crimes committed against the East Timorese people.[44]

At the same time, the report makes clear that it sees accountability going beyond a narrow legalistic notion. Drawing on customary systems of law from East Timor, for instance, the Commission implemented "Community Reconciliation Procedures" (CRPs) through which perpetrators of what were deemed as relatively minor acts of violence (such as killing a few livestock or burning one or two houses) were held accountable to their victims and by which perpetrators agreed to perform acts of restoration that are meaningful to direct victims and their communities. For example, the crime of burning a house down might have required the offender to rebuild that house.[45] The resulting "community reconciliation agreement" was registered at a district court, which was supposed to ensure acts of reconciliation were proportionate to the original crimes, were carried out, and did not violate human rights. The Commission was charged with referring what are called serious crimes (genocide, war crimes, torture, and crimes against humanity – irrespective of when committed – as well as murder and sexual offences perpetrated between

---

[43] Jakarta signed a memorandum of understanding with the United Nations, thus promising cooperation in terms of extradition among other matters. Later, however, Jakarta contended that the memorandum had no legal standing because Indonesia's parliament never ratified it. The United Nations in East Timor rejected this argument as valid.

[44] *Chega!*, part 11: 26.

[45] For a journalistic account of one such Community Reconciliation Procedure, see "East Timor's Example," *The Times of . India*, 5 January 2004, *http://timesofindia.indiatimes.com/articleshow/404228.cms*. While most participants expressed satisfaction with the CRPs, some victims felt that the punishments meted out were not sufficiently strong. See G Robinson, "Forgiveness in East Timor, But Where Is the Justice?" published online by the UCLA International Institute *http://www.international.ucla.edu/print.asp?parentid=11589*, 28 May 2004.

1 January and 25 October 1999), which were ineligible for CRPs, to East Timor's General Prosecutor for possible prosecution.

In terms of accountability beyond judicial proceedings for Indonesian military personnel and government officials responsible for atrocities committed in relation to the war and occupation, the Commission makes a number of recommendations. It calls upon the Indonesian government to send:

> a senior delegation to Timor-Leste to acknowledge the violations committed by its representatives during the occupation and to apologise to the victims and families of victims for these violations.[46]

It also asks Jakarta to revise official accounts and educational materials regarding its presence in East Timor, and to provide full disclosure of documents relating to military operations that resulted in atrocities against civilians. Moreover, it recommends that the Government of Indonesia and Indonesian businesses that profited from activities related to the war and occupation of the former Portuguese colony pay reparations to East Timor.[47]

In terms of external actors beyond Indonesia, the Commission recommends that the international community – especially within countries and institutions highlighted by *Chega!* – endeavour to ensure that the report receives wide circulation, but, unlike in the case of Indonesia, does not call upon these actors to revise their official accounts of their roles in the war and occupation. It also asks that all states that had military cooperation programmes (it says nothing about non-humanitarian economic assistance to Jakarta) with Indonesia in the 1974–1999 period – regardless of whether the assistance was directly employed in East Timor – formally apologise to the East Timorese people. And it calls upon the Permanent Members of the Security Council – particularly the United States, as well as Britain and France – to provide reparations to "victims of human rights violations suffered during the Indonesian occupation".[48] The report makes the same demand of businesses that profited from the sale of weaponry to Indonesia during that period. While the report surprisingly says nothing specific about Japan, Australia, and other Western countries in terms of reparations, it does recommend that "governments who provided military assistance ... during the occupation and business corporations who benefited" from weapon sales to Indonesia

46 *Chega!*, part 11: 31.
47 *Chega!*, part 11: 32 and 34.
48 *Chega!*, part 11: 4.

contribute to a reparations programme, one that will prioritise and target "the most vulnerable victims [individually and collectively] of human rights violations", those who live in extreme poverty, are disabled, or – due to continuing misunderstandings – are shunned or discriminated against by their neighbours (*e.g.*, women sexually enslaved by Indonesian troops), those "who still suffer daily from the consequences of the conflict and whose children will inherit the disadvantages their parents face as a result of their victimisation".[49]

Truth commissions often call for such amends, typically for specific victims of atrocities – a function of their tendency to focus on individual acts or events of violence, while ignoring systemic forms of injustice. In doing so, commissions help reify the notion that the worst injustices are those brought about by particular atrocities. In the case of South Africa, for example, one effect of the focus by the Truth and Reconciliation Commission (TRC) on individual acts and events was to downplay the fact that apartheid was a system, one in which certain groups and individuals – within South Africa, but also abroad – accrued substantial socio-economic benefits, while helping to dispossess and impoverish a far greater number. Although a few thousand victims, or families of those killed during the apartheid regime, received monetary compensation as a form of reparation, the TRC's form of justice did not help to restore the profound socio-economic deficiencies experienced by millions of South Africans as a result of apartheid as a political-economic structure. As such, many continue to suffer from what one might term post-apartheid apartheid – apartheid not as a political-institutional regime, but as a socio-economic system marked by deep race and class divides – as various South African analysts have suggested.[50]

East Timor's Commission's recommendations are more far-reaching, and move beyond a focus on individuals directly victimised in the conflict. In

---

[49] *Chega!*, part 11: 42 and 35.

[50] See, for example, H Marais, *South Africa: Limits to Change: The Political Economy of Transition*, (Zed Books Ltd, London and New York, and University of Cape Town Press, Cape Town, 2001); and T Bell with D Buhle Ntsebeza, *Unfinished Business: South Africa, Apartheid and Truth* (Verso, London and New York, 2003). According to Archbishop Desmond Tutu, the TRC's chair, the commission provided a restorative of justice, one that heals socio-psychological and spiritual wounds. But Tutu also sees this justice as insufficient. Speaking on the day marking the formal end of the TRC's work in March 2003, he asked rhetorically, "Can you explain how a black person wakes up in a squalid ghetto today, almost 10 years after freedom? Then he goes to work in town, which is still largely white, in palatial homes. And at the end of the day, he goes back home to squalor? I don't know why those people don't just say, 'To hell with peace. To hell with Tutu and the truth commission'". Quoted in G Thompson, "South African Commission Ends Its Work," *The New York Times*, 22 March 2003.

raising the need to aid those who live in extreme poverty, for example, the Commission highlights the collective and structural legacies of the war and occupation. But the Commission's analysis and thus its recommendations are not as structural as they could and should be – that is, if the goal is to achieve a justice that is commensurate to the multifaceted forms of damage wrought by the conflict. It is to this topic that I now turn.

Reconciliation

According to the Commission, reconciliation requires three components: truth, justice, and reparations.[51] What precisely the Commission means by "reconciliation", however, is not obvious. Nor is it sufficiently clear with whom East Timor's victimised population should reconcile and how.

When the report speaks of reconciliation, it sometimes associates it with the loose concept of "healing" – one that would implicitly involve all of East Timor. It also associates it with a restoration of dignity to those victimised by the conflict.[52] The Commission employed various methods to achieve this form of reconciliation.

One method utilised was the holding of public hearings, such as a four-day, nationally broadcast hearing in which leaders of the various East Timorese political parties of the conflict-ridden 1974–1976 period participated. The participants:

> publicly accepted responsibility for their actions, expressed regret for the harmful acts they or the institution they represented had done, and ... affirmed their solidarity in a moving closing ceremony.

At the same time, the Commission hosted numerous hearings at which victims from different sides of the conflict were able to recount their experiences.

---

[51] *Chega!*, part 11: 36 & 38.

[52] For examples of such associations, see *Chega!*, see part 11: 36 and 37. Such statements are manifestations of a frequent misconception about truth commissions: that they lead to group and personal "healing." For proponents of this position, participation in a truth commission is almost akin to therapy. Research on the "healing" effects of commissions is far from conclusive, however. In fact, there is much evidence that such bodies can actually heighten inter-group tensions. See Priscilla B Hayner, *Unspeakable Truths: Confronting State Terror and Atrocity*, New York: Routledge, 2000; also see Richard A Wilson, *The Politics of Truth and Reconciliation in South Africa: Legitimizing the Post-Apartheid State*, Cambridge, U.K. and New York: Cambridge University Press, 2001. Regarding the difficulties of "healing" in East Timor, see Margot Cohen, "Survivors In East Timor Find It Hard To Forgive," *Far Eastern Economic Review*, March 28, 2002. Available online at *http://www.etan.org/*

This, according to *Chega!*, "contributed to a more balanced and accurate public perception of shared history" while helping to "restore the dignity denied to individual victims" and to dispel "some of the residual anger that fuels continuing division".[53]

The Commission's Community Reconciliation Procedures (CRP) were also designed to achieve reconciliation. At a CRP, a person who had harmed his/her neighbours would admit his guilt, explain why and how he had committed such crimes, and then ask to be accepted back in the community. According to *Chega!*, a total of 1,371 perpetrators successfully completed a CRP, exceeding the Commission's initial target of 1,000 individuals. About 40,000 individual community members attended and participated in CRP hearings. Meanwhile, victims, perpetrators, and other participants in the hearings, according to assessments undertaken by the CAVR, generally indicated that the CRP made a "significant contribution" toward community-level reconciliation by providing opportunities for victims to express their anger and have it validated, and for perpetrators to demonstrate remorse directly to those they harmed.[54] Indeed, 96 percent of persons interviewed by the Commission said that "the CRP had achieved its primary goal of promoting reconciliation in their community".[55] That said, the Commission acknowledges that it simply did not have enough time and resources to allow everyone who wanted to participate in a CRP to do so: an additional 3,000 perpetrators could have participated had the programme continued.[56] Overall, however, the Commission judged its work in the area of the CRP to have been successful:

> [D]espite predictions of revenge attacks on perpetrators for their role in the violence of 1999, Timor-Leste has enjoyed a high level of peace and stability during the difficult initial years of nation building.[57]

Where the Commission and the overall process fell short, according to a number of the interviewees, was that individuals who perpetrated murders or rapes of people in the communities remained free in West Timor and hence did not have to face their communities or the courts in Timor-Leste.[58] Thus,

---

53 *Chega!*, part 9: 38.
54 *Chega!*, part 1: 32–33.
55 *Chega!*, part 9: 34.
56 *Chega!*, part 9: 47.
57 *Chega!*, part 9: 3.
58 Without saying so explicitly, the report implies that these perpetrators were East Timorese members of the TNI-affiliated militia groups.

although these interviewees "expressed satisfaction with the results of the CRP, they were dissatisfied with the progress that had been made towards achieving comprehensive justice."[59]

As such, a lack of "comprehensive justice" is inextricably linked to an absence of comprehensive reconciliation. The Commission could do nothing about reconciling the East Timorese with their compatriots who had been militia leaders and who have decided to remain in Indonesia. Likewise, the CAVR could do nothing concrete in terms of reconciling the East Timorese with Indonesian perpetrators and their supporters abroad. All that the CAVR could do was to recommend courses of action.

Chega! speaks of reconciliation in relation to Indonesia in Part 11, which contains the Commission's recommendations. There, the Commission makes clear that it sees reparations from Jakarta – discussed above – as one of the key factors related to reconciliation between East Timor and its giant neighbour.

Although the report does not discuss reconciliation with external actors beyond Indonesia, it would seem reasonable to infer that its call for reparations, among other things, from the Western powers that enabled Indonesia's war and occupation is related to a sense that reconciliation must take place in the international arena as well. Yet, it is a reconciliation that is insufficiently systemic.

As discussed above, the CAVR seems to have paid heed to Mahmood Mamdani's call – made in specific reference to South Africa's Truth and Reconciliation Commission – for truth commissions to move beyond legalistic frameworks that focus on individual victims and perpetrators to social justice frameworks concerned with victims and beneficiaries in a collective sense. Because the injustices were systemic, Mamdani asserts, not simply a set of ugly incidents, full reconciliation can only come about through systemic change. Failure to realise this severely limits the ability of those who benefited from the *ancien régime* to live in peace with the victims – individual and collective – as the structural injustices, and the associated social tensions, live on.[60]

Coffee, for example, East Timor's top export earner, helped to finance Indonesia's war and occupation as the TNI handed over control of the

[59] *Chega!*, part 9: 35.

[60] See Mahmood Mamdani, "Reconciliation Without Justice. *Southern African Review of Books* Issue 46, November/December 1996.

territory's coffee trade to an Indonesian businessman in exchange for his providing food and supplies to the invading forces. This arrangement eventually resulted in a 20-year deal (one that actually lasted only until 1992) by which PT Denok Hernandes became the sole buyer and exporter of the occupied territory's coffee. This military-backed monopoly consistently and systematically underpaid East Timorese coffee producers. In 1983 alone, East Timorese smallholders received only one-sixth the price paid in neighbouring West Timor, resulting in an $18 million dollar loss in income to East Timorese growers and the overall economy in that year.[61] Over the course of the occupation, such effective theft resulted in what were undoubtedly many tens of millions of dollars income, and a significant decapitalisation of the East Timorese economy that stunted its development and diversification.

Today, coffee remains East Timor's most important agricultural export commodity, but, as is the case for coffee smallholders throughout the world, it is a poverty crop for East Timorese farmers. This outcome is related not only to Indonesia's stealing of much of the country's coffee wealth during the occupation, but also to larger changes to the global coffee regime during the same period, ones that have resulted in a significant shift in coffee-related income away from producer countries (in the so-called Third World) to the major consumer countries (located in the global North), and ones brought about in no small part by a larger war against the "Third World" that the United States and it allies waged against countries in Asia, Africa, and Latin America – especially those that overtly challenged US and/or Western hegemony. In this regard, East Timor's coffee-related poverty is related to global structures and relationships that, in turn, are very much related to the East Timor-Indonesia conflict, but that extend beyond its confines. As such, reparations – if the goal is to achieve justice for those wronged – must also go beyond the strict boundaries of the conflict, and endeavour to see that those persons, groups, or institutions whose privilege is in part derived from East Timor's victimisation provide amends to those afflicted by their gains. Such an approach embraces the notion that reconciliation and redistributive justice are inextricably linked.[62]

Conclusion

While pragmatism on the part of South African beneficiaries of apartheid *might* potentially lead them to redistribute their privilege, there is little need

[61] *Chega!*, part 7, section 9: 11–14.

[62] This analysis is based on and expanded upon in Joseph Nevins, "Restitution over Coffee: Truth, Reconciliation and Environmental Violence in East Timor," *Political Geography*, Vol. 22, No. 6, August 2003: 677–701.

for the beneficiaries, direct and indirect, of the invasion and occupation of East Timor to do so. They live outside the country's boundaries and, given East Timor's very marginal status in the global political-economy and its relative geographic isolation, they have little to fear from East Timor. As such, the Indonesian elite and its international partners-in-crime have the luxury of forgetting, while the East Timorese population is condemned to remember: they will live with the physical, social, and psychological effects of the war and occupation for decades.[63]

As the violence that erupted in East Timor in April 2006 illustrates, this legacy of injustice makes for a dangerous chemistry. Contributing to this state of injustice is the report's effective burial: Indonesia has dismissed the report; Washington, London and their Western allies have ignored it; and the mainstream media in the West, following the lead of the officialdom, has largely paid it no heed. Soon after the report's release, East Timor's then-president, Xanana Gusmão, and then-foreign minister, José Ramos-Horta, felt compelled to reject the report's recommendations for reparations, as well as its calls for an international tribunal for fear of offending the sensibilities of its giant neighbour and Western backers.[64]

While the Bible says that the truth shall set us free, the aftermath of East Timor's truth commission report illustrates that freedom is often a prerequisite to be able to speak the truth: East Timor's leaders undoubtedly desire an international tribunal and reparations, but they fear the consequences of demanding them, given the political and economic vulnerability of their country. It also shows how immune many of us in wealthy Western countries have become to the truth's allegedly liberating effects.

Disclosure of Western participation in horrors abroad has become almost numbingly common. From American and British involvement in the 1965–66 slaughter of hundreds of thousands in Indonesia, to their long-standing support for the apartheid regime in South Africa, Britain's killing of tens of thousands

---

[63] These scars include the country's deep-seated poverty, the weakness of its state institutions, widespread unemployment, and pervasive socio-psychological trauma. Regarding the latter, according to the results of a study conducted throughout East Timor by the International Rehabilitation Council for Torture Victims (IRCT), ninety-seven percent of interviewees stated that they had experienced at least one traumatic event during the Indonesian occupation. The IRCT classified 34 percent of the respondents as suffering from post-traumatic stress disorder. See J Modvig *et al.*, "Torture and Trauma in Post-Conflict East Timor," *The Lancet*, Vol. 356, Nov. 18, 2000: 1763.

[64] See Jeffrey Kingston, "Balancing Justice and Reconciliation in East Timor," (2006) 38 *Critical Asian Studies*, 271.

in colonial Kenya in the 1950s, and effective US backing of the Guatemalan state's genocide against the indigenous population in the 1970s and 1980s, the documentation is extensive and irrefutable.[65] Yet, it is typically ignored by officialdom, or when forced to confront it, denied or explained away.

Denial or social distancing is not distinctive to those who govern powerful Western countries. What is unique is their ability to determine what becomes public debate on the international level, what information is effectively buried, and thus what we collectively know. As psychologist Judith Herman has observed, "The more powerful the perpetrator, the greater is his prerogative to name and define reality, and the more completely his arguments prevail".[66]

The costs of failing to ensure accountability for the West's crimes and complicity are high – and not only in victimised places such as East Timor. More broadly, it facilitates foreign policies that are all-too-often dismissive of international law. It helps explain why the United States and Britain led the way into the still-unfolding disaster in Iraq, for instance, and are the same external powers most responsible for facilitating Israel's ongoing crimes against the Palestinians.

It is for such reasons that, regardless of the pragmatism of *Chega!*'s recommendations, it is necessary to echo them. They help us to imagine the possibility that not only Suharto, now living in comfortable retirement, but also the likes of Henry Kissinger, Tony Blair, Bill Clinton, and George W Bush might some day be held accountable for their conduct and their ugly legacies, thus forcing policy-makers in Jakarta, Washington, London, and elsewhere to think twice about engaging in or backing state terror abroad again.

Championing the recommendations can also help give greater weight to truth commissions – especially those focusing on international crimes. "If done well", Priscilla Hayner asserts, "a truth commission can change how a country understands and accepts its past, and through that, if it is lucky, helps to

---

[65] See, for example, *Guatemala: Memory of Silence, Report of the Commission for Historical Clarification*, February 1999, available online at http://shr.aaas.org/guatemala/ceh/report/english/toc.html; Caroline Elkins, *Imperial Reckoning: The Untold Story of Britain's Gulag in Kenya*, New York: Owl Books, 2005; and John Roosa, *Pretext for Mass Murder: The September 30th Movement and Suharto's Coup d'État in Indonesia*, Madison, Wisconsin: University of Wisconsin Press, 2006.

[66] Judith Herman, *Trauma and Recovery: The Aftermath of Violence: From Domestic Abuse to Political Terror*, New York: Basic Books, 1997: 8.

fundamentally shape its future".[67] To the extent this is true, we need more truth commissions – especially ones that focus on the crimes of the world's most powerful states – as well as more international judicial proceedings. And to the extent that it is not, it is significantly due to an international context unfavourable to truths which challenge an unjust world order built in large part on colonial and neo-colonial atrocities of which East Timor is one small and painfully enduring example. In this regard, the quest for truth is inextricably linked to the struggle for global justice.

[67] Hayner, above, n.52, 2001: 248.

Human Rights, Justice and Reconciliation in Timor-Leste

Jeff Kingston

Most Timorese have come of age with no experience of living under the rule of law. In the absence of a functioning judiciary there is understandably widespread scepticism about prospects for justice. Despite considerable efforts to establish the rule of law and to nurture an effective judiciary, the human rights situation remains grim. This is a nation with abundant grievances and no redress. Most Timorese families have been wounded by human rights violations and most are still waiting, with increasing resentment and despair, for a reckoning. There are few signs of accountability in this troubled island and to the extent that perpetrators avoid justice, the prospects for reconciliation are fading.

Aniceto Neves, programme manager at Yayasan Hak (Association for Law, Human Rights and Justice) points out that the government of Timor-Leste has acceded to seven international treaties related to human rights since 2003, but has been unable to meet its obligations. On paper the commitment to human rights appears strong, but he says, "At issue is implementing the standards that have been adopted".[1] He says that the police and military have frequently been implicated in human rights violations since independence in 2002 and attributes this to a lack of training, education, and resources. In addition, the weakness of the judicial system and the bias of the judges and prosecution make it extraordinarily difficult to realise justice. In his view, the manipulation of the judiciary by Fretilin, the ruling party, has significantly hindered justice and accountability. Political intervention to block investigations and sideline or delay prosecutions has stifled the development of the judicial system and calls into question whether the government has the political will to enforce the human rights obligations it has assumed. He asks, "How can we say the government respects human rights when it condones violations by promoting impunity for members of government?" In his view, the breakdown of law and order in 2006 and the escalation of gang violence are symptomatic of a failed judicial system.

[1] Interview, 18 December 2006.

The ebbing of respect for formal judicial mechanisms has created a dangerous situation. To restore respect for the justice system, he says, there is a dire need for developing the courage and capacity to prosecute the most serious cases, starting with the ruling political elite, and involving Indonesian's responsible for the crimes and violence surrounding the referendum in 1999. This is unlikely.

The cocoon of impunity and the mounting backlog of cases imperil the development of the judiciary and undermine public confidence in it. There is a need for more effective international assistance in developing the capacity of the judicial system, in addition to greater political will to prosecute elite criminals and reduce political intervention in the courts. The nascent judicial system is at risk of being swamped by high expectations, heavy demand, and low credibility. It is a work in progress that is in some significant ways being overtaken by events.

Justice is necessary to restore dignity to those who suffered gross indignities. Reconciliation is a process that cannot proceed without justice for human rights violations, and justice cannot begin until there is a rule of law enforced by the judicial system and security forces. This paper explores the nexus of justice, human rights and reconciliation in Timor-Leste.

Father Martinho Gusmao, Director of the Justice and Peace Commission in the Catholic Diocese of Bacau, believes there is a political agenda to maintaining a weak judiciary. He says, "This is part of a strategy to close the door on justice".[2] In his view, the government wants to bury the past and lacks political will to pursue justice despite the public's overwhelming desire for accountability. He insists that the CAVR findings will not be forgotten and that the government cannot escape its obligations to meet public expectations for a reckoning.[3] The weak judiciary, he says, has become a convenient excuse for the government. As a result, many people are seeking mediation by traditional and religious leaders, but this is not slaking the people's thirst for justice. By failing to prosecute perpetrators the government has sent the wrong message and encouraged young people to resort to violence and illegal activities. They are emboldened by government-sanctioned impunity. The political leadership has set the tone through its expedient approach to human

---

[2] Interview, 19 December 2006.

[3] For a summary of the testimony of 8,000 East Timorese witnesses who testified before the nation's truth commission and strong recommendations favoring accountability see, *Chega!*: The Report of the Commission for Reception, Truth and Reconciliation in Timor-Leste (CAVR) (CAVR, Dili, 2005), *http://www.etan.org/news/2006/cavr.htm* (last accessed July 21, 2007).

rights violations and what he characterises as an overly zealous concern for reconciliation. By evading and undermining formal mechanisms and institutions, the government bears responsibility for nurturing and sustaining a cycle of impunity. He warns that the government is also stoking vigilantism, because, "What people can't find in the courts they will find on the streets in the form of dark justice".

International Justice?

> Four concepts represent what was missing most from the justice process in East Timor and should, instead, have been its mantra: political will, leadership, management, and accountability. *David Cohen*[4]

There is still widespread desire for international justice and renewed hope in some quarters that the UN may make this possible. UNMIT officials spoke of appointing a special prosecutor to look into the violence in 2006 and examined in detail in the UN Report of the Commission of Inquiry (COI).[5] They also spoke of reopening the Serious Crimes Unit investigation with an eye towards recommending prosecution in Timor-Leste courts, not a hybrid tribunal as suggested in a 2005 report by a UN panel of experts.[6] Given the shortcomings of the Timor-Leste judicial system, many interviewees expressed concern that this doomed the prospects for justice.

In the wake of the 1999 bloodletting, the UN developed hybrid tribunals that shared judicial functions between the UN and the national government.[7] These tribunals combine UN authority, funding, resources, judges, and prosecutors with local participation, creating a process that is potentially more meaningful to the victims, less politically divisive, and more effective in capacity-building. However, East Timor's hybrid tribunal never realised this potential.

---

[4] David Cohen, "Indifference and Accountability: The United Nations and the Politics of International Justice in East Timor" East-West Center Special Reports, No 9 (June 2006), p.111.

[5] Interview, 18 December 2006 with Finn Reske-Nielsen, Deputy Special Representative of the Secretary-General for Governance Support, Development and Humanitarian Coordination, UN Resident and Humanitarian Coordinator, and Eric Huck Gym Tan Deputy Special Representative of the Secretary-General for Timor-Leste, Security Sector Support and Rule of Law. December 18, 2006. The Report of the UN Independent Special Commission of Inquiry for Timor-Leste, (October 2, 2006), hereafter referred to as the COI Report, examines the reasons for and responsibility regarding the eruption of violence in 2006.

[6] Report to the Secretary-General of the Commission of Experts to Review the Prosecution of Serious Violations of Human Rights in Timor-Leste (then East Timor) in 1999 (26 May 2005).

[7] Suzanne Katzenstein, "Hybrid Tribunals: Searching for Justice in East Timor" (2003) 16 *Harvard Human Rights Journal* 245.

This is principally due to Indonesia's failure to cooperate with extradition requests or assist in investigating crimes. In addition, there was insufficient financial support. For example, the UN budget for the hybrid tribunal in East Timor amounted to $6.3 million in 2001 compared to $178 million for the International Criminal Tribunal for Rwanda and $223 million for the International Criminal Tribunal for Yugoslavia in 2002–2003.[8]

Aside from not holding those most responsible for the crimes accountable, the hybrid tribunal also failed to provide minimum standards of due process in the cases that it did try. In general, defenders did not get fair trials or competent defense and now that the tribunal has been shut down, prospects for appeals are uncertain.

The experiment in East Timor has undermined the UN's reputation; the sense of outrage at crimes against humanity that propelled support for justice at any cost was superseded by a penurious approach that casts doubt on the entire enterprise.[9] Is such tainted justice worth pursuing? If those most responsible for these crimes are not held accountable and only those from the lower echelons are prosecuted without a competent defence, what messages are being sent and what lessons learned? This sorry state of affairs has stoked justified and widespread scepticism about pursuing justice in the courts, and has undermined efforts to restore respect for the rule of law.

David Cohen calls on the UN to learn the lessons of the failures and shortcomings of the Special Panels for Serious Crimes (SPSC), the so-called hybrid tribunal.[10] He highlights the failure of capacity-building, the flawed jurisprudence, the inadequate defence counsel, cronyism in staffing, language obstacles, a lack of proper leadership, and inadequate resources.[11]

---

[8] As of November 2005, the International Criminal Court for Rwanda had spent a total of $1 billion while handing down a mere 25 judgements.

[9] For a scathing assessment, see David Cohen, " Seeking Justice on the Cheap: Is the East Timor Tribunal Really a Model for the Future?" (2002) *Asia Pacific Issues* No 61 (August 2002).

[10] Cohen, above, n.4.

[11] For a comparison of the origins, verdicts and impact of the Serious Crimes Panel for East Timor and the Indonesian Human Rights Court see SD Roper and LA Barria, "Assessing the Record of Justice: A Comparison of Mixed International Tribunals versus Domestic Mechanisms for Human Rights Enforcement" (2005) 4 *Journal of Human Rights* 521. The authors also focus on the shortcomings of these alternatives to International Criminal Tribunals and conclude that those responsible for the violence have not been brought to justice. However they find some redeeming benefits in the judicial training involved in the process.

Reverend Augustinho de Vasconselos, who serves on the CAVR, echoes the views of many Timorese in complaining that leaving justice to the courts of Timor-Leste means letting Indonesian perpetrators off the hook and perpetuating the injustice that only Timorese face accountability.[12] He continues to insist on an international tribunal because only such a proceeding will be credible and impartial. In order to restore public faith in justice, he calls for "shock therapy", meaning convictions of high-ranking perpetrators. Given the state of the Timor-Leste judiciary and the climate of intimidation and political intervention, he believes that only an international tribunal can provide the needed therapy. Joachim de Fonseca agrees that nothing will happen with the CAVR recommendations and SCU investigations unless the UN takes full responsibility and commits adequate resources to pursuing judicial redress.[13] Otherwise Indonesian perpetrators will continue to enjoy immunity.

Ousted PM Alkatiri spoke of the need to be realistic and told me that an international tribunal is a dream and one that is unlikely to come true given the reluctance of the international community to support such an initiative.[14]

President Gusmao has criticised the CAVR report for embracing what he terms "grandiose idealism" and the insistence on prosecution, retribution, and reparations.[15] He believes that rigorous prosecution may perpetuate cleavages and place human rights and peace at risk. He also maintains that it is not possible for the government to pursue justice given the absence of international support for such an endeavor. Dwelling on this agonising past carries the risk of finding reasons in old grievances for renewed violence. In his view, the priority must be on a process of reconciliation and healing the wounds of a traumatised society.

Current President Jose Ramos-Horta shares Xanana Gusmao's (his predecessor) emphasis on reconciliation. He rhetorically asked me, in 2005 when he was serving as Foreign Minister:

> Why didn't the UN establish a tribunal here back in 1999 when they had 7,000 PKO here who could have arrested the culprits in West Timor? There

[12] Interview, 19 December 2006.

[13] Interview, 20 December 2006. Fonseca serves as Assessor, Office of the Prime Minister, Office of the Advisor on Human Rights. He took this position in July 2006 after serving as Director of Yayasan HAK, a human rights NGO.

[14] Interview, 19 December 2006.

[15] Interview with President Xanana Gusmao, 16 December 2005. All quotes and attributions draw from this interview. This and following few paragraphs draw on Jeff Kingston, "Balancing Justice and Reconciliation in East Timor" (2006) 38 *Critical Asian Studies* 271.

> is not much we can do to bring Indonesians to trial by ourselves. This isn't only pragmatism. I sincerely believe that Indonesia is making progress on democratic reforms and strengthening the rule of law. However this takes a long time and the situation is fragile. SBY (President Susilo Bambang Yudhoyono) is weak and does not fully control the military and can't challenge them in this way without risking that his opponents would gang up on him. It is important that we do not destabilize the slow process of democratization in Indonesia because it is our best guarantee. They have shown the courage to accept our independence. Knowing that the situation is so difficult and that the UN Security Council doesn't want an International Tribunal it doesn't make sense for us to pursue it.[16]

Eduardo Gonzalez, Senior Associate at the International Center for Transitional Justice (ICTJ), observes:

> The geopolitical setting has changed dramatically since 9/11. Now Indonesia is a valued ally in the global war on terror. Because of that there is little inclination in the international community to press Indonesia hard on what happened in 1999. Sadly, such geopolitical considerations create double standards of justice.[17]

Unlike East Timor's leaders, he strongly supports prosecution of perpetrators, arguing that the failure to do so erodes the quality of independence and democracy in East Timor.[18]

A Dili-based US diplomat said that Xanana Gusmao has set a "terrible precedent" in emphasising reconciliation at the expense of justice. His desire to improve relations with Indonesia "makes sense", but this "creates a long-term dilemma for East Timor".

Helena Cobban succinctly states the case against international tribunals in Foreign Policy, raising important questions about whether such courts facilitate peace, justice and human rights, and if they deter future war crimes.[19] However, she also correctly insists that it is important to listen to the survivors

---

[16] Interview with Foreign Minister Jose Ramos-Horta, 13 December 2005.

[17] Interview, 28 December 2005.

[18] In Bacau, I spoke with a man on 22 December 2006 who echoed these remarks, asking, "If we don't pursue justice for what these people did to us, how can we be sure the government won't do the same to us?"

[19] Helena Cobban, "International Courts" (March/April 2006) *Foreign Policy* 22.

of atrocities and address their concerns rather than imposing international agendas. In Timor-Leste the people have made their wishes clear both in front of the truth commission and in media polls – they want formal prosecution of those suspected of serious crimes against humanity.

Former President Gusmao thinks this is unwise and told me in 2005 that he is inspired by the example of South Africa where amnesty was exchanged for truth.[20] Truth commissions may facilitate impunity but they do guard against collective amnesia. Moreover, they can induce a healing catharsis, but only if the testimonies are forthright and accepted by the victims as a credible account of what they experienced.

Chega!, the CAVR's final report represents a start, giving voice to the victims and establishing a historical record for this horrible epoch. However, it is an incomplete record because those most responsible for orchestrating the atrocities from Indonesia have not yet testified. Moreover, many of those indicted by the Serious Crimes Unit have not been prosecuted

CAVR Reconsidered

What a difference six months makes. In December 2005 in interviews I conducted with top political leaders including then President Xanana Gusmao and Foreign Minister Jose Ramos-Horta, the findings and recommendations of the CAVR report were dismissed as "grandiose idealism". *Chega!* was not warmly welcomed by a leadership that clearly values reconciliation over accountability.[21] Both Gusmao and Ramos-Horta emphasised the need to build strong relations with Indonesia and were very public with their reservations about pursuing justice. There was widespread disappointment among many Timorese that their leaders had unnecessarily conceded too much to the perpetrators of serious crimes, and doubts were expressed that reconciliation without justice was either desirable or viable. There were concerns that not holding perpetrators accountable would send the wrong message and would encourage further violence and retribution.

The violence that erupted in the late spring of 2006 demonstrated the costs of sanctioning impunity. In the wake of this mayhem, the political leadership has

[20] Eduardo Gonzalez of the ICTJ notes that relatively few of those who testified at South Africa's Truth Commission received amnesty because criteria were very strict. Interview, 28 December 2005.
[21] For further analysis of justice and reconciliation drawing on interviews with President Gusmao and PM Jose Ramos-Horta, see Jeffrey Kingston, "Balancing Justice and Reconciliation in East Timor", above, n.15; and Jeff Kingston, "Regaining Dignity: Justice and Reconciliation in East Timor (2003) 13 *Brown Journal of World Affairs* 227.

changed its tune on the CAVR report, and now extols its embrace of justice and accountability as a necessary step towards reconciliation. Pat Walsh argues that this about face is driven by political turmoil and the belated recognition that promoting the conclusions of the CAVR can strengthen the basis for reconciliation, human rights, and community confidence-building measures. Referring to the descent into violence in 2006, Walsh said, "We've seen the consequences of the absence of accountability". Political leaders discovered that they cannot easily give away people's right to seek justice nor stifle their desire for accountability.

Former PM Mari Alkatiri confided he had been wrong to downplay the need for a reckoning, and at the end of 2006 said he supports the conclusions and recommendations of the CAVR report but, as noted above, does not expect the international community to support an international tribunal.[22] The public about face of Alkatiri, Gusmao and Ramos-Horta provides vindication to members of the CAVR, but they and others want these leaders to follow through with concrete actions. When the CAVR travelled throughout the country collecting testimony from some 8,000 witnesses to the horrors they endured between 1975–1999, it raised the hopes of victims, and their communities, for justice. These expectations have turned into disappointment and resignation, as it is evident to everyone that in terms of government priorities, the dictates of reconciliation have trumped accountability. The CAVR provided a false hope to a people who have become inured to their dismal fate, but still have a need for justice.

I visited a coffee-farming area at the end of 2006 and spoke with one of the farmers and the man who organised them into a cooperative. This Japanese-sponsored venture nearly collapsed because the organiser had not reckoned with history, and had included farmers who had committed various crimes against their neighbours during the Indonesian era. After independence, these farmers has been ostracised from the community and forced to build their own hamlet, visible across the valley. When they were allowed into the cooperative, the other farmers withdrew; reconciliation was not going to come so easily and without a reckoning. The cooperative then regrouped and now only includes the pro-independence farmers and those who they approve.

I discussed the CAVR process with one of the cooperative's farmers and he wondered why nothing had happened to the perpetrators. He and others had given testimony with the expectation that the accused would go to jail. In his

[22] Interview with Dr Mari Alkatiri, 19 December 2006.

mind, testifying was the same as convicting and it was hard for him to understand why the authorities were taking no action. Indeed, many find the short-circuiting of justice unfathomable and feel betrayed. For them, it is not a matter of disseminating the findings of the CAVR, currently the focus of the CAVR secretariat. They lived through and endured the findings, know who committed crimes, and want to see the malefactors pay. Time has not healed the anguish or dampened the desire for retribution. There is disappointment that the Indonesian perpetrators seem out of reach, but bitter incomprehension that Timorese who committed crimes and remain in the communities have not been held accountable. There seems to have been relatively little resort to vigilante justice, but it could be a time bomb, as people see their hopes for formal justice fade.

Under such circumstances it is little wonder that there is no faith in justice in Timor-Leste and the good intentions of the CAVR have roiled more than calmed communities by raising and then failing to meet expectations for justice.

UN Redux

There are good reasons why the collective mantra in the UN these days is to promise less and deliver more. There is a consensus in Timor-Leste and the international community that the UN left too soon. Finn Reske-Nielsen, who served as Acting Senior Representative of the Secretary General for UNMIT until mid-December 2006, spoke of a collective naivete about the difficulties of nation-building and over-confidence about how much progress had been made when the UN oversaw the transition to independence in May 2002.[23] He said:

> The fundamental problem was that everyone, including me, underestimated the time required to guide post-conflict Timor to a stable and firm footing. We were way too optimistic in 2002.

At the time, he pointed out, the international community had a lot on its plate, including Haiti, Sudan, and Lebanon and as a result Timor-Leste did not get the sustained assistance it needed. According to him, Secretary-General Kofi Annan publicly acknowledged that the UN had left too soon, and everyone involved with the UN mission at that time feels responsible for letting the Timorese down. The establishment of UNMIT in August, 2006 is, he said, recognition of both the UN's earlier failure and its responsibility to address the unfinished business of nation-building.

---

[23] Interview, 18 December 2006.

The problem, Fiske-Nielsen said, is that the government of Timor-Leste lacks the capacity to deliver on its broader plans and policies. One of the important lessons from the UN experience in Timor-Leste, he added, is the need for simplicity and decentralisation. In the past, he acknowledged that the UN tried to formulate programmes based on the highest standards, creating unrealistic policies given the context of limited capacity and human resources. It is clear that programmes and policies that are "good enough" are preferable to "best practices" that cannot be delivered. The key, he says, is to provide and gradually improve basic services. He laments that by all criteria people are worse off now than when the UN took over the task of nation-building. He says there is sufficient funding to implement necessary programmes to improve people's standard of living, but the key is sensibly spending this money. This depends on promoting greater decentralisation and greater involvement of local communities in designing and delivering services.

Aniceto Neves of Yayasan HAK (Association for Law, Human Rights and Justice) says that the premature departure of the UN left the judicial system vulnerable to political manipulation.[24] In his opinion, had the UN stayed longer and nurtured stronger government institutions, including the judicial system, it would have been possible to lessen the overt political control of the judiciary that has brought it into such disrepute. This missed opportunity by the UN has been a critical factor in undermining public faith in the judicial system.

It is clear that the UN presence serves as a lightning rod. They are criticised all around for what they did do (did not do), are criticised for leaving too soon, and criticised on their return for not making faster progress in the midst of political turmoil. Clearly the detractors have some compelling arguments, but on the other hand, with a few exceptions there is a consensus that an imperfect UN mission is better than none at all. And, the UN presence facilitated peaceful and fair elections in 2007. In a society where cleavages are deep and peace is fragile, the UN is a reassuring presence that may not always live up to high expectations, but does make a significantly positive difference. The UN officials I interviewed were chastened and eager to seize this new opportunity to get it right. The renewal of UNMIT's mandate in February 2007 reflects the international community's strong support and recognition that it needs to help address the still fragile and volatile security, political, social, and humanitarian situation.

---

[24] Interview, 18 December 2006.

Political Will and Justice

> "The problems in the Timor-Leste court system run deep, and securing justice for crimes in 2006 may prove as difficult as for the violence that wracked the country in 1999." *International Crisis Group*[25]

Maria Vasconselos, the Acting Director of the Judicial System Monitoring Programme (JSMP), told me that as a practising lawyer, often as a public defender, she is frustrated with a minimally functioning judicial system, one that has capacity to accomplish much more than it does.[26] She has tried to bring her own case to court – she was burned out of her house in 1999 and 2006 and has evidence against the perpetrators – but is always told by court officers to wait because they are "too busy". Thus, even those who are well connected to the legal system and know the ropes are frozen out. She shakes her head in disbelief about the excuse of being "too busy", saying that the courts are usually empty and not in session. For her, it is not so much a case of capacity as it is of political will. She is baffled at the lack of progress in creating a functional judiciary and wonders why the international and local judges are not doing more and why the prosecution seems stuck in low gear.

Expectations for justice have not been met because of a lack of political will to vigorously pursue justice regardless of status or borders. Everywhere people complain that there is no justice for the elite, only for the common people. People openly complain that those who have good political connections and who commit crimes need not fear justice.

Joaquim da Fonseca, the government advisor on human rights, asks, "How can we talk of human rights in East Timor? Respect for human rights requires the proper context and we do not have that".[27] Fonseca admits feeling more influential as an outside critic where there are many channels to exercise influence whereas inside government he is isolated by his lack of political ties and constrained in what he can say because of his position. He rues the weakness of his office in the face of other ministries all asserting their own competing agendas and claims on limited resources. In trying to promote greater attention to human rights issues at cabinet meetings, he confesses frustration at hearing the "echo of one hand clapping".

---

[25] International Crisis Group, Asia Report No 120, 10 October 2006, p.17.
[26] Interview, 20 December 2006.
[27] Interview, 20 December 2006.

The justice system suffers from a credibility gap because it is widely believed to be under the control of the ruling party, Fretilin.[28] Weak procedures and weak implementation fuels the impression that the system is rigged. Blatant political manipulation of the justice system discredits it in the public's eyes. Fonseca laments that, "Equality before the law is not fully observed. Those with political importance are given privileged treatment". And so a jaded public grows more jaded, hoping for a justice that does not come.

I arrived in Dili shortly after the proceedings against Rogerio Lobato, the Interior Minister under PM Alkatiri, were postponed. The postponement of this widely anticipated trial was on everyone's minds and was taken as a barometer of the ruling political elite's willingness to prosecute their own; political interference in the trial was expected and the postponement was all the proof anyone needed.

Lobato was accused of providing weapons to hit squads for use against political opponents and Dr Alkatiri's ouster from office on June 26, 2006 is popularly ascribed to his knowledge of, and acquiescence to, this weapons transfer. President Gusmao forced the issue after he had seen damning evidence of Dr Alkatiri's complicity.

Fonseca, like everyone else in Dili, seemed to expect that Lobato's alleged co-conspirator, ousted Prime Minister Mari Alkatiri, would not be prosecuted.[28A] Alas, in the court of public opinion, Dr Alkatiri has already been found guilty so the justice system received yet another black eye by exonerating him in early February 2007.

Fonseca described the high profile Rogerio Lobato case as a golden opportunity for the government to restore some credibility to the judicial system. If the ruling class can convict one of its own, he asserted, it would go a long way in reassuring the people that justice is not only for the poor and powerless. The trial against the former Interior Minister resumed in January 2007, and in March he was found guilty and sentenced to seven and a half years in prison. In addition to the weapons transfer charges Lobato, still deputy chairman of Fretilin, was also found criminally negligent in the deaths of nine policemen, killed by soldiers in Dili, on 24 May 2006. As of writing, his judicial fate remains uncertain.

---

[28] *ibid.*

[28A] *ibid.*

One diplomat told me that the habits and inclinations of the political elite were formed during the long struggle for independence. Due the exigencies of the time, they did what they had to do and there was no recourse to formal mechanisms of justice. Among the current leadership, she says there is a:

> gravitational pull away from going through the institutions and formal processes and when faced with obstacles there is a continued inclination to go outside the system and work informally.

These inclinations, and impatience with working through an imperfect system, undermine the development of government institutions and formal mechanisms. She adds:

> When push comes to shove, if the leaders can't go through formal channels they tend to fall back on informal solutions and personal networks. This practice doesn't allow institutions to develop and undermines them at every stage.

There is concern that the "court of public opinion" is a dangerous factor because there is little popular knowledge about, or commitment to abstract principles of law. There is no presumption of innocence and little appreciation for rules of evidence or legal procedures. Courts are seen as public forum to confirm guilt and mete out punishment.

This situation requires public education about the role of law and respect for judicial mechanisms. Any such efforts face a significant obstacle given the desperation for "justice" and the thirst for retribution; the desire for results trumps all other concerns.

Judicial Training Centre

Outside of UN staff, it is hard to find anyone expressing a positive opinion about the work of the JTC. There is a consensus that judicial training is a priority for a country desperately trying to build a judicial system from scratch under extremely difficult circumstances. Since it began operating in 2001, the JTC has recorded impressive statistics, but according to Aniceto Neves, the quality is not there.

International legal professionals have had to play a major role in all aspects of the judicial system because of the lack of human resources. Critics suggest that overall the level of these international legal professionals ranges from poor to mediocre with a few brilliant exceptions. One of the factors frequently cited is the limiting of the pool of applicants to those fluent in Portuguese, one of the national languages (Tetum is the other).

Language is a major issue, as most Timorese legal professionals are not fluent in Portuguese and the focus of much of their legal training has been on developing language abilities rather than knowledge of the law. The problems of the language barrier were evident when all of the Timorese judges who sat a qualifying exam in 2005 failed.

David Cohen observes:

> This event suggests the complete ineffectiveness of five years of UN support for the justice system of East Timor. The failure of every single one of the judges, prosecutors, and public defenders in a minimum competency examination is itself an indictment of the UN and Timorese government's joint efforts at capacity building in the judiciary.[29]

Cohen further argues that political considerations may have been more important than language skills in the collective failure. There is a widespread sense that the exam was not graded impartially and that certain of the judges in question had excellent track records in the courts and compared favourably to some of the international judges. Cohen asserts and local sources confirm, that Fretilin has tried to "stack" the courts and ensure a pliable judiciary.[30] In doing so in such an obvious way, however, it reinforces the sense that the courts are not independent and are bastions of political bias and favoritism. In addition, by calling into question the professional qualifications and competence of these judges, and all of the other local court actors, inevitably there are now doubts about the outcomes of the cases in which they were involved.

Commission on Truth and Friendship (CTF)

In an attempt to get Indonesian perpetrators to add their testimony to the record, the CTF was launched in the summer of 2005 with Indonesia covering two thirds of expenses.[31] Political leaders in both nations hope that by establishing a common, conclusive truth about what happened in Timor-Leste in 1999, that Indonesia and Timor-Leste will be able to put the past behind them and move forward without further recrimination. However, there is widespread concern among Timorese that the CTF emphasises reaching closure, has no judicial mandate, and only ensures impunity for ranking

---

[29] Cohen, above, n.4, at p.94.

[30] Interview, Aniceto Neves, Yayaysan HAK, 18 December 2006.

[31] The official website is *www.ctf-ri-tl.org*. See also ETAN webiste for critical commentary on the CTF, *http://etan.org/timor/default.htm*.

perpetrators. Under its terms of reference, the CTF can make recommendations for amnesty that must be approved by the Timor-Leste Parliament.

The CTF's mandate has been extended to early 2008. In its first 12 months it did not hold a single public hearing, called no witnesses, and failed to issue a progress report on its review and evaluation of the evidence presented by the CAVR or the SCU. This lack of transparency and progress sparked widespread criticism of the CTF. Many critics see no reason to continue with a charade aimed at providing Indonesian perpetrators with immunity from prosecution.

In February 2007, the CTF held its first of five hearings and it called some 70 witnesses in a series of hearings up to June 2007 aimed at reconciling former foes and getting beyond recrimination. The first high-profile witness to testify was former Foreign Minister Ali Alitas, long the most prominent apologist for Indonesia's occupation of Timor-Leste during the Suharto era. He claimed he was unaware of evidence that the Indonesian military was behind most of the 1999 slaughter, and blamed Australia for being overzealous in sending troops to calm the strife. Performances like this – hedged and misleading more than forthright – and significant differences in the type of questioning by commissioners from both nations, led to a disappointing outcome. The question is how to establish the truth if those testifying are less than brutally honest.

The Timorese commissioners are disappointed in the exercise. Commissioner Aniceto Guterres from Timor-Leste described the initial session as "imperfect". He said:

> Actually, if you take a closer look there are still differences between Indonesia's commissioners and East Timor's. When all the information is gathered and we formulate the substance of our report, that will be a problem.[32]

There are strong doubts about whether the truth alone will be enough to promote reconciliation without further prosecution of those responsible for human rights abuses and other crimes.

The Timor-Leste commissioners face significant political pressures at home and know that the findings of the CTF and its recommendations for amnesty

---

[32] 20 February 2007, The West.

will come under critical scrutiny. The Church, the CAVR Secretariat, and civil society organisations have repudiated the CTF and thus if it is to have any credibility it must come up with the goods – truthful and comprehensively forthright testimony by the witnesses – considered in light of the evidence collected by the SCU in its indictments and the rulings of Indonesia's *ad hoc* Human Rights Court.[33]

Critics believe that the ten-member commission's main task is to improve bilateral relations rather than find the truth and promote justice. John Miller of the East Timor Action Network refers to the CTF as a "whitewash", while Father Gusmao dismisses it as an exercise in "collective amnesia". He says the problem is not that Timor-Leste needs state-sponsored reconciliation with Indonesia, rather Timorese people need justice for the crimes committed, and this means holding perpetrators accountable for their actions and choices.

Fonseca, Ramos-Horta's human rights advisor, says the arguments in favor of the CTF are deeply flawed and it is a "farce". It will not produce conclusive proof or credible accountability and he believes that the TNI (Indonesian military) will emerge as the only beneficiary. The leadership in Dili, he says, has frankly admitted that the CTF is a political tool to achieve reconciliation and does not serve the justice system in any way. In his view, the parallels that President Gusmao draws with postponed justice for General Augusto Pinochet are not valid. He says, "We are in a completely different situation. Years from now we won't have control over the Indonesian generals". He adds that the global political situation does not favour accountability for serious violations of human rights, pointing to the watered down human rights bodies of the UN.

Walsh and Reverend Vasconselos from the CAVR believe that the CTF will not close the window on justice because the public rejects it; there is no popular support for a rush to closure, especially given a lack of credible accountability by those deemed most responsible for the most serious crimes.

The Asia Foundation's Kim Hunter also doubts that the CTF will deliver the truth and without that it is hard to imagine it promoting real friendship. She suggests that the CTF is inadvertently useful in keeping the issue of accountability alive and high on the radar screen of public discourse, confounding government efforts to reach premature closure.

---

[33] See Roper and Barria, above, n.11. Ten high-ranking Indonesian perpetrators out of 17 defendants were found guilty in this court, but the verdicts were subsequently overturned by the Supreme Court.

Newly elected President Ramos-Horta gave his endorsement to the CTF and praised its work but he is a lonely voice in Dili. The end of the hearings in June vindicated the critics because the Indonesian witnesses did not provide credible testimony, and instead tried to shift blame onto the UN for the violence in 1999. This outcome was expected, but as a consequence, the path towards reconciliation has grown much steeper. There is little hope that the extension of the mandate to early 2008 will enable the CTF to retrieve any credibility or promote reconciliation.

The problem with truth commissions, despite their proliferation, is that the findings and process don't promote reconciliation. Public opinion polls in South Africa, arguably the most famous and "successful" truth commission, indicated that two thirds of the public was angrier about the past after the process concluded.[34] The search for a unifying *truth* is elusive, opens old wounds, and raises expectations that finding out what happened to whom and why will lead to consequences for the perpetrators. Public disappointment with the lack of government action on the findings of the CAVR indicates that the truth has not set the Timorese free, nor created a consensus about forgiving those who committed crimes if they are not held accountable.

Amnesty in exchange for testimony is not always acceptable to those affected by the crimes. It must meet very strict criteria or run the risk of discrediting the process. The CTF's conditions for amnesty are not clear, and the granting of immunity may spark recrimination rather than contribute to a healing process. There is also a danger, as in Guatamala, that the results of truth commissions can be ignored and drop off the political agenda.[35]

Timor-Leste is a new state and has limited capacities, enormous problems, and competing agendas. The CTF can only help the Timorese turn the page if it sheds more light on the planning by Indonesian military commanders, their Timorese militias, and Indonesian government officials for the referendum in 1999 that led to the widespread violence; what they knew about this violence as it escalated; and how they responded to the situation as it evolved. And, naturally, in looking at what happened, people will be eager to learn why it happened and why it was allowed to happen.

Truth commissions do not usually individualise responsibility, whereas the investigations and indictments prepared by the SCU under UN auspices have

---

[34] For this statistic and an assessment of truth commissions, see J Tepperman, "Truth and Consequences", (2002) 81 *Foreign Affairs* 128.

[35] *ibid*.

fingered individuals who have testified at the CTF. To the extent that the CTF process "trumps" the SCU process and the CAVR recommendations, justice, human rights and reconciliation in Timor-Leste stand to suffer. Under such circumstances it is hard to imagine a social consensus advocating harmony and creating greater trust within Timor-Leste and with Indonesia.[36] There should be no rush to closure on a tight timetable according to political dictates. It is clear that such an initiative is doomed because it is out of synch with public opinion in Timor-Leste and does not reflect the Timorese desire for accountability. Xanana Gusmao may be right that given all the current problems associated with poverty and inadequate governance, finding something approaching justice in a courtroom is neither a priority or viable – at least for now. The window on justice remains open, and for now the task is to assemble as complete a record as possible to prepare for the time when the constellations of opportunity, circumstance, and political will come into alignment.

Truth commissions are imperfect because they emerge from imperfect situations and flawed compromises, Thus they can be most helpful as a step in a longer process, rather than serving as an end to the search for justice. In the case of Timor-Leste, given the current reluctance of the international community to back an international tribunal, the choice is not between the CTF and trials, it is the alternative to doing nothing. On its own, Timor-Leste cannot force the Indonesian government to prosecute its own perpetrators, nor ensure their extradition to face trial in Dili. What it can do is place the onus on the international community to eventually support an international tribunal by demonstrating good faith and exhausting available alternatives such as the CTF.

Reconciliation

The lack of justice is the major obstacle to reconciliation among Timorese and between Timor-Leste and Indonesia. Victims feel frustrated that those who harmed them have not been held accountable and are demoralised that the prospects for justice are remote given the state of the judicial system. Having no recourse against perpetrators leaves victims feeling that their human rights have been doubly violated.

Maria Vasconselos, the Acting Director of the Judicial System Monitoring Program (JSMP), told me that the absence of accountability and the failures

---

[36] For a discussion of how truth commissions can nurture trust, see A Boraine, "Transitional Justice: A Holistic Interpretation", (2006) 60 *Journal of International Affairs* 17.

of the judicial system to dispense justice is creating a social malaise that undermines the foundations of civil society. Many Timorese are disappointed in the government's emphasis on reconciliation and wonder when if ever they can look forward to justice.

Whether or not justice postponed is justice lost remains to be seen. The Church and civil society organisations will continue to give a voice to the victims and lobby for justice. They are keeping the issue of accountability alive and preserving an option important for many traumatised victims.

Modest satisfaction for victims entails recognition of their suffering, acceptance of responsibility by Indonesia, clear signs of contrition and atonement, and cultivating a common historical memory of what happened in Timor-Leste in the final quarter of the twentieth century.

Reconciliation is difficult because the aggressor nation must humble itself by acknowledging wrongdoing and demonstrating sincere contrition in ways that confront national pride and identity.[37] Germany demonstrates that this is possible and beneficial, Japan that it is difficult, but decidedly problematic if neglected. The onus is on Indonesia; reconciliation will depend on its political choices and actions. However, the Timorese must also be ready to accept meaningful, symbolic gestures of responsibility and atonement that will fall short of a full reckoning.[38] Reconciliation thus also requires the wronged nation to act with restraint such that the victimising nation can atone while retaining some dignity.

Ultimately, the ongoing failure of justice in Timor-Leste and the recent violence serve as an indictment of the international community and bestow a responsibility to facilitate both reconciliation and justice. As elsewhere around the world, those who bear the greatest responsibility for human rights violations are the least likely to face accountability. This is not an encouraging basis for reconciliation and unlikely to address even the most modest needs of

[37] For further discussion of reconciliation issues, see JW Yamazaki, *Japanese Apologies for World War II: A Rhetorical Study* (Routledge, London, 2005); S Saaler, *Politics Memory and Public Opinion: The History Textbook Controversy and Japanese Society* (Deutsches Institut fur Japanstudien, Munich, 2005); and A Horvat, "Overcoming the Negative Legacy of the Past: Why Europe is a Positive Example for East Asia" in (2004) 11 *Brown Journal of World Affairs* 137.

[38] In this context, to facilitate reconciliation there is a "need" for high profile convictions of Indonesian perpetrators. The UN suggests a targeting of prosecutions focusing on those most responsible for the most serious crimes. See Report of the Secretary-General, "The Rule of Law and Transitional Justice in Conflict and Post-Conflict Societies" (23 August 2004) S/2004/616*.

victims. It is important to recognise that it is not too late – the evidence has been gathered and is available – and that the window of opportunity remains open. Targeted prosecution of those who orchestrated excesses can send a powerful message to perpetrators and victims. A collective shrug of the shoulders is equally eloquent.

Realists dismiss efforts at international justice as a "false hope", and certainly Timorese know all too well what it is like to be forsaken, but they patiently await a reckoning. Why not? For 24 years under Indonesian occupation, these people nurtured a "false hope" for self-determination against the odds, and in the end managed to prevail over pragmatism and power. As both nations consolidate democracy and the rule of law, the basis for a reckoning may improve. This trend merits sustained and generous international support.[39] The failures of justice in Timor-Leste are obstacles to reconciliation among a people hungry for justice and do not justify abandoning efforts to get it right. Regaining dignity for Indonesia and the people of Timor-Leste hangs in the balance.

Alexander Boraine, who was a key player in the South African Truth Commission, reminds us that in the search for justice and reconciliation it is not an either/or situation and that the balancing of these imperatives must be informed by the "political space for accountability".[40] Pursuing accountability cannot ignore the limits of a fragile emerging democracy as in Timor-Leste, but neither can this search be abandoned without undermining and distorting the nation-building process. Reconciliation at all costs is a recipe for disaster, a course that would bankrupt the government's credibility while denying victims redress and the dignity this confers.

Prospects

In his remarks to the UN Security Council in February 2007, then Prime Minister Jose Ramos-Horta explained that, "... the violence of today was part of a collective trauma deriving from the violence of the country's past".[41] To achieve justice, he spoke of a, "... two-fold battle: delivery of quick, efficient and impartial justice; and the long-term endeavor of forming a judicial system from scratch". In his view, the key is "dedicated and disciplined institution

[39] Call argues that international justice can be redeemed and is essential to a stable and just global order. CT Call, "The Future of Transitional Justice", (2004) 11 *Brown Journal of World Affairs*, 101.
[40] Boraine, above, n.36.
[41] UN Security Council SC/8952, 12 February 2007.

building", a task measured in decades rather than years. He chided the UN for its hasty downsizing in 2002, saying that, "... even a Manhattan take-out restaurant needed at least a year or two to establish itself; it was reasonable to think it would take much longer to build a nation".

Timor-Leste shows that there are no quick fixes in nation-building or in addressing the problems of post-conflict nations. Timorese are still traumatised and scarred by the collective experience of degradation, fear, and loss under a brutal Indonesian occupation from 1975 to 1999. Most Timorese have no experience with the rule of law and have been influenced by the ways and means of military occupation. Systematic violence and abuse of civil liberties and human rights was the norm that shaped the Timorese people. Richard Lloyd-Parry, Asia Editor for *The Times*, likens Timor-Leste to an abused person who has been locked up and beaten over nearly three decades, one that is collectively suffering from post-traumatic stress syndrome.[42] The eruptions of violence in contemporary Timor-Leste are part of the Indonesian legacy. History is not destiny but it does powerfully influence inclinations, options, and choices.

Achieving independence in 2002 was a dream come true that has fallen well short of popular expectations. The struggle for self-determination was a unifying experience that focused on ousting a common enemy. Now the Timorese are grappling with all of the divisions and competing agendas that were suppressed for so long, as the go through the convulsions of nation-building. The leaders who led the struggle for freedom are also facing tasks and demands to which they are not accustomed, and in some important ways may not be well-suited. The shining promise of independence has not delivered a better life for many, and their frustrations can be seen in the piles of burning tyres and barricades sprinkled around Dili on the eve of presidential elections in 2007. The political leadership also faces the problems of reining in their own inclinations, honed as freedom fighters, and also those of the opportunists who are swelling the ranks of political parties. This is a fragile transition era of nation-building when much has been achieved, but even more remains to be done in trying conditions, where impatience for results vies with the need for patient institution-building and cultivating of good governance.

Timor-Leste was left to fend for itself far too soon by the international community, and has paid the cost in terms of mediocre governance and an upsurge in violence. According to the UNDP, welfare among the people has

---

[42] Lecture at Temple University, Japan Campus, 22 February 2007.

declined since independence. Poverty remains endemic; some 20 percent of the nation's one million citizens live on less than $1 a day.[43] These are all signs of a faltering state, one that is perilously close to the abyss. And yet, in some important ways, President Ramos-Horta is right in pointing out that there have been important successes against high odds. And he is also right in describing as Herculean the challenges facing Timor-Leste. The problem is that the successes have not been in the justice sector, have not improved the human rights situation, and have had a very limited impact on reconciliation.

Fonseca, the government's human rights advisor, agrees, saying that, "The number one human rights problem affecting Timor-Leste is the lack of justice and accountability. It is so serious that it weakens public administration". There is no deterrent to crime, and so it spins out of control because, "The culture of impunity has entered into the consciousness of the people".[44]

The problem is that the process of establishing a judicial system from scratch is being overtaken by events and burdened with a growing backlog of cases. The court system provides no redress to victims and it thus has a long uphill battle to regain public trust. Ineffective law enforcement and a dysfunctional court system nurture a sense of impunity and encourage "street justice". Those who are arrested also confront a lack of justice and infringement on their human rights. Fonseca admits that detainees are poorly treated and often languish in prison waiting for a trial date that never comes. The denial of lawyer visits and due process are also breaches of their constitutional rights. In addition, police frequently abuse their powers of detention.

It is hard to escape the conclusion that the prospects for justice in Timor-Leste are remote. My interviews produced a staggering set of obstacles that include the following: politicisation of the judicial system; the lack of established judicial procedures; the lack of human resources; the questionable quality of international judicial assistance; the failure to prioritise cases; the inadequacy of the Judicial Training Centre; low respect for human rights; gender bias; institutional mediocrity in the UN; and the lack of commitment to abstract principles of law and due process among the police. In addition, it is difficult and dangerous to prosecute in the absence of a witness protection programme.

Aniceto Neves of Yayasan HAK notes that, "People think it is a waste of time to go to court. They know they need to solve the problem by themselves".[45]

---

[43] For recent UNDP figures, see *http://www.laohamutuk.org/reports/06HDIslips.htm*.

[44] Interview, 20 December 2007. Following quotes for Fonseca also draw on this interview.

[45] Interview, 18 December 2006.

In some respects the failure of the judicial system has opened up space for civil society organisations to step in, mediate, and promote dispute resolution. However, the sheer magnitude of the needs overwhelms the capacity to provide such services.

The Church is perhaps the strongest and best organised institution in Timor-Leste, and has a long record in defending human rights and promoting justice. Indeed, the Church has been an outspoken critic of the government's rush to reconciliation, arguing that there can be none until there is justice. Father Gusmao, Director of the Justice and Peace Commission in the Catholic Diocese of Bacau, says the government needs to create the conditions for economic and social justice, describing poverty as the most prevalent infringement on basic human rights throughout the island. He worries that the "blessing" of oil and gas revenues will do little to alleviate endemic poverty and will only serve the interests of the wealthy and powerful. In order to improve prospects for justice in Timor-Leste he calls for sustained and massive international intervention. In the frustrations of the growing middle class he sees hope, because it is their yearning for justice and stability that can bring significant domestic pressure to bear on the government.

The UN must promise less and deliver more to overcome its declining credibility and to become more effective. The UN leadership is painfully aware that it failed Timor-Leste in leaving too soon, and its staff are very open and contrite about this mistake. They now admit that they had been naïve to imagine that nation-building could be accomplished on a tight timetable, and are collectively embarrassed that they hurriedly declared their mission accomplished, eager to have a "success" story. The UN now has a second chance to get things right. Nowhere is this more pressing than in restoring the rule of law, promoting accountability, and in nurturing the human resources needed to make the judicial system function.

The JTC, under the auspices of the UNDP, is part of the larger Herculean task of building functioning institutions and instilling good governance. It has not earned much kudos in capacity-building for the judiciary and must learn from the criticism directed at it from all quarters; it has become a symbol of mediocrity and political manipulation. It is within the capacity of the UNDP to improve standards and practices at the JTC and to provide relevant and competent legal training. This will take more than a decade and considerable resources. What is not within the purview of the JTC is the systematic political intervention that threatens the establishment of a sound judicial system.

The breakdown of law and order, vigilante justice, and the escalation of gang violence are symptomatic of a failed judicial system. Time is running out, Fonseca says, and "The government has to give more than lip service to justice and human rights". The rule of law is the foundation of a secure nation just as accountability and justice are crucial to lasting peace and reconciliation.

Combining Community Reconciliation and Local Justice: A Modest Proposal for Reform

*Spencer Zifcak**

Despite the best efforts of many, and notably Timor-Leste's Commission for Reception, Truth and Reconciliation (CAVR), it is an unfortunate fact that the nation's justice system remains in a continuing state of crisis. The crisis has both political and administrative dimensions. Politically, the absence of prosecutions of those militia leaders involved in provoking the troubles of 1999 is a serious and extensive problem that remains largely unaddressed. Most of those involved in serious criminal activity at that time escaped from the country. Of the many prosecutions commenced within the country by the UN's Serious Crimes Unit, however, only very few proceeded prior to that Unit's closure in 2005. Subsequently, the Fretilin Government did not consider the remaining prosecutions to be a high priority.

To this has now been added the dilemma of whether, and in what way, the leaders of the most recent rebellion, which culminated in the assassination attempts upon the President and Prime Minister of the country, should be brought to justice. This is a complex question, made all the more so by the evident desire of the political leadership not to provoke any further violent backlash and, for that reason, to proceed wherever possible and cautiously through a process of political reconciliation and settlement rather than by initiating criminal prosecutions.

Further, it is clear that almost all middle level perpetrators of the violence in the post-1999 period have not been dealt with by the courts and nor are they likely to be. These perpetrators fell between the cracks of the Serious Crimes Unit's investigations of murder, rape and similar offences on the one hand and the CAVR's community reconciliation process which was designed to deal with minor criminal behaviour such assault, arson and theft on the other. In

* The author wishes to acknowledge the contribution of the Asia Foundation in funding the research on the basis of which this chapter was written.

theory, they were to be dealt with by the police and in the District Courts. In practice, the District Court system, under-resourced as it was, simply did not have the capacity to deal with such complex political prosecutions as may have come forward. Even if it had, the capability of the local police to investigate the alleged criminal activity and prepare adequate prosecution briefs would similarly have been negligible.[1]

One consequence of all this has been a continuing residue of resentment within local communities about this failure to act. Their citizens perceive rightly that justice has not been done, that their emotional injuries have not been healed and that their desire for prosecution and punishment is unlikely to be addressed. There is little prospect that this situation will change. Too much time has passed and, in any case, the present government is too distracted and divided to address the matter seriously. The District court system too is overwhelmed, having thousands of criminal and civil cases pending. Consequently, there is little scope for any immediate relief or improvement.

It seems to me, nevertheless, that while waiting for the kind of large scale judicial reforms that are so evidently required to address the crisis, small steps may still be taken to make the justice system work better. While the bigger picture may be dispiriting, at the local level there have been successes that may constructively be built upon. The most significant of these, in my view, has been the conduct of the CAVR's community reconciliation process. There is a general consensus that, within its given parameters, the reconciliation process in local communities worked surprisingly well.[2] It recognized, incorporated and built upon traditional justice to produce a system of local dispute resolution that, for the most part, produced reasonable results for both perpetrators and victims alike. Certainly, it had its drawbacks. On balance, however, these were outweighed by its positive outcomes. These outcomes, particularly those of a procedural nature, suggest that one modest answer to the present justice mire, at least at the local level, may be to meld what was learnt from the CAVR's community interventions with the best features of

---

[1] For a more detailed consideration of the problems of the courts with respect to the prosecution and hearing of alleged human rights abuse see Judicial System Monitoring Project *Justice in Practice: Human Rights in Court Administration*, (2001) JSMP and recent updates on the Project web site at www.jsmp.minihub.org.

[2] P Pigou *The Community Reconciliation Process of the Commission for Reception, Truth and Reconciliation*, UNDP Timor Leste (2004); L Kent *Participants' Perspectives on the CAVR's Community Reconciliation Process*, Judicial System Monitoring Program, Timor Leste (2004).

Timor-Leste's traditional justice system so as to provide a framework within which at least local justice may become fairer and more effective.

In the remainder of this chapter, I want to sketch how such a melding might occur. To do that, I turn first to a brief evaluation of the CAVR's community reconciliation process. I then summarize some relevant features of traditional law. Finally, I draw the two together in a series of proposals that could represent one incremental but nevertheless worthwhile way forward.

THE COMMUNITY RECONCILIATION PROCESS

The CAVR's principal objectives as set down in its governing regulation were these[3]:

1. to inquire into human rights violations that took place in the context of East Timor's political conflicts;
2. to establish the truth with respect to alleged widespread violations;
3. to refer specific violations to the Office of the General Prosecutor with recommendations for prosecution where appropriate;
4. to promote reconciliation and to assist in reception and reintegration of individuals guilty of minor offences into their local communities.

A Community Reconciliation Process (CRP) in the last category could be initiated where a person made a full admission of responsibility for their actions. Once having received and accepted an admission in written form, the Commission could convene a reconciliation hearing. This hearing brought together the perpetrator and his or her victims in a public forum, the purpose of which was to determine whether the two parties may be reconciled and, if so, what reparation if any should occur to effect that reconciliation. Where an agreement to reconcile was reached its terms would be lodged with the Office of the General Prosecutor. A failure by the perpetrator to fulfil the terms of the agreement opened that party to prosecution in the formal court system for the offences admitted.

A reconciliation hearing was normally conducted in the following way:

1. The Chair of the local reconciliation panel would introduce the reconciliation process, explain how events would and place the proceedings within their proper legal context. Introductory remarks were also made by village leaders

[3] UNTAET Regulation 2001/10, 13 July 2001, *On the Establishment of a Commission for Reception, Truth and Reconciliation in East Timor,* Section 3.

and sometimes by the traditional elders. The Catholic Church was represented by the local priest who introduced the Church's perspective and then led a prayer for the success of the proceedings.

2. The perpetrator/deponent was then asked to read his statement to those present at the hearing. These would include the victims of the crimes concerned and members of the local community who had chosen to attend. Following the reading, the deponent might make any further oral statement that he or she wished by way of elaboration, explanation or apology. The deponent's statement was followed by questions from the Panel seeking further clarification. These questions were addressed to issues such as the identity of others involved in the acts disclosed, the chain of command that was in operation during the criminal activity with which the hearing was concerned.
3. The victims present were then asked to respond to the statements made by detailing the impact of the crimes committed against them or members of their families. They were also invited to ask questions of the perpetrator to clarify his or her precise role and responsibility.
4. The members of the community present were then invited to make any statements or ask any questions of the perpetrator in relation to the matter.
5. At the end of questioning, which could be extensive, a conciliation conference is convened, chaired by the Regional Commissioner. The conference consisted of the members of the panel, the perpetrator or perpetrators and the victims present. The purpose of the conference was to determine the nature of the reparation that the perpetrator should be required to make.
6. The outcome of the conciliation process was embodied in a Community Reconciliation Agreement which would be registered with the Dili District Court.

This process was followed and complemented by a reconciliation ceremony conducted in accordance with traditional law and custom. The ceremonials varied from district to district and even from village to village. They tended to be more elaborate in rural constituencies and less so in urban ones. All, however, involved the traditional practice of rolling out the mat upon which customary rites and forms of reconciliation would take place. Rolling the mat up at the conclusion was the principal symbolic representation of the successful conclusion of the proceeding.

Evaluating the Process

(i) Community Reconciliation Agreements

The primary outcome of the process was the successful conclusion of community reconciliation agreements between many hundreds of individuals and their victims or, where no victims were identifiable, with members of their wider communities. Very few hearings broke down. In this the role of community reconciliation panels was critical. The panels handled a hearing process in which frequently sensitive subject matter was spoken about, and in which the prospect of angry if not violent exchange was always a possibility, with very considerable skill. This was particularly the case given that panel members had no prior experience of mediation of this kind, were given brief but effective training and then had to learn what to do in effect as they went along. It is notable but unsurprising in this regard, that panels were considerably more effective in their conduct of hearings towards the end of the process than they were at its beginning.

In the course of the process, the wider community came better to recognise what had occurred in their locality, how individuals there had acted wrongly, and what responsibility might properly be attributed to the perpetrators and to the community leadership.

At its conclusion, there was a sense in which the CRP has become a victim of its own success. 200 hearings were conducted and over 1500 perpetrators came forward. Approximately 30,000 people attended the hearings across the country. It became apparent that there were many more individuals who had engaged in minor politically motivated crime who wished to come forward. On a rough estimate, it may reasonably be suggested that only one-third of those who expressed an interest in facing their communities with a view to reintegration were able to do so in the fifteen months during which the process was conducted.

(ii) Integration with Formal Justice System

A further, very significant product of the process was the successful manner in which it was integrated with the formal and informal justice systems. There were some administrative difficulties initially with the process of registering Community Reconciliation Agreements with the District Courts. Nevertheless giving force and effect to agreements reached, thus tying them into the formal justice system, was a good innovation that added a measure of gravity and consequence to the community process.

(iii) Melding with the Traditional Justice System

The mesh between community reconciliation and the informal, traditional justice system was no less important and constructive. The addition of adat processes at the conclusion of the regular mediation proceedings enhanced the understanding and acceptability of community reconciliation across the country. There were, of course, differences in the degree to which these processes were regarded as significant in different localities. Overall, however, it is clear that in designing the process to incorporate elements of traditional justice, its founders made it more likely that the reconciliation process would achieve its objectives and that agreements made would endure.

(iv) Legislative Shape and Sanction

The detailed regulatory framework that governed the conduct of the CRP provided legal certainty to the process and was of very considerable assistance in defining the relationship between the Commission and other institutions, such as the Serious Crimes Unit, which were designed to implement a comprehensive strategy for achieving transitional justice. One might quarrel with the content of parts of the regulation but to have these interrelationships embodied in law was clearly beneficial.

Not every product of the CRP was positive however. It revealed a number of problems in its wake. I deal now briefly with the most significant of these.

(i) Uncovering the Truth?

In observing the reconciliation hearings it became apparent that however much the truth was desired, it was not in the end the principal consideration upon which reconciliation would be founded. Rather, a decision by victims or the community to re-embrace and reintegrate a perpetrator appeared to rest more upon the level of contrition he had demonstrated and upon the panel's and the community's judgment of their character and social acceptability. The conclusion that community reconciliation was a success, therefore, needs to be tempered by the knowledge that the truth did not always win out. In its absence, then, forgiveness and the community's desire to leave a conflicted past behind became the key.

(ii) Looking after Victims' Interests

The desire to leave the past behind and by doing so commence the process of rebuilding interpersonal and community relationships had another problematic effect. In significant numbers of hearings it had the effect of putting individual victims' interests to one side in favour of the wider community interest. Consequently, it left some victims unhappy and unresolved. Having been brought into the process by the desire of the perpetrator to reconcile, some victims left it with their antagonists in a better social situation and legal position but with their own feelings still mixed and troubled.

(iii) Victim Compensation?

Similarly, and more generally, it became evident in the course of my study that the provision of financial compensation to victims was an exceptionally important issue. A universal program of compensation, even if only symbolic in monetary terms, was supported by almost everyone interviewed. Such a program, if it had been implemented, would have made a valuable contribution to national reconciliation by affording tangible, public recognition to those who had suffered. Regrettably, a comprehensive program of compensation remained beyond the financial capacities of a Government and nation whose economic plight remains grave.

It would be wrong, however, to focus in too concentrated a manner on the weaknesses. Because taken overall the process, in my view, was a considerable success. Much was achieved in a very short time frame. And many innovations introduced, particularly that of the community reconciliation panels, proved their value against expectation.

As foreshadowed previously, therefore, it seems to me that the positive experiences of the CRP could contribute to the constructive adaptation of the existing Timorese local justice system. A modified local justice system, incorporating the best features of the CRP and traditional mechanisms of community justice could provide an appropriate complement to the formal court system. The effective combination of the two, in turn, might do much to ease the present crisis in the courts while, in the longer term, enhancing the justice system's credibility in the wider community.

To explore this idea further, the following discussion proceeds in three stages. First, I provide a concise summary of the existing system of local, community justice and the principles that underlie it. Next, I summarise my interviews with members of local communities and senior governmental and judicial officials to illuminate their attitudes to the local system and prospect of its combination with more formal justice mechanisms. Then, I take four innovations introduced within the framework of the CRP and apply them to generate several proposals for compatible and complementary reforms to the existing practice of local justice.

TRADITIONAL JUSTICE: THE LEGAL FRAMEWORK

As is remarked in many studies of traditional justice in East Timor, no one system of traditional justice exists in the country. There are in fact many such systems. One study of local mediation by the Peace and Democracy Foundation, for example, identified no less than 63 different forms based on different dialects and places.[4] Having said that, however, it is possible to

[4] Peace and Democracy Foundation, Dili, *Preliminary Report: Research on Customary Dispute Resolution and a Draft Mediation Model for Timor Leste* (2003).

identify certain underlying principles and practices common to most existing systems. This identification is not easy because what is described derives from an oral rather than written tradition. Nevertheless, there have been several recent academic studies of the subject and what follows here is a précis of their findings, combined with my own observations of customary law and ritual in the reconciliation context.[5]

The system of local, customary justice derives from two principal sources: the first is ancient narratives including ancient myths and rituals. The second is stories founded in more recent historical experience recited by the *lian nain*, that is the customary elders whose role is as holders of the law. These stories provide what might loosely be described as precedents of proper behaviour.

Since law is 'held' by traditional elders, it follows that behavioural rules at village level are founded principally upon respect for one's elders and the primacy of one's family's interests. Traditional courts then consist of an elder or a council of elders who are respected as having the authority and wisdom to make decisions concerning disputes that arise between individuals and families in the village. This authority is crystallised in a series of 'metaphors for living'. These metaphors in turn provide the foundation for making decisions with respect to what constitutes right or wrong behaviour. Not unlike modern legal systems, the traditional court, then, is expected to make its decisions on the basis of the facts before it and the metaphors or principles that have guided proper conduct in cases of a similar kind in the past.

It is important to note in this regard that the composition of local tribunals has changed somewhat in recent years, partly in response to the incursion of colonial systems of law. To a significant degree, the responsibility for local dispute resolution has now shifted from the traditional 'holders of the law', to chiefs of the villages, the *chefe de suco* and the *chefe d'aldeia*. While the two act frequently in concert, it has become increasingly the case that substantive decision-making, albeit on a similar foundation, has shifted to the chiefs, while ritual and ceremony remains the province of the *lian nain*.

[5] See for example J J Fox (Ed) *The Flow of Life*, Canberra: Australian National University Press; J J Fox and C Sather *Origins, Ancestry and Alliance*, Canberra: Australian National University Press (1996); D Babo-Soares *A Brief Overview of the Role of Customary Law in East Timor*, Paper presented to a symposium on East Timor, Indonesia and the Region, Universidade Nova de Lisboa (2000); D Babo-Soares *Nahe Biti: The Philosophy and Process of Grassroots Reconciliation (and Justice) in East Timor*, Judicial System Monitoring Project (2002); D Mearns *Looking Both Ways: Models for Justice in East Timor*, Australian Legal Resources International (2002).

The system of traditional law operates hierarchically. Disputes between families, whether over marriage, property or other matters, will generally be left to the families themselves to resolve. The family elders will convene to endeavour to reach an appropriate compromise. If individuals or families are unsuccessful in resolving their disagreements, the matter will then be referred to the *chefe d'aldeia* (neighbourhood chief) who will seek to mediate. Should this attempt fail, the dispute is referred upwards again, this time to the *chefe de suco*, the head of the village. He may convene a council of elders consisting of the members of the traditional and administrative leadership. The local priest may also become involved. The Council is more likely to be convened if the matter in dispute is one concerning local custom or tradition, therefore having some value as a precedent of sorts in similar future cases. An inability to resolve the disputation in the village, depending on the continuing seriousness of the disagreement, may then be referred to the police and the engagement with the civil authorities begins. The police will also become involved if there are disagreements between neighbourhoods or villages, particularly where there appears to be the risk of disorder. This, in turn, may lead to the disagreement being taken before the courts.

Customary law and practice is founded upon certain guiding principles. The principles most relevant to the present study are the following. First, a strong emphasis is placed in local justice systems upon reciprocity and exchange. In western systems of law, evidence is considered, a determination made and a penalty determined, all in an arbitral fashion. In traditional law, by contrast, a determination is made but remains contestable by the parties. Further, the penalty is one that is negotiated between the tribunal and the parties, in a manner seeks not only to punish the guilty party but also to place all parties in a position that equates roughly to that which prevailed before the misconduct took place. This reflects the belief that the wrongdoing creates a debt that must be repaid not only to the person harmed but also to the wider community if the matter in question is to be finalised. Sanctions, therefore, have both a personal and social dimension. In the personal dimension, the offender may incur social isolation or exclusion. However, such a consequence may not necessarily follow if suitable reparation can be made which compensates not only the victim for the harm he or she has suffered but also restores a sense of balance to the community as a whole. This constitutes the social dimension of the sanction.

Secondly, consistent with the principal of reciprocity, every effort is made to mediate proceedings whether civil or criminal. The essential precondition for successful mediation is a full and frank admission of responsibility by the perpetrator concerned. If such an admission is made, it is then expected that the victim or opposing party will act in a forgiving manner and seek to agree upon the terms of an exchange.

Thirdly, the notion of justice has a strong temporal dimension. Decisions are made and suitable reparations are decided upon. Both decision and reparation, however, are designed to achieve not only a mediated settlement in the present between the specific parties to the dispute but also to contribute to the well-being of the wider community in the future. The idea is to heal past mistakes and by so doing promote future harmony.

Fourthly, the process has a strong spiritual as well as secular aspect. It follows that local dispute resolution proceedings will normally be followed by the taking of oaths and the conduct of appropriate rituals. These are believed to legitimise the proceedings in the transcendent realm. The failure to take an oath is widely believed to invalidate the preceding proceedings. The failure to abide by the oath, is thought to bring down substantial adverse consequences not only upon the relevant participant but on their families and, perhaps, through generations. Bobo-Soares has described the significance oath and ritual graphically in the following terms[6]:

> "The objective of the Oath is twofold. First, it demonstrates that social stability has been recovered and the status of the previously deemed social malefactor has been re-established. Likewise, the balance between cosmos and secular world has also been re-established. Secondly, it provides protection and closes down the chapter of that specific conflict. Social order, indeed social life, is therefore restored."

Fifthly, the idea of reconciliation is deeply embedded within local systems of justice. This follows from the significance attached to reciprocity and exchange as the foundation for an agreement that will settle matters between the parties so that they may resume normal social relations. The resumption of normal social relations in turn has the effect of contributing to the continuing social and spiritual well-being of the community as a whole. This is why the punishment of an offender by a distant, formal court and the service of their sentence in a distant penal institution seems so unsatisfactory. It makes no advance either in the process of individual reparation or community healing.

Nahe Biti, or grassroots reconciliation, is well known and translated literally means the laying down of the mat. It is accompanied by its own special set of

6 Bobo-Soares, note 5 *supra*.

customs and rituals. As noted previously, when the mat on which participants are asked to sit is unfolded the process of reconciliation begins. It is not concluded until the mat is taken up by the local religious leader and folded. The participants may also chew on beetle nut share a meal together and drink from common vessels to signify that they intend to place their conflicted past behind them. More elaborately in some areas, the throats of chickens and pigs are cut, the blood is poured into cups of tua and the parties drink from the cups to signal their concurrence with the decision that has been mediated. It is important to note that each of these rituals has a meaning, significance and binding effect that travels very much further the simple acknowledgement of an accord. These rituals also signify and cement the community's assent within a traditional legal and religious framework. As one CAVR Commissioner put it to me:

> "it is ancestral tradition, spirituality, magic that provides the most important binding element to these agreements. If these are transgressed, then the community is wronged...the person who breaks the agreement may be punished under traditional law or by 'the other.'"[7]

It with an understanding of these structures and principles that we may proceed to consider how the traditional justice system may constructively be adapted to enable it to take its place as an integral part of the administration of democratic Timor Leste's overall system of justice.

Before doing so, however, I give some introductory consideration to the attitude of senior governmental and judicial officers, and the attitudes of local people more generally, to community justice and the prospect that it might provide an appropriate and effective alternative to the existing formal court system.

Attitudes to the Local Justice System

(i) The Local Community

The perceptions and opinions of local people about the administration of justice in their country, have been well summarized in a survey undertaken by the Asia Foundation, published in February 2004. Here, I summarise the results relevant to this study, combined with additional observations obtained during my own research.

[7] Personal Interview.

Unsurprisingly, in the light of what has been delineated above, the participants in the survey stated that access to the formal court system was a matter of considerable concern. They believed that the quality of justice and the level of service provided by the system was plainly inadequate. Local people's perception of the justice system in the country as a whole, however, embraced both the formal court system and traditional 'adat' processes. There was a strong view that both systems had their contribution to make and that each contribution should be utilized appropriately. The proper role of the two systems, however, should be distinguished.

Reflecting the almost universal view of those interviewed for this study, participants in the Foundation survey indicated clearly that the formal court system was the system most appropriate for the resolution of serious crimes, contractual disputes, disputes with governmental agencies and police abuse. On the other hand, the local, community justice system was the most appropriate for the resolution of minor crime and for solving neighbourhood and familial disputes. Of the two systems, those surveyed indicated that they felt more comfortable with the systems of local justice than they did with engagement with the formal court system.

Participants said that they were generally positive about the way in which the formal system operated. They believed that for the most part it operated fairly and provided equal treatment across the country. At the same time they identified an extensive list of problems with it. The principal problems identified in the Foundation study and this one were these.

The formal courts were regarded as both inaccessible and dysfunctional. The cost of proceedings in the system operated as a substantial disincentive to its use. Its use of Portuguese as the official language was also seen as alienating. Local people had little knowledge or experience of the system and did not understand the law and procedure that governed its practice. There was a strong residual feeling, deriving from the experience of colonial rule, that the formal court system may not operate in the people's best interests. It was likely that it would operate in the interests of the rich and powerful rather than giving equal weight to the situation and argument of ordinary citizens. Almost a third of the respondents believed that court personnel were open to corruption.

The formal courts were regarded as distant. Their proceedings lacked relevance to the affairs of the local community. There was no sense in which the proceedings were owned by the local community. In this context, it was felt by many that while the courts might be successful in delivering individual justice, communal understandings of justice more consonant with traditional culture and values were insufficiently influential in determining the form and outcome of legal proceedings.

Speaking generally, the traditional system of justice was favoured. Most survey respondents indicated that they were comfortable in bringing a problem to either the *chefe de suco* or to traditional adat leaders for consideration. The adat system was widely considered as fair and accessible. It was efficient and affordable. The system was also regarded as more accurately reflecting people's culture and values than the formal court system did. It was better understood and more familiar not least because its proceedings were conducted in the local language and in a manner that most people had already known and experienced. Consonant with traditional values its emphasis was more conciliation than arbitration. Compensatory exchange operated as its principal currency. In the traditional system a strong emphasis was placed on achieving lasting reconciliation. This reconciliation was not only effected between the perpetrator and victim but between their families and within the community at large. This emphasis on community in the view of many made it more likely that decisions would be respected and observed.

Participants, however, acknowledged that the system of traditional justice had its own problems. Different decisions might be reached in similar cases. Decision makers may on occasions be biased, either because of their own interests or because they may rely too heavily on prior, personal knowledge of the matters in dispute. Some participants also felt that the decisions of village chiefs may be subject to political influence and interference. A significant minority of interviewees in the Foundation survey believed that decisions made in accordance with customary law may breach human rights standards. Again, a significant minority believed that the system of traditional justice resulted in the unfair treatment of women, particularly in relation to cases of domestic violence. Nevertheless, over half of the interviewees still believed that such cases should be handled in accordance with the local custom and process rather than by the formal court system. Cases of rape, in contrast, were sufficiently serious to be referred to that system for prosecution and trial.

Taking all this into consideration it was significant that 75% of the participants in the Foundation survey indicated that the traditional system of justice required reform if it was to operate more effectively.

(ii) Ministers and Jurists

In senior governmental and judicial circles, reservations were held about the co-optation of customary law and justice. These were both similar and different from those expressed immediately above.

The primary reservation held by many was that, consonant with the development of a modern, functioning democracy, Timor Leste should devote its full attention to ensuring that the formal court system operated in a unified, comprehensive and fair way and in a manner that was consistent with the rule of law. The idea of developing parallel systems of law was unattractive in this context, particularly because systems of local justice varied considerably between districts, sub-districts, towns and villages across the country. The problems associated with having varying procedures and standards in criminal proceedings were of particular concern in this regard.[8]

> "We must have short, medium and long term policy goals. These must all be directed in one way or another towards our formal justice system operating effectively. We cannot simply hand justice back to traditional leaders acting in accordance with local culture...If minor crimes are to be dealt with locally, then strict preconditions must apply and there must be consistency across the board." (Justice Minister)

This view is commendable. The problem, however, is that pure reliance on the formal court system seems impractical in present circumstances. The personnel, skills and resources are simply not there to provide it with adequate support. Consequently, there is an acknowledgment that, at least for an interim period that may stretch for some years, formal and traditional justice must operate in tandem. If this is the case, however, politicians, judges and representatives of NGO's alike are clear that the manner in which local justice is conducted must be defined by law and that significant adaptations must be made to ensure procedural fairness and consistency of outcomes[9]:

> "The District Courts are not functioning. This is owing to the number and skill of judges, to logistics and the fact that local people are still unfamiliar with formal court processes. People are not sufficiently informed of procedures for bringing cases to permit the system to work. So, it may be desirable that the formal court system be supplemented by traditional justice mechanisms. Until the district system is functioning effectively, then systems of traditional justice may be necessary to provide part of the answer to unmet need. Of course, matters like judicial independence are things we understand but cannot readily be transposed into the traditional justice arena...We must be careful if we intervene to introduce some measure of consistency in local systems that we do not destroy the process.

[8] Personal Interview.
[9] Personal Interview.

What might be desirable is some amalgam of traditional justice and the reconciliation processes now begun. It would provide a good beginning if the crimes to be dealt with by the formal court system and the crimes by reconciliation/traditional justice could be defined by law" (Judge of the Court of Appeal).

There was a keen appreciation among actors in government, the judiciary and in NGOs that a local justice system that remained fixed and unreformed would be an unsuitable partner for the national courts. The principal concern here was that solutions arrived at locally might be in breach of human rights standards to which the government and country was committed[10]:

"Serious crimes could not be dealt with by the local justice system. To take just one example, rape is unacceptable. But in some local communities the crime may be swept aside simply by the families concerned throwing a party and making up. We could not allow this to happen." (Justice Minister)

The interviewees in this study wrestled with the question of what additional measures needed to be grafted onto the local community justice system in order to ensure that it operated fairly, consistently, comprehensively and in accordance with the rule of law. Several very constructive suggestions were made, a number of the most important of which were encapsulated in the following statement from a Judge of the District Court[11]:

"As a jurist I don't favour handling criminal cases through the traditional system. However because of limited resources, if a viable alternative were to exist one may consider its use. However, there would need to be preconditions. The government would have to review the situation carefully. There would have to be legislation to govern and legitimate the process, to ensure common standards across the country for specific classes of cases both civil and criminal. There needs to be some guarantee of justice as equal for all. One could also create CAVR type panels across the country to complement existing local justice systems. But even then it would be best if there were some direct connection with the formal justice system. Perhaps there should be judicial oversight of the system by judges within each district."

This would appear to me to be an appropriate set of adaptations with which to begin. I explore them and others in the section that follows.

---

[10] Personal Interview.
[11] Personal Interview.

Community Justice and Reconciliation: Proposals for Adaptation and Coherence

This consideration of a modest series of proposals with respect to traditional justice needs to begin with a caveat. I am not an expert in customary law and practice nor would I pretend to be. Consequently, the proposals here ought to be read as preliminary and suggestive rather than concluded. They might serve as one point of departure among many in a continuing deliberation and dialogue about Timor Leste's justice system. That more research needs to be undertaken is I think evident. The view is shared at the most senior levels of Government. In discussing the matters dealt with here, the nation's Minister for Justice told me that:

> "It may be that we need to constitute local tribunals. Certainly, the local system must operate in a way that is consistent across the country. To determine how we should approach this is something that I think now requires considerable new research and consultation."[12]

It is perhaps best then to begin by making clear the underlying principles upon which these proposals are based. They are as follows:

1. The existing system of customary law and justice, which has evolved over many centuries, should be modified to the minimum extent possible consistent with the values of a newly democratic polity;
2. The local justice system should be conducted in a manner that reflects the importance of adherence to due process;
3. The local justice system similarly should be concerned with the achievement of substantive fairness so that, for example, its outcomes should as far as possible be consistent with international and national, constitutionally based human rights standards;
4. The local justice system's present emphasis upon grassroots reconciliation should be preserved and enhanced;
5. In the spheres of both criminal and civil law, an operational distinction should continue to be drawn between serious matters and non-serious matters. Serious matters should remain within the province of the formal court system. Non-serious matters may be dealt with by the local, community justice system;
6. To as great an extent as possible, given existing inter-regional, legal and customary differences, the local justice system should promote national consistency in both procedures and outcomes;

---

[12] Personal Interview.

7. The local justice system should be regulated by law. A legal framework endorsed by the parliament should provide the foundation for its operation;
8. To as great an extent as possible, adaptations made to the local justice system should be such as have been demonstrated to work in practice in related contexts.

It is from the last principle that I move now to a consideration of how the positive experience of the CRP may contribute to further discussion and deliberation upon local justice reform.

There are four positive aspects of the experience of the CRP which, in my view, may be of particular significance in the development of a reformed local justice system. First, the CRP managed successfully to set in place its practices and procedures in a manner that was complementary to and supplemented by those characteristic of existing customary law and practice. This is a complementarity that ought also to be sought when considering the melding of the existing formal and informal justice systems.

Secondly, perhaps the major innovation of the CRP was the creation of community reconciliation panels. These operated at a village level throughout the country in a way that was widely accepted by local communities. In so doing, the panels introduced a measure of representativeness, impartiality and procedural fairness into local reconciliation proceedings. Their re-creation in the context of the administration of local justice may bring with it similar benefits and advantages.

Thirdly, the CRP was connected directly to the formal court system and to the national prosecution service. This relationship was crucial and for the most part operated effectively. A similar linkage should also be created in the future between the formal justice system and its local counterpart.

Fourthly, the CRP operated within the context of legislation that regulated its workings in some detail. Generally considered, the governing legislation was appropriate and well adapted to local situations and circumstances. The legislation also gave legal force and effect to the outcomes of local reconciliation proceedings, giving them weight and import. It would seem to be an essential prerequisite for the reform of the existing system of local justice that it be contained similarly within a national legal framework determined and endorsed by the national government and parliament.

In the remainder of this section of the report, I explore the implications of each of these four positive innovations in more detail.

(i) Complementarily between the CRP and Traditional Law and Custom

It will be apparent from the preceding discussion that the process of community reconciliation was one that resonated with local communities, being familiar to them from its resemblance to *Nahe Biti*. While some of the structural and procedural aspects of the CAVR's community reconciliation process were novel, its designers sought consciously to embrace existing custom and tradition within the new form. This developed in harmony with the principles, processes and rituals of *Nahe Biti* and in doing so gathered significant local credibility. It accorded important formal roles to village chiefs and the *lian nain*. It adopted traditional ritual and ceremony as an active and significant supplement to the legislatively mandated mediation procedures. It provided for participation by the entire local community. And, as importantly, as anything, by embracing traditional rites, it added a gravity to agreements reached that is likely to add significantly to their enduring effect.

The lesson is clear. In the future development of any modified, legislatively sanctioned local justice system, all of these components should similarly be adopted and incorporated. So, for example, it may be appropriate to provide that village heads preside over, or at least participate actively, in the hearing and determination of local disputes. Similarly, the *lian nain* should continue to play their ceremonial role. Provision should be made for community involvement in the proceedings and in the negotiation of their outcomes. If these things are done, the decisions that are made are likely to be accorded their proper respect.

It should be noted that the implementation of these suggestions, may to different eyes, be regarded as inconsistent with certain fundamental legal principles, for example, the separation of executive and judicial power. Nevertheless, the principles of minimum interference and prior operational success would appear to dictate that some modification of the fundamental principle is appropriate and workable.

(ii) Community Justice Panels

Without doubt, the key innovation of the CRP was the creation of community reconciliation panels. Their acceptance and success suggests that the panel idea might also constructively be extended into the operation of the local system of justice.

There are several important considerations that tend to towards this conclusion. The first is concerned with ensuring that local proceedings are conducted in a way that is procedurally as fair as possible. Significant weight needs to be attached therefore to making the person or body conducting local proceedings as impartial as possible. It is one of the principal criticisms of the existing system of local justice that the decision-maker or decision-makers may be biased. The problem was summarised aptly by Dr David Mearns in his research on models for justice in East Timor:

> "In many districts, the arbitrariness of the judgments and the potential for bias and the exercise of vested interest were seen as real problems with the local system. Since most local systems relied on strong political leaders who were often not descended from customary leaders and were not 'traditional' anyway, this was considered a particularly difficult problem."[13]

There are many potential sources of bias in present local systems. Village heads may be biased on the basis of their political affiliation, as noted above. Bias may be introduced by virtue of the decision-maker's familial, tribal or cultural ties. Favourable treatment may be procured by corruption. In small communities, proceedings may tend towards predetermined outcomes, simply by virtue of the decision-makers' prior knowledge of and attitude towards the disputants or the circumstances of the dispute. Local people's experience of justice under the Indonesian regime, which was notoriously corrupt and politically influenced, still makes them cautious about embracing any new system whether formal or informal.

So, it is clearly critical to eliminate bias introduced in these ways. It is also crucial to minimise or remove any and every other source of partisanship if the local justice system is to be perceived as a credible complement to the formal courts. The reinvention of community reconciliation panels as community justice panels may provide one proven and effective means of achieving this outcome.

The interposition of community justice panels into systems of local justice could provide a number of very important benefits in this and other respects. The panels broaden the range of decision-makers beyond one person. This makes it far more difficult for those seeking to bribe or improperly influence the local tribunal. Procuring one vote is much easier than procuring five.

The establishment of a central or regional body to monitor and vet local appointments also lessens the prospect that inappropriate candidates will be

[13] D Mearns *Looking Both Ways: Models for Local Justice in East Timor*, Australian Legal Resources Institute (2002), pp.53–54.

selected. In the CRP, panel members were chosen by the CAVR's regional commissioner in consultation with the local community. Some similar process of district based selection, perhaps by the District Administrator in consultation with local communities, could serve the same purpose.

If modelled on community reconciliation panels, local panels are likely to be more representative of the plurality of community interests than one village chief would be. The requirement in the CRP that female representation be included and the suggestion that there be a representative of the younger members of the local community added significantly to the quality of judgments made and the credibility of the process.

The panels were given important early training in applying relevant law and ensuring fair procedure. Their sophistication in doing so increased significantly during the course of the CRP. A similar program of education for new members of community justice panels could be expected to reap similar, significant rewards.

The representativeness of the panels and their progressively greater skill in conducting hearings also drew the wider community into the process. Community members, particularly for minority groups felt that their interests were better represented, and the effective conduct of hearings allowed for extensive and appropriately moderated involvement in proceedings by community members who chose to participate in them. Consequently, the sense of community ownership of the process was enhanced.

For all these reasons, it would seem sensible to incorporate panels into local systems of justice. The panels would usually be chaired by the village chief, thereby acknowledging his (or her) role and position. The chief would be surrounded however by other community leaders, representing important interests according to their significance and distribution in the local community. The benefits of such an arrangement may be very substantial indeed.

I note that without the positive experience of the CRP, such a proposal might have been regarded as too radical an alteration to the existing system of local justice. That experience, however, and the credibility attached to it during the course of the process by local people across all districts, suggests that this reform's time may well have arrived. Of course, its commencement could be hastened and its credibility enhanced, if former members of the community reconciliation panels formed the kernel of the membership of the new community justice panel structure.

(iii) Connection with the Formal Court System

The CRP was connected directly to the formal court system and the prosecution service. The Office of the Prosecutor General was responsible for determining whether cases fell into a class that was appropriate for reconciliation. It could also withdraw cases from reconciliation where it appeared that a deponent had participated in serious crime. The formal court system exercised a supervisory jurisdiction. It was required to register Community Reconciliation Agreements. In doing so, it was responsible for determining whether the reparation proposed in the agreements was proportionate to the circumstances and in accordance with human rights principles. If not, the agreement would not take effect.

In exploring constructive adaptations to the local justice system, it would seem sensible and appropriate for a similar linkage between it and the formal court system to be made. There are several reasons for this.

First, the intention in permitting the local justice system to play a complementary role in the administration of justice is not that local justice should operate separately but rather that it should be fully integrated so that a unified system of justice is created. Consistent with the rule of law, all people should be treated equally before the law. The creation of separate systems of justice would severely undermine this principle.

Secondly, therefore, appropriate linkage mechanisms should be created. These should allow the ready movement of cases from one jurisdiction to the other where this is in the interests of achieving justice. At the same time, there should be no confusion about which jurisdiction should be approached in the first instance.

Thirdly, therefore, in criminal cases a vetting process similar to that conducted by the Office of the Prosecutor General might constructively be set in place to determine which cases were appropriate for resolution at local level and which should be handled at district level through the courts. A similar process would need to be constructed for civil matters. Effective vetting would streamline justice administration considerably. The broad criteria for making such decisions would be defined by law.

Fourthly, the court's supervisory jurisdiction with respect to proportionality and the observance of human rights principles was not used during the CRP. This was because the system of registration broke down. But in any case, the agreements mediated tended towards leniency rather than harshness. Nevertheless, the requirement that the courts should be the final arbiters in relation to serious matters such as the observance of human rights is a good one. Given that human rights are protected explicitly by the Constitution, in accordance with democratic principle it should be the judicial arm of government which takes ultimate responsibility for ensuring their protection.

For similar reasons a further link should also be created. Cases determined in the system of local justice should be subject to appeal to the courts by the party whose interests have adversely been affected. Consideration might also be given to allowing village chiefs or panels to refer matters to the courts where matters are too complex or where the appropriate decision is uncertain.

If a unified system of justice is desired, then a path should be open to litigants to have their cases determined in the final instance by the highest court in the land upon the law applicable throughout the land. The appellate mechanism would ensure that this possibility was open and that national law could develop on the basis of knowledge of and experience with the full range of legally contested matters that arose within Timorese society.

(iv) A Regulatory Framework

It follows, finally, from what has just been said that the local justice system's operation and its relationship to the formal court system should be determined and regulated by law. The weight and importance attached to the CRP was in part owed to the legislative authority upon which it rested. The relevant regulation set out in detail the way in which the reconciliation process was to operate. It provided a measure of clarity to implementation. It ensured procedural fairness and consistency across the country. It made the outcomes legally enforceable in the courts. These are all matters that should also properly been governed by law in devising an adapted local justice system.

An overarching regulation, debated by and adopted by the national parliament, might then govern the following matters, among others:

1. The general and specific jurisdictions of the local justice system including:
   (i) The definition of serious and non-serious crimes and the mechanism to be used to determine the appropriate category;
   (ii) The definition of serious and non-serious civil matters and the mechanism to be used to determine the appropriate category.
   The composition of local courts, however constituted, including:
2. The method of selection of local chairpersons and panel members, if panels are to be used;
   (i) The qualifications required of chairpersons and panel members;

   (ii) Their terms and conditions of office including provisions for their appointment and removal;
   (iii) The composition of local courts for particular kinds of case, for example in relation to more serious criminal offences or more complex civil matters;
   (iv) The method of decision-making to be adopted, *e.g.*, consensus, majority decision etc.
3. The powers of local courts including:
   (i) The power to summon witnesses;
   (ii) The power to penalise witnesses providing untruthful evidence;
   (iii) The penalties for non-observance of decisions;
   (iv) The method by which decisions may be enforced; and
   (v) Whether any of the powers listed above should be exercised exclusively by the formal courts rather than local tribunals.
4. The procedural rules to be adopted at local hearings including:
   (i) The general requirement to act in accordance with due process;
   (ii) The requirement that all parties, including members of the wider community, be entitled to be heard;
   (iii) The requirement that the person or persons constituting the local court act impartially and independently;
   (iv) The circumstances appropriate to referring a case for resolution by reconciliation and those appropriate for referral for resolution by some form of arbitral process;
   (v) The particular process to be adopted for reconciliation and arbitration respectively;
   (vi) The role to be assigned to traditional elders, traditional law and traditional ritual and ceremony.
5. The supervisory jurisdiction of the formal courts including:
   (i) The power to review cases on the grounds that the decisions reached are disproportionate to the circumstances or in conflict with international and national human rights standards, for example in relation to their treatment of women;
   (ii) The power to resolve inconsistencies between national and customary law and the criteria in accordance with which such inconsistencies should be resolved;
   (iii) The power to hear appeals from decisions of the local courts;
   (iv) The power to review the legality of decisions taken; and
   (v) The power to review the constitutionality of decisions taken.

Conclusion

This list, like all the proposals contained in this section is, as I emphasised at the outset, only suggestive. My hope is that the proposals made, founded as they are on the positive experience of the CRP, may act to enliven discussion and debate on the future shape of Timor Leste's justice system.

This is but one, tentatively suggested, way forward. It may not be the best way, and in the course of devising it, much may have been missed. If, however, the proposals contained here serve to contribute to a wider debate in the Timorese community about how the justice system in Timor might best be constituted then this research will have achieved its modest purpose.

Index

N

O